# Studies in Latin American Ethnohistory & Archaeology

Joyce Marcus
General Editor

Volume I       *A Fuego y Sangre: Early Zapotec Imperialism in the Cuicatlán Cañada, Oaxaca*, by Elsa Redmond, Memoirs of the Museum of Anthropology, University of Michigan, No. 16. 1983.

Volume II      *Irrigation and the Cuicatec Ecosystem: A Study of Agriculture and Civilization in North Central Oaxaca*, by Joseph W. Hopkins, Memoirs of the Museum of Anthropology, University of Michigan, No. 17. 1984.

Volume III     *Aztec City-States*, by Mary G. Hodge, Memoirs of the Museum of Anthropology, University of Michigan, No. 18. 1984.

Volume IV      *Conflicts over Coca Fields in Sixteenth-Century Peru*, by María Rostworowski de Diez Canseco, Memoirs of the Museum of Anthropology, University of Michigan, No. 21. 1988.

Volume V       *Tribal and Chiefly Warfare in South America*, by Elsa Redmond, Memoirs of the Museum of Anthropology, University of Michigan, No. 28. 1994.

Volume VI      *Imperial Transformations in Sixteenth-Century Yucay, Peru*, transcribed and edited by R. Alan Covey and Donato Amado González, Memoirs of the Museum of Anthropology, University of Michigan, No. 44. 2008.

Volume VII     *Domestic Life in Prehispanic Capitals: A Study of Specialization, Hierarchy, and Ethnicity*, edited by Linda R. Manzanilla and Claude Chapdelaine, Memoirs of the Museum of Anthropology, University of Michigan, No. 46. 2009.

Volume VIII    *Yuthu: Community and Ritual in an Early Andean Village*, by Allison R. Davis, Memoirs of the Museum of Anthropology, University of Michigan, No. 50. 2011.

Volume IX      *Advances in Titicaca Basin Archaeology–III*, edited by Alexei Vranich, Elizabeth A. Klarich, and Charles Stanish, Memoirs of the Museum of Anthropology, University of Michigan, No. 51. 2012.

Memoirs of the Museum of Anthropology
University of Michigan
Number 51

Studies in Latin American Ethnohistory & Archaeology
Joyce Marcus, General Editor

Volume IX

# Advances in Titicaca Basin Archaeology—III

edited by

Alexei Vranich

Elizabeth A. Klarich

and

Charles Stanish

Ann Arbor, Michigan
2012

©2012 by the Regents of the University of Michigan
The Museum of Anthropology
All rights reserved

Printed in the United States of America
ISBN 978-0-915703-78-4

Cover design by Katherine Clahassey

The University of Michigan Museum of Anthropology currently publishes two monograph series, Anthropological Papers and Memoirs, as well as an electronic series in CD-ROM form. For a complete catalog, write to Museum of Anthropology Publications, 4013 Museums Building, 1109 Geddes Avenue, Ann Arbor, MI 48109-1079, or see www.lsa.umich.edu/umma/publications.

Library of Congress Cataloging-in-Publication Data

Advances in Titicaca basin archaeology-III / edited by Alexei Vranich, Elizabeth A. Klarich and Charles Stanish.
    p. cm. -- (Latin American Ethnohistory & Archaeology ; vol. 9.)
 Includes bibliographical references and index.
 ISBN 978-0-915703-78-4 (alk. paper)
1. Indians of South America--Titicaca Lake Region (Peru and Bolilvia)--Antiquities. 2. Tiwanaku culture--Titicaca Lake Region (Peru and Bolilvia) 3. Excavations (Archaeology)--Titicaca Lake Region (Peru and Bolilvia) 4. Titicaca Lake Region (Peru and Bolilvia)--Antiquities. I. Vranich, Alexei, 1968- II. Klarich, Elizabeth A., 1973- III. Stanish, Charles, 1956-
  F3319.1.T57A38 2012
  984'.12--dc23
                          2012021393


The paper used in this publication meets the requirements of the ANSI Standard Z39.48-1984 (Permanence of Paper)

# Contents

List of Illustrations — viii
List of Tables — xvi
Preface, *by Alexei Vranich, Elizabeth A. Klarich, and Charles Stanish* — xvii

1 Andean Archaeology in the Twenty-First Century — 1
   *Joyce Marcus*

2 The Earliest Ceramic Sequence at the Site of Pukara, Northern Lake Titicaca Basin — 13
   *David Oshige Adams*

3 Archaeological Excavation at Balsaspata, Ayaviri — 49
   *Henry Tantaleán*

4 Ceramic Changes and Cultural Transformations at Paucarcolla-Santa Barbara — 77
   *Ilana Johnson*

5 Variation in Corporate Architecture during the Early Middle Formative Period: New Data from Cachichupa, Northeastern Lake Titicaca Basin — 91
   *Aimée M. Plourde*

6 Scale and Diversity at Late Formative Period Pukara — 105
   *Elizabeth A. Klarich and Nancy Román Bustinza*

7 Prehispanic Carved Stones in the Northern Titicaca Basin — 121
   *Charles Stanish*

8 Spatial and Temporal Variations in Stone Raw Material Provisioning in the Chivay Obsidian Source Area — 141
   *Nicholas Tripcevich and Alex Mackay*

9 Human Skeletal Remains from Taraco, Lake Titicaca, Peru — 163
   *Francine Drayer-Verhagen*

| 10 | Ritual Use of Isla Tikonata in Northern Lake Titicaca<br>*Cecilia Chávez Justo and Charles Stanish* | *183* |
|---|---|---|
| 11 | Late Tiwanaku Mortuary Patterns in the Moquegua Drainage, Peru: Excavations at the Tumilaca la Chimba Cemetery<br>*Nicola Sharratt, Patrick Ryan Williams, María Cecilia Lozada, and Jennifer Starbird* | *193* |
| 12 | Above-Ground Tombs in the Circum-Titicaca Basin<br>*Charles Stanish* | *203* |
| 13 | The Ancient Raised Fields of the Taraco Region of the Northern Lake Titicaca Basin<br>*D. Michael Henderson* | *221* |
| 14 | The Archaeology of Northern Puno: Late Sites in Sandia and Carabaya, Peru<br>*Luis Flores Blanco, César Cornejo Maya, and Daniel Cáceda Guillén* | *265* |
| 15 | The Late Intermediate Period Occupation of Pukara, Peru<br>*Sarah J. Abraham* | *283* |
| 16 | The Development of Society and Status in the Late Prehispanic Titicaca Basin (circa AD 1000–1535)<br>*R. Alan Covey* | *299* |
| Index | | *311* |

# Contributors

Sarah J. Abraham
*University of California, Santa Barbara*

Daniel Cáceda Guillén
*Independent Investigator*

Cecilia Chávez Justo
*Proyecto Collasuyu, Puno, Peru*

César Cornejo Maya
*Independent Investigator*

R. Alan Covey
*Dartmouth University, Hanover*

Francine Drayer-Verhagen
*University of California, Santa Barbara*

Luis Flores Blanco
*Proyecto Arcaico Ramis, Puno, Peru*

D. Michael Henderson
*University of California, Los Angeles*

Ilana Johnson
*University of California, Los Angeles*

Elizabeth A. Klarich
*Smith College, Northampton*

María Cecilia Lozada
*University of Chicago, Chicago*

Alex Mackay
*The Australian National University, Canberra, Australia*

Joyce Marcus
*University of Michigan, Ann Arbor*

David Oshige Adams
*Pontificia Universidad Católica del Perú*

Aimée M. Plourde
*University College London, England*

Nancy Román Bustinza
*San Sebastián, Cusco, Peru*

Nicola Sharratt
*University of Illinois, Chicago*

Charles Stanish
*University of California, Los Angeles*

Jennifer Starbird
*University of Illinois, Chicago*

Henry Tantaleán
*University of California, Los Angeles*

Nicholas Tripcevich
*University of California, Berkeley*

Alexei Vranich
*University of California, Los Angeles*

Patrick Ryan Williams
*The Field Museum, Chicago*

# Illustrations

1.1. Map of Lake Titicaca, showing sites around the lake, *2*
1.2. Burial in Collasuyu, *6*
1.3. Reconstruction of a stone burial structure, *8*

2.1. Chronological chart for the Lake Titicaca Basin, *14*
2.2. Map with Pukara and other major Formative sites within Lake Titicaca Basin, *15*
2.3. View of front of the Qalasaya pyramid, *16*
2.4. View of sunken court excavated by Kidder and the Copesco Project, *16*
2.5. View of front of the Qalasaya pyramid with main staircase visible, *17*
2.6. Sectors of the Qalasaya pyramid, *18*
2.7. Profile of the North 44 Axis, Sector BF, *18*
2.8. Profile of the North 42 Axis, Sector BG, *19*
2.9. Plan of Sector BB, *19*
2.10. Western profile of Unit N2-3 E17-18, Sector BB, *20*
2.11. Profile of the Cross Section 4 North Sector BB, *21*
2.12. Profile of East 22 Axis, Sector BB, with profile of Unit N6-7 E23-24, *22*
2.13. Morphological classification of open vessels, *24*
2.14. Morphological classification of plates, *25*
2.15. Morphological classification of bowls (cuencos), *25*
2.16. Morphological classification of bowls (tazones), *26*
2.17. Morphological classification of closed vessels, *27*
2.18. Morphological classification of ollas, *28*
2.19. Morphological classification of jars, *29*
2.20. Bowls with painted decoration on interior, *30*
2.21. Bowls with painted and incised decoration on interior, *31*
2.22 Bowls with painted and incised decoration on interior, *31*
2.23. Vessels with painted and incised decoration on interior, *32*
2.24. Bowls with painted and incised decoration on interior, *33*
2.25. Body fragments with painted decoration on exterior, *34*
2.26. Vessels with painted decoration on exterior, *34*
2.27. Vessels with painted decoration on exterior, *35*
2.28. Vessels with painted decoration on exterior, *35*
2.29. Vessels with incised decoration on exterior, *36*
2.30. Body fragments with incised decoration on exterior, *36*
2.31. Vessels with incised decoration on exterior, *37*
2.32. Vessels with incised decoration on exterior, *37*
2.33. Body fragments with incised decoration on exterior, *38*
2.34. Body fragments with incised decoration on exterior, *38*
2.35. Vessels with incised decoration on exterior, *39*
2.36. Vessels with painted and incised decoration on exterior, *39*
2.37. Vessels with painted and incised decoration on exterior, *40*
2.38. Vessels with painted and incised decoration on exterior, *40*
2.39. Body fragments with painted and incised decoration, *41*

2.40. Body fragments with appliqué and incised decoration, *41*
2.41. Body fragments with appliqué and incised decoration, *41*
2.42. Vessels with appliqué and incised decoration, *42*
2.43. Bowls with painted decoration on interior and exterior, *42*
2.44. Bowls with painted decoration on interior and exterior, *43*
2.45. Bowl and body fragment with painted, incised, and appliqué decoration, *43*

3.1. Location of Balsaspata and other archaeological sites in the area of Ayaviri, *50*
3.2. Photo of the site at the time of excavations, September 1998, *51*
3.3. Sketch map of the site area, *51*
3.4. Unit 01, south profile, *52*
3.5. Ceramic key, *53*
3.6. Qaluyu-style Incised tazón from surface of Unit 01, *53*
3.7. Fragments of Collao-style vessels, *53*
3.8. Formative period vessels, *54*
3.9. Formative jar forms, *54*
3.10. Formative period vessels, *55*
3.11. Formative period tazones, *55*
3.12. Formative period tazones, *56*
3.13. Formative period tazones, *56*
3.14. Formative period vessels, *56*
3.15. Formative period vessels, *56*
3.16. Fragments of Qaluyu Incised, *57*
3.17. Formative tazón, *57*
3.18. Formative vessels, *57*
3.19. Formative vessels including Qaluyu Incised, *58*
3.20. Formative vessels including Qaluyu Incised, *58*
3.21. Base of Formative vessel with painted decoration, *58*
3.22. Formative vessels including Qaluyu Incised and Painted, *59*
3.23. Formative vessels, *59*
3.24. Formative vessels, *59*
3.25. Formative vessels including Qaluyu Incised, *60*
3.26. Formative vessels including Qaluyu Painted, *60*
3.27. Formative vessels including Qaluyu Incised, *60*
3.28. Formative period neckless ollas, *61*
3.29. Formative period neckless ollas and tazón base, *61*
3.30. Formative vessels including Incised and Painted Qaluyu, *61*
3.31. Formative vessels including Qaluyu, *61*
3.32. Qaluyu-style tazones, *62*
3.33. Fragments of Qaluyu Incised vessels, *62*
3.34. Formative period neckless ollas, *62*
3.35. Formative period neckless olla, *62*
3.36. Formative vessels including a neckless olla, *63*
3.37. Formative period tazones and neckless ollas, *63*
3.38. Qaluyu Painted vessels, *64*
3.39. Qaluyu-style tazón with incised decoration, *64*
3.40. Fragments of Formative vessels, *64*
3.41. Fragments of Qaluyu Incised, *65*

3.42. Formative tazones, jar and neckless olla, *65*
3.43. Fragments of Formative vessels including Qaluyu Painted and Incised, *65*
3.44. Formative tazón and two neckless ollas, *65*
3.45. Qaluyu-style tazón, *66*
3.46. Qaluyu-style tazón, *66*
3.47. Qaluyu-style tazón with incised decoration, *66*
3.48. Formative tazones with painted decoration, *67*
3.49. Qaluyu Incised vessel, *67*
3.50. Qaluyu-style tazón, *67*
3.51. View of the excavation of Unit 04, *68*
3.52. Surface fragments, *68*
3.53. Qaluyu-style tazón, *69*
3.54. Qaluyu-style fragment, *69*
3.55. Qaluyu-style vessel with painted decoration, *69*
3.56. Local Inca-style vessels, *70*
3.57. Formative vessels including Qaluyu, *70*
3.58. Formative vessels including Pukara, *71*
3.59. Formative vessels including Qaluyu Painted and Incised, *71*
3.60. Base of Unit 07, *72*
3.61. Fragments of a ceramic style called Ayacwira, *72*
3.62. Inca arybalo found at Balsaspata, *73*
3.63. Inca-style plate found at Balsaspata, *73*

4.1. Map of the Lake Titicaca Basin, *79*
4.2. Photo of the site of Paucarcolla-Santa Barbara, *80*
4.3. Formative period ceramic distribution, *82*
4.4. Qaluyu and Pucara ceramics, *83*
4.5. Possible Kalasasaya Complex, *84*
4.6. Tiwanaku ceramics, *86*
4.7. Tiwanaku period ceramic distribution, *87*
4.8. Late Intermediate period ceramic distribution, *87*
4.9. Slab-cist tomb, *88*
4.10. Inca period ceramic distribution, *88*
4.11. Inca and Sillustani-Inca ceramics, *89*

5.1. The Lake Titicaca Basin, showing selected locations, *92*
5.2. Titicaca Basin chronology, *93*
5.3. The Huancané-Putina River valley, *95*
5.4. Location of Cachichupa in the upper Huancané-Putina valley, *96*
5.5. Schematic site map of Cachichupa, *97*
5.6. Photo of Cachichupa, *98*
5.7. Support wall for Terrace K, *98*
5.8. Profile of strata in Terrace K-2, *99*
5.9. Examples of pottery recovered from K-1, *101*

6.1. Map of Lake Titicaca Basin with Formative period sites and modern towns, *106*
6.2. Regional chronology, *107*
6.3. Location of Pukara and Pucará, indicating excavated areas, *108*

6.4. Proposed limits of Pukara, *109*
6.5. Map of Pukara center and periphery, *110*
6.6. Air photo of the four survey areas from 2006, *110*
6.7. Project areas from 2000 and 2001, *111*
6.8. Data collector screen running TerraSync, and data dictionary, *112*
6.9. Zones 1 and 4 on georeferenced air photo with surface collections marked, *113*
6.10. Zone 2 on georeferenced air photo, indicating Lagunita and Northern Mounds, *114*
6.11. Zone 3 on georeferenced air photo, with surface artifact collections marked, *116*
6.12. Zone 4, view of artificial platform on Pucaorqo, *116*
6.13. Zone 4, Formative period monolith on Pucaorqo, *117*
6.14. Preliminary maximum limits of Pukara based on 2006 survey, *118*

7.1. Lake Titicaca in South America, *122*
7.2. Map of entire Titicaca Basin, *123*
7.3. Low, bulky statue found in Taraco, Peru, *124*
7.4. Slightly decorated sandstone statue, Taraco, Peru, *126*
7.5. Cornejo stela found at site TA-1039, *126*
7.6. Fragment of statue with frog motif, Taraco, *126*
7.7. Carved statue fragment dredged from river Ramis, Taraco, *126*
7.8. Possible tenon or standing statue fragment from site TA-1057, *127*
7.9. Field drawing of opposite side of statue in Figure 7.8, *127*
7.10. Two limestone monoliths on surface of site AR-1245, *127*
7.11. Smaller of two statues on AR-1245, *127*
7.12. Larger of two statues on AR-1245, *127*
7.13. Broken upright statue at Huancanewichinka near Huancané, *128*
7.14. Uncarved statue in streets of modern Taraco, Peru, *128*
7.15. Uncarved statue in streets of modern Taraco, Peru, *128*
7.16. Uncarved statue in streets of modern Putina, Peru, *128*
7.17. Uncarved statue in streets of modern Putina, Peru, *129*
7.18. Site of Qaluyu with numerous carved stones on the surface, *129*
7.19. Sunken court at the site of Machacamarca in the upper Huancané Valley, *129*
7.20. Notched, sandstone statue at Machacamarca, *129*
7.21. Close-up of notched, sandstone statue at Machacamarca, *130*
7.22. Uncarved statue in Taraco, *130*
7.23. Sunken court at AR-626, *131*
7.24. Uncarved statue at site AR-626, *131*
7.25. Close-up of uncarved statue at site AR-626, *131*
7.26. Uncarved limestone statue at site HU-521, *131*
7.27. Large uncarved statue and other carved stones at site HU-291, *132*
7.28. Uncarved statue at HU-220, *132*
7.29. Uncarved limestone statue at AR-1249, *132*
7.30. Huge, solitary limestone block shaped into a statue-like form, *132*
7.31. Close-up of block, with cupules on the surface, *132*
7.32. One of the great sunken courts at Pucara, *133*
7.33. Carved slabs in the sunken court at Pucara, *133*
7.34. The Aguirre 1 carved stone slab from site TA-934, *134*
7.35. Field drawing of the Aguirre 1 carved stone slab, *134*
7.36. The Aguirre 2 carved stone slab from site TA-934, *134*

7.37. Carved statue at the Pucara Museum, *134*
7.38. The Tacca "stela" located near TA-1047, *135*
7.39. Field drawing of the Tacca stela, *135*
7.40. Slab with opposing felines, Taraco Municipal Museum, *136*
7.41. Uncarved andesite slab in Taraco, *136*
7.42. Uncarved red sandstone slabs in plaza, Taraco, *136*
7.43. Large uncarved sandstone slabs at TA-1042, *136*
7.44. Fine-grained basalt lintel from AR-1023, *137*
7.45. The Yaya-Mama stela, Taraco Municipal Museum, *137*
7.46. The lintel from AR-1023 with foot impression, *137*
7.47. Close-up of lintel from AR-1023, *137*
7.48. Small andesite head from TA-1034, *138*
7.49. Drawing of small andesite head from TA-1034, *138*
7.50. A carved head from TA-1056, *139*
7.51. A carved limestone head from TA-1042, *139*
7.52. A large carved block at TA-725, *139*

8.1. Chivay type obsidian in the south-central Andes, *142*
8.2. Comparison of the consumption site altitudes of three major obsidian types, *143*
8.3. Chivay obsidian source showing Maymeja zone and obsidian lag, *144*
8.4. Upper Colca Project Area: 2003 intensive survey and reconnaissance blocks, *145*
8.5. Test excavations in the debris pile at the Maymeja quarry pit, *146*
8.6. Obsidian surface lag gravels east of Cerro Hornillo, *146*
8.7. Temporal charts with projectile point typology data, *147*
8.8. Temporally diagnostic artifacts by block from the Upper Colca 2003 survey, *148*
8.9. Diagnostic projectile points by survey block, *149*
8.10. Radiocarbon dates from Upper Colca 2003 test excavations, *154*
8.11. Flake metrics for obsidian from the quarry area, *155*
8.12. Cores from the Chivay source workshop and obsidian artifacts from Qillqatani, *156*
8.13. Changing morphology of complete obsidian flakes from the workshop test unit, *156*

9.1. Excavation plot showing locations of Burials 1, 2 and 3, *164*
9.2. Burials 1 and 2, *166*
9.3. Burial 3, *168*
9.4. Burial 3. Frontal view of cranium, showing broad nasal indices, *170*
9.5. Burial 3. Mandible, showing differential molar wear, *171*
9.6. Burial 3. Maxilla, showing differential molar wear, *171*
9.7. Burial 3. Lateral view of cranium, *172*

10.1. Map of Lake Titicaca showing location of Isla Tikonata, *184*
10.2. Google image of the Capachica Peninsula and precise location of Isla Tikonata, *184*
10.3. Maize growing on the east side of the island during March, *185*
10.4. The cave entrance where the mummies were found, *186*
10.5. Two of the mummies found in the cave, *186*
10.6. A typical, well-preserved basket, *187*
10.7. Tiwanaku incensario found on the eastern side of the island, *187*
10.8. Tiwanaku-style kero found on the eastern side of the island, *188*

10.9. A possible Tiwanaku- or Pucara-style puma head from an incensario, *188*
10.10. Detail of an incensario fragment found on the island, *188*
10.11. Altiplano period-style kero found on the eastern side of the island, *188*
10.12. Altiplano period-style olla found on the eastern side of the island, *189*
10.13. Altiplano period-style jars found on the eastern side of the island, *189*
10.14. Fiber cap reportedly found on this mummy, *190*
10.15. Inca-style mace head found on the island, *190*

11.1. Map of the Moquegua Valley, *194*
11.2. Site of Tumilaca la Chimba, *195*
11.3. Map of Tumilaca la Chimba, *196*
11.4. Stone-lined tomb, Tomb 4, *197*
11.5. Stone-lined tomb, Tomb 15, *197*
11.6. Partially stone-lined tomb, Tomb 24, *198*
11.7. Partially stone-lined tomb, Tomb 16, *198*
11.8. Tomb with no stone lining, Tomb 20, *198*
11.9. Tomb with no stone lining, Tomb 20, *198*
11.10. Outer rings surrounding Tombs 21 and 22, *199*
11.11. Outer rings surrounding Tombs 21 and 22, *199*
11.12. Individual facing east, Tomb 1, *200*
11.13. Kero with black and orange geometric design, Tumilaca la Chimba, *201*
11.14. Kero with depiction of stylized trophy head, Tumilaca la Chimba, *201*

12.1. The south central Andes, *204*
12.2. The Titicaca Basin, *205*
12.3. Chulpa at the site of Cutimbo, Puno, *206*
12.4. Chulpa at the site of Cutimbo, Puno, *206*
12.5. Fieldstone chulpa at the site of AR-1062, near Arapa, Peru, *206*
12.6. Large fieldstone chulpa at the site of Yacari-Tuntachawi, near Juli, *207*
12.7. Roofed chulpa from Carabaya, above Ollachea, *207*
12.8. Small chulpa in the high puna, near Mazocruz, *207*
12.9. Adobe chulpas from Sillustani, *208*
12.10. Adobe chulpa from the site of AR-1374, near Arapa, Peru, *208*
12.11. Adobe chulpa from the site of AR-1172, near Arapa, Peru, *208*
12.12. Adobe chulpa from the site of AR-1374, near Arapa, Peru, *209*
12.13. Chulpa from the site of HU-532, near Huancané, Peru, *209*
12.14. Collar tomb from the site of P-4, Otora, Peru, *210*
12.15. Large slab-cist tomb near the town of Caya Caya, Peru, *210*
12.16. Several slab-cist tombs on the site of AR-1100, near Arapa, Peru, *211*
12.17. A modest slab-cist tomb at the site of TA-706, near Taraco, Peru, *211*
12.18. Slab-cist tombs on a ridge at the site of AR-1104, near Arapa, Peru, *211*
12.19. Hillside graves in a rockshelter at the site of AR-1112, near Arapa, Peru, *212*
12.20. Hillside graves in a rockshelter at the site of AR-1112, near Arapa, Peru, *212*
12.21. The location of the Otora Valley, Peru, *214*
12.22. Sites located on survey in the Otora Valley, Peru, *215*
12.23. Site of P-8 with three collar tombs located next to a cluster of rooms, *216*
12.24. Modern cemetery from the Mazocruz area, *217*

13.1. Lake Titicaca region showing the district and town of Taraco, *222*
13.2. View looking south across the alluvial plain, *224*
13.3. Contemporary sod block structures found throughout the alluvial plain, *224*
13.4. Satellite image of the Taraco region showing major geographical features, *225*
13.5. Annual rainfall statistics for the Tararco region for the period 1964–2006, *226*
13.6. Annual flow for the Río Ramis near Tararco from 1956 to 2006, *227*
13.7. Massive levee located alongside Río Ramis near the town of Taraco, *227*
13.8. Three views of raised fields around Taraco district, *229*
13.9. Enlargements of an aerial photo showing contemporary fields scanned with three different scan densities, *231*
13.10. Aerial photos of a typical region of relict raised fields, *232*
13.11. Examples of relict raised fields, *233*
13.12. Terrain features that meet the criteria for relict raised fields, *234*
13.13. Identifying relict fields in highly disturbed areas, *234*
13.14. Relict raised fields north of Río Ramis, identified with high confidence, *236*
13.15. Enlargement of region showing raised field patterns within individual qochas, *237*
13.16. Relict raised fields south of Río Ramis, *238*
13.17. Photograph of author among very large raised fields, *239*
13.18. Comparison between wavelength characteristics of inland and lakeshore fields, *239*
13.19. Enlargement of photo of fields showing the close spatial relationship of small and large wavelength components, *240*
13.20. Composite map showing the location of major hydrological features, *241*
13.21. Identified relic raised field areas overlaid on map of hydrological features, *242*
13.22. Evidence of meander scarring in three different areas around Taraco, *244*
13.23. Evidence of natural watercourses that once flowed across the alluvial plain, *245*
13.24. Canals in use today in controlling the runoff from Cerro Imarocus, *245*
13.25. Comparison between deeper Qocha Camilaca and shallower Qocha Quechuata in the dry season, *246*
13.26. Aerial photograph of the area below Cerro Imarocus showing major canals, *247*
13.27. Two views of Canal Ramis, *248*
13.28. Offshore canals supplied by Canal Ramis, *249*
13.29. Occupation sites identified around Taraco, *251*
13.30. Flow chart of hydrological calculations, *252*
13.31. Calculation of seasonal rainfall runoff for the Granja Salcedo region, *254*
13.32. Precipitation and runoff in the Taraco region, *254*
13.33. Estimated area of raised fields supplied by runoff from Cerro Imarocus, *255*
13.34. Elevation profile of levees alongside Río Ramis at the location of Canal Ramis, *257*
13.35. The normal discharge of Río Ramis at Puente Ramis, *257*
13.36. Aerial photo showing entrance of Río Ramis into the lake, *259*

14.1. Location map of the sites registered in Carabaya and Sandia, *266*
14.2. Plan of Maukallacta, *268*
14.3. Circular structures (chulpas) in Maukallacta, *268*
14.4. Quadrangular structures with niches in Maukallacta, *269*
14.5. Plan of Chunchulacalloc, *269*
14.6. Semi-subterranean structure in Chunchulacalloc, *270*
14.7. Quadrangular structure in Chunchulacalloc, *271*
14.8. Complex of chulpas in Huancasayan, *272*
14.9. Plan of Colocolo, *272*
14.10. View of a pair of structures in Colocolo, *273*
14.11. Photograph of archaeological material in Municipal Museum of Usicayos, *274*
14.12. Panoramic view of Quilli-Quilli covered with grass, *275*
14.13. Plan of Chichaccori, *275*
14.14. One of the chullpas at Chichaccori, *276*
14.15. Quadrangular structure in Chichaccori, *277*
14.16. Plan of Pitumarka, *278*
14.17. General view of the lower sector at Pitumarka, *278*
14.18. Plan of Marka Marka III, *279*
14.19. View of the entrance at Marka Marka III, *280*

15.1. Map showing location of Block 1 in relation to Kalasaya and other sites, *286*
15.2. Block 1 showing architectural subdivisions, *287*
15.3. Profile of Collao wall in Block 1, *287*
15.4. Collao bowls, *288*
15.5. Collao jars, *289*
15.6. Collao Black on Red bowls, *290*
15.7. Collao Black on Red jars, *291*
15.8. Collao pottery: rim tics and punctates, *291*
15.9. Asillo pottery, *292*
15.10. Transitional period bowls, *293*
15.11. Transitional period jars, *293*
15.12. Bowl rim diameter distribution, *294*

16.1. The Titicaca Basin, *301*
16.2. Altiplano period ceramic styles, *302*
16.3. Major pukara locations, *303*
16.4. Important Inka sites, *306*
16.5. Inka period local ceramic styles, *307*

# Tables

2.1. Distribution of wares by strata, Sector BB, *46*
2.2. Distribution of wares by strata, Sector BF, Platform 2, *46*
2.3. Distribution of wares by strata, Sector BF, Platform 3, *46*
2.4. Distribution of wares by strata, Sector BG, Platform 3, *46*

5.1. Summary of radiocarbon dates from Terrace K, *99*

8.1. Obsidian is prevalent in surface collections from all three survey blocks, *154*
8.2. Obsidian: clear and with inclusions, by survey block, *154*

9.1. Comparison of cranial indices, *169*
9.2. Molar wear comparison with other Altiplano groups, *170*
9.3. Comparison of molar wear differentials with other Altiplano groups, *170*

13.1. Comparison of three aerial photographic surveys of northern Lake Titicaca, *230*
13.2. Summary of relict raised field areas, specifying water source and delivery means, *250*
13.3. Hydraulic parameters for Canal Ramis for assumed flow heights, *256*

15.1. Surface treatment by ceramic type, *288*
15.2. Temporal distribution of the Pukara ceramic assemblage, *295*
15.3. Distribution of vessel forms by ceramic types, *295*
15.4. Temporal distribution of vessel forms, *295*

16.1. Major Titicaca Basin survey regions, with site counts for Tiwanaku, Altiplano, and Inka period occupations, *301*

# Preface
*by Alexei Vranich, Elizabeth A. Klarich, and Charles Stanish*

The purpose of the Advances in Titicaca Basin Archaeology series is to provide a peer-reviewed publication venue for empirical studies in the circum-Titicaca region. Advances I was published in 2005; Advances II is in press and will come out shortly. The present volume, Advances III, is a collection of research papers providing theoretically-informed data from archaeological research from the northern Titicaca Basin region and western slopes of the south central Andes. This book complements Advances II, which focuses on the southern Titicaca area. We defined the circum-Titicaca region in Chapter 1 of Advances I and continue to use that definition. This region is defined as the area of maximum distribution of Tiwanaku objects over the south central Andes, from roughly San Pedro de Atacama in the south to the Arequipa area in the north, and east into the Carabaya and Larecaja regions.

We are pleased to present this new collection of empirical research from the northern Titicaca region here in Advances III. Our fieldwork continues, and these reports contribute to the canon of irreplaceable archeological knowledge of this impressive region. These data are not only invaluable in and of themselves as testimony to the rich cultural history of the region and the people who created it, but also add to our knowledge of this region where archaic chiefdoms and states formed, collapsed and reformed. As such, these data add to our comparative database of archaeology as a comparative behavioral and social science.

We thank many people for the help and advice. We particularly thank Joyce Marcus, Director of the Museum of Anthropology at the University of Michigan, and a longtime friend, for her help, counsel and work on this book. Jill Rheinheimer of the Museum of Anthropology Publications shepherded the manuscript through its many phases and produced an outstanding product, for which we are very grateful.

We also thank our colleagues at UCLA and Smith College for their support over the years and the many participants in our field projects over the last two decades. A number of foundations and individuals have sponsored our research. We gratefully acknowledge the National Science Foundation, the Cotsen Endowments at UCLA, the Wenner-Gren Foundation, the Howard Heinz Endowment for Archaeological Field Research in Latin America, the Dumbarton Oaks Research Library, the Centro de Investigación de Arqueología Andina (CIARA) and the National Endowment for the Humanities. Individual donors include Charles Steinmetz, Deborah Arnold, Harris Bass, and David Boochever. The help of all is greatly appreciated.

# Chapter 1

# Andean Archaeology in the Twenty-First Century

*Joyce Marcus*

Twenty years ago, the University of Michigan announced a job opening for a Great Lakes archaeologist. One memorable applicant asserted, "I work near a *great* lake, indeed one of the greatest." As it turned out, he was referring to Lake Titicaca. Unfortunately for him, Michigan was seeking someone who worked near Lakes Michigan, Ontario, Huron, Superior, and Erie.

Other than his desire to get a job, why did that enterprising applicant consider Titicaca a *great* lake? Well, it lies at 3812 m (12,530 ft), making it one of the highest and coldest large bodies of water in the world. It is one of the deepest, with a maximum depth of 281 m. It has one of the longest shorelines of any lake (1125 km). Most importantly, that superficially inhospitable high-altitude environment supported a long developmental sequence that climaxed in impressive villages, towns, and cities (see Fig. 1.1).

## The Years of Exploration

Like today's archaeologists, the early explorers—whether European or American—were fascinated by the Titicaca Basin's ability to support farming, dense populations, and large settlements such as Qaluyu, Taraco, and Pukara (north of the lake) and Chiripa, Lukurmata, and Tiwanaku (south of the lake). The first Europeans who arrived in the region were part of Francisco Pizarro's conquering army. Popular interest surged in the nineteenth century when naturalist Alexander von Humboldt reported on the Titicaca area. He wrote about the landscape, geology, and natural resources.

Humboldt was followed by Ephraim George Squier, whose monumental work *Peru: Incidents of Travel and Exploration in the Land of the Incas* (1877) included drawings of Tiwanaku's buildings, monuments, and carved stones, the great Inka ruins near Hatuncolla, and the monuments on the Islands of the Sun and Moon (Julien 1983; Bauer and Stanish 2001; Stanish and Bauer 2004). Multiple generations of naturalists and archaeologists—including Alexander Agassiz, Max Uhle, Weston La Barre, Adolph Bandelier, Wendell C. Bennett, Stig Rydén, Arturo Posnansky, Alfred Kidder II, Luis Valcárcel, Carlos Ponce Sanginés, Gregorio Cordero Miranda, Luis Lumbreras, David Browman, Karen Mohr Chávez, Sergio Chávez, Alan Kolata, Catherine Julien, Clark Erickson, Oswaldo Rivera Sundt, Elías Mujica, Juan Albarracin Jordan, John Hyslop, Eduardo Pareja, Mario Núñez, Rolando Paredes, Max Portugal, Johan Reinhard, Brian Bauer, Mark Aldenderfer, Charles Stanish, Christine Hastorf, Marc Bermann, John Janusek, Elizabeth Klarich, Nathan Craig, Cecilia Chávez, and Elizabeth Arkush—have added to our understanding of the region.

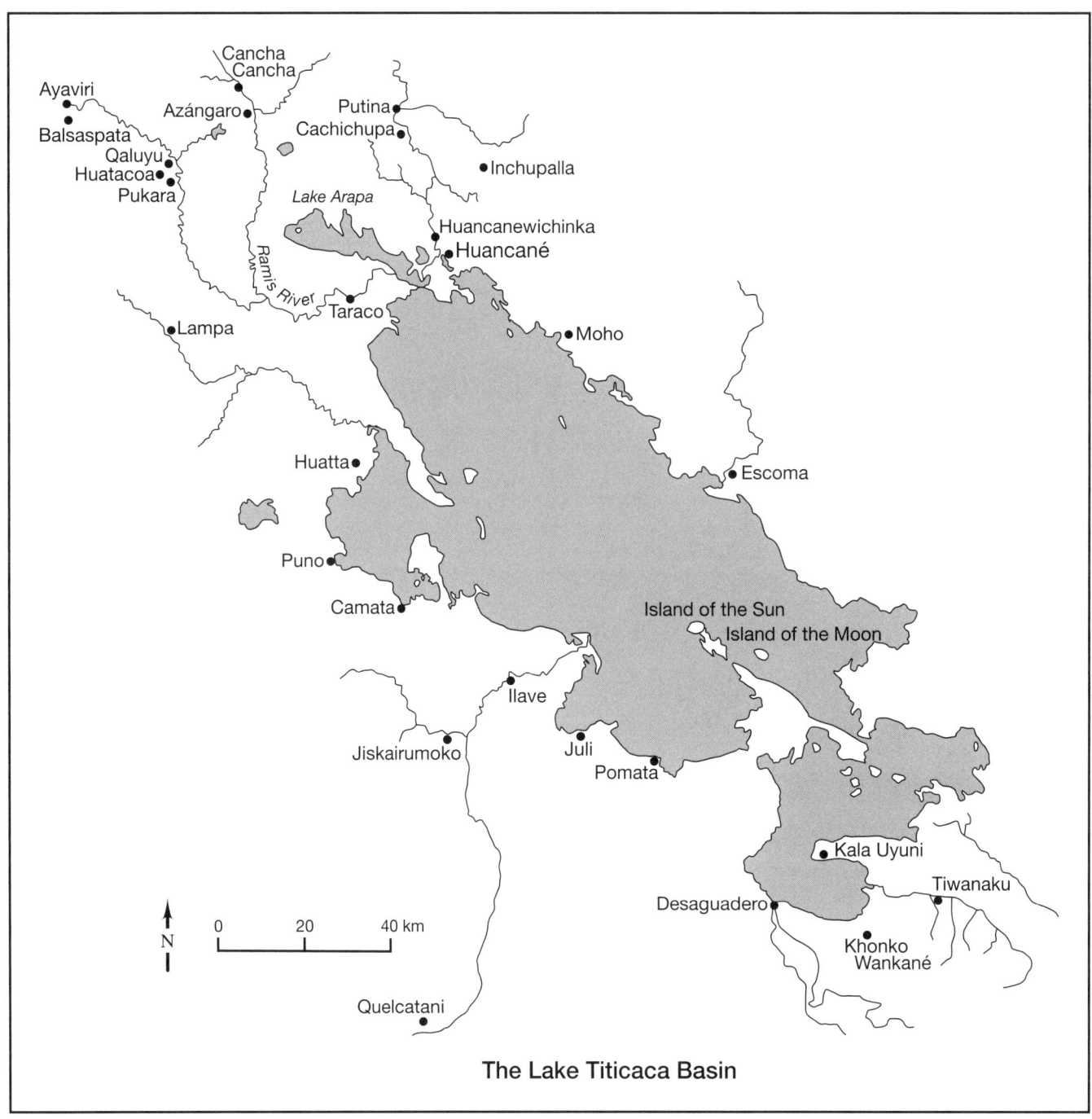

Figure 1.1. Map of Lake Titicaca, showing sites around the lake (adapted from Stanish and Bauer 2004: Fig. 1.3).

## The Northern Titicaca Basin

The focus of this volume is the northern Titicaca Basin, an area occupied by the dominant Colla ethnic group. The quarter of the Inka Empire called Collasuyu, in fact, drew its name from the Colla (Rostworowski and Morris 1999; Rowe 1946). The recent explosion of archaeological projects in the Titicaca Basin—an area covering more than 50,000 km$^2$—is reflected in the data-packed chapters of this book. These new data will not only advance our understanding of sociopolitical evolution within the Titicaca Basin, but in areas well beyond Peru and Bolivia.

The Titicaca Basin shows continuous occupation from the Early Archaic period onward (Aldenderfer 1989; Cipolla 2005; Klink and Aldenderfer 2005). Every period is becoming better known as a result of the flurry of recent surveys and excavations (e.g., Arkush 2005a; Bandy 2001; Cohen 2010; Klarich 2005; Plourde 2006; Stanish 2011; Stanish and Levine 2011; Tantaleán 2008).

For millennia prior to 1500 BC, the Titicaca Basin was home to hunting and gathering societies, people who hunted deer and wild camelids and an array of small animals. They also fished in the lake and gathered edible wild plants, as well as *Scirpus*, canes, and reeds from around the lake. Even after agriculture took hold in the basin, subsistence strategies probably involved a mix of hunting, herding, and gathering along with the increased reliance on domestic plants and animals.

By 1300 BC one can see the beginnings of rank society in the northern Titicaca Basin (Cohen 2010; Plourde 2006). Among the largest Middle Formative sites in the northern basin were Qaluyu and Cancha Cancha (see Fig. 1.1). The numerous stone stelae at these sites first attracted the attention of archaeologists.

Some Middle Formative centers ultimately became large Late Formative political centers, featuring stone enclosures called sunken courts (Cohen 2010). They seem to have hosted ceremonies that attracted people from smaller villages in the area. The villagers of this era do not seem to have been overly concerned with defense. We infer this from their non-defensible settlement locations and from the lack of any evidence of conflict in their skeletal remains or the scenes they painted.

At about 500 BC this era of peaceful village life seems to have ended. We see new themes on carved stone stelae, textiles, and ceramics that indicate a bellicose era, a time when leaders began to be admired for military prowess. Depictions of trophy heads appeared in the northern Titicaca Basin (Arnold and Hastorf 2008), and excavations in one sunken court yielded the actual trophy skulls. The movement of communities to defensible localities suggests elevated levels of warfare.

Major centers with sunken courts include Taraco, Pukara, Balsaspata, Qaluyu, Cancha Cancha, Arapa, and Huancanewichinka (see Fig. 1.1). Stanish and Levine (2011) have identified several political centers—including Taraco and Pukara—that competed for domination of the northern Titicaca region during the latter part of the first millennium BC. Both Taraco and Pukara reached at least 100 ha. Eventually, a high-status residential sector at Taraco was burned, after which its population and economic activity dropped precipitously. Coincident with the burning of the high-status sector at Taraco came the rise of Pukara, making it plausible that the latter community was the aggressor. Pukara's apparent victory over Taraco ultimately led to the former's new position as the capital of a regional polity. Pukara then embarked on a program of territorial expansion, subjugating and incorporating populations up to 100 km distant.

This Andean scenario is similar to one detected earlier in Mexico's Oaxaca Valley, providing us with an invaluable comparative perspective. Roughly 2500 years ago the Oaxaca Valley was occupied by at least three rank societies, seemingly in conflict with each other. To the north lay San José Mogote. To the south lay San Martín Tilcajete. To the east lay Yegüih. Despite differences in population, none of these rank societies were able to subjugate their rivals; the three therefore left a sparsely occupied buffer zone between the territories each controlled (Marcus and Flannery 1996). Periodically, however, they burned each other's temples or used stone monuments to portray the sacrifice of enemy leaders.

At roughly 500 BC the leaders of San José Mogote acted decisively to gain an advantage. Gathering up at least 2000 people from their paramount center and many of its satellite villages, the leaders of San José Mogote moved to the summit of a mountain located in the buffer zone (Marcus 2008a). On the more easily climbed slopes, the new arrivals began to build 3 km of defensive walls. They were in the act of creating the largest nucleated community in the valley and turning it into a stronghold from which they could launch attacks on their rivals.

Some 200 years after its founding, this community had grown to 5000 people. The mountaintop center ultimately became Oaxaca's first city, which we now call Monte Albán (Blanton 1978; Marcus 2008a, 2009).

We know a lot about Monte Albán's conflicts with San Martín Tilcajete, a rival chiefly center (Redmond and Spencer 2012; Spencer and Redmond 2001a, 2001b, 2004, 2006). Tilcajete's response to the population growth of Monte Albán was to double in size. Nevertheless, about 2280 years ago, Monte Albán attacked Tilcajete and torched the buildings on Tilcajete's plaza. Tilcajete refused to capitulate. Between 2250 and 2000 years ago, Tilcajete increased in size again and moved its plaza uphill to an even more defensible ridge. Tilcajete also added defensive walls to its most easily climbed slopes.

Monte Albán was prepared for a long campaign. Its leaders concentrated thousands of farmers, craftsmen and warriors into a ring of 155 satellite villages, most within a half-day's walk of Monte Albán. Eventually Monte Albán attacked Tilcajete again, burning its major temple and its ruler's palatial multiroom residence. Tilcajete did not recover from this second attack. The site was abandoned and on a mountaintop not far away, its conquerors built an administrative center linked to Monte Albán. By this point in time, Monte Albán appears to have subdued the entire Valley of Oaxaca and turned its former rivals into the political subjects of a first-generation state. During this same period,

Monte Albán carved a series of stone monuments that reflected its military unification of the valley (Marcus and Flannery 1996).

One of the most important structures was on the west side of Monte Albán's plaza; its façade was covered with a display of slain enemies analogous to those at Cerro Sechín in the Casma Valley of northern Peru (Marcus 2007; Samaniego et al. 1985; Tello 1956). The largest of these 300 carved stones depicted sprawling corpses, some with evidence of decapitation, heart removal, or genital mutilation. A few of the smaller stones showed severed heads. Some monuments included the hieroglyphic names of important victims.

## The Chronology of the Titicaca Basin

Archaeologists who work in poorly known regions often spend years trying to establish a reliable chronology. The early archaeologists who worked in the Titicaca Basin were no different. While today's chronology is more reliable, Chapter 2 of this volume shows that refinements are still being made. Here, David Oshige Adams reports on his refinements using the unstudied collections of the Pukara museum. He combines his own analysis with information from the work of Cecilia Chávez (2008), John Rowe and Catherine Brandel (1971), Lee Steadman (1995), and others.

In addition to Oshige Adams' refinement of the Pukara chronology, various chapters show renewed attention to the households and social organization of Formative period settlements. Formative period population in the northern Titicaca Basin increases significantly at key sites, such as Qaluyu and Pukara, as well as at some satellite sites (Kidder 1943; Klarich 2005). Later in Tiwanaku times and during the Late Intermediate period, there is also evidence for significant population increase. During the Late Horizon, there is a massive Inka presence throughout the northern Titicaca Basin.

In Chapter 3 Henry Tantaleán reports on his excavations at Balsaspata (also known as Pueblo Libre), a site near Ayaviri (see Fig. 1.1). Occupation there begins at 1500 BC, when the local population was still using Archaic projectile points along with early Qaluyu pottery. This settlement seems to be contemporaneous with nearby Qaqachupa, a site located just across the Ayaviri River. Of great significance are the raised fields discovered near Balsaspata. Their early date confirms Erickson's (1987, 1988) and Stanish's (1994, 2003) suspicion that raised fields were in use as early as the Qaluyu period. At Balsaspata, Tantaleán recovered pottery similar to Marcavalle pottery (Mohr Chávez 1977), as well as obsidian from the Chivay source in Arequipa.

Given that Balsaspata is located between Cusco (to the north) and Lake Titicaca (to the south), it is not surprising that this site shows contact with, and influence from, both areas. The Formative occupants at Balsaspata built stone buildings with walls made from large cut blocks, similar to those discovered by Amanda Cohen (2010:150–57) at Huatacoa, a site in the lower Ayaviri Valley (Fig. 1.1). Local villagers digging at Balsaspata also discovered a stela carved in Pukara style. As suggested by Tantaleán and Pérez Maestro (1999), this Pukara-style stela probably reflects a religious iconography shared by many communities.

In Chapter 4 Ilana Johnson discusses the Formative period at the site of Paucarcolla-Santa Barbara. Although Paucarcolla-Santa Barbara never became a major center in the northern basin, it was an important node on the ancient road that linked the eastern and western cordilleras, and a key locale for monitoring long-distance trade. Johnson suggests that the earliest elites at Paucarcolla-Santa Barbara relied on alliances with other elites to maintain and increase their high status, and that such connections enabled elites to participate in an emergent ideology and to gain access to exotic goods (and see Plourde 2005). Changes in ceramic styles apparently reveal changing inter-elite affiliations and shifts in trading partners.

During the Middle and Late Formative periods, these elite evidently did not have the ability to coerce people to nucleate, so they used persuasion and gifts to attract followers to their religious events and to join their social groups. The inducements offered to loyal followers included exotic trade goods, reliable security and protection, and the chance to participate in religious rites and feasts.

Even though there is evidence throughout the Titicaca Basin that status was enhanced through competition, warfare, and the taking of trophy heads, the enduring control of subject peoples and places was successfully sustained and reinforced by having subject communities participate in ceremonial and religious rites. By giving feasts in which exotic goods and intoxicating substances were generously given to commoners, elites kept their followers content. This, of course, anticipated later Inka practices.

Long-distance exchange was one source of the goods given to commoners. As noted by Stanish and Levine (2011), both trade and war led to high levels of in-group cooperation and brought in outside resources that fueled a cycle of internal faction building as well as territorial expansion.

In Chapter 5 Aimée Plourde reports on Cachichupa in the Putina Valley, a site that has a series of terraces overlooking sunken courts below (Fig. 1.1). She gives us a good view of the corporate architecture of the Middle Formative. The settlement at Cachichupa, which lies along the road leading to the tropics, was in a good position to monitor the movement of resources to and from the highlands. Plourde provides a model for the formation of urbanism: the act of creating terraces was a labor-intensive strategy to concentrate labor (and later houses) into a single location. Data from excavations at Cachichupa provide some novel insights into the timing and character of corporate architecture during the Formative period.

The terraces at Cachichupa may constitute the earliest monumental terracing in the Titicaca Basin, predating the platform complexes seen on the Taraco Peninsula and the monumental terracing known from the site of Pukara. The precociousness of corporate architecture in the Huancané-Putina Valley suggests that processes of increasing collective action and politico-religious activities began much earlier in the northern basin than previously thought.

In Chapter 6 Elizabeth Klarich and Nancy Román Bustinza summarize their recent work at Pukara itself. Their mapping and survey provide the first systematic effort to determine the site's limit, as well as the extent of its habitation and ceremonial areas. Previous estimates of Pukara have ranged from 1.5 km² to 6 km². Learning that Pukara was 2.0 km² at its height is important, because its large size has implications for understanding social evolution and the rise of urbanism in the Titicaca region. Indeed, Pukara appears to be the same size as Tiwanaku at this time.

An earlier generation tended to focus on the carved stone monuments at Pukara, Taraco, Arapa, and Hatunqolla. The systematic surveys conducted in the region over the last two decades have located many new monuments. Those discoveries indicate an even greater variety of carving styles than formerly appreciated.

In Chapter 7 Stanish lays the groundwork for a typology of carved stones for the Titicaca Basin as a whole. Not surprisingly, the two traditional centers of complex culture—the southern Tiwanaku/Huatta area and the northern Huancané/Juliaca area—contain the greatest number of carved stones. Most monuments were originally associated with hilltop sites and sunken courts; monuments, however, were captured by victorious political groups, who brought them to their respective political centers.

In Chapter 8, Nicholas Tripcevich and Alex Mackay provide an important analysis of obsidian from the Chivay source near Arequipa. This source is now considered to yield the finest obsidian and it was, not surprisingly, widely sought and highly valued. In Chapter 9 Francine Drayer-Verhagen provides the first analysis of human remains from excavated contexts from the Late Formative at the site of Taraco.

In Chapter 10 Cecilia Chávez and Charles Stanish introduce us to the Island of Tikonata near the Capachica Peninsula and the Island of Amantaní. People now living on the island have found ancient caves with mummies and Tiwanaku pottery, and this chapter describes the mummies in some detail.

In Chapter 11 we read about the Tumilaca la Chimba cemetery in the Moquegua Valley of southern Peru. The authors of this chapter—Nicola Sharratt, Patrick Ryan Williams, María Cecilia Lozada, and Jennifer Starbird—present a bioarchaeological analysis of a Middle Horizon cemetery. For millennia the Moquegua region was closely tied to the large polities controlling the Titicaca region. Though the cemetery has been looted and damaged by irrigation, Sharratt et al. salvage key information that contributes to our understanding of the Tiwanaku polity before and after it collapsed.

Stanish deals with Titicaca Basin burial traditions in Chapter 12. For millennia throughout the south-central Andes, local people were burying their dead in tombs below ground. Beginning around the third century BC, some highland people experimented with above-ground earthen tumuli, an initially rare practice that continued for many centuries. Around the twelfth century AD, larger numbers of people began to bury their ancestors in above-ground stone tombs. Stanish synthesizes the survey data from the northern Titicaca Basin, then combines them with data from above-ground tombs in the Titicaca region and excavations in a *chullpa* in the Moquegua region.

It is now evident that placing burials above ground began in the Late Formative, long before Tiwanaku expanded. During Tiwanaku times the use of above-ground tombs appears to have been restricted to elite individuals, perhaps the political and religious elite. The use of above-ground tombs actually increased after the collapse of Tiwanaku. The available data indicate that cists, collar tombs, and stone chullpas were burial structures that usually contained multiple interments. The chullpas are best interpreted as the burial locales of corporate groups that emerged after Tiwanaku took control of the area.

Chullpas varied considerably in architectural style, but the essential principle behind chullpa building remained constant: above-ground tombs became a locus of offerings and ritual performances, a place where corporate groups could continue to communicate with their ancestors (Fig. 1.2). The presence of doors and wall niches in chullpas suggests that (unlike below-ground cist tombs) chullpas were designed for ongoing ceremonial use. They witnessed the insertion of new interments, a practice similar to that documented for the Zapotec of the Valley of Oaxaca, Mexico. The Zapotec are known to have reopened family tombs or mausolea on multiple occasions to add new family members (Marcus 2006, 2008b). The relationship between the Zapotec living and dead could continue without interruption so long as the descendants of nobles held up their end of the bargain. Noble descendants had a vested interest in asserting genealogical ties. The descendants placed vessels with beverages near the tomb entrance, where the names and images of their ancestors were placed. Communicating with one's ancestors by keeping their tombs accessible was important for the Maya as well. For example, following the death of a royal woman at the city of Copán, Honduras, the Maya kept her tomb open. When they revisited her tomb, they covered her skeleton with bright red cinnabar and placed new offerings with her.

In Peru, the traditional below-ground cist tombs were used for one event and then permanently covered, often sealed under a floor or placed in a cemetery. Stanish convincingly shows that the development of above-ground tombs in the south-central Andes is best understood as part of larger political and cultural processes operating in the region after the retreat of the Tiwanaku expansionist state.

The more humble above-ground tombs marked areas on the landscape to which corporate groups could periodically return, reaffirming their social ties with the ancestors. Some scholars have interpreted these tombs as ayllu-based reactions to supra-community pressures, particularly those of the state. For his part, Stanish shares Paul Goldstein's view: that the chullpa phenomenon was a way in which newly-emergent societies of the post-Tiwanaku era drew on earlier elite burial practices in order to establish links across political units and cultural space. Goldstein (2005) notes that the spread of post-Tiwanaku collared tombs represents the appearance of status markers used by a local elite in the face of state collapse. These practices were clearly centered

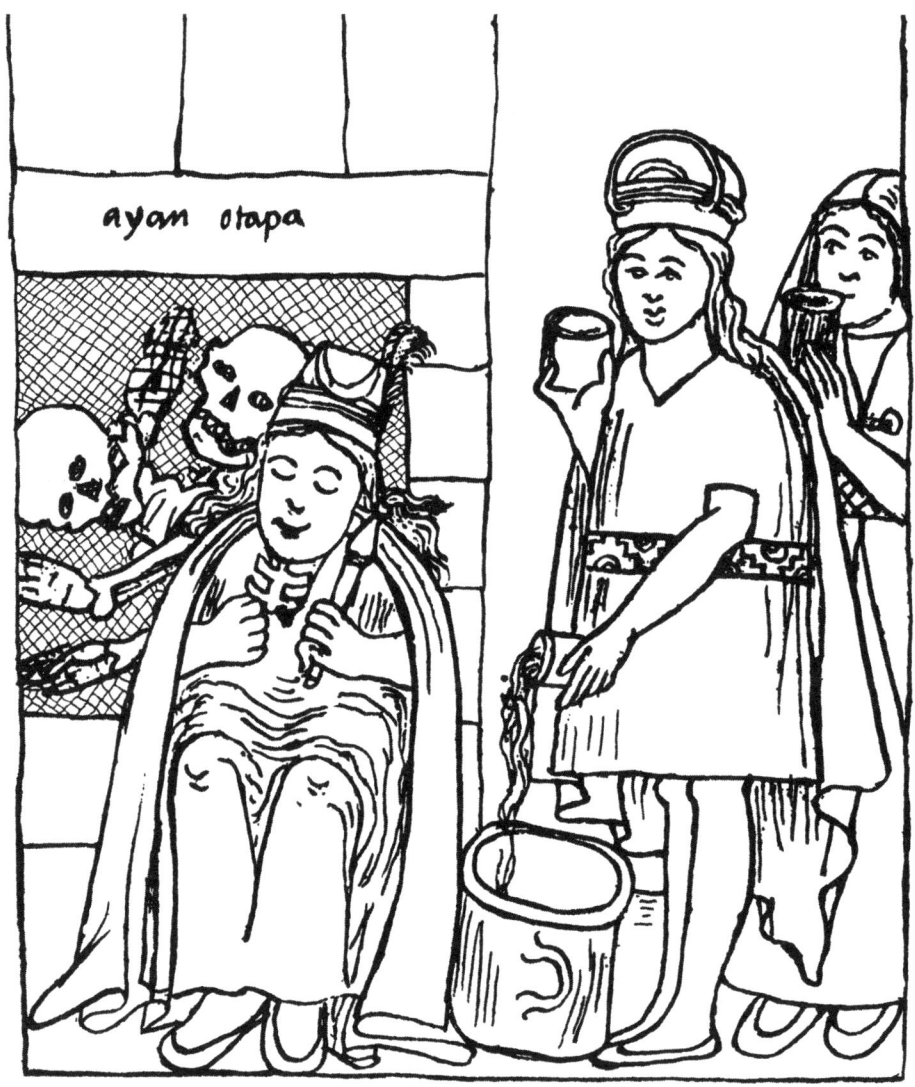

Figure 1.2. Burial in Collasuyu, showing the stone structure where bones of the deceased were buried. It also shows the attendees who offered maize beer in rites commemorating the recently deceased person shown in seated position (redrawn from Guaman Poma de Ayala 1980:268–69).

on ancestor worship, as the dead were constantly revisited and the tombs were reopened to witness new rites and offerings.

The post-Tiwanaku political landscape may be viewed as one in which smaller political units sought to reestablish regional exchange alliances after the collapse of a state system. From this perspective, chullpas represent a status-validation marker for prominent lineage heads seeking to establish regional exchange. The mutual adoption of similar above-ground burial practices can be understood as one means of reinforcing new alliance systems between emergent elite lineages, most likely by drawing on, and intensifying, the tradition of ancestor worship by prominent families.

Tiwanaku remains occur on several islands in Lake Titicaca. The largest and most famous are the Islands of the Sun and Moon (Bauer and Stanish 2001; Stanish and Bauer 2004). Numerous residential sites and ceremonial centers are known. The pilgrimage centers on the Islands of the Sun and Moon were first established during Tiwanaku times. The associated ceramic assemblages had a number of incense burners and finely made drinking beakers or *keros*.

Other islands in the lake have Tiwanaku remains. Included are Pariti, Amantaní, Khoa, Isla Estéves in the Puno Bay, Isla Paco or Suriqui, and possibly Isla Soto. Late Intermediate and Inka period remains are also found on these islands, plus a number of others such as Taquile, Amantaní, and some smaller islands such as Pallalla and Chuyu near the Island of the Sun.

It is significant that Tikonata does not have any chullpas. Tiwanaku evidently created a series of ceremonial sites on some islands as part of a ritual pilgrimage circuit. These pilgrimages may connect to the Andean duality called *uma* and *urco*, a concept the Titicaca peoples still believed in at the time of Spanish conquest (Bouysse-Cassagne 1986).

The fact that maize could be grown on the Islands of the Sun, Pariti, Amantaní, and Tikonata is significant. Maize grown on these islands was considered sacred during the Inka period, and this may have been true of earlier periods as well. The procurement of sacred maize would be one reason to visit Tikonata. Another reason might be the belief that these islands were sacred places to be visited during ritual pilgrimage circuits. Such visits might explain the burning of incense and the consumption of maize beer in keros. Stanish and Chávez suggest that some Tiwanaku elite chose to be buried on Tikonata, Pariti, or the Island of the Sun.

Burial customs also varied in each quarter (*suyu*) of the Inka Empire. Felipe Guaman Poma de Ayala describes the burial practices of each quarter—Chinchaysuyu, Antisuyu, Collasuyu, and Cuntisuyu—as well as those reserved for the Inka emperor himself (Guaman Poma de Ayala 1980:262–71). For Collasuyu, he says that burial rites took place five days after death. If the individual was rich, the deceased was richly dressed, placed in a seated position, and given vessels of gold, silver, and pottery. If the individual was poor, abundant food was offered. To mourn and to celebrate the life of the deceased, the living came back after ten days to offer food and liquid, especially corn beer and water. As was the case with the Zapotec (mentioned earlier in this chapter), the commemorative funerary rites conducted in Collasuyu were performed in front of the tomb. In this quarter of the Inka Empire, the rites were repeated after six months and again after one year (Fig. 1.2).

In Chapter 13 Michael Henderson analyzes the distribution of raised fields in the Taraco area, presenting new data from the first extensive survey of such relict fields. He combines aerial photos from 1970 with digital scanning techniques available today, and is able to identify raised fields across a much larger area.

Prior to Henderson's survey, the Taraco area was not recognized as a major location for raised field agriculture, in contrast to the extensive areas of fields near Juliaca, Pomata, Tiwanaku, Catari, and Desaguadero. This lack of recognition was due to the high rainfall levels in the region that left groundwater that obscured the fields. Also, the higher erosion rates in this area obscured many of the fields in low-altitude photographs. Henderson's data force us to reevaluate our understanding of the role of raised field agriculture in the rise of the state. Earlier theories held that the raised fields were associated with major states capable of managing complex engineering tasks. Henderson's data, however, suggest that raised fields came into being much earlier and were used throughout the cultural sequence, up to the point at which they became unusable due to climatic change.

Our understanding of the size and complexity of the water management system around Taraco is increased by Henderson. He examined hydraulic features on the alluvial plain (river courses, canals, meander scars, and *qochas*) using aerial photographs, satellite imagery, ground surveys, and interviews with local farmers, the result being that a new picture of the canals and natural watercourses has emerged. For example, we can now see similarities between the Ramis canal around Taraco and the Waña Jawira canal around Tiwanaku.

The new information on ancient raised field farming and water resource management will certainly contribute to ongoing research on the evolution of sociopolitical complexity. The idea that raised fields played a central role in the formation and maintenance of the archaic state had become received wisdom. Henderson's work will revitalize the debate about the role of raised fields by providing new data from aerial photography, as well as actual calculations of labor effort and the distribution of water.

In Chapter 14 Luis Flores Blanco, César Cornejo Maya, and Daniel Cáceda Guillén report on the North Basin survey carried out in Sandia and Carabaya in the lower elevations of the Department of Puno. The Toledo *Tasa* of 1572 (Toledo 1975) asserts that towns in the region were required to provide gold, presumably from this region's eastern slopes. The towns of the northern Titicaca region are said to have provided fish, cloth, wool, chuño and other commodities.

It is noteworthy that towns such as Taraco, Samán, and Azángaro were required to provide maize. Maize normally does not grow well in the highland region surrounding the lake, except on islands such as Island of the Sun, Amantaní and Tikonata.

In Chapter 15, Sarah Abraham describes the Late Intermediate period at the site of Pukara, using ceramic and architectural data. This period appears to last longer in the north than does the Late Intermediate period in the south, for reasons that remain to be explained.

In Chapter 16, R. Alan Covey reviews settlement patterns, architectural forms, burial patterns, production and trade from the period of the Tiwanaku collapse to the eve of the Spanish Conquest. Covey focuses on the manner in which social relations expand and contract as a means of both risk management and reaction to foreign incursion. He shows that from AD 1000 to 1535, the Titicaca region experienced a widespread rejection of state institutions and the local accommodation and opportunistic handling of foreign rule. At the time of the European invasion the Titicaca Basin was one of the wealthiest provinces, and its imperial administrators and local elites were responsible for managing camelid herds and labor tribute (Murra 1956).

Inka site planning is documented for the largest administrative centers in the Titicaca Basin, clustered in the Colla and Lupaqa territories (Hyslop 1976, 1977, 1990; Murra 1956). At 50 to 80 ha, the largest Inka sites (Hatunqolla and Chucuito) are substantially larger than earlier sites and exhibit the kind of central planning that is absent in previous periods. While little architecture remains at the largest sites, researchers have noted the presence of formally laid out plaza spaces and principal roadways, establishing a new urban grid. Storage structures, typically present at Inka administrative centers, are not well documented for Inka sites in the Titicaca Basin. However, storehouses have been identified on the hillside above Hatunqolla (Hyslop 1990:196).

A grid plan was established at Hatunqolla and Chucuito, as well as at some other important administrative sites (e.g., Carpa, Paucarcolla). In the areas most heavily affected by imperial occupation, new settlements were established near the imperial highway, with central plazas at each site center. Most small villages lacked formal planning.

Circular houses continued to be common during the Inka occupation, but some rectangular houses were also seen. The rectangular form was also used for special religious and administrative architecture. The production of cut stone masonry was also reestablished during the Inka occupation for use in special-purpose buildings and elite tombs (Fig. 1.3). Masonry blocks are noted both at Inka administrative centers and lower-order sites (e.g., Albarracin Jordan and Mathews 1990:162–64). Carved rock outcrops and minor shrine sites were distributed throughout the basin (Arkush 2005b).

Most local groups seem to have maintained their existing burial patterns. Under Inka rule, however, Colla elites constructed larger mortuary towers at the site of Sillustani, incorporating Inka masonry techniques in the monumental constructions (see Fig. 1.3). Lupaqa elite residing at Chucuito continued to bury their dead in mortuary towers at Cutimbo. Studies of chullpa architecture (e.g., Arkush 2005a) have reported instances of Inka pottery and masonry in the mortuary sectors of fortified hilltop sites, indicating continued use of burial facilities under imperial rule.

Under Inka rule the Titicaca Basin featured Inka polychromes at all levels of the settlement hierarchy. Colonial documents report specialized potters at certain locations in the basin. The proliferation of Inka motifs and vessel forms did not replace local ceramic traditions. For example, the Sillustani, Chucuito, and Pacajes Inka styles show considerable continuity from earlier ceramic traditions. The two former styles cluster around the administrative sites where the Colla and Lupaca resided.

Colonial documents describe the Inka use of Titicaca Basin labor for mining gold on the Amazonian slope. The incorporation of the Titicaca Basin into the imperial economy appears to have increased local access to metal objects, which are found in burials and offerings.

Archaeological evidence for an Inka occupation of the Titicaca Basin complements the rich Colonial documentary record (Covey 2009; Julien 1983; Murra 1956; Rostworowski and Morris 1999; Rowe 1946). Imperial occupation wrought profound changes to settlement systems, local hierarchies, and the expression of social and ethnic identities. Under imperial rule, the Inka state promoted centralized herding and integrated the Titicaca Basin's human population into a broader imperial political economy. These developments permitted some local elites to become wealthier, adopting Inka construction techniques and material culture styles to assert their status. Some used imperial administrative policies to extend their kin and ethnic networks to the Pacific and Amazonian slopes.

Figure 1.3. Reconstruction of a stone burial structure like that depicted by Guaman Poma de Ayala (see Fig. 1.2). This Sillustani chullpa, a composite image drawn by Kay Clahassey, was adapted from examples illustrated in Gasparini and Margolies (1980:149, 151–53).

The source of local elite power shifted from resource management and defense to savvy exploitation of imperial policies and hegemony (Covey 2006a, 2006b, 2009). The diversity of the provinces comprising the Titicaca Basin and the increasingly varied opportunities for expressing status and identity appear to have accentuated ethnic differences and shaped local interaction with the empire.

The long-term archaeological perspectives displayed in this book demonstrate the capacity of local leadership to adapt to (and even take advantage of) new state policies (Covey 2006b; Julien 1993). They were able to formulate new arrangements as alternatives to state-imposed practices (Arkush 2005a, 2006; Covey 2006b). Where conditions favored conservative management of resources by elite leaders, the local kin groups assumed greater importance and political divisions and social statuses were not emphasized in material culture. Conversely, conditions promoting surplus production and regional trade sustained sharper social divisions and broader opportunities to gain social status.

## The Future of Titicaca Basin Archaeology

The contributions in this book increase our archaeological knowledge of the northern Titicaca Basin and suggest productive directions for future research in the area. Those directions include (1) documenting the rise of early villages and hereditary inequality; (2) documenting cycles of conquest, incorporation, and secession, which are followed by the emergence of new central places that repeat that sequence of behaviors; (3) documenting the evidence for competition, violence, and warfare; and (4) establishing the major spheres of interaction achieved through alliance and autonomy.

## References Cited

Albarracin Jordan, Juan, and James E. Mathews
1990  *Asentamientos prehispánicos del valle de Tiwanaku, Volume I*. Producciones CIMA, La Paz, Bolivia.

Aldenderfer, Mark
1989  Archaic period settlement patterns in the high sierra of the Osmore Basin. In *Ecology, Settlement, and History in the Osmore Drainage, Peru*, edited by Don S. Rice, Charles Stanish, and Phillip R. Scarr, pp. 129–66. British Archaeological Reports, International Series, Oxford, U.K.

Arkush, Elizabeth N.
2005a Colla Fortified Sites: Warfare and Regional Power in the Late Prehispanic Titicaca Basin, Peru. PhD dissertation, Department of Anthropology, University of California, Los Angeles.
2005b Inca ceremonial sites in the southwest Titicaca Basin. In *Advances in Titicaca Basin Archaeology–1*, edited by Charles Stanish, Amanda B. Cohen, and Mark S. Aldenderfer, pp. 209–42. Cotsen Institute of Archaeology, University of California, Los Angeles.
2006  Collapse, conflict, conquest: The transformation of warfare in the late prehispanic Andean highlands. In *The Archaeology of Warfare: Prehistories of Raiding and Conquest*, edited by Elizabeth N. Arkush and Mark W. Allen, pp. 286–335. University Press of Florida, Gainesville.

Arnold, Deborah Y., and Christine Hastorf
2008  *Heads of State: Icons, Power, and Politics in the Ancient and Modern Andes*. Left Coast Press, Walnut Creek, CA.

Bandy, Matthew S.
2001  Population and History in the Ancient Titicaca Basin. PhD dissertation, Department of Anthropology, University of California, Berkeley.

Bauer, Brian S., and Charles Stanish
2001  *Ritual and Pilgrimage in the Ancient Andes: The Islands of the Sun and Moon*. University of Texas Press, Austin.

Blanton, Richard E.
1978  *Monte Alban: Settlement Patterns at the Ancient Zapotec Capital*. Academic Press, New York.

Bouysse-Cassagne, Thérèse
1986  Urco and uma: Aymara concepts of space. In *Anthropological History of Andean Polities*, edited by John V. Murra, Nathan Wachtel, and Jacques Revel, pp. 201–27. Cambridge University Press, Cambridge.

Chávez, Cecilia
2008  Análisis de la cerámica del sector medio y bajo de la sub-cuenca del Río Huancané, Puno-Perú, 2008. Electronic document, http://www.sscnet.ucla.edu/ioa/collasuyu/.

Cipolla, Lisa M.
2005  Preceramic period settlement patterns in the Huancané-Putina River Valley, northern Titicaca Basin, Peru. In *Advances in Titicaca Basin Archaeology–1*, edited by Charles Stanish, Amanda B. Cohen, and Mark Aldenderfer, pp. 55–63. Cotsen Institute of Archaeology, University of California, Los Angeles.

Cohen, Amanda B.
2010  Ritual and Architecture in the Titicaca Basin: The Development of the Sunken Court Complex in the Formative Period. PhD dissertation, Department of Anthropology, University of California, Los Angeles.

Covey, R. Alan
2006a Intermediate elites in the Inca heartland, AD 1000–1500. In *Intermediate Elites in Pre-Columbian States and Empires*, edited by Christina M. Elson and R. Alan Covey, pp. 112–35. University of Arizona Press, Tucson.
2006b *How the Incas Built Their Heartland: State Formation and the Innovation of Imperial Strategies in the Sacred Valley, Peru*. University of Michigan Press, Ann Arbor.
2009  Inca agricultural intensification in the imperial heartland and provinces. In *Andean Civilization: A Tribute to Michael E. Moseley*, edited by Joyce Marcus and Patrick Ryan Williams, pp. 365–77. Cotsen Institute of Archaeology, University of California, Los Angeles.

Erickson, Clark
1987  Dating of raised-field agriculture in the Lake Titicaca Basin, Peru. In *Pre-Hispanic Agricultural Fields in the Andean Region*, edited by William Denevan, Kent Mathewson, and Gregory Knapp, pp. 373–84. British Archaeological Reports, International Series, Oxford, U.K.
1988  An Archaeological Investigation of Raised Field Agriculture in the Lake Titicaca Basin of Peru. PhD dissertation, Department of Anthropology, University of Illinois, Urbana-Champaign.

Gasparini, Graziano, and Luise Margolies
1980 *Inca Architecture*, translated by Patricia J. Lyon. Indiana University Press, Bloomington and London.

Goldstein, Paul S.
2005 *Andean Diaspora: The Tiwanaku Colonies and the Origins of South American Empire*. University Press of Florida, Gainesville.

Guamán Poma de Ayala, Felipe
1980 [1614] El primer nueva corónica y buen gobierno, 3 vols, edited by John V. Murra, Rolena Adorno, and Jorge L. Urioste. Siglo Veintiuno, Mexico City.

Hyslop, John
1976 An Archaeological Investigation of the Lupaca Kingdom and Its Origins. PhD dissertation, Department of Anthropology, Columbia University, New York.
1977 Chulpas of the Lupaca zone of the Peruvian high plateau. *Journal of Field Archaeology* 4:149–70.
1990 *Inka Settlement Planning*. University of Texas Press, Austin.

Julien, Catherine J.
1983 *Hatunqolla: A View of Inca Rule from the Lake Titicaca Region*. University of California Publications in Anthropology, vol. 15. University of California Press, Berkeley.
1993 Finding a fit: Archaeology and ethnohistory of the Incas. In *Provincial Inca: Archaeological and Ethnohistorical Assessment of the Impact of the Inca State*, edited by Michael Malpass, pp. 177–233. University of Iowa Press, Iowa City.

Kidder, Alfred II
1943 *Some Early Sites in the Northern Lake Titicaca Basin*. Papers of the Peabody Museum of American Archaeology and Ethnology, Harvard University, vol. 27, no. 1. Cambridge, MA.

Klarich, Elizabeth
2005 From the Monumental to the Mundane: Defining Early Leadership Strategies at Late Formative Pukara, Peru. PhD dissertation, Department of Anthropology, University of California, Santa Barbara.

Klink, Cynthia J., and Mark S. Aldenderfer
2005 A projectile point chronology for the south-central Andean highlands. In *Advances in Titicaca Basin Archaeology–1*, edited by Charles Stanish, Amanda B. Cohen, and Mark Aldenderfer, pp. 25–54. Cotsen Institute of Archaeology, Los Angeles, California.

Marcus, Joyce
2006 Identifying elites and their strategies. In *Intermediate Elites in Pre-Columbian States and Empires*, edited by Christina M. Elson and R. Alan Covey, pp. 212–46. University of Arizona Press, Tucson.
2007 Early great art styles and the rise of complex societies. In *Gordon R. Willey and American Archaeology: Contemporary Perspectives*, edited by Jeremy A. Sabloff and William L. Fash, pp. 72–104. University of Oklahoma Press, Norman.
2008a *Monte Albán*. Fondo de Cultura Económica, Mexico City.
2008b The archaeological evidence for social evolution. *Annual Review of Anthropology* 37:251–66.
2009 How Monte Albán represented itself. In *The Art of Urbanism: How Mesoamerican Kingdoms Represented Themselves in Architecture and Imagery*, edited by William L. Fash and Leonardo López Luján, pp. 77–110. Dumbarton Oaks, Washington, D.C.

Marcus, Joyce, and Kent V. Flannery
1996 *Zapotec Civilization: How Urban Society Evolved in Mexico's Oaxaca Valley*. Thames and Hudson, London and New York.

Mohr Chávez, Karen
1977 Marcavalle: The Ceramics from an Early Horizon Site in the Valley of Cuzco, Peru, and Implications for South Highland Socioeconomic Interaction. PhD dissertation, Department of Anthropology, University of Pennsylvania, Philadelphia.

Murra, John V.
1956 The Economic Organization of the Inca State. PhD dissertation, Department of Anthropology, University of Chicago.

Plourde, Aimée
2006 Prestige Goods and Their Role in the Evolution of Social Ranking: A Costly Signaling Model with Data from the Formative Period of the Northern Lake Titicaca Basin, Peru. PhD dissertation, Department of Anthropology, University of California, Los Angeles.

Redmond, Elsa M., and Charles S. Spencer
2012 Chiefdoms at the threshold: The competitive origins of the primary state. *Journal of Anthropological Archaeology* 31:22–37.

Rostworowski, María, and Craig Morris
1999 The fourfold domain: Inka power and its social foundations. In *South America*, edited by Frank Salomon and Stuart B. Schwartz, pp. 769–863. Cambridge University Press, Cambridge.

Rowe, John H.
1946 Inca culture at the time of the Spanish conquest. In *Handbook of South American Indians*, vol. 2, edited by Julian H. Steward, pp. 183–330. Smithsonian Institution, Washington, D.C.

Rowe, John H., and Catherine Brandel
1971 Pucara style pottery designs. *Ñawpa Pacha* 7/8(1969–1970):1–16.

Samaniego, Lorenzo, E. Vergara, and H. Bischof
1985 New evidence on Cerro Sechín, Casma Valley, Peru. In *Early Ceremonial Architecture of the Andes*, edited by Christopher B. Donnan, pp. 165–90. Dumbarton Oaks, Washington, D.C.

Spencer, Charles, and Elsa M. Redmond
2001a Multilevel selection and political evolution in the Valley of Oaxaca, 500–100 B.C. *Journal of Anthropological Archaeology* 20:195–229.
2001b The chronology of conquest: Implications of new radiocarbon analyses from the Cañada de Cuicatlán, Oaxaca. *Latin American Antiquity* 12:182–201.
2004 Primary state formation in Mesoamerica. *Annual Review of Anthropology* 33:173–99.
2006 Resistance strategies and early state formation in Oaxaca, Mexico. In *Intermediate Elites in Pre-Columbian States and Empires*, edited by Christina Elson and R. Alan Covey, pp. 21–43. University of Arizona Press, Tucson.

Squier, Ephraim George
1877  *Peru: Incidents of Travel and Exploration in the Land of the Incas*. Harper and Brothers, New York.

Stanish, Charles
1994  The hydraulic hypothesis revisited: A theoretical perspective on Lake Titicaca Basin raised field agriculture. *Latin American Antiquity* 5(4):312–32.
2003  *Ancient Titicaca: The Evolution of Complex Society in Southern Peru and Northern Bolivia*. University of California Press, Berkeley.
2009  The Tiwanaku occupation of the northern Titicaca Basin. In *Andean Civilization: A Tribute to Michael E. Moseley*, edited by Joyce Marcus and Patrick Ryan Williams, pp. 145–64. Cotsen Institute of Archaeology Press, University of California, Los Angeles.
2011  *Lake Titicaca: Legend, Myth and Science*. Cotsen Institute of Archaeology Press, University of California, Los Angeles.

Stanish, Charles, and Brian S. Bauer (editors)
2004  *Archaeological Research on the Islands of the Sun and Moon, Lake Titicaca, Bolivia: Final Results from the Proyecto Tiksi Kjarka*. Monograph no. 52. Cotsen Institute of Archaeology Press, University of California, Los Angeles.

Stanish, Charles, and Abigail Levine
2011  War and early state formation in the northern Titicaca Basin, Peru. *Proceedings of the National Academy of Sciences* 108(34):13901–6.

Steadman, Lee H.
1995  Excavations at Camata: An Early Ceramic Chronology for the Western Titicaca Basin, Peru. PhD dissertation, Department of Anthropology, University of California, Berkeley.

Tantaleán, Henry
2008  Ideología y realidad en las primeras sociedades sedentarias (1400 ANE–350 DNE) de la Cuenca Norte del Titicaca, Perú. PhD dissertation, Departamento de Prehistoria, Universidad Autónoma de Barcelona, Spain.

Tantaleán, H., and C. Pérez Maestro
1999  Pukara y el surgimiento de la civilización en el altiplano Andino. *Revista de Arqueología* 215:32–42.

Tello, Julio C.
1956  *Arqueología del Valle de Casma. Culturas: Chavín, Santa o Huaylas Yunga u sub-Chimú*. Publicación Antropológica del Archivo "Julio C. Tello" de la Universidad Nacional Mayor de San Marcos, Lima, Perú.

Toledo, Francisco de
1975 [1572]  *Tasa de la visita general de Francisco de Toledo*. Universidad Nacional Mayor de San Marcos, Lima, Perú.

Chapter 2

# The Earliest Ceramic Sequence at the Site of Pukara, Northern Lake Titicaca Basin

*David Oshige Adams*

## Introduction

This chapter presents preliminary results from an investigation of the earliest pottery recovered from the site of Pukara, northern Lake Titicaca Basin. The collection analyzed is from excavations conducted by Proyecto Copesco (or Plan Copesco) during the second half of the 1970s.[1] Due to the passage of time, it was not always possible to locate the exact excavation contexts or specific details of those contexts from which the pottery was recovered. Nevertheless, this pottery serves as an important contribution in discussions of the first occupations in the site of Pukara.

The Formative period in the Lake Titicaca Basin (ca. 2000 BC–AD 450) has received much attention from archaeologists over the last several years due to its importance as one of the few regions of autonomous early state development (e.g., Bandy 2001; Beck 2001; Hastorf 2005; Janusek 2001, 2004, 2005; Klarich 2002, 2003, 2005a, 2005b; Plourde and Stanish 2006; Stanish 2001, 2003). This process corresponds to the actions of groups of individuals within larger groups with interest in accumulating wealth, power and prestige within a social context where others try to maintain their individual autonomy (Stanish 2001:195).

One of the sites that is fundamental to understanding this long and complex process is Pukara—Pukara and Tiwanaku emerged as the two most important regional centers during the Late Formative. However, the earliest documented occupations in Pukara correspond to the Middle Formative, which spans from approximately 1400 to 500 BC (Fig. 2.1).

## Location and Description of the Site

The site of Pukara is located in the northern part of the basin, approximately 80 km northwest of Lake Titicaca, on Km. 106 of the Puno-Cusco highway in the Pucara River Valley (Fig. 2.2). The composition of the site, following Elías Mujica (1979:186–87, 1991:278–80, 1996:19–20), has two different architectural components: the monumental sector with at least six truncated pyramids (the Qalasaya to the west, one to the north, two to the east near the river, the Lagunita Mound to the south and one on the peak of Cerro Pucaorqo), and residential zones with rustic structures made of river and field stones held together with adobe. Due to the density of middens—remains of food and ceramics, worked bone and stone and other artifacts—it is inferred that there was a dense, permanent occupation, which was identified by Franco Inojosa (*densísima población*, 1940:129) as extending to the limits of rubbish dumps. Following early studies, Elizabeth Klarich (2005a:57) adds that Pukara has two general areas: a central area with monumental constructions such as the Qalasaya complex, surrounding pyramids, and central pampa, and a peripheral area near the river where domestic constructions and extensive middens are located.

The Qalasaya is the most impressive of the pyramids and has received the most attention from archaeologists. It is a monumental construction that measures 315 m in length (north-south), 300 m east-west, and 32 m in height (Mujica 1996:20). It is composed of artificial platforms, forming a stepped, truncated

*13*

| Years | Northern Basin | Southern Basin | Western Basin | Ica Valley |
|---|---|---|---|---|
| 1540 / 1450 | INCA | INCA-PACAJES | INCA | LATE HORIZON |
| 1100 | COLLA | PACAJES | LUPAQA | LATE INTERMEDIATE PERIOD |
| 1000 | Late Huaña (AD 600-1100) | LATE TIWANAKU V | EXPANSIVE TIWANAKU | MIDDLE HORIZON |
| 800 | EXPANSIVE TIWANAKU | EARLY TIWANAKU V | | |
| 600 | | LATE TIWANAKU IV | | |
| | Early Huaña (AD 380-600) | EARLY TIWANAKU IV | | |
| 400 | | LATE FORMATIVE 2 Tiwanaku III/ Qeya | | EARLY INTERMEDIATE PERIOD |
| 300 | Late Pukara (AD 100-380) | LF 1B/ Tiwanaku II | LATE FORMATIVE Late Sillumocco | |
| 100 | LATE/UPPER FORMATIVE | LATE FORMATIVE 1 | | |
| 0 | Middle/Classic Pukara (200 BC-AD 100) | LF 1A/ Tiwanaku I/ Qalasasaya | | |
| 200 | Initial Pukara (500-200 BC) | Late Chiripa 2 | Early Sillumocco | EARLY HORIZON |
| 500 | Cusipata (800-500 BC) | MIDDLE FORMATIVE | | |
| | MIDDLE FORMATIVE | Late Chiripa 1 | | |
| 800 | | Early Formative 2/ Middle Chiripa | MIDDLE FORMATIVE | INITIAL PERIOD |
| 1000 | Qaluyu (1400-800 BC) | EARLY FORMATIVE | | |
| 1300 | | Early Formative 1/ Early Chiripa | | |
| 1500 | EARLY FORMATIVE | | Pasiri EARLY FORMATIVE | |
| 2000 | | | | |

Figure 2.1. Chronological chart for the Lake Titicaca Basin.

pyramid with a stone façade on the east and south; the surrounding hilltops of Calvario and Pucaorqo serve as the Qalasaya's western and northern edges, respectively. On top of the pyramid are three ceremonial enclosures aligned north-south and facing east (Mujica 1991:280–81) (Fig. 2.3).

The enclosures have received the most attention due to their similarities to constructions at the site of Chiripa in the southern Lake Titicaca Basin. Of the three, the central enclosure (or White and Red Temple) is the most studied to date, beginning with Alfred Kidder II's excavations of an area of approximately 1796.5 m$^2$, which exposed the entire structure (Chávez 1992:78). This U-shaped structure is composed of a square plaza surrounded by a wall of white stone slabs. Surrounding the plaza and one level higher is a platform marked by walls made of red rocks

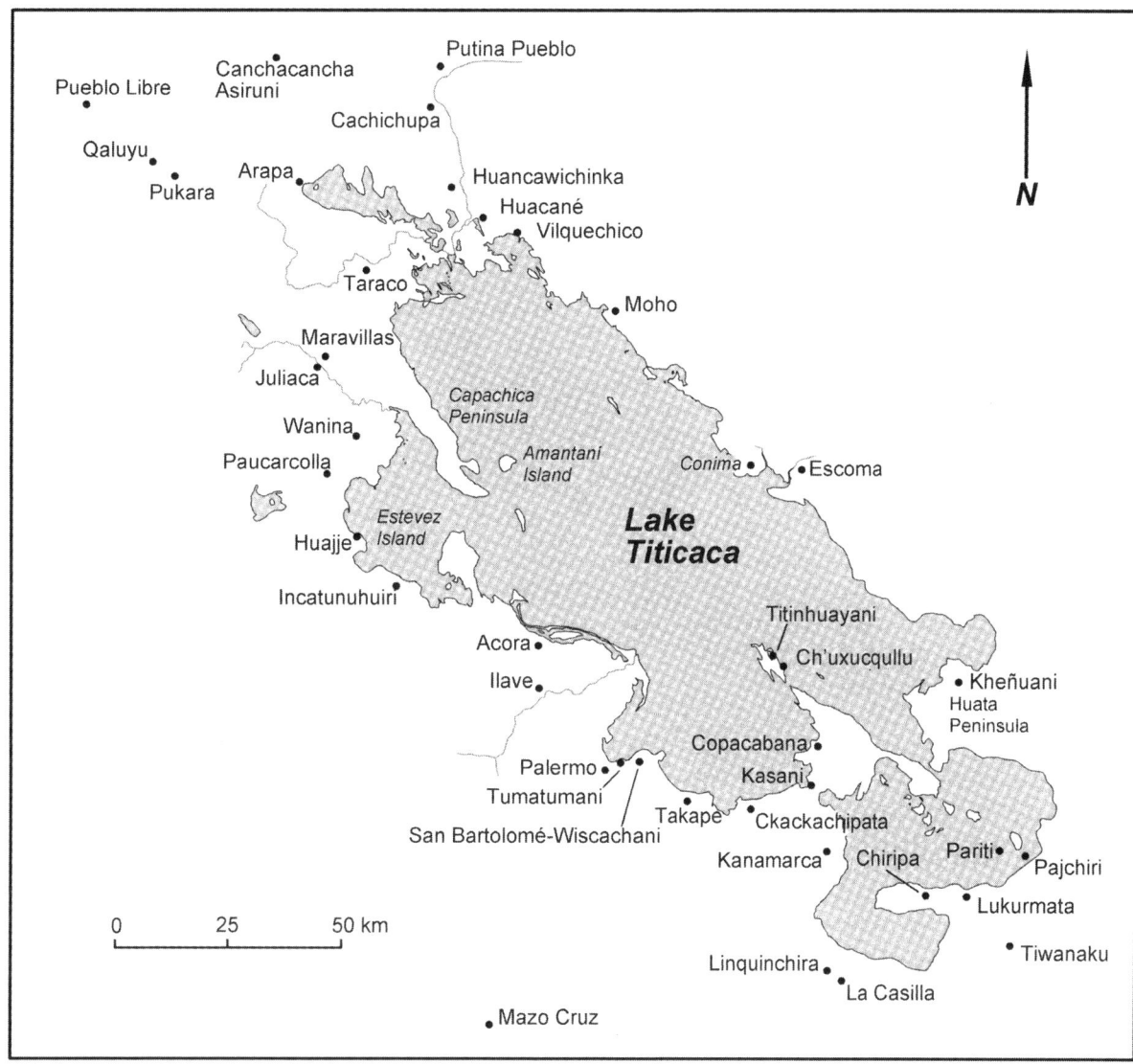

Figure 2.2. Map with Pukara and other major Formative sites within the Lake Titicaca Basin (adapted from Stanish 2003).

that form small rooms (Mujica 1991:282). Kidder (1942:343–44) indicated that in total the structure measured 50 m by 40 m while the sunken plaza measures 15 m² and 1.5 m in depth (Fig. 2.4). The Copesco Project, directed by Mujica and Nakandakari, also excavated in this plaza hundida (sunken plaza or sunken court), which they designated as Sector BB. As discussed below, these excavations continued until they reached bedrock, producing the majority of the material analyzed here.

The pyramid's façade is composed not of a single wall, but of groups of platforms with different characteristics that form three blocks or sectors associated with the ceremonial enclosures described above (Fig. 2.5). Furthermore, in the lower part of the pyramid is a large platform that measures 160 m long by 60 m wide; it is connected to the upper platform through a central stairway (Mujica 1991:281). The site's monumental zone includes other structures—less known due to lack of research—that provide evidence for major corporate labor. Klarich (2005a:59) notes that the Lagunita Mound and the Northern Mound serve as the limits of the site's monumental sector.

Figure 2.3. View of the front of the Qalasaya pyramid (from northeast).

Figure 2.4. View of the sunken court excavated by Kidder (White and Red Temple) and the Copesco Project (Sector BB).

Figure 2.5. View of the front of the Qalasaya pyramid with the main staircase visible (from the east).

**Original Contexts of the Analyzed Materials**

The ceramic materials for this study were recovered from excavations in three sectors. In Sector BB, Mujica and Nakandakari excavated in grid units and in areas within the sunken court while in BF and BG they primarily excavated in trenches on the terraces along the front edge of the Qalasaya pyramid (Fig. 2.6). Given that it was impossible to find all the necessary documentation for Sectors BF and BG, we relied solely on drawings of general profiles. These drawings correspond to cuts that show the construction fill of the platforms that form the stepped pyramid; although the excavation units are identified, there is no stratigraphic information available (Figs. 2.7, 2.8). In regard to Sector BB, while the strata are not described in detail and many of the profiles are not available, the recovered information is of value. Visible in Figure 2.9 are a plan view of this sector, the grid system, and the location of the profiles that are detailed below.

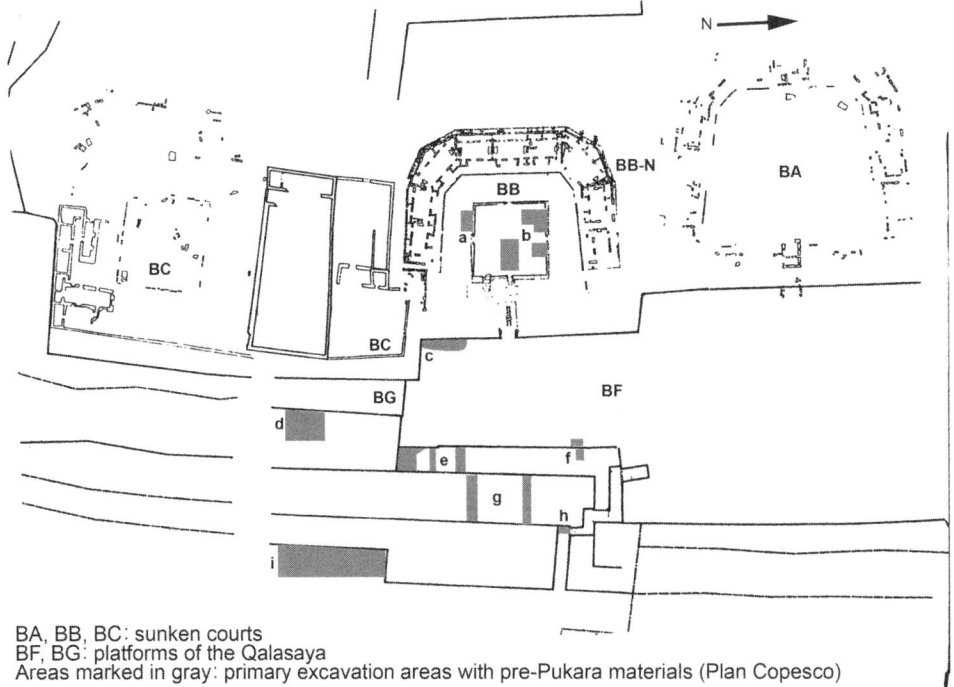

Figure 2.6. Sectors of the Qalasaya pyramid (adapted from Wheeler and Mujica 1981).

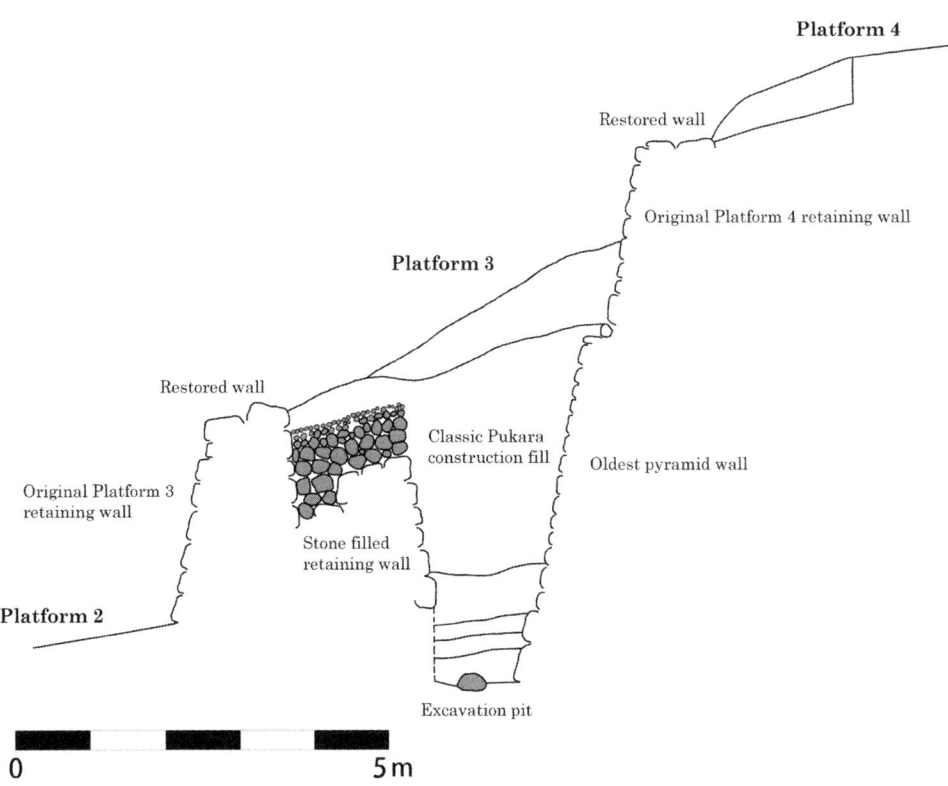

Figure 2.7. Profile of the North 44 Axis, Sector BF, with the detail of Platform 3 (adapted from Wheeler and Mujica 1981).

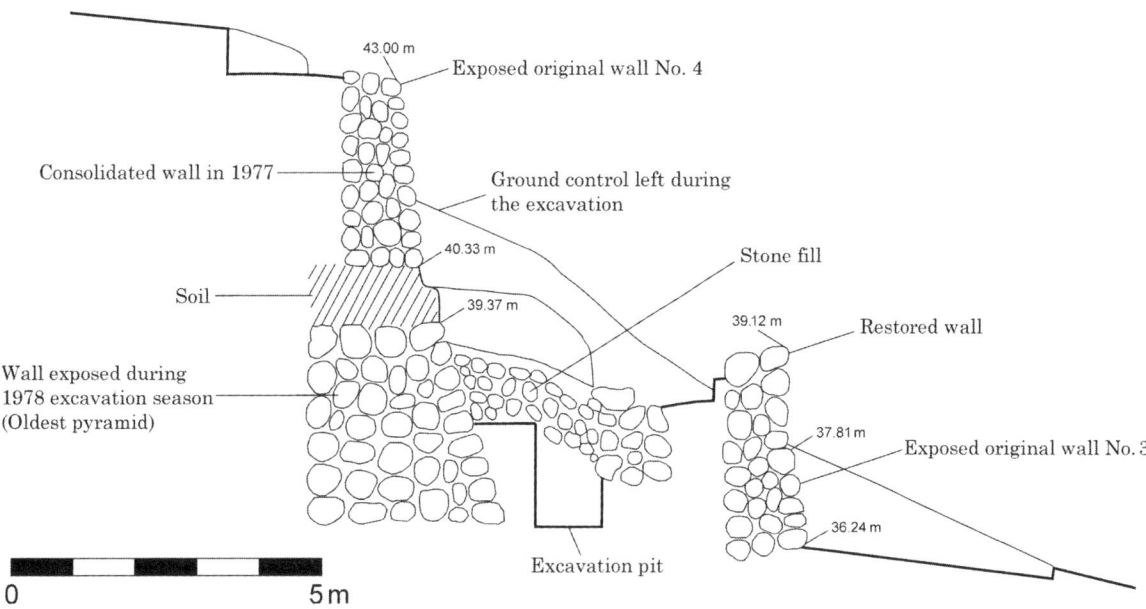

Figure 2.8. Profile of the North 42 Axis, Sector BG, with the detail of Platform 3 (adapted from Wheeler and Mujica 1981). Note that the metric designations refer to Copesco datum levels.

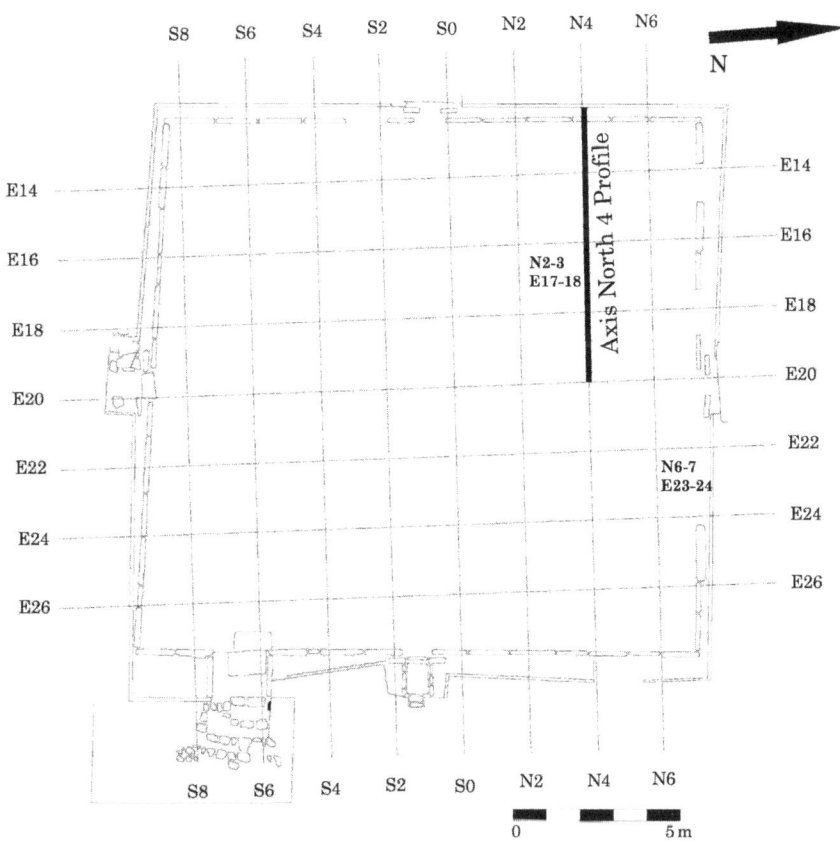

Figure 2.9. Plan of Sector BB with the location of the excavation units and the profiles cited in text (adapted from drawings of the Proyecto Copesco).

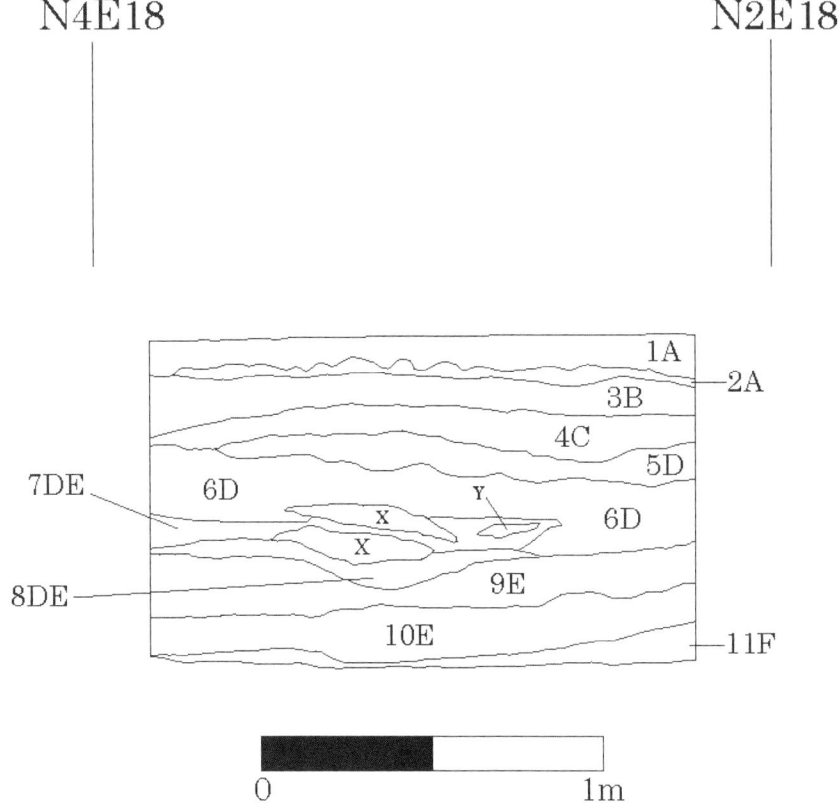

Figure 2.10. Western profile of Unit N2-3 E17-18, Sector BB (adapted from drawings of the Proyecto Copesco).

*Strata Descriptions, Sector BB, Unit N2-3 E17-18 (Fig. 2.10)*

2A: Black soil. Fragments from this stratum were not analyzed because they pertain to the Middle/Classic Pukara period.

3B: Red soil with gravel. Fragments from this stratum were not analyzed because they pertain to the Middle/Classic Pukara period.

4C: White soil. Fragments from this stratum were not analyzed because they pertain to the Middle/Classic Pukara period.

5D: Red soil. A large bowl (tazón) with straight, diverging walls and a flat, beveled rim was found.

6D: Black soil. The following objects were recovered: a small bowl (cuenco) with diverging walls and round rim; a large jar (cántaro) with slightly concave, diverging neck and externally thickened, rounded rim; a medium-necked olla with slightly concave, vertical walls and a beveled rim; a neckless olla with steeply inclined walls and round, internally thickened rim; and a large bowl (tazón) with straight, diverging walls and a flat, inclined rim.

7DE: No description of the stratum was found and the following objects were recovered: a medium-necked olla with slightly concave vertical walls and an externally thickened rim; a medium-necked olla with slightly concave, converging [?] walls and an externally thickened rim; two medium bowls [tazones] with straight, diverging walls and rounded rims; a medium jar (cántaro) with a slightly concave, vertical neck and beveled border; and a small jar (cántaro) with a slightly concave, diverging neck and an externally thickened, round border.

8DE: Black soil. A medium bowl (tazón) with straight, diverging walls and a flat, inclined border was recovered.

9E: Red soil with gravel. No diagnostic rims were encountered.

10E: Yellow, sandy soil. No diagnostic rims were encountered.

11F: Black, sandy soil. No diagnostic rims were encountered.

X: Red lenses. No diagnostic rims were encountered.

Y: Black, sandy soil. No diagnostic rims were encountered.

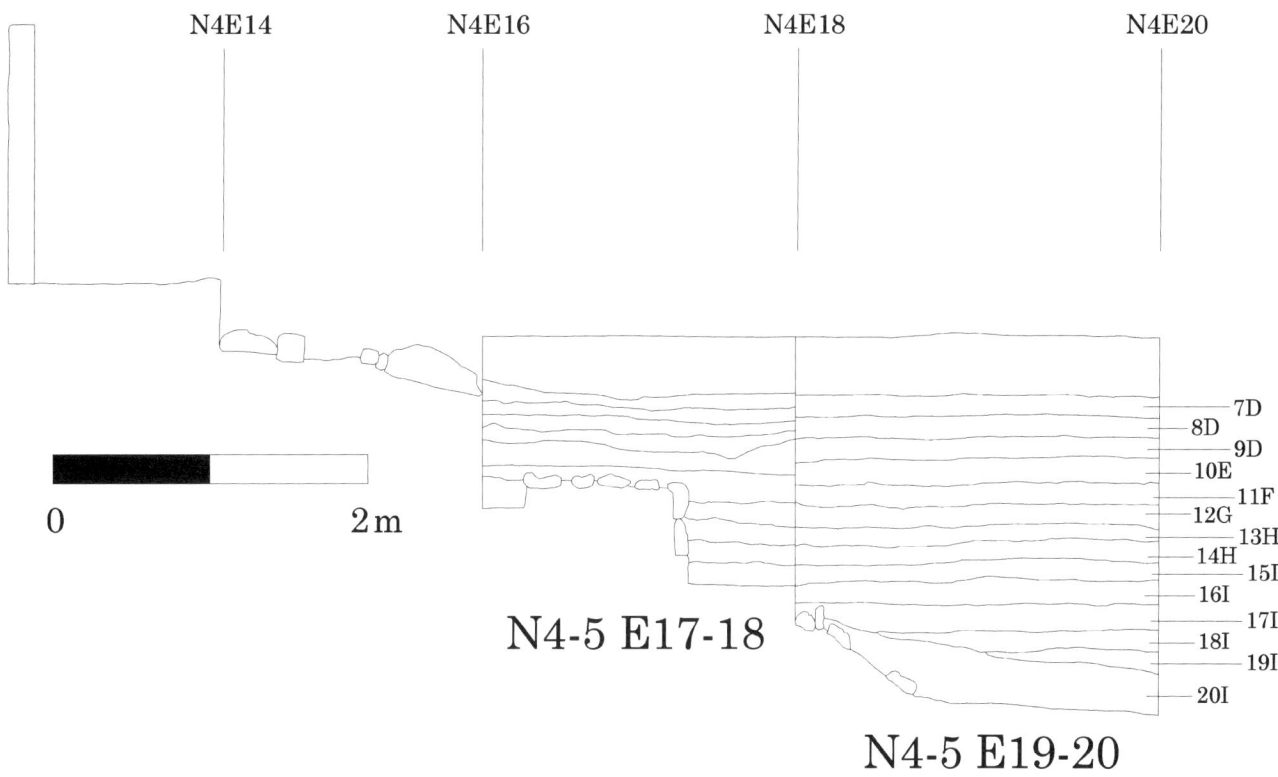

Figure 2.11. Profile of the Cross Section 4 North Sector BB (adapted from drawings of the Proyecto Copesco).

*Strata Descriptions, Sector BB, Cross Section 4 North, Units N4-5 E17-18 and N4-5 E19-20 (Fig. 2.11)*

7D: Black soil with red lenses and gravel. The following artifacts were recovered: a medium plate (plato) with an externally thickened rim; a vertical, short-necked olla with an externally thickened rim; a medium-necked olla, slightly concave and converging, with a rounded rim; large jar (cántaro) with a slightly concave, diverging neck and horizontal, flat, externally thickened rim; medium bowl (tazón) with straight, vertical walls and a flat, horizontal rim; and a large bowl (tazón) with straight, diverging sides and a slightly rounded rim.

8D: Black soil with white, sandy lenses. The following artifacts were recovered: small jar (cántaro) with concave, diverging neck and externally thickened, rounded rim; medium jar (cántaro) with concave, diverging neck and externally thickened, rounded rim; large jar (cántaro) with slightly concave, diverging neck and flat, horizontal, externally thickened rim; and a medium bowl (tazón) with straight, diverging sides and rounded rim.

9D: Red soil with compact, sandy gravel. A neckless olla with inclined walls and pointed, rounded rim was recovered.

10E: Red soil interspersed with sandy black and white soil. A medium bowl (tazón) with straight, diverging sides and rounded rim and a large bowl (tazón) with straight, diverging sides and a slightly rounded rim were recovered.

11F: Soil that was half red with gravel and half white and sandy. A medium-necked olla, slightly concave and vertical with a rounded rim, was recovered.

12G: Black soil with sandy yellow lenses. A vertical, short-necked olla with a horizontal, flattened rim was recovered.

13H: Red soil with sandy gravel with black sandy lenses. No diagnostic rims were identified.

14H: Soft gray sandy soil. A large bowl (tazón) with straight, vertical walls and rounded rim was recovered.

15I: Black, compact sandy soil. No diagnostic rims were identified.

16I: No description of the stratum was found. The following artifacts were encountered: a neckless olla with inclined walls and an elongated, rectangular rim; a large jar (cántaro) with a slightly concave, vertical neck and externally thickened rim; and a medium bowl (tazón) with straight, diverging walls and an inclined, flat rim.

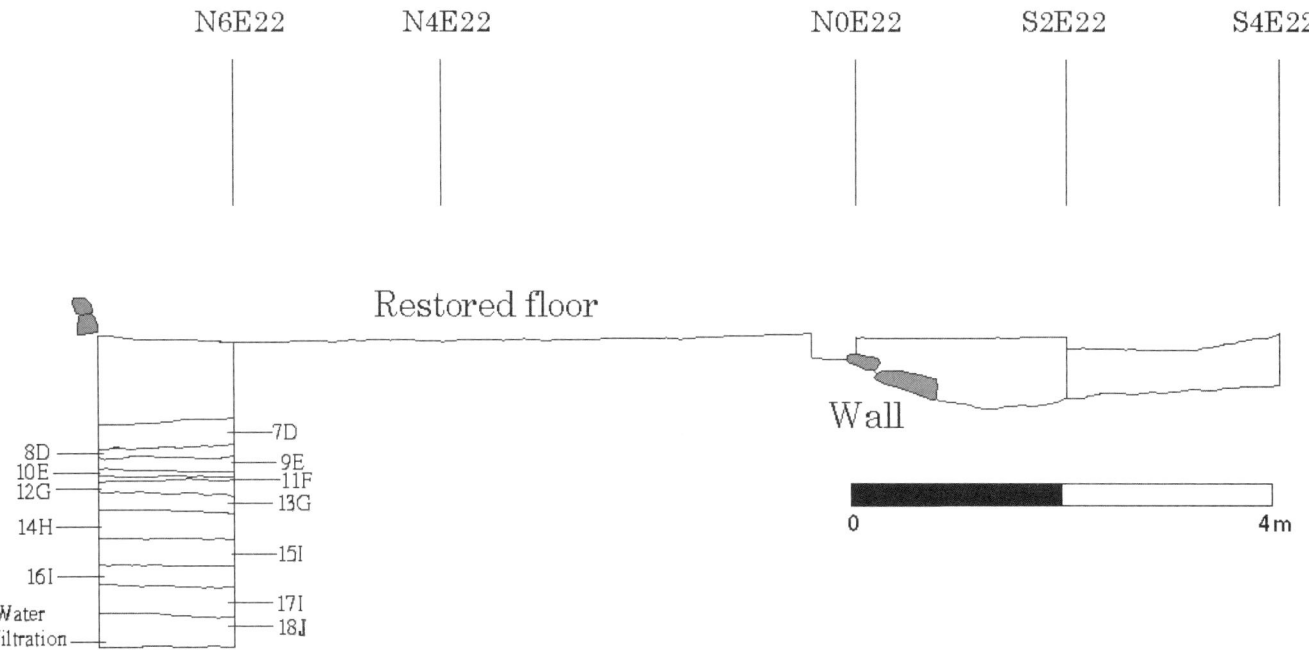

Figure 2.12. Profile of the East 22 Axis, Sector BB, with the profile of Unit N6-7 E23-24 (adapted from drawings of the Proyecto Copesco).

17I: No description of the stratum was found. A medium bowl (tazón) with straight, diverging walls and an externally thickened rim and a medium bowl (tazón) with diverging, concave walls and rounded border were recovered.

18I: No description of the stratum was found. The following artifacts were encountered: a small plate with a rounded border; a small bowl (tazón) with convex, diverging walls and a rounded rim; a medium bowl (tazón) with straight, vertical walls and a slightly rounded rim; a large bowl (tazón) with straight, vertical walls and a horizontally flattened rim; and a large bowl (tazón) with convex, diverging walls and rounded rim.

19I: No description of the stratum was found. A neckless olla with slightly inclined walls and flat, inclined rim and a large bowl (tazón) with straight, diverging walls and an externally thickened rim were recovered from this context.

20I: No description of the stratum was found. A medium bowl (tazón) with straight, diverging walls and a rounded rim was recovered.

*Strata Descriptions, Sector BB, Unit N6-7 E23-24 (Fig. 2.12)*

7D: Black soil with red lenses and gravel. A small bowl (cuenco) with diverging sides and a rounded border was recovered.

8D: Black soil with sandy, white lenses. No diagnostic rims were identified.

9E: Red soil with compact, clay-rich gravel. No diagnostic rims were identified.

10E: Red soil interspersed with black and white sandy soil. No diagnostic rims were identified.

11F: Context composed of half red soil with gravel and half sandy white soil. A medium plate (plato) with an externally thickened rim was recovered.

12G: Black soil with yellow, sandy lenses. A neckless olla with inclined walls and a round, elongated rim and a neckless olla with slightly inclined walls and a flat, horizontal rim were recovered.

13G: Red soil with clayey-gravel with black, sandy lenses. No diagnostic rims were identified.

14H: Smooth, sandy gray soil. No diagnostic rims were identified.

15I: Compact, sandy black soil. The following artifacts were recovered: a small jar (cántaro) with slightly diverging, concave neck and rounded rim; two neckless ollas with slightly inclining walls and rounded rim; and a small bowl (tazón) with straight, diverging walls and an externally thickened rim.

16I: No description of the stratum was found. A large plate (plato) with a rounded rim was encountered.

17I: No description of the stratum was found. The following artifacts were recovered: a large bowl (cuenco) with diverging walls and rounded rim; a small jar (cántaro) with slightly concave, diverging neck and elongated, flattened, inclined rim; neckless olla with very inclined walls and an internally thickened, rounded rim; neckless olla with slightly inclined walls and externally thickened rim; a medium plate (plato) with rounded rim; a large bowl (tazón) with vertical, convex walls and rounded rim; and a large bowl (tazón) with straight, diverging walls and externally thickened rim.

18J: No description of the stratum was found. A large bowl (tazón) with diverging, convex walls and a rounded rim was recovered. They halted excavation at this level due to the filtration of water.

## The Ceramics

In the morpho-functional analysis, open vessels such as plates (platos) and bowls (cuencos and tazones) and closed vessels such as neckless ollas, necked ollas and jars (cántaros) were identified. A total of 4582 sherds were analyzed, but the majority of these were too small to identify as part of a specific vessel form. Therefore, pottery sherds were included in this analysis when over 5% of the rim was present, which totaled 300 identifiable vessels.

*Open Vessels (N = 150, 50% of total) (Fig. 2.13)*

*Plates/Platos* (N = 5, 1.67% of total). These vessels have a flat base with very short, very steep sides. Despite the fact that the number of samples is very limited and therefore not representative, their manufacture is consistent. The interior surface was smoothed, the exterior was burnished and both surfaces were slipped, but not decorated. Very few examples were recovered, but they have been classified, according to their size and the form of the lip, into three categories (Fig. 2.14).

*Bowls/Cuencos* (N = 8, 2.67% of total). These vessels have convex walls and a rounded base and the maximum diameter can be found on the rim or the body. The interior surface was generally smoothed or burnished while the exterior was smoothed and burnished. However, in the majority of the cases it was difficult to determine the type of surface finish because of erosion. Both surfaces were slipped and undecorated. There were few total specimens, but they were classified based on size, shape of the walls, and form of the lip; one group had two subcategories (Fig. 2.15).

*Bowls/Tazones* (T) (N = 137, 45.48% of total). These vessels have a flat base and the maximum diameter is at the rim. Interior surfaces were generally smoothed or polished. The internal wiping was likely done with some type of cloth based on the marks, although in many cases a blunt object was used, such as a corncob or simply a hand. The exterior surfaces were generally polished or burnished. In the case of a polished exterior, the interior surface was also polished while in the cases where the exterior was burnished the interiors were wiped. Both surfaces were slipped and almost always undecorated. When there was decoration present, in the vast majority, it was only on the interior or exterior surface, very few on both surfaces.

The primary classification of these vessels is based on the diameter. Three sizes are defined based on data collected during this study regarding size ranges and from previous classifications of ceramics from the same site (e.g., Klarich 2005b) (Fig. 2.16).

(A) *Small bowls/Tazones pequeños* (T1) (N = 16, 5.35% of total). These bowls have a diameter between 5 and 10 cm with the median at 9 cm. They were divided into five categories based on the orientation and form of the walls and into thirteen subcategories based on the lip.

(B) *Medium bowls/Tazones medianos* (T2) (N = 61, 20.06% of total). These bowls have a diameter between 11 and 16 cm with the median at 14 cm. They were divided into four categories based on the orientation and form of the walls and into eighteen subcategories based on the form of the lip.

(C) *Large bowls/Tazones grandes* (T3) (N = 60, 20.06% of total). These bowls have a diameter between 17 and 29 cm with the median at 20 cm. They were divided into six categories based on the orientation and form of the walls and twenty-one subcategories based on the form of the lip.

*Closed Vessels (N = 150, 50% of total) (Fig. 2.17)*

*Neckless ollas/Ollas sin cuello* (N = 21, 7.02% of total). The vessels are typically globular with medium-sized mouths, convex walls, and a narrow base. The majority of the vessels were wiped on the interior with a cloth and one-third of the samples were not slipped. On the exterior surfaces the great majority were burnished and almost all were slipped. Neckless ollas were classified into three categories based on the orientation of the walls and eleven subcategories were developed based on the form of the lip (Fig. 2.18).

*Necked ollas/Ollas con cuello* (N = 42, 13.71% of total). Necked ollas are mostly globular with wide mouths, convex walls, and narrow bases.[2] The majority of the interiors were wiped with cloth and slipped. Of the exterior surfaces, almost an equal number were wiped with a cloth or polished although in various cases it was difficult to determine due to erosion. These were classified into three categories based on the length of the neck and the form and orientation of the walls, and into twenty subcategories based on the form of the lip (Fig. 2.18).

*Jars/Cántaros* (Ca) (N = 87, 29.09% of total). These are necked vessels, with a narrow base, that are typically between globular and elliptical shapes. It is important to emphasize that because we are dealing only with rim fragments, it is possible that some of the examples designated as jars are actually ollas. The interior surfaces were generally wiped with a cloth and slipped. The exterior finish is almost equally divided between surfaces that have been wiped (with cloth), burnished and polished and all were slipped. There are three size categories based on diameter of the rim (Fig. 2.19).

(A) *Small jars/Cántaros pequeños* (Ca1) (N = 39, 13.04% of total). These jars have diameters between 5 and 11 cm with the median at 9 cm. They were classified into two categories based on the form and orientation of the walls of the neck and into thirteen subcategories based on the form of the lip.

(B) *Medium jars/Cántaros medianos* (Ca2) (N = 25, 8.36% of total). Medium jars have a diameter between 12 and 15 cm with the median at 13 cm. They were classified into three categories based on the form and orientation of the walls of the neck and into twelve subcategories based on the form of the lip.

(C) *Large jars/Cántaros grandes* (Ca3) (N = 23, 7.69% of total). Large jars have a diameter between 16 and 30 cm with the median at 19 cm. They were classified into three categories based on the form and orientation of the walls of the neck and into nine subcategories based on the form of the lip.

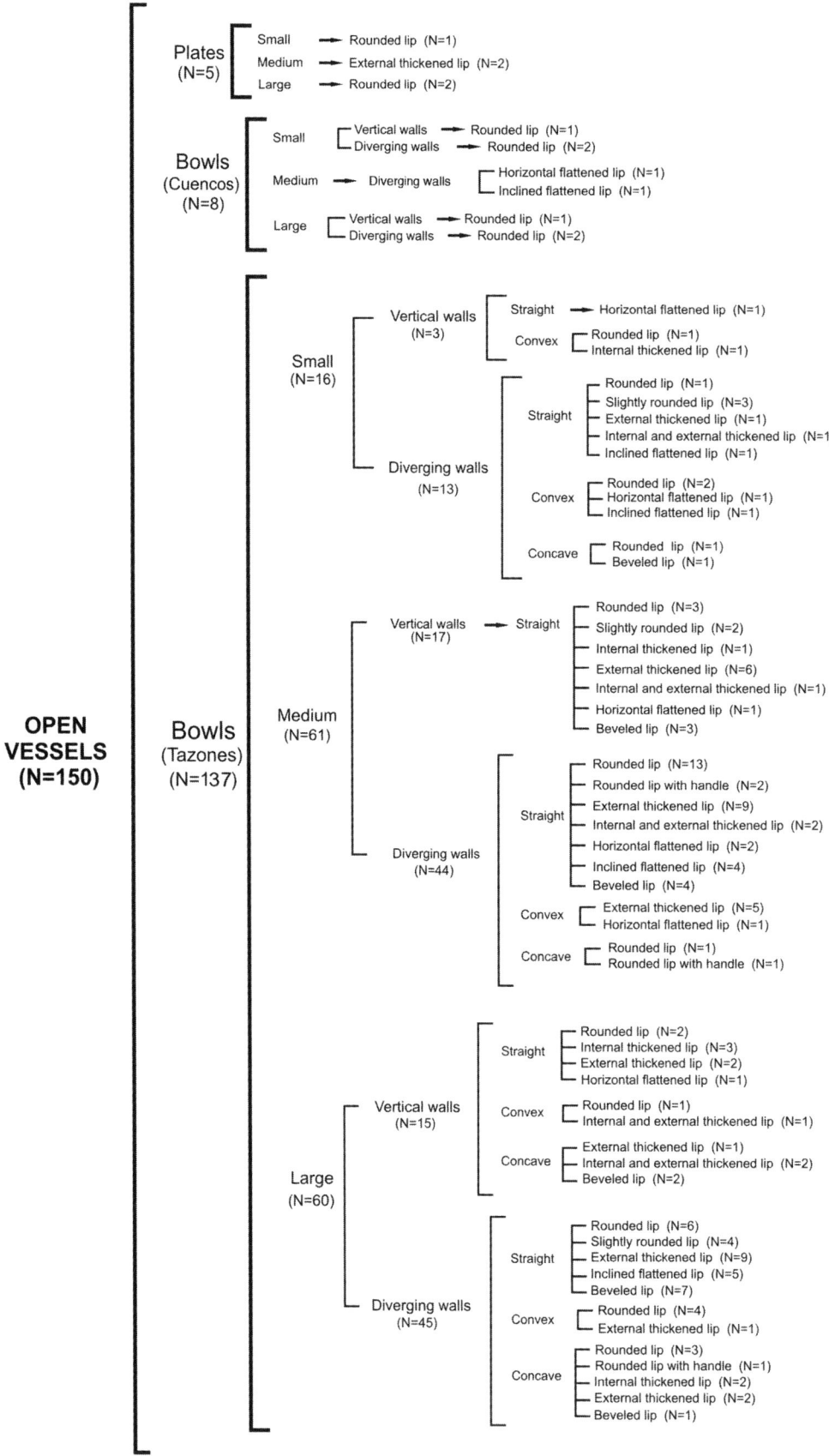

Figure 2.13. Morphological classification of open vessels.

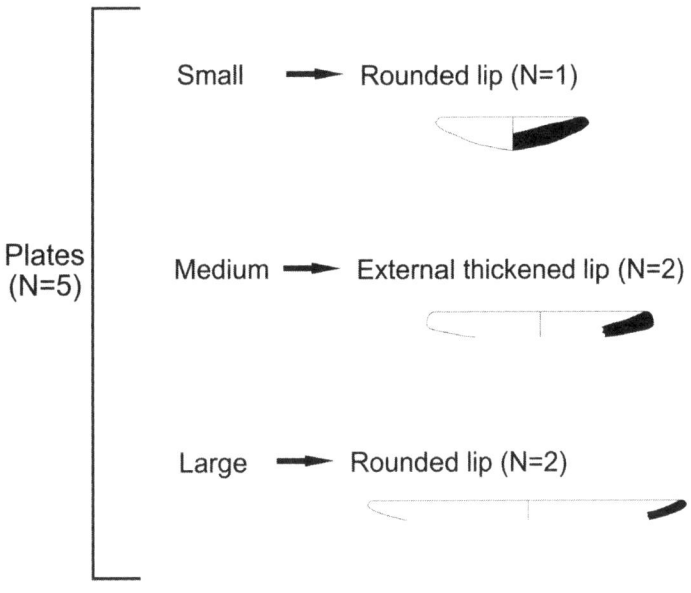

Figure 2.14. Morphological classification of plates.

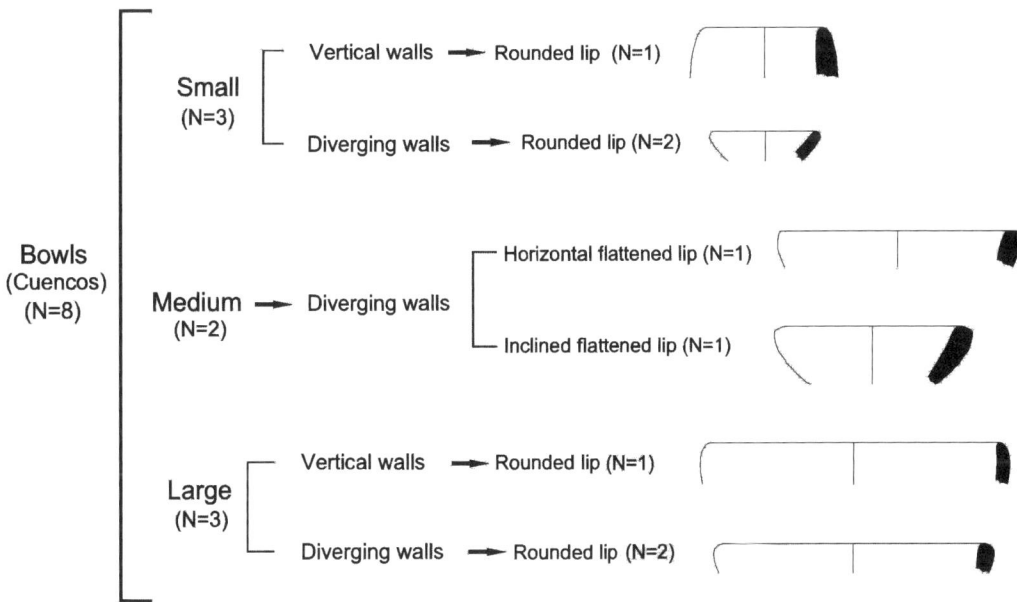

Figure 2.15. Morphological classification of bowls (cuencos).

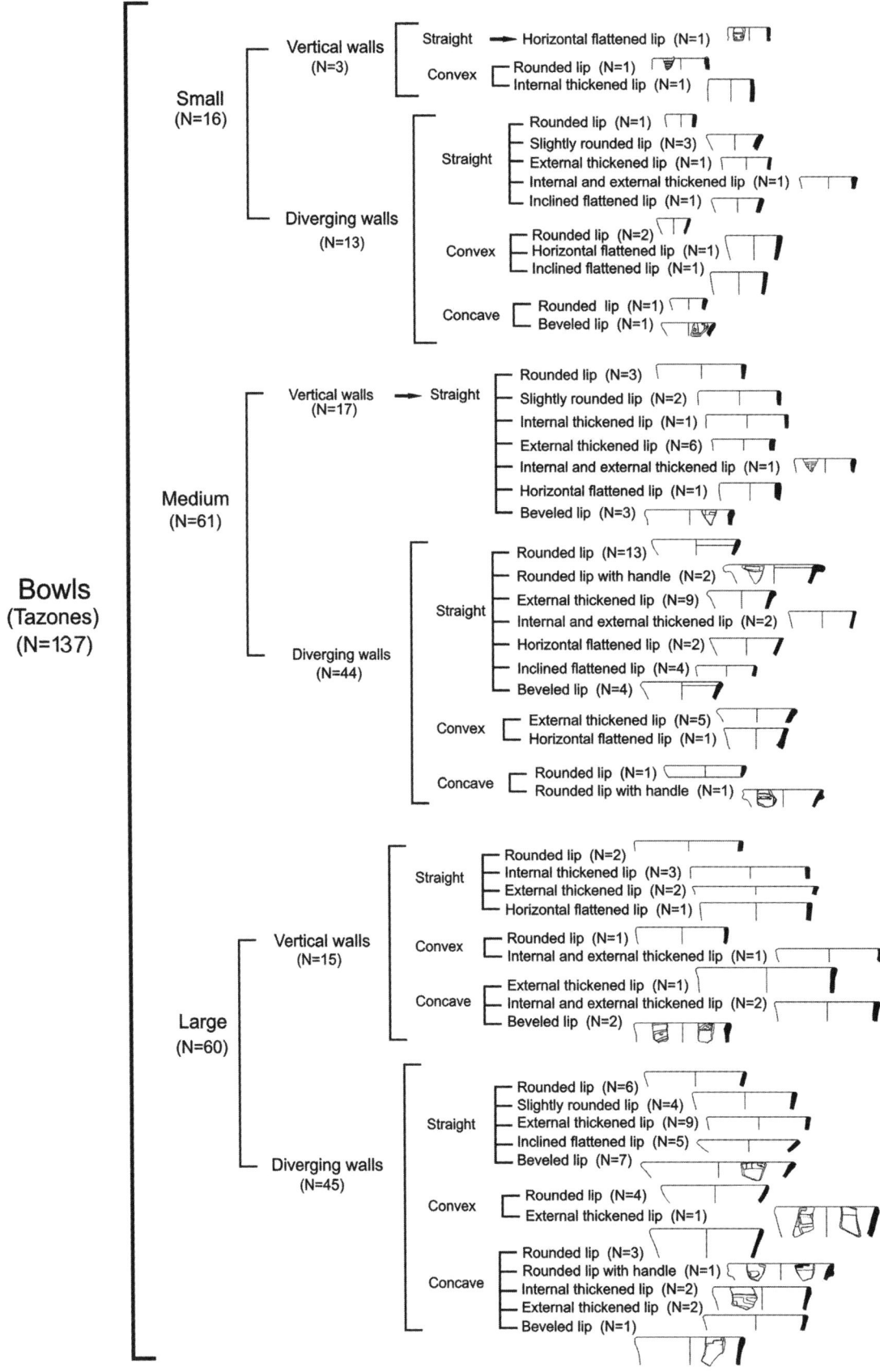

Figure 2.16. Morphological classification of bowls (tazones).

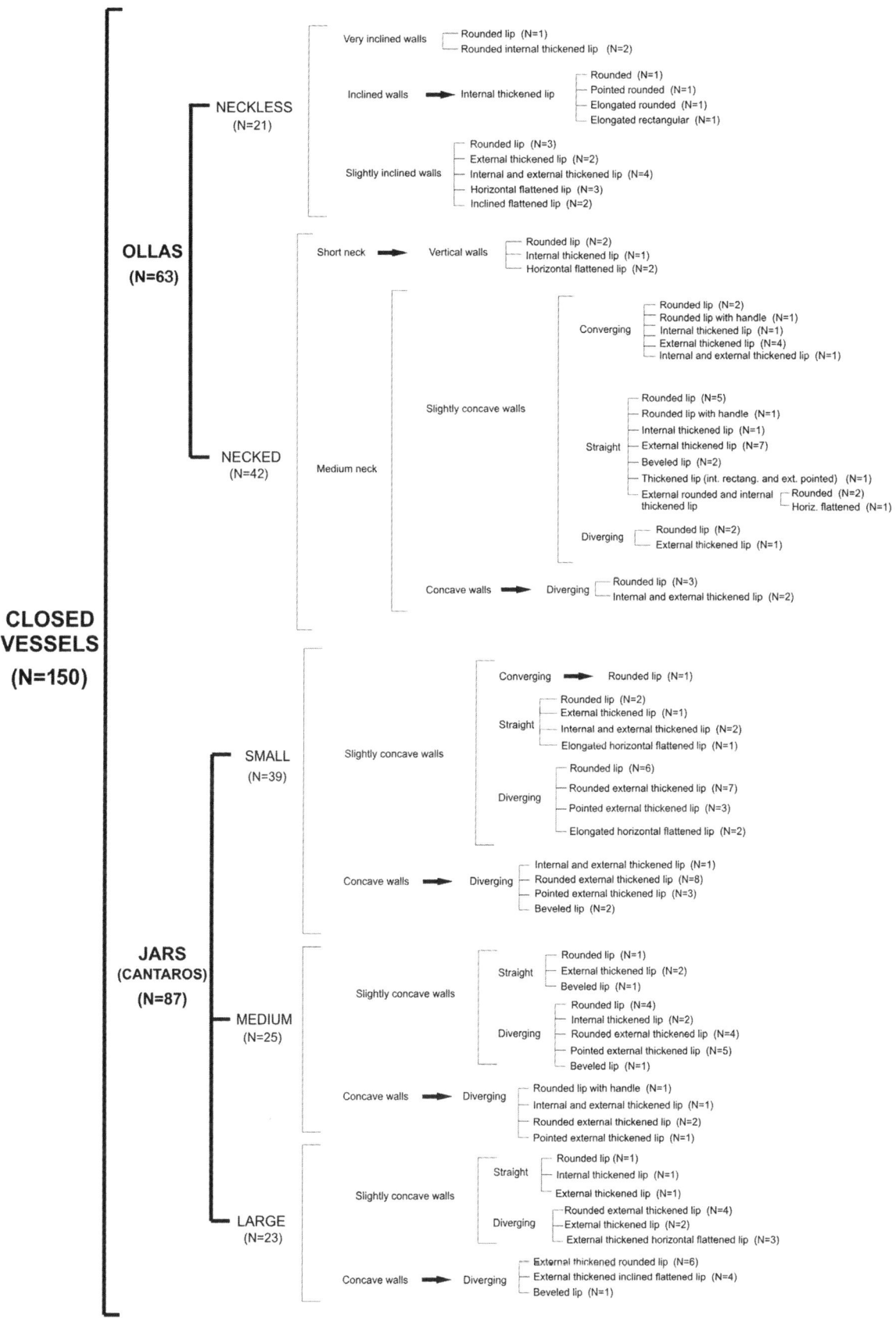

Figure 2.17. Morphological classification of closed vessels.

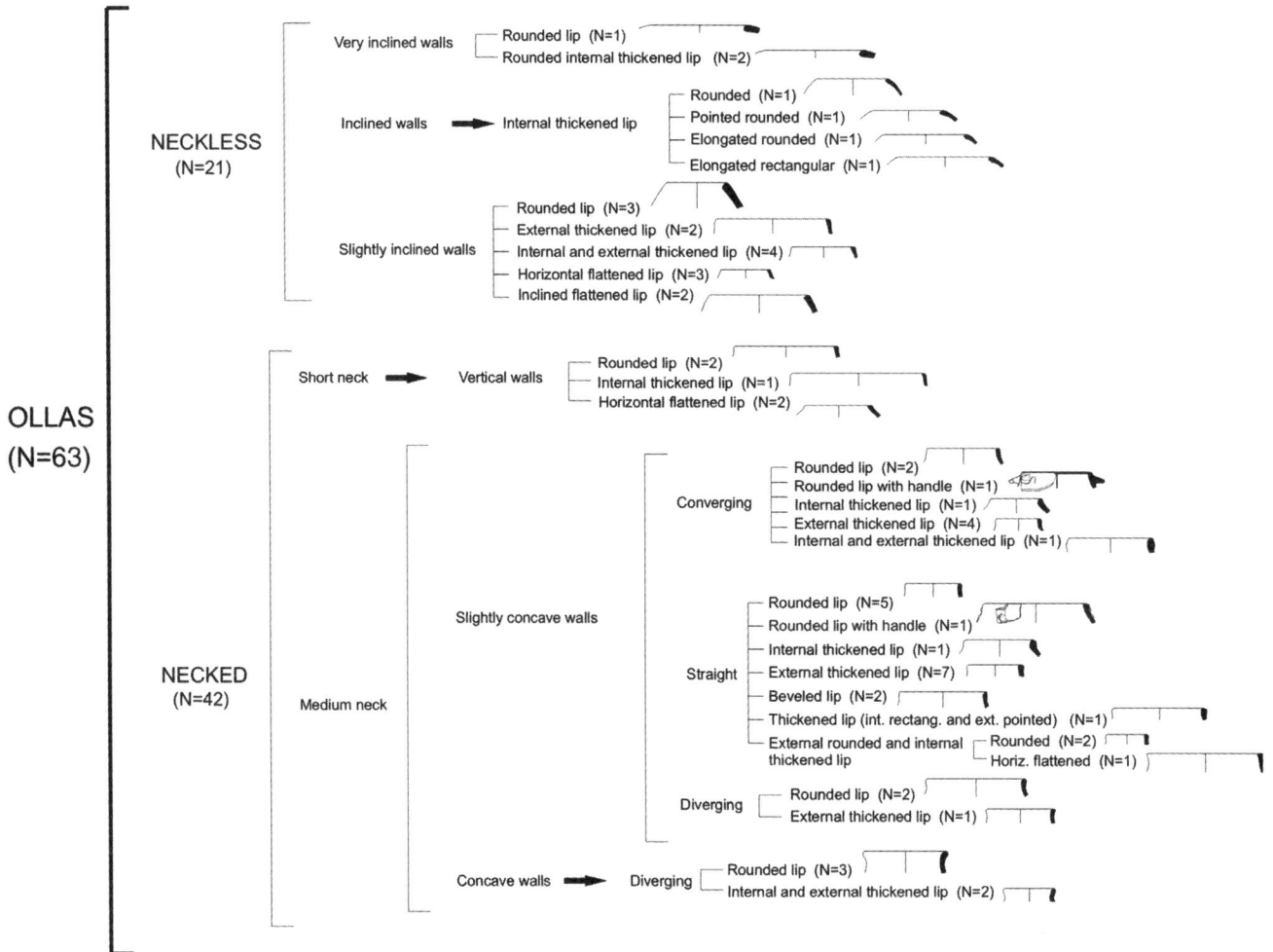

Figure 2.18. Morphological classification of ollas.

*Description of the Formal Variations in the Sequence*

Because the majority of the ceramics analyzed came from construction fill—often mixing fragments from different places and time periods—and not from contexts associated with architecture, it was very difficult to reconstruct a formal ceramic sequence. Despite these challenges, a number of trends can be noted.

First, the most ubiquitous formal category is the large bowl (tazón grande) with diverging walls. The frequency may signal the importance of consuming foods or liquids during public gatherings during the earliest occupations of the site.

Second, in the majority of the cases, neckless ollas are recovered in the earliest levels, which coincides with trends seen in the earliest sequences in the central Andes.

Third, in the deepest levels very few jars (cántaros) have been identified; they increase in frequency in intermediate levels, which are closer to the Middle or Classic Pukara phase. This may indicate that vessels for storage and/or transportation of liquids and solids were not common during the first occupations of the site.

Fourth, in Sector BB the following trends were observed, from earliest to latest levels: the lowest levels include primarily neckless ollas with slightly inclined walls and large bowls (tazones) with diverging walls; subsequently, medium and large bowls (tazones) became most popular and jars (cántaros) began to be used with more frequency; and in the most recent deposits, the most utilized forms were medium bowls (tazones) with diverging walls and small jars (cántaros).

Fifth, in Sector BG, Platform 3, in the deepest excavation levels the most popular form was the large bowl (tazón) with diverging walls, and the only neckless olla on this platform was found. In later contexts the large bowl remained popular, but many small jars were also used.

Sixth, in the lowest terrace of Sector BG, the same trends continued in the area where Copesco found a niched, stone enclosure with lithic sculptures associated with the earliest pyramid. In the earliest levels the most common forms were large bowls (tazones), and a neckless olla was identified. Subsequently, medium and large bowls (tazones) with diverging walls, medium-necked ollas, and small pitches (cántaros)

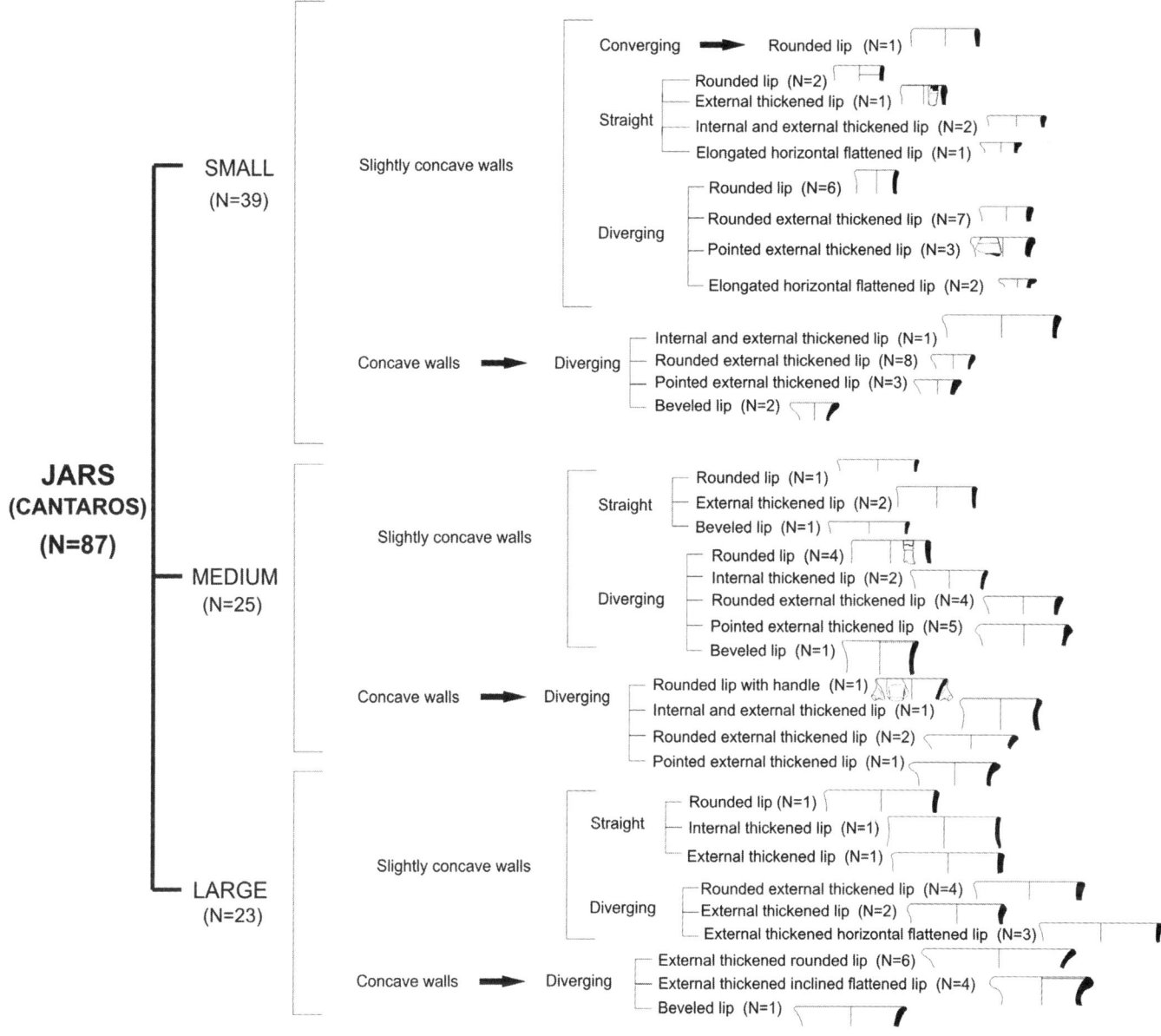

Figure 2.19. Morphological classification of jars (cántaros).

were most popular. In the most recent levels of the Formative sequence, large bowls (tazones) with diverging walls and jars (cántaros) were found.

Seventh, in the lowest levels of Platform 2 of Sector BF, medium bowls (tazones) and medium-necked ollas were found. In the following levels medium-necked ollas continued to be popular, along with jars (cántaros). Then, in the highest levels, this tendency continued, but small jars (cántaros) were predominant in the sample.

Eighth, in the earliest levels of Platform 3 of Sector BF, bowls (tazones) and medium-necked ollas were encountered. Subsequently, the most frequent forms were small and medium jars (cántaros), medium-necked ollas, and bowls (tazones).

## Decorative Categories

Decorative categories were defined based on the identification of a technique or a combination of techniques into five groups: painted; incised; painted and incised; appliqué and incised; appliqué, painted and incised. They were further organized based on the location of the decoration on the vessel—interior or exterior or both—resulting in the following classification:

*Internal Decoration: Painting*

Only three cases of paint on a vessel's interior were recorded, with all three pertaining to decoration on the lip of bevel-rimmed bowls (tazones). All three share the same paint colors, slip color, type of stepped design (with variations), and location of the decoration on the vessel (on the bevel). In the first case (Fig. 2.20a), an elongated black "step" with cream on red slip is observed, with a red slip on the vessel's exterior. On the second example (Fig. 2.20b), there is a more elaborate design; it is the only such case recorded in the sample. It is a "stepped" motif that is repeated using black or dark brown and cream, but in a negative technique. To accomplish this, the vessel was first slipped red on the interior and exterior, then painted on the bevel with a dark color; finally, the cream was added in a way to delimit the rectangular spaces, leaving an in-between space without paint in the form of a step, which is observed in the dark paint. The third case (Fig. 2.21a) corresponds to a simpler "step" motif than the others, combining black and white. This design is found painted on a red slip that was also applied to the vessel's exterior.

*Internal Decoration: Incisions*

Only one example was identified with this type of decoration (Fig. 2.21b). The design corresponds to a straight, thin line made with a sharp instrument before firing. The line is found on the upper part of the vessel, very close to the lip, and appears to surround the entire mouth of the vessel.

*Internal Decoration: Painting and Incisions*

There are few examples in this category, but all feature a "stepped" motif of different varieties, located on the upper part of the vessel. These designs were made when the vessel was leather-hard, although in some case the incisions were made when it was already dry. The instrument used in the decoration would have been thin, with a sharp point.

In all cases the design was made through incisions that form the "stepped" combination with paint filling these spaces. The paint is always black, white or cream, and red or orange and it is always found painted on a red slip, which is applied to the exterior of the piece (Figs. 2.22–2.24). Sometimes a space without paint was intentionally left in order to utilize the color of the slip in the formation of the decorative panels (Fig. 2.25a). In almost all cases, the incised lines that form the design are straight and show single, elongated "steps" (Fig. 2.25a, b); single, thickened "steps" (Fig. 2.22b); or double "steps" (Fig. 2.22a). However, there is a single example of a "step" motif that uses the method of combining incisions with painted spaces of distinct colors, but the line is curvilinear instead of straight (Fig. 2.23b).

*External Decoration: Painting*

Despite having the greatest variety of designs, painted designs on the exterior are exclusively geometric. To clarify, there are no "natural" decorations with anthropomorphic, plant, zoomorphic characteristics; they are limited to straight and curved lines,

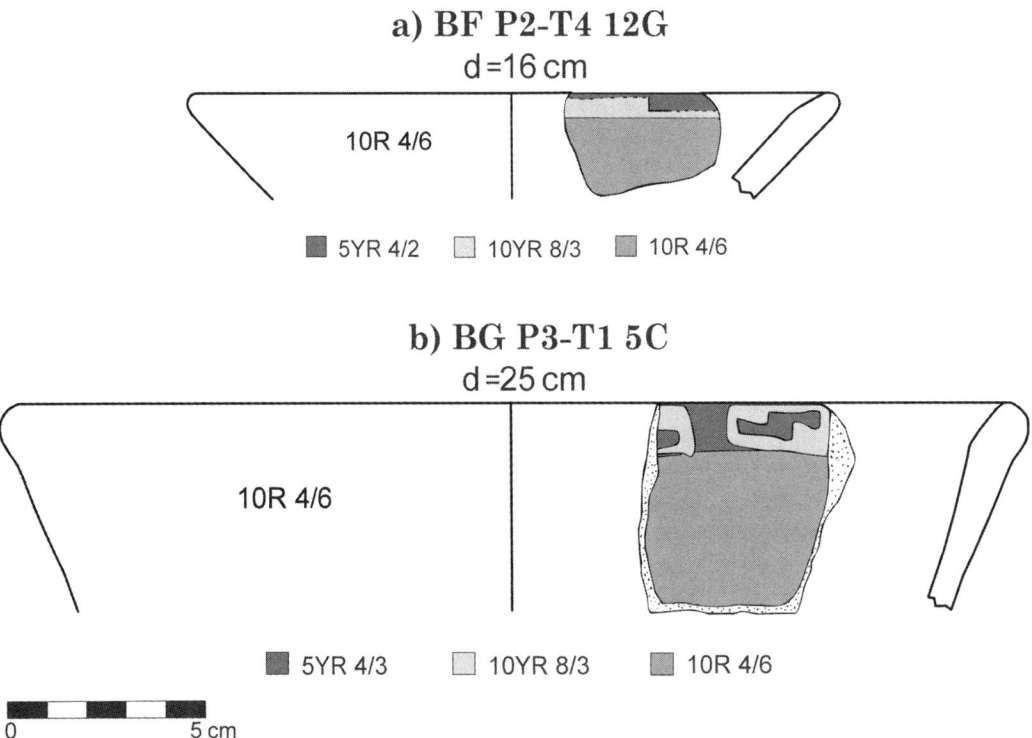

Figure 2.20. Bowls (tazones) with painted decoration on interior.

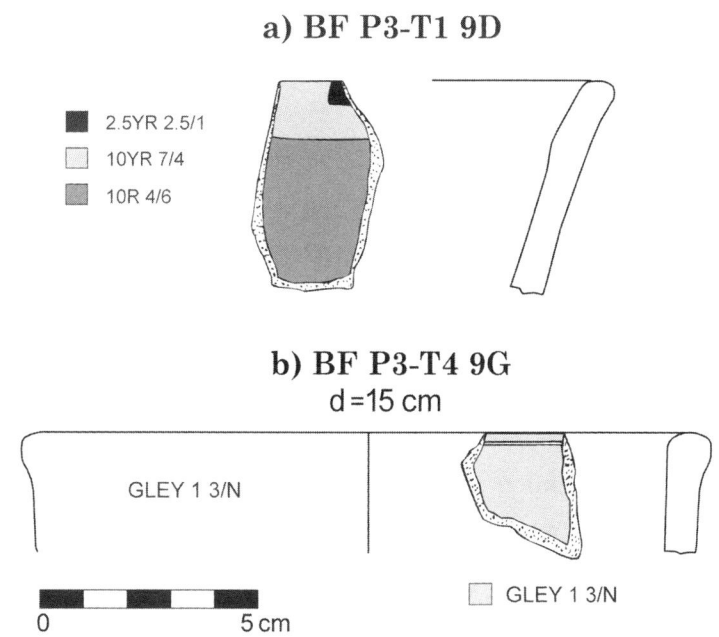

Figure 2.21. Bowls (tazones) with painted (*a*) and incised (*b*) decoration on the interior.

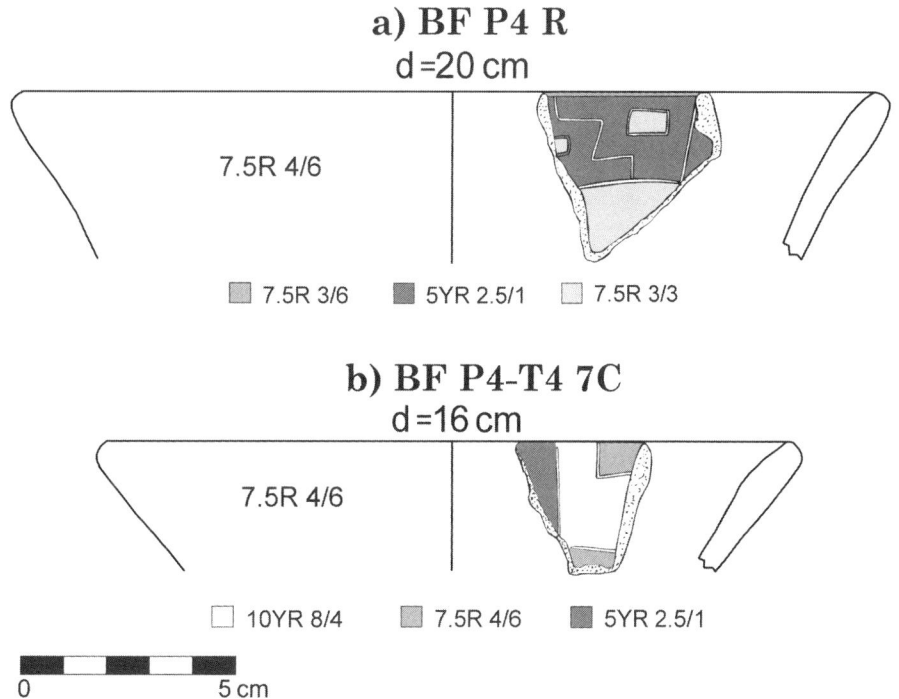

Figure 2.22. Bowls (tazones) with painted (*a*) and incised (*b*) decoration on the interior.

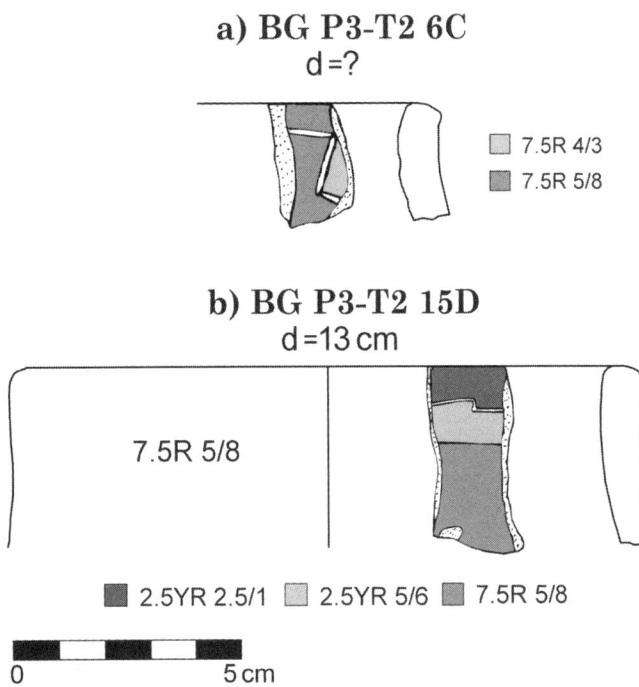

Figure 2.23. Vessels with painted and incised decoration on the interior. *a*, body fragment; *b*, jar (cántaro).

rhomboids, hatched and zone painted. In all cases, the paint was applied to the vessel before being fired and combined a maximum of three colors. The only design identified completely—and co-incidentally the most commonly occurring—features concentric rhomboids in cream paint on a dark brown or black background, overlying a red slip (Figs. 2.25*c*, 2.26*a*, 2.27*c*). In other cases, despite not being able to fully recognize the designs, it is possible to identify the same technique and combination of colors that were used for the vessels with the concentric rhomboids (Figs. 2.26*b*, 2.27*a*, *b*, 2.28*a*, *c*).

Apart from these examples that conform to a decorative style, other variants were identified, including thick cream lines painted on red slip (Fig. 2.25*h*), thick black lines painted on a red slip (Figs. 2.25*a*, 2.28*b*), thick cream lines painted over black (Fig. 2.25*i*), and a single case of a latticed design with two tones of black paint over a cream slip (Fig. 2.26*c*).

*External Decoration: Incisions*

Four stylistic groups have been identified in this category. The first corresponds to vessels with very thick, deep, straight horizontal and parallel incisions made with a blunt point while the vessel was leather-hard (Figs. 2.29*a*, 2.31*b*). The second group includes vessels with thick, curved lines or thick, deep lines that form concentric, elliptical designs in the form of a spiral, which were executed in the same manner as outlined above with a blunt tool (Figs. 2.29*b*, *c*, 2.31*a*, 2.32*a*). One unique example has a combination of the two types of incision; the technique above is paired with another using very fine lines that were made with a sharp tool when the vessel was dry before firing (Fig. 2.35*a*).

The third group corresponds to fragments with deep, wide incisions made with a sharp tool when the vessel was leather-hard. The incisions include lines, dots, circles and ellipses that form geometric figures that are not identifiable due to the size of the sherds (Figs. 2.32*c*, 2.33*a*, *c*, 2.34*a–d*). However, in two exceptional cases it was possible to deduce that the lines, ellipses and circles formed part of a plant image, which could be identified as the stem, branches, and upper part of the flower (Fig. 2.33*b*, *d*).

The fourth group does not share a coherent style, but is made up of fragments with the following characteristics that could not be classified within the other groups: shallow, thick lines forming a geometric design made with a blunt instrument when the vessel was leather-hard (Fig. 2.30*c*); shallow, thin lines made with a sharp instrument when the vessel was leather-hard (Fig. 2.30*a*, *d*); a design formed by a horizontal line and a wide, deep incision forming an elongated circle, which was made with a blunt tool when the vessel was leather-hard (Fig. 2.35*b*); and, lastly, thin, incised lines made with a sharp tool when the vessel was dry just before firing (Figs. 2.30*b*, 2.32*b*).

*External Decoration: Painting and Incisions*

Two groups of fragments share this form of decoration. The first, which is encountered in the majority of the cases, has thin, shallow incised lines that form geometric figures. These incisions are typically made when the vessel is leather-hard although in some cases they are made when the surface is already dry. The figures delimited by the incisions are then painted with the most frequently used color combinations of red and black or red, black and cream.

In terms of the designs, the majority of the fragments are too small to identify the entire decoration. Nevertheless, the following elements have been identified: "step" motifs (Fig. 2.36*b*); "simple squares" (Fig. 2.39*d*); "concentric squares" (Fig. 2.39*a*); and "small Xs" (Fig. 2.39*b*), among others. In the other group are fragments whose decoration consists of very thin, shallow, horizontal lines made with a sharp tool when the vessel was leather-hard. This incision is associated with a thick, wide horizontally painted band. In these cases, the black color of the band is combined with the red slip of the vessel below (Figs. 2.37*c*, 2.38*c*). There is a fragment with a slight variation to this technique included in the group; it also has a thin incised line made with a sharp instrument on leather-hard clay, but in this case the area covered by the painted horizontal band includes the rim and lip and is a slightly lighter color (Fig. 2.37*b*).

*External Decoration: Appliqué and Incisions*

In these cases, the incisions are generally thick and made on leather-hard clay before firing. The designs, which are typically

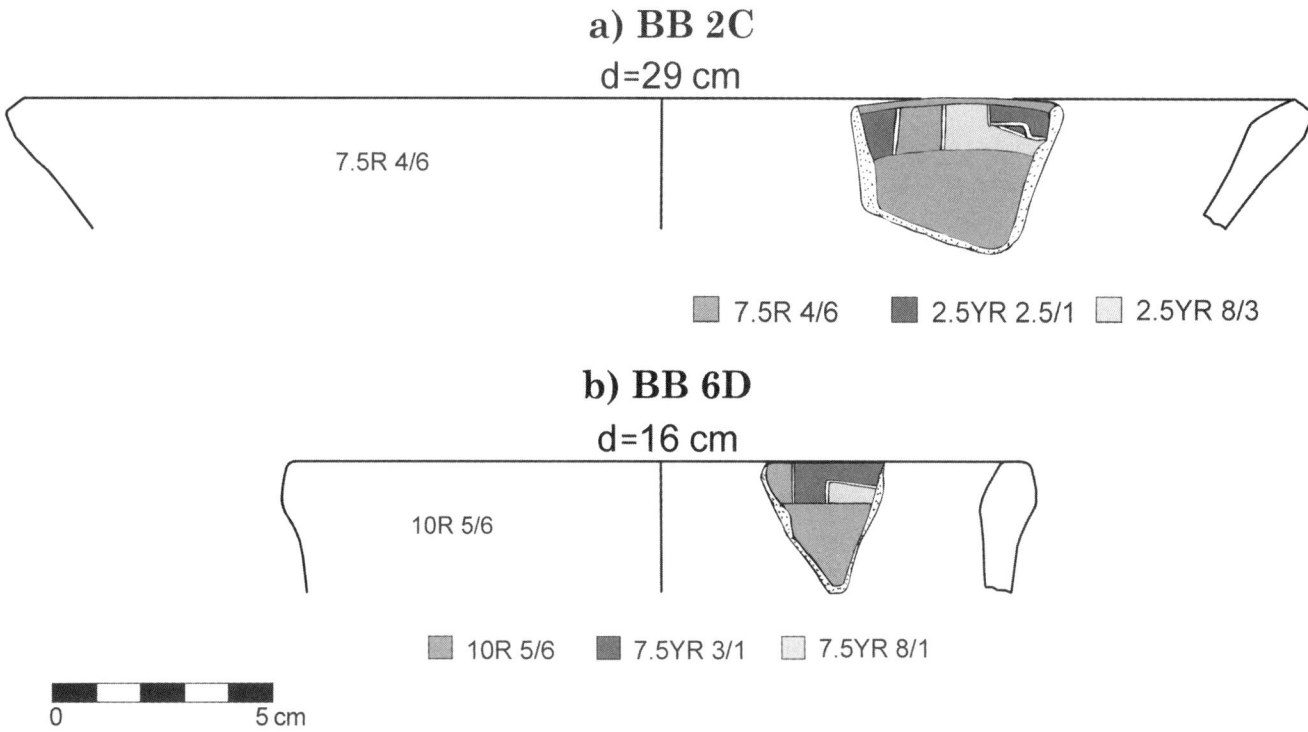

Figure 2.24. Bowls (tazones) with painted and incised decoration on the interior.

horizontal incisions, were likely made with a wide, blunt instrument. In the cases of diagonal or vertical incisions, they are thin or moderately thick and the tool used was probably a thin piece of wood with a sharp point. The incisions are always made into the appliqué element, which may be either a rounded nub or a strip of clay. An incised design with short lines has been identified in three variations: (a) vertical orientation (Figs. 2.40a, 2.41a); (b) diagonal orientation (Figs. 2.40c, e, 2.41b, c, 2.42a, b); and (c) horizontal orientation (Fig. 2.40b, d, f).

*External Decoration: Painting, Incisions and Appliqué*

Only one case was recorded in which all three techniques were used together on the exterior wall of a vessel. Black, red and yellow paint were added within two concentric circles, which were formed using thin incisions. Also, these painted, incised circles were on top of a raised area, giving volume to the design on the vessel wall (Fig. 2.45b).

*Internal and External Decoration: Painting*

In this category there are only four examples and three of them pertain to the same decorative style. Also, in two examples the internal decoration is limited to a band of color applied over the slip on the upper zone of the vessels. In one of these cases, the exterior decoration is made of thick lines forming a black figure over a red slip, which is unfortunately unidentifiable (Fig. 2.43b). On the other, the design is a square painted in thick cream-colored lines on a black background applied over a red slip (Fig. 2.44a).

In the other two cases, the decoration is located on the interior bevel of the rim and the design consists of thick, cream-colored lines painted on a black background applied over a red slip. The slip continues onto the vessel's exterior surface. In one of these the lines are wavy (Fig. 2.43a) while in the other the design is more elaborate, including a wide "raindrop" figure with thick, short lines on the interior (Fig. 2.44b).

*Internal and External Decoration: Paint, Incision and Appliqué*

There is only one example in the category, which is a combination of black and red paint and thin incisions forming a step pattern. The design is found applied onto a red slip on the interior of the vessel while on the exterior is a small handle (Fig. 2.45a).

*Correlation between Formal Categories and Decoration*

In spite of the limited numbers of decorated fragments and the difficulty of assigning many of them to formal vessel categories, a few trends have been identified. First, when there is decoration on the interior (painted or painted and incised), in the majority of

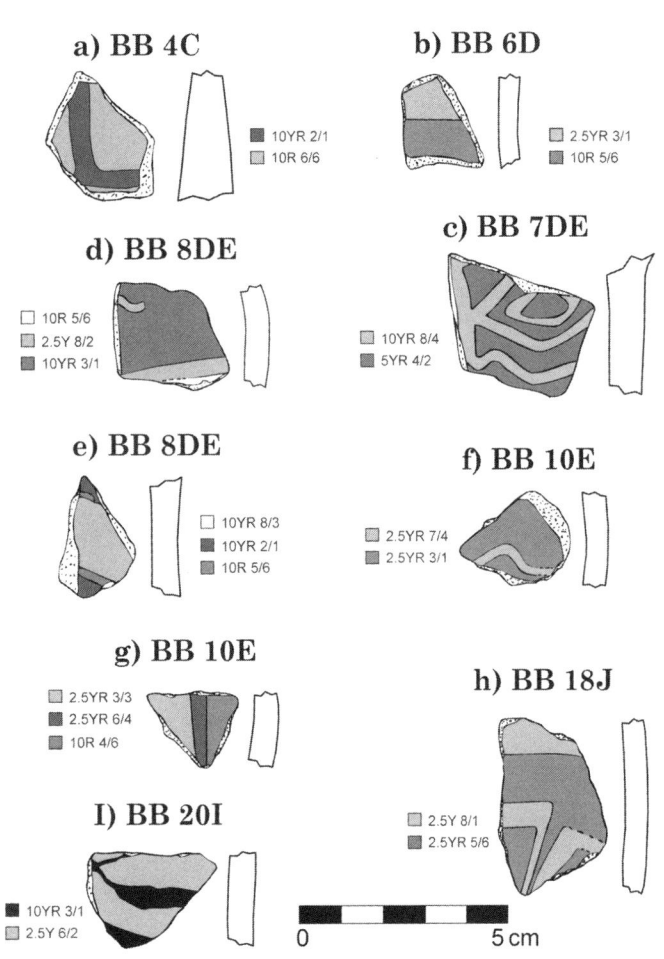

Figure 2.25. Body fragments with painted decoration on the exterior.

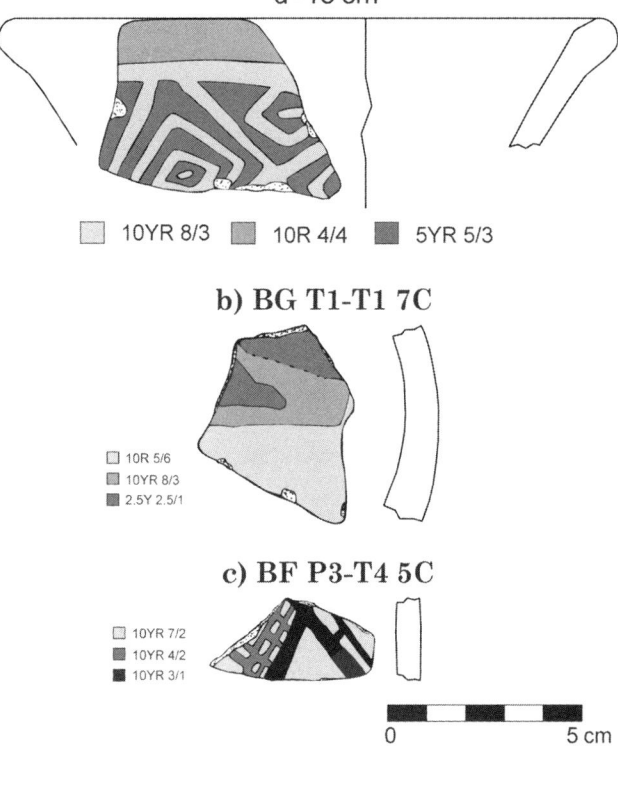

Figure 2.26. Vessels with painted decoration on the exterior. *a*, bowl (tazón); *b*, *c*, body fragments.

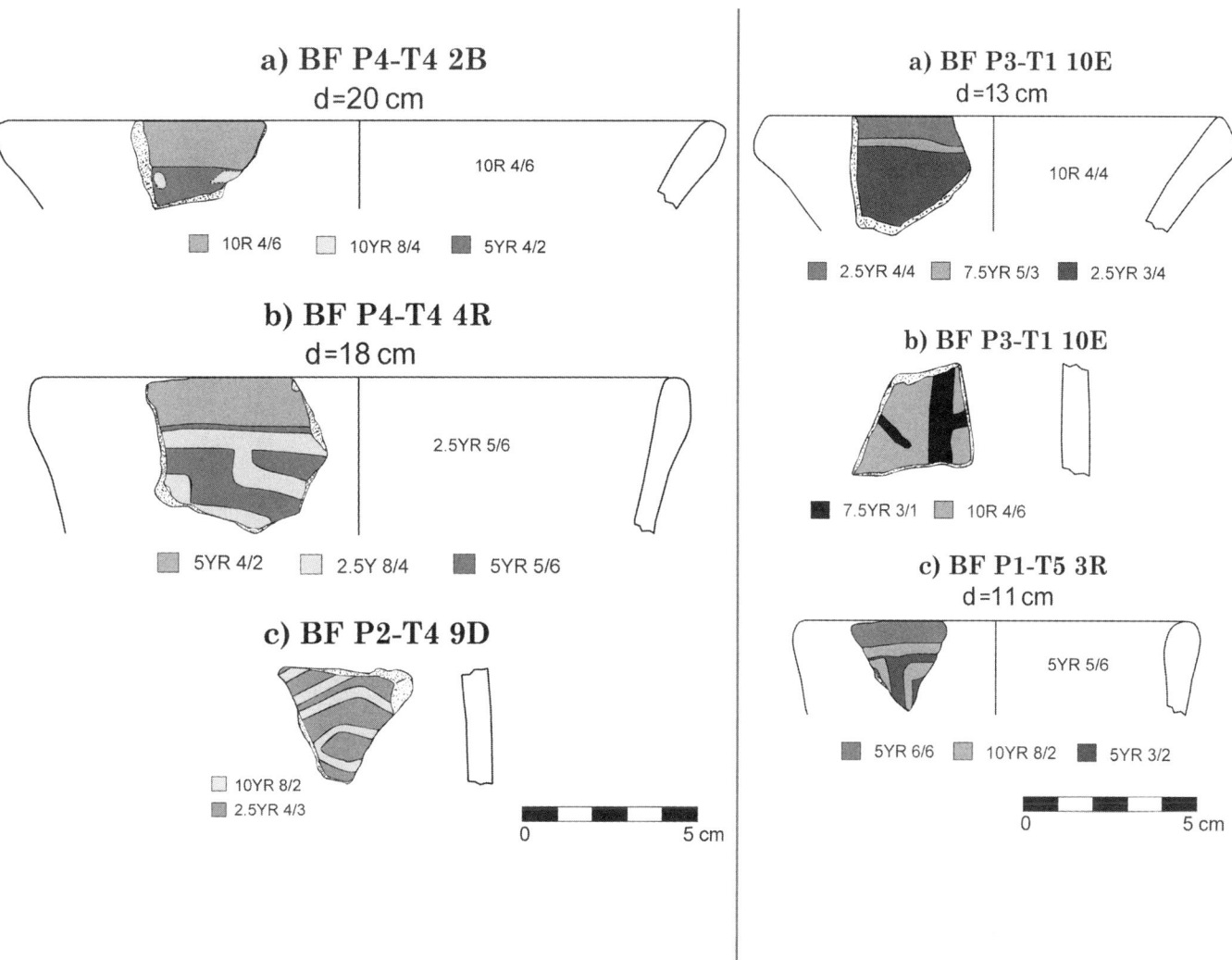

Figure 2.27. Vessels with painted decoration on the exterior. *a, b*, bowls (tazones); *c*, body fragment.

Figure 2.28. Vessels with painted decoration on the exterior. *a, c*, bowls (tazones); *b*, body fragment.

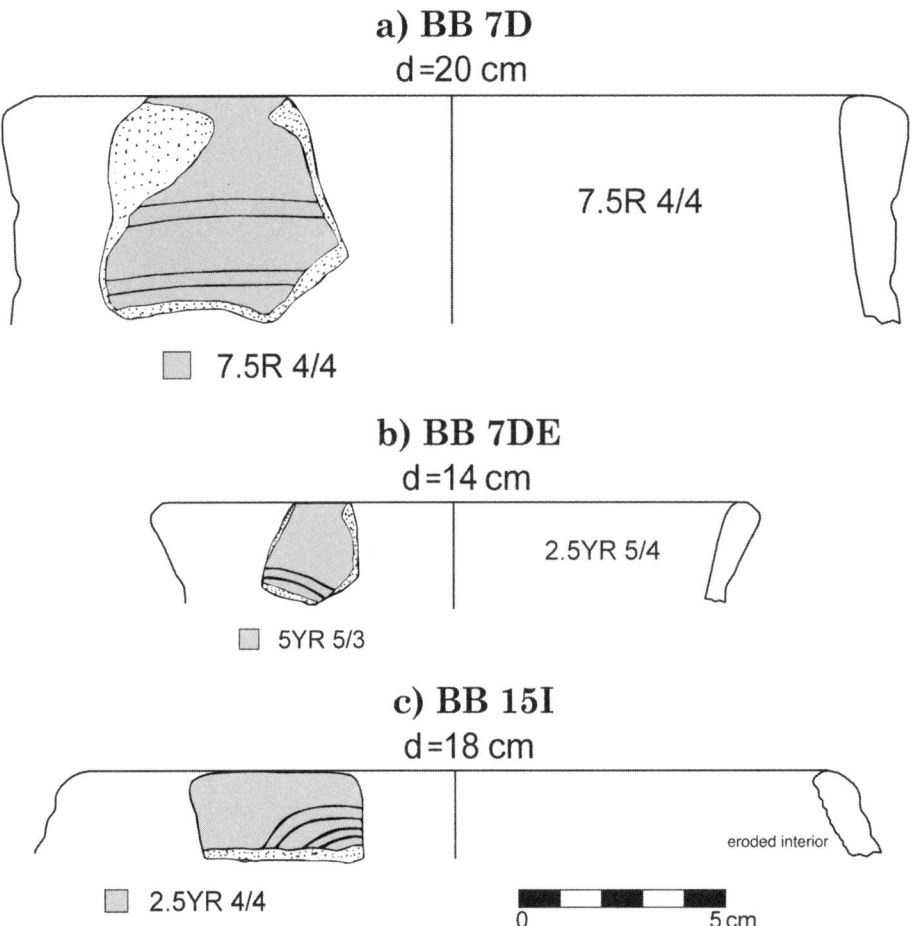

Figure 2.29. Vessels with incised decoration on the exterior. *a*, *b*, bowls; *c*, olla.

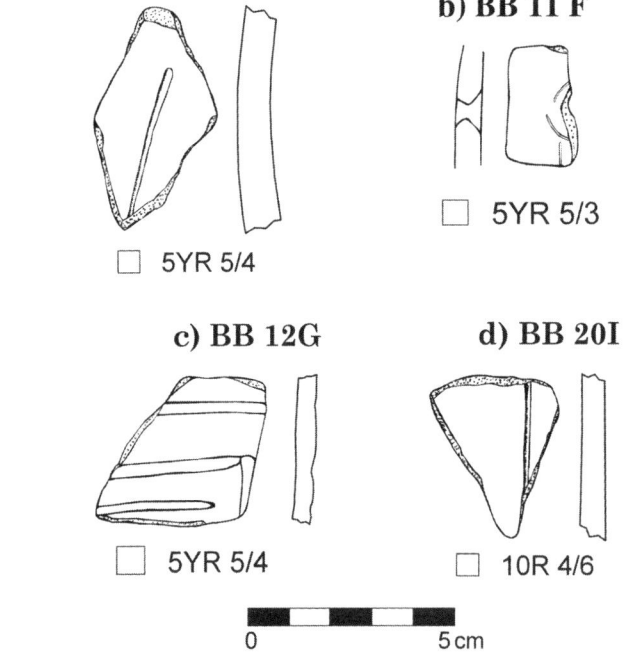

Figure 2.30. Body fragments with incised decoration on the exterior.

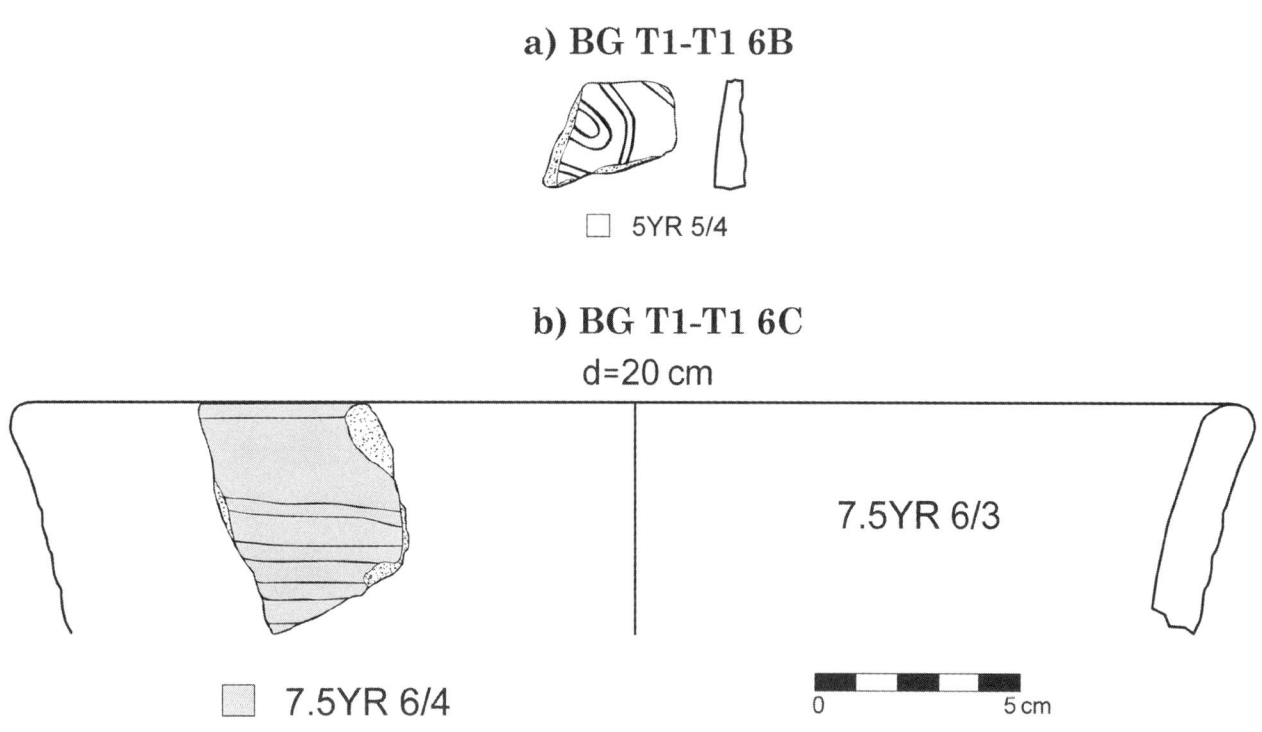

Figure 2.31. Vessels with incised decoration on the exterior. *a*, body fragment; *b*, bowl (tazón).

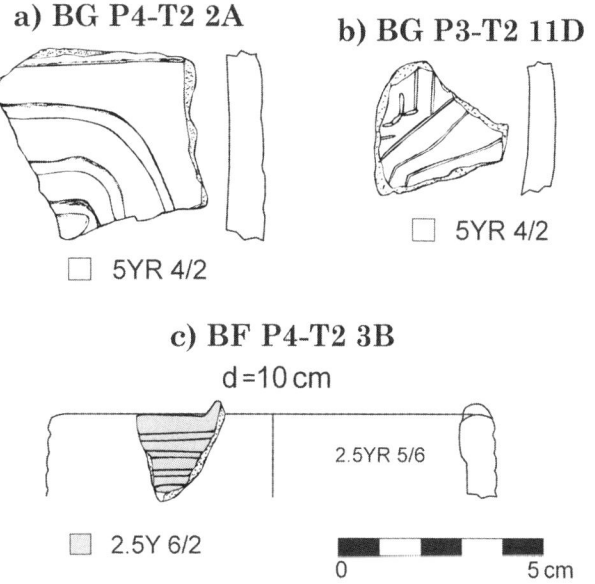

Figure 2.32. Vessels with incised decoration on the exterior. *a*, *b*, body fragments; *c*, bowl (tazón).

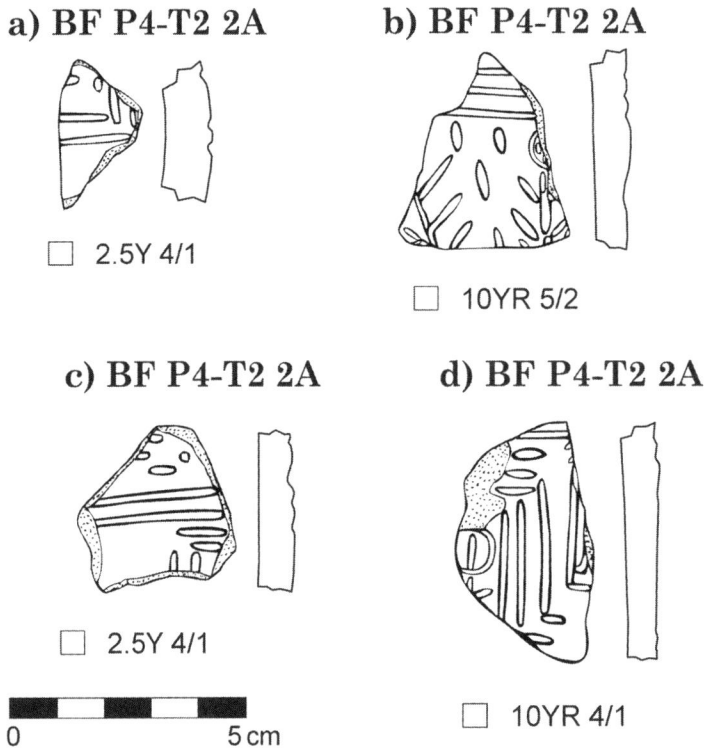

Figure 2.33. Body fragments with incised decoration on the exterior.

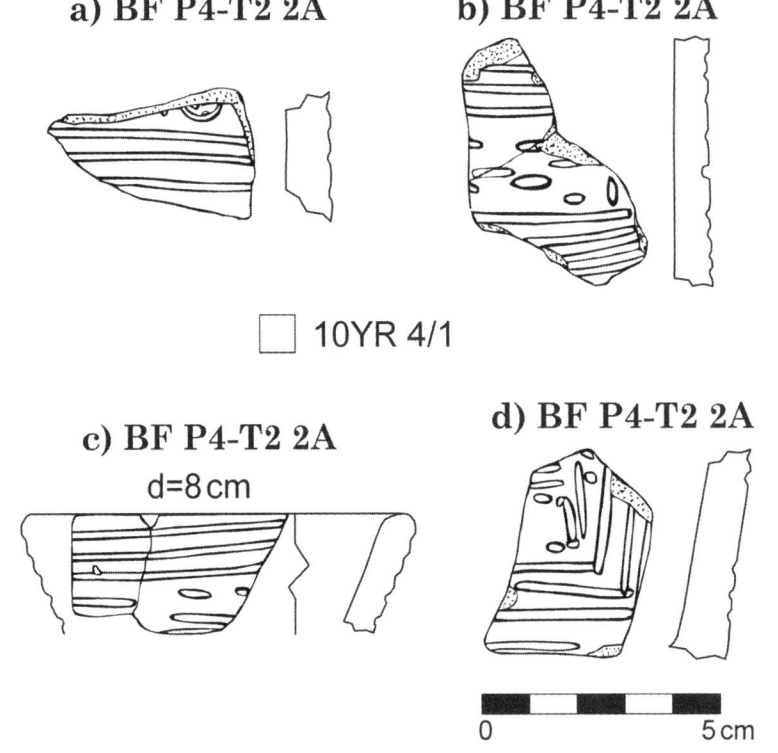

Figure 2.34. Body fragments with incised decoration on the exterior.

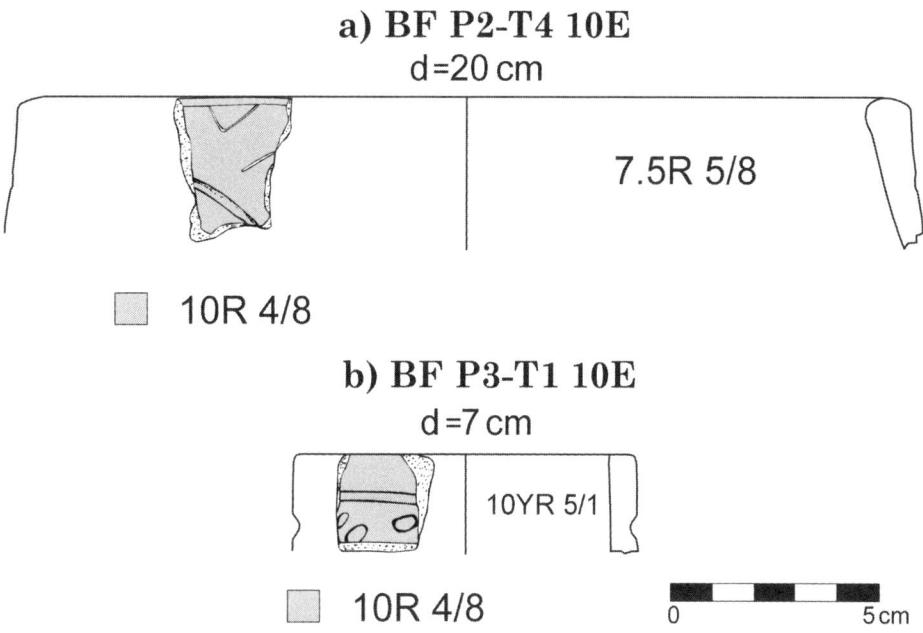

Figure 2.35. Vessels with incised decoration on the exterior. *a*, olla; *b*, bowl (tazón).

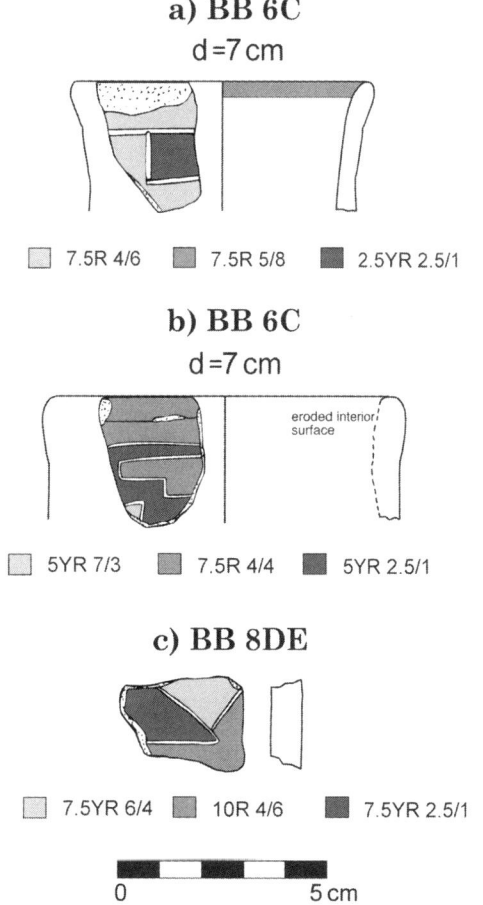

Figure 2.36. Vessels with painted and incised decoration on the exterior. *a*, *b*, bowls; *c*, body fragment.

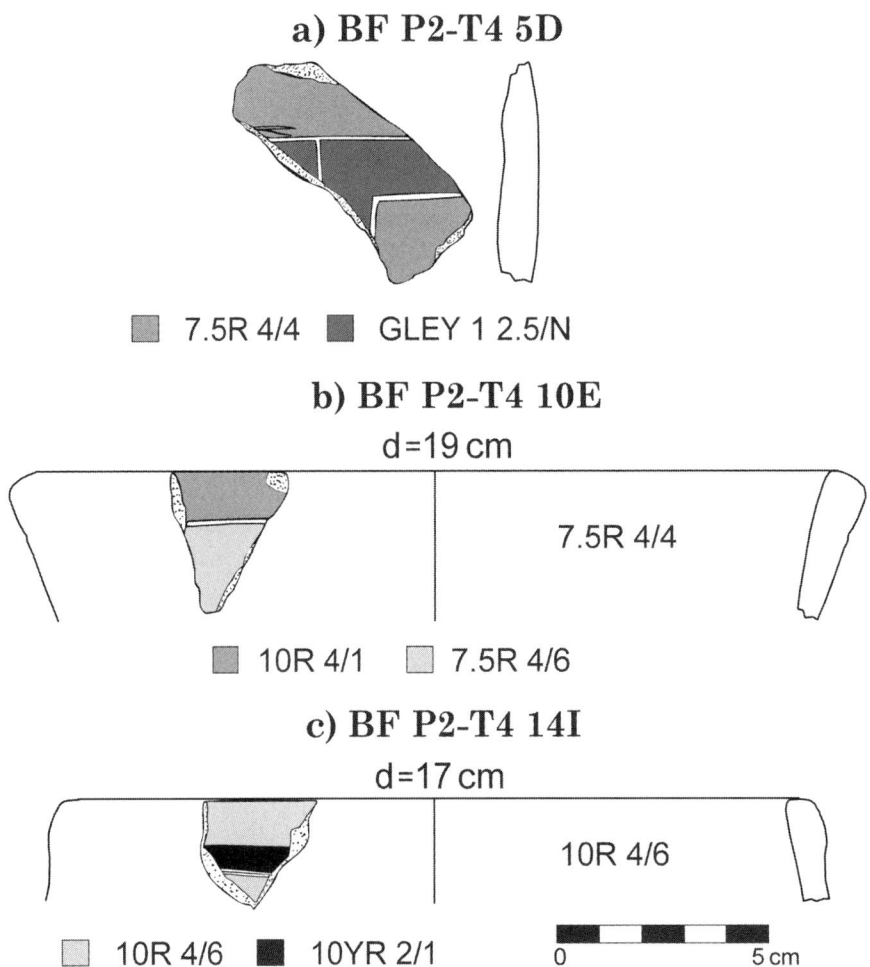

Figure 2.37. Vessels with painted and incised decoration on the exterior. *a*, body fragment; *b*, bowl (tazón); *c*, olla.

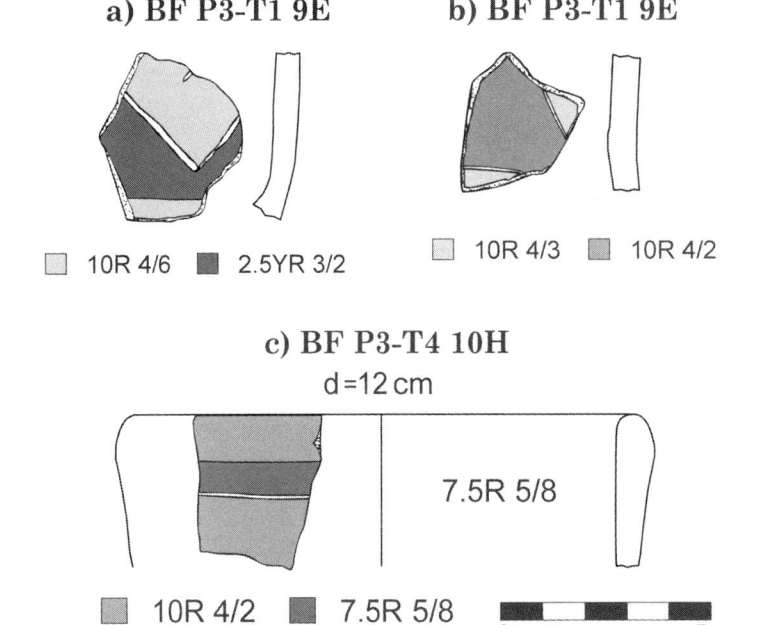

Figure 2.38. Vessels with painted and incised decoration on the exterior. *a*, *b*, body fragments; *c*, bowl (tazón).

Figure 2.39. Body fragments with painted and incised decoration.

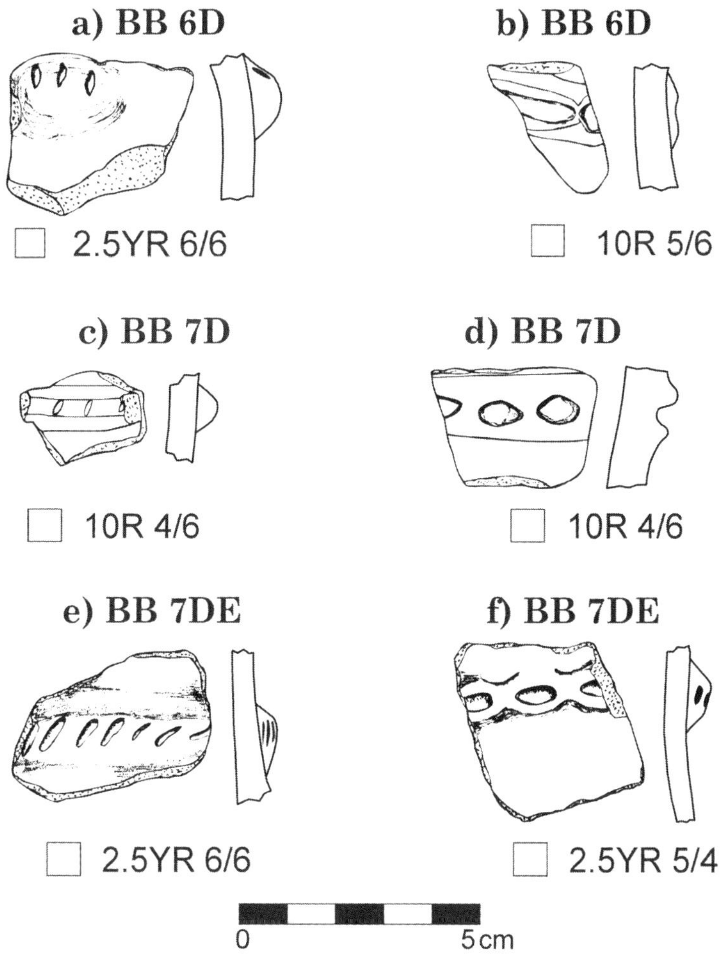

Figure 2.40. Body fragments with appliqué and incised decoration.

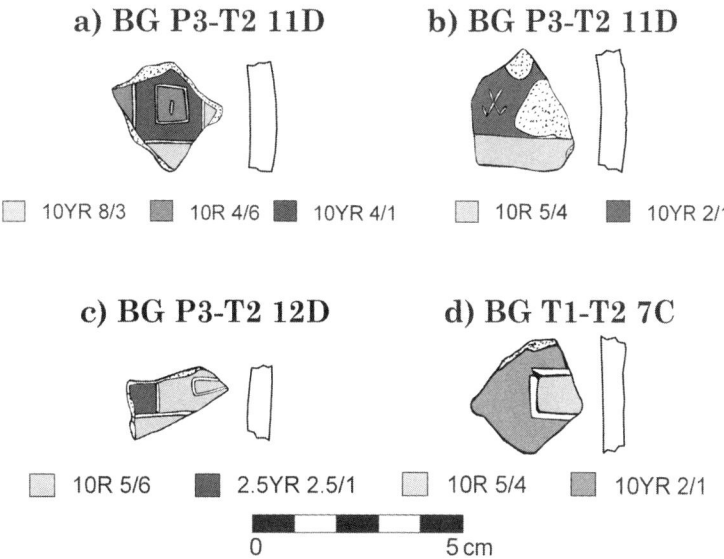

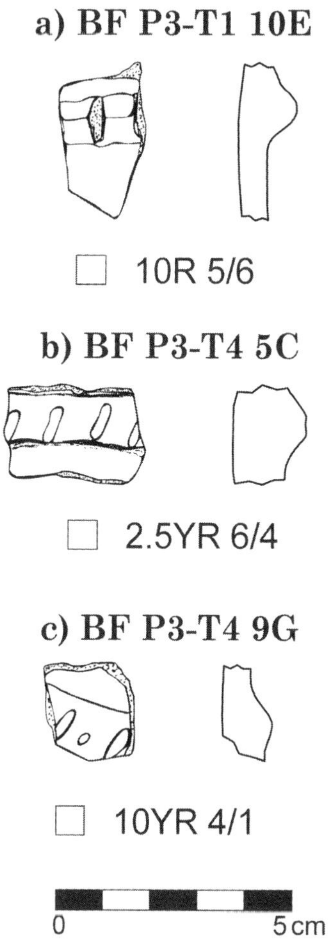

Figure 2.41. Body fragments with appliqué and incised decoration.

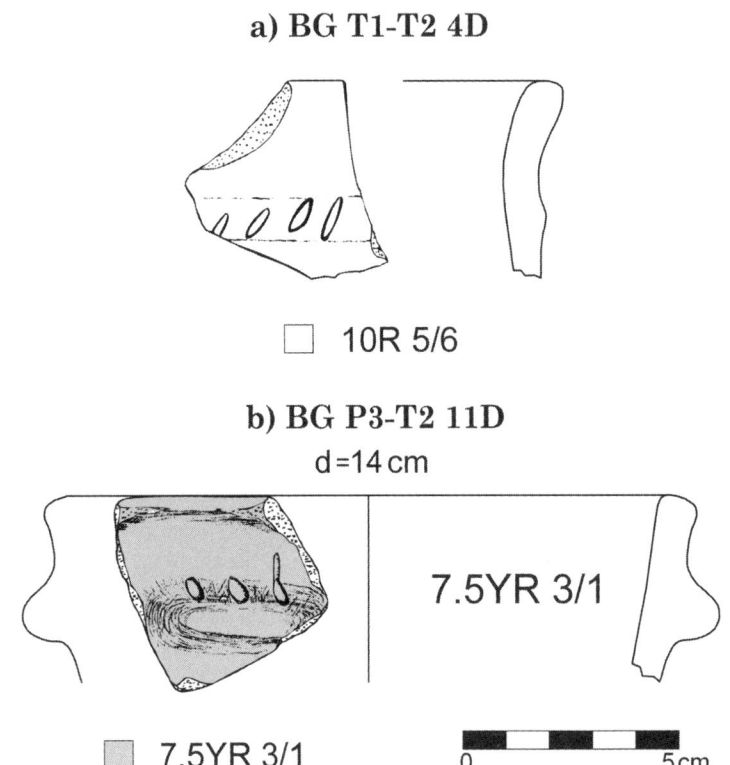

Figure 2.42. Vessels with appliqué and incised decoration. *a*, unidentified form; *b*, bowl (tazón).

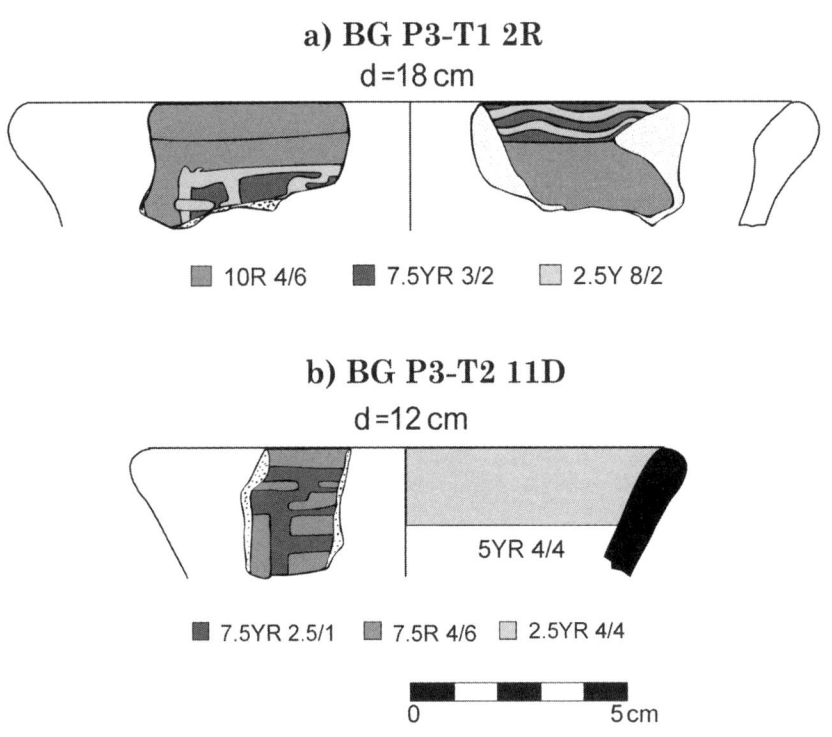

Figure 2.43. Bowls (tazones) with painted decoration on the interior and exterior.

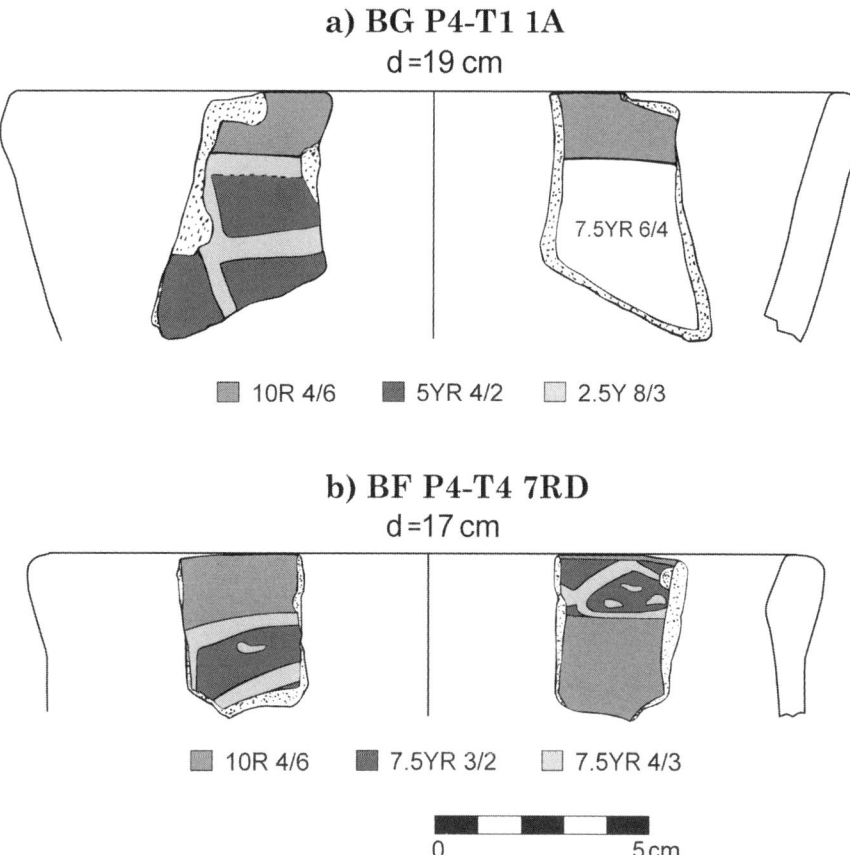

Figure 2.44. Bowls (tazones) with painted decoration on the interior and exterior.

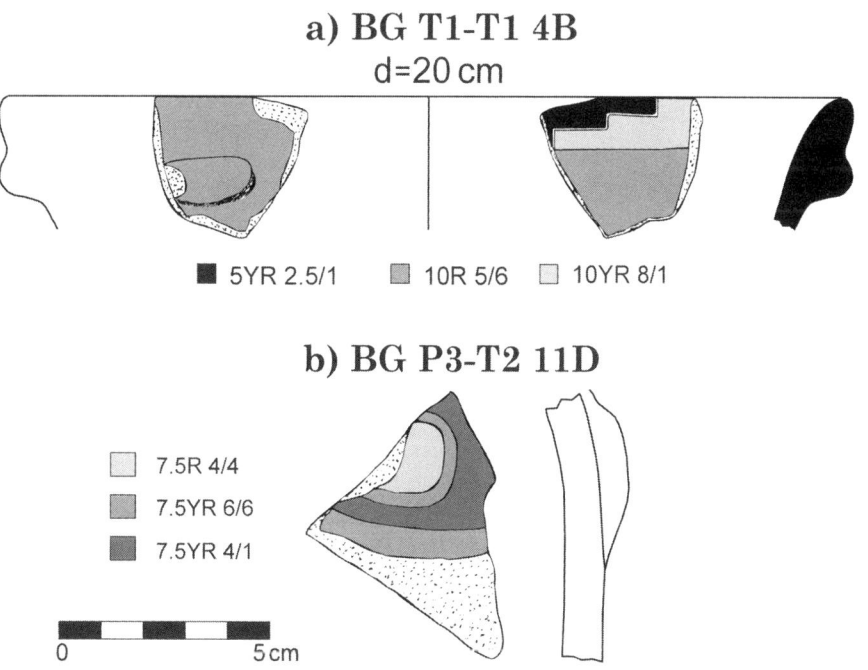

Figure 2.45. *a*, bowl (tazón) with painted and incised decoration on the interior and appliqué decoration on the exterior; *b*, body fragment with appliqué, painted and incised decoration.

these cases it is located on the interior beveled lip of a medium or large bowl (tazón) with diverging walls. The only case of an incised decoration on the interior was on a medium bowl (tazón) with vertical walls.

Second, when decoration is located on the vessel exterior, the majority of painted designs are found on medium and large bowls (tazones) with diverging walls. In the case of painted and incised decoration on the exterior, vessel types include: a medium bowl (tazón) with vertical walls; a large bowl (tazón) with diverging walls; a medium-necked olla with converging walls; and a small jar (cántaro) with a slightly concave, vertical neck. Incised decoration on the exterior is found on the following vessel types: two small bowls (tazones) with vertical walls; one small bowl (tazón) with diverging walls; a medium bowl (tazón) with diverging walls; a large bowl (tazón) with diverging walls and another with vertical walls; and a neckless olla with slightly inclined walls.

Lastly, in the case of vessels with both internal and external decoration, almost all are large bowls (tazones) with diverging sides. There is only one exception to this case, which is a small jar (cántaro) on which the internal decoration is limited to a small painted band near the rim.

*Stylistic Considerations*

This study has identified examples of four ceramic styles that have been preliminarily defined in the existing literature as Qaluyu, Cusipata, Initial Pukara or Incised Cusipata and Ramis. Additionally, there are examples that cannot be classified within these groups. Given that there is limited evidence, it is not possible to assert whether these unidentified sherds are new local styles, non-local styles, or variants within the styles already mentioned.

*Qaluyu*

First, in this sample there are examples of designs made with thick linear or curvilinear incisions on brown or grayish slipped bowls (tazones) (Figs. 2.29, 2.31), which are similar to designs assigned to the Qaluyu style in earlier publications (see Lumbreras and Amat 1968:103, Fig. 1*g*, *h*; Steadman 1995:588, Fig. 49*a–d*). Karen Mohr Chávez (1977:1025) noted that these designs had been found in the type site of Qaluyu and share similarities with ceramics recovered in her excavations at Marcavalle (Cuzco) within the early ceramic phases. Lee Steadman (1995:538) adds that in the site of Camata in the western Titicaca Basin, these decorations were also encountered in the "Late Qaluyu 1" phase, inserting them into the later part of the earliest sequence at that site.

The other case that is related stylistically to Qaluyu is a fragment with the painting technique labeled by Luis Lumbreras and Hernán Amat (1968:78) as Qaluyu "dark on light" (*oscuro sobre claro*) and by Steadman (1995:425) as "brown or black on cream." I have classified this example as "latticed," but given the small size of the sherd, it is not possible to identify the entire design (Fig. 2.26*c*). It is quite possible that this design is like the diamonds with interior latticing that Steadman (1995:577, Figs. 37*f*, 38*f*) identified as the most common design found in the earliest periods at Camata. Mohr Chávez (1977:1024–25) also encountered this design on vessels from Pikicallepata and Marcavalle.

*Cusipata*

Previous research by Elías Mujica (1987:26, Fig. 6*a–f*) includes the majority of cases that were analyzed in the present study. The fragments of this style that have yet to be published share with the others the combination of cream paint on a dark brown or black background, which is all painted over a red slip. The designs are the same, using either straight or undulating lines (Figs. 2.25*d*, *f*, 2.28*a*) or horizontal, concentric diamonds (Figs. 2.25*c*, 2.27*c*). Examples of ceramics of this style were also encountered in excavations of the central pampa at Pukara by Elizabeth Klarich (2005a:342, Fig. 10), but besides this example they have not been identified in excavations. Mohr Chávez (1977:1027) found various similarities between the Cusipata ceramic style and Marcavalle cream/brown, which merits further investigation to determine the nature of this relationship.

*Pucara Pampa, and So On*

The third ceramic style was originally defined as Pucara Pampa (Franquemont 1986:9), then as Initial Pukara (Wheeler and Mujica 1981:34), and finally as Incised Cusipata (Mujica 1987:24). Vessels of this style have incised decoration used to delimit the design area, which is then painted in black, white or red. The figures are generally geometric, including squares, rectangles, and step motifs (Figs. 2.22*a*, *b*, 2.23*b*, 2.24*a*, *b*, 2.36*a–c*, 2.45*a*). One example of this style has been published by Klarich (2005a:342, Fig. 2); it was recovered from excavations on the central pampa at Pukara.

*Ramis*

The final style, Ramis, has been previously defined and described by Jane Wheeler and Elías Mujica (1981:40). It is defined as poorly manufactured and fired black pottery with incised geometric designs and post-fire paint. This style would be contemporaneous with Painted Cusipata and Incised Cusipata and may come from the eastern valleys. In the present study, various fragments of this style were analyzed and likely correspond to serving vessels for food or liquids. This is based on the examples published by Wheeler and Mujica (1981:41, Fig. 25, 1 and 2) and our identification of two small bowls (Figs. 2.32*c*, 2.24*c*) and a possible bowl (tazón) with a pedestal base (Fig. 2.34*d*).

There are two important examples worth mentioning within the decorated wares. These are the only fragments from the earliest sequence from Pukara with naturalistic decorations, specifically a plant with a stem, branches, and flower on the upper part (Fig.

2.33*b*, *d*). Stylistically, these sherds are also Ramis. In all others analyzed, early fragments exclusively feature geometric designs.

It is important to note that because of erosion it was not possible to document the presence of post-fire painting in the present sample. However, Klarich (2005a:227) documents the presence of two post-fire painted sherds excavated from the central pampa at Pukara, as does Steadman (1995:446) from the "Initial Pucara" phases at Camata.

*Other Styles*

A distinct and little understood style is composed of vessels with appliqué decoration that have also been incised. Klarich (2005a:227) proposes that this ceramic style is non-local, like the Ramis style. There is a strong similarity between those published by Klarich (2005a:340, Figs. 2, 3) and those identified in this study (Fig. 2.40*c*, *e*).

*Technology: Paste Analysis*

Paste analysis[3] was done macroscopically and first considered color, then the characteristics of the inclusions (color, form, size, quantity, distribution), hardness, porosity and texture, and firing. Based on these preliminary analyses, 52 pastes, 15 paste groups and 8 wares were defined (Tables 2.1–2.4).[4] However, these groupings will need to be corroborated with future petrographic analyses.

*The Earliest Ceramic Sequence at Pukara*

Due to the fact that the analyzed ceramics were from a limited number of contexts and generally recovered from construction fill, the process of reconstructing the ceramic sequence was quite difficult. Typically, fill episodes are composed of trash from a variety of time periods, resulting in levels in which the recovered sherds were not necessarily used contemporaneously. Nevertheless, it was possible in some contexts to define a coherent sequence based on the study of ware categories.

In this analysis, it is first important to note that throughout the sequence almost all formal categories of vessels were produced with all wares, meaning that there was no exclusive production of particular ware categories. This is important because it could be an indicator of little centralization and/or hierarchical structuring of ceramic production at Pukara. This also may mean that ceramic producers were not specialists during this time period and that each productive unit was able to produce the whole range of vessel types. However, it is important to note in this analysis that bowls (tazones), especially medium and large bowls, are the vessel form found most commonly in all ware categories. Only in the case of Ware F are there more jars (cántaros) than bowls (tazones), which is interesting considering it is one of the earliest ware categories in the sequence.

As mentioned previously, ceramics in this analysis were recovered from three sectors at Pukara—BB, BF and BG—and due to a lack of secure contexts the reconstruction of the sequence has been challenging. However, there are a number of important chronological elements documented within this sample that were first noted from Sector BB and subsequently confirmed with the materials from Sectors BF and BG.

*Sector BB*. To begin, there are ceramic wares that appear throughout the entire Formative sequence, most notably Wares A and B. There are also wares that appear gradually over time and remain until the end of the Middle Formative. In Table 2.1 it is documented that Wares F and G are encountered primarily in the latest strata with Middle Formative materials, which corresponds to the transition to the Late Formative (Middle or Classic phase) at Pukara. However, it is notable that these wares also appear in the lowest level, corresponding to the earliest pottery at the site. This is important because Wares F and G generally fit the descriptions for Qaluyu ceramics, corresponding to the general chronology for the Titicaca Basin. Additionally, based on the results of the present study, it is possible to argue that this ceramic tradition was not restricted to the earliest levels of the site, but continued until the Middle or Classic Pukara transition. Finally, we also note that Ware C is encountered consistently throughout the sequence, which corresponds to Huaña I (Chávez Justo, n.d.). This would be a ceramic tradition that was not documented for this region, but has been tentatively defined as originating in the Middle Formative and continuing through the Altiplano period. It has been documented in areas such as Taraco and the zone of Huancané; with the present findings its range has been expanded west to Pukara.

*Sector BF*. In this sector the ware sequence is much clearer (Tables 2.2, 2.3). It is again clear that Wares A and B are present in almost the entire sequence while others, such as Ware H, are not encountered in the early levels but continue through the end. This suggests that some traditions were present from the earliest periods of occupation while others were incorporated or invented locally and continued to be used at least until the beginning of the Late Formative, if not for many years longer. In this sector, the wares or pastes that correspond to those described for Qaluyu appear in the middle of the sequence. It is noteworthy that their appearance is grouped and also that they were not present in the upper levels. This suggests that their use in this part of the site was not long term, which makes sense when considering that the analyzed ceramics were recovered from construction fill and not from occupation levels. Also, in spite of the possibility that the ceramics are mixed, it is important to note that sherds from the Huaña I tradition are present, appearing in the intermediate levels and continuing through the end of the sequence.

*Sector BG*. Analysis of pottery from this sector produces the same trends as Sectors BB and BF. For example, Ware A and Ware B to a lesser degree are present throughout the entire sequence while other traditions are limited to some levels (Table 2.4). This is the sector with the most potential for mixed levels and a smaller number of sherds. These contexts, like those of Sector BF, come exclusively from construction fills.

Table 2.1. Distribution of wares by strata, Sector BB.

| Level | Ware | | | | | | | |
|---|---|---|---|---|---|---|---|---|
| | A | B | C | D | E | F | G | H |
| C | X | X | X | X | X | X | X | X |
| D | X | X | X | X | X | X | X | X |
| DE | X | | X | X | X | | | X |
| E | X | X | | | X | | | |
| F | | | | | | | X | X |
| G | X | | X | | | X | | |
| H | X | | | | | | | |
| I | X | X | X | X | X | X | X | X |

Table 2.2. Distribution of wares by strata, Sector BF, Platform 2.

| Level | Ware | | | | | | | |
|---|---|---|---|---|---|---|---|---|
| | A | B | C | D | E | F | G | H |
| B | X | X | X | | | | | X |
| C | X | X | | | | | | X |
| D | | X | X | | | | | X |
| E | X | X | X | | | X | X | X |
| F | X | | X | | | | | |
| G | X | X | X | | | | | X |
| H | | | X | | | | | |
| I | X | X | | X | X | | | |

Table 2.3. Distribution of wares by strata, Sector BF, Platform 3.

| Level | Ware | | | | | | | |
|---|---|---|---|---|---|---|---|---|
| | A | B | C | D | E | F | G | H |
| D | X | | X | | X | | | X |
| E | X | X | X | X | X | X | X | X |
| F | X | X | X | | | | | X |
| G | | | X | | X | | | |
| H | X | | | | | | | |

Table 2.4. Distribution of wares by strata, Sector BG, Platform 3.

| Level | Ware | | | | | | | |
|---|---|---|---|---|---|---|---|---|
| | A | B | C | D | E | F | G | H |
| B | | X | X | | | | | X |
| C | X | X | X | X | X | | | |
| D | X | X | X | | X | X | | X |

## Conclusions

During the Middle Formative, the first complex societies emerged in the Lake Titicaca Basin, with corporate architecture. These sites were led by elites who competed for control of both local and non-local goods. When effective, elites could weave together disparate social groups and mobilize populations beyond the household level. Depending on the ability of the elites, they could attract large or small groups to their respective sites, resulting in differences in site size and complexity. Based on the offerings of the local elite, large sites would therefore have had populations with diverse origins, reflecting the greater number of people who migrated to these centers. The growth of such centers would also have included a number of coexisting traditions in many aspects of daily life, including, of course, ceramic production.

In the sample analyzed in this study, the interactions of contemporaneous, distinct traditions are reflected by the variety of paste types, paste groups and ware categories present in the contexts excavated at Pukara. This diversity indicates that, for example, there were various "Qaluyu styles" or various traditions within these categories that have been grouped together by archaeologists. With respect to this diversity, it is important to note the existence of the Huaña I style at Pukara during almost the entire sequence, confirming initial suspicions that this recently defined tradition was contemporaneous with Qaluyu and continued into later periods. Future studies at Pukara and surrounding sites will serve to refine the spatial and chronological distribution of these various ceramic types during the dynamic and still poorly understood Formative period in the Titicaca Basin.

## Acknowledgments

I want to thank the editors of this volume for inviting me to participate. Also I am in debt to a number of people without whom I would not have been able to complete this research: Elías Mujica, Elizabeth Klarich, Peter Kaulicke, Cecilia Chávez Justo, Edmundo de la Vega, Bárbara Carbajal and Honorato Ttaca.

## Notes

1. All information related to the Plan Copesco Project (maps, drawings and plans) was generously provided by Elías Mujica.

2. It is possible that necked ollas and jars (cántaros) were mixed during analysis due to the small size of the neck sherds.

3. The methods of ceramic analysis used were the same as those developed by Cecilia Chávez Justo in "Análisis de la Cerámica del Sector Medio y Bajo de de la Sub-cuenca del Río Huancané (Puno-Perú), 2008" (Chávez Justo 2008).

4. A detailed description of the ceramic pastes, paste groups, and ware categories are available in the author's Licenciatura thesis (Oshige 2010).

## References Cited

Bandy, M.
2001 ¿Por qué surgió Tiwanaku y no otro centro político del Formativo tardío? *Boletín de Arqueología PUCP* 5:585–604. Pontificia Universidad Católica del Perú, Lima.

Beck, R.
2001 Architecture and polity in the Formative Lake Titicaca Basin, Bolivia. *Latin American Antiquity* 15(3):323–43.

Chávez Justo, C.
2008 Análisis de la cerámica del sector medio y bajo de la sub-cuenca del Rio Huancané, Puno-Peru, 2008. Electronic document, http://www.sscnet.ucla.edu/ioa/collasuyu.

Chávez, S.
1992 The Conventionalized Rules in Pucara Pottery Technology and Iconography: Implications of Socio-Political Development in the Northern Titicaca Basin. PhD dissertation, Department of Anthropology, Michigan State University, East Lansing.

Franquemont, E.
1986 The ancient pottery from Pucara, Peru. *Ñawpa Pacha* 24:1–30.

Hastorf, C.
2005 The Upper (Middle and Late) Formative in the Titicaca region. In *Advances in Titicaca Basin Archaeology–1*, edited by C. Stanish, A. Cohen, and M. Aldenderfer, pp. 65–94. Cotsen Institute of Archaeology, University of California, Los Angeles.
2008 The Formative period in the Titicaca Basin. In *Handbook of South American Archaeology*, edited by H. Silverman and W. Isbell, pp. 545–61. Springer, New York.

Inojosa, J. M.
1940 Informe sobre los trabajos arqueológicos de la Misión Kidder en Pukara, Peru (enero a julio 1939). *Revista del Museo Nacional* 9(1):128–42.

Janusek, J.
2001 Diversidad residencial y el surgimiento de la complejidad en Tiwanaku. *Boletín de Arqueología PUCP* 5:251–94. Pontificia Universidad Católica del Perú, Lima.
2004 Tiwanaku and its precursors: Recent research and emerging perspectives. *Journal of Archaeological Research* 12(2):121–83.
2005 Residential diversity and the rise of complexity in Tiwanaku. In *Advances in Titicaca Basin Archaeology–1*, edited by C. Stanish, A. Cohen, and M. Aldenderfer, pp. 143–72. Cotsen Institute of Archaeology, University of California, Los Angeles.

Kidder II, A.
1942 Preliminary notes on the archaeology of Pucara, Puno, Peru. *Actas y Trabajos Científicos de XXVII Congreso Internacional de Americanistas* (Lima 1939) 1:341–45.
1943 *Some Early Sites in the Northern Lake Titicaca Basin*. Papers of the Peabody Museum of American Archaeology and Ethnology, Harvard University, vol. 27, no. 1. Cambridge, MA.

1948 The position of Pucara in Titicaca Basin archaeology. In *Reappraisal of Peruvian Archaeology*, edited by W. C. Bennett, pp. 87–89. Society for American Archaeology and the Institute of Andean Research, Menasha, WI.

Klarich, E.
2002 Occupation and offerings: Elite household organization at Pukara, Lake Titicaca Basin, Peru (200 BC–AD 200). Paper presented at the Society for American Archaeology 67th Annual Meeting, Denver, CO.
2003 Informe sobre las excavaciones de la temporada 2001 en Pukara, Peru: Una discusión sobre la organización del sitio, la cronología local y su posición en el Formativo Tardío. Paper presented at the 51st International Congress of Americanistas, Santiago, Chile.
2005a From the Monumental to the Mundane: Defining Early Leadership Strategies at Late Formative Pukara, Peru. PhD dissertation, Department of Anthropology, University of California, Santa Barbara.
2005b ¿Quiénes son los invitados? Cambios temporales y funcionales de los espacios públicos de Pukara como una reflexión acerca de las estrategias de liderazgo durante el Periodo Formativo Tardío. *Boletín de Arqueología PUCP* 9:185–206. Pontificia Universidad Católica del Perú, Lima, Perú.

Lumbreras, L., and H. Amat
1968 Secuencia arqueológica del altiplano occidental de Titicaca. *37th International Congress of Americanists* 2:75–106.

Mohr Chávez, K.
1977 Marcavalle: The Ceramics from an Early Horizon Site in the Valley of Cuzco, Peru, and Implications for South Highland Socioeconomic Interaction. PhD dissertation, Department of Anthropology, University of Pennsylvania, Philadelphia.

Mujica, E.
1978 Nueva hipótesis sobre el desarrollo temprano del altiplano, del Titicaca y de sus áreas de interacción. *Arte y Arqueología* 5/6:285–308.
1979 Excavaciones en Pucara, Peru. In *Arqueología Peruana*, edited by R. Matos Mendieta, pp. 184–97. Universidad Nacional Mayor de San Marcos, Lima.
1985 Altiplano-coast relationships in the south-central Andes: From indirect to direct complementarity. In *Andean Ecology and Civilization,* edited by S. Masuda, I. Shimada, and C. Morris, pp. 103–40. University of Tokyo Press, Tokyo.
1987 Cusipata: Una fase pre-Pukara en la cuenca norte del Titicaca. *Gaceta Arqueológica Andina* 13:22–28.
1991 *Pukara. Una sociedad compleja temprana en la cuenca norte del Titicaca. Los Incas y el Antiguo Perú. 3000 Años de Historia*, Tomo 1, pp. 272–97. Editorial Quinto Centenario, Madrid.
1996 La pirámide Qalasaya. *Medio de Construcción* 120:18–23.

Orton, C., P. Tyers, and A. Vince
1993 *Pottery in Archaeology*. Cambridge University Press, Cambridge.

Oshige, D.
2010 La secuencia más temprana en el sitio de Pukara, Cuenca norte del Lago Titicaca. Licenciatura Tesis, Facultad de Letras y Ciencias Humanas, Pontificia Universidad Católica del Perú, Lima, Perú.

Plourde, A., and C. Stanish
2006 The emergence of complex society in the Titicaca Basin: The view from the north. In *Andean Archaeology III: North and South*, edited by W. Isbell and H. Silverman, pp. 237–57. Springer, New York.

Rice, P.
1987 *Pottery Analysis: A Sourcebook*. University of Chicago Press, Chicago and London.

Rowe, J.
1942 Sitios históricos en la región de Pucara, Puno. *Revista del Instituto Arqueológico* 6(10/11):66–75.

Rowe, J., and C. Brandel
1971 Pucara style pottery designs. *Ñawpa Pacha* 7/8(1969–1970):1–16.

Rye, O. S.
1981 *Pottery Technology: Principles and Reconstruction*. Taraxacum, Inc., Washington, D.C.

Skibo, J. M.
1992 *Pottery Function: A Use-Alteration Perspective*. Plenum Press, New York.

Stanish, C.
1994 The hydraulic hypothesis revisited: Lake Titicaca Basin raised fields in theoretical perspective. *Latin American Antiquity* 5(4):312–32.
2001 Formación estatal temprana en la cuenca del lago Titicaca, Andes surcentrales. *Boletín de Arqueología PUCP* 5:189–215. Pontificia Universidad Católica del Perú, Lima.
2003 *Ancient Titicaca: The Evolution of Complex Society in Southern Peru and Northern Bolivia*. University of California Press, Berkeley and Los Angeles.

Steadman, L. H.
1995 Excavations at Camata: An Early Ceramic Chronology for the Western Titicaca Basin, Peru. PhD dissertation, Department of Anthropology, University of California, Berkeley.

Wheeler, J., and E. Mujica
1981 *Prehistoric Pastoralism in the Lake Titicaca Basin, Peru, 1979–1980 Field Season*. Report submitted to National Science Foundation, grant no. BNS 7015119.

# Chapter 3

# Archaeological Excavation at Balsaspata, Ayaviri

*Henry Tantaleán*

**Introduction**

The archaeological site of Balsaspata or Pueblo Libre, in Ayaviri, Department of Puno, was investigated by the author on September 8–30, 1998. The work was conducted as part of a salvage excavation by the Instituto Nacional de Cultura of Peru (INC) as a result of the rapid destruction of the site area. The importance of the site was suggested by the large quantities of decorated ceramic fragments, bone, lithics, and carved stone. With the objective to verify the site's actual size and chronology, the author and a small team composed of Carmen Pérez Maestro, Eduardo Arizaca and two local assistants conducted archaeological research at the site.

Although no information about the site existed in the literature, the people of Ayaviri recognized it as a site, and there was a museum in the municipality where objects from the site were collected. Likewise, Messrs. Italo Oberti and Jorge Calero Flores had requested that the INC declare the site as cultural patrimony of the nation. Moreover, the site's importance had been recognized by the then-students of archaeology at the Universidad Nacional San Antonio Abad del Cuzco Eduardo Arizaca and Jorge Calero (Arizaca et al. 1995:21; Calero 1998; Fernández 1998:38).

It was at this time that the property where the site was located was claimed by the homeowner's association "Pueblo Libre," aided by the municipality of Melgar. The municipality had sold lots to people in this association who threatened to construct houses. This was denounced by the local INC representative in Ayaviri and confirmed by the director of the INC-PUNO, Dr. Rolando Paredes, on September 4, 1998. Due to the circumstances, it was necessary to immediately intervene at the site and establish an effective presence. In reality, the site had already been badly disturbed by the mining of middens to make adobes. The site's northeast section had been badly dug for adobe materials, resulting in a number of archaeological remains left on the surface including fragments of ceramics, lithics, and animal bones.

The abundance of early ceramic sherds on the surface of the site indicated a major Formative period occupation, up to then poorly studied in the region. The diagnostic pottery suggested the existence of an intensive occupation from the first sedentary altiplano societies up to the Inca period. We had hoped that an excavation at the site, even a small one, would reflect the social and historical processes that developed in this zone. Here, I present a description of this work, a synthesis of the recovered materials, including the ceramics, and a reconstruction of the cultural occupations that we can infer from this small investigation.

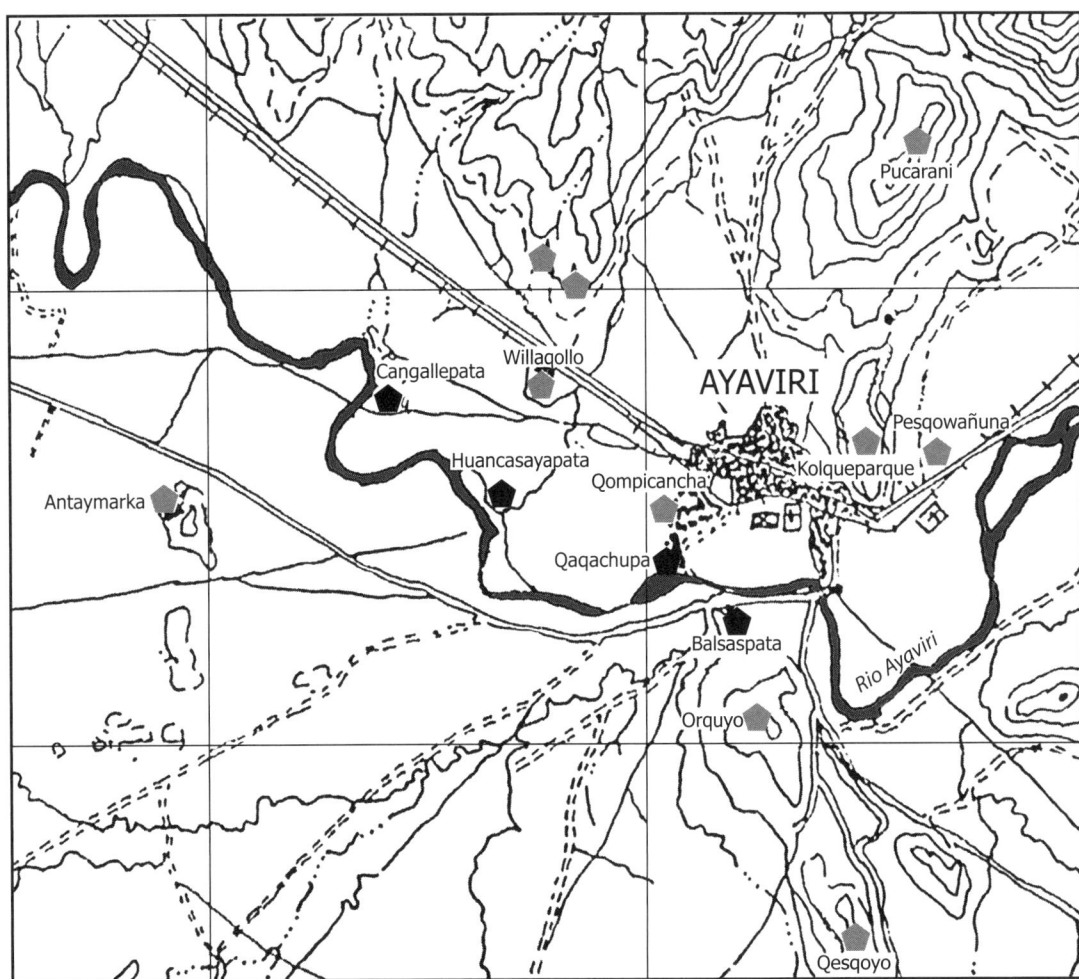

Figure 3.1. Location of Balsaspata and other archaeological sites in the area of Ayaviri. The black pentagons mark the Formative sites and the gray pentagons mark sites of another periods. The map blocks are 4.0 km on a side.

## Location and Geography of Balsaspata

The archaeological site of Balsaspata or Pueblo Libre is on the outskirts of the town of Ayaviri, at the edge of a new neighborhood called Pueblo Libre. It is on the right margin of the Río Ayaviri, in the province of Melgar (Fig. 3.1). The site is delimited on the east by the Pueblo Libre neighborhood, on the north by a dirt road that runs parallel to the river, and to the south and west by the asphalt Juliaca-Cuzco highway (Fig. 3.2). Later reconnaissance indicated that the site extends across the asphalt road to the hills such that the road cuts the site into two.

The site is in the area referred to by Luis Lumbreras (1981) as the South Central Andes. Although the definition of this cultural area has been questioned (Burger et al. 2000), we continue to use this framework. The name Balsaspata suggests that this area was where they crossed the river, perhaps with small boats. The area of Ayaviri, like Pukara to the south, forms part of the same hydrological drainage, a natural route between the Cuzco region and Lake Titicaca. Today, the site is a medium-sized mound that has been badly altered by modern soil mining and other human activities.

## Methodology

Work began in September 1998 with a surface collection of the diagnostic ceramic material from the entire site. The surface was so badly damaged that it was not necessary to carry out a systematic collection as originally planned. We made a sketch map of the site (Fig. 3.3) from which we were able to define and locate the zones where we would conduct investigations. We also drew the sectors that were obviously disturbed. This methodology was created to do an archaeological evaluation of the site—to assess its state of preservation, its extent, its func-

Figure 3.2. The site is located in the center of the image, between the river and the house compound in the foreground. Photograph taken by the author at the time of excavations, September 1998.

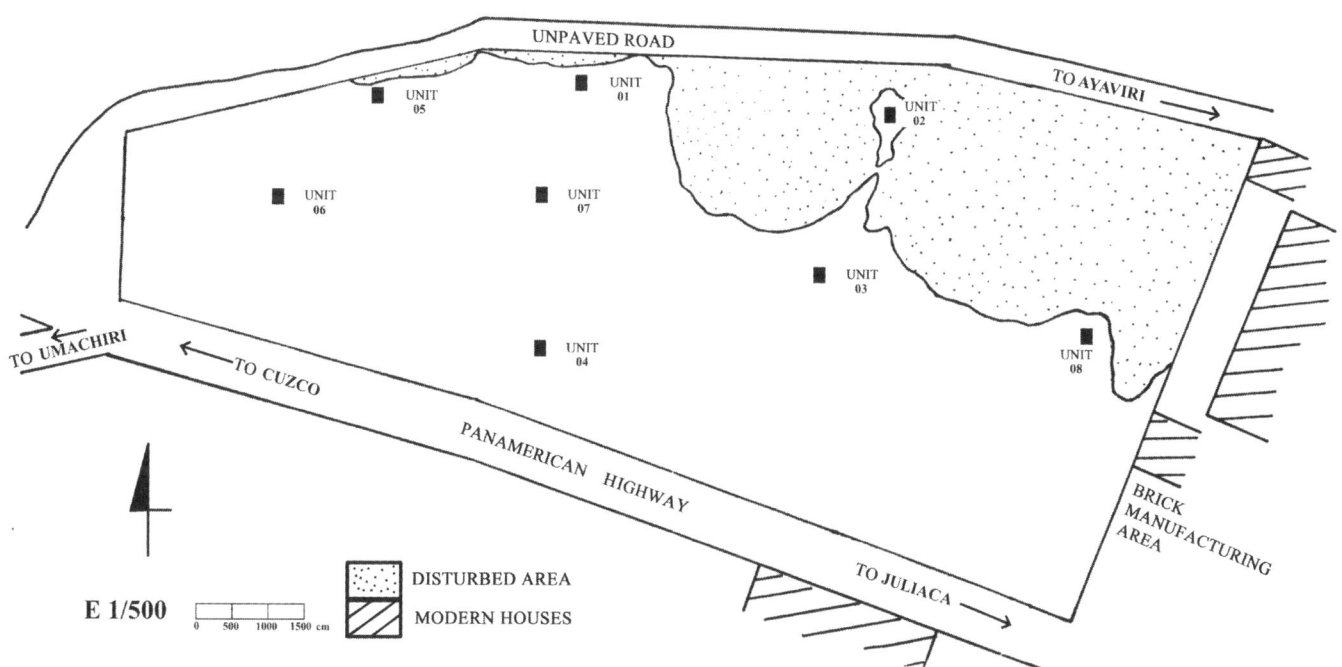

Figure 3.3. Sketch map of the site area.

tion, the existence of structures, and the relative age of these features, and to define the successive occupations through time.

We excavated test pits in areas with and without obvious cultural materials on the surface. The test pits were cardinally oriented and measured 1 × 1 m, with the exception of Unit 01, which was 1 × 2 m. This larger pit was intended to define the successive and superimposed prehispanic occupations (with the goal to get a good stratigraphic column), as well as to characterize these occupations from diagnostic pottery from each period. Even though this was an emergency rescue excavation, we were able to recover quite a bit of information from these excavations.

The units were excavated in natural levels. However, when we encountered the remains of structures or other features with ceramics or other associated materials, we immediately subdivided the natural levels into arbitrary ones in order to preserve chronological information.

## Description of the Excavated Units

Before we excavated the test units, we studied the profiles made by the road construction on the site's northern side. There, we could identify evidence of prehispanic occupation that included possible structures. We also took into account elevations of the mound, scatters of artifacts and so forth. With these observations, we excavated eight units (described below).

### Description of Unit 01

This unit was located in the profile on the north side of the site that was exposed by the road construction. The profile appeared to have cut through numerous structures and had a large quantity of cultural material. Even so, in this sector we found a major prehispanic occupation, defined by an immense quantity of midden that, overall, was part of a homogeneous level of high-density artifacts. In this unit, after removing a pair of levels, we found a very deep level with Formative pottery including Pukara (400 BC), Cusipata, and Qaluyu, the latter obviously indicating an earlier component. This excavation unit reached a depth of 3 m, ending with a sterile level of yellowish clay (Fig. 3.4).

*Surface level (registry number 101).* The surface materials include a large quantity of Qaluyu Incised pottery, along with worked bone, camelid bone and lithic debris (Figs. 3.5, 3.6).

*Stratum A (registry number 102).* Level A has little material, taking into account its size. It most likely represents the abandonment phase of the site (Fig. 3.7).

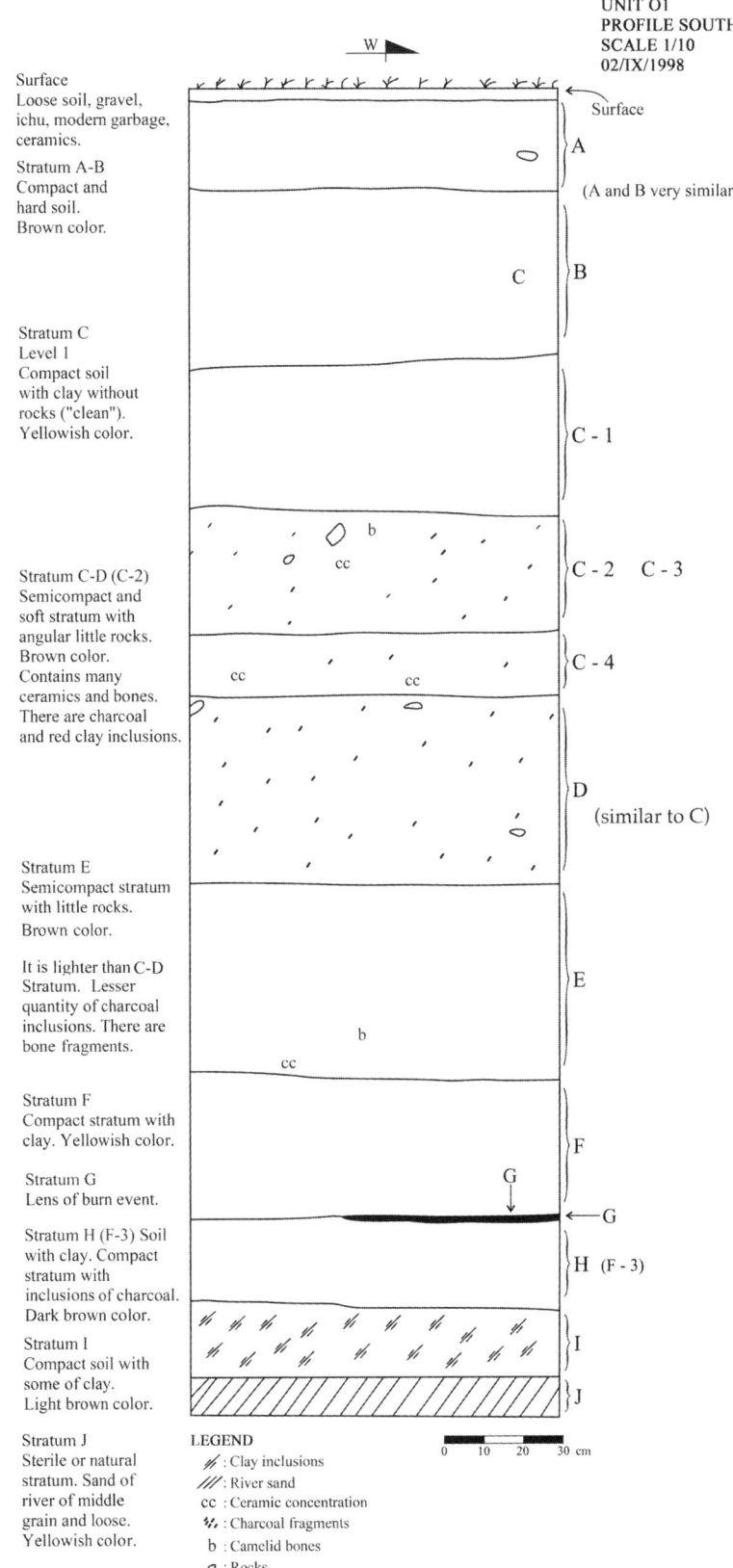

Figure 3.4. Unit 01, south profile.

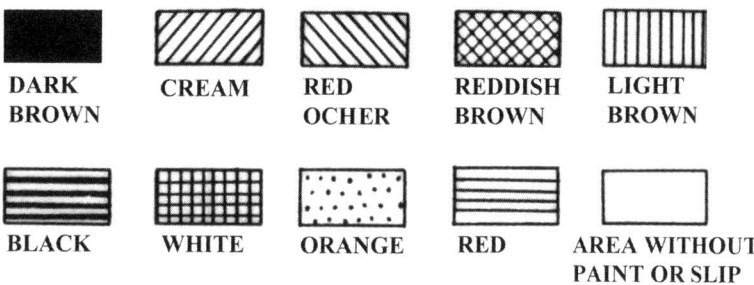

Figure 3.5. Ceramic key.

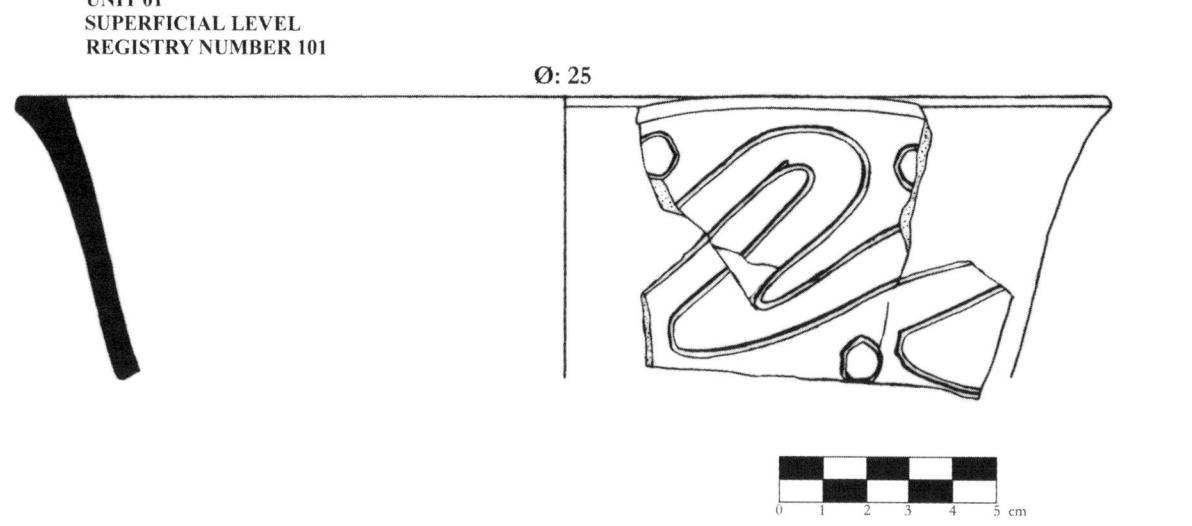

Figure 3.6. Qaluyu-style Incised tazón from surface of Unit 01.

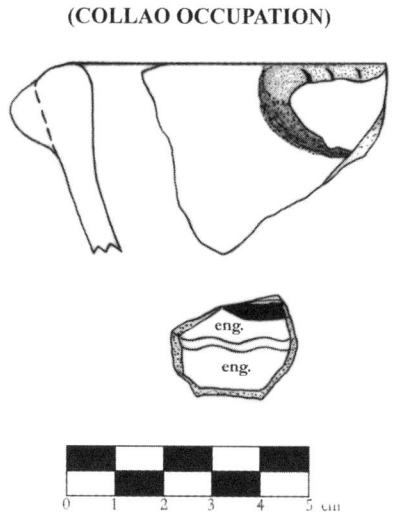

Figure 3.7. Fragments of Collao-style vessels.

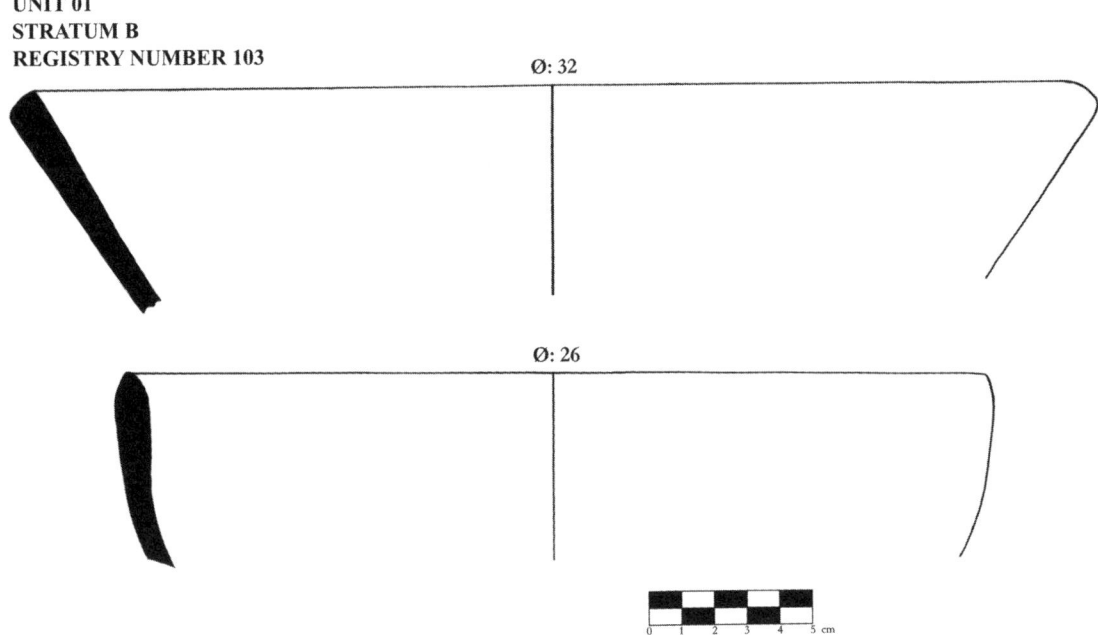

Figure 3.8. Formative period vessels.

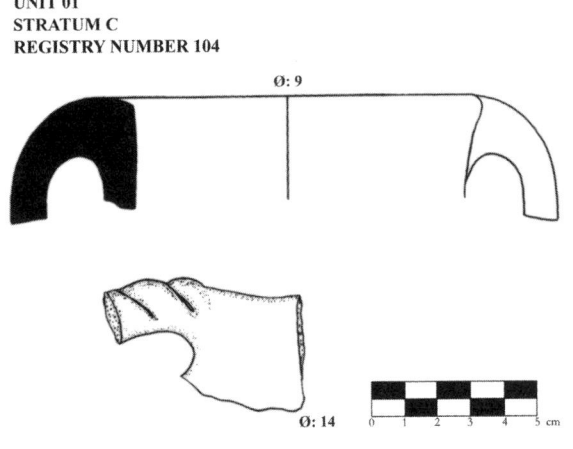

Figure 3.9. Formative jar forms.

*Stratum B (registry number 103)*. This level has undecorated pottery, ceramics with micaceous clay, lithics (obsidian and flint), camelid bones and lithic debris (Fig. 3.8).

*Stratum C, level 1 (registry number 104)*. This level has early Formative pottery characterized by red slip with mica. There is much burned camelid bone as well as post-fire burned pottery and a variety of lithic flakes (Fig. 3.9).

*Stratum C, level 2 (registry number 107)*. This level has Formative period Qaluyu and Pukara, camelid bones, obsidian and so forth. Many of the ceramic fragments are very large, including bases, rims and one bowl that is 40% complete. This is a classic Pukara occupation (Figs. 3.10–3.17).

*Stratum C, level 3 (registry number 111)*. This level has pottery, lithics and camelid bone. This level has some Qaluyu diagnostics (Figs. 3.18–3.21).

*Stratum C, level 4 (registry number 114)*. This level has incised and painted Formative pottery that is most likely Qaluyu but with some similarities to Cusipata. We also discovered a molded fragment and a dark surface fragment with incisions. The level also contained lithic debris (obsidian and flint), and worked bone (Figs. 3.22–3.25).

*Stratum D (registry number 116)*. This stratum has neckless ollas, painted and incised Formative fragments, obsidian, camelid bone in abundance, and obsidian (Figs. 3.26–3.31).

*Stratum E (registry number 125)*. This stratum does not have as much material as the preceding one, but there is a fair amount of neckless ollas as well as incised (fine and thick incisions) pottery (Figs. 3.32–3.35).

*Stratum F, level 1 (registry number 128)*. This stratum and level has plainwares, neckless ollas, lithics and one complete obsidian point, lithic flakes and cores and camelid bones (Fig. 3.36).

*Stratum F, level 2 (registry number 130)*. This level has plainware pottery, a low density of camelid bones, plus a lot of obsidian (Figs. 3.37, 3.38).

*Stratum G (registry number 131)*. There are virtually no artifacts in this level. There is some carbon and burned soil.

*Stratum F, level 3 (registry number 132)*. This level has small carbon flecks, pottery and bone although the density is quite low. This is an ash lens, the remains of burnt vegetal material.

*Stratum I (registry number 134)*. This has a small quantity of artifacts and carbon.

*Stratum J*. This is a sterile level.

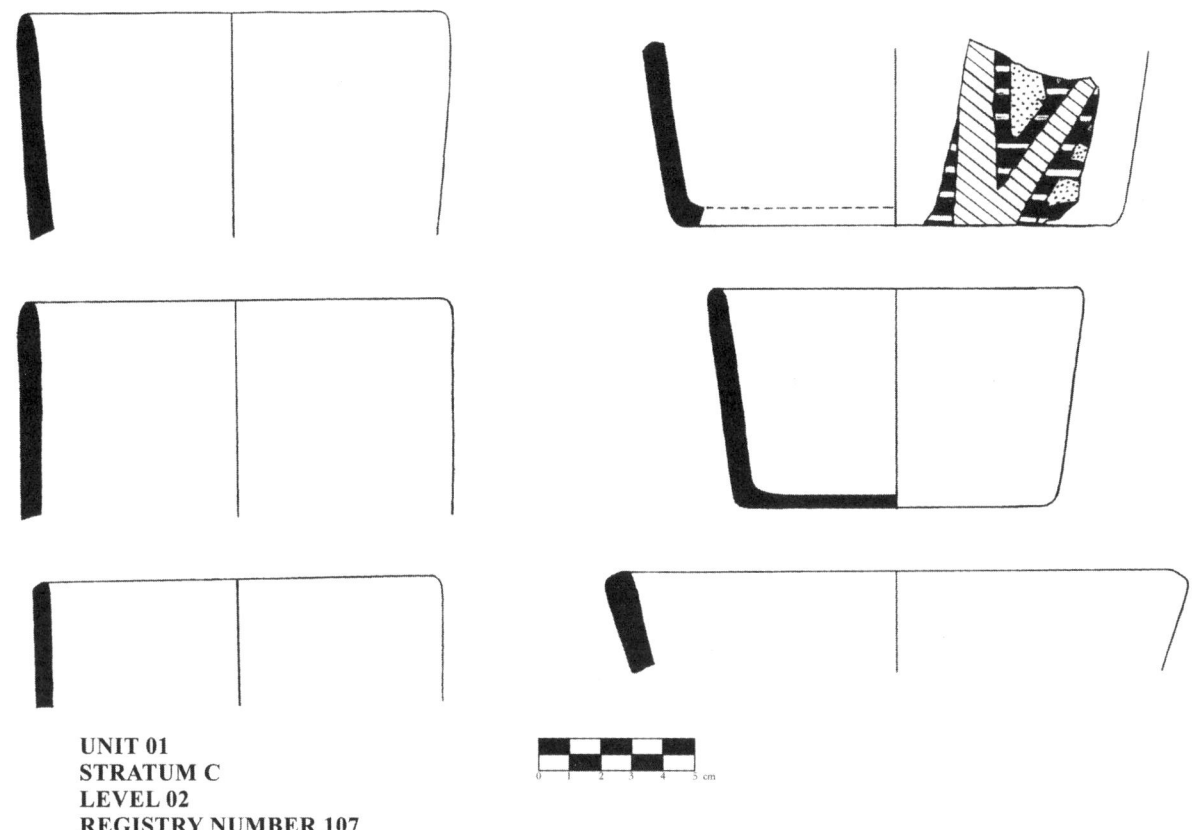

Figure 3.10. Formative period vessels.

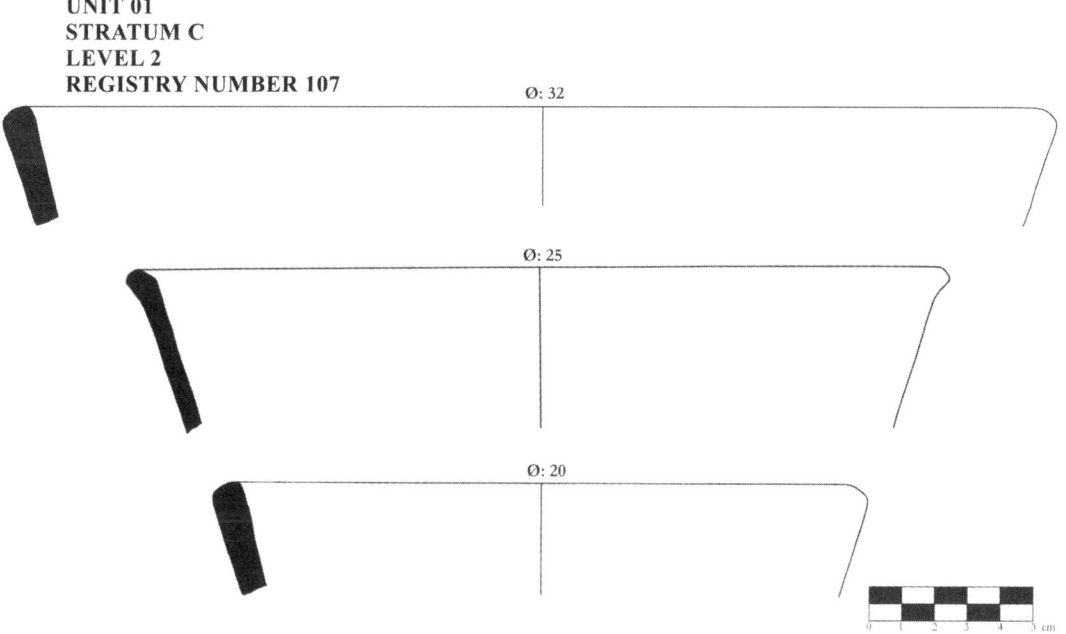

Figure 3.11. Formative period tazones.

56　　　　　　　　　　　　　　　*Advances in Titicaca Basin Archaeology–III*

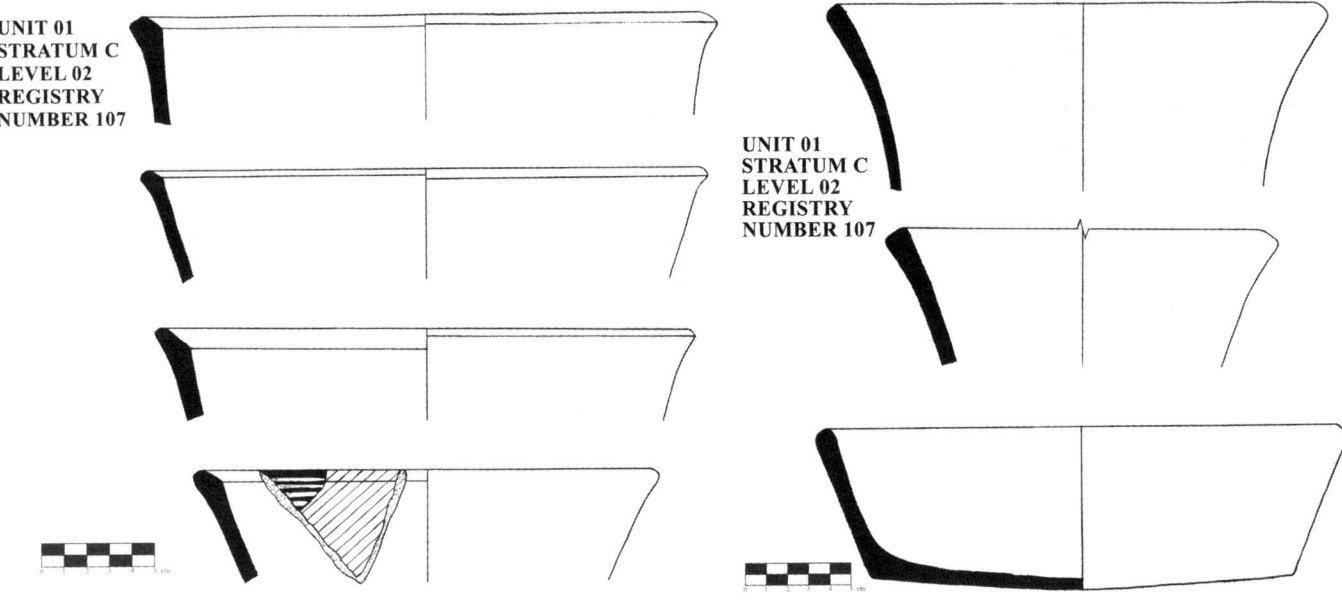

Figure 3.12.  Formative period tazones.

Figure 3.13.  Formative period tazones.

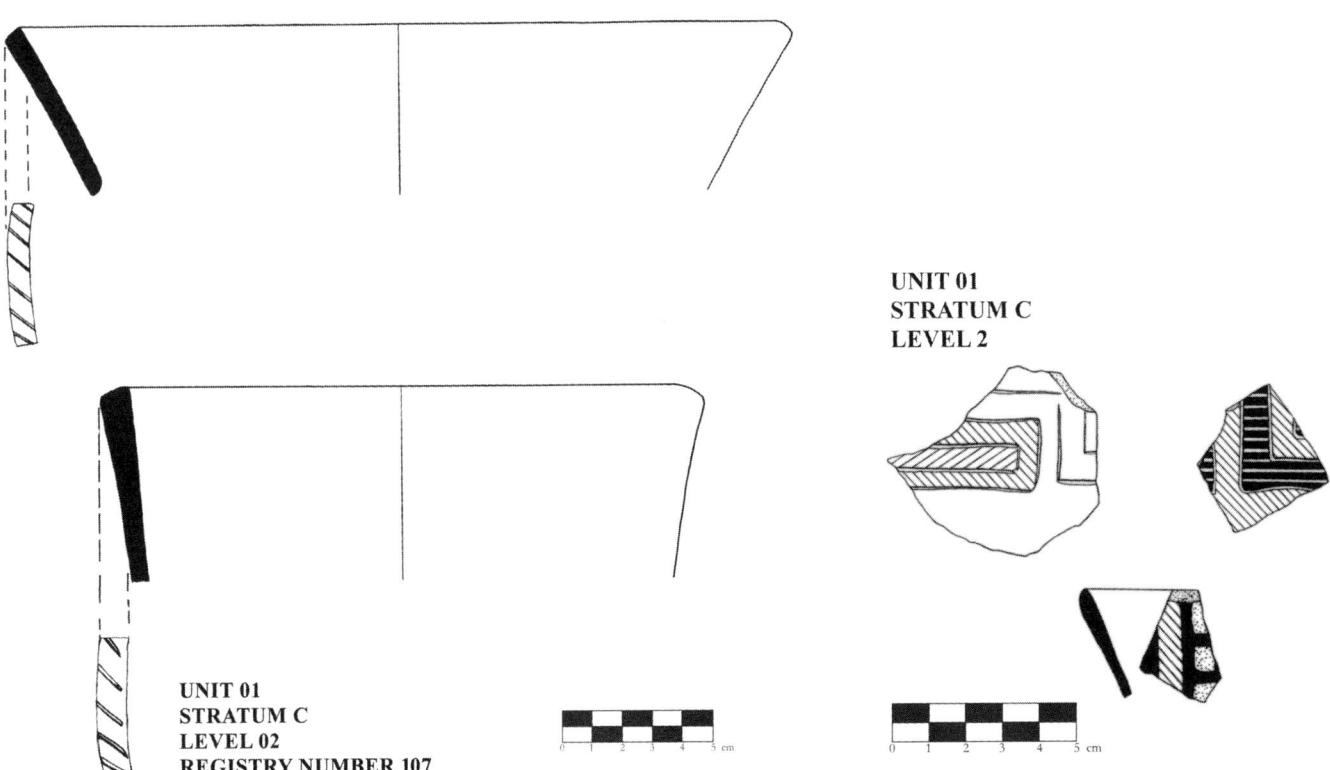

Figure 3.14.  Formative period vessels.

Figure 3.15.  Formative period vessels. The top two fragments are Pukara in style.

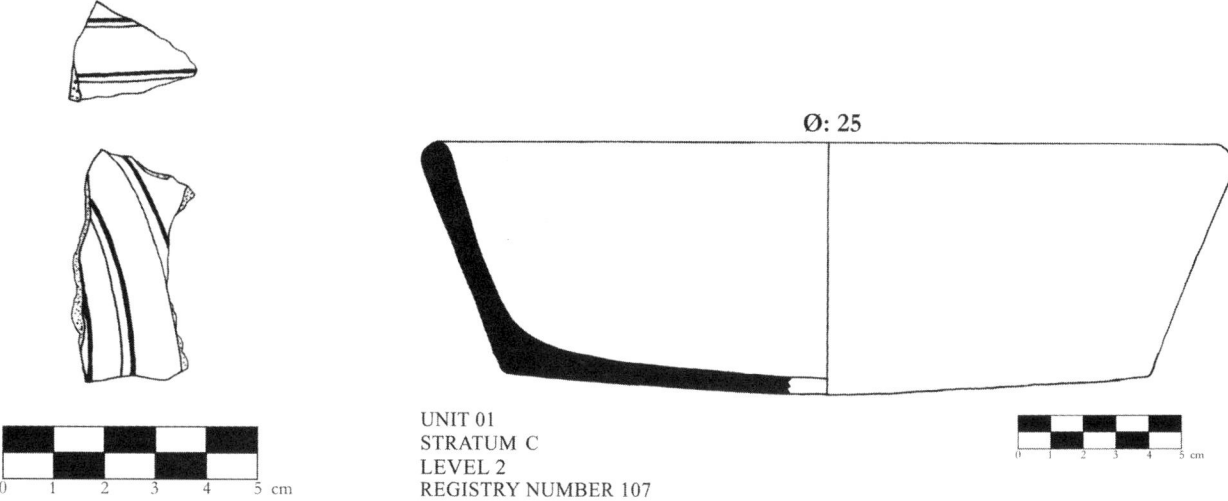

Figure 3.16. Fragments of Qaluyu Incised.

Figure 3.17. Formative tazón.

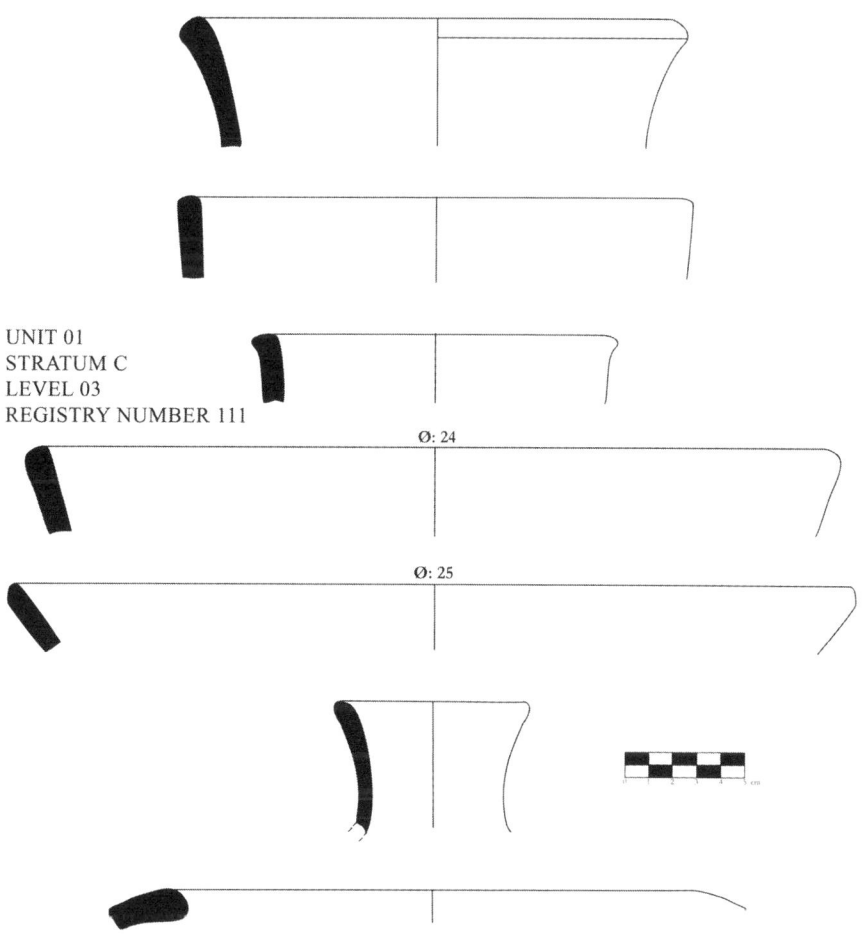

Figure 3.18. Formative vessels.

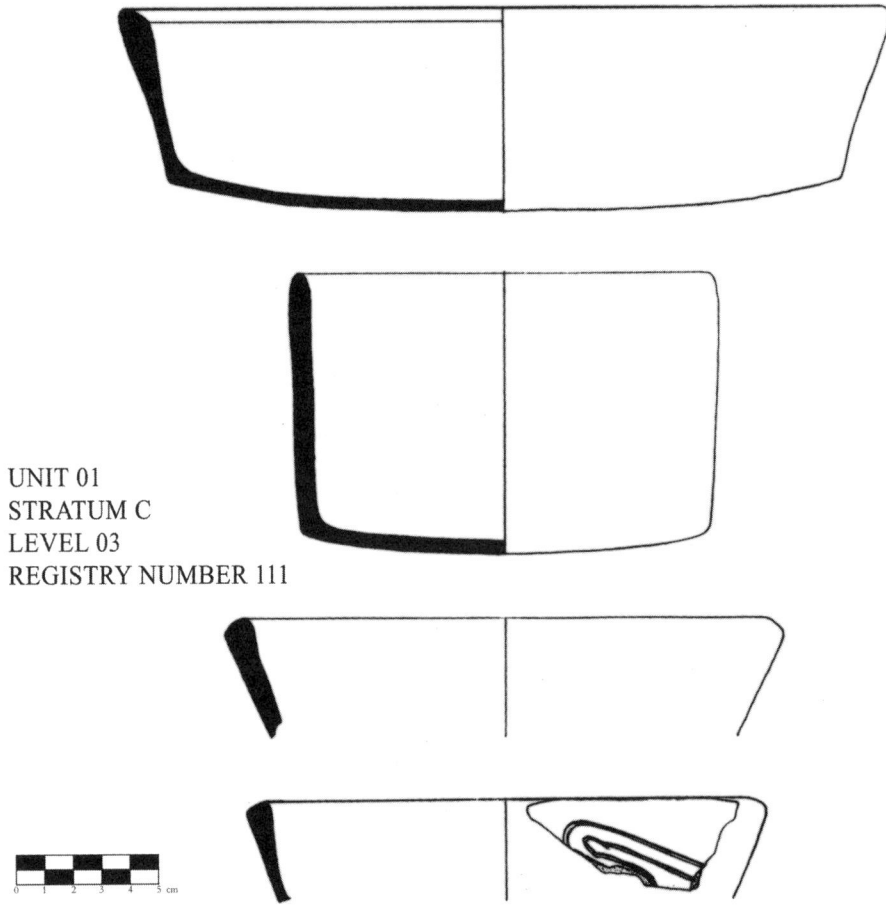

Figure 3.19. Formative vessels including Qaluyu Incised.

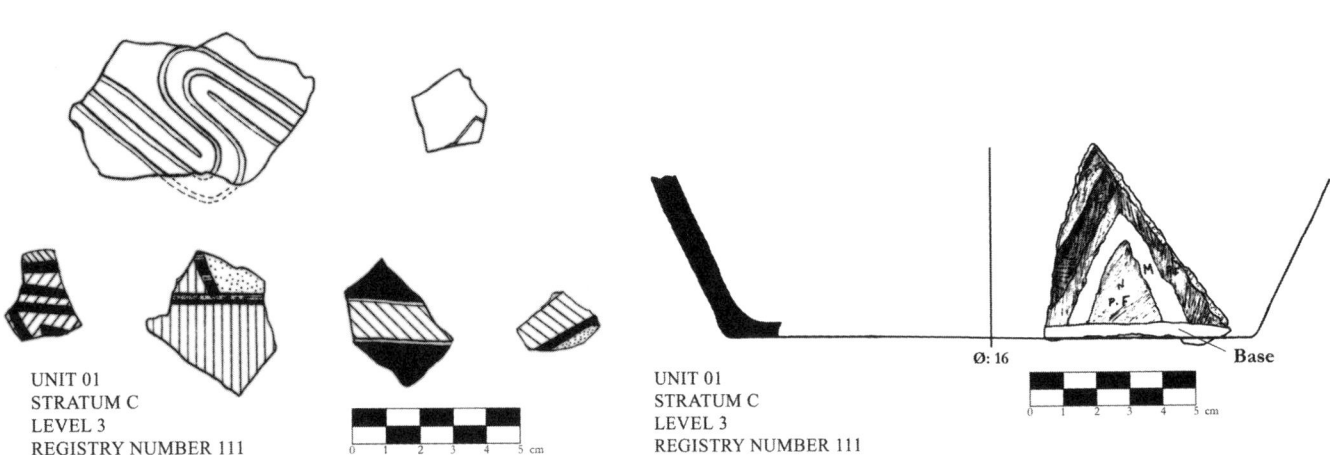

Figure 3.20. Formative vessels including Qaluyu Incised.

Figure 3.21. Base of Formative vessel with painted decoration.

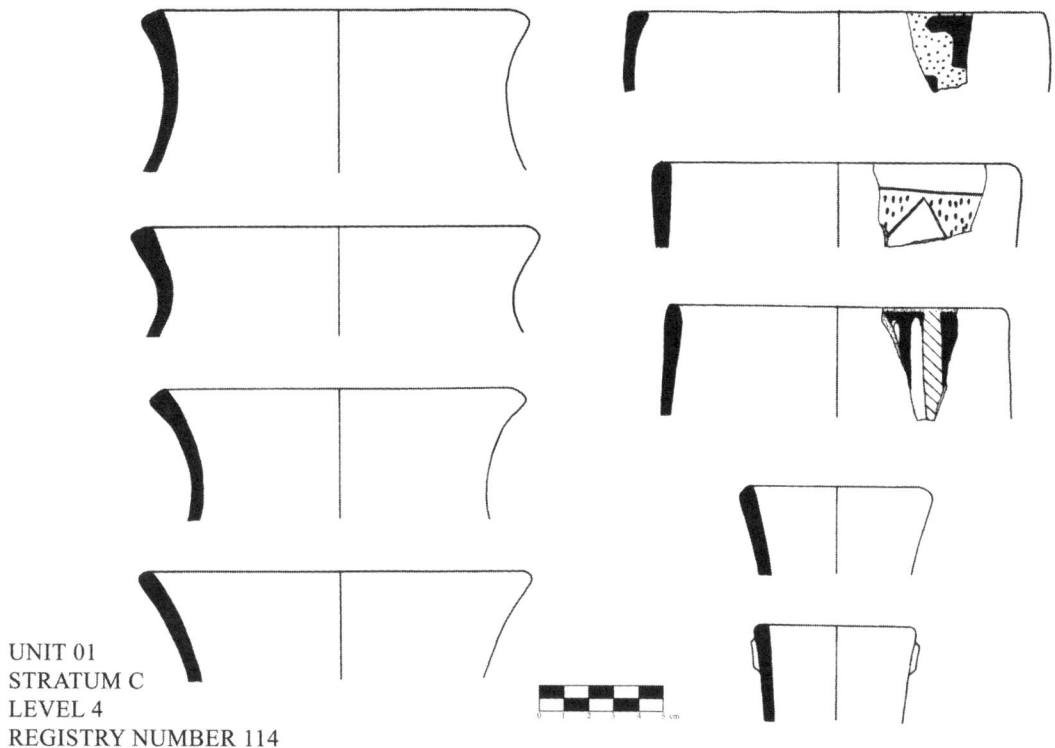

Figure 3.22. Formative vessels including Qaluyu Incised and Painted.

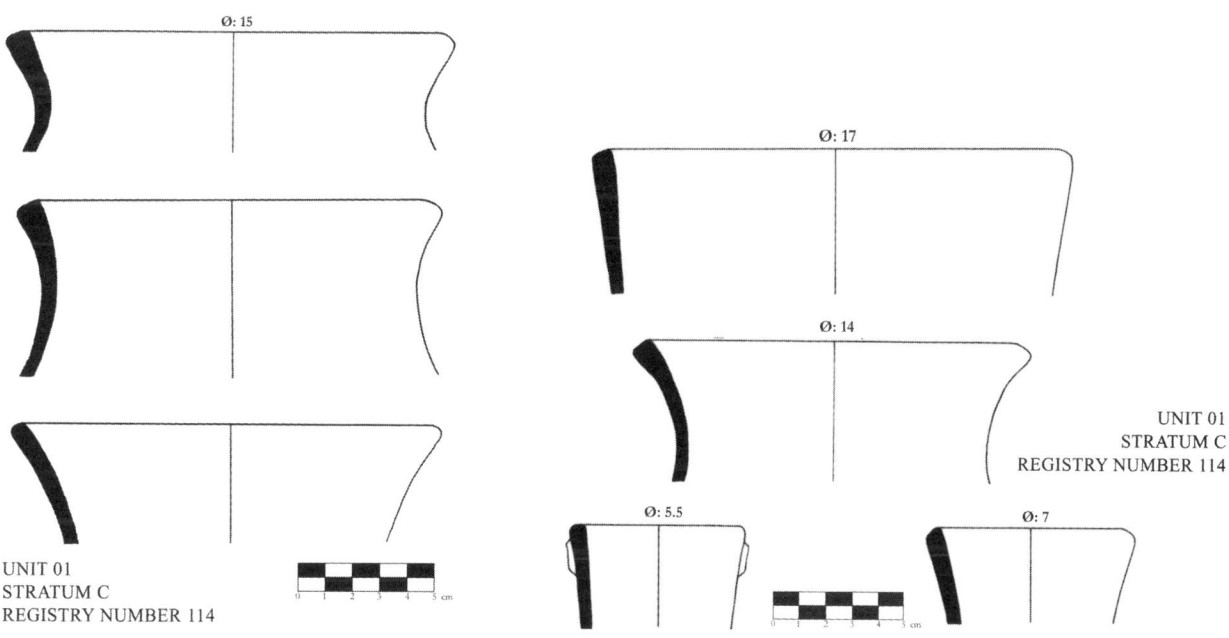

Figure 3.23. Formative vessels.

Figure 3.24. Formative vessels.

Figure 3.25. Formative vessels including Qaluyu Incised.

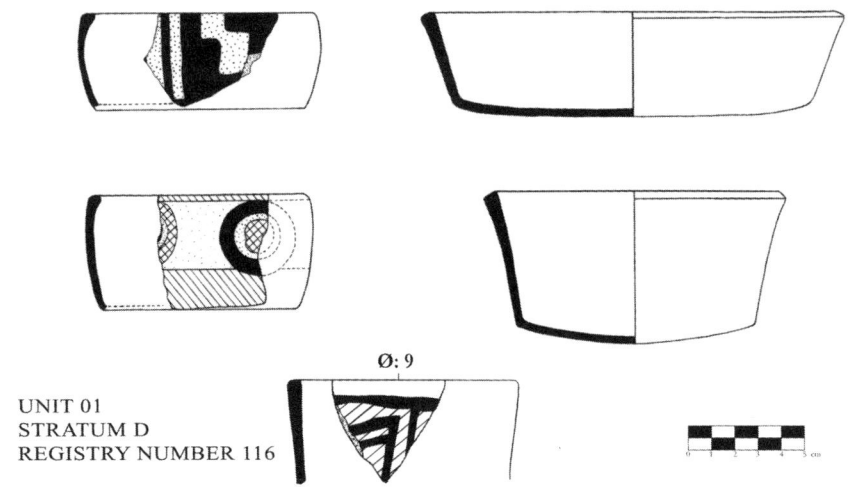

Figure 3.26. Formative vessels including Qaluyu Painted. The bottom fragment is defined by Calero (1998) as Ayacwira.

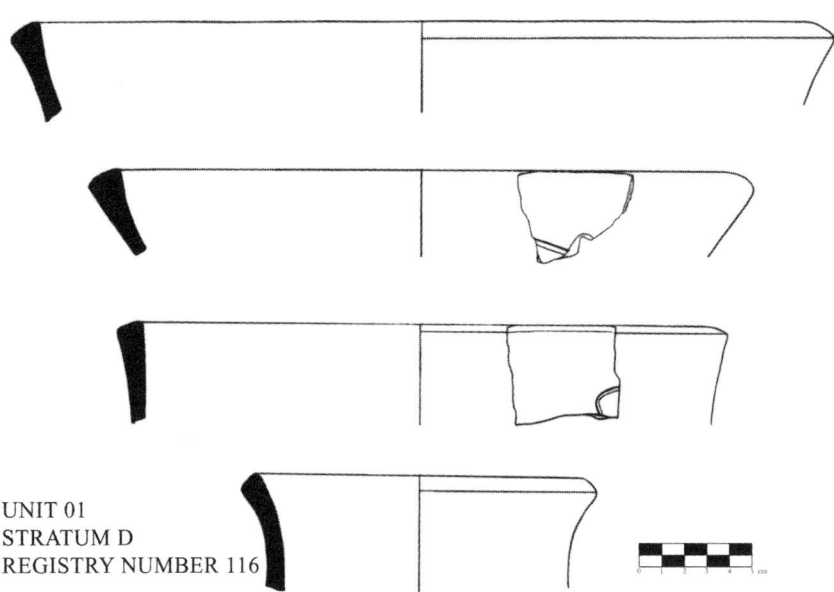

Figure 3.27. Formative vessels including Qaluyu Incised.

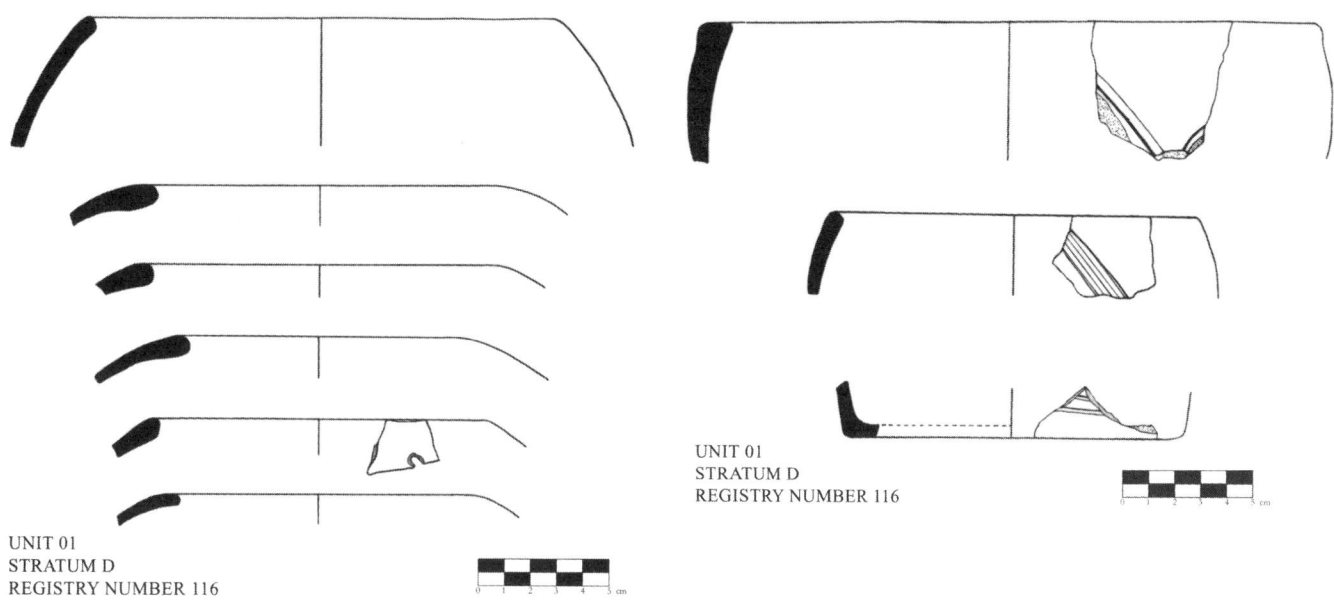

Figure 3.28. Formative period neckless ollas.

Figure 3.29. Formative period neckless ollas and tazón base.

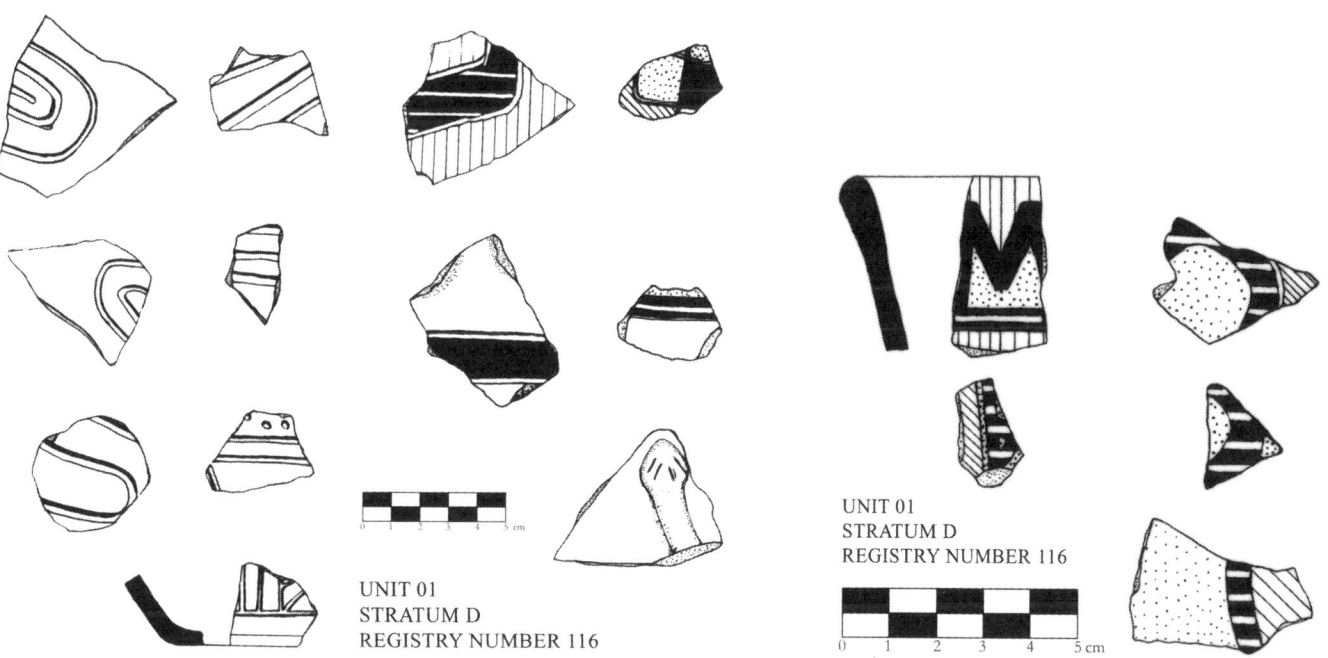

Figure 3.30. Formative vessels including Incised and Painted Qaluyu and possible Pukara vessels (the two in the upper right-hand corner).

Figure 3.31. Formative vessels including Qaluyu. Fragments of Qaluyu Painted vessels (except for the fragment in the upper left-hand corner) possibly related to Ayacwira style.

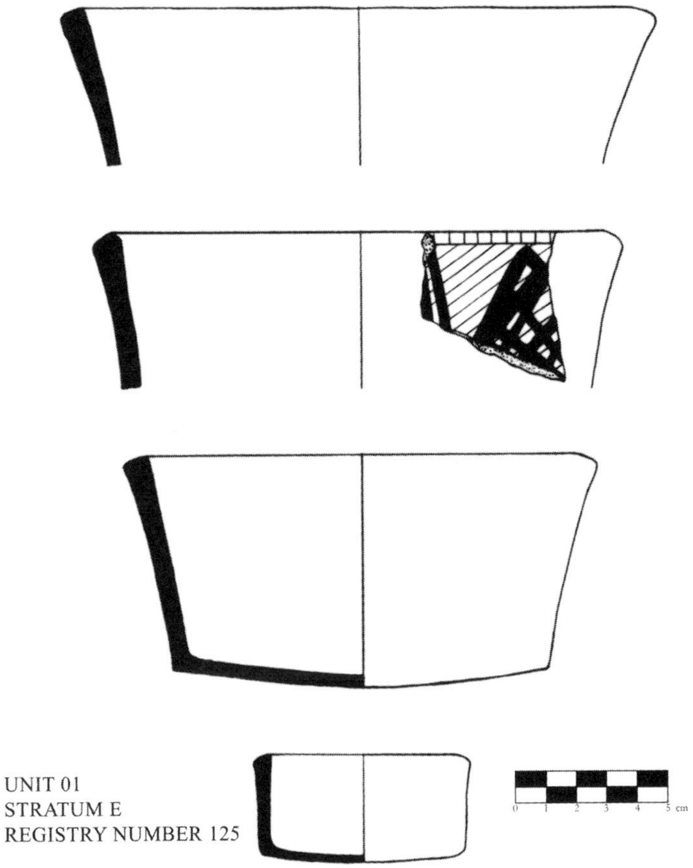

Figure 3.32. Qaluyu-style tazones.

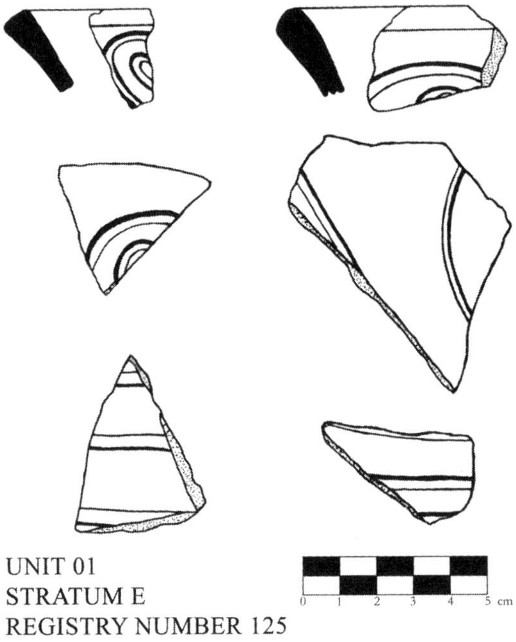

Figure 3.33. Fragments of Qaluyu Incised vessels.

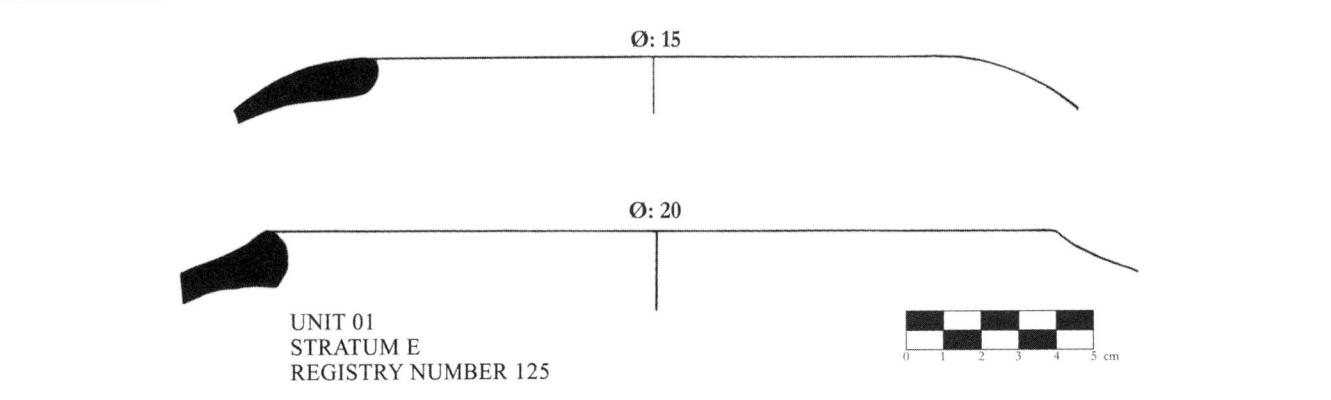

Figure 3.34. Formative period neckless ollas.

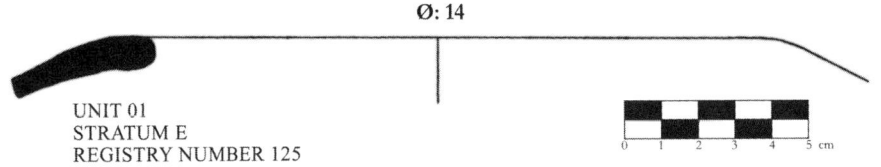

Figure 3.35. Formative period neckless olla.

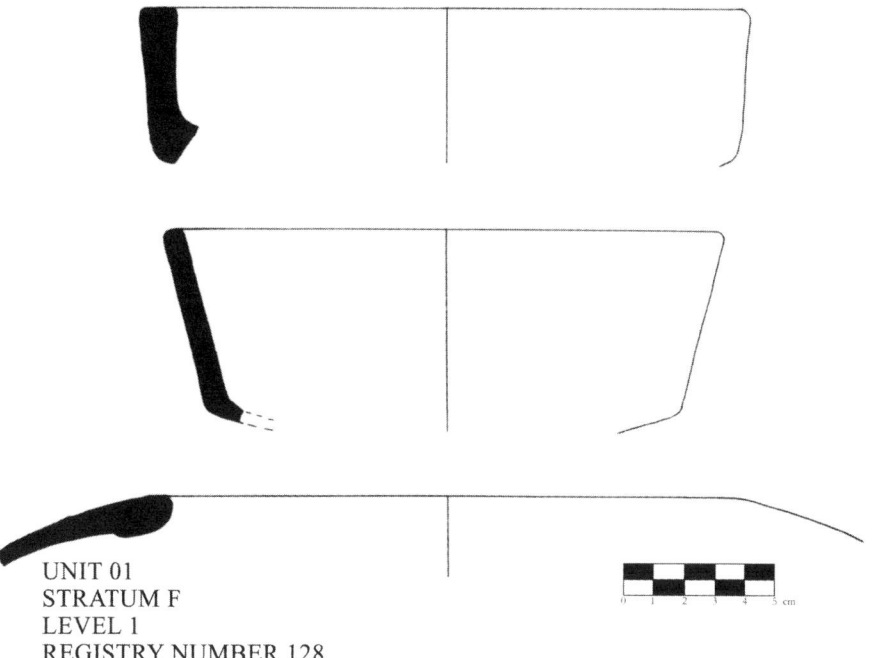

Figure 3.36. Formative vessels including a neckless olla.

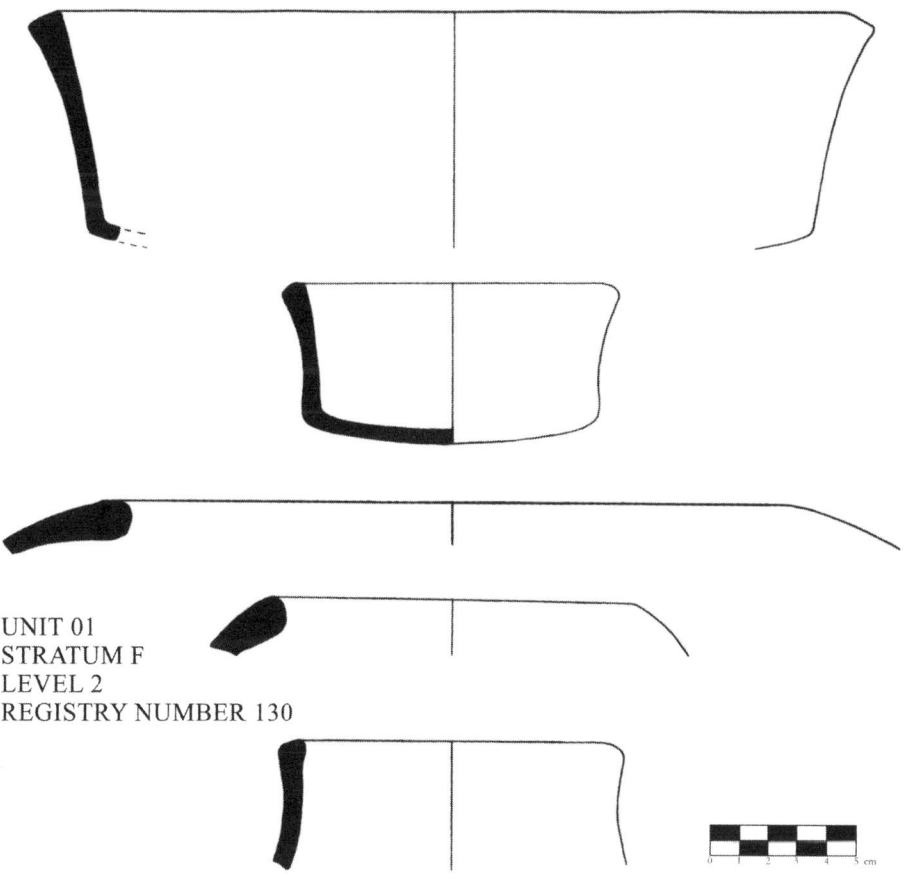

Figure 3.37. Formative period tazones and neckless ollas.

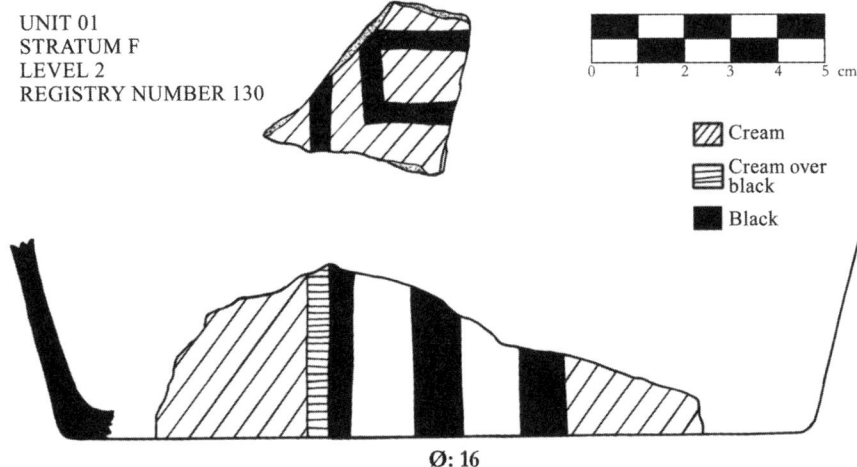

Figure 3.38. Qaluyu Painted vessels.

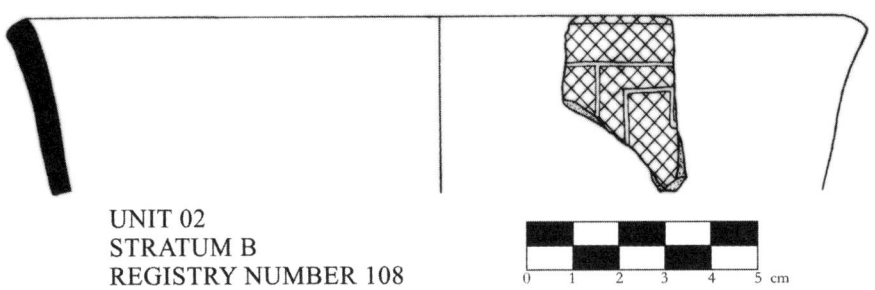

Figure 3.39. Qaluyu-style tazón with incised decoration.

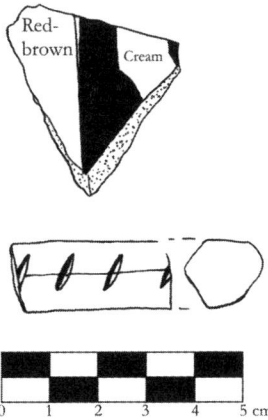

Figure 3.40. Fragments of Formative vessels including Qaluyu Painted and an appliqué with incisions.

*Description of Unit 02*

We put Unit 02 (1 × 1 m) in the north area of the site close to the road parallel to the river in a sort of "island" inside the disturbed area.

*Surface level (registry number 105).* There is abundant material including pottery, bone, camelid bones and some lithics.

*Stratum A (registry number 106).* This has a regular quantity of pottery and bone fragments. There is a camelid mandible.

*Stratum B (registry number 108).* This stratum has fragments of incised geometric Pukara pottery. There is also crude pottery with red slip as well as camelid bones and polishing stones (Figs. 3.39, 3.40).

*Stratum C (registry number 109).* This stratum has red slipped pottery. There are also some pieces of burned soil with grass impressions, camelid bones and chert flakes. We found some scoria of an unidentified metal (Fig. 3.41).

*Stratum D (registry number 110).* This stratum has coarse, burnt pottery, flakes, and a lot of camelid bone. There are also many small fragments of carbon (Fig. 3.42).

*Stratum E (registry number 112).* This stratum has pottery, broken bone, some lithic material, and a fragment of thick-incised blackware (Figs. 3.43, 3.44).

*Stratum F (registry number 113).* This has a fragment of a painted black and beige tazón, a lot of burned plainware with mica and large sand, camelid bones, obsidian flakes, and polished bone. There is very little carbon. There is a piece of clay with mica (Figs. 3.45, 3.46).

*Stratum G (registry number 115).* There is little cultural material here except for a large quantity of obsidian. There are some small fragments of carbon (Fig. 3.47). Below this stratum is the sterile sand of the river.

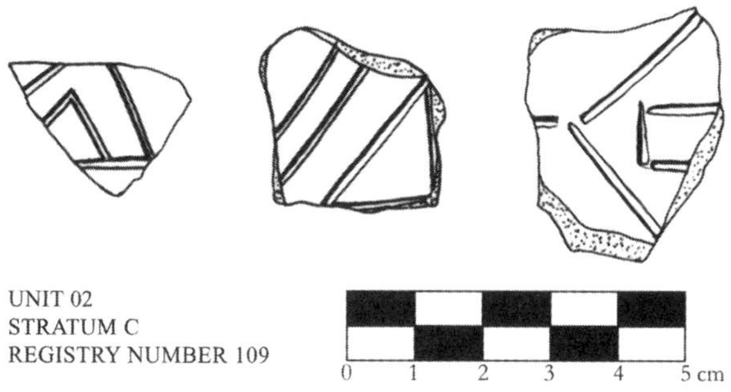

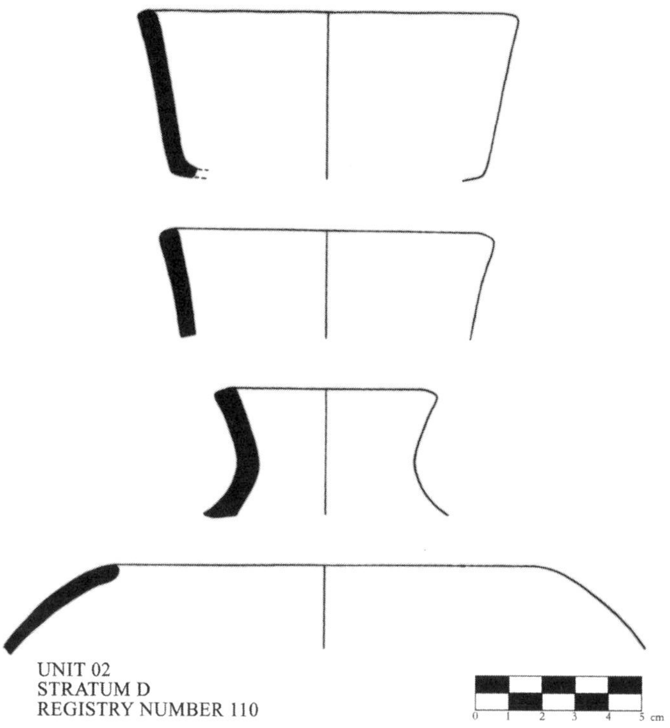

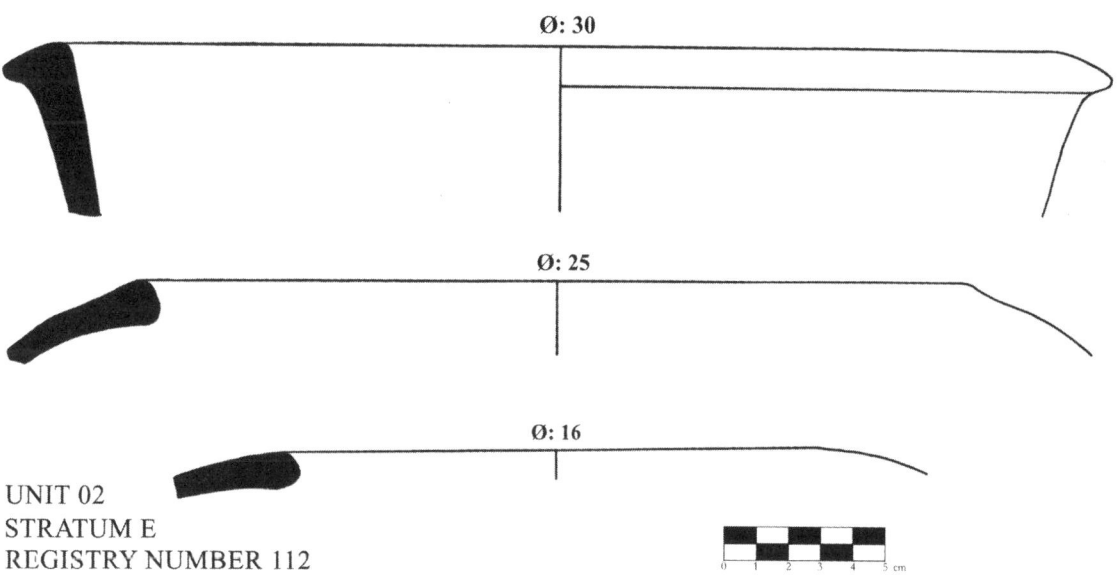

UNIT 02
STRATUM C
REGISTRY NUMBER 109

UNIT 02
STRATUM D
REGISTRY NUMBER 110

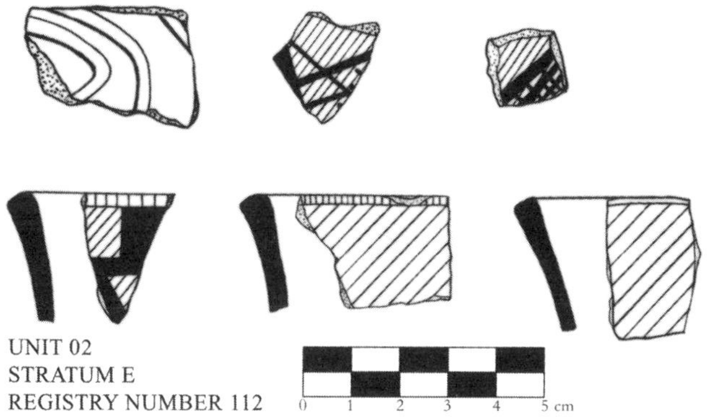

UNIT 02
STRATUM E
REGISTRY NUMBER 112

(*upper left*) Figure 3.41. Fragments of Qaluyu Incised.

(*above*) Figure 3.42. Formative tazones, jar and neckless olla.

(*left*) Figure 3.43. Fragments of Formative vessels including Qaluyu Painted and Incised.

Ø: 30

Ø: 25

Ø: 16

UNIT 02
STRATUM E
REGISTRY NUMBER 112

Figure 3.44. Formative tazón and two neckless ollas.

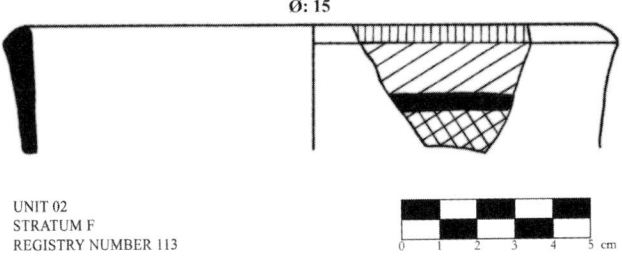

Figure 3.45. Qaluyu-style tazón.

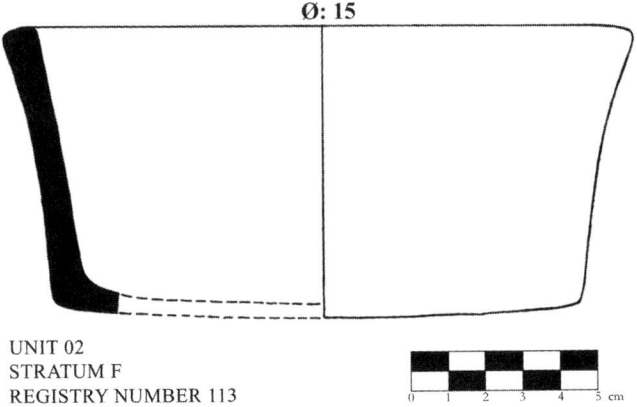

Figure 3.46. Qaluyu-style tazón.

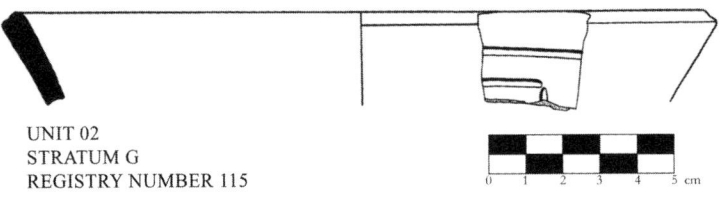

Figure 3.47. Qaluyu-style tazón with incised decoration.

*Description of Unit 03*

This was located in an elevated sector of the site. On the surface there is much evidence of looting of possible tombs. For this reason, we chose an area that was least disturbed. We wanted to confirm whether or not these elevations were in fact cultural mounds or if they were natural. This test pit was not deep; at around 20 cm we found a circular cist made in the form of a Collao-Inka tomb. We did not continue with this excavation.

*Description of Unit 04*

We placed this unit in the northern profile of the site to define the same characteristics as in Units 01 and 02. We also wanted to define a stratum of fieldstones and some semi-shaped stones that we noticed in the profile that corresponded to archaeological structures. This turned out to be disturbed stones with associated cultural materials, including some late (Collao) pottery fragments. This stratum represented a destruction episode on the highest part of the site. Below this stratum we found an intact stratum that had a cut stone wall associated with some Formative pottery.

*Surface level (registry number 119).* There are few lithic and ceramic materials. There is a cut stone approximately 22 × 26 cm.

*Stratum A (registry number 120).* This level had modern objects, prehispanic pottery and obsidian. There are fragments of Pukara Incised Geometric.

*Stratum B, level 1 (registry number 121).* This level has Collao pottery, Inca plates, and worked obsidian. In the lower part of the level there is a large quantity of Cusipata black-on-white pottery (Fig. 3.48).

*Stratum B, level 2 (registry number 122).* This level has incised Qaluyu and plainware pottery, camelid bone and obsidian (Fig. 3.49).

*Stratum C (registry number 123).* This level has plainware pottery and obsidian. There is one piece of worked bone, some bird bone and a lot of carbon.

*Stratum D (registry number 124).* This unit has small pieces of carbon mixed with the soil. There is a wall built with large stone. There is a compact floor made with yellow clay associated with the wall on one side. The floor was clean but on the other side there is Formative pottery including painted blackwares, possibly Cusipata. This is a semi-subterranean structure built with cut stones (Figs. 3.50, 3.51).

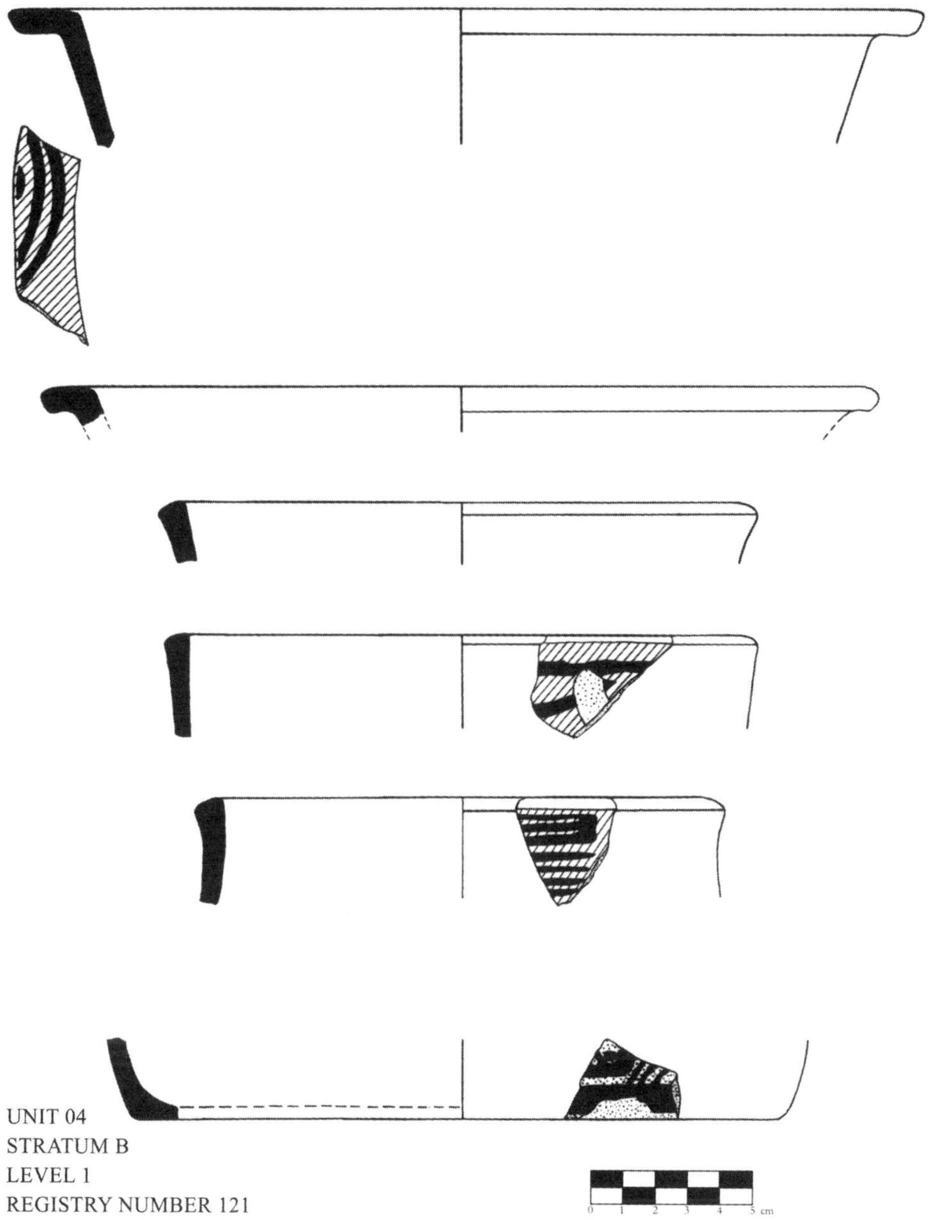
UNIT 04
STRATUM B
LEVEL 1
REGISTRY NUMBER 121
0 1 2 3 4 5 cm

Figure 3.48. Formative tazones with painted decoration.

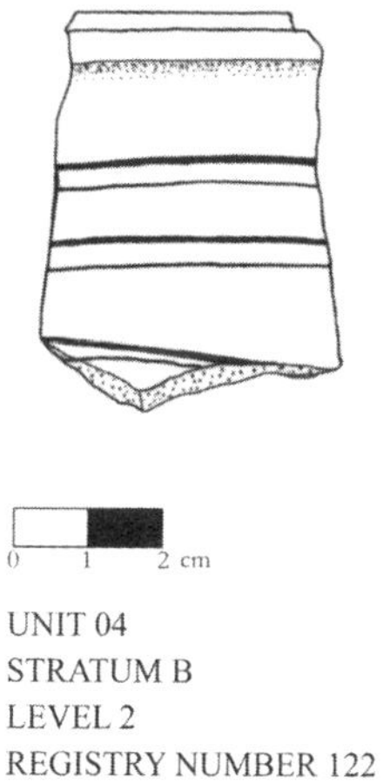
0 1 2 cm
UNIT 04
STRATUM B
LEVEL 2
REGISTRY NUMBER 122

Figure 3.49. Qaluyu Incised vessel.

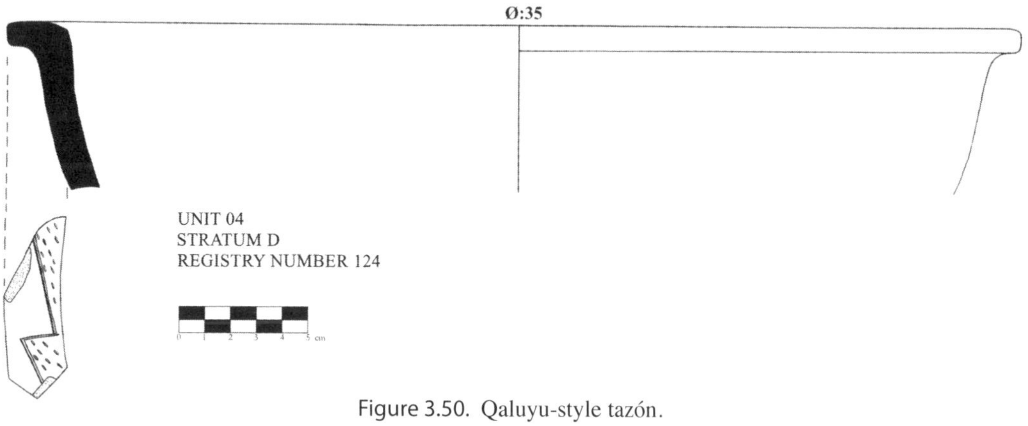
Ø:35
UNIT 04
STRATUM D
REGISTRY NUMBER 124

Figure 3.50. Qaluyu-style tazón.

Figure 3.51. View of the excavation of Unit 04. One can see the wall built with semi-cut stones and to the right a yellow clay floor (with the arrow). Qaluyu fragments were found on this floor; below the floor was sterile river sand. The scale is 20 cm.

Figure 3.52. Surface fragments including: *a*, local Inca; *b*, Collao plate; *c*, *d*, two Qaluyu Painted fragments; *e*, *f*, two Qaluyu Incised fragments.

*Description of Unit 05*

This is located on the northern part of the site. The first two layers or strata of the unit, down to 1 m below, were disturbed by heavy machinery. Below these disturbed levels, we find similar archaeological levels, though with lower densities than Units 01 and 02.

*Surface level (registry number 127).* This is a disturbed stratum with Inca and Cusipata vessel fragments. This is probably a modern dump mixed with archaeological midden (Fig. 3.52).

*Stratum A, level 1 (registry number 129).* This stratum has ceramic fragments, camelid bone and lithics (Fig. 3.53).

*Stratum A, level 2 (registry number 133).* This stratum has few ceramic fragments, animal bone, lithics, and small pieces of carbon (Fig. 3.54).

*Stratum B (registry number 135).* This stratum has a few ceramic fragments, animal bone, lithics, and small pieces of carbonized vegetal matter.

*Stratum C (registry number 137).* This was a very sparse level. There was one Qaluyu cream and black fragment with geometric motifs. There was also some obsidian (Fig. 3.55).

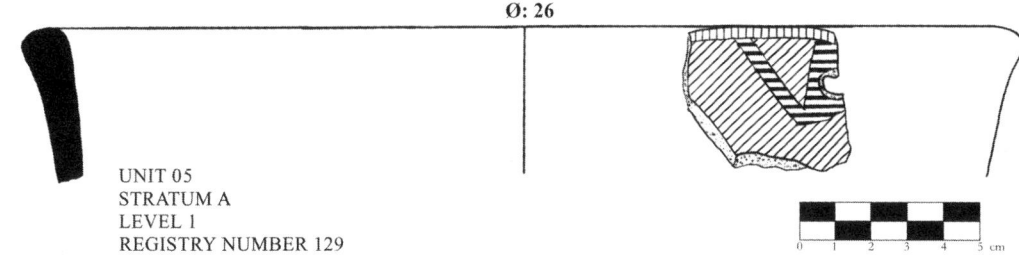

Figure 3.53. Qaluyu-style tazón.

Figure 3.54. Qaluyu-style fragment.

Figure 3.55. Qaluyu-style vessel with painted decoration.

*Description of Unit 06*

This unit was placed on the extreme west side of the site where there was evidence of heavy equipment disturbance. About 1.5 m were removed from the surface. The intent of this unit was to compare this area of the site with the other units. The unit was deep but it did not have much material and we found nothing significant. We were able to show that, along with Unit 04, this area was peripheral to the main occupation of the site.

*Description of Unit 07*

We put this unit on the high side of the second high spot on the site, located west of the other high area where Unit 03 was excavated. This unit coincided with the external southern side of a cist tomb, which was defined from a cut into the mound. It is typically Collao in style (AD 1100–1450), although it is possible that it was Inca in date. Below this stratum we found a Formative level that began with a mixture of Pukara and Qaluyu. In this last stratum we found a wall made with semi-cut stones that seems to be contemporary with Qaluyu in its earliest phase. This was associated with the wall in Unit 05. However, this structure did not have a related floor as in Unit 05 but there was some gray clay that could have functioned as a floor material. Under this gray stratum we found a sterile floor, made with alluvial sand probably obtained from the river that has a similar sand material composed of large-grained yellowish sand.

*Surface level (registry number 138)*. The surface here contained some late pottery.

*Stratum A (registry number 139)*. This stratum has fragments of local Inca pottery. In the north wall of the unit we see the tomb. This is a cist made with uncut fieldstones with an oval or circular form. The tomb was sealed with a slab and soil fill. The stones used in the tomb are calcareous (limestone) that do not appear near the site. The closest limestone is about 2 km from the site (Fig. 3.56).

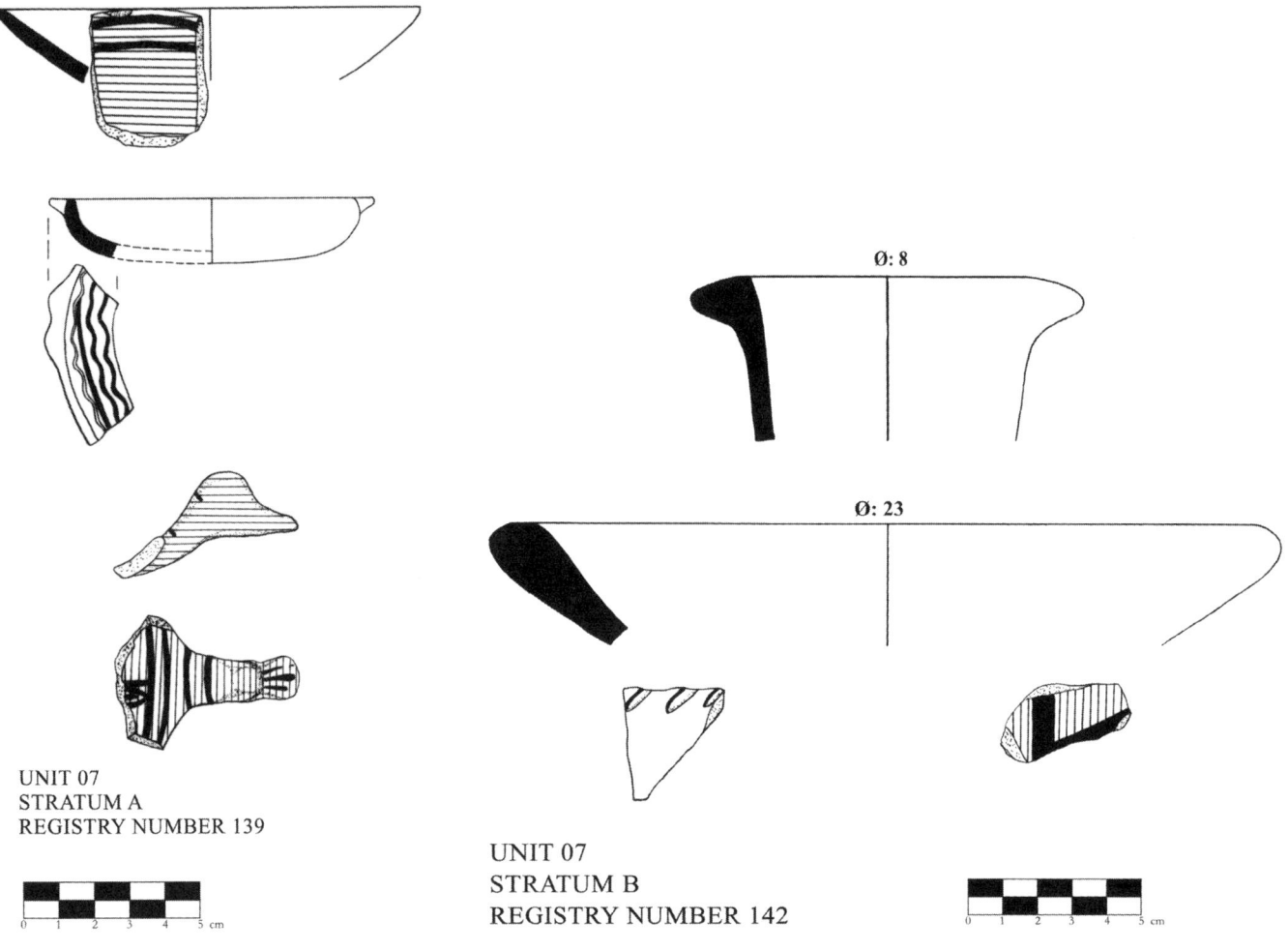

Figure 3.56. Local Inca-style vessels.

Figure 3.57. Formative vessels including Qaluyu.

*Stratum B (registry number 142)*. Just below stratum A there is Inca pottery and one fragment of Formative ware, camelid bone, and a fragment of a worked bone (Fig. 3.57).

*Stratum C (registry number 144)*. Pottery with red slip (Pukara), camelid bones, burned bones and a feline claw (Fig. 3.58).

*Stratum D, level 1 (registry number 145)*. This unit has the well-constructed wall made with uncut stones similar to the one in Unit 04. This stratum contains a lot of fragments of animal bones and chipped stone. There are some painted black over cream Qaluyu 2 (following Steadman 1995) fragments clearly associated with this level. There are also small fragments of carbon (Fig. 3.59).

*Stratum D, level 2 (registry number 147)*. Under the wall with the large stones was a supporting wall made with small rocks. There is virtually no cultural material associated with this stratum. A sterile level is found under the wall.

### Description of Unit 08

Unit 08 was excavated to verify if the eastern sector, which was mined for soil and where there was such a high concentration of materials, still retained some intact archaeological deposits. This unit confirmed that there was little remaining. This unit consisted of the first stratum with disturbed material and a second stratum with some Pukara. We unfortunately did not find that this area was very deep, reaching only 1 m; here we found the sterile stratum consisted of the yellowish river sand that was clean and loose.

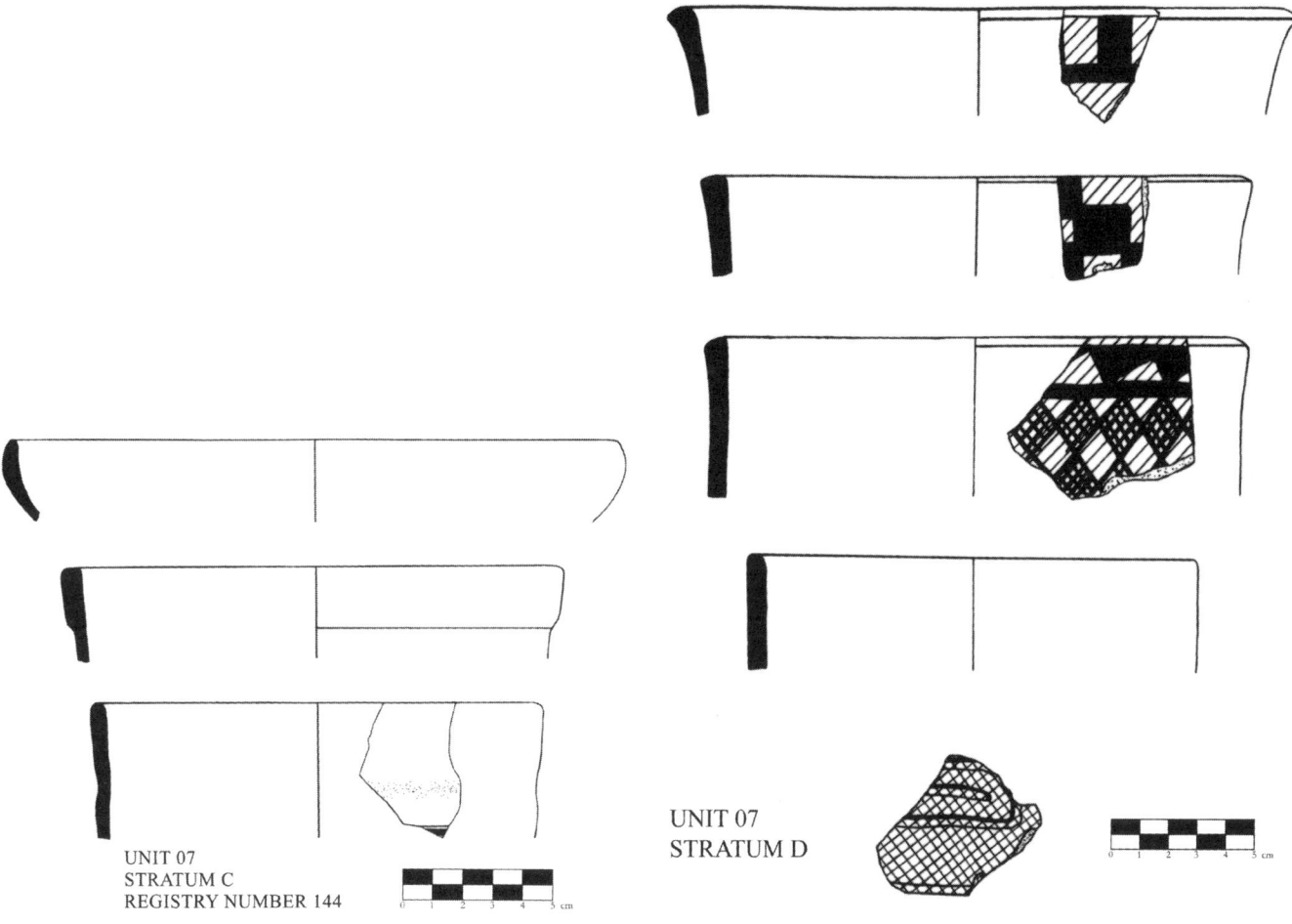

Figure 3.58. Formative vessels including Pukara.

Figure 3.59. Formative vessels including Qaluyu Painted and Incised.

## Human Prehispanic Occupation at Balsaspata

The occupation at Balsaspata began in the Early Formative circa 1500 BCE when the population was still using Archaic projectile points alongside early Qaluyu pottery (most notably neckless ollas). In this period, we see a settlement with a concentration of animal bones, such as camelid and deer, that we interpret as increased consumption of these resources. The site was emerging as a center in the region and was found near the river edge of Ayaviri. This possibly occurred simultaneously with the site of Qaqachupa (Burger et al. 2000), a site close to Balsaspata on the other side of the river.

Based upon the recovered materials, we can infer that during this early period there existed a division of labor for the production of diverse goods, such as textiles, indicated by the discovery of spindle whorls made from modified potsherds and camelid bone tools for weaving (Tantaleán 2005: Figs. 7, 8). We also found a large quantity of pottery polishers and other tools used for making incisions in pottery. Likewise, there is a proliferation of obsidian, including waste material most likely the result of point and other tool manufacturing. There were also a large quantity of cooking ollas and grinding stones. All of these diverse elements in the material culture indicate specialized production for internal consumption and external trade (Burger et al. 2000).

We also note that in the area of Balsaspata there are many raised fields. Our results agree with Erickson (1988) and Stanish (2006) in that this technology was most likely in use by the Qaluyu period. In the adjacent zone northeast of Balsaspata, we

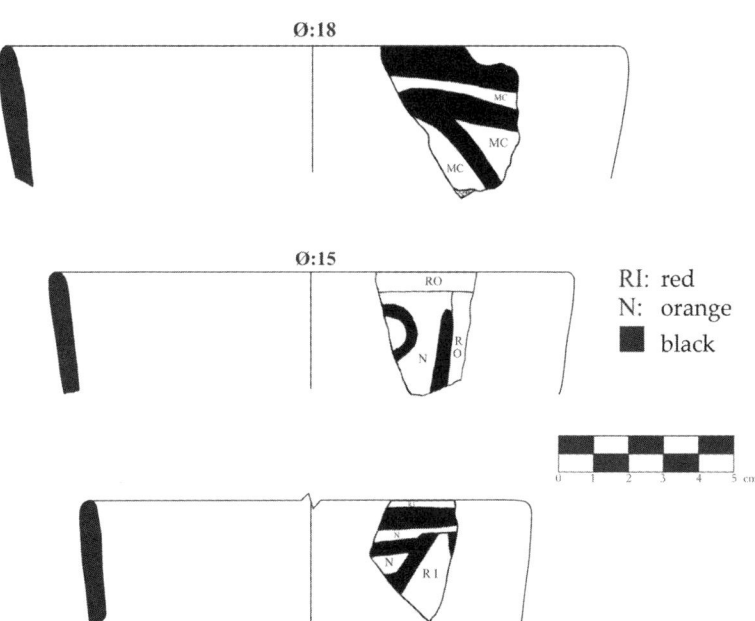

Figure 3.60. Base of Unit 07. One can see the wall built with semi-cut stones and to the right a yellow clay floor. Qaluyu fragments were found on this floor; below the floor was sterile river sand.

Figure 3.61. Fragments of a ceramic style called Ayacwira (Calero 1998), collected on the site's surface.

were able to recognize a large raised field area that indicates agricultural production for local consumption.

At Balsaspata, we also observe a large quantity of Qaluyu pottery and its variants, principally decoration with paint and incisions.[1] Here we note similarities with the Marcavalle style, also mentioned by other investigators (Mohr Chávez 1977; Lumbreras 1981; Burger et al. 2000). These investigators mention trade between these two polities as an explanation for this pattern. This also explains the presence of obsidian, a resource that comes largely from the Chivay source in Cotahuasi, Arequipa (Burger et al. 2000). This obsidian is abundant at Balsaspata during the Formative occupation (Tantaleán 2005: Fig. 9). As demonstrated by Burger et al. (2000), the Ayaviri zone was in an intermediate area between the Cuzco and Titicaca regions. As such, it was influenced by both areas, as indicated by the material remains.

As we have seen, the Formative period occupation at Balsaspata also documents important architectural structures with walls made from large cut stone blocks. The structures are rectangular in shape with yellowish and gray clay floors associated with Qaluyu pottery fragments (Figs. 3.51, 3.60). This pattern is similar to what Amanda Cohen has discovered in the site of Huatacoa, located in the lower Ayaviri Valley (Cohen 2010; Plourde 2006). The worked stone walls and carefully prepared floors indicate an intensive social activity apart from domestic labor. These constructions most likely were used for nondomestic, communal activities.

In this period, apart from the typical Qaluyu pottery styles, we found some atypical pieces that we are just beginning to understand (Fig. 3.26). During the time in which we excavated at Balsaspata, a local investigator (Calero 1998) named a style "Ayacwira," tentatively placed in the Early Regional Development period, following Pukara. This hypothesis is not supported by the stratigraphy. His studies were based upon typological analysis of surface materials. If this hypothesis is true, there would be a society later than Pukara that would explain the hiatus that one sees in the chronology of the northern basin. Our excavations do not confirm this proposition, as this style of pottery is associated with the latest Qaluyu pottery and closely linked with Pukara. This ceramic style comes in various forms at the site with the principal characteristic the use of painted decoration with black lines, almost always straight, that delimit spaces of yellow or red over an orange slip (Fig. 3.61). Based upon the stratigraphic evidence, I suggest that this is a style that

Figure 3.62. Inca arybalo found at Balsaspata. Recovered by Eduardo Arizaca.

Figure 3.63. Inca-style plate found at Balsaspata. Recovered by Eduardo Arizaca.

is contemporary with Late Qaluyu and Early Pukara. It is locally produced, but we do not know if it was produced at Balsaspata.

We also have fragments of a style called Cusipata (defined by Edward Franquemont, 1986). This is located chronologically between Qaluyu and Pukara although it has been found stratigraphically with the former (Mujica 1987:25). During our excavations, we did not find that Cusipata was associated with an isolated human occupation at the site. At Balsaspata, the majority of the Cusipata fragments were found mixed with the levels with the highest percentage of Qaluyu and Pukara polychromes. The best example of Cusipata pottery was recovered by Eduardo Arizaca, that, while found out of context, is the most complete find of this type in the region (Tantaleán 2005: Fig. 13).

There are Pukara materials found at Balsaspata but these were not recovered in particularly high quantities. The majority of these pieces were found mixed with the latest phases of Qaluyu. A big question is whether there is a Pukara domestic style that we have not identified that, if found in quantity, would be considered an indication of a Pukara occupation. On the other hand, the Pukara polychrome can be considered a prestige good shared by elites (Goldstein 2000) while Balsaspata would have been a minor village during this period.

Our colleague Eduardo Arizaca informs us that some time ago the people removed a carved stela from the site that was in Pukara style. It is locally referred to as Ñakaj or Decapitator, a sculptural style associated with this culture.[2] As we have described in an earlier article (Tantaleán and Pérez 1999), this and other material elements form part of a religious ideology that served the elite to justify and reproduce the material basis of society that supported them. This group utilized the labor of the population to construct the great religious and secular structures of Pukara and its satellites, to control trade routes on a large scale, for other large-scale production such as raised fields and cochas, and to produce sumptuary objects that utilized the "official" Pukara style. The elite used these activities to maintain control, in effect "naturalizing" social inequalities. This all occurred with the emergence of the theocratic state in the northern basin that continued up to approximately AD 350.

After this period there existed an apparent hiatus of 700 years until the appearance of cultural materials that are referred to as the Altiplano kingdoms that emerged around AD 1000. This hiatus—in which there is no archaeological occupation—has not been sufficiently studied although there are some hypotheses to explain this (Lumbreras and Amat 1968; Mújica 1990; Stanish

2003). In spite of the lack of research in the area, we can say that the majority of sites with Pukara occupations were abandoned, and we cannot find an "epigonal" period at sites like Balsaspata. The question is: where did the population that inhabited sites like Balsaspata and other Pukara settlements go?

Likewise, as Pukara fell, Tiwanaku expanded throughout the Titicaca Basin. However, the northernmost Tiwanaku site with Tiwanaku IV and V is found at the site of Maravillas (Mujica 1990), in the heart of Pukara territory.[3] The influence of Tiwanaku cannot explain the disappearance or invasion of territory that was formerly occupied by Pukara.

The explanation for the disappearance of Pukara materials in the region should be found in the society that produced them. We can explain the abandonment of these sites as a result of socio-economic reasons such as the collapse of Pukara from internal contradictions and the creation of a new lifestyle and mode of production. We can surmise a drop in economic production and a transformation in the elite classes. There would be a disruption in the exchange of goods throughout the region, which would disrupt the flow of Pukara materials. Stanish (2003:159) postulates that there was an epoch of drought that corresponds to the collapse of Pukara and, in turn, suggests the existence of a culture called "Early Huaña." Obviously, much more work must be done to test whether such a culture exists in the Ayaviri area.

Following the idea of drought postulated by Stanish, it is also possible that these ecological factors accelerated the change from a predominantly agricultural to a pastoral one. In this economic system, there were no population concentrations but rather smaller, dispersed settlements. In this respect, the lack of large sites does not negate the possibility of human occupation during this time period.

The last prehispanic use at Balsaspata was a mortuary one, with tombs placed at the top of the mound. In spite of the destruction of the site, we can say that about one-third of the mound was covered with intact and disturbed tombs on the higher areas of the site. While the tradition of cist tombs is pre-Inca, we found much material in Inca style associated with these tombs, including Inca-Cuzco style. Eduardo Arizaca has shown us Inca pottery with Imperial Cuzco forms from the site (Figs. 3.62, 3.63). It is possible that Balsaspata had been selected as a cemetery area because of its location above the pampa.

In conclusion, the site of Balsaspata and its previous human occupations that converted it into a cult place demonstrate the great continuity and success of the first human occupations of the Ayaviri-Pukara Valley. Although the site has almost disappeared, we were able to recover some of its most important archaeological features, and investigate how different societies occupied the site, and how its natural and social resources were produced and consumed. We believe strongly that our work here, humble as it is was, yielded valuable information that will help other researchers complete the intriguing puzzle that is the prehistory of the northern Titicaca Basin.

## Acknowledgments

I thank Chip Stanish for inviting me to publish this report and for translating it from my original in Spanish. Also, it is important to give thanks to Rolando Paredes Eyzaguirre (former director of Instituto Nacional de Cultura-Puno) who permitted me to excavate in Balsaspata. In the same way, Eduardo Arizaca and Carmen Pérez Maestro were the better company and brilliant archaeologists that I have there. My acknowledgments go also to Juan Roel who made the final drawings presented here. Finally, Jill Rheinheimer helped me in a great way to fix many mistakes on my original paper.

## Notes

1. See Chávez Ballón (1950), Lumbreras and Amat (1968), and Steadman (1995) for a good description of Qaluyu pottery.

2. These sculptures have been found in the type site of Pukara (Valcárcel 1932), in Altarane between Juliaca and Sillustani (Paredes 1984:13), in Chumbivilcas (Nuñez del Prado Béjar 1971), in the Isla de Sol (three examples are found in the Museum of Anthropology in La Paz) (Ponce Sanginés 1969:34–36), and in other places described by Kidder (1943), Rowe (1958), and Chávez (1988).

3. Burger et al. (2000) mention the presence of Tiwanaku material in Taraco but this does not prove its actual control over territory.

## References Cited

Arizaca, E., Jorge Calero, and J. Condori
1995 Prospección arqueológica del distrito de Ayaviri. *Revista cultural de Ayaviri* III(3):21–22. Ayaviri.

Burger, R., K. Mohr Chávez, and S. Chávez
2000 Through the glass darkly: Prehispanic obsidian procurement and exchange in southern Peru and northern Bolivia. *Journal of World Prehistory* 14(3):267–362.

Calero, J.
1998 *Ubicación cronológica e identificación de los procesos y técnicas de manufactura del material lítico, así como la posible función y uso de estos sociofactos*. Primer Cuaderno del Museo e Instituto de Arqueología y Antropología de Ayaviri-Melgar.

Chávez, S. J.
1975 The Arapa and Thunderbolt stelae: A case of stylistic identity with implications for Pucara influences in the area of Tiahuanaco. *Ñawpa Pacha* 13:3–25.
1988 Archaeological reconnaissance in the province of Chumbivilcas, south highlands Peru. *Expedition* 33(3):27–38.

Chávez Ballón, M.
1950 Arqueología del sur Andino. *Tradición. Revista Peruana de Cultura* 1(2):41–47. Cuzco.

Cohen, A.
2010   Ritual and Architecture in the Titicaca Basin: The Development of the Sunken Court Complex in the Formative Period. PhD dissertation, Department of Anthropology, University of California, Los Angeles.

Erickson, C.
1988   An Archaeological Investigation of Raised Field Agriculture in the Lake Titicaca Basin of Peru. PhD dissertation, Department of Anthropology, University of Illinois, Urbana-Champaign.

Fernández, M.
1998   *Qaluyo, Un estilo del Horizonte Temprano en el altiplano del sur. Aproximaciones en sus fases*. Primer Cuaderno del Museo e Instituto de Arqueología y Antropología de Ayaviri-Melgar.

Franquemont, E.
1986   The ancient pottery from Pucara, Perú. *Ñawpa Pacha* 24:1–30.

Goldstein, P.
2000   Exotic goods and everyday chiefs: Long-distance exchange and indigenous sociopolitical development in the south central Andes. *Latin American Antiquity* 11(4):335–61.

Kidder II, A.
1943   *Some Early Sites in the Northern Lake Titicaca Basin*. Papers of the Peabody Museum of American Archaeology and Ethnology, Harvard University, vol. 27, no. 1. Cambridge, MA.

Lumbreras, L. G.
1969   *De los Pueblos, las Culturas y las Artes del Antiguo Perú*. Moncloa Campodónico, Lima.
1971   Proyecto de investigaciones arqueológicas en Puno. *Pumapunku* 3:58–67. La Paz.
1981   *Arqueología de la América Andina*. Milla Batres, Lima.

Lumbreras, L. G., and H. Amat
1968   Secuencia arqueológica del altiplano occidental del Titicaca. *XXXVII Congreso Internacional de Americanistas. Actas y Memorias* 2:75–106. Buenos Aires.

Mohr Chávez, K.
1977   Marcavalle: The Ceramics from an Early Horizon Site in the Valley of Cuzco, Peru, and Implications for South Highland Socioeconomic Interaction. PhD dissertation, Department of Anthropology, University of Pennsylvania, Philadelphia.

Mujica, E.
1987   Cusipata: Una fase pre-Pukara en la cuenca norte del Titicaca. *Gaceta Arqueológica Andina* 13:22–28.
1990   Pukara: Une société complexe ancienne du bassin septentrional du Titicaca. In *Inca-Peru. 3000 ans d'histoire*, edited by S. Purin, pp. 156–77. Musées Royaux d'Arte et d'Histoire, Brussels.

Nuñez del Prado, J. V.
1971   Dos nuevas estatuas de estilo Pukara halladas en Chumbivilcas, Perú. *Ñawpa Pacha* 9:23–32.

Paredes, R.
1984   El "Degollador" (Nakaj) de Altarane, Puno. *Gaceta Arqueológica Andina* 11:13.

Plourde, A.
2006   Prestige Goods and Their Role in the Evolution of Social Ranking: A Costly Signaling Model with Data from the Formative Period of the Northern Lake Titicaca Basin, Peru. PhD dissertation, Department of Anthropology, University of California, Los Angeles.

Ponce Sanginés, C.
1969   *Tunupa y Ekako. Estudio Arqueológico Acerca de las Efigies Precolombinas de Dorso Adunco*. Academia Nacional de Ciencias de Bolivia, Publicación no. 19. La Paz.

Rowe, J.
1979 [1958]   The adventures of two Pucara statues. In *Peruvian Archaeology. Selected Readings*, edited by J. Rowe and D. Menzel, pp. 125–33. Peek Publications, Palo Alto.

Stanish, C.
2003   *Ancient Titicaca: The Evolution of Complex Society in Southern Peru and Northern Bolivia*. University of California Press, Berkeley.
2006   Prehispanic strategies of agricultural intensification in the Titicaca Basin of Peru and Bolivia. In *Agricultural Strategies*, edited by J. Marcus and C. Stanish, pp. 364–97. Cotsen Institute of Archaeology, University of California, Los Angeles.

Steadman, Lee
1995   Excavations at Camata: An Early Ceramic Chronology for the Western Titicaca Basin, Peru. PhD dissertation, Department of Anthropology, University of California, Berkeley.

Tantaleán, H.
2005   Balsaspata y las sociedades formativas en la cuenca nor-occidental del lago Titikaka. *Nuevos Aportes* 2:36–63.

Tantaleán, H., and C. Pérez Maestro
1999   Pukara y el surgimiento de la civilización en el altiplano Andino. *Revista de Arqueología* 215:32–42.

Tschopik, M.
1946   *Some Notes of the Archaeology of the Department of Puno, Peru*. Papers of the Peabody Museum of American Archaeology and Ethnology, Harvard University, vol. 27, no. 3. Cambridge, Massachusetts.

Valcárcel, Luis
1932   El personaje mítico de Pukara. *Revista del Museo Nacional* 1(1):18–31.

# Chapter 4

# Ceramic Changes and Cultural Transformations at Paucarcolla-Santa Barbara

*Ilana Johnson*

In the southern quarter of Tawantinsuyu, referred to by the Inca as Collasuyu, were several political and ethnic groups that occupied the region surrounding Lake Titicaca. These groups were Aymara speakers led by hereditary dynasties that controlled different areas, the two largest and most powerful being the Colla and Lupaca (Julien 1983). These two groups inhabited the northern and western portions of the Titicaca Basin. They lived on the hills and pampas around the lake and subsisted on fishing, camelid herding, and cultivation of quinoa (a native cereal grain) and tubers such as potatoes and oca. Although the chronicles provide many different, and sometimes conflicting, accounts of events that occurred during the reign of the Inca, they still supply important information. The Colla, ruled by a lord named Zapana, were centered at the town of Hatuncolla in the northern portion of the Titicaca Basin. The Lupaca leader, who was named Cari, resided at the city of Chucuito located south of the modern city of Puno on Lake Titicaca's western edge (Cieza de León 1959).

It is reported that the kingdoms of Colla and Lupaca were at war with each other. This is supported in the archaeological record by the abundance of hilltop fortifications, called pukaras, dating to the Altiplano period (AD 1100–1450) in the Titicaca Basin. According to the chronicles, word was brought to Inca Viracocha (the fifth Inca) that Zapana, lord of Hatuncolla, had become very powerful and was planning on marching against Cuzco (Cieza de León 1959). The Inca was pleased by the news because he wanted to find another lord who had the audacity to do battle with him (Betanzos 1996). Both leaders, Zapana and Cari, wanted to defeat the other and be the dominant Aymara leader of the Titicaca Basin, so each sent an emissary to the Incas to plead for their alliance and help in defeating their enemy. The Incas consulted their oracles and were told to go to the land of the Colla and seek the friendship of Cari and the Lupaca, but the Incas told both groups that they were coming to make an alliance with them. However, Zapana learned that the Incas had lied and had decided to wage war on the Colla with Lupaca's help. Tensions escalated and the two groups marched to the pampa near the village of Paucarcolla to wage battle:

> Cari, who must have been brave, marched his men to a village named Paucarcolla, and before it the two most powerful tyrants of the region met with a force said to have numbered 150,000. And they joined battle after their fashion, which is said was bitterly fought and over 30,000 Indians were killed. Cari won the victory and Zapana himself was killed in battle. [Cieza de León 1959:219]

After Zapana's death, Cari seized Hatuncolla and took all of the riches back to Chucuito, where he prepared lodgings for Viracocha Inca's arrival. Viracocha was very displeased with the outcome, for he secretly wished the two kingdoms to remain unstable so that he could conquer them and be the sole ruler of Collasuyu. He now realized that Cari and the Lupaca were too powerful to go up against and that he must make an alliance and quickly return to Cuzco so that no harm would befall him. Therefore, Viracocha told Cari that he was pleased he had won the battle and offered him one of his daughters as an alliance between the two kingdoms. Viracocha brought in a golden goblet from which the two leaders drank libations and the alliance was celebrated with feasting, dancing, and music. Viracocha returned to Cuzco, and the Titicaca Basin was not truly conquered until many years later during the reign of his son, Pachacuti Inca.

## Paucarcolla

The land around Paucarcolla was important during the Inca conquest, securing its place in the oral traditions as a result of the important battle that took place on its soil and the thousands of lives that were lost in the process. Paucarcolla is the name of the village settled by the Inca in the fifteenth century, and it is occupied to this day (Fig. 4.1). Paucarcolla-Santa Barbara refers to the hill adjacent to the modern city, currently used for farming and containing sparse habitation. Although the earlier inhabitants left no written records, we can reconstruct what may have occurred at Paucarcolla-Santa Barbara by examining the archeological record. It is obvious that the site was an important and strategic location to many polities throughout the prehistory of the Titicaca Basin because Paucarcolla-Santa Barbara has been continuously occupied for almost three thousand years and is one of the only sites in the Titicaca Basin that has ceramic refuse from all the major periods during that time. However, the nature of occupation at the site changed over time and the archaeological record provides some clues as to how these changes occurred. The ceramics and architecture that remain at the site tell us a story about the previous inhabitants at Paucarcolla.

The site of Paucarcolla-Santa Barbara is located on a large hill that stands out on the landscape and is near the lake's edge (Fig. 4.2). From the top of the hill, one can see for many kilometers in every direction and monitor traffic on the road or in the Puno Bay. The people who lived at Paucarcolla-Santa Barbara were farmers and herders who used the hillsides for terrace agriculture and the pampa below for herding and raised-field agriculture. At some point in the past, elites emerged at the site and a religious complex was built at the top of the hill. Elites must have considered Paucarcolla-Santa Barbara an important ritual and administrative center because the site was continually occupied for almost three thousand years and elites in each new polity realized the site's importance as part of their repertoire of administrative and religious centers. The question remains: Why was the site of Paucarcolla-Santa Barbara so important to the leaders of the earliest ranked and stratified societies in the Lake Titicaca Basin? Why did the site continue to be occupied generation after generation, even in the wake of repeated polity collapse?

### Data Recovery at Paucarcolla-Santa Barbara

This research attempts to gain an understanding of the political organization at the site of Paucarcolla-Santa Barbara and how the nature of power changed through time. Some of the questions I posed while conducting research at the site during the summer of 2002 included: Where does Paucarcolla stand within the regional framework of the Titicaca Basin? Was it a political center or a village of farmers and herders? What types of activities were occurring at the site in the past? Did the site have a ritual component? How did the demographic and social organization of the site change over time?

The best way to answer these questions was to thoroughly analyze the site on a regional level and look at the material remains for clues about the past. Since the majority of the site has been plowed due to its current use as agricultural fields, a systematic surface survey was conducted to recover diagnostic ceramics from the site's surface. In addition, ceramic and architectural remains were analyzed to provide a clear picture of the function of the site through time. By surveying the entire site, it was possible to see where occupation took place during different time periods and I was able to gain insight into the nature of that occupation.

The systematic survey of Paucarcolla-Santa Barbara covered an area of approximately 6.4 ha to include the entire hill and a small portion of the pampa at its base. Surface artifacts were collected and all time periods were represented on the surface due to generations of agricultural plowing. A team of three archaeologists conducted the survey. We walked the length of the site in transects set 40 m apart, and we stopped and collected artifacts every 40 m in a diameter of 1 m. Occasionally, very diagnostic ceramics were collected between stopping points. However, this was difficult to control due to language difficulties, so a density analysis would probably not yield reliable results. The entire hill was mapped using a total station to capture the site's complex topography. All visible pre-modern architecture was also recorded and later superimposed on top of the topography map.

### Data Analysis and Chronology

More than 2000 ceramic fragments from the survey were analyzed in a laboratory and the following features were recorded: slip color, paste color, paste type, design, rim type, munsell color, rim type, rim diameter, burnishing, wiping, incising, part of vessel, and vessel type. The ceramics were classified according to the existing typology for the northern Titicaca Basin (Stanish 2003). Each major epoch is associated with a political, cultural, and material change in the basin throughout its prehistory. The epochs within which ceramics have been found include the Early, Middle, and Upper Formative; Middle Horizon; Late Intermediate; Inca (Sillustani-Inca); and Colonial periods. The site of Paucarcolla-Santa Barbara had occupation in all these periods, all of which (except the Early Formative and Colonial periods)

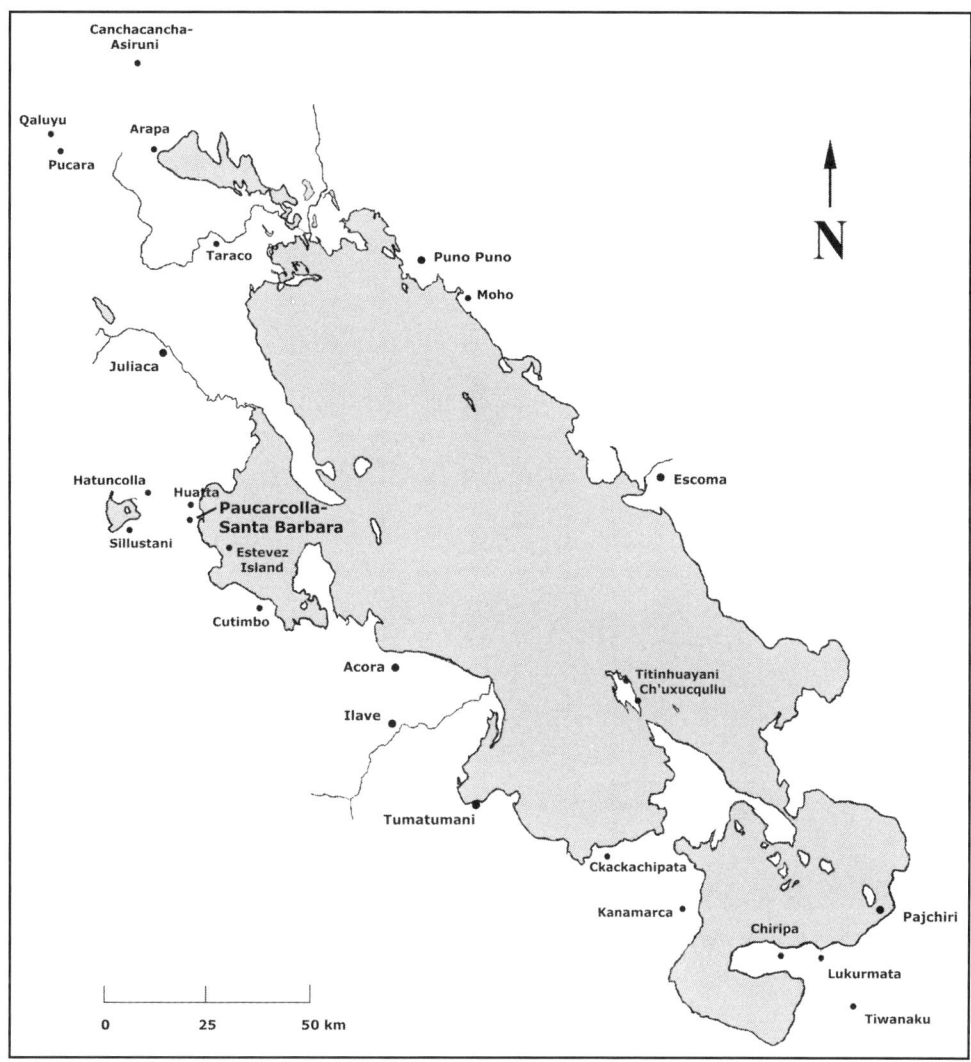

Figure 4.1. Map of the Lake Titicaca Basin.

are addressed here. The archaeological material typology for the northern Titicaca Basin is as follows:

*Middle Formative Period*

Ceramics from this period consisted mainly of plainwares that were medium thickness and had medium to large inclusions with dense mica. Some vessels were slipped, but most were not, and the majority of vessel shapes were bowls or ollas (Steadman 1995). The higher quality elite wares associated with the Qaluyu style were slipped with red tones and were highly polished. Many had raised bands, some with notches evenly spaced throughout the band. The main elite vessel shapes were bowls and trumpets, probably used in ritual contexts.

The period marks the emergence of sunken court complexes and carved stone stelae (Chávez and Chávez 1975). These architectural elements reflect the development of elite ideologies with economic ties and beliefs spanning a large area. Therefore, evidence of sunken courts, stelae, or ceramics from other sites with these elements would indicate a connection to the regional elite ideology.

*Upper Formative Period*

Plainwares from this period are indistinguishable from the earlier forms and also have large micaceous inclusions. The elite wares from this period are polychrome with bold colors such as red, black, orange, and cream. These colors were used on separate sections of the vessel, which were then separated by deep incised lines, called zone-incised (Steadman 1995; Stanish 2003). This technique can be seen throughout the Titicaca Basin and even into the western Andes in the valley of Paracas (Goldstein 2000).

Figure 4.2. Photo of the site of Paucarcolla-Santa Barbara.

However, each area is distinguishable from the rest due to their unique styles and motifs. Pukara zone-incised pottery is unique because of the linear incising and geometric shapes, such as L-shapes, rectangles, and triangles. The most prominent motifs include felines, running figures, llamas, birds, and bodiless rayed heads (Franquemont 1986).

The ritual architecture during this period consists of terraced walled compounds, sunken courts and artificial mountains or pyramids. This period marks the beginning of the Kalasasaya Complex, which can be seen at the primary ritual center of Pucara (Stanish 2003). This architectural complex provides evidence of an official religious cult with regulated traditions. Individuals or groups attempting to associate themselves with this religion would want to emulate the elements present at the main religious site in order to legitimize their power and connection to the supernatural (Goldstein 1993). Therefore, satellite religious and administrative centers would have these architectural elements at a reduced scale.

*Middle Horizon*

The Tiwanaku expansion into the northern basin was marked by the appearance of Tiwanaku elite ceramic vessels. Some of these vessels were imported directly from Tiwanaku, but most were made locally using nearby clay sources and imitating Tiwanaku imperial iconography and designs (Stanish 2003). The main vessel shapes of the Tiwanaku elite wares were keros (flared drinking cups), tazones (flared bowls), and incensarios (shallow bowls with pedestal feet). The presence of elite Tiwanaku wares suggests ritual and economic ties between Tiwanaku and satellite centers. These wares would have been used in rituals and feasts and served to tie individuals to the religious cult and to the leaders at Tiwanaku. The high quality of ceramics during this time period also suggests the presence of full-time craft specialists who were supported by the Tiwanaku elites (Janusek 1999). Local imitations of slightly lesser quality were produced at many of the satellite centers, suggesting that these sites had specialists of their own who were supported by local elites.

Keros were very standardized and almost all have a base measurement of 9 cm in diameter. These ceramics were used mainly in ritual contexts for drinking libations such as chicha beer or burning incense during ceremonies. These vessels were also painted with vibrant colors including red, black, orange, green, yellow, brown, and cream. Some of the most prominent patterns are the wavy line and step line. Motifs include felines, condors, llamas, trophy heads, and the staff god (Kolata 1993; Stanish 2003). Although the elite Tiwanaku wares stand out prominently in the archaeological record, Middle Horizon plainwares have not yet been identified or distinguished from earlier periods in the northern Titicaca Basin.

## Late Intermediate Period

Ceramics from this time period were much less standardized and did not require a great deal of skill or specialization. In the northwestern Titicaca Basin, the Colla-style ceramics were typically beige, brown, red-brown, or orange, and some had a washy slip. Vessel shapes include beakers, deep bowls, and ollas. The paste is very gritty with large angular rocky inclusions and no mica. Most tend to be undecorated, although some have thick black designs that were put on quickly and haphazardly (Carlevato 1988). Some ollas also have raised bands with punctates encircling the neck of the vessel. Many small ceramic figurines with cone-shaped heads were found to be associated with this period as well (Tschopik 1946).

The isolated clusters of slab-cist tombs during this period reflect a more dispersed settlement pattern as people began to increasingly rely on a pastoral lifestyle. The above-ground tombs suggest an emphasis on ancestor veneration. Also, at some sites they are located in different clusters, possibly reflecting moiety group organization.

## Inca Period

This period shows a marked increase in the quality of ceramics. Pastes tend to be much finer with little to no inclusions. The slips come in many colors and the decoration is very detailed and precise. Designs are made with very thin straight lines and include crosshatching, ovals, triangles, parallel lines, and the fern motif. Vessel shapes include thin plates (some with bird head handles) and aryballos (narrow-necked jar with a pointed base) (Carlevato 1988). Many of the vessels in the imperial Inca style were imported from Cuzco for the provincial elites; however, there is good evidence that many of the local pottery producers attempted to copy Cuzco-Inca styles by placing Inca motifs on crudely made, thick vessels. There is also a unique style that arose during this time period called Sillustani-Inca. This pottery employed many traditional Inca designs, such as linear patterns and crosshatching, but with a much narrower scheme of colors. These ceramics are usually plates painted cream or buff and their designs are typically black, brown, or red-brown (Tschopik 1946).

## Results

The site of Paucarcolla-Santa Barbara began as a small farming community manufacturing plain unslipped ceramics that were used for subsistence-related activities, such as cooking, storing, and eating. The inhabitants most likely practiced terrace agriculture on the hill itself and raised-field agriculture on the pampa below. They also probably tended herds of camelids on the pampa as the modern inhabitants continue to do. By the Middle Formative period, the people of Paucarcolla were aggregated into a nucleated village consisting of several households. The size of the occupation at the site during the Middle Formative period is difficult to assess because the plainwares are indistinguishable from those of the Upper Formative period (see Fig. 4.3 for a map of the ceramic distribution during the Middle and Upper Formative periods). It seems as though the occupation was dispersed during these periods and covered a large portion of the site.

Paucarcolla-Santa Barbara was most likely a large village complex during the Middle Formative period. However, the presence of high-quality elite ceramics of the Qaluyu style suggests that a more complex social organization was emerging at Paucarcolla-Santa Barbara. High-quality ceramics imported from other Qaluyu centers were used for rituals and feasts associated with the elite ideology (Fig. 4.4). Therefore, it is likely that Paucarcolla-Santa Barbara had a sunken court that was used by its inhabitants and neighboring communities during annual celebrations. Also, there were some families or individuals at Paucarcolla-Santa Barbara who became linked to the Qaluyu elite ideology and had access to valuable trade goods from throughout the Qaluyu sphere of interaction. These items would have been used during rituals and feasts and would have served to raise the status of those individuals who had access to them. Exotic items would have been symbols of these individuals' ties to the elite ideology and their ability to communicate with distant domains. These material symbols served to distinguish them from the rest of the population and to increase their status and power within their community at home.

Since there are no elaborate residences left on the surface and the ritual architecture is undated, it is difficult to speculate whether this was one of several Qaluyu ritual centers in the northern Titicaca Basin. The site is significantly larger than other nearby village sites, such as Huatta, that date to the same time period (Erickson 1987). There also does not seem to be a single primary regional center in the Titicaca Basin at this time, so Paucarcolla-Santa Barbara did not serve as a secondary center for a larger polity. Recent regional exploration has revealed that there are no other Middle Formative period centers located near Paucarcolla-Santa Barbara (Schultze 2008). However, previous research has identified several other centers in the northern and eastern part of the basin (Plourde 2006). It is therefore very tempting to speculate that this was a likely candidate for a Qaluyu center due to its location in the larger framework of Qaluyu-related sites.

The Upper Formative period at Paucarcolla-Santa Barbara does not show marked differences from the previous period and was most likely continually occupied without site abandonment. The site probably continued to grow in size due to natural population growth and migration from the surrounding areas as many Middle Formative period sites were abandoned. There is evidence of zone-incised elite pottery and ritual objects such as incensarios from the site of Pucara, implying that some individuals had ties to this large primary ritual center (Fig. 4.4). Pucara developed into a complex chiefdom during this time period and many smaller second-tier satellite centers also arose with strong ties to the elites at the ritual center (Stanish 2003). There is a possible area at Paucarcolla-Santa Barbara that could be a replication

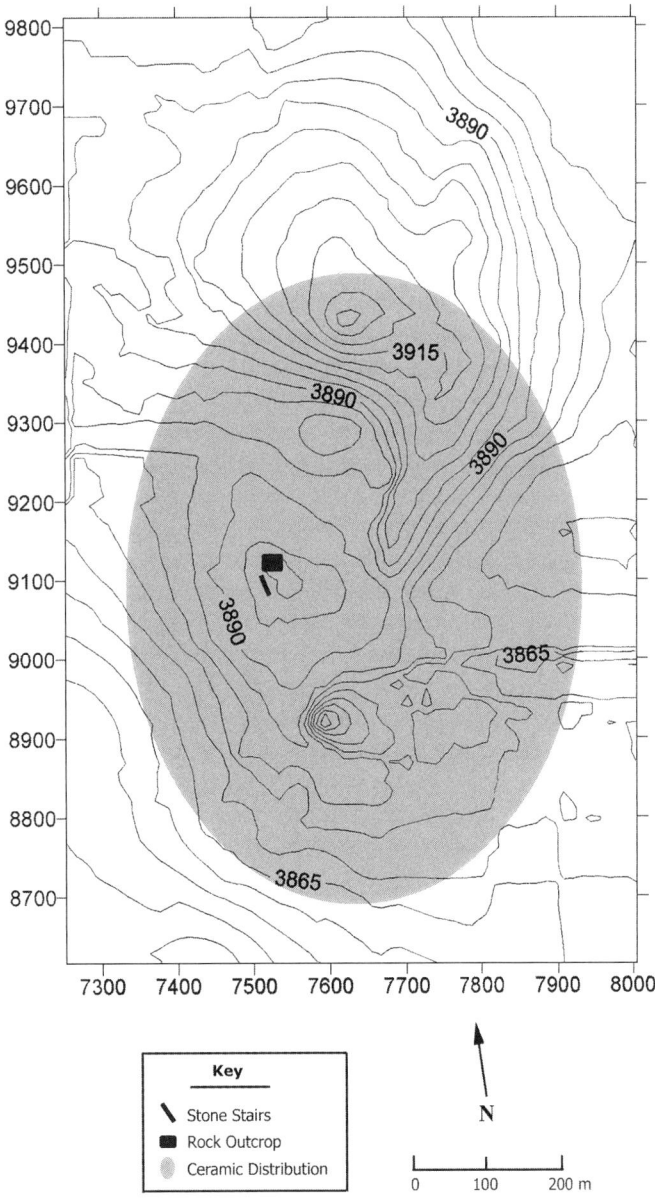

Figure 4.3. Formative period ceramic distribution.

of the Kalasasaya Complex (artificial mountain, sunken court, walled enclosure) that began to emerge in the basin at this time and was present at the site of Pucara.

At the top of the hill, there is a large natural stone outcrop that resembles a pyramid or artificial mountain and two lines of neatly placed stones nearby that could be the remnants of a semi-subterranean sunken court (Fig. 4.5). Although these features are undated, they seem to be in congruence with the architectural complexes of this time period. These features could also be one of the reasons that Paucarcolla-Santa Barbara was initially attractive to individuals looking for a sacred area in which to hold rituals. Since the components of the Kalasasaya Complex were important to the main religious traditions of the Formative and Tiwanaku periods, this may be the reason why the site was continually occupied in a similar manner during these time periods.

By the Upper Formative period, Paucarcolla-Santa Barbara was incorporated into the larger Pucara sphere of political and ideological influence. It is likely that there was a sunken court complex at the site during this time period, and it was probably a satellite center for the site of Pucara. The elites at Paucarcolla-Santa Barbara were linked to the elites at Pucara through shared ideology, religious iconography, and high-status Pucara ceramics that distinguished them from the rest of the population. Since the site of Paucarcolla-Santa Barbara is located on the ancient road in the middle of the eastern and western cordilleras, it must have been an important location for regulating trade. The site would have been an important satellite center for Pucara, and administration of the site would have proven crucial to controlling trade in the northern Titicaca Basin during this time period.

After the collapse of Pucara as a major center, the people of Paucarcolla-Santa Barbara most likely reverted to village life, subsisting on small-scale farming and herding. It was not until several hundred years later that the Tiwanaku state expanded into the northern Titicaca Basin. Because of the strategic location of Paucarcolla-Santa Barbara on the main road between the eastern and western slopes of the Andes, it was an attractive enclave to the Tiwanaku administrative elites. The village sites of Huatta and Cerro Cupe (Erickson 1987) were probably administered by the elites at Paucarcolla-Santa Barbara during this time period, and agriculture was intensified in order to pay tribute and taxes to the Tiwanaku elites. Since the site was an enclave of the Tiwanaku state, there were most likely Tiwanaku-affiliated elites settled at the site to ensure loyal administration of the area. However, the site was probably only a tertiary center within the greater Tiwanaku sphere, and the nearby site of Isla Estevez most likely served as a secondary center for the northwestern Titicaca Basin (Schultze 2008).

Paucarcolla-Santa Barbara also had a significant ritual component during the Middle Horizon. The Kalasasaya Complex that was developed in earlier periods became a symbol of imperial Tiwanaku control. These architectural components are found at the majority of Tiwanaku enclaves including sites as far away as Moquegua (Goldstein 1993). The fact that the natural rock outcrop and a sunken court may have already existed at the site from earlier periods could explain why it was an especially attractive site for Tiwanaku administration (Fig. 4.5). Since the Tiwanaku cult incorporated old ritual elements into their imperial ideology, the inhabitants at Paucarcolla-Santa Barbara may have been familiar with the elements and less opposed to an alliance with the new religious cult. The presence of elite and ritual Tiwanaku-style artifacts (such as keros, tazones, and incensarios) is a clear indicator that ritual practice was occurring at the site during this time period (Fig. 4.6). The number and quality of ar-

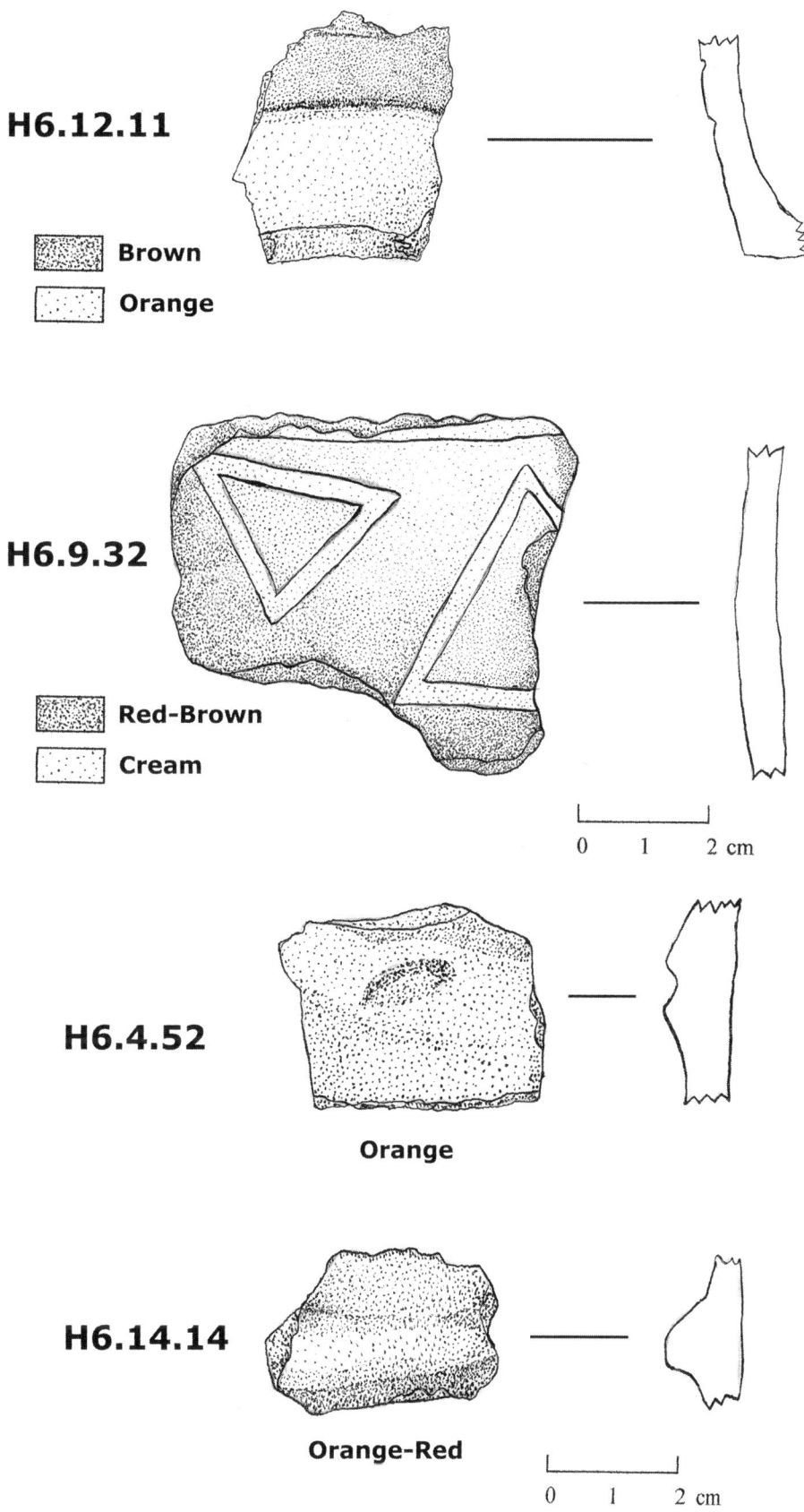

Figure 4.4. Qaluyu and Pucara ceramics.

Figure 4.5. Possible Kalasasaya Complex.

tifacts also indicate the importance of Paucarcolla-Santa Barbara within the Tiwanaku religious sphere (see Fig. 4.7 for ceramic distribution). The site was probably the religious center for the immediate region and people from neighboring villages traveled to Paucarcolla-Santa Barbara for rituals and festivals. During larger rituals and feasts, people from the area probably traveled to Isla Estevez or possibly to the center of Tiwanaku itself.

After the collapse of the Tiwanaku state, Paucarcolla-Santa Barbara ceased to be a center in the northern Titicaca Basin. The population at the site dispersed and the inhabitants returned to autonomous village life. There was no longer a nucleated settlement at Paucarcolla-Santa Barbara during the Late Intermediate period and the majority of ceramic refuse is found within or near the above-ground slab-cist tombs common during this period. There are nine tombs total, three located on the southern part of the hill, two to the east, and four located at the northern edge (Fig. 4.8). There were probably more tombs located at the site, but they were either looted long ago or the stones have been taken to build dividing walls for agricultural fields. Since the slab-cist tombs were small compared to some of the chulpa tombs found at neighboring sites, these probably represented corporate groups and were used in household ritual and ancestor veneration (Fig. 4.9).

The fact that there are few artifacts at the site dating to the Late Intermediate period indicates that settlement was very sparse. This is congruent with the pastoral subsistence pattern that dominated the basin following the collapse of Tiwanaku (Graffam 1992). The majority of groups were spread over the landscape and lived on hilltops near fortified pukaras for protection during frequent periods of warfare (Arkush and Stanish 2005). There was not a pukara at the site of Paucarcolla-Santa Barbara, but the inhabitants would have been very close to nearby fortified sites at Hatuncolla and Sillustani. Hatuncolla served as the center for the Colla ethnic group and the burial center at Sillustani housed the tombs of the elite lineages (Julien 1983). Families living at Paucarcolla-Santa Barbara during this period probably visited Hatuncolla on a regular basis for rituals and protection during battles. However, Paucarcolla-Santa Barbara did not serve as a secondary center and the inhabitants were most likely pastoralists who resided at the site on a permanent or semi-permanent basis.

When the Inca expanded into the Titicaca Basin, dismantling the warring Aymara chiefdoms, they installed strategic administration at many sites along the road system. Paucarcolla, located next to the road and near Hatuncolla, seemed to be a prime location to build a city. The Inca relocated groups from the hilltops into nicely aggregated urban cities along the road to ensure easy administration and control of the populations. People had to live in the Inca centers and walk to their fields located on the adjacent hills. This pattern can be seen at the site of Paucarcolla-Santa Barbara as the ceramic remains are almost exclusively located in the western part of the site near the modern, and presumably ancient, road (Fig. 4.10). There are few to no Late Horizon artifacts located on the top or sides of the hill. There are many Cuzco Inca ceramics, indicating the presence of Inca elites for administrating the production of surplus for the Inca Empire (Fig. 4.11). There are also a few Sillustani-Inca ceramic plate fragments, indicating that some households had ties to elites at Hatuncolla and Sillustani (Fig. 4.11).

Paucarcolla was a secondary urban center at this time, and was only slightly smaller than Hatuncolla and Chucuito. The Toledo *Tasa*, a document sent to the Spanish Crown, reported the population size and number of taxpayers in each community. This document reports that shortly after Spanish colonization, Paucarcolla had 1003 taxpayers (men between the ages of 20 and 60) and 4576 total individuals (men, women, and children). The inhabitants of Paucarcolla paid tribute in the form of meat, wool, dried fish, and salt (Cook 1975). The site is believed to be approximately 25 ha and was closely associated with Hatuncolla. "Paucarcolla may have been a provincial capital in its own right, or just a town subordinate to the capital at Hatunqolla" (Julien 1983:59). The sites appear to be contemporaneous and share several ceramic types made from the same clay source, suggesting a common ceramic production area. However, the size of the Inca period occupation at the site suggests that Paucarcolla was a separate and important provincial center.

## Conclusions

Although Paucarcolla-Santa Barbara never became a primary regional center in the northern Titicaca Basin, it was an important and strategic site to many expansive polities. It was located on the ancient road between the eastern and western cordilleras of the Andes, making it a key place for regulating long-distance trade. The first elites to emerge at Paucarcolla-Santa Barbara relied on alliances with other elites, connections to the emerging ideology, and access to exotic goods in order to increase their status and power. Paucarcolla-Santa Barbara is one of the few sites in the Titicaca Basin that was occupied for several consecutive time periods. Because of its strategic location on the road system and its widespread view of the surrounding area, it was a prime location for administration because it allowed for the regulation of traffic moving through the area.

Since the site was occupied by so many successive polities, it provides clues to the changing nature of power in the Titicaca Basin throughout time. The changes in ceramic styles at the site reveal the changing religious and political affiliation of the elites through time. Also, the distribution of ceramics reveals information about changes in the political and economic spheres, such as the dispersal of settlement and shift toward a pastoral economy after the collapse of Tiwanaku.

During the Middle and Upper Formative periods, the elites probably did not have coercive power and people were incorporated into the religious and political spheres through persuasion. There were many enticements to those who were affiliated, including exotic trade goods, information, a sense of belonging, protection, rituals, feasting, and an ideology that explained the natural and the supernatural. Even though there is evidence

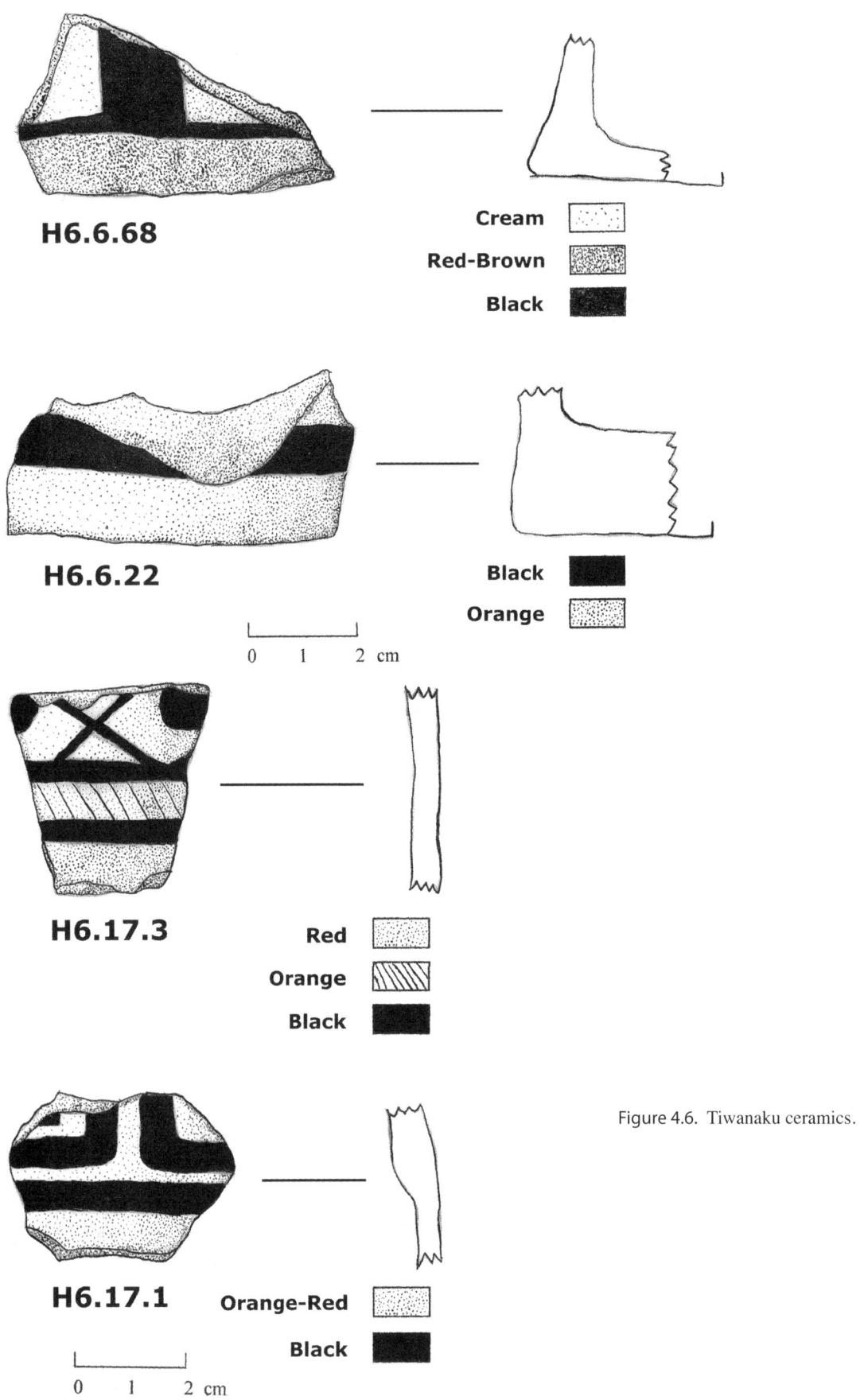

Figure 4.6. Tiwanaku ceramics.

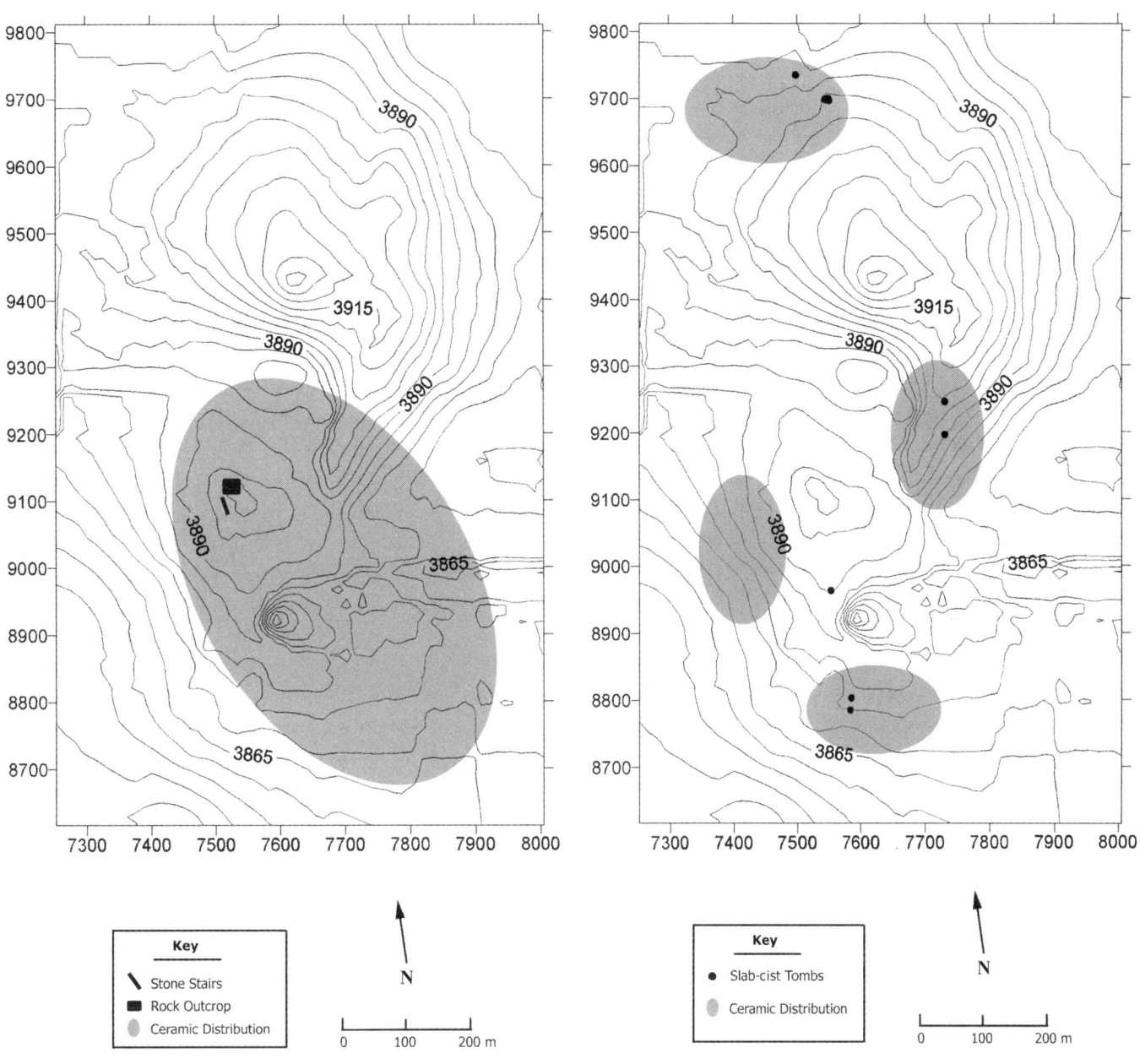

Figure 4.7. Tiwanaku period ceramic distribution.

Figure 4.8. Late Intermediate period ceramic distribution and location of slab-cist tombs.

88                                    *Advances in Titicaca Basin Archaeology–III*

Figure 4.9.
Slab-cist tomb.

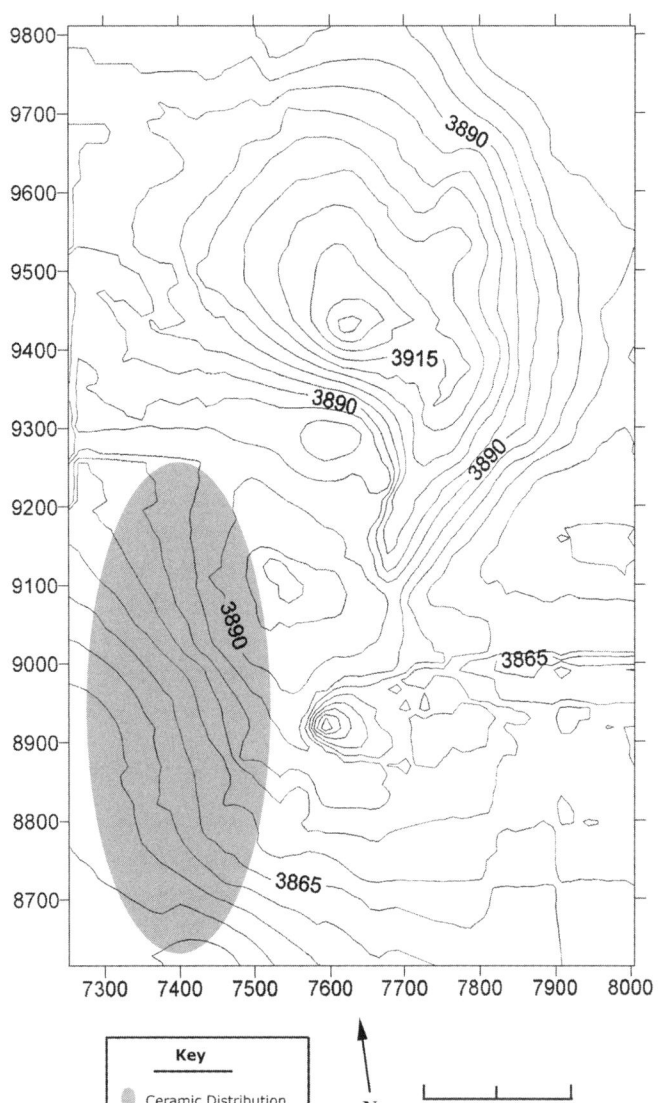

Figure 4.10.
Inca period ceramic distribution.

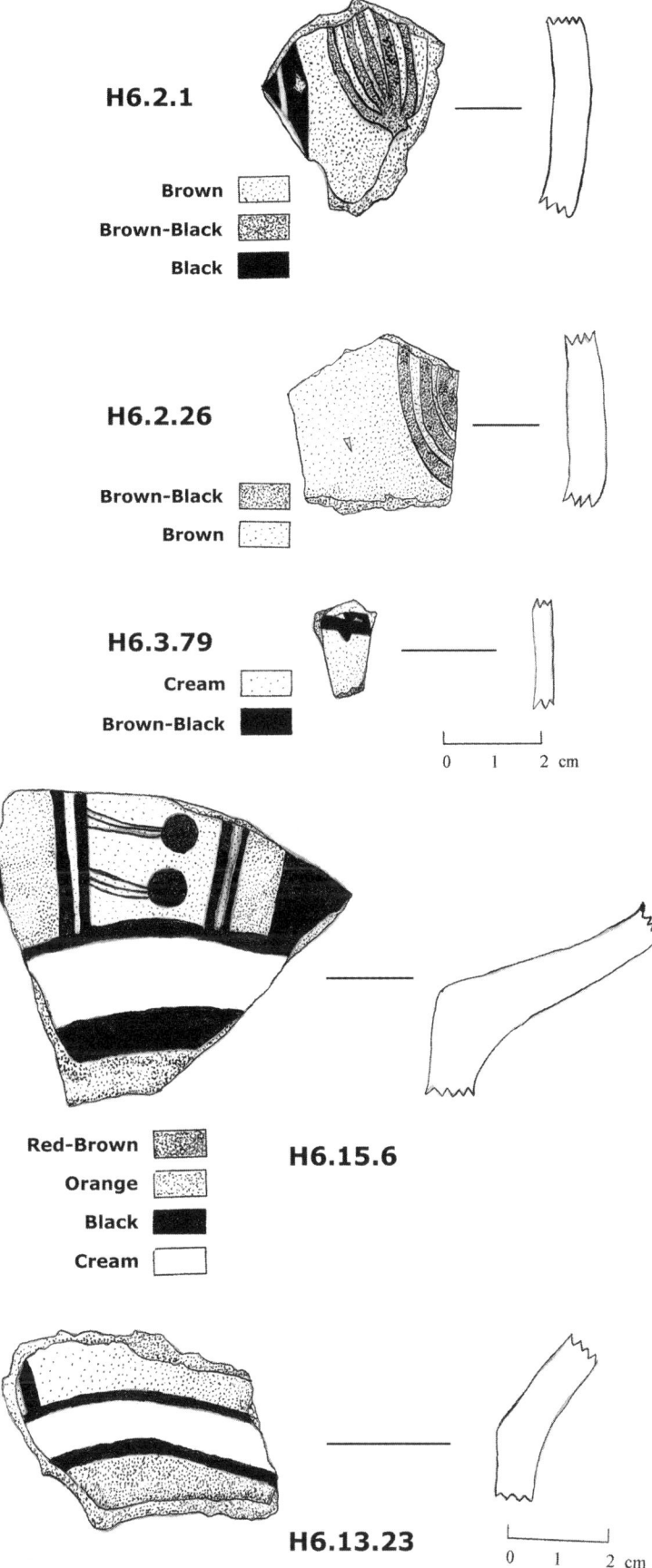

Figure 4.11.
Inca and Sillustani-Inca ceramics.

throughout the Titicaca Basin of power being gained through competition, warfare, and the taking of trophy heads, power and order was *sustained* through the incorporation of communities into the religious sphere. By giving feasts in which exotic goods and intoxicating substances were given to the commoner population, elites kept their followers content through the perceived benefits of their affiliation. Long-distance exchange arose as a necessary means for leaders to provide incentives to their followers so that they would continue to support the elites and provide them with surplus goods.

The data revealed here shed new light on the cultural sequence for the Andean highlands and the Lake Titicaca Basin. Several archaeologists currently working in the area are slowly beginning to assemble the various pieces of the prehistory of the Lake Titicaca Basin. Although this paper only outlines the site of Paucarcolla-Santa Barbara, each new project provides one piece of the larger puzzle. Hopefully, the research and results presented here will be useful in cross-cultural comparisons and will contribute to a better understanding of the role that ancient politics, economics, and ideology played in the ancient communities of the Titicaca Basin.

## References Cited

Arkush, E., and Charles Stanish
2005 Interpreting conflict in the ancient Andes: Implications for the archaeology of warfare. *Current Anthropology* 46(1):3–28.

Betanzos, Juan de
1996 *Narrative of the Incas*, translated and edited by R. Hamilton and D. Buchanan from the Palma de Mallorca manuscript. University of Texas Press, Austin.

Carlevato, D.
1988 Late ceramics from Pucara, Peru. *Expedition* 30(3):39–45.

Chávez, S. J., and K. L. Mohr Chávez
1975 A carved stela from Taraco, Puno, Peru and the definition of an early style of stone sculpture from the altiplano of Peru and Bolivia. *Ñawpa Pacha* 13:45–83.

Cieza de León, P. de
1959 *The Incas of Pedro de Cieza de León*, translated by Harriet du Onis. University of Oklahoma Press, Norman.

Cook, D. N.
1975 *Tasa de la visita general de Francisco de Toledo*. Universidad Nacional Mayor de San Marcos, Lima, Peru.

Erickson, C.
1987 Dating of raised-field agriculture in the Lake Titicaca Basin, Peru. In *Pre-Hispanic Agricultural Fields in the Andean Region*, edited by W. Denevan, K. Mathewson, and G. Knapp, pp. 373–84. British Archaeological Reports, International Series, Oxford, U.K.

Franquemont, Edward M.
1986 The ancient pottery from Pucara, Peru. *Ñawpa Pacha* 24:1–30.

Goldstein, Paul
1993 Tiwanaku temples and state expansion: A Tiwanaku sunken-court temple in Moquegua, Peru. *Latin American Antiquity* 4(1):22–47.
2000 Exotic goods and everyday chiefs: Long-distance exchange and indigenous sociopolitical development in the south central Andes. *Latin American Antiquity* 11(4):335–62.

Graffam, Gray Clayton
1992 Beyond state collapse: Rural history, raised fields, and pastoralism in the south Andes. *American Anthropologist* 94(4):882–904.

Janusek, John W.
1999 Craft and local power: Embedded specialization in Tiwanaku cities. *Latin American Antiquity* 10(2):107–31.

Julien, Catherine
1983 *Hatunqolla: A View of Inca Provincial Rule from the Lake Titicaca Region*. University of California Publications in Anthropology, vol. 15. University of California Press, Berkeley.

Kolata, Alan
1991 The technology and organization of agricultural production in the Tiwanaku state. *Latin American Antiquity* 2(2):99–125.
1993 *The Tiwanaku: Portrait of an Andean Civilization*. Blackwell Publishers, Massachusetts.

Plourde, A.
2006 Prestige Goods and Their Role in the Evolution of Social Ranking: A Costly Signaling Model with Data from the Late Formative Period of the Northern Lake Titicaca Basin, Peru. PhD dissertation, Department of Anthropology, University of California, Los Angeles.

Schultze, C.
2008 The Role of Silver Ore Reduction in Tiwanaku State Expansion into Puno Bay, Peru. PhD dissertation, Department of Anthropology, University of California, Los Angeles.

Stanish, C.
2003 *Ancient Titicaca: The Evolution of Complex Society in Southern Peru and Northern Bolivia*. University of California Press, Berkeley and Los Angeles.

Steadman, L.
1995 Excavations at Camata: An Early Ceramic Chronology for the Western Titicaca Basin, Peru. PhD dissertation, Department of Anthropology, University of California, Berkeley.

Tschopik, M. H.
1946 *Some Notes on the Archaeology of the Department of Puno, Peru*. Papers of the Peabody Museum of American Archaeology and Ethnology, Harvard University, vol. 27, no. 3. Cambridge, Massachusetts.

# Chapter 5

## Variation in Corporate Architecture during the Early Middle Formative Period

### New Data from Cachichupa, Northeastern Lake Titicaca Basin

*Aimée M. Plourde*

The construction of corporate, monumental architecture in prehistory is generally understood to represent—along with other factors, including the appearance of hierarchy in settlement patterning, differences in household and burial size and contents, and the appearance of prestige goods—the development of sociocultural practices and institutions integrating collective action above the level of the household that often involve increasingly hierarchical and formalized social relationships and leadership roles (e.g., Moseley 2001:114). The beginning of such processes marks the boundary for some scholars between the Early and Middle Formative periods (Fig. 5.2) in a developmental framework of the evolution of prehistoric society in the Lake Titicaca Basin, shown in Figure 5.1 (Klarich 2005:41–45; Stanish 2003:85–89). Data from the increasing volume of archaeological research taking place in the basin over the course of the last decade have begun to fill out the broad outline provided by this framework, providing a richer and more complex picture of prehistoric social dynamics, including an increased understanding of differences in intra-regional social trajectories within the basin. This chapter presents data on the discovery, at the site of Cachichupa, of a type of corporate architecture dating to the beginning of the Middle Formative period, formerly unknown from this date in the Titicaca Basin. This architecture takes the form of a series of massive terraces, much larger than needed for residence or agriculture, resembling somewhat the monumental terraces at the site of Pucara. Evidence regarding the construction and use of these terraces is presented, and possible ramifications for current understanding of sociopolitical process in the northern basin during the Middle Formative period are discussed.

### The Appearance and Development of Corporate Architecture in the Lake Titicaca Basin

The most common form of civic architecture to appear in the Titicaca Basin is a rectangular or trapezoidal enclosed space, demarcated either with walls or by being semi-subterranean, or a combination of the two. These enclosures, also termed plazas or temples, may further be placed on platforms or artificial terraces. As mentioned above, such architecture most commonly appears in the basin in the Middle Formative period, but is predated by a similar style of specialized architecture at the site of Asana, located in the upper reaches of the Moquegua Valley, just outside the Titicaca Basin to the west. Toward the end of its occupational sequence, from 4800 to 4400 BP (roughly 2800–2400 BC), a series of platform structures larger than the average house size were built, which Mark Aldenderfer (1998:228) interprets as areas for ceremonial activity.

The first evidence of such corporate or ritual architecture in the basin itself is indirect; Stanish (2003:104–5) suggests that the first evidence of sunken court architecture may come from the site of San Bartolomé-Wiskachani. He notes the presence of

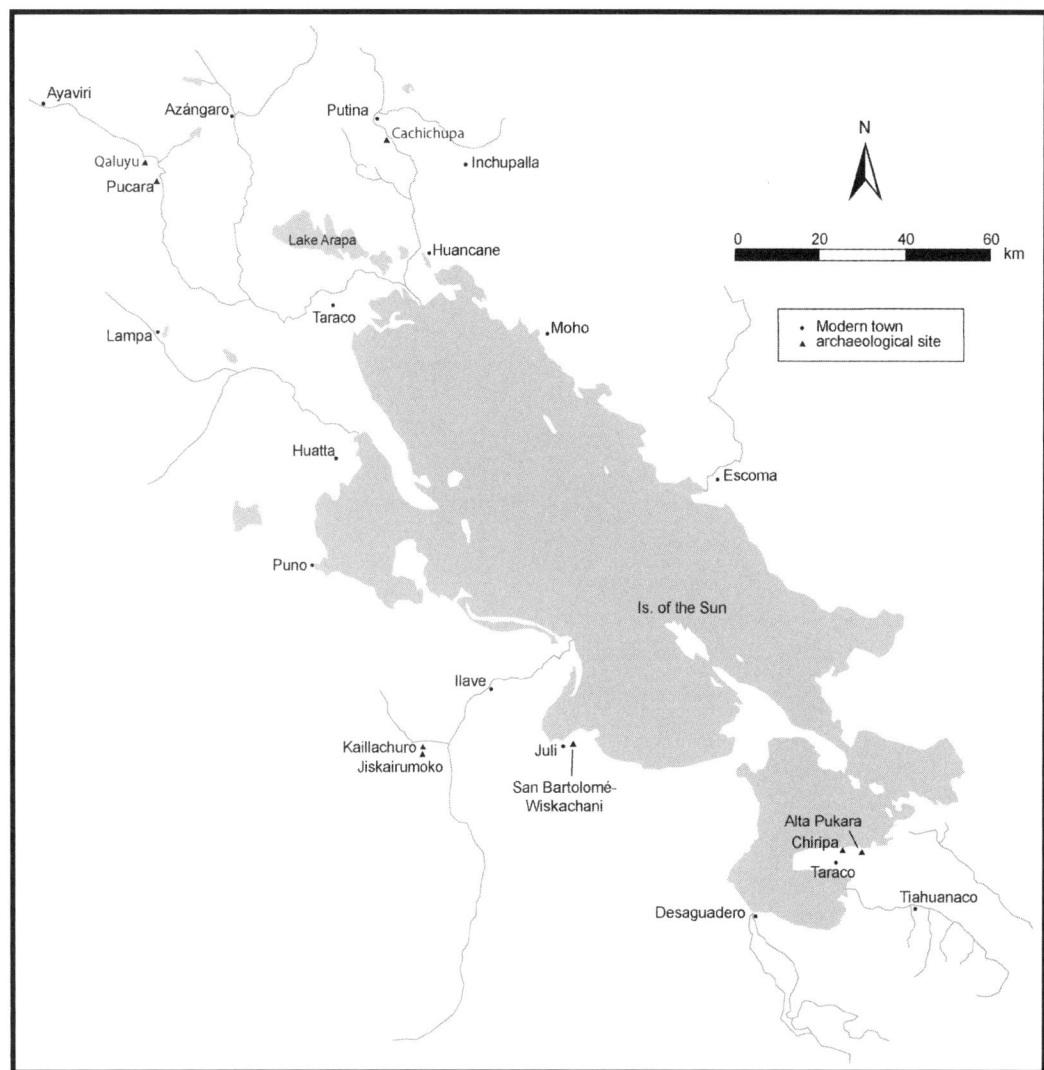

Figure 5.1. The Lake Titicaca Basin, showing selected locations and archaeological sites.

a petroglyph on the site whose figures could be interpreted as representing a ritual pathway going from a sunken court structure up the hill on top of which the site is located. Also located on the site are two carved stone protuberances that align visually with the highest peak in the eastern cordillera on the other side of the lake. He hypothesizes that this might constitute evidence for early mountain worship, a religious tradition commonly seen in historical and contemporary Andean society (Stanish 2003:105). Herhahn's (2004:19–20) excavations at the site discovered a substantial investment of tomb architecture as well, which reinforces the idea that the site had spiritual or religious associations.

To date, however, the earliest known sunken court in the Titicaca Basin is the Choquehuanca structure at Chiripa, in the southern basin, which was dated to approximately 1000 BC (Hastorf 2003), in the Middle Formative period as defined here. However, Hastorf, Emily Dean and others (Dean and Kojan 1999:40; Hastorf 2003:315) suggest that an area immediately adjacent to this structure—called the Santiago area, dating slightly earlier (1374–1131 cal BC)—may also have had some special-purpose function as well as a domestic one based on the presence of numerous burials and of decorated pottery. From these modest forms, corporate architecture on the Taraco Peninsula increased in elaboration and effort over the course of the Middle Formative period. Beck (2004a:327) has identified three major types of public architecture at Chiripa dating to the Middle Formative period: sunken enclosures (courts), located both on and off platforms; the Lower House structures located on a platform; and the more monumental version of this same combination, known as the Upper House complex, combining a sunken enclosure with the platform-chamber complex. Briefly, corporate architecture and ceremonial activity on the peninsula appear to have shifted from sunken enclosures to a more elaborate

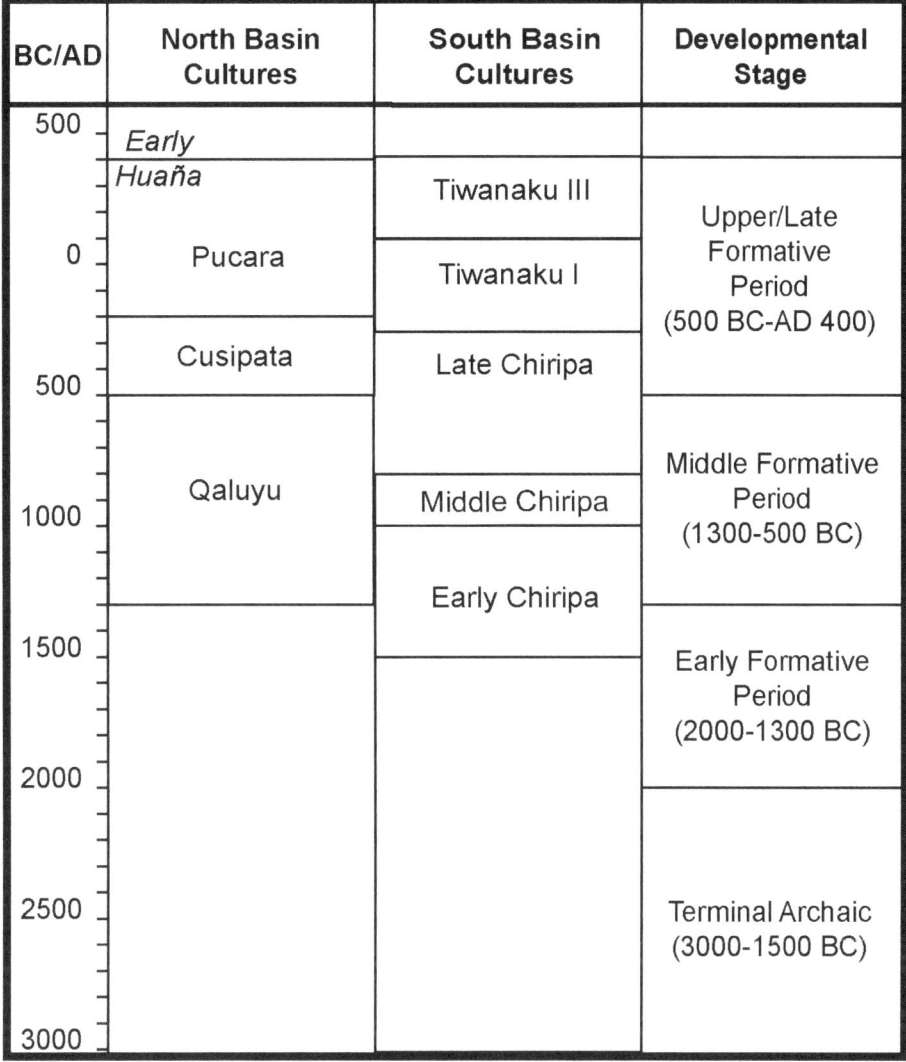

Figure 5.2. Titicaca Basin chronology.

complex, in which a plaza or enclosure was placed on an elevated mound and surrounded by special-purpose structures. Beck suggests that the shift to construction of much more labor-intensive platforms may have grown out of an Early and Middle Formative practice of terracing hillsides for residence and agriculture, and that platforms may have been viewed by Middle Formative peoples here as a special kind of terracing created for the dead (Beck 2004b:76, 109). Beck's characterization of possible Middle Formative perceptions of platform architecture is intriguing but currently difficult to assess.

Current understanding of Middle Formative social dynamics in the northern basin is not as detailed as that of the south basin. Work at the Upper Formative center at Pucara provided a glimpse into earlier corporate constructions at the site: excavations conducted by archaeologists working with the UNESCO project (Wheeler and Mujica 1981) discovered that Middle Formative occupations were located under the main temples at the site, leading them to suggest that the temple visible on the surface dating to the Upper Formative was built over an earlier one. Thomas Lynch (1981) reported that this earlier occupation dated to 800–200 BC, placing it at the transition between the Middle and Upper Formative periods and approximately contemporaneous with the construction of the Lower House platform complex at Chiripa (Plourde and Stanish 2006:248).

Nearby, Stanish and members of Programa Collasuyo conducted a brief inspection of the site of Qaluyu in 1998 (Plourde and Stanish 2006). Qaluyu is located in the river plain to the west of the Pucara River. The site's mounded area appears to have been built almost entirely of fill but it probably also made use of a natural rise in the river plain. While terracing on the northern and southern sides of the mounded area were likely to have been residential areas, the topography on top of the mound suggests that at minimum five sunken courts were present (Plourde and Stanish 2006:248), although Beck's excavations on top of the mound at Alto Pukara proved that the presence of a depression on the ground surface does not always correspond to a sunken court. Nevertheless, large, shaped stone blocks also present on the top of the mound are typical of the kind used to construct sunken courts in other sites in the Titicaca Basin. The layout of these courts does not suggest that they were constructed under any kind of architectural plan linking them; rather, it is more likely that courts were added to the mound over time. Notwithstanding the particular form as plaza or sunken enclosure, the presence of several ritual structures all located on top of the mound presents a range of possibilities. The considerable time span for the site from radiocarbon dates (1400–600 BC) suggests a long occupation at the site; it may be that, like at Chiripa, ritual structures were built and used at different times during the course of the Middle Formative. Alternatively, lineage/corporate groups at Qaluyu may have each simultaneously maintained their own ritual complex, instead of a structure within a single complex as hypothesized for Chiripa's House structures. These alternative scenarios have definite ramifications for our understanding of the nature and timing of social dynamics during this time and, in particular, the amounts of labor that civic/kin groups or elites were able to muster for politico-religious activity.

In summary, the sequence of the appearance and development of corporate architecture from the Taraco Peninsula in the southern basin suggests that the scale of politico-religious activity remained modest here until the end of the Middle Formative period (Bandy 2006; Hastorf 2003). In the northern basin the picture is much fuzzier. The monumental terracing and elaborate court structures at Pucara provide an excellent picture of the scale of later political activity, but data on earlier periods are still sparse. More data are needed on the first appearance and subsequent development of corporate architecture in the northern basin in order to understand political development here and the eventual rise of Pukara as a regional polity.

## Early Monumental Terracing at Cachichupa

Recent archaeological research at the site of Cachichupa, located in the Huancané-Putina River valley, provides new data on the development of corporate architecture in the northern Titicaca Basin during the Formative period. The Huancané-Putina River valley is located in the basin's northeastern corner, and contributes to one of the five major drainage systems feeding into Lake Titicaca (Fig. 5.1). Work here aimed to expand current knowledge of pre-Columbian settlement in the north basin in general and specifically to investigate the development of interregional trade between the basin and the lower slopes of the eastern cordillera descending into the tropical Amazonian lowlands (Plourde 2006; Stanish 1999). The valley runs northward from the lake edge some 34 km into the sierras, linking at the confluence of the Putina River with the Lloquecolla and the Pongongoni Rivers to a higher valley leading in turn to passes over the eastern cordillera, thus functioning as a corridor to the tropical lowlands beyond (Fig. 5.3). Today, the three major modern roads leading from the northern basin to the eastern slopes run through the Huancané-Putina Valley, intersecting in the city of Putina. The valley also is one of the last areas where agriculture and grazing are possible before crossing through the cordillera, as would be needed to support llama caravans for trading expeditions. In light of these facts, the valley is one of the most likely locations for a pre-Columbian exchange route from the northern basin to the eastern lowlands.

### Cachichupa

Cachichupa (site HU-14) was discovered during an initial reconnaissance of the valley in 1998 (Stanish 1999), which was performed in preparation for a later full-coverage survey of the valley. The site is located approximately three-quarters of the way up the valley in a strategic position where the sides of the valley narrow to an opening less than a kilometer in width, through which the river and the modern road pass (Fig. 5.4).

Cachichupa is situated on the southern slopes of a hill projecting out from the western side of the valley and at the hill base. The site measures minimally 5 ha in size and has two major components: a series of large, well-constructed terraces, and a series of compounds outlined on the surface by their stone foundations, located to the south and east of the terraces on a small plain or pampa formed by the last natural river terrace that abuts the river bed itself (Fig. 5.5). Systematic surface collections revealed that Formative pottery covers almost the entire site but is most dense on the larger terraces and in the area of stone foundations in the pampa. Excavations were conducted in both areas, revealing differences in both the nature and the dates of the occupations; while the lower area of foundations revealed relatively shallow deposits dating to the Upper Formative period, at least some of the terraces were constructed at the very beginning of the Middle Formative period.

### The Terraces at Cachichupa

Cachichupa's terraces extend from the base of the hill up between two large rock outcroppings of a reddish sandstone type material (Fig. 5.6). There are 35 terraces in total, designated with letters "A" through "Z" (some terraces were given a sub-designation using a number when distinctions in elevation or construction were apparent). The terraces vary considerably in size and form. Terraces A–D, located at the top of the hill, are relatively small, rectangular, and rather steeply inclined, and contained few cultural materials on their surfaces. Terraces E–H are somewhat larger, and possessed a low density of pottery on their surfaces but none dating to the Formative period. In contrast, the terraces from this point to the base of the hill are much larger and much deeper relative to their length. The retaining walls of the lower terraces are constructed of large, shaped stone blocks.

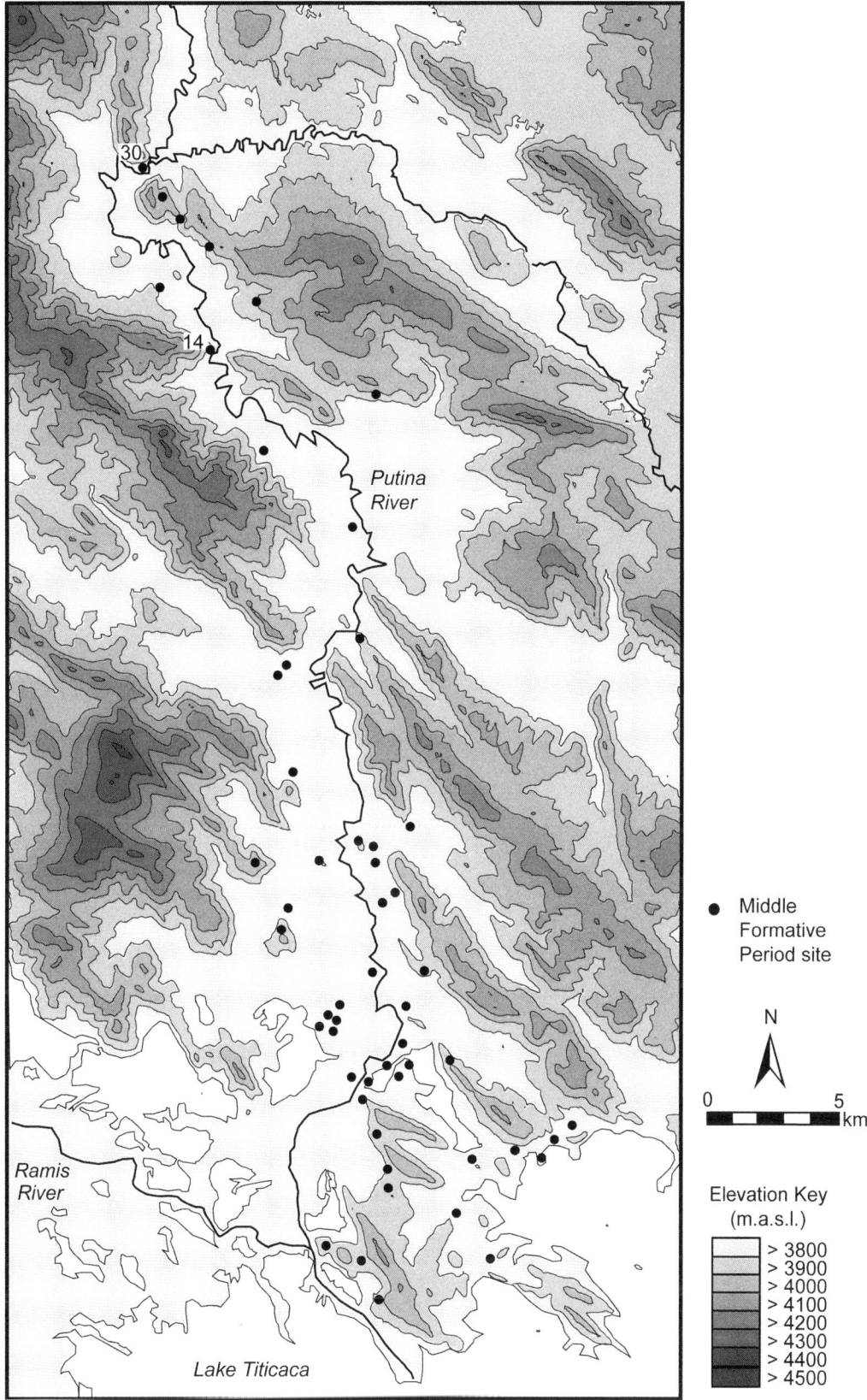

Figure 5.3. The Huancané-Putina River valley, showing sites dating to the Middle Formative period (approximated by C. Chávez' Formative I phasing; see Stanish et al., in press, for further detail).

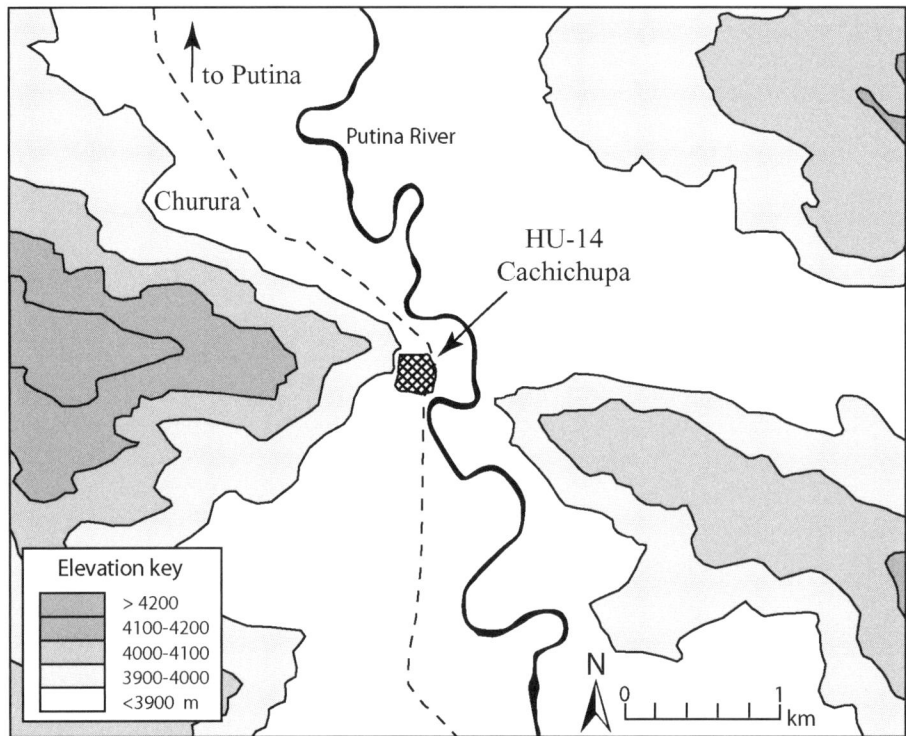

Figure 5.4. Location of Cachichupa in the upper Huancané-Putina Valley.

Most of these walls are still standing but many have been damaged by erosion and in a few isolated sections have fallen away completely. The density of pottery in general is much higher on the lower terraces, and of Formative period pottery in particular, although the difference in artifact concentration may be due in part to the use of the lower terraces for agriculture, leading to a higher turnover of artifacts to the surface. The highest concentrations of pottery diagnostic to the Formative period were found on Terrace K, Terrace U and Terrace W.

Of these, Terrace K was of particular interest for investigation, for several reasons. In addition to being one of the largest terraces, it is also the tallest; its support wall is approximately 6 m in height and was most likely taller at the time of construction given its current state of disrepair (Fig. 5.7). In profile (created where portions of it have fallen or been pulled down by local residents for easier access) it is possible to see that this support wall measures over a meter in thickness on average, and was constructed with large, finely shaped stones. Rectangular in shape, Terrace K is subdivided into two adjacent platforms, designated K-1 and K-2, which are separated by a low stone wall on the surface. Each of these is roughly square in shape, measuring an average of 30 m on a side. The combination of its form and height makes the surface of Terrace K an impressive expanse and gives it an imposing view of the rest of the site and of the valley to the south (Terrace K is clearly distinguishable in Fig. 5.6, midway up the slope of the hill).

To investigate how and when the terrace was constructed and to investigate its function, a 2 × 2 meter excavation unit was placed in the center of Terrace K-2. The stratigraphic sequence of Terrace K-2 consisted almost entirely of layers of fill, all of which contained cultural material until sterile soil was reached at almost 4.5 m from the surface (Fig. 5.8). The one possible exception is distinguished as Stratum III in the profile. The soil of this layer consists of a vibrantly-yellow sandy clay, contrasting sharply with the surrounding layers, containing small pieces of bone and charcoal and a low density of other cultural materials. The layer was compact like an occupational surface but its thickness and uneven surface call this interpretation into question. Instead, it may have been a special-purpose fill.

The rest of the strata represent layers of fill, containing a moderate amount of utilitarian pottery, stone tools, faunal remains and charcoal. In several instances the layers appear to interdigitate with one another, suggesting simultaneous deposition. This interpretation is strengthened by the nine radiocarbon dates obtained from throughout the stratigraphic sequence, given in Table 5.1. All the dates fall between 1040 and 1500 cal

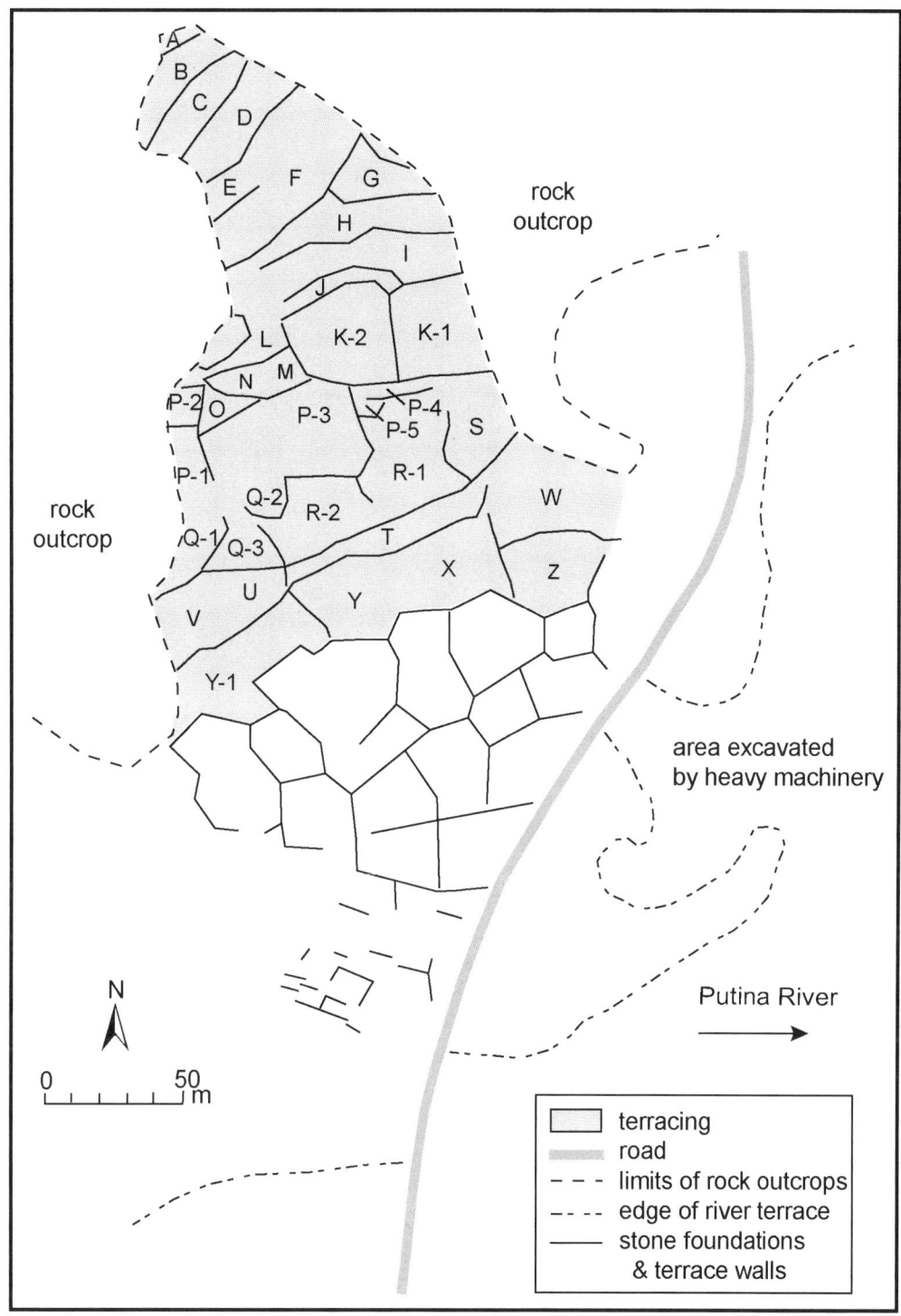

Figure 5.5. Schematic site map of Cachichupa.

Figure 5.6. Photo of Cachichupa, taken from the eastern side of the Putina River. Note that terraces K, I, and J are clearly visible midway up the slope of the hill.

Figure 5.7. A close-up photo of a section of Terrace K's support wall, illustrating its level of preservation. Note the person at the left-hand side of the photo for scale.

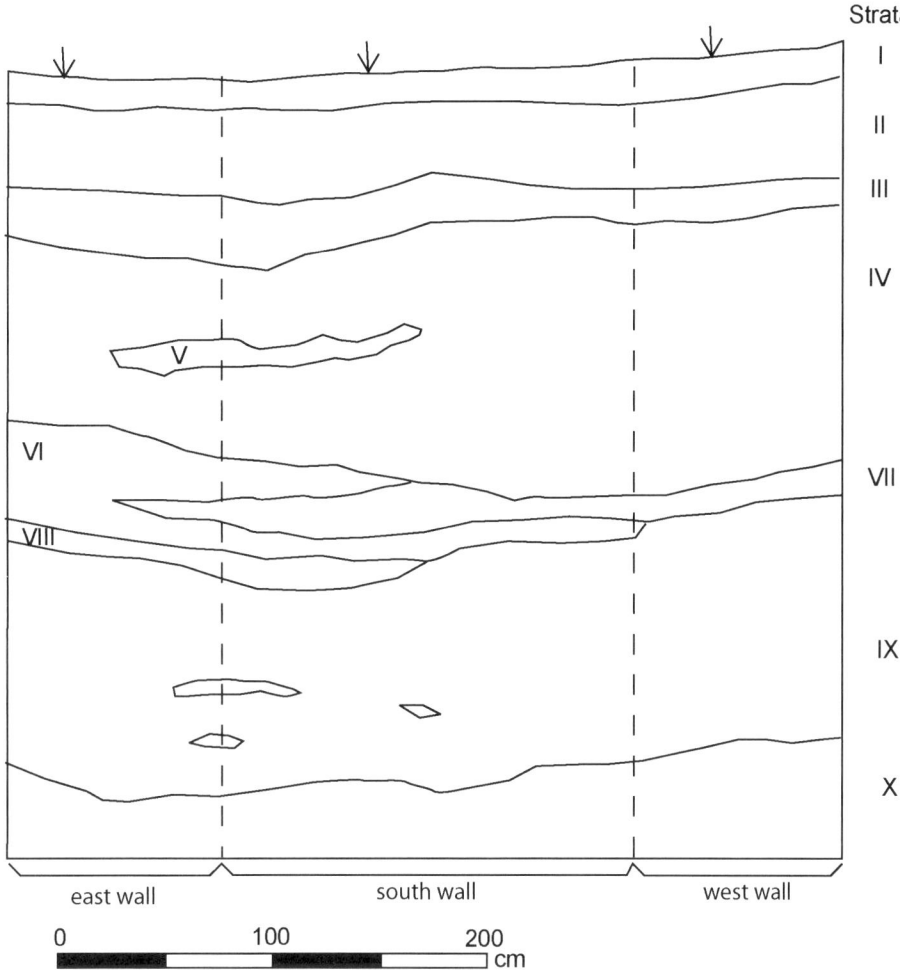

Figure 5.8. Profile of strata in Terrace K-2.

| Table 5.1. Summary of radiocarbon dates from Terrace K. | | | |
|---|---|---|---|
| **HU-14 Catalog Number** | **Excavation Provenience** | **Profile Affiliation** | **Calibrated Date** $(2\sigma)$ |
| 130 | Area A, Unit 1, Level 8 | Stratum III | 1500 BC–1260 BC |
| 161 | Area A, Unit 4, Level 10 | Stratum IV | 1420 BC–1050 BC |
| 224 | Area A, Unit 1, Level 13 | Stratum IV | 1380 BC–1040 BC |
| 320 | Area A, Unit 4, Level 16 | Stratum IV | 1380 BC–1040 BC |
| 389 | Area A, Unit 4, Level 18 | Stratum VII | 1430 BC–1130 BC |
| 446 | Area A, Unit 4, Level 20 | Stratum VIII | 1410 BC–1110 BC |
| 471 | Area A, Unit 4, Level 22 | Stratum IX | 1410 BC–1120 BC |
| 548 | Area A, Unit 1, Level 27 | Stratum IX | 1420 BC–1120 BC |
| 555 | Area A, Unit 1, Level 28 | Stratum IX | 1430 BC–1130 BC |
| 729 | Terrace K-1, Profile 6 | base of pit | 1130 BC–830 BC |
| 730 | Terrace K-1, Profile 6 | base of pit | 360 BC–50 BC |
| 731 | Terrace K-1, Profile 6 | base of pit | 1050 BC–820 BC |

BC, placing the entire construction around the beginning of the Middle Formative period. Further, all the dates almost completely overlap, suggesting that the entire terrace was constructed very rapidly, perhaps as a single episode. The small reversals between the dates from different strata—for instance, Stratum III near the top of the sequence produced the oldest date—reinforce this idea.

Valuable data on the possible functions of the terrace were also derived from the adjacent terrace, K-1. A community member initially pointed out a pit in this terrace that had been excavated by local residents some years previously. They had noticed a depression in the ground in the center of this terrace toward its western side, with several large, shaped stones appearing on the surface. According to our informant, similar indications in other areas of the site had, upon investigation, been found to indicate the presence of stone-lined canals, draining from the terraces to the base of the hill. Suspecting the presence of such a stone-lined canal here, the residents had dug, but the results were inconclusive. At the time of our project, the residents' abandoned pit measured over a meter in diameter, and was partially refilled with loose soil and plants. Several large, well-shaped stone blocks and a small pile of backdirt from their excavation lay at the pit's edge. While lack of time and resources prevented a full investigation of the feature, cleaning the pit's walls to create a profile (Profile 6) revealed the outline of a pit feature, filled with ash, concentrations of animal bone and charcoal, stone tools, and both utilitarian and decorated pottery. The latter included several serving vessels, tazones, decorated in both painted and incised Qaluyu styles (Rowe 1956:144), as well as a piece of pottery with the torso of a female figure molded in low relief on the exterior, strongly reminiscent of the Yaya-Mama style in the positioning of the arms (Fig. 5.9). Radiocarbon dates obtained from charcoal samples taken from the feature after cleaning, provided in Table 5.1, confirm the Middle Formative period date of the feature. Although one of the three dates is aberrant and may represent some contamination of the sample, the other two dates are chronologically close to one another at approximately 1000 BC. Given the pit's proximity to the modern surface of the terrace, these dates likely serve as a cap on the construction dates for the terrace.

Just beside and below the pit feature was a concentration of large, shaped rectangular stones, behind which an open space of some kind appeared to be located. The stones (which appeared similar to those currently lying on the surface that had evidently been removed by the community residents during their original excavation) were too large to move easily, and limited time prevented further investigation of the possibility that a collapsed canal was located here.

## Discussion

The data discussed above suggest several things about the construction and function of the terraces at Cachichupa, in turn casting light on the activities occurring at the site and more generally on social dynamics underway during the Formative period in the northern Titicaca Basin. Terrace K's size alone would suggest that its construction involved a considerable amount of effort, both in terms of transporting sufficient fill as well as the creation of its retaining wall from large, shaped stones. In addition to the terrace's size, the rapidity of construction strengthens the idea that a large amount of labor was required. While the preliminary nature of the investigations at Cachichupa limited the amount of excavation in other terraces, thus restricting our ability to speak to their construction and functions, a number of points nonetheless merit discussion. A profile of the stratigraphy of Terrace R was created where the supporting wall had fallen down. This profile revealed the presence of only a single stratum of fill. While Terrace R's height is only approximately 2 m, in overall surface area it is similar to Terrace K. Therefore, if it was constructed in a single episode, as implied by the single stratum in its profile, then it also would represent a substantial investment of labor. Many of the lower terraces are of a similar size and some considerable height as well, in total constituting evidence of substantial labor investment.

In terms of function, the sizes of the terraces are much larger than normally constructed for agriculture or residence, although it is worth noting that the majority of the terraces at the site—including Terrace K—are used for cultivation today, indicating the feasibility of such activity. The massive size of Terrace K instead suggests that it was built to serve a public function of some sort, as a public space where religious and political activities took place, and/or possibly with defensive capability in mind.

*Terrace Function*

### Ceremonialism

In addition to its generous size, several other pieces of evidence support the theory that Terrace K served some public, politico-ceremonial function. First, the contents of the large pit in Terrace K-1 strongly reinforce this idea. The pit contained what appear to be the remains of cooking and feasting, and possibly dedicatory offerings; loose ash, utilitarian and decorated pottery and lithic artifacts are likely the remains of the cooking process, and the lining of faunal remains and charcoal the remains of food or offerings. The presence of several finely made and decorated serving vessels supports the idea that the context for this activity was some sort of public, ceremonial function. At present it is not possible to say with certainty that the large rectangular stones lying partially under and alongside this pit constituted a tunnel or drain, or even more generally that whatever feature they do represent was associated with the excavation and filling of the pit, but nonetheless it seems likely that this is the case.

Excavations in Terrace K-2 also provide some evidence for nonresidential activity on the terrace, in the form of the possible occupation surface or fill layer, Stratum III. The layer's thickness and unevenness argue against its having been lain down as a floor surface but the presence of cultural materials within it

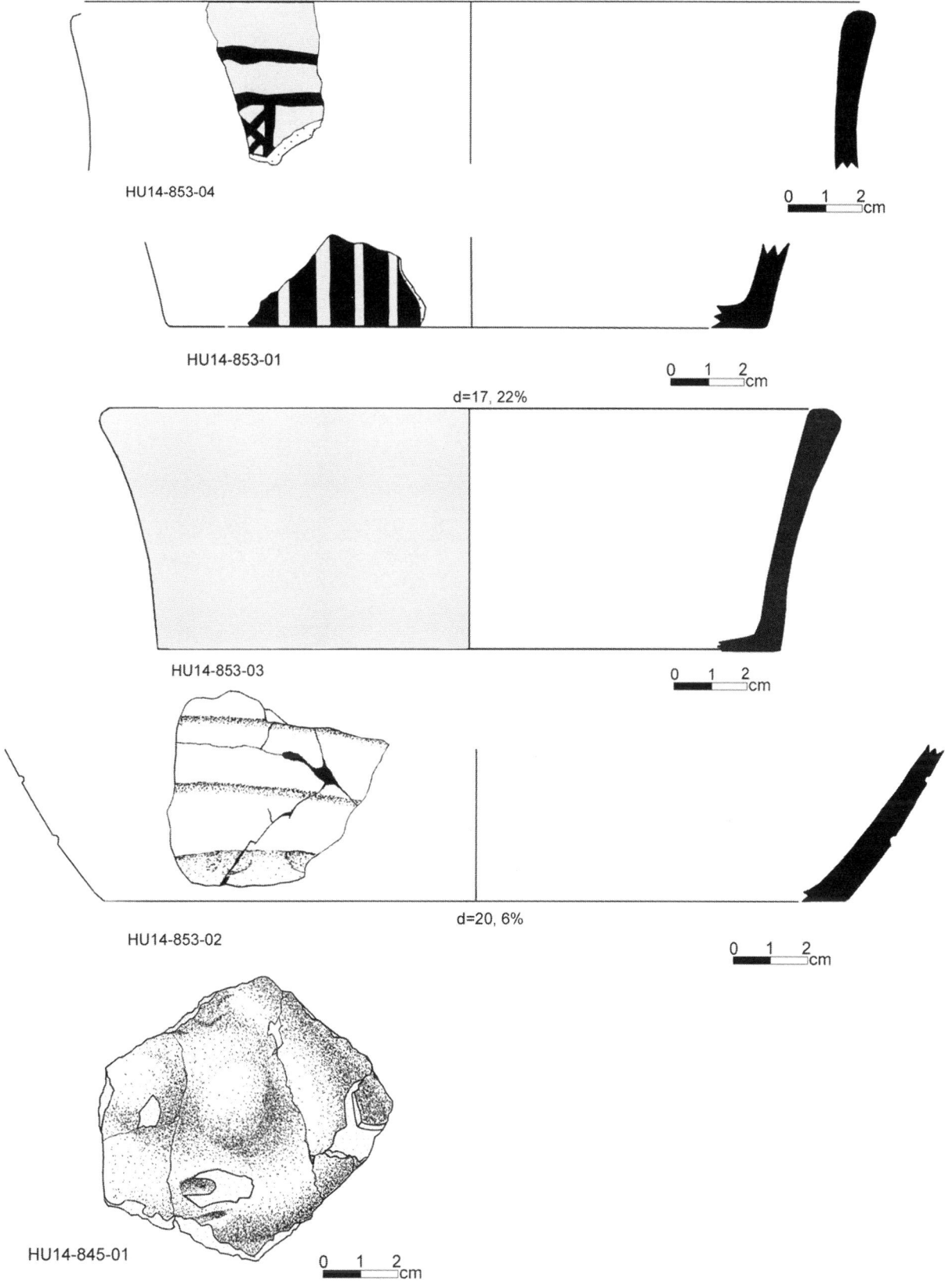

Figure 5.9. Examples of pottery recovered from K-1.

and its compactness leave no doubt that it is of cultural origin. Further, its distinctive yellow color implies that the soil was brought up to the terrace surface from some distance away. It seems possible, therefore, that this stratum represents some sort of special-purpose fill or cap, placed on top of the terrace by Middle Formative residents.

Finally, while conjectural, it must be noted that the placement of Cachichupa and of the terraces there bears some resemblance to the site of Pucara. Both sites are set on the western side of a valley, overlooking the river, and consist of a set of monumental terraces with residential and ceremonial compounds at their base; both sets of terraces are located between large rock outcroppings, a much larger outcropping on the left side. This passing resemblance with the Upper Formative regional center of Pucara may be no more than coincidence, but given the evidently very purposeful construction of the terraces at Cachichupa, and the later links to Pucara held by site residents (Plourde 2006), I do not think it can be discounted out of hand.

*Defense*

Defensive capability is another potential aspect of the terrace construction at Cachichupa. While not fortified with parapets or other defensive works, Terrace K could be considered defensible in that, at the very least, it would be difficult to ascend the terrace without the knowledge and consent of those residing above, and it certainly could have provided a refuge to site residents in case of attack. The site's placement on the hillside projecting out into the valley provides a good view both up and down the valley corridor, allowing for easy monitoring of approach to the site. The notion that defence may have been a factor in the use of the terraces is further strengthened by the settlement pattern in the upper valley (see Fig. 5.3). The majority of Middle Formative Period sites are located in defendable locations, and several have evidence of fortifications on the surface (Stanish et al., in press).

*Site Function*

The possible functions proposed above for Terrace K at Cachichupa, and potentially for others of the large terraces as well, provide a starting point from which to theorize about site function and about social developments in the region more generally. The considerable amount of labor required for the rapid construction of Terrace K suggests that Cachichupa may have been a local center of some kind during the Middle Formative period. In fact, the early date of such a large corporate construction is somewhat surprising; it represents substantially more labor investment than the construction of the Choquehuanca sunken court, for example, with which it is contemporaneous or may even slightly predate.

Why here, and why now? Again the settlement pattern in the Huancané-Putina Valley during the early part of the Formative period provides some insight. A complete and detailed analysis of settlement in the Huancané-Putina Valley is forthcoming (Stanish et al., in press) but an initial assessment suggests that settlement during this time was slightly concentrated in the lower portion of the valley and near the lake's edge, an unsurprising fact generally correlating with the overall distribution and richness of resources (Plourde 2006:451). However, as noted above, defence seems to have been of particular concern in site placement in the uppermost portion of the valley. At the same time, Cachichupa (HU-14) and HU-30, located under the modern town of Putina, are larger sites in locations that are defendable but also strategic for monitoring if not controlling traffic along the valley floor. These two sites also produced the most evidence of politico-ceremonial activity in terms of decorated Qaluyu pottery, stone sculpture and remains of civic architecture. HU-030 and Cachichupa are also within visible range of one another, further strengthening the idea that their positioning had defensive and/or controlling aspects. In this context, it is also interesting to note that no Formative occupations were located beyond this point in the adjoining valley, which links to passes through the eastern cordillera. Taken together, I suggest that the Middle Formative settlement at Cachichupa, and the construction of massive terraces there, was associated with the trafficking of goods from the eastern tropical lowlands into the northern basin through the Huancané-Putina Valley.

## Conclusions

The interpretation of developments in the northeastern lake basin given above remains to be tested more rigorously following the complete analysis of settlement data (Stanish et al., in press). It is nonetheless clear that the data from excavations at Cachichupa provide some novel insights on the timing and character of corporate architecture in the northern basin during the Formative period. First, the early date of Terrace K's construction in combination with the rapidity with which it was built suggest that greater variation in the timing of the appearance and development of corporate architecture and/or greater variability in its forms existed in the early Middle Formative than has been previously supposed. The terraces at Cachichupa may constitute the earliest monumental terracing presently known in the Titicaca Basin, presaging the platform-chamber complex on the Taraco Peninsula and the monumental terracing at the site of Pucara. In light of this, Beck's characterization of the development of corporate architecture during the Middle Formative period may need revision if applied to the basin as a whole.

The precocious appearance of corporate architecture in the Huancané-Putina Valley in turn can be interpreted as indication that processes increasing collective action and politico-religious activities also began earlier in the northern basin than previously thought. Hastorf (2005:65) observed that early centers in the Titicaca Basin are more often located on or near the lakeshore. The data from Cachichupa may stand as an exception to this rule, or may mark a divergence in development between the northern and southern regions of the basin; further research in other areas of the north (for example, Stanish and Levine 2010; Stanish and Umire 2002) will help to clarify this question.

## Acknowledgments

I gratefully acknowledge the support of the National Science Foundation, Wenner-Gren Foundation for Anthropological Research, Department of Anthropology at UCLA, Cotsen Institute of Archaeology at UCLA, Friends of Archaeology at UCLA, and Programa Collasuyu for different portions of this research. Thanks to Charles Stanish and Elizabeth Klarich for the invitation to contribute to this volume, and to them and my other colleagues in Andean archaeology for useful discussions on related issues.

## References Cited

Aldenderfer, M.
1998  *Montane Foragers: Asana and the South-Central Andean Archaic*. University of Iowa Press, Iowa City.

Bandy, M. S.
2006  Early village society in the Formative period in the southern Lake Titicaca Basin. In *Andean Archaeology III: North and South*, edited by W. H. Isbell and H. Silverman, pp. 210–36. Springer, New York.

Beck, R. A.
2004a  Architecture and polity in the Formative Lake Titicaca Basin, Bolivia. *Latin American Antiquity* 15(3):323–43.
2004b  Platforms of Power: House, Community, and Social Change in the Formative Lake Titicaca Basin. PhD dissertation, Department of Anthropology, Northwestern University, Evanston, IL.

Dean, E., and D. Kojan
1999  Santiago. In *Early Settlement at Chiripa, Bolivia*, edited by C. A. Hastorf, pp. 37–41. Contributions of the University of California Archaeological Research Facility, no. 57. Berkeley.

Hastorf, C. A.
2003  Community with the ancestors: Ceremonies and social memory in the Middle Formative at Chiripa, Bolivia [Review]. *Journal of Anthropological Archaeology* 22(4):305–32.
2005  The Upper (Middle and Late) Formative in the Titicaca region. In *Advances in Titicaca Basin Archaeology–1*, edited by C. Stanish, A. B. Cohen, and M. S. Aldenderfer, pp. 65–94. Cotsen Institute of Archaeology, University of California, Los Angeles.

Herhahn, C. L.
2004  Mixed Economy or Mosaic? Paper presented at the 69th Annual Meeting of the Society for American Archaeology, Montreal, Canada.

Klarich, E.
2005  From the Monumental to the Mundane: Defining Early Leadership Strategies at Late Formative Pukara, Peru. PhD dissertation, Department of Anthropology, University of California, Santa Barbara.

Lynch, T. F.
1981  Current research: Andean South America. *American Antiquity* 46(1):201–4.

Moseley, M. E.
2001  *The Incas and Their Ancestors: The Archaeology of Peru*, rev. ed. Thames and Hudson, New York.

Plourde, A. M.
2006  Prestige Goods and Their Role in the Evolution of Social Ranking: A Costly Signaling Model with Data from the Late Formative Period of the Northern Lake Titicaca Basin, Peru. PhD dissertation, Department of Anthropology, University of California, Los Angeles.

Plourde, A. M., and C. Stanish
2006  The emergence of complex society in the Titicaca Basin: The view from the north. In *Andean Archaeology III: North and South*, edited by W. H. Isbell and H. Silverman, pp. 237–57. Springer, New York.

Rowe, J. H.
1956  Archaeological explorations in southern Peru, 1954–55. *American Antiquity* 22(2):135–50.

Stanish, C.
1999  *Reconnaissance of the Lower Sectors of the Rámis and Putina River Valleys, Puno: Report on the 1998 Field Season Archaeological Investigations*. Submitted to the National Institute of Culture, Lima, Peru.
2003  *Ancient Titicaca. The Evolution of Complex Society in Southern Peru and Northern Bolivia*. University of California Press, Berkeley.

Stanish, C., and A. Levine
2011  War and early state formation in the northern Titicaca Basin, Peru. *Proceedings of the National Academy of Science* 108(34):13901–6.

Stanish, Charles, Cecilia Chávez J., Karl LaFavre, and Aimée Plourde
in press  *The Northern Titicaca Basin Archaeological Research Program–Volume I. The Huancané-Putina Survey*. Cotsen Institute of Archaeology, University of California, Los Angeles.

Stanish, C., and A. Umire
2002  *Prospección Arqueológica del Sector Bajo de la Cuenca del Rámis (Ríos Azángaro y Rámis), Puno*. Report submitted to the National Institute of Culture (INC).

Wheeler, J., and E. Mujica
1981  *Prehistoric Pastoralism in the Lake Titicaca Basin, Peru, 1979–1980 Field Season*. Report submitted to National Science Foundation, grant no. BNS 7015119.

Chapter 6

# Scale and Diversity at Late Formative Period Pukara

*Elizabeth A. Klarich and Nancy Román Bustinza*

**Introduction**

On May 9, 2011, the Pukara Archaeological Complex was declared cultural patrimony of the nation, as documented in the "Normas Legales" published in *El Peruano* (May 14, 2011:442445–46). Pukara was the first regional center in the northwestern Lake Titicaca Basin of Peru and its influence can be traced through much of the south-central Andes during the Late Formative period[1] (500 BC–AD 400[2]) (Fig. 6.1) (see Klarich 2005 for a summary). The Pukara[3] culture is characterized by its elaborately decorated polychrome pottery, intricately carved stone sculpture, and monumental architectural complexes (Chávez 1992; Franquemont 1986; Mohr Chávez 1988; Mujica 1978; Paredes 1985; Stanish 2003; Wheeler and Mujica 1981). The early growth of Pukara is contemporaneous with the initial occupations of Tiwanaku in the southeastern Lake Titicaca Basin (Stanish et al. 1997). However, unlike Tiwanaku, subsequent occupations did not obscure or heavily modify Late Formative Pukara, except in limited areas that were reoccupied by the Colla and Inca during the Altiplano period and Late Horizon, respectively (Abraham and Balasalle 2011; Hyslop 1990; Wheeler and Mujica 1981) (Fig. 6.2).

In 1939, Alfred Kidder II of the Peabody Museum at Harvard University conducted large-scale excavations and identified a variety of areas with Late Formative occupations within the site (Fig. 6.3): the central sunken court located on the Qalasaya architectural complex, a truncated step-pyramid with stone-faced terraces (Area VI); a probable residential area and production zone on the site periphery (Areas I, II and III); and fragments of buildings in the central district of unclear scale and function (Areas IV and V) (Chávez 1992; Inojosa 1940; Kidder 1942). In the 1970s, Plan Copesco (Comisión especial para coordinar y supervigilar el plan turístico y cultural Perú-Unesco) worked for over four years at Pukara (Paredes 1985; Wheeler and Mujica 1981). The project included extensive horizontal and vertical excavations of the central sunken court first excavated by Kidder and reconstruction of the stone-lined terraces and stairways of the Qalasaya.

Even with data accumulated through excavation and mapping projects in the architectural core and site periphery over the last century, archaeologists have not arrived at a consensus regarding the most basic characteristics of Pukara—the scale, site organization and diversity of areas within the site (Fig. 6.4) (see Klarich 2005 for summary). Site size estimates, for example, range from 1.5 km[2] (Chávez 1992; Cohen 2010:67) to 2 km[2] (Stanish 2003:142) to 4 km[2] (Erickson 1988:12; Tantaleán 2010:54, citing Mujica 1978:290) to up to 6 km[2] (Mujica 1991:276). The smaller size estimates include the central ceremonial district and

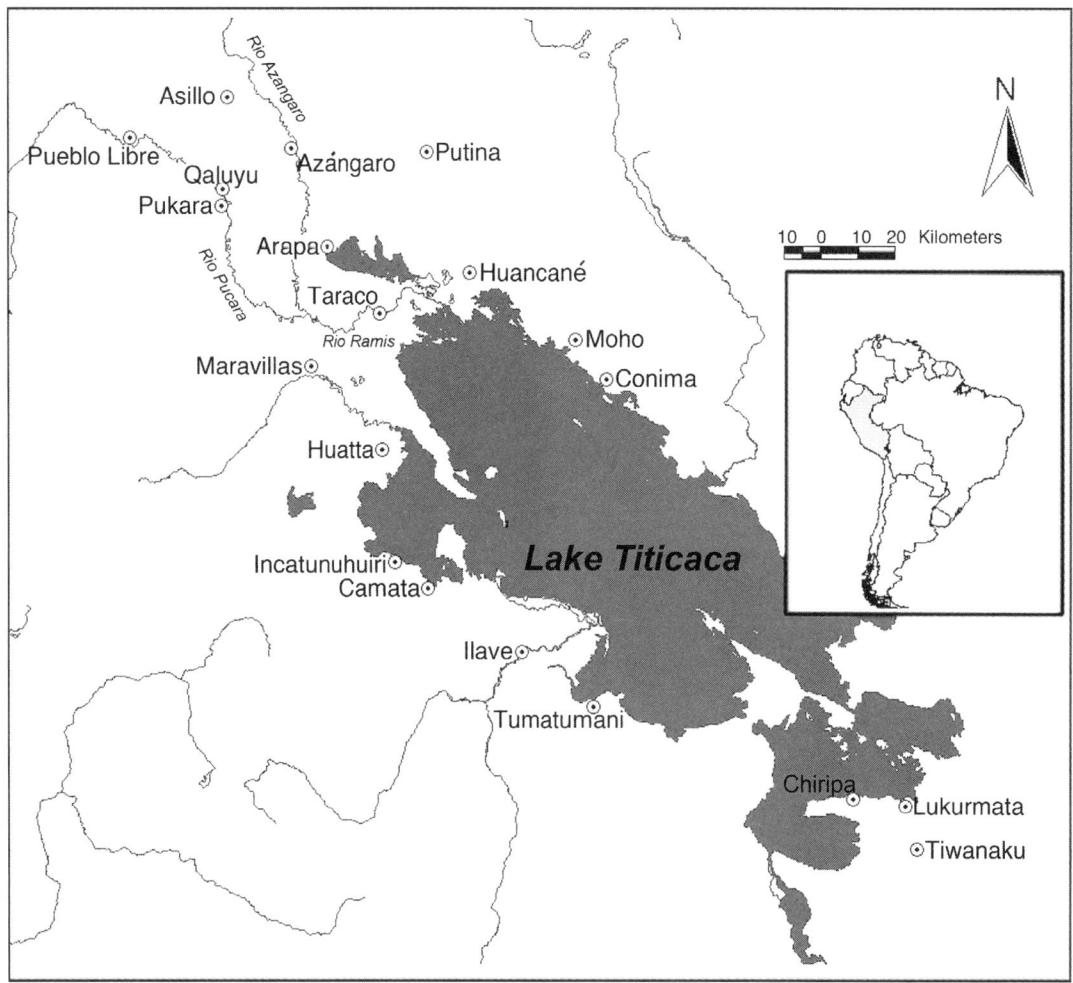

Figure 6.1. Map of the Lake Titicaca Basin with Formative period sites and modern towns.

some of the area under the modern town of Pucará, as outlined by Stanish (2003:142–43):

> This estimate includes the central architectural core and the surrounding area with surface materials. Consistent with the observations of Franco Inojosa (1940), several areas appear not to have Upper Formative occupations, which account for the lower estimate of habitation area size than given by other researchers. The upper limit of my estimate includes all areas with possible buried Upper Formative occupations. There are additional mounds and other refuse areas near the river, as mentioned by Kidder, but these were not counted in my total habitation area estimate given the existence of nonoccupied areas between these mounds and the central architectural core.

In contrast, the larger estimates include the architectural core and extend the boundaries to the riverbank to the east and to the Formative period site of Qaluyu to the north. It is unclear if these larger site size estimates were based on systematic survey of Pukara and its surrounding areas or gleaned from informal site visits and information regarding surface materials provided in excavation reports by Kidder, Plan Copesco, and others.

## Project Methods

In 2006, a survey was conducted with the goal of systematically defining the site boundaries while recording the distribution of surface architecture and artifacts from all occupations, including modern impact on the site. Pre-fieldwork project development entailed obtaining and integrating three types of complementary spatial data: historic air photos of Pukara and its surrounding areas from the national air photo service in Peru (SAN, Servicio Aerofotográfico Nacional); field notes and informal maps drawn by Alfred Kidder II during his 1939 excavation project (see Chávez 1992) and by the members of Plan Copesco from the 1970s (Wheeler and Mujica 1981); and base maps of the region downloaded and subsequently organized into a GIS database.

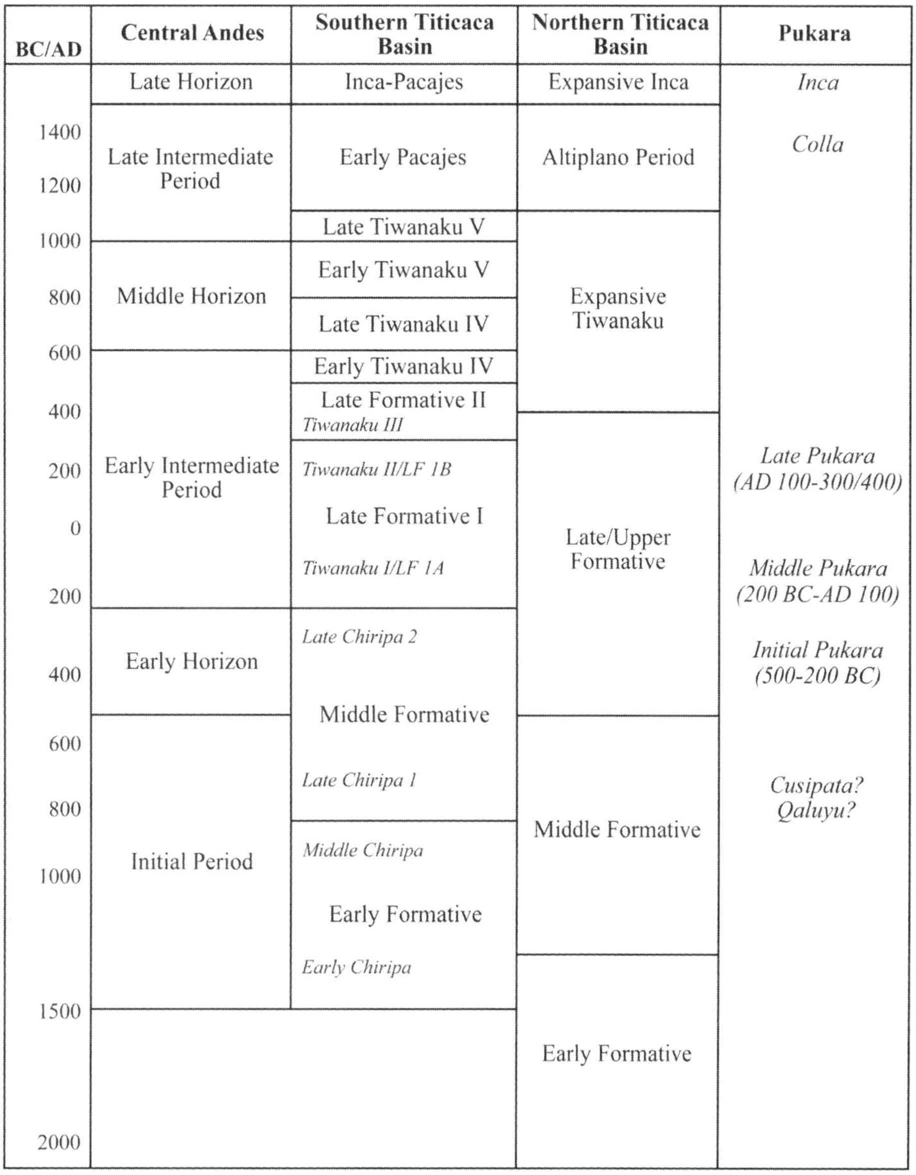

| BC/AD | Central Andes | Southern Titicaca Basin | Northern Titicaca Basin | Pukara |
|---|---|---|---|---|
| | Late Horizon | Inca-Pacajes | Expansive Inca | *Inca* |
| 1400 | Late Intermediate Period | Early Pacajes | Altiplano Period | *Colla* |
| 1200 | | | | |
| 1000 | Middle Horizon | Late Tiwanaku V | Expansive Tiwanaku | |
| 800 | | Early Tiwanaku V | | |
| | | Late Tiwanaku IV | | |
| 600 | Early Intermediate Period | Early Tiwanaku IV | Late/Upper Formative | *Late Pukara (AD 100-300/400)* |
| 400 | | Late Formative II *Tiwanaku III* | | |
| 200 | | *Tiwanaku II/LF 1B* | | |
| 0 | | Late Formative I | | |
| 200 | | *Tiwanaku I/LF 1A* | | *Middle Pukara (200 BC-AD 100)* |
| 400 | Early Horizon | *Late Chiripa 2* | Middle Formative | *Initial Pukara (500-200 BC)* |
| 600 | | Middle Formative | | |
| 800 | Initial Period | *Late Chiripa 1* | Middle Formative | *Cusipata? Qaluyu?* |
| 1000 | | *Middle Chiripa* | | |
| | | Early Formative | | |
| | | *Early Chiripa* | | |
| 1500 | | | Early Formative | |
| 2000 | | | | |

Figure 6.2. Regional chronology (compiled from Janusek 2004, Rowe 1960, Stanish 2003, and Mujica 1988).

For the pedestrian survey, the site was divided into four principal zones: Zone 1 to define the northern site boundary; Zone 2 to define the southern boundary; Zone 3 to clarify the eastern boundary; and Zone 4 to document prehistoric use of Pucaorqo, a peak just north (and overlooking) the architectural core (Figs. 6.5, 6.6). In each of these areas, the crew was spaced between 1 m and 5 m depending on ground cover, and the presence and distribution of surface architecture and diagnostic artifacts were recorded. It was likely, based on a systematic survey and 100% surface collection of 32 blocks (5 m × 5 m each) in the central pampa area in 2000 (Klarich and Diaz 2001), that surface remains would primarily reflect later prehistoric (Colla) and modern occupations (Fig. 6.7). Therefore, special attention was paid to areas with intrusive modern activities, such as mining for clay or plowing for agriculture, as Formative period remains are typically located 30 to 50 cm below the modern ground surface. In addition to the chief surveyor carrying the GPS unit and the data collector, crew members were responsible for taking photos, written descriptions, and artifact collections.

Field observations were recorded using a sub-meter accuracy GPS unit (Trimble Pro-XR) and organized in-field using a data collector unit (Recon) running the program TerraSync. The entire process is quite flexible; the data are collected and categorized through project-specific data dictionaries developed in TerraSync

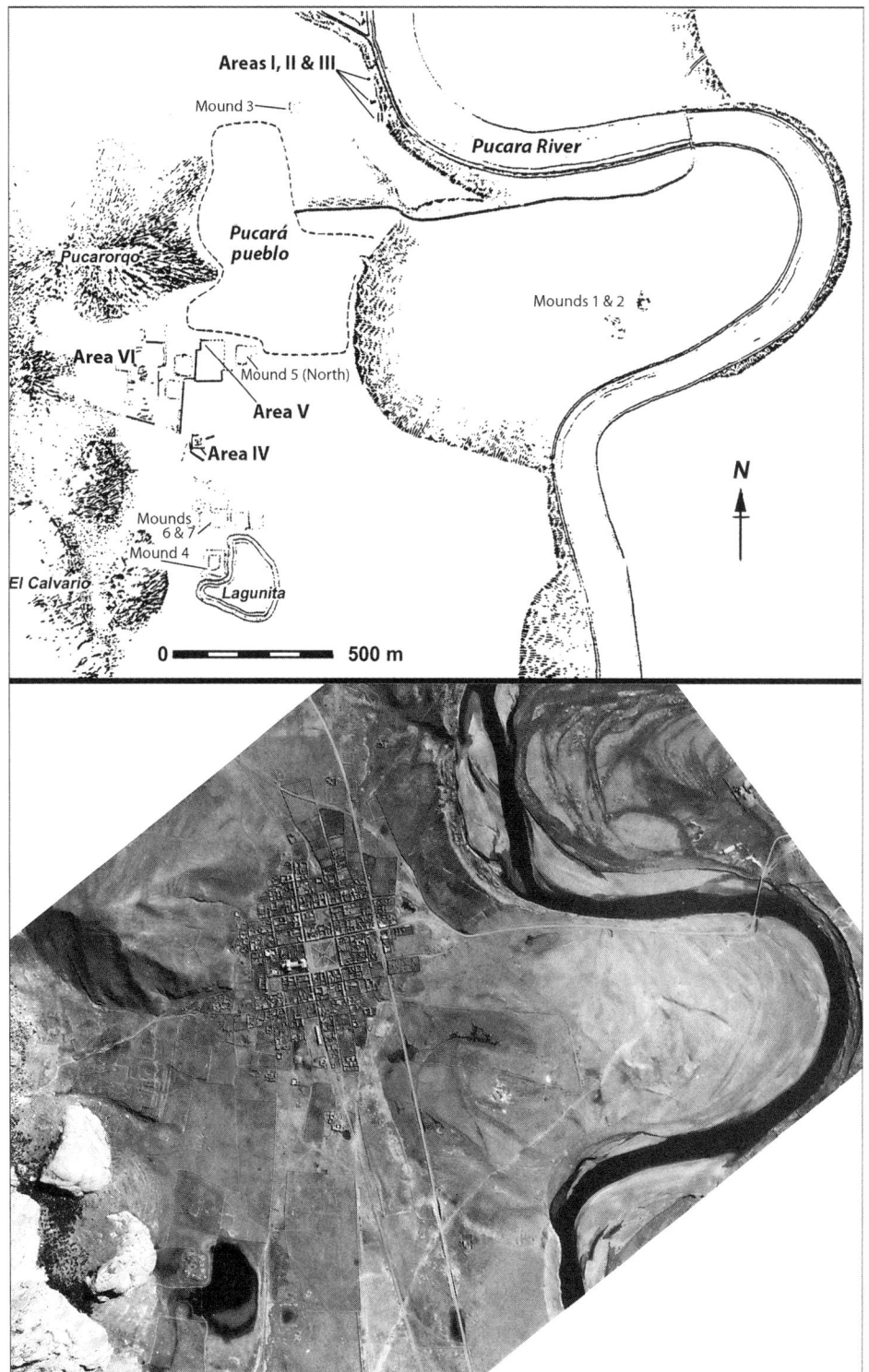

Figure 6.3. Location of Pukara (the site) and Pucará (the town), indicating areas excavated (Areas I–VI) and mounds observed (Mounds 1–7) by Kidder in 1939 (map adapted from Mohr Chávez 1988; air photo courtesy of SAN, Peru).

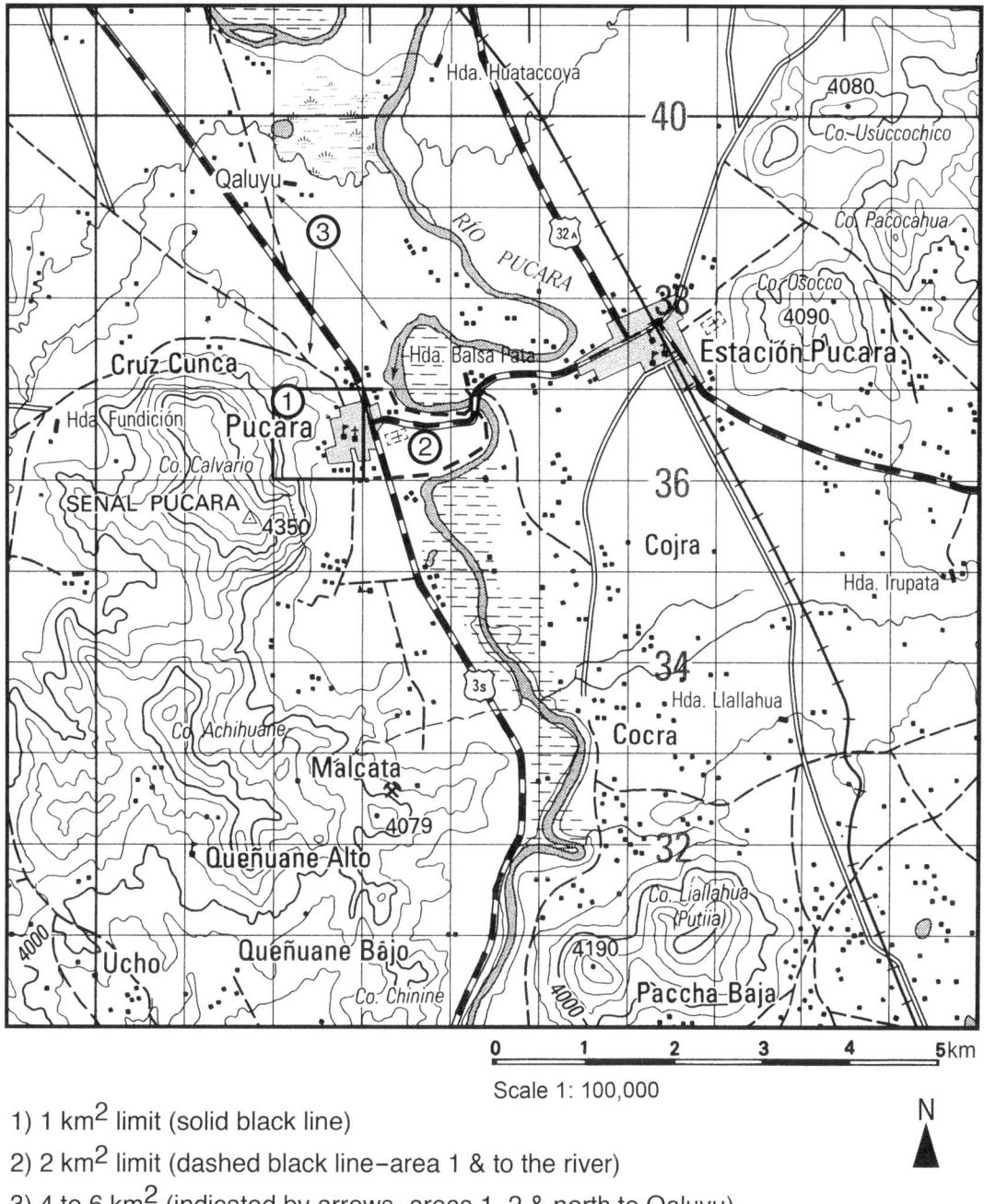

1) 1 km² limit (solid black line)
2) 2 km² limit (dashed black line—area 1 & to the river)
3) 4 to 6 km² (indicated by arrows—areas 1, 2 & north to Qaluyu)

Figure 6.4. Proposed limits of Pukara.

Figure 6.5. Map of Pukara center and periphery (adapted from Wheeler and Mujica 1981), indicating the mounds observed by Kidder (1939) and by Plan Copesco (1970s). Four areas from the 2006 survey are noted (Zones 1–4).

Figure 6.6. Air photo of the four survey areas from 2006 (SAN, Peru). The architectural core is within the area outlined in black and overlapping Zone 2.

Figure 6.7. Project areas from 2000 and 2001. Kidder's Area IV excavations are visible to the west and south of Block 3.

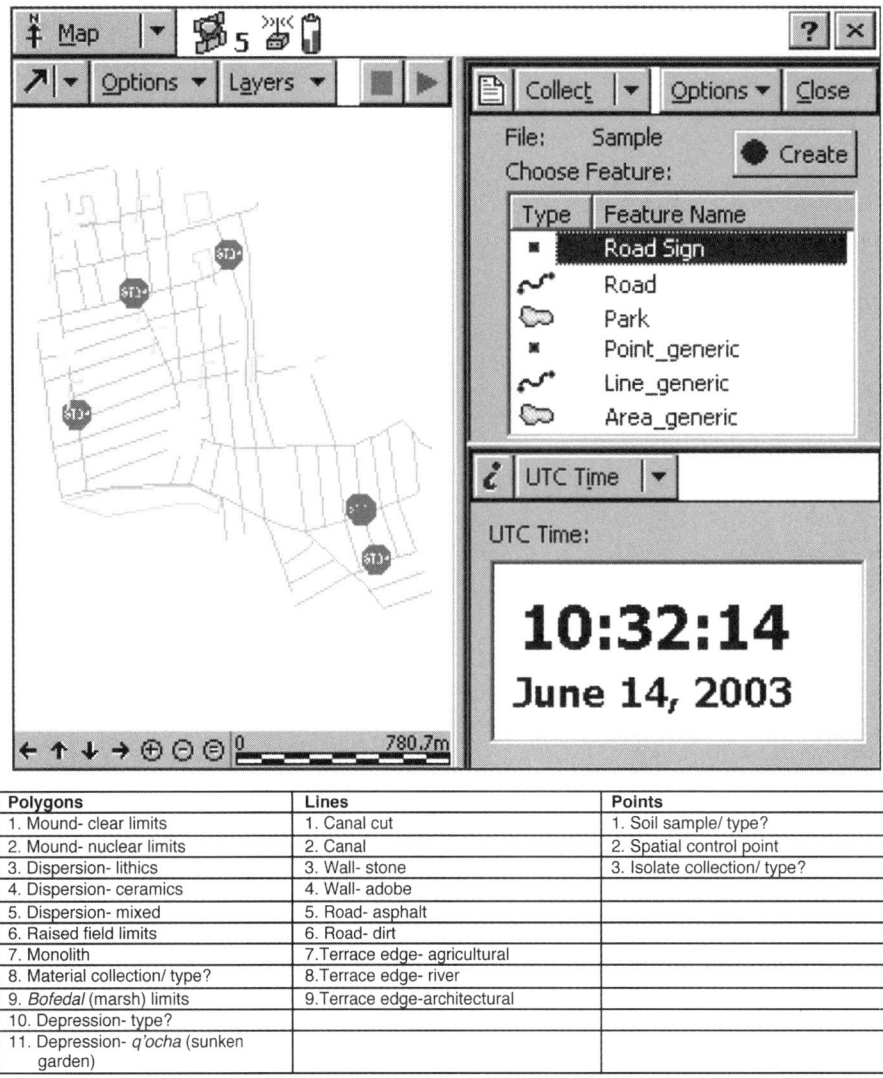

Figure 6.8. Data collector screen running TerraSync, Version 2.40 (*upper*) (Trimble Navigation Limited 2003:8) and table with data dictionary developed for recording polygons, lines and points during 2006 survey (*lower*).

(Fig. 6.8). Features are recorded as "wall fragment," "ceramic scatter," or "mound perimeter" and are noted as prehistoric, modern or unclear in order to facilitate analysis and map production using GIS software (ESRI ArcMap).

At the end of each day, the field data were downloaded from the hand-held Recon unit into the project laptop, copied, and transferred into the project GIS database. A key step was the differential correction of the raw survey field data, which improves the accuracy of the GPS from approximately 3-meter to sub-meter recording intervals. This was accomplished by first downloading GPS data recorded by a permanent base station in Arequipa, Peru, and operated by the International GNSS Service (IGS).[4] Each weekend, the crew downloaded the Arequipa base station data from the IGS webpage that corresponded to the time each day during which the Pukara data were being collected in the field. Using GPS Pathfinder Office it was possible to use the data from the Arequipa base station to correct the newly collected field data and produce more accurate site maps.

In addition to the GPS, historic air photos from 1968 were essential for navigating Pukara on foot and provided different views that highlighted changes in the location of structures, pits, agricultural field walls, and other clear surface and sub-surface

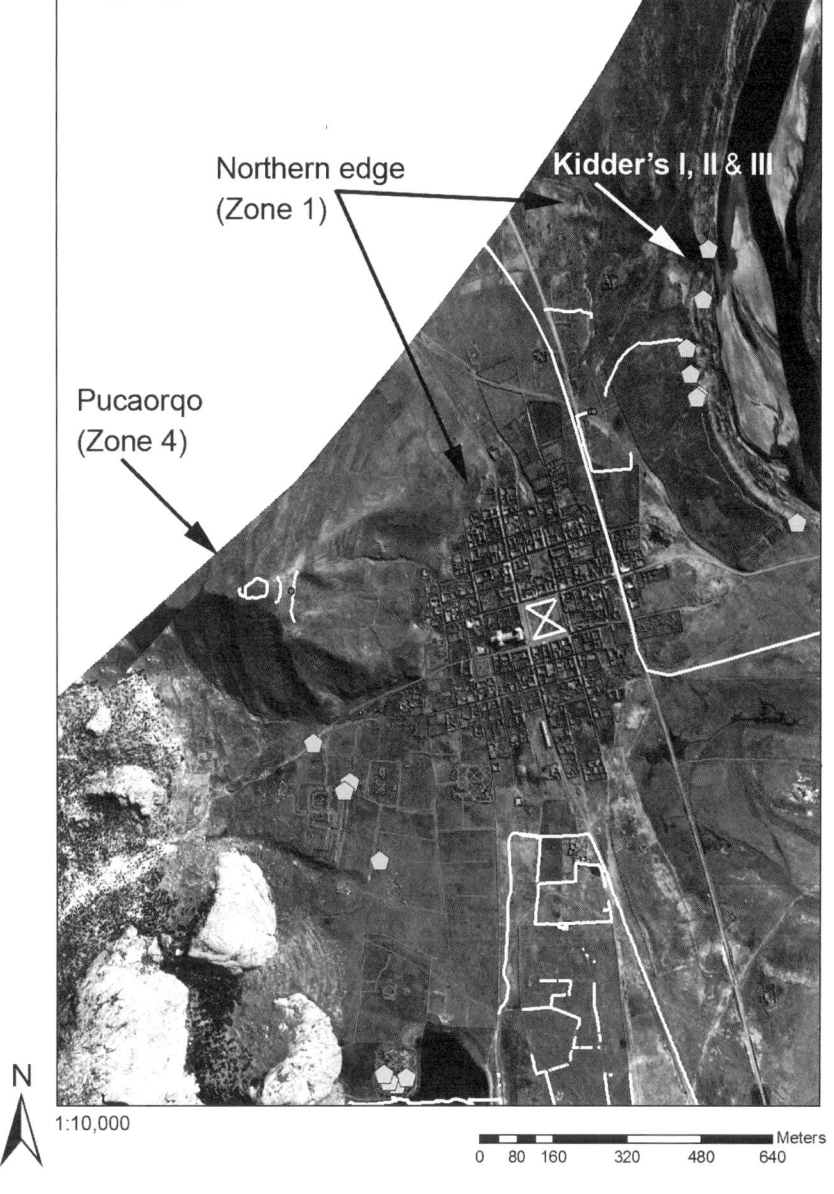

Figure 6.9. Zones 1 and 4 on georeferenced air photo (SAN) with surface collections marked in solid white pentagons. Variety of linear features recorded with GPS, indicating modern and prehistoric surface remains.

modifications from the last 40 years of town expansion. The survey crew also relied on the air photos for locating features in the central architectural district as they appeared before the Plan Copesco excavation and restoration project in the 1970s and early 1980s.

**Results**

For the survey project, Zone 1 included the area between the northern edge of the modern town of Pucará and the archaeological site of Qaluyu, located approximately 4 km to the north. Because both sites include significant Formative period occupations, including mounds with sunken courts, some have argued that Qaluyu served as the northern boundary of Pukara during the Late Formative, extending the site boundaries to 6 km$^2$ (Wheeler and Mujica 1981: Fig. 10; Mujica 1991). Starting at the edge of town, the survey was relatively straightforward because hundreds of meter-deep holes were present in the area due to modern clay mining practices for making adobes, in addition to open large fields that have been plowed deeply using agricultural machinery and foot plows (Fig. 6.9). Based on the 2006 survey, the Formative period occupation of Pukara does

Figure 6.10. Zone 2 on georeferenced air photo (SAN), indicating the Lagunita and Northern Mounds and a variety of semi-buried features in the architectural core recorded in 2006.

not appear to extend much beyond the northern boundaries of the modern town.[5] However, due to issues with a local landowner, the crew was not able to survey the area just south of Qaluyu, but did visit the site for preliminary mapping.

Zone 2 was directly south of the monumental architecture at Pukara; it focused on defining the area around the Lagunita Mound (Fig. 6.10). A lagoon surrounds this mound and its southern limit has been treated as the southern border of the site, but this area had not been documented in any detail. It was evident from the historic air photo, the Copesco maps, and previous visits to the site that this area was covered with semi-buried walls and surface artifacts. Also, Manuel Chávez Ballón excavated in this general area in 1949: "los resultados obtenidos fueron muchos miles de fragmentos de alfarería y sólidos conocimientos sobre la Cultura Pukara"[6] (Chávez Ballón 1950:42). A final report of these excavations has not been published, but local residents report that he excavated near the Lagunita Mound.

The survey of Zone 2 began with the mound, which measures several meters in height and was looted before Kidder's 1939 excavation project. The trench cut through the middle of the mound is visible today and, unfortunately, local landowners continue to use the area as a source of stone blocks for construction projects.⁷ The edges of the mound were mapped, a number of distinct construction terraces were recorded, and surface artifacts were collected, including obsidian flakes and incised Classic Pukara pottery. To the south and east of the mound is a lagoon area that fluctuates seasonally in size. The water table is very high in this area and there is runoff from the nearby hills, resulting in many marshy zones; presumably this area was naturally inundated and expanded as a borrow pit for the mound's construction. Along the periphery of the lagoon and to the south there were no surface artifacts or evidence of semi-buried walls, indicating that the Formative period occupation of Pukara did not extend much beyond the previously discussed south boundary.

During field recording on Pukara's southern edge, the crew took advantage of the opportunity to further document a number of important architectural features in the site's central area. The Qalasaya dominates the site core; it is a 30-m-tall structure with stone-lined terraces on its eastern face, a central staircase, and an upper platform with three semi-subterranean buildings or sunken courts (Wheeler and Mujica 1981). It is located at the base of the Peñon, a massive pink sandstone outcrop visible throughout the valley that serves as the western boundary of the site; a number of lower artificial terraces and mounds extend to the northeast and southeast, forming a U-shaped area designated as the central district.

At the base of the Qalasaya terraces is the central pampa, an area excavated by Kidder in 1939 (designated Area IV) and Klarich in 2001 (Klarich 2005), which featured a variety of constructions during the Formative and Altiplano periods (see Fig. 6.7). In 2006, the first area re-mapped was the Northern Mound, a structure approximately the same size as the Lagunita Mound, located on the northern edge of the central architectural district. The mound has been heavily affected by modern activities, particularly related to mining for stones and adobe materials, and merits additional investigation to determine the presence of a sunken court on the uppermost platform. Located between the Qalasaya and Northern Mound is the largest single platform constructed at the site, which has a number of exposed large stone slabs forming structures around a central, sunken area. In 1939, Kidder excavated a single wall of one of these stone structures, designated as Area V, but the exact location and layout of the surface architecture had yet to be mapped.⁸ Additionally, a number of semi-buried walls visible in the historic air photos were identified by the survey crew and recorded using the GPS. Lastly, the crew mapped a few architectural features of the Qalasaya, including the central sunken court and several terrace edges, to assist in the process of accurately georeferencing the historic air photo in the project GIS.

Zone 3 included the areas along the banks of the Pucara River, which apparently served as the site's eastern border (Fig. 6.11). Zone 3 was subdivided into the northern area, a relatively entrenched area of river with a high terrace located just east of town, and the southern area, a low-lying zone highly affected by the meanderings of the river. In the northern area, the crew identified a number of archaeological deposits, including the excavation scars and back dirt piles from Kidder's excavations of Areas I, II and III (see Chávez 1992; Inojosa 1940; Kidder 1942). Based on exposed archaeological contexts in the riverbank profile, this area was used extensively for dumping Late Formative period trash. On the open terrace area directly west of the riverbank there was limited surface material, but a trench recently excavated for a sewer line exposed dense deposits of Late Formative material directly behind the grade school, approximately 30 to 50 cm below the ground surface. These finds were a surprise, challenging models that posit a noncontinuous occupation between the architectural core of the site and the extensive middens located on the periphery excavated by Kidder.⁹ Additional test excavations and geophysical survey would provide valuable insights into whether occupations on the site periphery were ephemeral or continued relatively uninterrupted from areas of visible architecture and surface remains. Lastly, there was no indication that the Formative period occupation extended north of the large *quebrada* in this area. It was clear from the survey along the riverbank that the prehistoric deposits have been heavily affected by riverine cutting and depositing, processes that need to be documented by a trained geomorphologist during subsequent projects at the site.

To the south, a major goal of surveying near the riverbank was to relocate a series of large mounds documented by Kidder and Plan Copesco (Fig. 6.11). The limits and general characteristics of two mounds were recorded near the modern river course. They measure only a meter in height and have few surface artifacts, but the presence of large cut stone blocks at their bases and in the general vicinity are characteristic of Late Formative constructions and there were few surface indications of later materials. Several community members have mentioned that this area had more numerous blocks in the past that have been removed to build field walls and modern constructions. Lastly, along both the northern and southern areas of Zone 3 the crew collected various clay samples under the direction of Honorato Ttacca, a project member and experienced Pucará potter.

Finally, Zone 4 included Pucaorqo and the surrounding hills (see Fig. 6.9), which are located north and overlooking the architectural core of Pukara. At the top of Pucaorqo is an artificially leveled platform with a large carved monolith and a series of stone terraces (Fig. 6.12). While the construction date of the terraces is unclear and there are few surface artifacts, the monolith is clearly Formative (Fig. 6.13). Today the peak is a pilgrimage destination and the monolith is covered with modern burned offerings and ash deposits. The crew continued to survey along the spine of the hills to the north and south, including the area directly west of the Qalasaya. There are few Formative period artifacts on these upper slopes and along the eroding stone terraces. Instead, the area is covered with Collao sherds from the Altiplano period, which were first mentioned by John Rowe during a visit to Pukara (Rowe 1942).

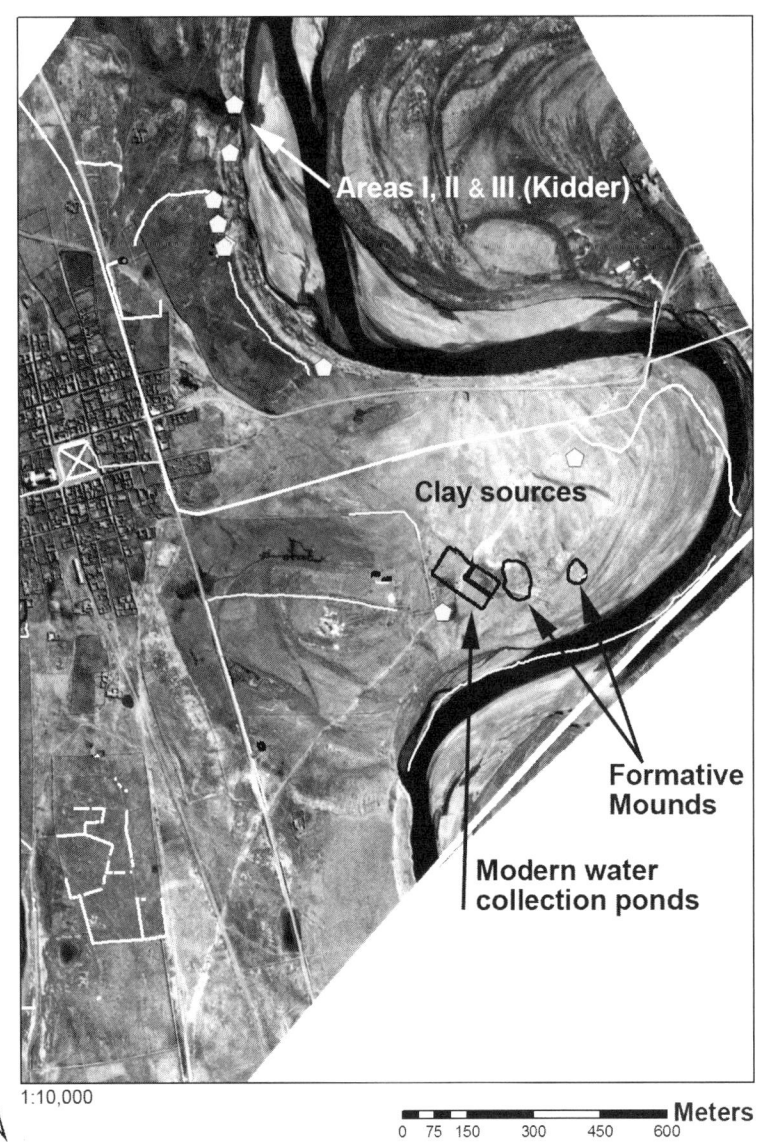

(*left*) Figure 6.11. Zone 3 on georeferenced air photo (SAN), with surface artifact collections and samples from clay sources marked in solid white pentagons. Remains of mounds recorded by Kidder and Copesco relocated (see Figs. 6.3, 6.5).

(*below*) Figure 6.12. Zone 4, view of artificial platform on Pucaorqo. Photo taken from Pucará main square, facing west. Modern cross is located on peak next to Formative monolith (photo courtesy of Matt Wilhelm).

Figure 6.13. Zone 4, Formative period monolith on Pucaorqo. Photo taken facing west (photo courtesy of Matt Wilhelm).

## Future Directions

Data from the 2006 survey were used to develop a preliminary delimitation for Pukara, providing further evidence for the smaller site size estimates discussed above (Fig. 6.14). If occupation was spatially continuous during the Late Formative—from the central architectural district and extending under Pucará and to the riverbank—the largest extent of the site measures 2.2 km². As noted by Stanish (2003) and further noted during our survey, it is likely that there were clusters of occupation, possibly with dense residential and activity areas clustered on the western and eastern limits of the site. However, geophysical survey and further excavations are necessary to determine the relationship of surface and sub-surface remains, as both cultural and natural factors continue to modify the landscape of the site and its surrounding areas.

Unfortunately, the lack of Formative period surface remains across much of prehistoric Pukara and modern Pucará makes it difficult to discuss the nature of site organization and the diversity of site areas beyond very general divisions between the "architectural core" and "periphery." Excavations in 2009 (Flores 2009) and 2010 (Carbajal 2010) targeted areas within both areas to clarify how different areas of the site were being used, with a particular focus on refining the site chronology and determining the directionality of growth and development of Pukara during the Formative period.

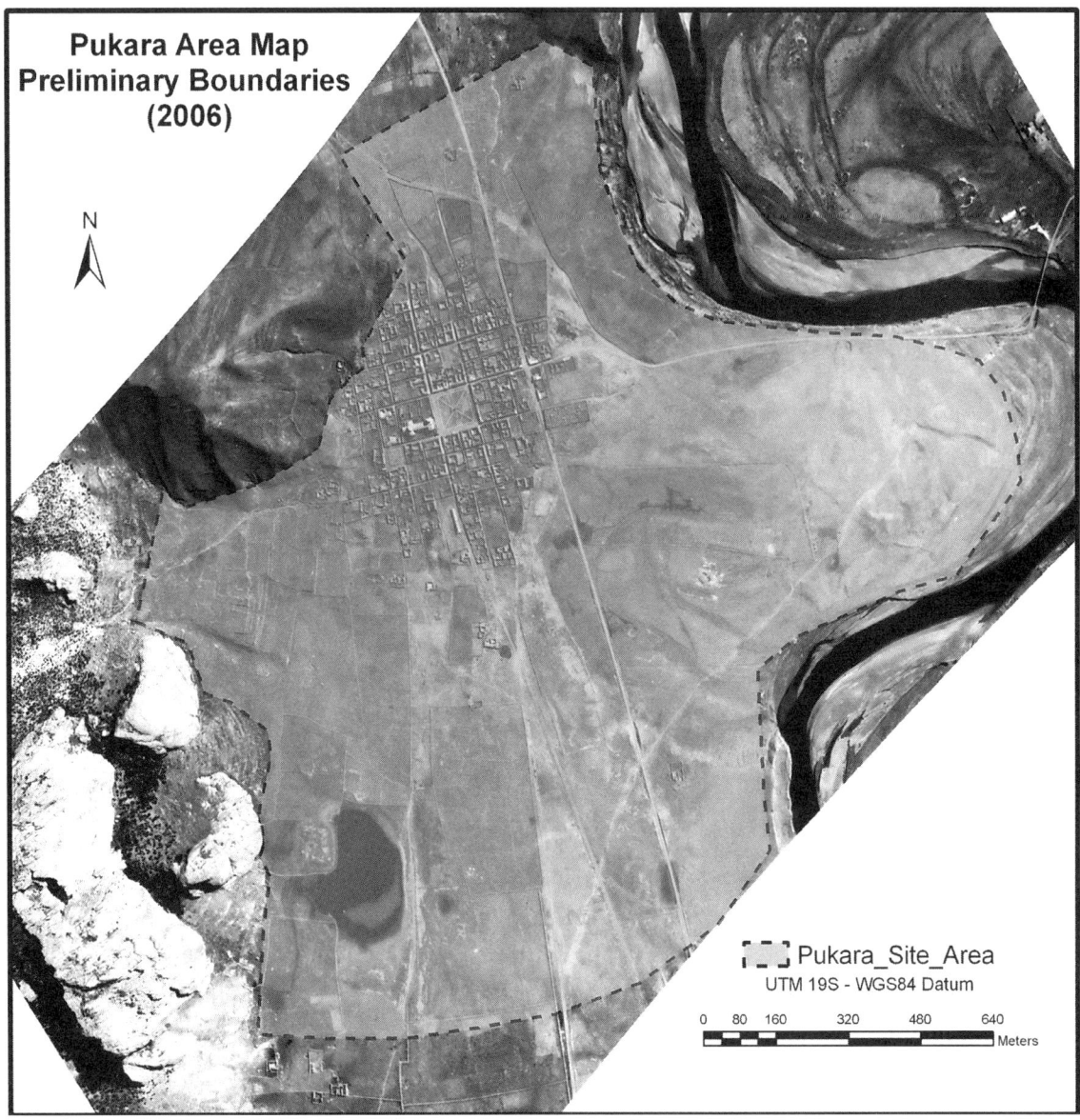

Figure 6.14. Preliminary maximum limits of Pukara based on 2006 survey (2.2 km$^2$).

At Pukara, debates have primarily centered on whether the site functioned as an urban center, a ceremonial site, or a regional political center within the Lake Titicaca Basin (see Klarich 2005 for summary). These "top down" approaches, which focus on elite guided activities as central to site development and social change, neglect to consider the role of non-elites in social, economic, and political change. By further documenting the temporal and spatial organization of both the site periphery and monumental constructions of the site core, it will be possible to formulate a more complete picture of Pukara. In turn, the insights gained at Pukara will contribute to the growing body of archaeological and anthropological literature addressing early centers across the globe.

## Acknowledgments

Funding was received from the Howard Heinz Endowment for Archaeological Field Research in Latin America for *Scale, Layout and Diversity: Documenting the Regional Center of Pukara, Lake Titicaca Basin, Peru* (Project No. 704177). The project was co-directed by the authors during the summer of 2006 (Proyecto Arqueológico Pukara, Resolución Directoral Nacional No. 1347) and was greatly facilitated by the Puno office of the National Institute of Culture. Logistical support was provided by Programa Collasuyu and a special thanks to Mark Aldenderfer for loaning us his Trimble Pro-XR unit and to Charles Stanish for the use of his vehicle. The field crew—David Oshige, Barbara Carbajal, Matthew Wilhelm and Honorato Ttacca—formed an incredible team that showed no fear in the face of stampeding llama herds, the freezing cold Río Pucara, and precarious clay sources. Lastly, thank you to Nathan Craig and Nico Tripcevich for answering countless tech questions over the years; to Margaret Brown Vega for collecting valuable spatial data for the project in 2009; and to Matt Wilhelm for his help with the maps.

## Notes

1. The Late Formative is also called the Upper Formative (e.g., Stanish 2003).
2. Following Mujica (1988), the Pukara period is divided into Initial Pukara (500–200 BC), Middle Pukara (200 BC–AD 100) and Late Pukara (AD 100–300).
3. The archaeological site and culture are spelled "Pukara" by the Peruvian Ministry of Culture (formerly the National Institute of Culture) and the modern town where the site is located is spelled "Pucará."
4. See http://igscb.jpl.nasa.gov/network/site/areq.html.
5. In future projects we hope to document the presence of prehistoric architecture and/or artifacts within the modern town of Pucará. Many local people have mentioned finding monoliths or broken pottery in their house compounds or fields, but these occurrences have yet to be systematically recorded.
6. "The results obtained were many thousands of ceramic sherds and solid knowledge about the Pukara Culture."
7. The mound is highly disturbed and limited excavations in 2009 recorded additional looting since 2006.
8. In 2009 and 2010, this area was mapped and further excavations were conducted by the Pukara Archaeological Project.
9. Luis Flores directed additional excavations of this area in 2009 (Flores 2009), with publications forthcoming.

## References Cited

Abraham, S., and A. Balasalle
2011  The Architecture of La Quinta: Interpreting Colonial Strategies of Conquest and Conversion at Pukara, Peru. Poster presented at the 76th Annual Meeting of the Society for American Archaeology, Sacramento.

Carbajal Salazar, B.
2010  *Informe Final, Proyecto de Investigación Arqueológica Pukara 2010*. Submitted to the National Institute of Culture, Peru (available from author).

Chávez, S. L.
1992  The Conventionalized Rules in Pucara Pottery Technology and Iconography: Implications of Socio-Political Development in the Northern Titicaca Basin. PhD dissertation, Department of Anthropology, Michigan State University, E. Lansing.

Chávez Ballón, M.
1950  Arqueología del sur andino. *Tradición* 1(2):41–48.

Cohen, A.
2010  The Significance of Sunken Court Architecture to the Development of Sociopolitical Complexity. PhD dissertation, Department of Anthropology, University of California, Los Angeles.

*El Peruano*
2011  *Normas Legales* 11 May:442445–442446, No. 11398. Lima, Peru.

Erickson, C.
1988  Raised field agriculture in the Lake Titicaca Basin: Putting ancient agriculture back to work. *Expedition* 30(3):8–16.

Flores Blanco, L. A.
2009  *Informe Final, Excavaciones Arqueológicas en Pukara 2009, Puno-Peru*. Submitted to the National Institute of Culture, Peru (available from author).

Franquemont, E.
1986  The ancient pottery from Pucara, Peru. *Ñawpa Pacha* 24:1–30.

Hyslop, J.
1990  *Inka Settlement Planning*. University of Texas Press, Austin.

Inojosa, J. M.
1940  Informe sobre los trabajos arqueológicos de la Misión Kidder en Pukara, Peru (enero a julio 1939). *Revista del Museo Nacional* 9(1):128–42.

Janusek, J. W.
2004  Tiwanaku and its precursors: Recent research and emerging perspectives. *Journal of Archaeological Research* 12(2):121–83.

Kidder II, A.
1942  Preliminary notes on the archaeology of Pucara, Puno, Peru. *Actas y Trabajos Científicos de XXVII Congreso Internacional de Americanistas* (Lima 1939) 1:341–45.

Klarich, E. A.
2005  From the Monumental to the Mundane: Defining Early Leadership Strategies at Late Formative Pukara, Peru. PhD dissertation, Department of Anthropology, University of California, Santa Barbara.

Klarich, E. A., and R. Diaz Montalvo
2001 *Informe Preliminar: Proyecto de Arqueología Doméstica de Pukara (C/097-2000), Prospección Geofísica y Recolección de Superficie del Sitio de Pucará*. Submitted to the National Institute of Culture, Peru, permit no. C/097-2000 (available from the authors).

Mohr Chávez, K. L.
1988 The significance of Chiripa in Lake Titicaca Basin developments. *Expedition* 30(3):17–26.

Mujica, E.
1978 Nueva hipótesis sobre el desarrollo temprano del altiplano, del Titicaca y de sus áreas de interacción. *Arte y Arqueología* 5/6:285–308.
1985 Altiplano-coast relationships in the south-central Andes: From indirect to direct complementarity. In *Andean Ecology and Civilization*, edited by S. Masuda, I. Shimada, and C. Morris, pp. 103–40. University of Tokyo Press, Tokyo.
1988 Peculiaridades del proceso histórico temprano en la cuenca norte del Titicaca: Una propuesta inicial. *Boletín del Laboratorio de Arqueología* 2:75–122.
1991 Pukara: Una sociedad compleja temprana en la cuenca norte de Titicaca. In *Los Incas y El Antiguo Peru: 3000 Años de Historia*, pp. 272–97. Tomo 1. Sociedad Estatal Quinto Centenario, Madrid.

Paredes, R.
1985 Excavaciones arqueológicas en Pukara, Puno. Licenciatura tesis, La Universidad Nacional San Antonio Abad del Cuzco, Peru.

Rowe, J. H.
1942 Sitios históricos en la región de Pucara, Puno. *Revista del Instituto Arqueológico* 6(10/11):66–75.
1960 Cultural unity and diversification in Peruvian archaeology. In *Man and Cultures: Selected Papers of the Fifth International Congress of Anthropological and Ethnological Science*, pp. 627–31. Philadelphia.

Stanish, C.
2003 *Ancient Titicaca: The Evolution of Complex Society in Southern Peru and Northern Bolivia*. University of California Press, Berkeley and Los Angeles.

Stanish, C., E. de la Vega M., L. Steadman, C. Chávez J., K. L. Frye, L. O. Mamani, M. T. Seddon, and P. C. Chuquimia
1997 *Archaeological Survey in the Juli-Desaguadero Region of Lake Titicaca Basin, Southern Peru*. Fieldiana Anthropology, New Series 29. Field Museum of Natural History, Chicago.

Tantaleán, H.
2010 *Ideología y Realidad en al Primeras Sociedades Sedentarias (1400 ANE–350 DNE) de la Cuenca Norte del Titicaca, Perú*. Series 2150. British Archaeological Reports, Oxford.

Trimble Navigation Limited
2003 TerraSync Operation Guide, Version 2.4, Revision A, September 2003. Accessed online (http://www.trimble.com/terrasync_ts.asp?Nav=Collection-30232).

Wheeler, J., and E. Mujica
1981 *Prehistoric Pastoralism in the Lake Titicaca Basin, Peru, 1979–1980 Field Season*. Report submitted to National Science Foundation, grant no. BNS 7015119.

# Chapter 7

# Prehispanic Carved Stones in the Northern Titicaca Basin

*Charles Stanish*

The study of the stone carving traditions of the pre-Colonial northern Titicaca Basin (Figs. 7.1, 7.2) remains in its infancy. We have of course the seminal work of Valcárcel (1925, 1932, 1935, 1938), Kidder (1943), and Sergio Chávez and Karen Mohr Chávez on the Yaya-Mama tradition (Chávez and Chávez 1975). Valcárcel's work demonstrated the sophistication of this stone working tradition in the pre-Tiwanaku periods. He showed that this Andean carving tradition extended from Colombia to Bolivia and was richly represented in the northern Titicaca Basin. Chávez and Chávez defined the Yaya-Mama religious tradition with monoliths having male and female icons being central in the material expression of this ideology. They also demonstrated that the famous Arapa stela was actually the missing half of the Thunderbolt stela in Tiwanaku, providing an early case of huaca capture in the Titicaca Basin.

The work of these pioneers focused on the beautifully carved monolithic statues found largely at Pucara, Taraco, Arapa and Hatuncolla. The systematic reconnaissances and surveys that have been conducted in the region in the last two decades indicate that there is a much greater quantity and variety of stone carving in the region than is apparent by a focus on the carved statues alone. Along with these impressive monoliths are large numbers of carved stone pieces, utilized in a variety of ways throughout the centuries.

The purpose of this brief report is primarily to illustrate some new finds from the Northern Titicaca Basin Archaeological Survey. Carved stones in the region come in a number of varieties that can be classified with several different features, including morphology, stylistic motifs, and raw material. I refrain from creating a formal typology until we have additional data; new stone carvings are constantly discovered and our sample, while magnificent, is still far too small for meaningful statistical samples. This chapter should instead be viewed as the beginning of the construction of a typology for the Titicaca Basin as a whole.

At the present time, we can therefore offer the following classification of stone carving in the northern Titicaca Basin based upon the following morphological and functional types: carved statues, undecorated statues, carved architectural slabs, uncarved architectural slabs, lintels/building stones, smaller carved portable stones, and finally, as a temporary category, "miscellaneous" pieces.

## Carved Stones in the Northern Titicaca Basin

### Carved Statues (Stelae)

The most prominent carved stones of course are the large monoliths or statues that formerly graced the sunken courts and possibly other buildings in the ancient political centers of the northern Titicaca Basin. Some of the morphological types that seem to be emically meaningful include statues with notches,

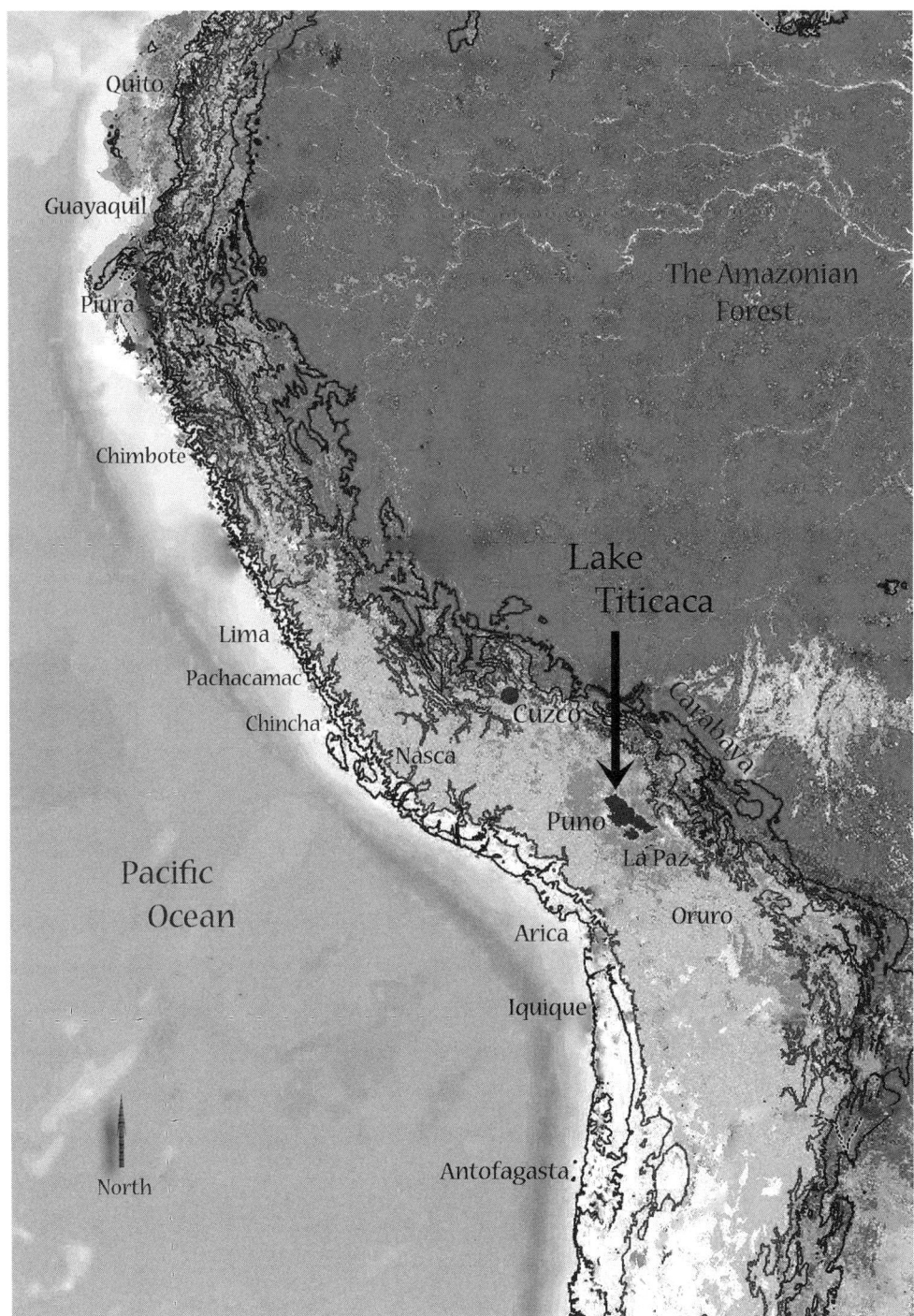

Figure 7.1. Lake Titicaca in South America.

statues without notches, bulky, squared and anthropomorphic statues. Based upon iconographic motifs, some statues are clearly Pucara (ca. 400 BC–AD 300) while others have motifs that have been described as Qaluyu. Qaluyu is a long period, beginning by 1400 BC and ending around 200 BC.

The broad categories of motifs include geometric, animal, and human. Within these categories are elements like crosses, steps, felines, rings, flamingos, snakes, frogs, decapitators, trophy heads, and so forth. When found in situ, carved statues are usually associated with large Middle and Upper Formative period

Figure 7.2. Map of the entire Titicaca Basin. (Sites are designated simply by number.)

political centers in the northern Titicaca Basin. This places the statues firmly within this broad tradition of Qaluyu and Pucara in the north, and in the Chiripa and Early Formative periods in the south (see Bandy and Hastorf 2007).

The Middle and Upper Formative time periods are huge, beginning circa 1400 BC and ending in the fourth century AD. Such a chronological designation is admittedly of little utility when used without some kind of qualification. We can date the carvings a bit more precisely using several lines of evidence. It is likely that the use of small, uncarved stones began around 1400 BC, more or less simultaneously with the development of the sunken court tradition (Stanish 2003; Cohen 2010). The earliest courts probably did not have carved stone, but instead used the polished andesite or basalt "huancas" that were possibly painted periodically and were placed upright in the courts.

The carving tradition of statues probably began around 1000–800 BC, though this remains very speculative. It is possible that some of these carved statues could have been used during Tiwanaku times (ca. AD 650–950) in the northern Titicaca Basin, as in the south, but the evidence is thin at this point. In the greater Titicaca Basin, carved statue tradition continued unabated through the Tiwanaku period and was found sporadically in the Inca and even in the early Spanish Colonial period. We have no statues that are known from Altiplano (Late Intermediate) period contexts, but we have indirect evidence that earlier monoliths were used through that time and into the present as huacas or sacred objects.

Within this broad swath of time, we can identify some chronologically sensitive motifs and carving techniques, particularly Pucara and Qaluyu ones. Some possible candidates for a pre-Pucara date are the bulky, seated anthropomorphic ones, as seen in Figure 7.3 and in Kidder (1943: Plate III, 1-6). These limestone statues were found in the plaza of Taraco and have been noted for quite some time around the region. Similar ones are found in Titimani on the Huata Peninsula in Bolivia (Portugal 1981, 1988a, 1988b; Lémuz 2001). Evidence that they are pre-Pucara is speculative. First, they do not have the motifs as seen in Pucara carvings. Second, the faces are vaguely reminiscent of Chiripa styles from the south, placing the statues early in the Titicaca Basin sequence.

The pieces are also poorly executed, prompting speculation by some that this means that they are early. Frankly, we do not really have a good idea as to how old these statues are. Very few have been found in secure professional excavation contexts in situ and properly published, with the exception of Chiripa and possibly Tiwanaku. Furthermore, there is no comparable iconography on excavated pottery, with the possible exception of some figurines found in Sillumocco (C. Chávez, pers. comm.) and possibly in Bolivia. What we can say is that some figurines with similar faces in the south are fiber-tempered. Fiber-tempering begins with the first pottery around 1400 BC and most likely ends around 200 BC (Steadman 1995), giving us an unsuitably large bracket of time for any systematic analysis of statue dynamics. It is important to keep open the possibility that the stylistic variation as seen in these blocky anthropomorphic statues may very well not be chronological, but regional. We can also state with some certainty that the Yaya-Mama tradition, as described by Chávez and Chávez (1975:65), is in fact pre-Pucara in date as these two scholars assert (and see Tantaleán 2008). This conclusion is based upon iconographic analyses between the Yaya-Mama and Pucara styles.

One of the few scientific excavations to uncover a standing, in situ monolith is from the work of the Taraco Archaeological Project in the southern Titicaca Basin at the site of Kala Uyuni. Here, Cohen and Roddick (2007) report an intact standing sandstone monolith in the center of one of two sunken courts. The court, according to Bandy and Hastorf (2007), dates to the Late Chiripa period circa 800–200 BC. These data accord extremely well with the observations of our work in the northern Titicaca Basin reported here regarding the nature and kinds of courts associated with statues. The statue in the Kala Uyuni court was not decorated. Its raw material, size and shape are typical of undecorated statues found throughout the entire Titicaca Basin (see below).

Carved statues come in most types of raw material, including limestone, andesite, sandstone and basalt. Given our current data set, there does not appear to be any pattern between morphology, motifs and raw material, at least for carved statues. Raw material sourcing studies and the expansion of our database will allow us to make more precise statements in the future.

The most famous of the northern Titicaca Basin carved statues come from just a handful of sites. This is most likely not just

Figure 7.3. A low, bulky statue found in Taraco, Peru, in the northern Titicaca Basin. This limestone statue is now in the municipal museum.

an artifact of archaeological work, but a real pattern in which only the political centers actually had the majority of monoliths while the smaller centers and sites did not have many or had none at all. It is also possible that in the highly competitive environment of the Upper Formative, many stelae from smaller sites were captured and placed as trophies in courts. We know, for instance, that the Arapa stela was captured by the Tiwanaku peoples and half of it was moved 175 km to the capital (Chávez and Chávez 1975).

In rough order of importance, the sites with significant numbers of statues are Pucara, Taraco, Arapa, Hatuncolla and Cancha-Cancha Asiruni (Tintiri). Ephraim Squier and other early travelers commented on a few of the more prominent statues. The first serious publications on the Pucara pieces were by the celebrated Luis Valcárcel (1925, 1932, 1935, 1938). He advanced his famous interpretation of the "gato de agua" motif and demonstrated similarities between Pucara statue motifs with other cultures such as Tiwanaku and Nasca. Alfred Kidder II (1943) referenced the Pucara sculptures and tried to contextualize them with some statues from around the region. Cancha-Cancha Asiruni was scientifically discovered by Chávez Ballón and described by Sergio Chávez. The site has a number of carved statues on the surface that were placed in the numerous sunken court complexes on the settlement (Stanish 2003; Tantaleán and Leyva 2010).

In the town of Taraco, we discovered a number of statues not previously reported. The vast majority of the statues were uncarved (see below). One complete sandstone piece, however, has a distinctive carving on its upper face. The motif appears to be some kind of stylized toad or fish though it is very worn (Fig. 7.4). At over 4 m in height, this statue is typical of the many uncarved ones found throughout the region, but in this case it has a very modest carving. It is very similar to the monolith fragment found in TA-1039 that we have called the Cornejo stela after the landowner on whose property we found the piece (Fig. 7.5). Site TA-1039 is located about 200 m from the Ramis River; it is composed of a low and very small mound about 10 × 15 m in size. This sandstone statue measures about 87 × 41 × 20 cm. It is broken on both ends so we do not know if it was notched. The anthropomorphized frog motif looks like one seen in the Taraco Museum today (Fig. 7.6).

Another fragment with crossed hands (seen in Fig. 7.7) is almost certainly part of a statue that was originally much larger. The piece was found (during dredging operations to build a bridge) in the river next to the town of Taraco and is currently in the Taraco Museum. The river has indeed cut into the ancient town over the centuries. The fragment came from an area with considerable architecture, as indicated by excavations in the area, and was originally part of a complex sunken court area.

The small statue in TA-1057 (Figs. 7.8, 7.9) may have been a tenon or a freestanding carved statue. It has a *suche* or serpent motif carving typical of the region. It was at least 1 m high, and was probably much larger originally.

Two statues (one small, the other large) were found at site AR-1245 (Fig. 7.10), one that is typical of many more in the region. The site is a classic sunken court complex in the northern Titicaca Basin. The small limestone piece (Fig. 7.11) is about 111 cm long and measures about 28 cm in diameter. There is a damaged carving that may be a frog, lizard, fish or other naturalistic motif. The second, larger, limestone statue was found nearby. It is over 200 cm in height, and some 80 cm wide at its greatest width (Fig. 7.12). Most significant is the fact that the stones were only minimally carved in antiquity. The limestone in the area naturally forms into these elongated shapes, and the carvings on the pieces were effectively added on to what was natural stone. The carving iself is a crude rendition of a snake or lizard motif with the ubiquitous oval or "donut" shape typical of Formative period carvings. Their shapes clearly suggest their use as typical statues, but they appear to have been natural limestone rocks selected for their shape and modified with a modest carving on a natural surface.

Farmers and construction workers have discovered a few carved statues in sites, at least according to various unsubstantiated reports. One intact but broken statue was discovered by farmers near the town of Huancané at the site of Huancanewichinka (Fig. 7.13). This Formative statue was set perfectly upright in virtually the middle of the court when we visited the area in 1998. Whether the stones were left exactly as they were during the use of the court (unlikely) or were maintained by locals as a huaca well after the courts were abandoned (much more likely) is not known. What is clear is that the statue was broken long ago, as evidenced by the heavy weathering on the cracked faces.

*Undecorated Statues*

While the carved statues have captured the archaeological imagination, uncarved statues are far more common throughout the region. Uncarved stelae are found in scores of sites in the area, almost always associated with Formative period pottery. Uncarved statues are morphologically very similar to carved ones. They are carved from sandstone, limestone, basalt and andesite. Some have steps or notches at the top, while many others do not.

The towns of Taraco and Putina, both major Formative period centers, are replete with uncarved statues throughout the streets. These statues are today incorporated into buildings and streets and used as steps or as building materials. Dozens of such statues were incorporated into the foundations of the Colonial period churches in each town.

The statues shown in Figures 7.14 and 7.15 are typical of those found in the streets of Taraco; the statues in Figures 7.16 and 7.17 are found in the streets of Putina. There is now little question that the uncarved stelae were originally located in or at least very near the sunken courts. Figure 7.18 shows several such stelae at the iconic site of Qaluyu. These were thrown on the surface as debris from looting activities. Our extensive surveys in the region have discovered a number of sunken court sites with uncarved, as well as carved, stelae.

The site referred to as Hu-316, also locally called Machacamarca in the upper Huancané Valley, has a classic notched, undecorated stela (Figs. 7.19–7.21). This is one of the principal Formative and Huaña I period centers with a sunken court and monolith; it is part of the complex that includes several domestic habitation sites below the sunken court area. The site covers most of the east side of Cerro Machacamarca with artificial terraces. The court is trapezoidal with a "key-shaped" entrance. It is impossible to precisely measure the court, but it is about 17 m on a side with some variation for the trapezoidal effect. An uncarved stela is found in the center of the court, apparently very close to its original location. The sandstone monolith is 2.30 m long, and

Figure 7.4. Slightly decorated sandstone statue on the northern side of Taraco, Peru.

Figure 7.5. The Cornejo stela found at site TA-1039.

Figure 7.6. A fragment of a statue with a frog motif found in the municipal museum in Taraco.

Figure 7.7. A carved statue fragment dredged from the river Ramis at Taraco.

Figure 7.8. A possible tenon or standing statue fragment from the site TA-1057.

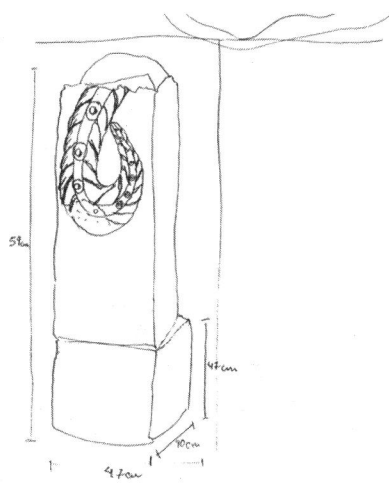

Figure 7.9. A field drawing of the opposite side of the statue in Figure 7.8. Drawing by Adán Umire.

Figure 7.10. Two limestone monoliths on the surface of site AR-1245.

Figure 7.11. The smaller of two statues on AR-1245.

Figure 7.12. The larger of two statues on AR-1245.

Figure 7.13. Broken upright statue at the site of Huancanewichinka near Huancané. The statue appears to be in its original location.

Figure 7.14. Uncarved statue in the streets of modern Taraco, Peru.

Figure 7.15. Uncarved statue in the streets of modern Taraco, Peru.

Figure 7.16. Uncarved statue in the streets of modern Putina, Peru.

Figure 7.17. Uncarved statue in the streets of modern Putina, Peru.

Figure 7.18. The site of Qaluyu with numerous carved stones on the surface.

Figure 7.19. The sunken court at the site of Machacamarca in the upper Huancané Valley.

Figure 7.20. A notched, sandstone statue at Machacamarca. The notch is adjacent to the arrow scale in the photograph.

Figure 7.21. Close-up of a notched, sandstone statue at Machacamarca.

Figure 7.22. Uncarved statue in Taraco (site TA-725).

about 35 cm wide. We cannot measure the third side because it is buried. Virtually all the pottery on the surface in the sunken court area is Formative and Huaña I period in date. It is therefore likely that the court was built in the Formative with associated occupations on the sides and below the hill.

Machacamarca is typical of dozens of sites in the northern Titicaca Basin. Uncarved stelae are found throughout the area, usually associated with sunken courts and almost always in association with Formative period pottery. The stelae found at the sites of TA-725 (Fig. 7.22), AR-626 (Figs. 7.23–7.25), Hu-521 (Fig. 7.26), Hu-291 (Fig. 7.27) and Hu-220 (Fig. 7.28) are typical of this pattern as well. The statue at Hu-291 is made of limestone and appears to be less worked than those made of sandstone. It is similar in style and appearance to those in AR-1245. Even more emblematic of these kinds of limestone statues are those such as the one seen in Figure 7.29 from the site of AR-1249. This 2-m-long piece appears to be largely a natural fracture, with some obvious shaping on one end and a protuberance at the base reminiscent of other carved statues. The most spectacular in size is the giant limestone found at AR-1385 (Figs. 7.30, 7.31). At over 6 m high, this piece was decorated with small, carved depressions. It is found alone, in a field next to the modern and ancient road. There is evidence of shaping of the limestone to achieve a statue-like effect but nothing like this has been reported in the literature in this area. It is most likely that the piece was set upright in the pampa, but the precise site with which it was affiliated is unknown. Not surprisingly, the piece is called "balsarumi" or "stone balsa," balsa referring to the reed boats that are used on the lake.

*Carved Architectural Slabs*

One of the sunken courts at the iconic site of Pucara is shown in Figure 7.32. The sunken court is faced on the interior with large and heavy slabs, almost all of them carved from the relatively soft red sandstone found in the area. One of the niches, as seen in Figure 7.33, is faced with a carved slab creating a stepped pattern. It is likely that many other carved slabs were at the site and have since been removed.

More elaborate slabs have been described in the southern Titicaca Basin for the Chiripa cultures (Chávez and Chávez 1975:49). In the Northern Titicaca Basin Survey, we discovered several bas-relief slabs that almost certainly were used to face sunken courts. The Aguirre stelae, named after the owner of the land on which they were first recorded, are seen in Figures 7.34–7.36. These sandstone stelae are in the pampa, moved from a site where there was most certainly a sunken court. We do not know where that site was, but it is possibly covered by pampa mounds and natural soil accumulations. Both stelae have snakes or other serpent-like creatures that are very similar to one found in the Pucara Museum (Fig. 7.37). Both slabs are around 60 × 60 × 20 cm in size, with variation across all the axes due to the uneven surfaces.

Another badly worn red sandstone decorated slab is found at the intersection of two roads in the pampa, not associated with any nearby archaeological site. Residents of the area call it the Tacca stela. According to informants, it is used today as a marker (*hito*) between two communities (Fig. 7.38). The slab appears to have the characteristic Formative period crossed hands with two crosses below, and a stylized step or lightning bolt motif as

Figure 7.23. The sunken court at AR-626.

Figure 7.24. Uncarved statue at site AR-626.

Figure 7.25. Close-up of uncarved statue in Figure 7.24 at site AR-626.

Figure 7.26. A uncarved limestone statue at site HU-521.

Figure 7.27. Large uncarved statue and other carved stones at site HU-291.

Figure 7.29. Uncarved limestone statue at AR-1249.

Figure 7.28. Uncarved statue at HU-220.

Figure 7.30. A huge, solitary limestone block that was shaped into a statue-like form. This stone had cupules on the surface.

Figure 7.31. Close-up of the huge, solitary limestone block shown in Figure 7.30. This stone had cupules on the surface.

Figure 7.32. One of the great sunken courts at the site of Pucara.

Figure 7.33. Carved slabs in the sunken court at Pucara.

Figure 7.34. The Aguirre 1 carved stone slab from site TA-934.

Figure 7.35. Field drawing of the carved stone slab seen in Figure 7.34. Drawing by Adán Umire.

Figure 7.36. The Aguirre 2 carved stone slab from site TA-934.

Figure 7.37. Carved statue at the Pucara Museum. The view from the top mimics the experience of a viewer on top of an uncovered sunken court.

seen in the drawing by Adán Umire (Fig. 7.39). The size is 48 × 50 × 17 cm.

A pair of opposing felines is seen in a carved decorative slab in the Taraco Museum (Fig. 7.40). These most likely decorated some kind of sunken court or other building. The iconography is decidedly Pucara in style, placing this piece a bit later than the other decorated slabs described above.

Given that these slabs are relatively light and artistically interesting, many have been moved to indoor places, particularly churches, where they were incorporated into Colonial period buildings.

### Uncarved Architectural Slabs

Uncarved slabs were used to line the great sunken courts at Pucara (see Fig. 7.33). They are also found on the surface or incorporated into buildings in Taraco. The slab shown in Figure 7.41 is typical of many andesite slabs found in the town. The Colonial period church that dominates the plaza was built with many sandstone slabs that look very much like those found at Pucara. Figure 7.42 shows a number of red sandstones that are used as steps in the church side entrance. Likewise, site TA-1042 (Fig. 7.43) has stone slabs, near a house, that are used today as a bench.

### Lintels/Building Stones

We assume that the narrow and long carved stones are lintels, as opposed to statues, by their shape. In reality, we have little direct evidence to suggest that they were lintels other than simple analogy to later Inca and Colonial period buildings. It is perfectly possible that they were not lintels at all, but rather were building stones or even monoliths.

A classic and beautiful fine-grained basalt lintel is seen in Figure 7.44 at the site of AR-1023. It is reminiscent of the famous Yaya-Mama stela now found in the Taraco Museum (Fig. 7.45) but without the carving. The lintel from AR-1023 seen in Figures 7.46 and 7.47 is an enigmatic foot impression in an otherwise undecorated piece that is 2.25 × 0.45 × 0.22 m in dimension.

### Carved Portable Stones

As mentioned, one of the few portable stones to be excavated scientifically is that from the Taraco Archaeological Project in the southern Titicaca Basin. Cohen and Roddick report finding a small "lightning stone" (Chávez 1975) in a Late Chiripa (ca. 800–200 BC) context. Several portable or at least small stone carvings were found in the Northern Titicaca Basin Archaeological Survey. A small head found in the north is seen in Figures

Figure 7.38. The Tacca "stela" located near TA-1047.

Figure 7.39. Field drawing of the Tacca stela in Figure 7.38. Drawing by Adán Umire.

Figure 7.40. Slab with opposing felines currently in the Taraco Municipal Museum.

Figure 7.41. Uncarved andesite slab in Taraco.

Figure 7.42. Uncarved red sandstone slabs in the main church in the plaza of Taraco.

Figure 7.43. Large uncarved sandstone slabs at TA-1042.

Figure 7.44. A fine-grained basalt lintel from AR-1023.

Figure 7.45. The Yaya-Mama stela now at the Taraco Municipal Museum.

(*left*) Figure 7.46. The lintel from AR-1023 with foot impression.
(*above*) Figure 7.47. Close-up of the lintel from AR-1023 seen in Figure 7.46.

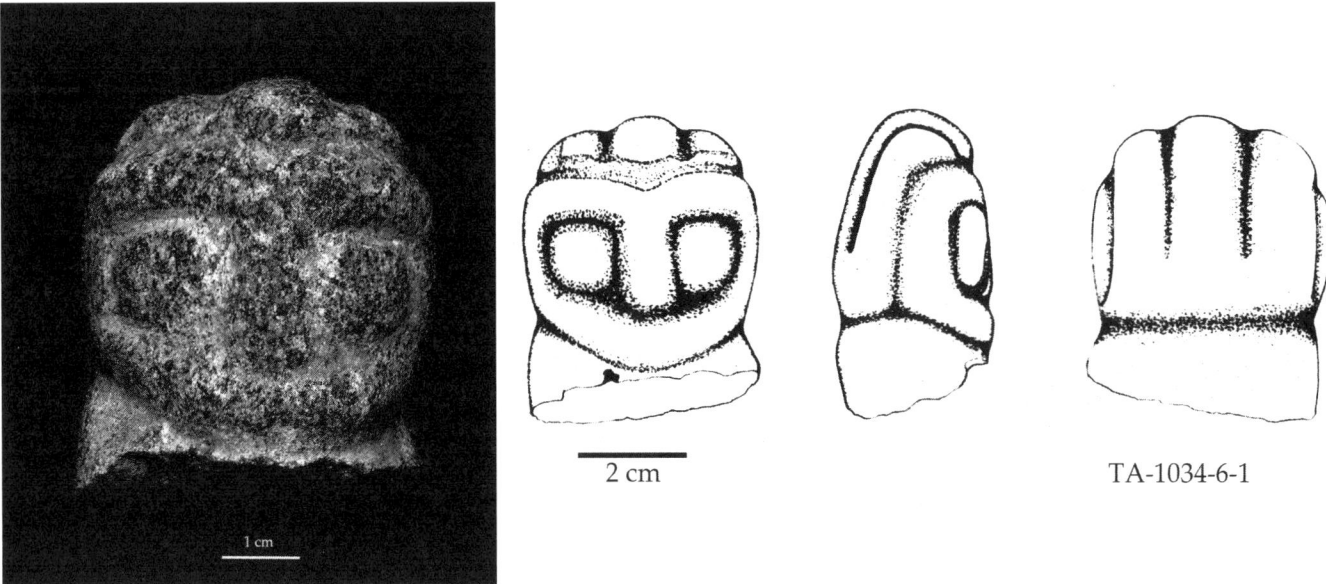

Figure 7.48. Small andesite head from TA-1034.

Figure 7.49. Drawing of the head seen in Figure 7.48. Drawing by Cecilia Chávez.

7.48 and 7.49. Made of a coarse-grained andesite, the head is carved in a classic Formative style and was found at the site of TA-1034. Figure 7.50 likewise depicts a head carved in andesite (from TA-1056) while the head shown in Figure 7.51 (from TA-1042) is carved in limestone.

*Miscellaneous Pieces*

The category of miscellaneous pieces contains stone carvings of unknown function. The massive carved block at Taraco (Fig. 7.52) is a huge piece that is referred to by people today in the region as an "altar." At present, we have no idea of how it functioned. It seems unlikely that the piece has been moved from its original location.

**Conclusion**

Our knowledge, both empirical and theoretical, continues to grow with each passing research season. It is clear that the two traditional centers of complex cultural development—the southern Tiwanaku/Huatta area and the northern Titicaca region that arcs from Huancané across Lake Arapa to Juliaca—also contained the greatest density and diversity of carved stone. Statues, both carved and uncarved, are associated with mounded pampa or hilltop sunken court sites and political centers. It is likely that many of the stone statues and other stone "huacas" throughout the region were captured by victorious political groups and moved to these political centers. Such a fact obviously complicates interpretation on one hand, but creates exciting new challenges for Titicaca Basin archaeology.

Figure 7.50. A carved head from TA-1056.

Figure 7.51. A carved limestone head from TA-1042.

Figure 7.52. A large carved block at TA-725.

# References Cited

Bandy, M. S., and C. A. Hastorf
2007 Introduction. In *Kala Uyuni. An Early Political Center in the Southern Titicaca Basin*, edited by M. Bandy and C. Hastorf, pp. 1–11. Contributions of the Archaeological Research Facility, University of California, Berkeley, no. 64. Berkeley.

Chávez, S.
1975 The Arapa and Thunderbolt stelae: A case of stylistic identity with implications for Pucara influences in the area of Tiahuanaco. *Ñawpa Pacha* 13:3–26.
1981 Notes on some stone sculpture from the northern Lake Titicaca Basin. *Ñawpa Pacha* 19:79–91.
1988 Archaeological reconnaissance in the province of Chumbivilcas, south highland Peru. *Expedition* 30(3):27–38.

Chávez, S. J., and K. L. Mohr Chávez
1970 Newly discovered monoliths from the highlands of Puno, Peru. *Expedition* 12(4):25–39.
1975 A carved stela from Taraco, Puno, Peru and the definition of an early style of stone sculpture from the altiplano of Peru and Bolivia. *Ñawpa Pacha* 13:45–83.

Cohen, A.
2010 Ritual and Architecture in the Titicaca Basin: The Development of the Sunken Court Complex in the Formative Period. PhD dissertation, Department of Anthropology, University of California, Los Angeles.

Cohen, A., and A. Roddick
2007 Excavations in the AC (Achachi Coa Kkollu) sector. In *Kala Uyuni. An Early Political Center in the Southern Titicaca Basin*, edited by M. Bandy and C. Hastorf, pp. 41–65. Contributions of the Archaeological Research Facility, University of California, Berkeley, no. 64. Berkeley.

Kidder II, A.
1943 *Some Early Sites in the Northern Lake Titicaca Basin*. Papers of the Peabody Museum of American Archaeology and Ethnology, Harvard University, vol. 27, no. 1. Cambridge, Massachusetts.

Lémuz Aguirre, C.
2001 Patrones de asentamiento arqueológico en la Península de Santiago de Huata, Bolivia. Licenciatura de Arqueología, Universidad de San Andrés.

Portugal Ortiz, M.
1981 Expansión del estilo escultórico Pa-Ajanu. *Arte y Arqueología* 7:149–59.
1988a Excavaciones arqueológicas en Titimani (II). *Arqueología Boliviana* 3:51–81. Instituto Nacional de Arqueología, La Paz.
1988b Informe de la prospección a Pacajes (Etapa I). *Arqueología Boliviana* 3:109–17.

Stanish, C.
2003 *Ancient Titicaca. The Evolution of Complex Society in Southern Peru and Northern Bolivia*. University of California Press, Berkeley.

Steadman, L.
1995 Excavations at Camata: An Early Ceramic Chronology for the Western Titicaca Basin, Peru. PhD dissertation, Department of Anthropology, University of California, Berkeley.

Tantaleán, H
2008 Ideología y realidad en las primeras sociedades sedentarias (1400 ANE–350 DNE) de la Cuenca Norte del Titicaca, Perú. PhD dissertation, Departamento de Prehistoria, Universidad Autónoma de Barcelona, Spain.

Tantaleán, H., and M. Y. Leyva
2010 De la huanca a la estela: La formación de los asentamientos permanentes tempranos (1400 ANE–350 DNE) de la cuenca norte del Titicaca. *Bulletin de l'Institut Français d'Études Andines* 40(2):1–30.

Valcárcel, L. E.
1925 Informe sobre las exploraciones arqueológicas en Pukara. *Revista Universitaria del Cuzco* XV(48):14–21.
1932 El personaje mítico de Pukara. *Revista del Museo Nacional* 1(1):18–30, 122–23.
1935 Litoesculturas y cerámica de Pukara. *Revista del Museo Nacional* IV(1):25–28.
1938 Los estudios peruanistas en 1937. *Revista del Museo Nacional* 7(1):6–20.

Chapter 8

# Spatial and Temporal Variations in Stone Raw Material Provisioning in the Chivay Obsidian Source Area

*Nicholas Tripcevich and Alex Mackay*

Research into the prehistoric procurement of widely circulated raw materials provides an opportunity to investigate changes in the mechanisms of exchange through time and the impact of regional demand on local provisioning systems. Raw material sources are often exploited to meet both local and regional needs, but parsing the effects of local from regional demand at a lithic source can be complex. By focusing on the relationship between the artifacts found at raw material source workshops and at local sites, archaeologists can gain information about exploitation of the lithic source, as well as local and regional provisioning in prehistory. This chapter focuses on lithic artifacts found in the vicinity of the Chivay obsidian source that lies above the Colca Valley of Arequipa and the documented regional consumption of obsidian from this source in prehispanic times. Comparisons of local obsidian consumption with production at the source indicate that quarrying in the principal obsidian source area was not carried out by local residents for local consumption. This suggests the operation of two distinct procurement and distribution systems: (1) embedded procurement for a down-the-line exchange mode of distribution, disseminating relatively small nodules of Chivay obsidian into local and regional consumption zones, and (2) direct procurement by caravans of large nodules at the source, specifically for regional consumption.

The Chivay obsidian source is located at 4900 m above sea level (masl) on the slopes of two adjacent volcanic vents high above the Colca Valley in southern Peru (Brooks et al. 1997; Burger, Asaro, Salas et al. 1998; Tripcevich 2007, 2010; Tripcevich and Mackay 2011; Tripcevich et al. 2012). The data presented here reveal the operation of both targeted and embedded procurement systems at the Chivay source area (sensu Binford 1979; Gould and Saggers 1985). Data from a workshop at the obsidian source indicate that targeted long-distance procurement of large obsidian nodules for non-local consumption increased during the Terminal Archaic and Early Formative periods. As we discuss below, the regional distribution of Chivay obsidian at this time was at its peak both geographically and in diversity of sites, suggesting that the demand for obsidian was relatively high, and that regional economic integration around the Titicaca Basin had not yet coalesced into a distinctive exchange sphere.

The Chivay/Cotallaulli[1] obsidian was formerly known as the "Titicaca Basin Type" (Burger and Asaro 1977) because proveniencing research begun thirty-five years ago showed that over 90% of the obsidian artifacts analyzed from the Titicaca Basin are of this type (Fig. 8.1). In the mid-1990s, the geological source of this type was finally documented in the Colca Valley and the obsidian type was renamed (Brooks et al. 1997; Burger, Asaro, Salas et al. 1998; Burger et al. 2000). The prevalence of non-local obsidian in the Titicaca Basin is noteworthy when one considers that high-quality cherts are available in much of the region, including the Titicaca Basin, and small and often low-quality[2] nodules of obsidian are available in flows and lag

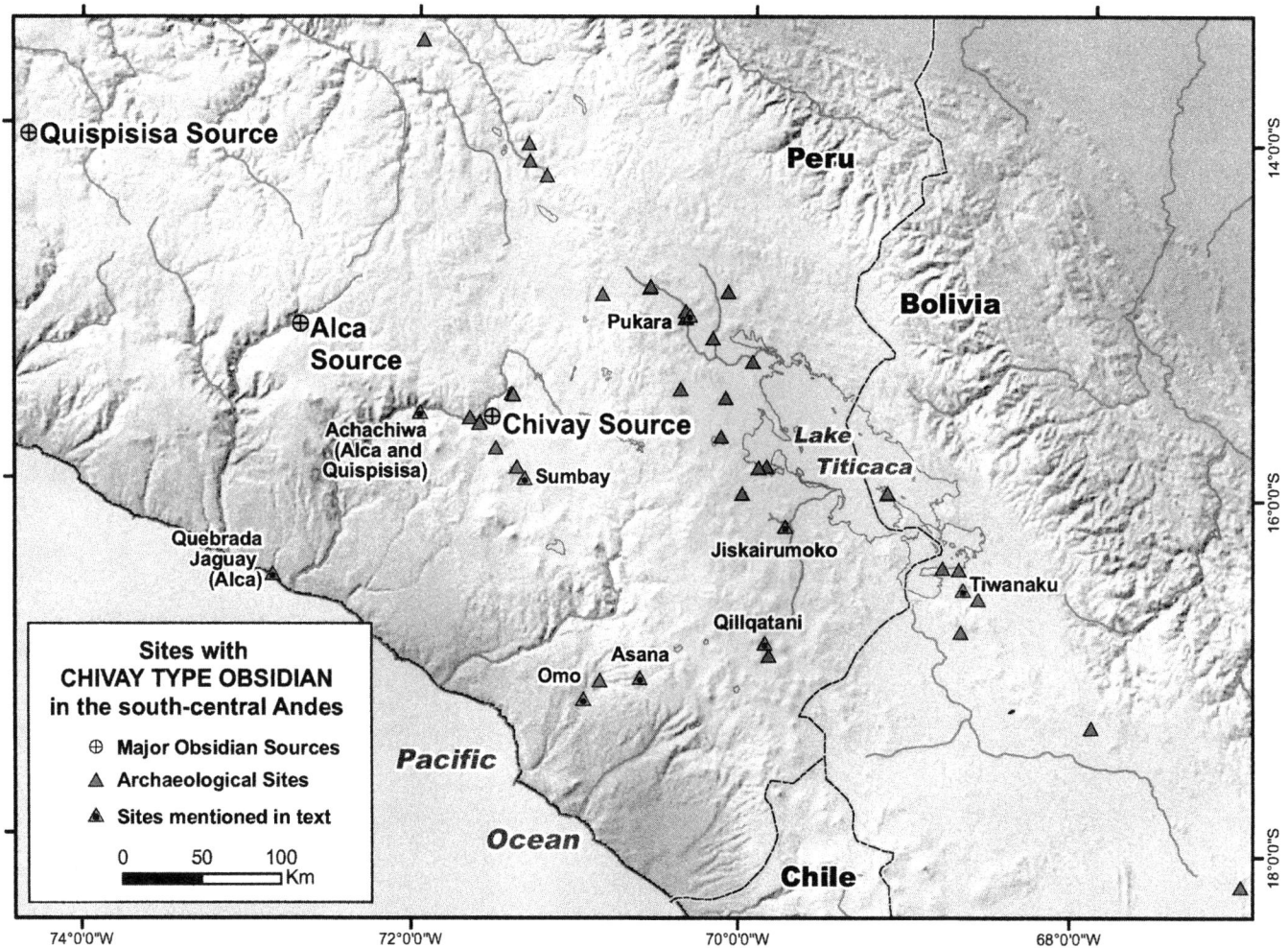

Figure 8.1. Chivay type obsidian in the south-central Andes (from data principally in Burger et al. 2000).

gravels in more easily accessible locations on the slopes of Cerro Hornillo.

The use of Chivay obsidian in the south-central Andes spans a ten-thousand-year time period. As compared with other widely distributed obsidian types in the central Andes, the consumption of Chivay obsidian is almost entirely confined to the high-altitude altiplano of Peru and Bolivia (Fig. 8.2). Obsidian artifacts produced from this source material are known for having the characteristics of a homogeneous and relatively transparent glass (Brooks et al. 1997). As discussed in further detail below, the earliest evidence of human use of the Chivay source area dates to the Early Archaic period (9000–7000 BCE). The obsidian sourcing literature indicates that the distribution of Chivay obsidian increases significantly through time from the Terminal Archaic until the Middle Formative when it reaches its largest geographical extent, and then it occurs exclusively in the areas occupied by Titicaca Basin polities during the Late Formative and Middle Horizon. There is evidence of reduced use in the Late Intermediate period and the Late Horizon (Burger et al. 2000).

Here, we examine the local and regional importance of the Chivay source in three parts. First, we review both the local and regional obsidian distribution data and explore the changing use of the Chivay source area through time by way of the spatial distributions of temporally diagnostic materials. Next, we investigate the role of obsidian within the local economy by comparing obsidian consumption at local sites (less than one-day's travel from the source) with production at a site identified as the probable source workshop. Finally, we discuss what our data reveal about the contexts of regional demand for obsidian that guided production at the source workshop, and the implications of these changes in regional demand for obsidian through time.

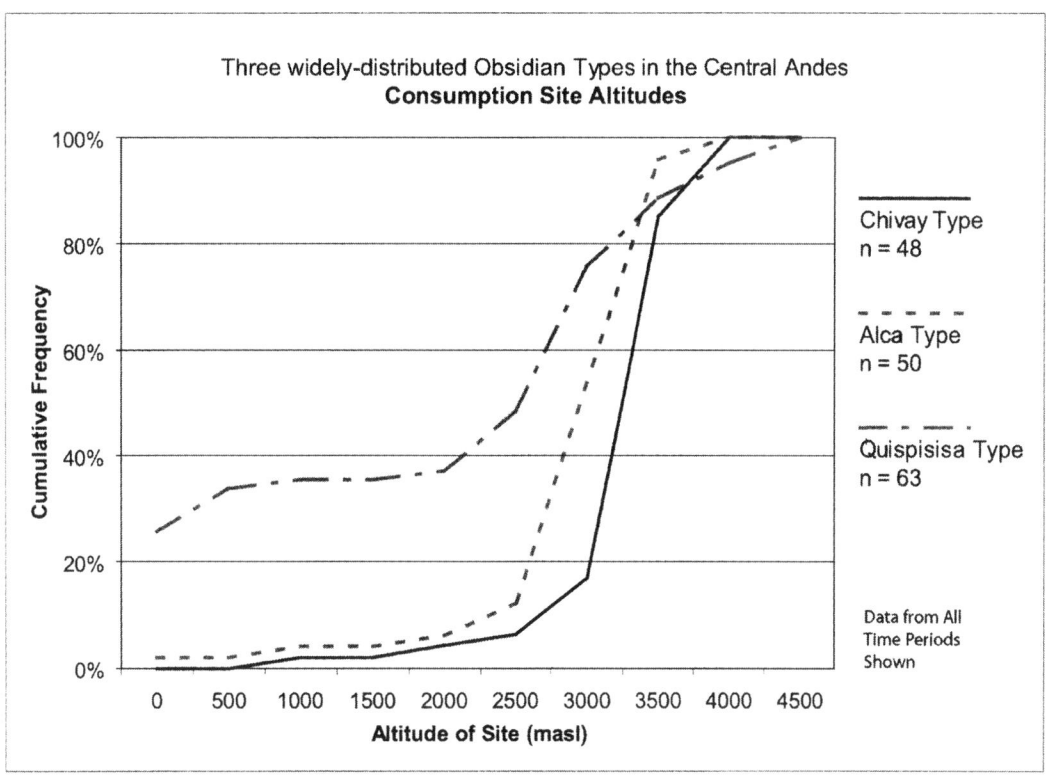

Figure 8.2. Comparison of the consumption site altitudes of three major obsidian types in the Andes (source: Brooks et al. 1997; Burger et al. 2000; Craig 2005; Frye et al. 1998; Stanish et al. 2002).

We discuss the local use of Chivay obsidian in terms of contrasting ecological zones in the Colca area. Agro-pastoral land use patterns that are common in the Andes are apparent in the Colca Valley in both prehispanic and modern subsistence activities (Guillet 1992; Browman 1990). Intensive agriculture in the lower elevation valley grades into a herding economy in the higher altitude puna ecozone, and Colca Valley communities maintain access to products from higher altitude areas either through exchange or by direct access (Casaverde R. 1977; Guillet 1992:133–39; Markowitz 1992:69–76; Shea 1987:81–85). Such systematic local movement created an excellent context for embedded procurement of lithic raw materials in the past. This procurement of obsidian, embedded into local travel between valley and puna, can be contrasted with targeted procurement by regional caravan networks. At least one historically important travel route ("Quebrada Escalera" on Fig. 8.3) passes close to the Chivay obsidian source (Casaverde R. 1977).

For the purposes of field research in 2003 the study region was divided into six blocks, four of which were surveyed intensively (Fig. 8.4), while the more remote Blocks 4 and 5 were inspected on reconnaissance trips. The nature and distribution of resources in the intensive survey blocks are as follow:

**Block 1** is an oval volcanic depression known as "Maymeja" (Fig. 8.3) by the local herders, and it is where the largest and highest quality obsidian nodules are located. In general, Maymeja is a rocky and barren high-altitude environment but it also contains productive *bofedal* grazing land that currently supports a herder and approximately 200 animals for part of the year. Altitude range of survey: 4070–5160 masl.

**Block 2** is a puna environment featuring very large bofedales, and intensive pastoralism. Departing from the Chivay source, this block lies one-day's travel to the southeast, and it is the first grazing area of significant size that could support large herds in the direction of the Lake Titicaca Basin. Altitude range: 4350–4530 masl.

**Blocks 3 and 6** are primarily in the *suni* zones of the upper Colca River valley close to a river confluence that forms a crossroads in the regional transportation system. There is abundant evidence of former agricultural activity in this area, although

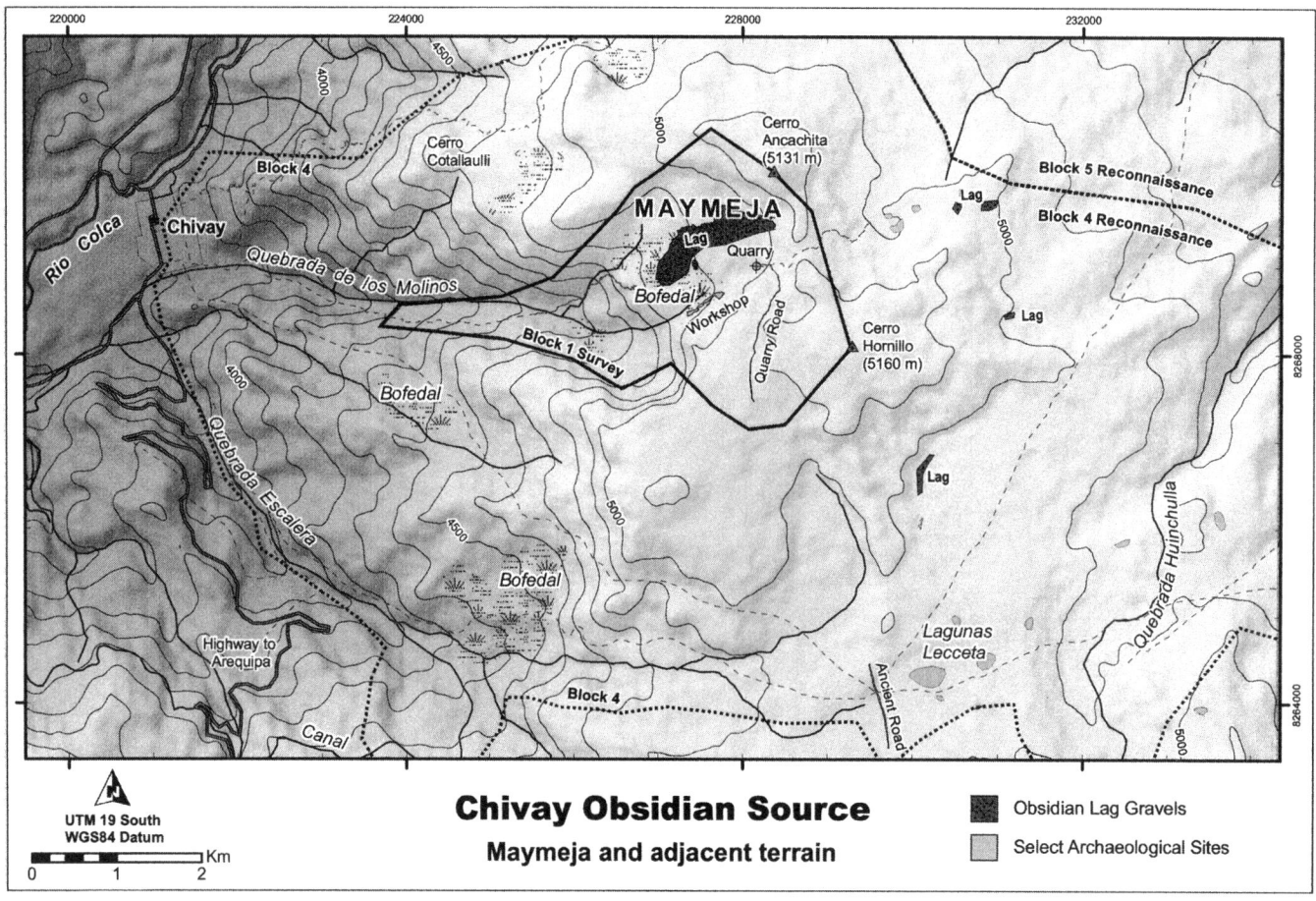

Figure 8.3. Chivay obsidian source showing Maymeja zone and obsidian lag in surrounding terrain.

today the maximum altitude of intensive agricultural activity seems to have shifted another 100 vertical meters down valley to the vicinity of Tuti. Altitude range: 3830–4300 masl.

**Blocks 4 and 5** are extensive zones of lava flows and tephritic soils, with modern pastoral settlements concentrated around water sources. Due to the difficulty of access and the low density of archaeological features in this area, we conducted a prospective rather than a systematic survey in these survey blocks (Banning 2002). Altitude range: 3870–5160 masl.

Our intensive survey areas (Blocks 1, 2, 3, and 6) totaled 33 km² with a surveyor interval of 10–15 m, while in our reconnaissance work (Blocks 4 and 5) we targeted areas that were judged from imagery and maps to have a high likelihood of archaeological sites and geological obsidian exposures. During the course of the project we dug eight 1 × 1 m test units in three of the survey blocks. Using a mobile GIS system based on ESRI Arcpad 6 customized for archaeological feature recording (Tripcevich 2004), 1100 separate archaeological loci were located and mapped during the survey and reconnaissance work.

A quarry pit and a nearby workshop were identified in the course of the survey of the Maymeja area of Block 1, in the obsidian source zone (Fig. 8.3). The quarry pit was found in association with the largest, high-quality obsidian nodules, and was at an altitude of 4950 masl. The quarry pit is now mostly filled in, but remains 2 m deep and 4 m × 5 m across (Fig. 8.5). The quarry is exposed on a ridge and is a difficult place to work. A workshop site was found 600 m downslope in a warmer, sheltered location and close to the only perennial water source in Maymeja as well as to a bofedal. In this discussion of raw material procurement, it is important to note that the quarry pit is not the only source of obsidian in the area. Smaller nodules of variable quality obsidian also occur as marekanites or surface lag gravels (Fig. 8.6) throughout Maymeja as well as just below 5000 masl around the shoulders of the rhyolitic southern dome, Cerro Hornillo. No high-quality obsidian was available in either Block 2 or Block 3, though chert, chalcedony, quartzite and aphanitic, fine-grained volcanic stone (andesite and basalt) did occur locally.

Departing from the quarry was a prehispanic road that is 3–4 m wide and cleared of most rocks (see Fig. 8.3 map). This

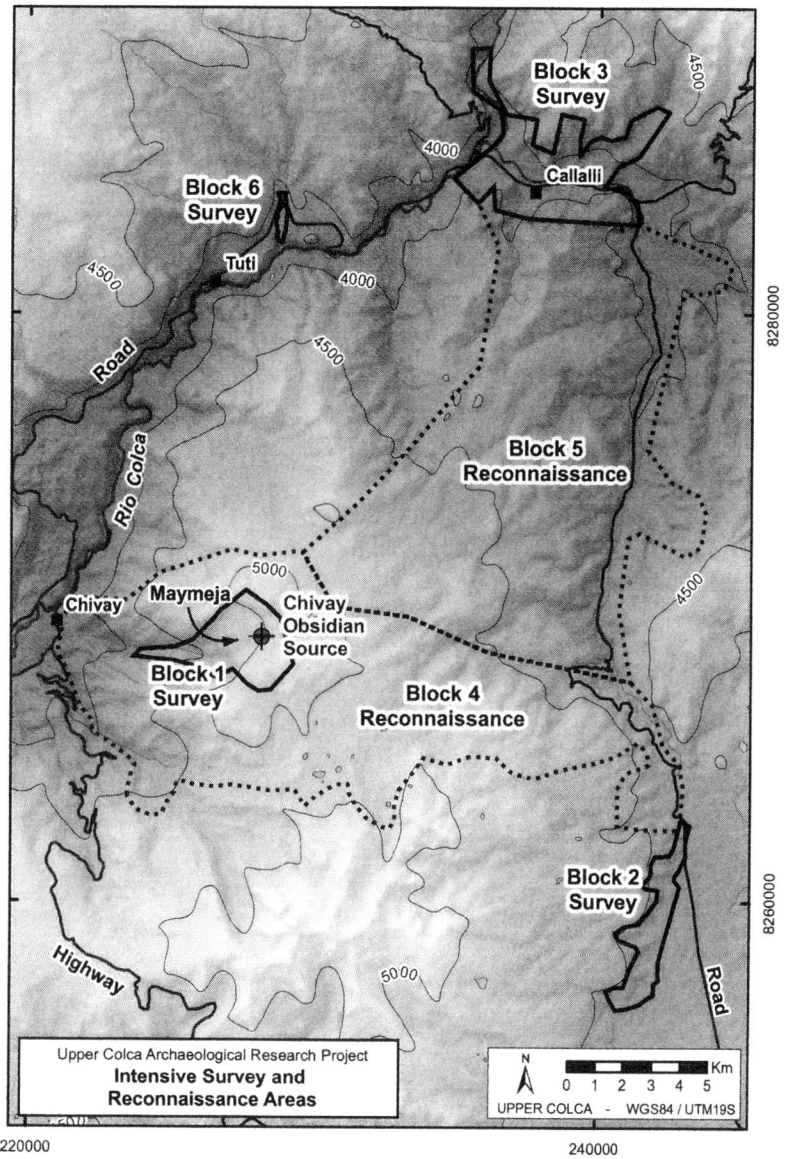

Figure 8.4. Upper Colca Project Area: 2003 intensive survey and reconnaissance blocks.

road departs the Maymeja area toward the south, following the route with the lowest gradient out of the volcanic depression and avoiding difficult talus areas. We were able to follow two sections of this road for a total of 3 km, and it can be described as of the "*Cleared Road type:* . . . systematically cleared of all stones or other debris" (Beck 1991:75–76). At 4 km from the quarry pit this trail joins "Escalera," a major thoroughfare climbing steeply out of the Colca Valley to the puna and off toward the east-south-east (the direction of Lake Titicaca). Today, the route of the modern Chivay-Arequipa highway has shifted traffic to Patapampa and around the south side of Cerro Huarancante and so currently these more ancient travel routes see little use.

## I. Surface Survey: Temporal Distributions Around the Obsidian Source

General patterns in the prehistoric use of the obsidian source region can be explored by examining the spatial distributions of temporally diagnostic archaeological features that we documented in the course of our survey work. Temporal control was difficult to achieve with our surface survey data: the rugged volcanic terrain and infrequent water sources of the Upper Colca Project survey area present few suitable residential locations, leading to a high percentage of reoccupation sites.

We have the benefit of recently published time-sensitive chronologies for both projectile points and pottery styles appli-

Figure 8.5. Test excavations in the debris pile at the Maymeja quarry pit with the workshop and bofedal 600 m downslope on the left side of the photo.

Figure 8.6. Obsidian surface lag gravels or marekanites east of Cerro Hornillo. These deposits are accessible but consisted of smaller nodules with bubbles and ash inclusions, and lacked an adjacent bofedal.

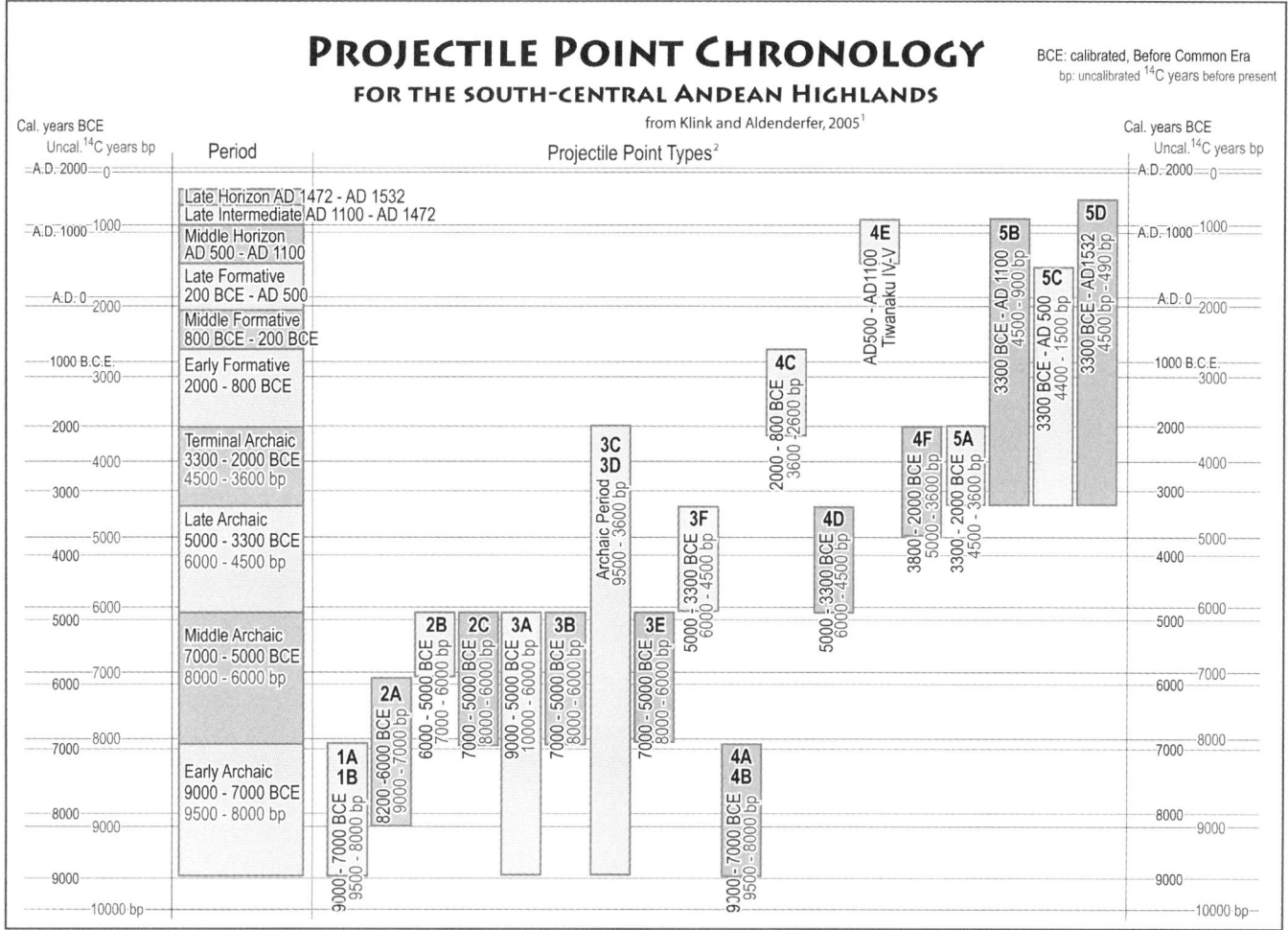

Figure 8.7. Calibrated and uncalibrated temporal charts with projectile point typology data from "Projectile Point Chronology for the South-Central Andean Highlands" (Klink and Aldenderfer 2005; Bronk Ramsey 2003; Stuiver et al. 1998).

cable to the Colca region (Klink and Aldenderfer 2005; Wernke 2003:447–537). The south-central Andean projectile point chronology was published by Klink and Aldenderfer (2005) in the first volume of this book series using uncalibrated Before Present dates. In Figure 8.7 shown here, the uncalibrated date ranges for each projectile point type were calibrated in Oxcal v3.9 (Bronk Ramsey 2003) and the mean was rounded to no more than 100 years to arrive at a general reference for projectile point types against calibrated Before Common Era dates.

The limitations of typological approaches notwithstanding (Mackay 2005), the chronological pattern in our survey data shows relatively steady occupation through the Archaic and then a marked increase in frequency of finds associated with the Terminal Archaic and onward (Fig. 8.8). We found consistent occupation of the Block 2 puna area in all time periods, and relatively few diagnostic artifacts near the Chivay obsidian source as compared with those found in Block 2.

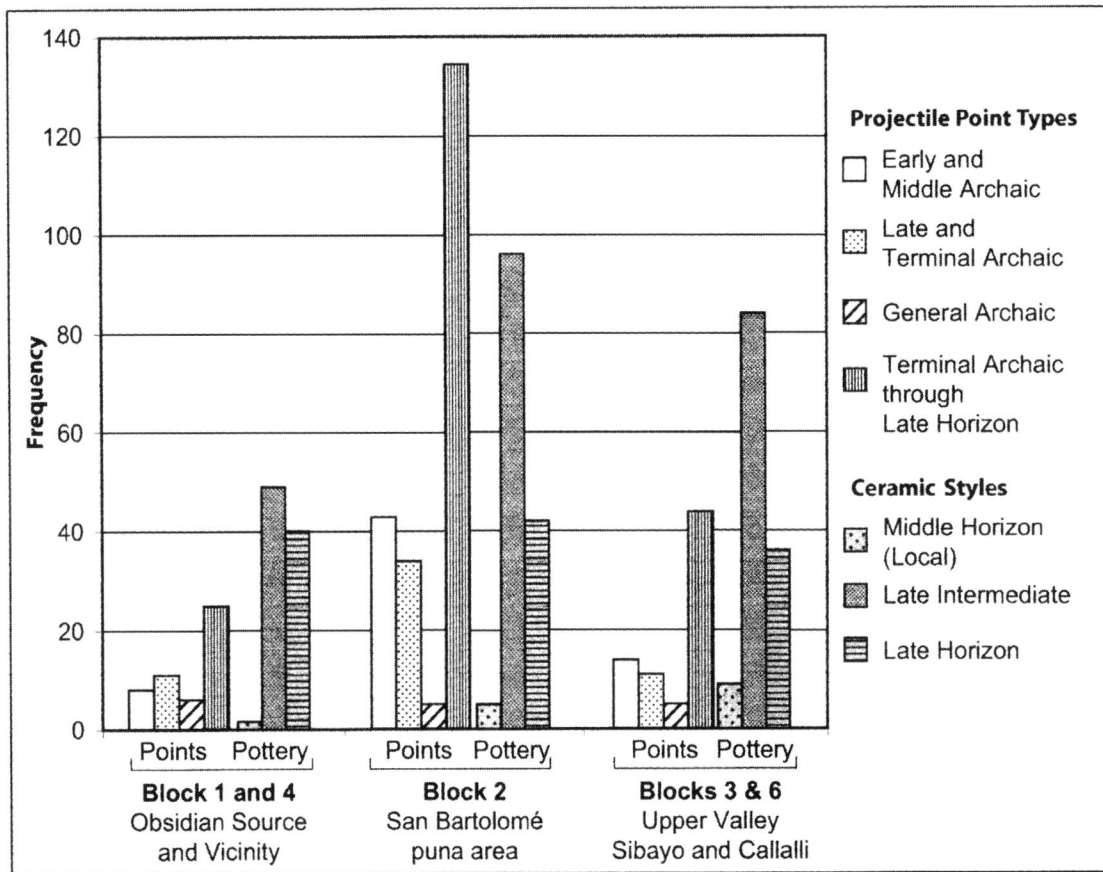

Figure 8.8. Temporally diagnostic artifacts by block from the Upper Colca 2003 survey.

### Early Use of the Chivay Source

*Regional Use during the Early and Middle Archaic*

The earliest documented use of Chivay obsidian falls during the Early Archaic. During this period human groups in the south-central Andes have been characterized as living in small foraging groups with high mobility and relatively egalitarian social structure (Aldenderfer 1989, 1999). Obsidian exchange between neighboring groups may have been in the context of both maintaining access to resources and risk reduction (e.g., Wiessner 1982). From a subsistence perspective, Spielmann (1986:281) describes these as *buffering*, a means of alleviating periodic food shortages by physically accessing them directly in neighboring areas, and *mutualism*, where complementary foods and other goods that are procured or produced are exchanged on a regular basis. Finished obsidian tools may have served as tokens representing mutual access to territory, or as markers of intergroup or interindividual relationships (Brown 1985:223). Another likely context for obsidian distribution in the Archaic period is at periodic aggregations. Seasonal aggregations have been well documented among foragers living in low population densities, where gatherings are the occasion for trade and consumption of surplus food as well as for maintaining social ties and for ceremonial obligations (Birdsell 1970:120; Steward 1938). If analogous gatherings were occurring among foragers in the south-central Andes, it have would created an excellent context for the distribution of a highly visible material like obsidian that was irregularly available in the landscape.

*Evidence from Obsidian Procurement*

In our survey we recovered sixteen Early Archaic type obsidian points in the vicinity of the Chivay source, but all of them were found outside the Maymeja source area, either in the lower reaches of Block 1, or in Block 2 to the east, so there is no Early Archaic evidence from the quarry area itself. At the site of Asana in Moquegua, more than 200 km to the southeast, Aldenderfer (1998:157, 163) recovered Chivay obsidian flakes in levels belonging to the Asana II/Khituña phase, or Early Archaic levels. One flake was found stratigraphically above a $^{14}$C sample dated to 9820 ± 150 BP (Beta-40063) 10,000–8700 cal BCE. Eleven other flakes were found in a level dating to 8720 ± 120 BP (Beta-35599) 8250–7550 cal BCE. At the rockshelter of Qillqatani, obsidian from a still unidentified source was found in levels dating to around 7100 ± 130 BP (Beta-18926) 6230–5720 cal BCE. Chivay obsidian is not found at Qillqatani until approximately 1500 years later. What is interesting about

| Temporal Period<br>Projectile Point Type | Survey Blocks 1 & 4<br>Chivay Source<br>and vicinity (B4) | | Survey Block 2<br>San Bartolomé | | Survey Block 3 & 6<br>Callalli area and<br>Upper Valley (B6) | | Total |
|---|---|---|---|---|---|---|---|
| Middle Horizon<br>Type: 4E | | | Obsidian: | 1 | | | 1 |
| Term. Archaic -<br>Late Horizon<br>Types: Series 5, 5D | Volcanics:<br><br>Obsidian: | 1<br><br>32 | Volcanics:<br>Chalcedony:<br>Chert:<br>Obsidian: | 1<br>1<br>2<br>117 | Obsidian: | 1 | 155 |
| Term. Archaic -<br>Middle Horizon<br>Type: 5B | Obsidian: | 2 | Volcanics:<br>Obsidian: | 1<br>11 | | | 14 |
| Term. Archaic -<br>Late Formative<br>Type: 5C | | | Obsidian: | 1 | | | 1 |
| Archaic Period<br>(general)<br>Type: 3D | Volcanics:<br><br>Obsidian: | 2<br><br>2 | Volcanics:<br>Chert:<br>Obsidian: | 2<br>1<br>2 | Chalcedony:<br>Chert: | 1<br>1 | 11 |
| Terminal Archaic<br>Type: 5A | Obsidian: | 2 | Obsidian: | 2 | Chert: | 1 | 5 |
| Later Late Archaic<br>and Term. Archaic<br>Type: 4F | Obsidian: | 2 | Volcanics:<br>Chalcedony:<br>Obsidian: | 2<br>1<br>7 | Obsidian: | 1 | 13 |
| Late Archaic<br>Types: 3B, 3F, 4D | Volcanics:<br><br><br>Obsidian: | 1<br><br><br>3 | Volcanics:<br>Chalcedony:<br>Chert:<br>Obsidian: | 12<br>1<br>2<br>7 | Volcanics:<br>Chalcedony:<br>Chert:<br>Obsidian: | 1<br>1<br>2<br>1 | 31 |
| Later Middle Archaic<br>Type: 2B | Obsidian: | 1 | | | | | 1 |
| Middle Archaic<br>Types: 2C, 3A,<br>3B, 3E | Volcanics:<br>Chert:<br><br>Obsidian: | 1<br>1<br><br>7 | Volcanics:<br>Chert:<br>Obsidian:<br>Quartzite: | 5<br>3<br>12<br>1 | Volcanics:<br>Chert:<br>Obsidian: | 1<br>2<br>1 | 34 |
| Early - Middle<br>Archaic<br>Type: 2A | | | Obsidian: | 2 | | | 2 |
| Early Archaic<br>Types: 1A, 1B | | | Volcanics:<br>Chalcedony:<br>Chert:<br>Obsidian: | 3<br>1<br>2<br>14 | | | 20 |
| Total | | 57 | | 217 | | 14 | 288 |

Figure 8.9. Diagnostic projectile points by survey block from the Upper Colca 2003 survey.

the use of obsidian at Asana and at Qillqatani is that an obsidian source (the Aconcagua source [Frye et al. 1998]) of material of lower knapping quality is nearby—but that source is used only briefly by pastoralists at Asana, and much later in the sequence. Evidently, the quality of Chivay material was preferred even at these early dates.

Sandweiss et al. (1998:1832) observe that the Chivay source may have been covered by a glacial readvance during the Younger Dryas (ca. 10,800–9800 cal BCE) and they propose that this is why the earliest confirmed site in coastal Peru, Quebrada Jaguay (Fig. 8.1), had obsidian only from the Alca source despite being nearly equidistant from the Chivay source. At the Chivay source, the Maymeja area was perhaps glaciated during the Early Archaic while the eastern and southern flanks of the Cerro Hornillo were exposed, but contained smaller obsidian nodules. The Early Archaic obsidian points recovered from Block 2 (Fig. 8.9) were relatively small (length for 13 complete points = 34.96 mm +/- 6.72 mm) and it appears that the material could have been obtained from lag deposits of smaller obsidian nodules around the east side of Cerro Hornillo (Fig. 8.6) or from secondary deposits in glacial moraines. The earliest points found in the Maymeja source area were three Middle Archaic points, which leaves open the possibility that the Maymeja sector of the Chivay source area was glaciated as late as 7000 BCE.

### Late Archaic and Terminal Archaic Periods

In the Late and Terminal Archaic periods, obsidian continues to be used in flake form, for projectile point production, and occasionally for other bifacial tool types. Although obsidian has many functional applications, especially among pastoralists, it is also visually unusual and may have served as a marker of ethnic affiliation or had symbolic significance in some cases, particularly in zones where it does not occur naturally (Tripcevich 2010:69). In the context of sociopolitical change and early social ranking that begins in the Late and Terminal Archaic, obsidian was perhaps one of a number of materials of limited availability that served as status indicators.

### Regional Use at the End of the Archaic

In the Late Archaic period, obsidian continues to be used as flakes and as bifacially flaked tools, especially projectile points, both locally and regionally. The regional database is somewhat limited for the Late Archaic because many of the samples that are potentially from the Late Archaic contexts described in Burger et al. (2000) are surface collected from multicomponent rockshelter sites. A few samples were gathered from diagnostic Late Archaic projectile point types, providing a stronger temporal affiliation. Interestingly, the obsidian types Tumuku and Chumbivilcas, chemical types with less extensive circulation in the past (the geological sources are still unlocated), are relatively abundant in the Late Archaic.

Chivay obsidian continues to be found throughout the Titicaca Basin but regional evidence indicates that obsidian circulated slightly less during the Late Archaic. This situation is reversed in the Terminal Archaic when Chivay obsidian returns and is found in relative abundance in the south-central Andes.

Buffering and mutualism strategies (described above) likely continued to serve as a means for the exchange of goods between foragers, and these strategies continued to be relevant with early pastoralists. On a subsistence level, hunters benefit from the fracture predictability and the penetration and cutting capacity of obsidian tools. Obsidian has advantages and disadvantages over other available lithic materials like chert or andesite for both hunters and herders performing their subsistence tasks. With the advent of pastoralism around 3500 BCE, obsidian distribution and use expanded significantly in the south-central Andes. These changes are probably the result of some combination of the following phenomena: population growth, increased regional interaction and exchange by pastoralists, the functional properties of obsidian tools for herders, or the social and symbolic value of obsidian in a time of emerging social hierarchy. Among herders, obsidian functions as a practical cutting tool for both shearing wool and butchering (Gilmore 1950:446). The best caravan llamas are castrated males and obsidian or broken bottle glass continue to serve pastoralists as a sharp implement for this procedure because glass or stone remain non-oxidized and are less likely to cause infection than castrating with a metal knife (Timoteo Valdevia, pers. comm., 5 Sept 2003). With expanding herds, the demand for obsidian for all of the above pastoral procedures would have increased during this time. Simultaneously, obsidian was heavily used for series 5 type projectile points. Increased regional interaction from the Terminal Archaic period and onward is further suggested from the wider distribution of projectile point types in this time period. Less pronounced differences in regional projectile point forms has been observed as Type 5B and 5D projectile points were circulated widely within the pastoral zone of highland south-central Andes in the Terminal Archaic and onward (Klink and Aldenderfer 2005:47–53).

In the consumption zone far from the source area, the possession of Chivay obsidian—a visible and often transparent non-local product—may have served as a means of differentiating oneself for the local context or indicating affiliation or trade with distant groups (Tripcevich 2010:69). Exotic materials like gold pendants and non-local sodalite beads are found in the Chivay obsidian consumption zone (Aldenderfer et al. 2008). Such objects, along with obsidian in some cases, belong to a class of artifact used to demarcate commonplace from supernatural referents, or were at least part of a constellation of practices associated with the use of objects that signal status difference.

Further evidence of obsidian from secure contexts is needed to gain a better understanding of how non-local items figured into ritual and ceremonial practices in the Late and Terminal Archaic. Some researchers describing ranked societies have assigned long-distance traders great importance, as Helms (1992:159) argues that "we should consider long-distance travelers or contact agents as political-religious specialists, and include them in the company of shamans, priests, and priestly chiefs and kings as political-ideological experts or 'heroes' who contact cosmically distant realms and obtain politically and ideologically useful materials therefrom." However, in the south-central Andean highlands—where many households own cargo llamas starting perhaps during the Terminal Archaic, and where debt relationships or barter (non-market exchange) is argued to have been widespread in prehistory (Browman 1990; Nuñez and Dillehay [1979] 1995)—the actual kilometers implied by "long-distance" may need adjustment in this discussion. Traversing social boundaries and the risks of travel from changing political configurations probably represented greater obstacles to long-distance exchange than the physical distance across the puna once cargo-bearing camelids were available.

The degree to which this concept of ritual power accruing with distance is applicable in the south-central Andean highland would probably return to the articulation between the economy of exclusive, status-conferring goods and economies of other non-exclusive, reciprocity-based means of circulating goods. For sacredness or exotic power to be conferred through possession of non-local goods like obsidian, those goods cannot be widely available or mutable in economic circles accessible to just anyone (Clark and Blake 1994; Goldstein 2000).

Availability of materials often changed diachronically in the past, be it obsidian in the prehispanic Andes or glass drinking vessels in ancient Rome, and availability is a principal factor in ascribing value to its consumption (Appadurai 1986:38; Smith 1999:113–14). If this was the case in the Colca Valley, we should expect fewer ritual or ceremonial contexts for obsidian in the vicinity of the source area than has been observed in the consumption zone that includes the Titicaca Basin. Obsidian accessibility was linked to technological changes such as camelid domestication, allowing for cargo transport by llamas, and ultimately the emergence of sustained long-distance contact through caravan transport. Obsidian may have become relatively obtainable to everyone in the north Titicaca Basin from the Middle Formative onward as one of a number of items circulating among people sharing common ideological and economic bases.

*Late and Terminal Archaic Evidence from the Chivay Source Area*

In our Chivay source survey work we found that Late Archaic projectile point distributions are notable for the increased use of fine-grained volcanic rocks (andesite and basalt), particularly in the Block 2 puna area. There was perhaps a functional basis for this heavy use of fine-grained volcanics, as 56% of the large and stemmed 4D type points (Klink and Aldenderfer 2005:44–45) in our study are made of fine-grained volcanics while only 10% of the overall projectile points are made from fine-grained volcanics. Furthermore, projectile points made from the volcanics are consistently large and heavy (= 6.3 g +/- 2.88) while projectile points of other material types are much more variable, perhaps because the reduction constraints on volcanics result in larger points. The adoption of obsidian for small point production during the Terminal Archaic could therefore be linked to technological changes like the adoption of bow and arrow (Klink and Aldenderfer 2005:54). Additional support for the introduction of the bow at this time comes from Chinchorro burials in coastal northern Chile dating to circa 3700–1100 cal BCE, or the Terminal Archaic and Early Formative (Bittmann and Munizaga 1979).

The most pronounced temporal pattern observed in the vicinity of the Chivay source is the abundance of obsidian projectile points in the unstemmed, unshouldered triangular forms referred to as series 5 types (Klink and Aldenderfer 2005:47–53). The point chronology is not very time sensitive for these later periods with our data because over 90% of the series 5 points that we recovered were type 5D (Fig. 8.9), spanning the time period from the Terminal Archaic through the Inka period. In the Upper Colca Project area these points are most prevalent in the Block 2 puna area of our survey area where it appears that the points were being manufactured (Fig. 8.4). In the Block 2 area, the 130 projectile points we recovered belonging to series 5 were associated with quantities of advanced stage reduction debris, while in Block 3 the 22 obsidian series 5 points we identified were frequently isolates and, in general, obsidian tools were rarely associated with obsidian chipping debris.

*Ceramic Period Distributions from Survey*

The marked changes that occurred in the south-central Andes in the Formative period (ca. 2000 BCE) are summarized here with respect to lithic provisioning in the Colca Valley. Throughout the Formative and Middle Horizon the regional demand for obsidian is sustained, and then during the Late Intermediate period and Late Horizon the production and circulation of Chivay obsidian appear to diminish. Here we summarize the regional distributions and then discuss the ceramic period use of the Chivay source.

*Regional Context*

Early and Middle Formative distributions were larger in quantity and also geographically more extensive than during earlier times; however, distributions did not expand evenly in every direction. Chivay obsidian use was confined to the highland area (Figs. 8.1, 8.2). By the Early Formative period, distributions of Chivay obsidian have been found in excavations from at least six different sites ranging from the Cuzco Valley to southern Lake Titicaca Basin and the Island of the Sun, and also westward to Qillqatani on the headwaters of the Osmore River (Aldenderfer, in press; Burger et al. 2000:288–89; Shackley 2005; Stanish et al. 2002).

During the Middle and Late Formative, and the Middle Horizon, the relationships between obsidian distributions, stylistic traits, and accelerating political changes in the Lake Titicaca Basin have been explored elsewhere (Burger, Asaro, Salas et al. 1998; Burger et al. 2000). First emerging during the Late Formative period, Titicaca Basin regional centers appear to have commanded increasing influence over regional exchange. Investigations in the Titicaca Basin, including excavated obsidian samples collected predominantly from regional centers (Burger et al. 2000:322–23; Giesso 2003:323), have led investigators to propose that regional exchange with neighboring areas was controlled in some form by the Titicaca Basin centers, though the nature of this regional control is indistinct (Bandy 2005; Stanish 2003:156–64). If ethnography can serve as an example for the developing herder-agriculturalist relationship, modern pastoralists of the western Lake Titicaca Basin have long-standing mutualistic ties with the warm, productive farming areas of the western slope, such as the Colca Valley (Flores Ochoa 1968:129–37). Such accounts show that exchange between such areas was mediated by social ties between communities or individuals, and that even in modern circumstances, the transactions took place in private patios using barter medium where exchange values are typically fixed through tradition (Browman 1990; Nielsen 2001). During the subsequent Middle Horizon, obsidian in the Titicaca Basin continues to originate in the Colca Valley (Burger et al. 2000:324–43; Giesso 2003). Given the well-demonstrated pattern of Tiwanaku exercising control over distant resource areas such as Moquegua and Cochabamba, one might expect Tiwanaku materials in the vicinity of the Chivay source. Instead, we find no Tiwanaku affiliation, but rather Wari influence in the main

Colca Valley. Finally, during the Late Intermediate period and Late Horizon, the circulation of obsidian declined. Despite the evidence for conflict during the Late Intermediate period (Arkush 2005), and the close ethnohistoric ties between the Colla and the Aymara-speaking Collagua ethnic group in the upper Colca Valley (Julien 1983; Lumbreras 1974), demand for Chivay obsidian appears to have declined on a regional scale.

*Ceramic Period Evidence from the Colca*

The Formative through Late Horizon economy activities in the area of the Chivay source and adjacent suni and puna zones were principally devoted to pastoralism that complemented agricultural intensification projects occurring in the main Colca Valley. A principal question about raw material procurement in complex societies is the issue of circumscribed access to resources (Torrence 1984, 1986:98–110). At the Chivay source, we found no evidence of significant walls or major sites along access routes; however, there were natural barriers in the form of steep walls that ring this glaciated volcanic depression and that effectively limit access to the Maymeja area to six entry points. Furthermore, there is no evidence for there ever having been a supply and demand-based market economy in the south-central Andes (La Lone 1982; Stanish 2003:20–21, 69), precluding the commercial profit incentive for monopolizing access.

Our survey data are based largely on distributions of ceramic types. The Formative and Middle Horizon pottery styles for the Colca Valley are still being refined, but the Late Intermediate period (LIP) and Late Horizon (LH) pottery are well documented (Brooks 1998; De la Vera Cruz 1987; Malpass 1987; Wernke 2003). In our 2003 survey work we found sherds from grit-tempered, unslipped, neckless ollas in abundance, particularly in the Block 2 puna area. Despite the frequent use of Chivay obsidian in the Titicaca Basin, ceramics in styles belonging to the Titicaca Basin are few in the Colca Valley prior to the Late Intermediate period. In the course of our survey we located three sherds that resembled Qaluyu and Pukara styles in Block 3; however, sherds of Colla ($n = 26$) and Chucuito-Inka ($n = 8$) styles were identified in the course of our survey. While conducting an extensive survey in the main Colca Valley, Wernke (2003:135–39) located one sherd of diagnostic Pukara design.

During our survey work in 2003, the Middle Horizon evidence was even more enigmatic than the Formative. No Tiwanaku or Wari sherds were found during our survey despite the Colca region having spatial associations with both Middle Horizon states. In the case of the Tiwanaku polity, obsidian from the Chivay source was widely used both in the urban core of Tiwanaku and at affiliated sites throughout the south-central Andes. Colca Valley obsidian accounts for 90% of the obsidian artifacts ($n = 29/32$) that have been analyzed from Tiwanaku's civic-ceremonial area, and microdebitage of obsidian predominates in the fill of a number of ceremonial mounds in the Tiwanaku heartland (Brooks et al. 1997; Giesso 2003:367–70). To date, the only sample of Chivay obsidian collected from a site below 2000 masl is at the Tiwanaku colony of Omo (Goldstein 1989) at 1250 masl in Moquegua (Figs. 8.1, 8.2), and, interestingly, it was mixed in roughly equal portions with all the major Peruvian obsidian types: Alca, Quispisisa, and Andahuaylas A type obsidian (Burger et al. 2000:332, 338). In the Colca Valley, there are Wari-influenced settlements but in the Wari sphere people appear to have not used obsidian from the Chivay source, even when those people were residing in the Colca Valley. Large, Wari-influenced settlements have been identified at Charasuta (Doutriaux 2004:212–23) near Lari about 25 km down valley from the Chivay source, and at the site of Achachiwa (Doutriaux 2004:202–7; Vera Cruz 1987, 1988), 46 km down valley near Cabanaconde (Fig. 8.1). At Achachiwa, a predominantly Middle Horizon site with Wari architectural features, Brooks (1998:447) reports that she collected seven obsidian flakes for analysis and, surprisingly, none of the flakes were of Chivay type obsidian. Six of the flakes were from the Alca source (96 linear km away) and one was from the Quispisisa source (300 linear km away). Regional relationships during the Middle Horizon at the Chivay source are unresolved because no Tiwanaku or Wari ceramics were found at the source, yet the obsidian was being transported to the Titicaca Basin at the same time that the adjacent Colca Valley itself exhibited strong Wari influences, if not outright Wari control. This paradox might illuminate aspects of the relationship of Tiwanaku with its peripheral resource areas, complementing the emphasis on direct control through vertical complementarity that dominated regional research on the Middle Horizon.

Our survey results show that during the Late Intermediate period and Late Horizon, the Block 1 terrain around the obsidian source reflects a relatively high density of use as compared with earlier periods, but the emphasis appears to have been on pastoral grazing opportunities and water control projects rather than on obsidian procurement. The Block 2 puna was intensively occupied in the late prehispanic period, and again the spatial associations of Late Intermediate period and Late Horizon ceramics in Block 2 are predominantly with pastoral activities.

*Summary of Our Survey Evidence*

Our survey data indicate that the area surrounding the Chivay source was integrated into local economic subsistence throughout prehistory. Obsidian procurement was probably embedded in hunting forays into the mountainous terrain of the source area from the earliest human use of the region and through the most recent prehispanic periods. Our evidence from survey and excavation indicates that an emphasis on obsidian procurement, primarily in the form of nodules and blanks, appears to have peaked during the Terminal Archaic, Formative, and Middle Horizon. Procurement through direct access to the Chivay source—either embedded in foraging behavior or associated with caravan travel through intentional quarrying and production—appears to have been a dominant means of Chivay obsidian distribution. A second principal form of distribution is through down-the-line or local, reciprocity-based exchange networks, a process supported by regional evidence of obsidian appearing in diminishing numbers and smaller sizes with distance from the Chivay source. Differentiating these forms of production from obsidian production in the area of the Chivay source is the subject of the remainder of this chapter.

## II. A Comparison of Local Obsidian Consumption and Workshop Production

In the course of our 2003 fieldwork, test units were excavated at sites in each of the three survey blocks. The workshop pit returned Terminal Archaic and Early Formative dates, those from the puna were Late Formative, while those from the valley were Middle Horizon (Fig. 8.10).

Obsidian made up a large part of the stone artifact assemblages throughout the survey region. In Block 2, the puna of San Bartolomé, obsidian artifacts represented over 80% of collected artifacts, while in the Block 3 Callalli area obsidian was 35% of the artifacts (Table 8.1).

In Blocks 2 and 3, the nearest source of obsidian was over 15 km away. Obsidian appears to have served an important role in local raw material consumption, particularly in the pastoralist zone of Block 2 (San Bartolomé). Obsidian was being reduced throughout the survey region, though in Block 3, as mentioned above, obsidian reduction sites are few. The consumption pattern in Block 3 appears more akin to the distant consumption areas in the Titicaca Basin where obsidian has been found predominantly in the form of retouched tools and, especially, projectile points.

Given the density of obsidian in the local consumption zone, we may ask: Did the Block 2 and Block 3 obsidian come from the Maymeja quarry area, or from the more easily accessible cobbles occurring as surface lag around the east side of the Hornillo vent? This question connects to the issue of attempting to determine who invested the labor in excavating the quarry at Maymeja and reducing obsidian at the nearby workshop. If sufficient chemical variability were present at the Chivay source, then chemical analysis could aid in identifying more precisely the subsource origin of individual obsidian artifacts (Eerkens and Rosenthal 2004). Fourteen geological obsidian samples from throughout the Chivay source area were sent to the Missouri University Research Reactor for analysis and it was confirmed that, unlike the neighboring Alca source, there is little chemical variability at the Chivay obsidian source (M. D. Glascock, pers. comm., 2005; Burger, Asaro, Trawick et al. 1998; Jennings and Glascock 2002). The Chivay obsidian, known for its clarity, is aphyric throughout the source region but the surface lags observed on the east and south-east flanks of Cerro Hornillo had two apparent limitations. First, the nodules were smaller, with nodule sizes not exceeding 15 cm. Second, the material contained inclusions of gas bubbles or ash particles around which crystals would form as the magma was quenched. These inclusions rendered the glass either cloudy or occluded with very small inconsistencies that appeared to impact the visual quality and, in some cases, the fracture mechanics of the glass. Thus we were able to address the issue of subsource provenience by comparing the morphology and visual characteristics of complete obsidian flakes from the Maymeja workshop with those from Block 2 and those from Block 3.

The length and mean thickness of cortical and non-cortical complete flakes are shown in Figure 8.11. Early stage reduction flakes, taken here to be those with more than 20% cortex, made up 5% of all obsidian flakes in Blocks 2 and 3. The presence alone of such flakes indicates that some obsidian cobbles were being transported from the source region and reduced in Blocks 2 and 3. We note that there is a relatively clear distinction between the upper size limits of these early stage reduction flakes from Maymeja, and those appearing in Block 3, and, more strikingly, in Block 2 (Fig. 8.11, dashed line). Cortical flakes over 40 mm in length were common at the source workshop, but no cortical flakes at Block 2 were this length, and few cortical flakes in Block 3 exceeded 40 mm in length. These data do not support the reduction of large cobbles, such as those available in the Maymeja quarry, in the puna (Block 2) and in the upper valley (Block 3).

We can extend this analysis to all complete obsidian flakes, in case initial reduction (and decortication) of larger cobbles was occurring elsewhere with only later processing present in Blocks 2 and 3. With all complete flakes included, we find that these limits on flake size are reinforced, again most markedly in Block 2. Thus, there are no flakes discarded in Blocks 2 or 3 that approach the flake size potential offered by the quarry source, even after initial decortication. We preclude distance decay as an explanation of this pattern for two reasons. First, the early stages of cobble reduction, as represented by cortical flakes, are present on site. Thus, complete or near-complete cobbles were being reduced locally, but the maximum size of flakes attainable from these cobbles had an upper limit (an absolute upper limit in the case of Block 2) of 40 mm, substantially smaller than those produced in Block 1. Second, in our reconnaissance of Blocks 4 and 5, we found that there was a lack of significant intermediary consumption zones between the source and our puna and valley consumption zones.

The second piece of evidence for the use of these more accessible deposits is the visual characteristics of obsidian artifacts. Looking at the spatial distribution of obsidian with and without inclusions across all obsidian artifacts in our collections (primarily flakes) shows that those with inclusions are present in all parts of the survey. Obsidian artifacts containing inclusions are especially prevalent in Block 3, where they make up approximately one-half of the obsidian artifacts (Table 8.2).

These results have implications for comprehending the relationship between the quarried source and the local consumption of obsidian. If large cobbles of obsidian from the Maymeja quarry were being distributed to the region through down-the-line exchange, we would expect pieces from the quarry in the flaked artifacts from adjacent Colca Valley settlements. The data seem to preclude local consumption of the larger obsidian cobbles available in Maymeja. Such nodules appear to have played a minimal role in the local raw material consumption economy. This suggests to us that the extraction at the quarry was being carried out by non-locals specifically for the purposes of export.

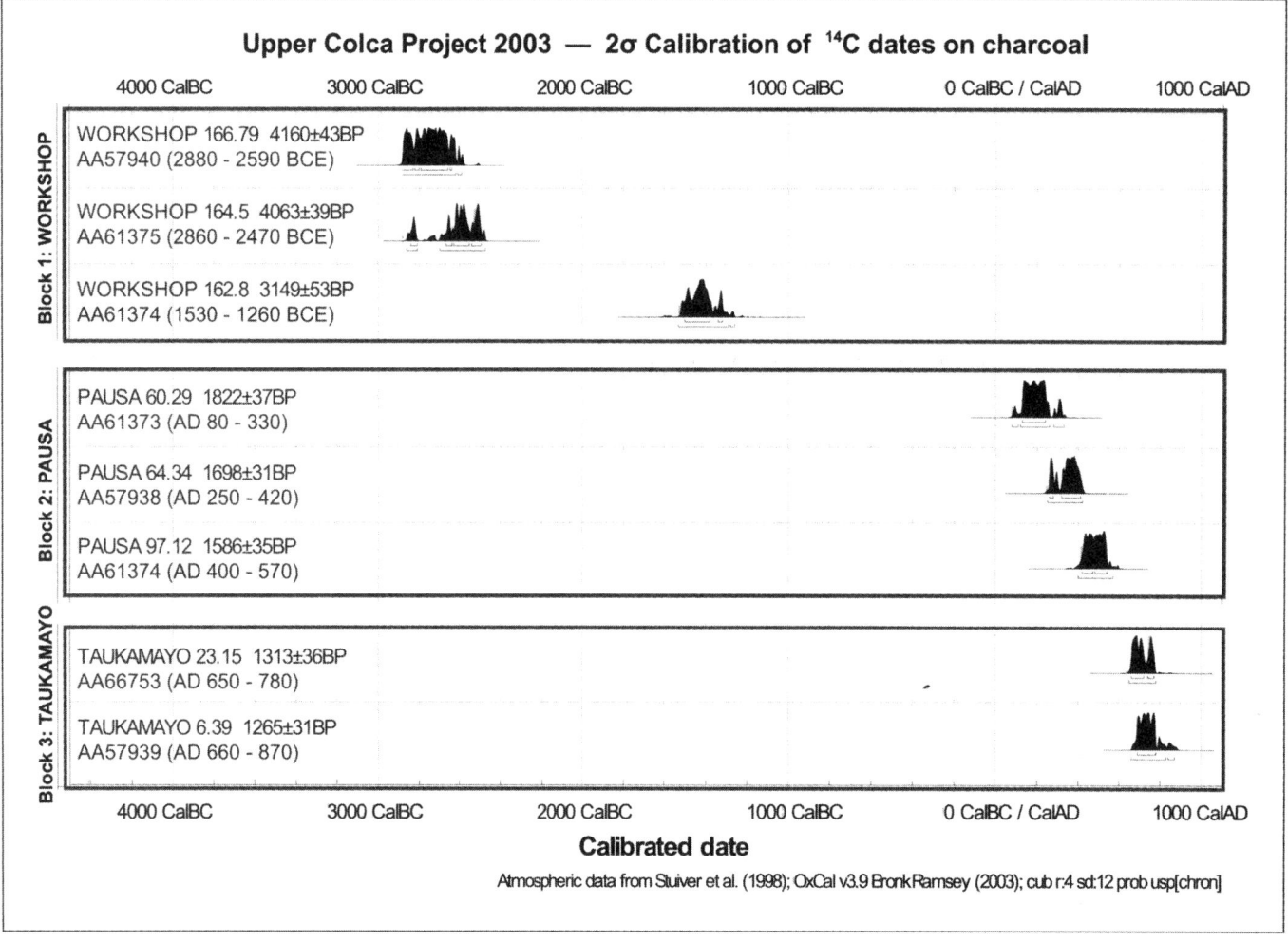

Figure 8.10. Radiocarbon dates from Upper Colca 2003 test excavations.

Table 8.1. Obsidian is prevalent in surface collections from all three survey blocks.

|  | Block 1 | | Block 2 | | Block 3 | |
|---|---|---|---|---|---|---|
|  | number | percent | number | percent | number | percent |
| obsidian | | | | | | |
| unretouched flakes | 4180 | 93.2 | 4810 | 93.8 | 1928 | 95.1 |
| retouched | 172 | 3.8 | 267 | 5.2 | 81 | 4.0 |
| cores | 132 | 2.9 | 52 | 1.0 | 18 | 0.9 |
| total | 4484 | 100.0 | 5129 | 100.0 | 2027 | 100.0 |
| non-obsidian | | | | | | |
| unretouched flakes | 90 | 84.1 | 958 | 86.9 | 3571 | 95.2 |
| retouched | 13 | 12.1 | 91 | 8.3 | 74 | 2.0 |
| cores | 4 | 3.7 | 54 | 4.9 | 105 | 2.8 |
| total | 107 | 100.0 | 1103 | 100.0 | 3750 | 100.0 |
| percentage obsidian | | 97.7 | | 82.3 | | 35.1 |

Table 8.2. Obsidian: clear and with inclusions, by survey block.

| Block | Obsidian Clear | Obsidian Inclusions | Total |
|---|---|---|---|
| 1 | 1922 | 99 | 2021 |
| 2 | 698 | 116 | 814 |
| 3 | 213 | 228 | 441 |
| 4 | 163 | 50 | 213 |
| 5 | 172 | 63 | 235 |
| 6 | 17 | 5 | 22 |
| total | 3185 | 561 | 3746 |

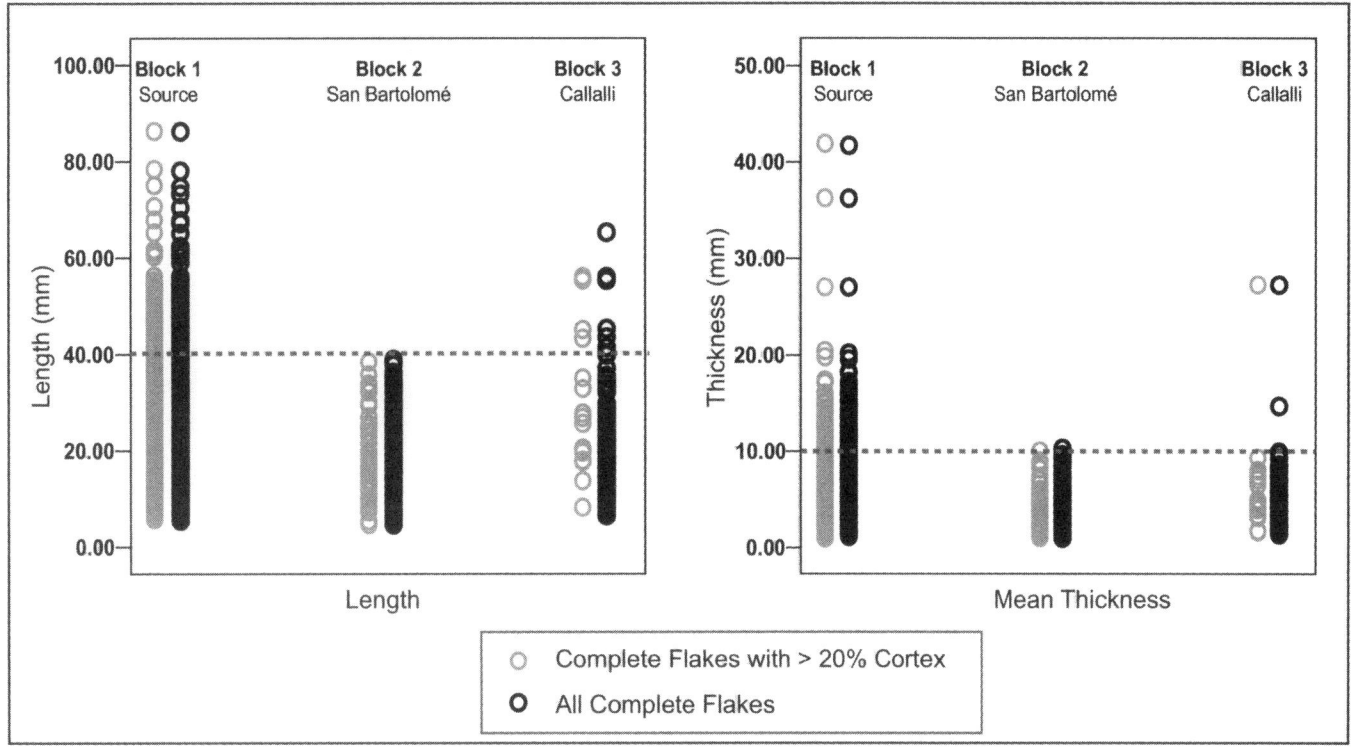

Figure 8.11. Flake metrics for obsidian from the quarry area, and consumption zones (Blocks 2 and 3).

### III. What Were the Contexts of Demand That Guided Production at the Source Workshop through Time?

To explore the contexts of consumption and demand for obsidian, we turn to the excavated data from the Maymeja workshop site (for further details on workshop and quarry stratigraphy see Tripcevich and Mackay 2011 and Tripcevich et al. 2012). At the workshop site (Q02002u3) we excavated a 1 × 1 m test unit to a depth of 70 cm in the center of a low mound of obsidian flaking debris that measured 3 m × 4 m. This test unit was clearly in a production context as it contained 339 cores (all with no positive percussive features) and overall we excavated over 750 kg of cultural material from this unit.

The analysis of a sample of flakes and cores from each level of this test unit revealed three important patterns.

1. *Mode of production*. Broken bifaces and bifacial thinning flakes are a relatively consistent feature of all levels. Combined, they account for about 5% of artifacts examined in each level. This indicates both that non-local consumers were commonly being provisioned with artifacts in biface form, and that this system was relatively consistent through time.

2. *Number of cores per level*. The basal level of the pit, dating to the middle of the Terminal Archaic (Fig. 8.10, Lot 166.79), contains relatively few artifacts in general and few cores specifically, as does the level that supersedes it, level 6 (Fig. 8.12). From level 5 the number of cores increases considerably, reaching a peak in level 4 and subsequently tailing off, albeit in a stochastic fashion. The peak in level 4 is important because it dates to circa 1400 BCE—and is thus contemporaneous with a known peak in Chivay obsidian frequency in at least one non-local consumption site: the rock shelter of Qillqatani (Aldenderfer 2005:22). This gives us reason to believe that this particular workshop site is in fact one source of the Chivay obsidian manufactured for use in distant locations. A second conclusion we can draw from this is that subsequent fluctuations in core prevalence per level may be indicative of changing demand for obsidian in other non-local consumption areas.

3. *Reduction sequence at the workshop test unit*. A notable pattern occurs in level 4 of the workshop test unit (Fig. 8.13) where a peak in core prevalence correlates with an increase in size of early stage reduction flakes. The error-bar figures present size data on flakes with more than 20% cortex from the last 5 levels

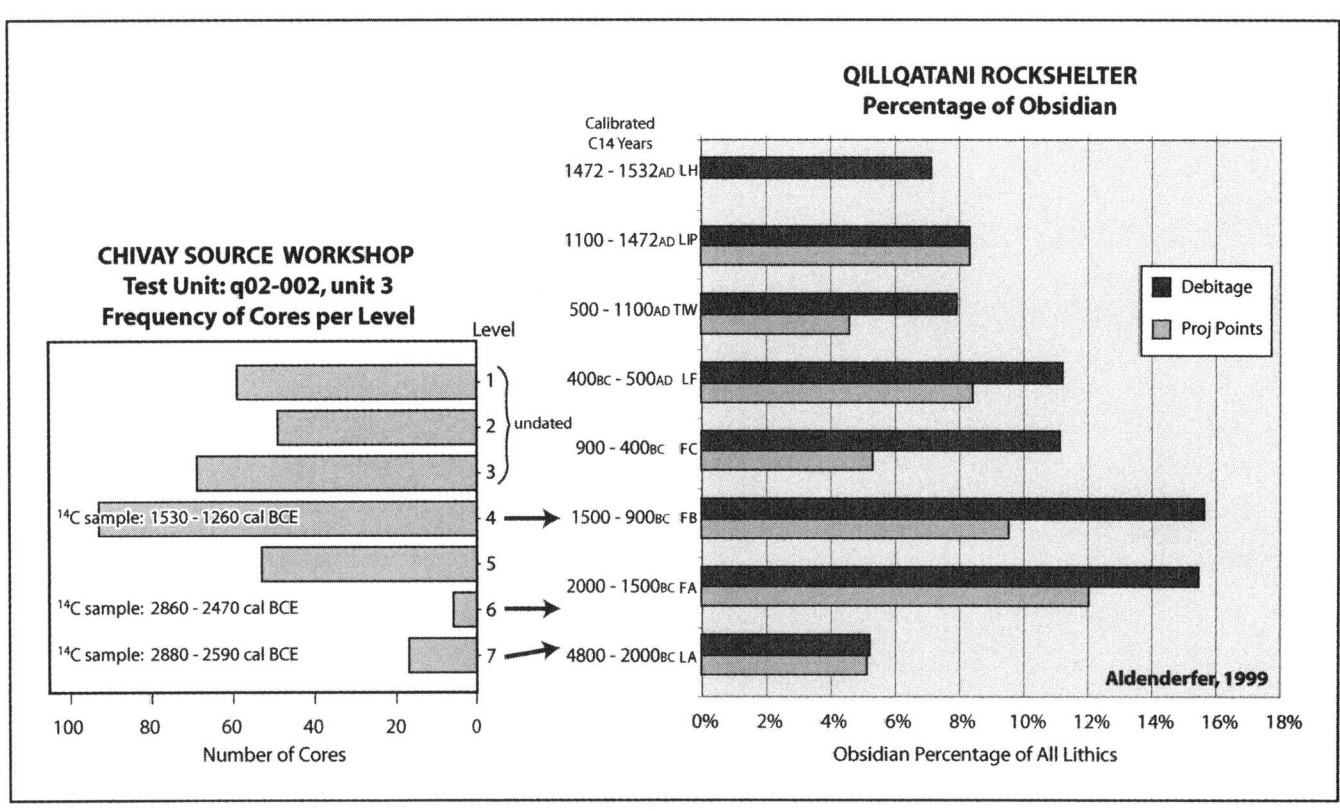

Figure 8.12. Cores from the Chivay source workshop and obsidian artifacts from Qillqatani (Aldenderfer 2005:22; Frye et al. 1998).

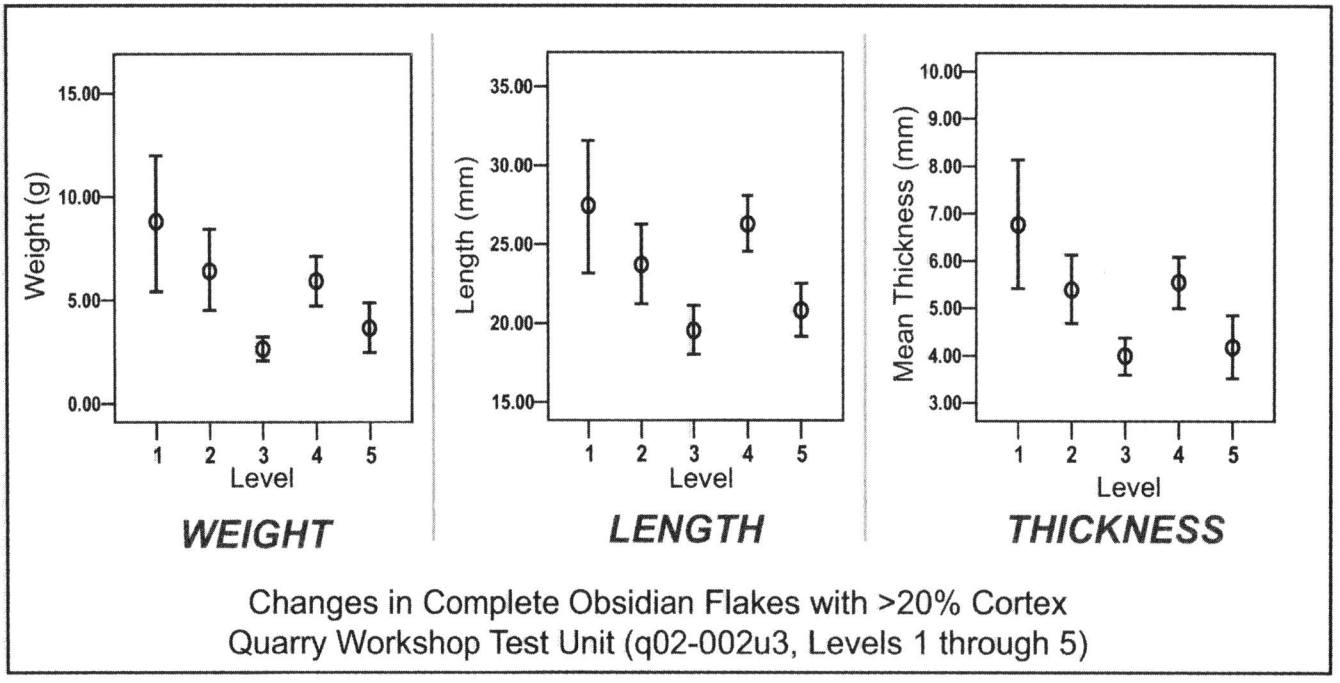

Figure 8.13. The changing morphology of complete obsidian flakes from the workshop test unit.

of the pit. Again, we take such flakes to be a reasonable indicator of initial cobble size. We see clear peaks in the size of early stage reduction flakes in levels 4, 2 and 1. In all instances, early stage reduction flakes from these three levels are significantly larger, statistically speaking, than those in levels 5 and 3. These data indicate that at certain times either demand or quarrying techniques led to the acquisition and reduction of larger cobbles. These interpretations are preliminary as few comparable datasets are available in the consumption zone against which to test our model of local versus regional consumption.

## Discussion and Conclusion

The regional demand for obsidian from Chivay throughout the prehispanic period resulted in distinctive archaeological patterns in both the Chivay source area and the larger consumption zone. Viewed diachronically, geographical changes in Chivay obsidian distributions provide some insight into the development of economic and social linkages across distance in the region. Obsidian use in the area adjacent to the source shows that, through most of preceramic time, obsidian, along with chert and fine-grained volcanic stone, was used for projectile point production and in the form of simple flakes.

### Obsidian Procurement

During the Early and Middle Archaic, during times of high residential mobility and in a context of relative social equality, obsidian procurement and exchange probably took place through direct access by mobile foragers or through down-the-line exchange. Beginning in the Terminal Archaic several changes occur in concert that influenced the production and regional consumption of obsidian at the Chivay source. First, the costs associated with regional exchange were lowered in a formal sense with the availability of cargo animals. The increased circulation of obsidian during the Terminal Archaic and through the Formative period serves as a measurable proxy of an overall reduction in the cost of moving products, from exotic or ceremonial goods, to perishable consumables like coca or *ají* pepper that were perhaps more widely available and more relevant to the non-elite segment of the altiplano population (Browman 1981). Using obsidian as a surrogate for inferring larger exchange patterns in perishable goods introduces its own problems, particularly given that (1) demand for the specific lithic properties of obsidian changed in prehistory, and (2) there were only a few geographical origin places of obsidian relative to the dispersed sources of perishable agricultural goods (Clark 2003:23). A pattern observed by ethnographers in the Andes is for altiplano residents to descend to adjacent agricultural regions in neighboring lowland valleys on the east or west sides to acquire products not available in the highlands (Custred 1974; Lecoq 1987; Nielsen 2001; West 1983), much as the pastoralists of Paratía acquire goods predominantly from the Colca (Flores Ochoa 1968:129–37). In the case of the north Titicaca Basin, a symmetrical relationship existed between herders and sierra agriculturalists in Arequipa. Herders would provide animal products, salt, and other goods circulating on the altiplano and they would acquire corn, peppers and other mid-altitude products in exchange. With obsidian available on a short detour from the Escalera caravan route climbing out of the Colca (Fig. 8.3), a caravan leaving the area with less than the anticipated load of sierra products (due to low crop yields or some other contingency) could recover some of the loss from the journey by transporting obsidian to the pastoral communities where it is widely used. Such an embedded mechanism, as a secondary and reliable Colca product in demand regionally, could account for a substantial proportion of obsidian circulation since caravan transport became established.

### Variability at the Chivay Source

In the course of our research in the environs of the Chivay obsidian source, we established that procurement and production of most obsidian for local use was sufficiently distinct to distinguish it from regional production activities at the obsidian source. Local needs for obsidian appear to have been satisfied with relatively small, easily available nodules. Therefore, material entering down-the-line trade networks from local communities were relatively small pieces of obsidian unless the social distance of exchange systems were sufficiently intimate to reciprocate regional demands for specific characteristics, such as larger, more homogeneous, or visually transparent nodules (Ericson 1984:6; Sahlins 1972:191).

On a practical level, flakes produced from small obsidian nodules easily available on the surface throughout the Chivay source region are probably adequate to meet the majority of requisite tasks (such as shearing and butchering). Relatively small projectile points can also be produced from such nodules. In contrast, a directed effort to obtain large, homogenous nodules was undertaken at the Maymeja quarry area, and the artifactual evidence of this production is not apparent in the local economy. If this quarrying activity were stimulated by down-the-line exchange, we would expect some portion of Blocks 2 and 3 obsidian flakes to exhibit traits of having come from the Maymeja quarry area. Instead, we see evidence that intensified production at the workshop associated with the Maymeja quarry commenced just as evidence for expanded consumption appears in faraway parts of the south-central Andean highlands.

Simultaneously, evidence for the Late and Terminal Archaic beginnings of political dynamism in the Titicaca Basin appears in the form of ritual structures, differential status in burials, precious metals, and other "transegalitarian" traits of incipient social ranking. The benefits of such material to individuals in the Titicaca Basin could be modeled in terms of improved relative social position, or increased reproductive success. The importance of regional interaction in the preceramic can be difficult for archaeologists to appraise because stylistic indicators of interaction are relatively few. We believe that camelid herds were expanding, caravan transport was probably flourishing, and the maintenance of regional social relationships was as relevant as ever to people in the Titicaca Basin. Prior to the sedentism and seed-plant agriculture that characterized early village life at the beginnings of the Formative period, access to semi-exotic obsidian may have visible and symbolic value because it was associated with exchange relationships and alliances between the Titicaca Basin and the western slope of the Andes. Demonstrating and maintaining these regional social relationships through possession of Chivay obsidian may have presented opportunities to aggrandizers in the Titicaca Basin. Our conclusions regarding the influence of obsidian exchange remains tempered with the recognition that in addition to being a remarkable, natural glass, obsidian has basic utility to pastoralists that would guarantee some degree of regional distribution regardless of its social or political significance.

## Notes

1. Brooks et al. (1997) refer to this obsidian source as "Cotallaulli," while Burger, Asaro, Salas et al. (1998) refer to it as "Chivay."

2. We use the term "low-quality" lithic material to refer to what we perceive as poor or unpredictable knapping characteristics caused by the presence of ash or gas inclusions, phenocrysts, microfissures or joints in the stone.

## References Cited

Aldenderfer, Mark S.
1989 The Archaic period in the south-central Andes. *Journal of World Prehistory* 3(2):117–58.
1998 *Montane Foragers: Asana and the South-Central Andean Archaic*. University of Iowa Press, Iowa City.
1999 The Pleistocene/Holocene transition in Peru and its effects upon human use of the landscape. *Quaternary International* 53(4):11–19.
2005 Preludes to power in the highland Late Preceramic period. In *Foundations of Power in the Prehispanic Andes*, edited by Kevin J. Vaughn, Dennis Ogburn, and Christina A. Conlee, pp. 13–35. American Anthropological Association, Arlington, VA.
in press *Winaypach aka markan Jaqipxtwa: Qillqatani and the Evolution of Andean Pastoralism*. University of Arizona Press, Tucson, Arizona.

Aldenderfer, Mark, Nathan M. Craig, R. Jeffrey Speakman, and Rachel Popelka-Filcoff
2008 Four-thousand-year-old gold artifacts from the Lake Titicaca Basin, southern Peru. *Proceedings of the National Academy of Sciences* 105(13):5002–5.

Appadurai, Arjun
1986 Commodities and the politics of value. In *The Social Life of Things: Commodities in Cultural Perspective*, edited by Arjun Appadurai, pp. 3–63. Cambridge University Press, Cambridge.

Arkush, Elizabeth
2005 Colla Fortified Sites: Warfare and Regional Power. PhD dissertation, University of California, Los Angeles.

Bandy, Matthew S.
2001 Population and History in the Ancient Titicaca Basin. PhD dissertation, University of California, Berkeley.
2005 Trade and social power in the Titicaca Basin Formative. In *Foundations of Power in the Prehispanic Andes*, edited by Kevin J. Vaughn, Dennis Ogburn, and Christina A. Conlee, pp. 91–111. American Anthropological Association, Arlington, Virginia.

Banning, E. B.
2002 *Archaeological Survey*. Manuals in Archaeological Method and Theory. Plenum, New York.

Beck, Colleen
1991 Cross-cutting relationships: The relative dating of ancient roads on the north coast of Peru. In *Ancient Road Networks and Settlement Hierarchies in the New World*, edited by Charles D. Trombold, pp. 66–79. Cambridge University Press, Cambridge, England.

Binford, Lewis R.
1979 Organization and formation processes: Looking at curated technologies. *Journal of Anthropological Research* 35(3):255–73.

Birdsell, J. B.
1970 Local group composition among the Australian aborigines: A critique of the evidence from fieldwork conducted since 1930. *Current Anthropology* 11(2):115–42.

Bittmann, B., and J. R. Munizaga
1979 El arco en América: Evidencia temprana y directa. *Indiana* 5:229–51.

Bronk Ramsey, Christopher
2003 Oxcal radiocarbon calibration program, version 3.9. http://www.rlaha.ox.ac.uk/O/oxcal.php.

Brooks, Sarah O.
1998 Prehistoric Agricultural Terraces in the Rio Japo Basin, Colca Valley, Peru. PhD dissertation, University of Wisconsin, Madison.

Brooks, Sarah O., Michael D. Glascock, and Martín Giesso
1997 Source of volcanic glass for ancient Andean tools. *Nature* 376:449–50.

Browman, David L.
1981 New light on Andean Tiwanaku. *American Scientist* 69(4):408–19.
1990 Camelid pastoralism in the Andes: Llama caravan fleteros, and their importance in production and distribution. In *Nomads in a Changing World*, edited by Philip Carl Salzman and John G. Galaty, pp. 395–438. Istituto Universitario Orientale, Naples.

Brown, James A.
1985 Long term trends to sedentism and the emergence of cultural complexity in the American Midwest. In *Prehistoric Hunter-Gatherers: The Emergence of Cultural Complexity*, edited by T. Douglas Price and James Allison Brown, pp. 201–34. Academic Press, Orlando.

Burger, Richard L., and Frank Asaro
1977 *Trace Element Analysis of Obsidian Artifacts from the Andes: New Perspectives on Pre-Hispanic Economic Interaction in Peru and Bolivia LBL6343*. Lawrence Berkeley Laboratory, University of California.

Burger, Richard L., Frank Asaro, Guido Salas, and Fred Stross
1998 The Chivay obsidian source and the geological origin of Titicaca Basin type obsidian artifacts. *Andean Past* 5:203–23.

Burger, Richard L., Frank Asaro, Paul Trawick, and Fred Stross
1998 The Alca obsidian source: The origin of raw material for Cuzco type obsidian artifacts. *Andean Past* 5:185–202.

Burger, Richard L., and Michael D. Glascock
2000 Locating the Quispisisa obsidian source in the Department of Ayacucho, Peru. *Latin American Antiquity* 11(3):258–68.

Burger, Richard L., Karen L. Mohr Chávez, and Sergio J. Chávez
2000 Through the glass darkly: Prehispanic obsidian procurement and exchange in southern Peru and northern Bolivia. *Journal of World Prehistory* 14(3):267–362.

Casaverde R., J.
1977 El trueque en la economía pastoril. In *Pastores de puna: Uywamichiq punarunakuna*, 1st ed., edited by Jorge A. Flores Ochoa, pp. 168–91. Estudios de la sociedad rural, vol. 5. Instituto de Estudios Peruanos, Lima.

Clark, John E.
2003 A review of twentieth-century Mesoamerican obsidian studies. In *Mesoamerican Lithic Technology: Experimentation and Interpretation*, edited by Kenneth G. Hirth, pp. 15–54. University of Utah Press, Salt Lake City.

Clark, John E., and Michael Blake
1994 Power of prestige: Competitive generosity and the emergence of risk in lowland Mesoamerica. In *Factional Competition and Political Development in the New World*, edited by Elizabeth M. Brumfiel and John W. Fox, pp. 17–30. Cambridge University Press, Cambridge, England.

Craig, Nathan M.
2005 The Formation of Early Settled Villages and the Emergence of Leadership: A Test of Three Theoretical Models in the Rio Ilave, Lake Titicaca Basin, Southern Peru. PhD dissertation, University of California, Santa Barbara.

Custred, H. Glynn
1974 Llameros y comercio interregional. In *Reciprocidad e intercambio en los Andes Peruanos*, vol. 10, edited by G. Alberti and E. Mayer. Instituto de Estudio Peruanos, Lima.

De la Vera Cruz, Pablo A.
1987 Cambios en los patrones de asentamiento y el uso y abandono de los andenes en Cabanaconde, Valle del Colca, Perú. In *Pre-Hispanic Agricultural Fields in the Andean Region*, edited by William M. Denevan, Kent Mathewson, and Gregory W. Knapp, pp. 89–128. British Archaeological Reports, International Series, Oxford, U.K.
1988 Estudio Arqueológico en el Valle de Cabanaconde, Arequipa. Bachiller thesis, Universidad Católica Santa María.

Doutriaux, Miriam
2004 Imperial Conquest in a Multiethnic Setting: The Inka Occupation of the Colca Valley, Peru. PhD dissertation, University of California, Berkeley.

Eerkens, Jelmer W., and J. S. Rosenthal
2004 Are obsidian subsources meaningful units of analysis?; Temporal and spatial patterning of subsources in the Coso volcanic field, southeastern California. *Journal of Archaeological Science* 31(1):21–29.

Ericson, Jon E.
1984 Towards the analysis of lithic production systems. In *Prehistoric Quarries and Lithic Production*, edited by Jonathon E. Ericson and Barbara A. Purdy, pp. 1–10. Cambridge University Press, Cambridge, England.

Flores Ochoa, Jorge A.
1968 *Los pastores de Paratía: Una introduccíon a su estudio*, 1st ed. Instituto Indigenista Interamericano, México.

Frye, Kirk L., Mark Aldenderfer, and Michael D. Glascock
1998 The Aconcahua Obsidian Source and Its Relation to South-Central Andean Exchange Systems. Paper presented at the Institute of Andean Studies conference, Berkeley, CA.

Giesso, Martín
2003 Stone tool production in the Tiwanaku heartland. In *Tiwanaku and Its Hinterland: Archaeology and Paleoecology of an Andean Civilization, Vol. 2*, edited by Alan L. Kolata, pp. 363–83. 2 vols. Smithsonian Institution Press, Washington, D.C.

Gilmore, R. M.
1950 Fauna and ethnozoology of South America. In *Handbook of South American Indians*, edited by Julian H. Steward, pp. 345–464, vol. 6. Smithsonian Institution, Bureau of Ethnology, Washington, D.C.

Goldstein, Paul S.
1989 Tiwanaku occupation of Moquegua. In *Ecology, Settlement, and History in the Osmore Drainage, Peru*, edited by Don Stephen Rice, Charles Stanish, and Phillip R. Scarr, pp. 219–56. British Archaeological Reports, International Series, vol. 545(i), Oxford, U.K.
2000 Exotic goods and everyday chiefs: Long-distance exchange and indigenous sociopolitical development in the south central Andes. *Latin American Antiquity* 11(4):335–61.

Gould, Richard A., and S. Saggers
1985 Lithic procurement in central Australia: A closer look at Binford's idea of embeddedness in archaeology. *American Antiquity* 50(1):117–36.

Guillet, David W.
1992 *Covering Ground: Communal Water Management and the State in the Peruvian Highlands. (Linking Levels of Analysis).* University of Michigan Press, Ann Arbor.

Helms, Mary W.
1992 Long-distance contacts, elite aspirations, and the Age of Discovery in cosmological context. In *Resources, Power, and Interregional Interaction*, edited by Edward M. Schortman and Patricia A. Urban, pp. 157–74. Plenum Press, New York.

Jennings, Justin, and Michael D. Glascock
2002 Description and method of exploitation of the Alca obsidian source, Peru. *Latin American Antiquity* 13(1):107–18.

Julien, Catherine J.
1983 *Hatunqolla: A View of Inca Rule from the Lake Titicaca Region.* University of California Publications in Anthropology, vol. 15. University of California Press, Berkeley.

Klink, Cindy, and Mark S. Aldenderfer
2005 A projectile point chronology for the south-central Andean highlands. In *Advances in Titicaca Basin Archaeology–1*, edited by C. Stanish, A. Cohen, and M. Aldenderfer, pp. 25–54. Cotsen Institute of Archaeology, Los Angeles, California.

La Lone, D. E.
1982 The Inca as a nonmarket economy: Supply on command versus supply and demand. In *Contexts for Prehistoric Exchange*, edited by Jonathon E. Ericson and Timothy K. Earle, pp. 292–316. Academic Press, New York.

Lecoq, Patrice
1987 Caravanes de lamas, sel et échanges dans une communauté de Potosi, en Bolivie. *Bulletin de l'Institut Français d'Etudes Andines* 16(3/4):1–38.

Lumbreras, L. G.
1974 *The Peoples and Cultures of Ancient Peru*, translated by Betty J. Meggers. Smithsonian Institution Press, Washington, D.C.

Mackay, Alex
2005 Informal movements: Changing mobility patterns at Ngarrabullgan, Cape York, Australia. In *Lithics 'Down Under': Australian Perspectives on Lithic Reduction, Use and Classification*, edited by Christopher Clarkson and Laura Lamb. British Archaeological Reports, vol. 1408. Archaeopress, Oxford.

Malpass, Michael
1987 Prehistoric agricultural terracing at Chijra in the Colca Valley, Peru: Preliminary report II. In *Pre-Hispanic Agricultural Fields in the Andean Region*, edited by William M. Denevan, Kent Mathewson, and Gregory W. Knapp, pp. 45–66. British Archaeological Reports, International Series, vol. 359(i), Oxford, U.K.

Markowitz, Lisa B.
1992 Pastoral Production and Its Discontents: Alpaca and Sheep Herding in Caylloma, Peru. PhD dissertation, University of Massachusetts.

Nielsen, Axel E.
2001 Ethnoarchaeological perspectives on caravan trade in the south-central Andes. In *Ethnoarchaeology of Andean South America: Contributions to Archaeological Method and Theory*, edited by L. A. Kuznar, pp. 163–201. Ethnoarchaeological series, vol. 4. International Monographs in Prehistory, Ann Arbor, Michigan.

Nuñez, Lautaro, and Tom D. Dillehay
1995 [1979] *Movilidad giratoria, armonía social y desarrollo en los Andes meridionales: Patrones de tráfico e interacción económica.* Universidad de Chile, Antofagasta.

Sahlins, Marshall
1972 *Stone Age Economics.* Aldine Publishers, New York.

Sandweiss, D. H., H. McInnis, R. L. Burger, A. Cano, B. Ojeda, R. Paredes, M. del Carmen Sandweiss, and M. D. Glascock
1998 Quebrada Jaguay: Early South American maritime adaptation. *Science* 281:1830–32.

Shackley, M. Steven
2005 Source provenance of obsidian artifacts—Jiskairumoko (189), Peru. University of California Berkeley Archaeological XRF Laboratory. *In* The Formation of Early Settled Villages and the Emergence of Leadership: A Test of Three Theoretical Models in the Rio Ilave, Lake Titicaca Basin, Southern Peru, by Nathan M. Craig, pp. 908–16. PhD dissertation, University of California, Santa Barbara.

Shea, D.
1987 Preliminary discussion of prehistoric settlement and terracing at Achoma in the Colca Valley, Peru. In *Pre-Hispanic Agricultural Fields in the Andean Region*, edited by William M. Denevan, Kent Mathewson, and Gregory W. Knapp, pp. 67–88. British Archaeological Reports, International Series, vol. 359(i), Oxford, U.K.

Smith, Monica L.
1999 The role of ordinary goods in premodern exchange. *Journal of Archaeological Method and Theory* 6(2):109–35.

Spielmann, Katherine A.
1986 Interdependence among egalitarian societies. *Journal of Anthropological Archaeology* 5:279–312.

Stanish, Charles
2003 *Ancient Titicaca: The Evolution of Complex Society in Southern Peru and Northern Bolivia.* University of California Press, Berkeley.

Stanish, Charles, Richard L. Burger, Lisa M. Cipolla, Michael D. Glascock, and E. Quelima
2002 Evidence for early long-distance obsidian exchange and watercraft use from the southern Lake Titicaca Basin of Bolivia and Peru. *Latin American Antiquity* 13(4):444–54.

Steward, Julian
1938 *Basin-Plateau Aboriginal Sociopolitical Groups.* U.S. Government Printing Office, Washington, D.C.

Stuiver, M., P. J. Reimer, and T. F. Braziunas
1998  High-precision radiocarbon calibration for terrestrial and marine samples. *Radiocarbon* 40(3):1127–51.

Torrence, Robin
1984  Monopoly or direct access? Industrial organization at the Melos obsidian quarries. In *Prehistoric Quarries and Lithic Production*, edited by Jonathon E. Ericson and Barbara A. Purdy, pp. 49–64. New Directions in Archaeology. Cambridge University Press, Cambridge.
1986  *Production and Exchange of Stone Tools Prehistoric Obsidian in the Aegean*. Cambridge University Press, Cambridge.

Tripcevich, Nicholas
2004  Interfaces: Mobile GIS in archaeological survey. *The SAA Archaeological Record* 4(3):17–22.
2007  Quarries, Caravans, and Routes to Complexity: Prehispanic Obsidian in the South-Central Andes. PhD dissertation, University of California, Santa Barbara.
2010  Exotic goods, Chivay obsidian, and sociopolitical change in the south-central Andes. In *Trade and Exchange: Archaeological Studies from History and Prehistory*, edited by Carolyn Dillian and Carolyn White, pp. 59–73. Springer, New York.

Tripcevich, Nicholas, and Daniel A. Contreras
2011  Quarrying evidence at the Quispisisa obsidian source, Ayacucho, Peru. *Latin American Antiquity* 22(1):121–36.

Tripcevich, Nicholas, J. W. Eerkens, and Tim R. Carpenter
2012  Obsidian hydration at high elevation: Archaic quarrying at the Chivay source, southern Peru. *Journal of Archaeological Science* 39(5):1360–7.

Tripcevich, Nicholas, and Alex Mackay
2011  Procurement at the Chivay obsidian source, Arequipa, Peru. *World Archaeology* 43(2):271–97.

Wernke, Steven
2003  An Archaeo-History of Andean Community and Landscape: The Late Prehispanic and Early Colonial Colca Valley, Peru. PhD dissertation, University of Wisconsin.

West, Terry L.
1983  Suffering we go: A llama caravan in Bolivia. *Llama World* Spring:10–15.

Wiessner, Polly
1982  Risk, reciprocity and social influences on !Kung San economics. In *Politics and History in Band Societies*, edited by E. Leacock and R. B. Lee, pp. 61–84. Cambridge University Press, Cambridge.

# Chapter 9

# Human Skeletal Remains from Taraco, Lake Titicaca, Peru

*Francine Drayer-Verhagen*

This chapter describes the skeletal remains of four individuals recovered from Taraco near Lake Titicaca, Peru, during September 2004. The individuals were interred at the base of a wall that was destroyed around AD 50 (see Stanish and Levine 2011). All of these burials are part of this wall/structure context and are most likely contemporary. They are dated to the Pucara-related occupation at the site.

Burials 1 and 2 are the remains of two children, each approximately four years old at time of death; Burial 2a is an infant (6–9 months); and Burial 3 consists of the almost complete skeleton of a young adult woman (20–24 years). The two four-year-old children were buried next to each other, apparently in the same position and presumably at the same time. Burial 2a was associated with Burial 2, suggesting that these may be secondary burials; however, that hypothesis is rejected because of the careful arrangements of Burials 1 and 2. Burial 3 was separated from the other individuals by a partial wall, making it, at this point, impossible to determine if these burials were part of a single event (Fig. 9.1). However, the evidence suggests that all individuals were interred at roughly the same time.

The skeletons are incomplete, yet the bones that are preserved are in excellent condition and there is no evidence of deterioration, discoloration due to soil chemicals, roots, burning, carnivore and/or rodent gnawing, cut marks or cultural modification. Differential preservation according to age and sex as described by Walker et al. (1988) was not observed.

A brief overview of the methods used for the bioarchaeological analysis is followed by an in-depth description of each individual and a discussion and comparative analysis with other human remains from the Altiplano. The Upper Formative and Late Intermediate collections consist of approximately two hundred individuals and originate from cave tombs located north of the Río Ilave. The Upper Formative skeletons are contemporary with the Taraco burials and are dated to AD 40–128. Cave burials from Quelcatani (dated from 2000 BC to AD 1640) are also used. In addition, data from the literature are used when appropriate. Because of the small number of individuals from Taraco, the comparative analysis is necessarily limited.

### Methods Used for Analysis

*Aging*. For children, dental development (crowns and roots) and eruption stages are used since the calcification and eruption of the teeth follow a fairly predictable curve (Gustafson and Koch 1974; Moorrees et al. 1963; Ubelaker 1989). Fusion stages of the vertebrae may also be helpful (Steele and Bramblett 1988). In addition, long bone measurements may be used to determine

Figure 9.1. Excavation plot showing locations of Burials 1, 2 and 3. Burial 3 is partly exposed and only the cranium is visible in this view. Photo: Javier Chalca.

children's ages (Ubelaker 1989b). For young adults the pubic bone is the preferred method (Brooks and Suchey 1990; Todd 1921a, 1921b), in addition to epiphyseal fusion stages (Lovejoy, Meindl, Pryzbeck, and Mensforth 1985; Greulich and Pyle 1959; Bass 1995; Krogman and Isçan 1986; Isçan et al. 1985).

Compared to the relative ease of aging children and young adults (< 22–24), determining the age at death of adults remains difficult (Aykroyd et al. 1999; Jackes 1992; Roth 1992). Using a combination of age indicators is preferred but this is possible only if the entire or majority of the skeleton is available for analysis (Acsádi and Nemeskéri 1970; Lovejoy, Meindl, Pryzbeck, Barton, Heiple, and Kotting 1985). Dental wear may also be used for aging; however, wear rates are diet and group specific and this method should be used within a group only (Powell 1985; Walker et al. 1991).

*Sex determination.* The os coxae are preferably used for sexing adults (Krogman and Isçan 1986; Phenice 1969), but cranial sexual dimorphic features (nuchal crest, glabella, mastoid process, supraorbital margin and mental eminence) are also widely used. However, these cranial traits work well for some groups but not for others. For instance, my prior research found that only the mastoid process and mental eminence of the Altiplano people conform to the Walker scale (in Buikstra and Ubelaker 1994; Drayer n.d.), which is most probably related to the artificial cranial deformation. Long bone dimensions, such as the diameters of the femoral and humeral heads (Dittrick and Suchey 1986; Reichs 1986), the tibial shaft at the nutrient foramen (Isçan and Miller-Shaivitz 1984), proximal tibia (Holland 1991; Kieser et al. 1992), and distal radius (Allen et al. 1987), also vary between the sexes. As is true for cranial sexual dimorphic traits, these measurements should preferably be compared within a group.

Sexing of children is problematic due to the absence of reliable sex indicators. It is true that the greater sciatic notch of the ilium can already be observed in fetal and infant remains but the large degree of overlap between males and females makes this characteristic rather useless (Boucher 1955; Fazekas and Kosa 1978; Schutkowski 1987; Souri 1959; Weaver 1980). Nevertheless, studies by Holcomb and Konigsberg (1995) revealed that the maximum depth of the notch was located more anteriorly in male fetuses. In addition, promising studies have shown that mandibular shapes also differ between boys and girls. These studies determined sex correctly in 70–90% of children of known sex (Schutkowski 1993). Although both these techniques—the sciatic notch and the mandibular shape—are still somewhat controversial, for lack of better methods I applied these to the two children in this collection.

*Osteometrics*. Postcranial measurements are immensely useful in determining age, sex, stature and activity patterns (Bridges 1989; Krogman and Isçan 1986; Larsen 1997; Trotter and Gleser 1958; Ubelaker 1989; Genovés 1967). The methods and measurements used are those recommended by Buikstra and Ubelaker (1994).

*Odontometrics*. The dentition supplies valuable information on age at death, health, genetic affiliation and diet (Brothwell 1989; Hinton 1981; Miles 1962, 1963, 1978; Smith 1984; Walker et al. 1991). The mesiodistal diameter of the teeth was measured as the maximum distance between the mesial and distal contact points. The buccolingual diameter was taken as the maximum distance between buccal and lingual surfaces of the tooth measured perpendicular to the mesiodistal dimension.

*Health and disease*. All skeletal remains were examined for abnormalities in size and shape, indicative of pathological conditions, such as periosteal lesions, porotic hyperostosis, cribra orbitalia, osteoarthritis, osteomyelitis, trauma and miscellaneous conditions (Ortner and Putschar 1985). These conditions are important indicators of nutritional status, physiological stress, activity patterns, sexual division of labor, and violence.

*Dental health and disease*. Studies show that in contemporary and ancient groups, dental decay increases dramatically with high sugar and/or carbohydrate consumption (Allison 1984; Brothwell 1959; Kelley et al. 1987; Leigh 1937; Milner 1984; Stewart 1931; Turner 1979). For this study I checked for the following dental conditions: carious lesions, abscesses, antemortem tooth loss, congenital absence, enamel hypoplasias and periodontal disease.

*Dental attrition*. The most important cause of dental wear is the coarseness of the diet (Brothwell 1989; Walker et al. 1991). Hunter-gatherers are believed to have had a coarser diet and temporal studies of teeth dating from foraging to agricultural communities show a decrease in wear over time (Patterson 1984). In addition, comparative analysis of occlusal wear patterns of the first mandibular molars has shown that agriculturists had cup-shaped wear patterns and greater wear plane angles while wear patterns of hunter-gatherers were generally flat with a slighter wear plane angle (Smith 1984). Dental wear was recorded by the E. Scott (1979a) method for the molars; the Smith (1984) system was used to score the anterior dentition.

*Artificial cranial deformation*. The practice of intentional remodeling of the cranium is a worldwide phenomenon (Gerszten and Gerszten 1995; Hoshower et al. 1995; Hrdlička 1912) and has been associated with status distinctions (Garrett 1988; Vlahos 1979), sex differences (MacCurdy 1923; Ossenberg 1970), regional or tribal affiliations (Cobo [1653] 1983:197; Hoshower et al. 1995; Shapiro 1928; Stewart 1943; Tello 1928; however, see Sutter and Mertz 2003) and cultural practices (Kroeber 1926; Imbelloni 1950; Stewart and Newman 1950). Attempts to classify deformation types have been unsuccessful and at the present time in Peru, types range from only two main classifications (the tabular-oblique and the circumferential or Aymara type [Anton 1989; Hrdlička 1912, 1914; MacCurdy 1923]) to fourteen types, which result from eleven types of deforming devices (Allison et al. 1981). For purposes of this analysis I used the types as recommended by Buikstra and Ubelaker (1994).

*Cranial nonmetric traits* are minor skeletal variations, such as extra foramena and wormian bones or ossicles within the sutures of the skull (Berry and Berry 1967; Corruccini 1972; Hauser and De Stefano 1989). Some of these traits can be used to reconstruct genetic relationships and may provide information on migration patterns (Bennett 1965; Buikstra et al. 1990; Cheverud 1982; Sjøvold 1984). Nonmetric cranial traits are also affected by the environment. Artificial cranial deformation is an extreme form of environmental stress and changes in nonmetric traits (such as an increase in extrasutural bones) have been reported in deformed crania (Dorscy 1897; Gottlieb 1978; Ossenberg 1970; Pucciarelli 1974). However, Konigsberg et al. (1993) found that artificial cranial deformation cannot affect discrete traits that develop during the fetal period, but that traits in active growth areas such as cranial sutures are indeed affected. The procedures used to score nonmetric traits are those recommended in Buikstra and Ubelaker (1994).

## Description of the Human Remains

### Burial 1 (Age: Approximately 4 Years)

These remains consist of a fragmented cranium, mandible and four cervical vertebrae. All deciduous teeth are present with the exception of the maxillary left central and lateral incisors, which have been lost postmortem. The cranium was positioned on the right side, oriented to the south and facing east (Fig. 9.2). Since the body was absent, its exact position could not be determined.

The superior view of the mandible shows that the chin protrusion is angular, the dental arcade is wide anteriorly, the alveoli of the canines protrude and the gonion areas are everted. Although the use of these characteristics is still controversial, the fact that all sexual dimorphic traits scored male suggests this may be a boy.

Figure 9.2. Burials 1 (*left*) and 2 (*right*). Burial 2a was associated with Burial 2. Photo: Javier Chalca.

Based on dental eruption, crown formation and completion of occipital and vertebral fusion stages, I suggest that this child was approximately four years old at time of death. All deciduous teeth have erupted and, as far as can be determined, the roots are complete. The first permanent mandibular and maxillary molars, which usually erupt between the ages of five and seven, have started to erupt through the alveolar bone. However, there is no degree of union of the lateral parts of the occipital bone, suggesting that this child is younger than four years (Redfield 1970). Union of the neural arches of the vertebrae occurs between the ages of one and three (although this process may be delayed until seven years) and fusion of the vertebral bodies and neural arches between the ages of three and seven (Bass 1995; Steele and Bramblett 1988). The few cervical vertebrae of this child are in variable stages of fusion; for instance, while some neural arches remain unfused, the body of one cervical vertebra has partially united with the arch.

This child has no evidence of cribra orbitalia, periostitis or osteomyelitis but there is some ectocranial pitting near the sagittal suture. Porotic hyperostosis usually presents in the form of pitting and spicules, and expansion of the diploë of the parietal bosses (Stuart-Macadam 1985), but the pitting on this cranium does not resemble that condition. The absence of cribra orbitalia and porotic hyperostosis suggests that this child had an adequate diet and an absence of physiological stress such as diarrhea and parasite infestation.

The cranium is highly fragmented and although some fractures are clearly the result of excavation procedures, the majority of the breaks occurred prior to that event. However, it is not known if the cranium was fractured perimortem and was the cause of death or if postmortem depositional forces were responsible.

Dental health was good and there are no carious lesions, abscesses, antemortem tooth loss, crowding or hypoplasias. The absence of enamel defects confirms that this child's diet was most probably sufficient and that levels of developmental stress and trauma were low, at least during the gestation period and the first year of life. The wear of the teeth (especially of the canines and molars) is substantial for such a young child and it is somewhat more severe than that of the other juvenile, Burial 2. In addition, the wear pattern of this child is asymmetric and the left teeth show more wear than the right.

This child does not have a metopic suture. There are right and left complete supraorbital notches, a left supraorbital foramen and a left infraorbital suture. The only intrasutural bone that was noted is the apical bone but the exact number of wormian bones could not be determined because of the cranium's fragmented condition. Both right and left temporal bones exhibit large tympanic dehiscences. The flexure of the superior sagittal sulcus is to the right and the mandible has one mental foramen. The cranium is deformed and the type of deformation is circumferential (Fig. 9.2). The pitting near the sagittal suture may be related to the deformation.

The absence of the postcranial skeleton is suggestive of a trophy or severed head burial, yet no evidence to support this hypothesis (such as cut marks on the cranium or on the vertebrae) was found. Nonetheless, in view of the longstanding practice of ritual and sacrificial burial practices in the Andes—especially considering the presence of a second child of approximately the same age—this possibility cannot be ruled out (Browne et al. 1993; Chávez 1992; Stanish 2003; Hastorf 2005; Coelho 1972; Drusini and Baraybar 1989; Proulx 1989; Verano 1995).

*Burial 2 (Age: Approximately 4 Years, Possibly Male)*

The second set of remains excavated from this site also belongs to a young child. These remains consist of the cranium and mandible, twenty teeth (visible), five cervical and eleven thoracic vertebrae, manubrium, right and left clavicles and partial scapulae, right and left humeral shafts and right ulna and radial shafts, ulna distal epiphysis, right ilium, four metacarpals and three hand phalanges, the left and right first ribs and fifty-four rib fragments. The legs, sacrum and most of the os coxae are missing.

This child was buried next to Burial 1, apparently in the same position. The distance between the chin of this child and the posterior cranium of Burial 1 was approximately 10 cm (Fig. 9.2). Commingled with these remains were the partial remains of an infant, approximately six to nine months old. Also included were two pottery sherds, two beads and an animal rib.

The shape of the mandible has the typical male characteristics similar to Burial 1 (Schutkowski 1993). In addition, when viewed from the ventral aspect, the sciatic notch describes an angle smaller than 90 degrees, which is characteristic for male ilia. However, more importantly, the position of the maximal depth of the sciatic notch is located more anteriorly (Holcomb and Konigsberg (1995).

Stages of crown formation and dental eruption and vertebral and occipital fusion suggest that this child was also approximately four years old at time of death. All deciduous teeth have erupted, the roots are complete and the first permanent mandibular and maxillary molars are partly visible through the alveolar bone. The lateral parts of the occipital bone are completely unfused and the fusion stages of the cervical vertebrae appear to be similar to those of the other child.

All deciduous teeth are present, except the mandibular left lateral and right central incisors and these have been lost postmortem. Although dental wear is substantial, it is not as severe as that of the other child. However, the wear is also asymmetric and the left teeth are more worn than are the right.

This child has severe periostitis of the endocranial surface of the greater wing of the sphenoid bone, and the exterior surface of the occipital bone exhibits some pitting near the lambdoid suture. The cranium is disarticulated due to non-fusion of the cranial sutures and several bones have been fractured (for instance, the mandible, parietal and frontal bones). Some of these fractures appear to be the result of excavation procedures but it is not known what caused the other fractures.

Dental health was good and there are no carious lesions, abscesses or antemortem tooth loss. As is true for the other child, the absence of enamel defects suggests adequate nutrition and low levels of physiological stress and trauma during gestation and the first year of life.

This individual has a complete metopic suture, which remains fully unfused. The right supraorbital notch is present but the supraorbital foramen is absent. There are right and left infraorbital sutures but no foramena. The left temporal bone has a small tympanic dehiscence and the mandible has one right and one left mental foramen.

The cranium of this child has been remodeled to a remarkable degree and the deformation is much more severe than that of the other individuals (Figs. 9.2, 9.7). The frontal, parietal and occipital bones are extremely elongated, resulting in the long, loaf-like Aymaran type of deformation. It is possible that the pitting and periostitis of the sphenoid and the occipital bone are associated with the deformational forces and are related to this child's demise.

*Burial 2a (Age: 6–9 Months)*

This burial was associated with Burial 2. The skeleton is very incomplete and consists only of the squamous and basilar parts of the occipital bone, six vertebral bodies, the proximal epiphysis of the left humerus and the right deciduous upper central incisor. The occipital bone is fractured and this appears to have occurred prior to excavation. Completion of the incisor root suggests that this infant was approximately six to nine months old at time of death. The occipital bone shows evidence of artificial deformation.

Very little can be concluded from these remains. The commingling of this individual with Burial 2 suggests that these remains may be secondary interments; however, as mentioned above, the careful arrangements of Burials 1 and 2 are typical of primary burials. I also reject the possibility that this infant's skeleton has deteriorated (see Walker et al. 1988) because of the excellent preservation of the few bones that are present. I suggest that it is more likely that most of this infant was removed during construction, reconstruction or destruction of the building, which would also explain the absence of the postcranial skeleton of Burial 1, the lower limbs of Burial 2 and parts of Burial 3.

*Burial 3 (Age: 20–24 Years, Probably Female)*

These are the well-preserved, fairly complete remains of a young adult. The burial consists of the cranium, mandible, vertebrae (with the exception of one thoracic and one lumbar vertebra), ribs, sternum, right and left clavicles, the right and left humeri, radii and ulnae, right ilium, the right femur, tibia and fibula, three left and four right carpals, ten metacarpals and thirteen phalanges, the right talus and calcaneous and five foot phalanges. Notably absent are the entire left and most of the right os coxae and the left leg and foot bones, suggesting that part of the skeleton was removed during prehistory. This person was buried in a flexed position, lying on the back but leaning slightly to the right, and the head was bent forward with the chin resting on the chest (Fig. 9.3). The orientation of the cranium was to the northeast.

Pelvic sex was ambiguous since only the greater sciatic notch and the preauricular sulcus of the ilium could be evaluated and these scored 3 on the Walker scale (Milner 1992 in Buikstra and Ubelaker 1994). In addition, the pubic bone could not be examined for postpartum scarring.

However, based on a combination of sexual dimorphic cranial traits, discriminate function analyses of the cranium and tibia, and average long bone measurements, I suggest that this individual is most probably a female. All sexual dimorphic cranial traits scored 2 (on the Walker scale; see Buikstra and Ubelaker 1994). As mentioned previously, my research has shown that most sexual dimorphic cranial traits do not work for the Altiplano people, probably because of cranial deformational forces. However, the mastoid process (a reliable sex indicator and usually not affected by cranial deformation) of this individual is rather feminine.

Discriminant function analysis of cranial and tibial measurements also suggests that this is a female (Howells 1969a, 1969b, 1973; Isçan and Miller-Shaivitz 1984). In addition, all long bone dimensions that are preferably used for sexing (such as femoral and humeral heads, calcaneous and maximum and transverse diameters of the tibia at the nutrient foramen) scored feminine when compared with the average dimensions of skeletal remains dating from the Upper Formative and Late Intermediate periods (Drayer n.d.).

The absence of the pubic symphyses of the os coxae prevented observation of age-related changes of the pubis; however, incomplete fusion of the iliac crest and changes of the auricular surface of the os coxae suggest an age of approximately 20–24 years at time of death (Suchey et al. 1984; Lovejoy, Meindl, Pryzbeck, and Mensforth 1985). All epiphyses of the long bones have united but traces of fusion lines are still visible on the proximal humerus, distal ulna and radius and proximal tibia, suggesting an age between 17 and 24 years (Greulich and Pyle 1959; Johnston 1961). The secondary centers of the vertebrae have united but fusion lines are noticeable on all five centers (superior and inferior rings of the centra, tips of the spinous processes and both tips of the transverse processes). These epiphyses fuse between the ages of 17 and 25 years (Bass 1995). In contrast, the medial clavicles, which are usually the last to fuse, have completely united; however, a large range of fusion ages have been recorded for this element (Krogman and Isçan 1986; Mensforth and Lovejoy 1985; Webb and Suchey 1985). The ossification phase of the sternal rib end is 2, also suggesting an age of 20.8 to 23.1 years (Isçan et al. 1985), and the basicranial suture, which usually fuses by the age of 26, remains completely unfused. The third molars have erupted (Mincer et al. 1993). Thus, based on a combination of age indicators (epiphyseal union stages, auricular surface and sternal rib end phases and

Figure 9.3. Burial 3. Photo: Javier Chalca.

dental eruption), I suggest that this individual was between 20 and 24 years old at time of death.

The facial indices of this individual are different than those of the Upper Formative and Late Intermediate people (Table 9.1). For instance, the nose is very broad (nasal index is 59.6) (Fig. 9.4) relative to the average nasal indices of the other two groups (47.4 and 49.8, which range from narrow nasal apertures to average or medium). In contrast, the orbits are narrower than the orbits of the Upper Formative and Late Intermediate people. The upper facial index is average or medium for all individuals but it is largest in the Taraco individual. The maxilloalveolar index is 111, indicative of an average or medium palate, in contrast to the other groups who have broad palates that range from 123 for the Late Intermediate to 126 for the Upper Formative people.

Postcranial measurements reveal that this woman was taller and more gracile than the average women of the other groups. Stature was derived from the maximum lengths of the femur and tibia and calculated by the Genovés (1967) method for Mexican females. This person was surprisingly tall (approximately 1.51–1.53 m). Average stature for Upper Formative females was 1.45 m and for Late Intermediate women, 1.43 m (Drayer n.d.).

The morphology and indices of the femur and tibia are similar to those of the Upper Formative and Late Intermediate people, suggesting that this woman was quite active and had the typical locomotion of the other Altiplano people. The platymeric index is 60, very broad and flat, and the neck-shaft angle is low. However, the femoral robustness index is only 10.9, in contrast to an average of 12.0 of the Upper Formative and Late Intermediate women.

The upper incisors are shoveled and this feature scored 2 on the Dahlberg and trace on the Hrdlička scales (Dahlberg 1956 in Turner et al. 1991). The mesiodistal and buccolingual dimensions of the teeth are small, especially when compared to the Late Intermediate teeth. The smaller teeth of this individual are consistent with the average dimensions of the Upper Formative people. The E. Scott (1979a) system was used to determine molar wear (Table 9.2) and the Smith (1984) system for wear of the anterior dentition. Calculations of wear differences between the first molars (eruption age six years) and second molars (eruption age twelve years) resulted in wear differentials of 12 for the mandibular, and 15 for the maxillary molars, suggestive of a very tough, fibrous diet and/or specific food preparation techniques (Table 9.3). Wear differentials are excellent age indicators since teeth erupt at certain ages. The time interval between the eruption of the first and second permanent molars is approximately six years and this means that the wear difference between these teeth was acquired during that time span. On the other hand, if the wear differential were high for only one antimere, mechanical or technological activities such as tool preparation might be responsible (Miles 1963, 1978).

Dental wear of this young adult is obviously much more severe than that of the other groups (Figs. 9.5, 9.6) (Tables 9.2, 9.3). Average wear differentials for the Upper Formative and Late Intermediate people are 4 and 5 respectively for the mandibular molars, and 7 and 8 for the maxillary dentition. The relatively

Table 9.1. Comparison of cranial indices.*

| | Taraco | Upper Formative (200 BC– AD 400) | | Late Intermediate (AD 1300–1450) | |
|---|---|---|---|---|---|
| | | n | mean | n | mean |
| nasal index | 59.6 | 47 | 47.3 | 38 | 49.7 |
| orbital index | 94.7 | 48 | 97.5 | 40 | 96.7 |
| facial index | 52.7 | 36 | 54.3 | 33 | 54.8 |
| cranial length/height index | 72.1 | 29 | 73.4 | 24 | 75.2 |
| cranial breadth/height index | 113.2 | 28 | 104.9 | 23 | 105.2 |
| cranial index | 63.7 | 43 | 71.8 | 39 | 73.1 |
| maxilloalveolar index | 111 | 46 | 126.5 | 32 | 123.1 |

*In Bass 1995

low wear rates, but especially the low wear differentials, during the Upper Formative are not unexpected since these people practiced intense agriculture. However, the Late Intermediate people are believed to have been agro-pastoralists (Stanish 2003; Drayer n.d.; Frye and de la Vega 2005) and although wear differentials during this period are indeed higher, differences between the two groups are small. The first mandibular molars of Burial 3 are slightly cup-shaped, which is typical of agriculturists but occlusal wear plane angles are absent (Hinton 1981; Smith 1984).

This individual appeared to be in good health and there is no evidence of cribra orbitalia, porotic hyperostosis, cranial trauma, nasal and/or parry fractures. However, the proximal end of the right fibula has a small bone spur, which may be the result of a muscle injury. More importantly, this person had sustained an injury to the seventh rib. The fracture is complete and no union had occurred at time of death. There is no evidence of a cloaca but the rib ends near the fracture are covered with thick layers of periostitis, suggesting that the injury was active at time of death and may have been of longstanding nature (8 weeks or longer). A wound to the chest to this degree may have resulted in a systemic infection; however, generalized periosteal lesions suggestive of septicemia or staphylococcus are absent.

There is no evidence of arthritis and this may simply be because of the young age and absence of additional trauma. Nonetheless, any kind of repetitive or strenuous activity would have left some osseous evidence, such as lipping. In contrast, severe arthritis of both right and left elbows was very common in the women of the Upper Formative period.

Dental health was good and there are no carious lesions, abscesses, pulp exposures, antemortem tooth loss, calculus or periodontal disease. However, the mandibular left third molar has a hypoplastic defect, suggesting that this person suffered from acute trauma or disease between the ages of nine and twelve years. The crowding near the upper right incisors is caused by the retention of the deciduous lateral incisor, which has migrated

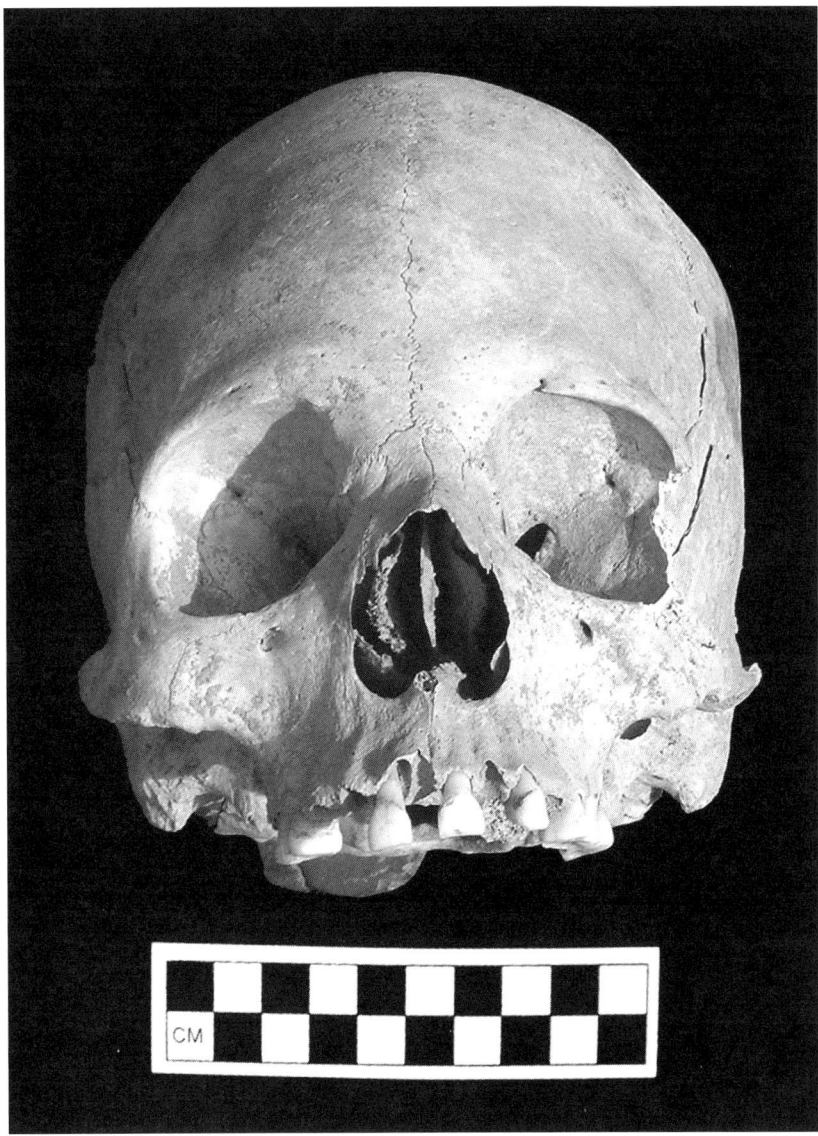

Figure 9.4. Burial 3. Frontal view of cranium, showing broad nasal indices. Photo: Cecilia Chávez Justo.

Table 9.2. Molar wear* comparison with other Altiplano groups.

|  | Taraco (AD 150) | Upper Formative (200 BC– AD 400) | | | | Late Intermediate (AD 1300–1450) | | | |
|---|---|---|---|---|---|---|---|---|---|
|  | wear | n | min | average wear | max | n | min | average wear | max |
| mandible |  |  |  |  |  |  |  |  |  |
| molar 1 | 29 | 34 | 16 | 29 | 38 | 30 | 18 | 30 | 40 |
| molar 2 | 17 | 30 | 13 | 25 | 36 | 14 | 8 | 25 | 38 |
| molar 3 | ? | 24 | 6 | 17 | 30 | 11 | 12 | 17 | 21 |
| maxilla |  |  |  |  |  |  |  |  |  |
| molar 1 | 32 | 28 | 16 | 28 | 40 | 20 | 20 | 29 | 40 |
| molar 2 | 17 | 23 | 11 | 21 | 40 | 18 | 10 | 21 | 33 |
| molar 3 | 12 | 11 | 4 | 13 | 28 | 14 | 4 | 13 | 24 |

*After E. Scott 1979a:214

Table 9.3. Comparison of molar wear* differentials with other Altiplano groups.

|  | Taraco | Upper Formative | | Late Intermediate | |
|---|---|---|---|---|---|
|  | wear | n | wear | n | wear |
| mandible |  |  |  |  |  |
| molar 1 | 29 | 34 | 29 | 15 | 30 |
| molar 2 | 17 | 30 | 25 | 14 | 25 |
| wear differential | *12* | *4* | | *5* | |
| maxilla |  |  |  |  |  |
| molar 1 | 32 | 28 | 28 | 20 | 29 |
| molar 2 | 17 | 23 | 21 | 18 | 21 |
| wear differential | *15* | *7* | | *8* | |

*Scott wear analysis (1979a)

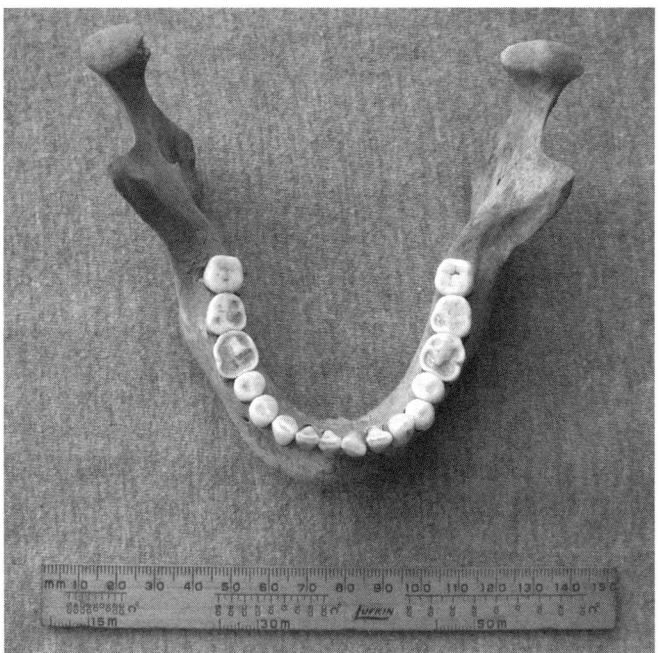

Figure 9.5. Burial 3. Mandible, showing differential molar wear. Photo: Cecilia Chávez Justo.

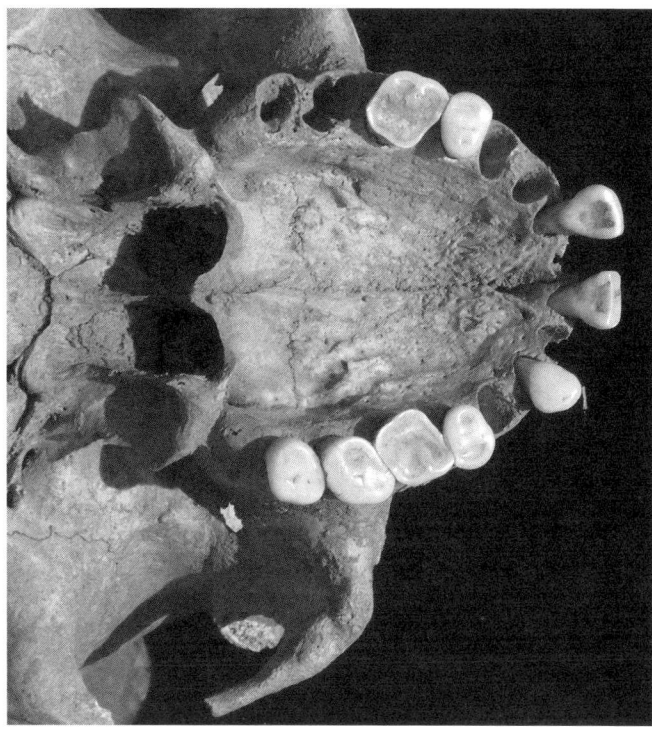

Figure 9.6. Burial 3. Maxilla, showing differential molar wear. Photo: Cecilia Chávez Justo.

labially in front of the permanent central incisor, causing this tooth to be offset laterally. The permanent right upper lateral incisor appears to be congenitally absent but no definitive conclusion can be reached without an X-ray. There is no evidence of temporomandibular joint disease.

This individual retains the metopic suture. In addition, the supraorbital notch and foramen and the infraorbital suture and foramen are present and the left temporal bone has a tympanic dehiscence. The frontal and occipital bones are slightly flattened and the skull is high (Fig. 9.7), but the cranium does not have the typical shape of the fronto-occipital deformation that is coastal in origin. I suggest instead that this is a variation of the circumferential or Aymara type of deformation with an erect orientation (Anton 1989).

## Discussion

Analyses of the Taraco skeletons reveal that three of the four individuals are young children, two of whom may have been twins. The young adult has been classified as a female based on sexual dimorphic cranial traits, discriminant function analysis of the cranium and tibia, and comparative analyses of other long bone dimensions with the Upper Formative and Late Intermediate individuals. Since sexing of young children is still controversial, the sex of the two four-year-old children could not be determined with certainty. However, mandibular and iliac sexual dimorphic traits scored male.

### Osteometrics and Activity Patterns

Cranial deformation affects many measurements, which makes comparative analysis with other individuals or groups difficult, if not impossible. Of more interest are those measurements that are not, or only minimally, affected by this practice. For instance, the face is usually not affected by remodeling practices to the extent that the cranial vault and cranial base are (Harris et al. 1973, however, see Kohn et al. 1993). Comparison of the nasal, orbital and palatal indices of Burial 3 with the Upper Formative and Late Intermediate remains suggests that she may have belonged to a different ethnic group (Table 9.1).

In addition, this woman is taller and more gracile relative to the women of the Río Grande Basin. Flattening of the subtrochanteric area of the femur (platymeria) and the degree of mediolateral flatness of the tibia (platycnemia) vary between different groups and this has been subscribed to miscellaneous causes (such as nutritional deficiencies, posture, gait and biomechanical loading and activities). It is believed that smaller cross sections are characteristic of more mechanically stressed and/or primitive groups (Bass 1995; Buxton 1938; Larsen 1997;

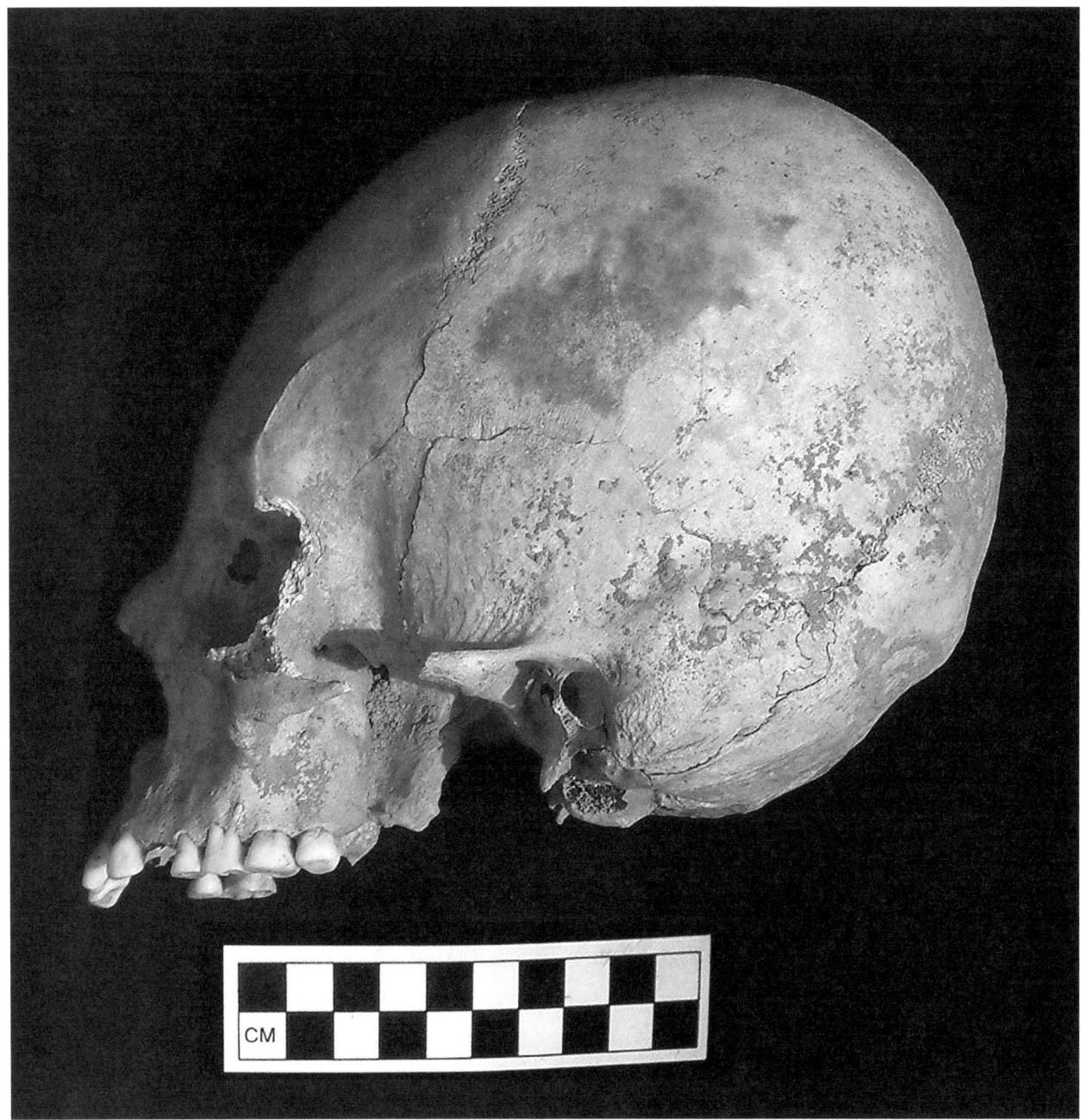

Figure 9.7. Burial 3. Lateral view of cranium. Photo: Cecilia Chávez Justo.

Lovejoy et al. 1976; Ruff and Hayes 1983a, 1983b). An increase in the subtrochanteric index (indicative of more circular cross sections) and the mid-shaft diameters of these bones is found with the transition to sedentism and agriculture (Bennett 1973; Brothwell 1981; Larsen and Thomas 1982; Larsen 1984).

The low platymeric and platycnemic indices of this woman are consistent with those of the Upper Formative and Late Intermediate people. In addition, the general shape of the femur is quite similar (low neck/shaft angle and arched shaft anteriorly/posteriorly). I have suggested (Drayer n.d.) that this may be due to the manner of locomotion of the people from this area, and to strenuous activities such as carrying very heavy loads.

*Odontometrics*

All dental measurements of Burial 3 are smaller than the average dimensions of the two other groups, especially when compared to the Late Intermediate teeth. An interesting trend was observed from the Upper Formative to the Late Intermediate periods. During the 1600 years that separate these groups, tooth dimensions *increased*, a trend that was also observed in a Peruvian coastal sample, spanning 9000 years (Scott 1979b). This is in direct contrast to the evolutionary theory that teeth reduce in size over time in response to natural selection and cultural changes associated with agriculture and food production techniques (Brace 1962; Calcagno and Gibson 1988; Macho and Moggi-Cecchi 1992). Allison (1990) also noted that the decrease in mandibular and maxillary dimensions of the Andean people over time has not been accompanied by a reduction in tooth size.

*General Health*

It is premature to draw any conclusions about the socioeconomic conditions from such a small sample; however, the lack of general stress indicators in these people (such as cribra orbitalia, porotic hyperostosis and hypoplasias) suggests nutritional sufficiency and an absence of infectious diseases, diarrhea, anemia and parasite infestations. It will be interesting to see if future research of additional skeletal material will bear out this trend.

In contrast, cribra orbitalia and porotic hyperostosis were common during the Upper Formative period, supporting the hypothesis that these people practiced intense agriculture. The prevalence of porotic hyperostosis and cribra orbitalia decreased dramatically during the Late Intermediate and these agro-pastoralists may have had access to a more varied diet. However, I suggest that it is more likely that the movement away from the densely populated villages that occurred during this period (Frye and de la Vega 2005) was instrumental in the decline of these conditions. The resettlement and relocation to small villages most probably greatly improved sanitation and overall living conditions.

The periostitis of the sphenoid of Burial 2 may have been caused by an inflammation or infection as a result of the extreme remodeling of the cranium. In addition, both children had small areas of ectocranial pitting near either the sagittal or lambdoidal sutures. The pitting does not resemble porotic hyperostosis and I suggest that this may also be related to the cranial deformation. Periostitis and pitting of the interior surfaces of the sphenoids and endocranial surfaces of children and infants were especially common during the Late Intermediate period (26.1% vs. 14.3% during the Upper Formative), suggesting that remodeling of children's crania may have had dire consequences more often than suspected (Drayer n.d.).

The rib fracture of Burial 3 was most likely the result of an accident or violence and the small spur at the proximal fibula may have been caused by a muscle injury. Except for these injuries, there is no evidence of trauma in any of the individuals. The crania of the children are fragmented and some of the breaks were clearly caused by excavation procedures; however, it is impossible to determine if the children suffered perimortem cranial trauma.

Osteoarthritis or degenerative joint disease may develop in response to infectious diseases or metabolic disturbances but is most often the result of trauma, occupational activities or old age (Jurmain 1977, 1980; Larsen 1997). The condition is widespread in archaeological populations (Drayer 1992; Walker et al. 1996; Jurmain 1977; Bridges 1992). Surprisingly, the young woman (Burial 3) does not have any evidence of degenerative joint disease in the elbows or wrists. Arthritis at these locations is almost always caused by occupational activities and most women of the other two groups, especially the Upper Formative women, suffered from severe, bilateral arthritis of the elbows and wrists, suggesting strenuous use of the arms.

At present time, between 50 and 80% of the American people suffer from some form of temporomandibular joint dysfunction and the condition is believed to be closely associated with mechanical forces, attrition and antemortem tooth loss (Christensen and Ziebert 1986; Hylander 1975; Sheridan et al. 1991). Because of the relative heavy dental wear of Burial 3 (at least for such a young person), some degree of osseous remodeling at the temporomandibular joint would not be unexpected, especially since the condition was quite common during the Upper Formative and Late Intermediate periods (50% and 45% respectively). However, there is no evidence at all of osseous changes at this joint.

Hypoplasias are enamel defects, caused by temporary cessation of enamel formation in response to malnutrition or developmental stress (Goodman and Rose 1990). The hypoplastic defect of the mandibular third molar of Burial 3 suggests that this person suffered from acute disease or trauma between the ages of nine and twelve years. Interestingly, this is the only tooth in the collection with an enamel defect. The absence of hypoplastic defects, porotic hyperostosis and cribra orbitalia strongly suggests that the diet of these three people was sufficient and that levels of developmental stress during early childhood were low.

In contrast, hypoplasias are common in the other two groups, but the ages at which the defects formed differ. For instance, my data of the Late Intermediate remains suggest that life was difficult from the age of one to two until at least twelve to fourteen years. In contrast, during the Upper Formative, people suffered from physiological and/or nutritional stress between birth and eight years. Analysis of the Quelcatani remains reveals that all four individuals from the Late Horizon period suffered developmental stress throughout childhood.

*Dental Development and Health*

These people had good dental health and there are no carious lesions, abscesses or antemortem tooth loss. The Upper Formative and Late Intermediate people had very few caries and dental health was relatively good, especially two thousand years ago. In contrast, the people from Quelcatani had many carious lesions and abscesses (Drayer and Aldenderfer 1998).

The dental wear rates of the Taraco individuals are much more severe than those of the Upper Formative agriculturists and Late Intermediate agro-pastoralists (especially the first molars) (Table 9.2, Figs. 9.5, 9.6), which may have led to pulp exposures, caries and abscess formations and antemortem loss at fairly young ages. It is believed that heavier wear results from a coarser diet, which may be aggravated by grinding stones or manos and metates made of specific rocks or stones (Benfer and Edwards 1991; Molnar et al. 1983; Walker et al. 1991). Severe attrition has also been linked to periodontal and temporomandibular joint disease but both these conditions are absent in the young adult and I would not expect to find these in the children.

The slightly cupped wear patterns of the mandibular first molars of Burial 3 are suggestive of an agricultural subsistence mode; however, a definite labial wear plane angle is absent. The retention of the deciduous upper right lateral incisor of Burial 3 caused the displacement of the permanent central incisor. The retention of deciduous teeth in adulthood (usually of the canines) often resulted in displacement or suppression of the permanent teeth; this condition was common in prehistoric groups from the Cuzco area (MacCurdy 1923).

*Cranial Deformation*

The process of intentional cranial deformation was usually started during infancy because this is the only time that the skull can be molded. The potential disastrous consequences of exerting strong pressure to the infant's head have been investigated but no evidence has been found of brain injury or decreased intellect (Wells 1964; Moss 1958; Bjørk and Bjørk 1964). Nonetheless, it is not unrealistic to assume that restraining the growth and remodeling of the infant's head may sometimes have resulted in accidental death and injuries (Gerszten and Gerszten 1995).

My research has shown that the Aymara or circumferential deformation type was most common in the people living west of Lake Titicaca during the Upper Formative and Late Intermediate periods. However, the severity of the remodeling and the positions of the bindings differed, which resulted in either oblique or erect orientations. In contrast, cranial deformation types of the people from Quelcatani varied and included the typical, bilobate deformation of the coastal type.

The deformation type of the Taraco individuals is circumferential. However, the crania show variations in remodeling techniques. For instance, the deformation type of the young adult appears to be "annular erecta," or circumferential with an erect orientation (Fig. 9.7). The cranium of Burial 2 is extremely elongated and typical of the long, loaf-like Aymara deformation while the remodeling of the other child, although also circumferential, is less severe (Fig. 9.2). If these children were twins, as their ages and burial positions suggest, then the difference in the severity of the deformations is puzzling. The question of sex differences arises here since the type of deformation (or the presence of deformation in general) may have been gender specific. However, my research of the other Altiplano groups reveals that severe cranial deformation in women was the norm and not the exception (Drayer n.d.). In addition, mandibular (and sciatic notch) characteristics suggest that both children were boys. It is not known if the infection of the sphenoid and the pitting near the lambdoid suture of Burial 2 and the parietal suture of Burial 1 were due to deformational practices.

*Discrete Cranial Traits*

Two of the three individuals (that could be examined) retain a metopic suture. I found this to be a common trait in the Upper Formative (18%) and Late Intermediate (24%) people. In addition, the supraorbital notch and foramen, and the infraorbital suture and foramen are present; these traits were also common during those time periods.

All three Taraco individuals have tympanic dehiscences. Tympanic dehiscences were very common during the Upper Formative (73.8%), but the frequency dropped slightly during the Late Intermediate (57.4%). I have suggested that these defects, especially in older people, may be due to recurrent sinus and/or ear infections (Drayer n.d.). Otitis media is one of the most common diseases that afflict people from this area at present time (Diaz et al. 1978). However, if this is so, the decline of the condition over time is puzzling.

Burial 3 has the typical shovel-shaped incisors that are believed to be genetically transmitted because of the high frequencies in Mongoloid groups. The condition is very common in Native Americans (Dahlberg 1951; Scott 1973; Blanco and Chakraborty 1976; Devoto et al. 1968).

*Trophy Heads*

Trophy heads and sacrificial burials are a pan-American phenomenon as evidenced by skeletal remains and iconographic representations (Tello 1918; Uhle 1914). Trophy heads are rarely found in graves and therefore the burial context is important in interpreting this phenomenon (such as interment near ceremonial structures and architectural features) (Browne et al. 1993; Coelho

1972; Verano 1995). So far, no resolution has been reached on whether these heads (including crania of women and children) were members of the same tribe, suggesting ancestor worship or human sacrifice, or were taken in battle or ritual warfare (Arkush and Stanish 2005; Browne et al. 1993; Platt 1986; Coelho 1972; Guillén 1993; Drusini and Baraybar 1989; Proulx 1989; Williams et al. 2001).

It is possible that Burial 1 is a trophy head. The severed head motif was well established in the Pukara style by this time (Chávez 1992; Hastorf 2005). However, there is no evidence of preparation, such as cut marks or other treatment (Klarich 1995; Williams et al. 2001), and I suggest that it is more likely that the entire postcranial skeleton (except for the first four cervical vertebrae) was removed in prehistory during building activities. This would also explain the absence of the legs of Burial 2 and the pelvis and left leg of Burial 3. The commingling of the cranial fragments of Burial 2a with Burial 2 is puzzling, but the humeral epiphysis of the infant is a strong argument against ritual or sacrificial trophy head interment.

## Conclusions

Analysis of the skeletal remains of the four individuals, buried at the base of a wall dated to the Pucara occupation, provides important and much needed bioarchaeological information. The preponderance of children in this sample is most probably an artifact of sample size and does not necessarily represent child mortality rates. The composition of the collection—a young woman and three young children—suggests that they may have been part of a family that succumbed to a disease or an enemy attack, although if the latter were true I would have expected to find evidence of skeletal trauma. On the other hand, if these burials were sacrificial in nature, I propose that initially the entire bodies were interred since there is no evidence of cut marks. More importantly, except for Burial 1, all individuals retain parts of the postcranial skeletons.

This study raises important questions regarding differences in socioeconomic conditions, subsistence modes, dietary compositions and genetic affiliations between people from the same time period and from the same general area, and in changes in these conditions over time. These questions will hopefully be addressed and answered in the near future when additional human remains are recovered.

## References Cited

Acsádi, G., and J. Nemeskéri
1970 *History of Human Life Span and Mortality*. Akademiai Kiado, Budapest.

Allen, J. C., M. F. Bruce, and S. M. McLaughlin
1987 Sex determination from the radius in humans. *Human Evolution* 2(4):373–87.

Allison, M., E. Gerszten, J. Munizaga, C. Santoro, and G. Focacci
1981 La práctica de la deformación craneana entre los pueblos andinos precolombinos. *Chungará* 7:238–60.

Allison, M. J.
1984 Paleopathology in Peruvian and Chilean populations. In *Paleopathology at the Origins of Agriculture*, edited by M. N. Cohen and G. J. Armelagos, pp. 525–29. Academic Press, Orlando, Florida.
1990 Paleopathology. In *The Aymara: Strategies in Human Adaptation to a Rigorous Environment*, edited by W. J. Schull and F. Rothhammer, pp. 49–61. Kluwer Academic Publishers, The Netherlands.

Anton, S. C.
1989 Intentional cranial vault deformation and induced changes of the cranial base and face. *American Journal of Physical Anthropology* 79:253–67.

Arkush, E., and C. Stanish
2005 Interpreting conflict in the ancient Andes: Implications for the archaeology of warfare. *Current Anthropology* 46(1):3–28.

Aykroyd, R. C., D. Lucy, A. M. Pollard, and C. A. Roberts
1999 Nasty, brutish, but not necessarily short: A reconsideration of the statistical methods used to calculate age at death from adult human skeletal and dental age indicators. *American Antiquity* 64(1):55–70.

Bass, W. M.
1995 *Human Osteology*, 4th ed. Missouri Archaeological Society, Columbia, MO.

Benfer, R. A., and D. S. Edwards
1991 The principal axis method for measuring rate and amount of dental attrition: Estimating juvenile or adult tooth wear from unaged adult teeth. In *Advances in Dental Anthropology*, edited by M. A. Kelley and C. S. Larsen, pp. 325–40. Wiley-Liss, New York.

Bennett, K. A.
1965 The etiology and genetics of wormian bones. *American Journal of Physical Anthropology* 23:255–60.
1973 *The Indians of Point of Pines, Arizona: A Comparative Study of Their Physical Characteristics*. Anthropological Papers of the University of Arizona 23. University of Arizona Press, Tucson.

Berry, A. C., and R. J. Berry
1967 Epigenetic variation in the human cranium. *Journal of Anatomy* 101:361–79.

Bjørk, A., and L. Bjørk
1964 Artificial deformation and cranio-facial asymmetry in ancient Peruvians. *Journal of Dental Research* 43:353–62.

Blanco, R., and R. Chakraborty
1976 The genetics of shovel shape in maxillary central incisors in man. *Journal of Physical Anthropology* 44:233–36.

Boucher, B. J.
1955 Sex differences in the foetal sciatic notch. *Journal of Forensic Medicine* 2:51–54.

Brace, C. L.
1962 Cultural factors in the evolution of the human dentition. In *Culture and the Evolution of Man*, edited by A. Montagu, pp. 343–54. Oxford University Press, New York.

Bridges, P. S.
1989 Changes in activities with the shift to agriculture in the southeastern United States. *Current Anthropology* 30:385–94.
1992 Prehistoric arthritis in the Americas. *Annual Review of Anthropology* 21:67–91.

Brooks, S. T., and J. M. Suchey
1990 Skeletal age determination based on the os pubis: A comparison of the Acsádi Nemeskéri and Suchey-Brooks methods. *Human Evolution* 5:227–38.

Brothwell, D. R.
1959 Teeth in earlier human populations. *Proceedings of the Nutrition Society* 18:59–65.
1981 *Digging Up Bones: The Excavation, Treatment and Study of Human Skeletal Remains*, 3rd ed. Cornell University Press, Ithaca.
1989 The relationship of tooth wear to aging. In *Age Markers in the Human Skeleton*, edited by M. Y. Isçan, pp. 303–18. Charles C. Thomas, Springfield.

Browne, D. M., H. Silverman, and R. García
1993 A cache of 48 Nasca trophy heads from Cerro Carapo, Peru. *Latin American Antiquity* 4(3):274–94.

Buikstra, J. E., and D. H. Ubelaker (editors)
1994 *Standards for Data Collection from Human Skeletal Remains: Proceedings of a Seminar at the Field Museum of Natural History*. Arkansas Archeological Survey, Fayetteville, Arkansas.

Buikstra, J. E., S. R. Frankenberg, and L. W. Konigsberg
1990 Skeletal biological distance studies in American physical anthropology: Recent trends. *American Journal of Physical Anthropology* 82:1–7.

Buxton, L. H. D.
1938 Platymeria and platycnemia. *Journal of Anatomy* 73:31–36.

Calcagno, J. M., and K. R. Gibson
1988 Human dental reduction: Natural selection or the probable mutation effect. *American Journal of Physical Anthropology* 77:505–17.

Chávez, S.
1992 The Conventionalized Rules in Pucara Pottery Technology and Iconography: Implications for Socio-Political Development in the Northern Lake Titicaca Basin. PhD dissertation, Department of Anthropology, Michigan State University, East Lansing.

Cheverud, J. M.
1982 Phenotypic, genetic and environmental morphological integration in the cranium. *Evolution* 36:499–516.

Christensen, L. V., and G. J. Ziebert
1986 Effects of experimental loss of teeth on the temporo-mandibular joint. *Journal of Oral Rehabilitation* 13:587–98.

Cobo, B.
1983 [1653] *History of the Inca Empire*, translated by Roland Hamilton. University of Texas Press, Austin.

Coelho, V. P.
1972 Enterramentos da cabeças da cultura Nasca. PhD dissertation, Universidad de São Paulo, Brazil.

Corruccini, R. S.
1972 The biological relationships of some prehistoric and historic Pueblo populations. *American Journal of Physical Anthropology* 37:373–88.

Dahlberg, A. A.
1951 The dentition of the American Indian. In *The Physical Anthropology of the American Indian*, edited by W. S. Laughlin, pp. 138–76. Viking Fund, New York.
1956 *Materials for the Establishment of Standards for Classification of Tooth Characteristics, Attributes and Techniques in Morphological Studies of the Dentition*. Zoller Laboratory of Dental Anthropology, University of Chicago, IL.

Devoto, F. C. H., N. H. Arias, S. Ringuelet, and N. H. Palma
1968 Shovel-shaped incisors in a northwestern Argentine population. *Journal of Dental Research* 47(5):820–23.

Diaz, B., D. Gallegos, F. Murillo, V. L. Lenart, W. H. Weidman, and R. I. Goldsmith
1978 Disease and disability among the Aymara. In *Multinational Andean Genetic and Health Program II*, pp. 219–35, vol. 12. Bulletin American Health Organization.

Dittrick, J., and J. M. Suchey
1986 Sexual dimorphism of the femur and humerus in prehistoric central California skeletal samples. *American Journal of Physical Anthropology* 70:3–9.

Dorsey, G. A.
1897 Wormian bones in artificially deformed Kwakiutl crania. *American Anthropologist* X:169–73.

Drayer, F.
1992 Evaluation of Joint Disease in the Hotchkiss Population (CCO-138). Paper presented at the American Association of Physical Anthropologists, Paleopathology Section, Las Vegas, Nevada.

n.d. Human Remains from Lake Titicaca. A Comparative Bioarchaeological Analysis of the Upper Formative and Late Intermediate Periods. Working paper, in possession of author.

Drayer, F., and M. Aldenderfer
1998 Human Remains from Quelcatani. Paper presented at the annual meeting of the American Anthropological Association, Chicago, IL.

Drusini, A. G., and J. P. Baraybar
1989 Anthropological study of Nasca trophy heads. *Homo* 41:251–65.

Fazekas, I. G., and F. Kosa
1978 *Forensic Fetal Osteology*. Akademiai Kiado, Budapest.

Frye, K. L., and E. de la Vega
2005 The Altiplano period in the Titicaca Basin. In *Advances in Titicaca Basin Archaeology–1*, edited by C. Stanish, A. B. Cohen, and M. S. Aldenderfer, pp. 173–84. Cotsen Institute of Archaeology, University of California, Los Angeles.

Garcilaso de la Vega
1961 [1609] *The Incas: The Royal Commentaries of the Inca*, translated by M. Jolas. Orion Press, New York.

Garrett, J.
1988 Status, the warrior class and artificial cranial deformation. In *The King Site: Continuity and Contact in Sixteenth-Century Georgia*, edited by R. L. Blakely, pp. 35–46. University of Georgia Press, Athens, Georgia.

Genovés, S.
1967 Proportionality of long bones and their relation to stature among Mesoamericans. *American Journal of Physical Anthropology* 26:67–78.

Gerszten, P. C., and E. Gerszten
1995 Intentional cranial deformation: A disappearing form of self-mutilation. *Neurosurgery* 37(3):374–82.

Goodman, A. H., and J. C. Rose
1990 Assessment of systematic physiological perturbations from dental enamel hypoplasias and associated histological structures. *Yearbook of Physical Anthropology* 33:59–110.

Gottlieb, K.
1978 Artificial cranial deformation and the increased complexity of the lambdoid suture. *American Journal of Physical Anthropology* 48:213–14.

Greulich, W. M., and S. I. Pyle
1959 *Radiographic Atlas of Skeletal Development of the Hand and Wrist*. Stanford University Press, Stanford, CA.

Guillén, A. C.
1993 Women, rituals and social dynamics at ancient Chalcatzingo. *Latin American Antiquity* 4(3):209–24.

Gustafson, G., and G. Koch
1974 Age estimation up to 16 years of age based on dental development. *Odontologisk Revy* 25:297–306.

Harris, J. E., C. J. Kowalski, and S. S. Watnick
1973 Genetic factors in the shape of the craniofacial complex. *Journal of Dental Research* 4:107–11.

Hastorf, C. A.
2005 The Upper (Middle and Late) Formative in the Titicaca region. In *Advances in Titicaca Basin Archaeology–1*, edited by C. Stanish, A. B. Cohen, and M. S. Aldenderfer, pp. 65–94. Cotsen Institute of Archaeology, University of California, Los Angeles.

Hauser, G., and G. F. De Stefano
1989 *Epigenetic Variants of the Human Skull*. Schweizerbart, Stuttgart.

Hinton, R. J.
1981 Form and patterning of anterior tooth wear among aboriginal human groups. *American Journal of Physical Anthropology* 54(4):555–64.

Holcomb, S. M. C., and L. W. Konigsberg
1995 Statistical study of sexual dimorphism in the human fetal sciatic notch. *American Journal of Physical Anthropology* 97:113–25.

Holland, T. D.
1991 Sex assessment using the proximal tibia. *American Journal of Physical Anthropology* 85:221–27.

Hoshower, L. M., J. E. Buikstra, P. S. Goldstein, and A. D. Webster
1995 Artificial cranial deformation at the Omo M10 site: A Tiwanaku complex from the Moquegua Valley, Peru. *Latin American Antiquity* 6(2):145–64.

Howells, W. W.
1969a Criteria for selection of osteometric dimensions. *American Journal of Physical Anthropology* 30:451–58.
1969b The use of multivariate techniques in the study of skeletal populations. *American Journal of Physical Anthropology* 31:311–14.
1973 *Cranial Variation in Man*. Papers of the Peabody Museum of Archaeology and Ethnology, Harvard University, no. 67. Cambridge, MA.

Hrdlička, A.
1912 *Artificial Deformations of the Human Skull with Special Reference to America*. Actas del XVII Congreso Internacional de Americanistas, Buenos Aires.
1914 Anthropological work in Peru in 1913. *Smithsonian Miscellaneous Collection* 61:1–69.
1939 *Practical Anthropology*. Wistar Institute of Anatomy and Biology, Philadelphia.

Hylander, W. L.
1975 The human mandible: Lever or link? *American Journal of Physical Anthropology* 43:227–42.

Imbelloni, J.
1950 Cephalic deformations of the Indians in Argentina. *Handbook of the South American Indians* 6:53–55.

Isçan, M. Y.
1988 Rise of forensic anthropology. *Yearbook of Physical Anthropology* 31:203–30.

Isçan, M. Y., and P. Miller-Shaivitz
1984 Discriminant function sexing of the tibia. *Journal of Forensic Sciences* 29:1087–93.

Isçan, M. Y., S. R. Loth, and R. K. Wright
1985 Age estimation from the rib by phase analysis: White females. *Journal of Forensic Sciences* 30:853–63.

Jackes, M.
1992 Paleodemography: Problems and techniques. In *Skeletal Biology of Past Peoples: Research Methods*, edited by S. R. Saunders and M. A. Katzenberg, pp. 189–224. Wiley-Liss, New York.

Johnston, F. E.
1961 Sequence of epiphyseal union in a prehistoric Kentucky population from Indian Knoll. *American Journal of Physical Anthropology* 20:249–54.

Jurmain, R. D.
1977 Stress and etiology of osteoarthritis. *American Journal of Physical Anthropology* 46:353–66.
1980 The pattern of involvement of appendicular degenerative joint disease. *American Journal of Physical Anthropology* 53:143–50.

Kelley, M. A., T. G. Barrett, and S. D. Saunders
1987 Diet, dental disease, and transition in northeastern Native Americans. *Man in the Northeast* 33:113–25.

Kieser, J. K., J. Moggi-Cecchi, and H. T. Groeneveld
1992 Sex allocation of skeletal material by analysis of the proximal tibia. *Forensic Science International* 56:29–36.

Klarich, E. A.
1995 Nasca and Paracas Trophy Heads: A Study of Skeletal Remains and Associated Iconography in Pre-Columbian South Coastal Peru. Bachelor's thesis, Department of Anthropology, University of Chicago, IL.

Kohn, L. A. P., S. R. Leigh, S. C. Jacobs, and J. M. Cheverud
1993 Effects of annular cranial vault modification on the cranial base and face. *American Journal of Physical Anthropology* 90(2):147–69.

Konigsberg, L. W., L. A. P. Kohn, and J. M. Cheverud
1993 Cranial deformation and non-metric trait variation. *American Journal of Physical Anthropology* 90:35–48.

Kroeber, A.
1926 *Archaeological Exploration in Peru. Part I. Ancient Pottery from Trujillo*. Memoir vol. 2, no. 1. Field Museum of Natural History, Chicago, IL.

Krogman, W. M., and M. Y. Isçan
1986 *The Human Skeleton in Forensic Medicine*, 2nd ed. Charles C. Thomas, Springfield, Illinois.

Lallo, J. W., G. J. Armelagos, and R. P. Mensforth
1977 The role of diet, disease and physiology in the origin of porotic hyperostosis. *Human Biology* 49:471–83.

Larsen, C. S.
1984 Health and disease in prehistoric Georgia: The transition to agriculture. In *Paleopathology at the Origins of Agriculture*, edited by M. N. Cohen and G. J. Armelagos, pp. 367–92. Academic Press, Orlando, FL.
1997 *Bioarchaeology: Interpreting Behavior from the Human Skeleton*. Cambridge University Press, Cambridge.

Larsen, C. S., and D. H. Thomas
1982 *The Anthropology of St. Catherines Island 3. Prehistoric Human Biological Adaptation*. Anthropological Papers of the American Museum of Natural History 57(3). New York.

Leigh, R. W.
1937 Dental morphology and pathology of pre-Spanish Peru. *American Journal of Physical Anthropology* 22:267–96.

Lovejoy, C. O., A. H. Burstein, and K. G. Heiple
1976 The biomechanical analysis of bone strength: A method and its application to platycnemia. *American Journal of Physical Anthropology* 44:489–506.

Lovejoy, C. O., R. S. Meindl, T. R. Pryzbeck, and R. P. Mensforth
1985 Chronological metamorphosis of the auricular surface of the ilium: A new method for the determination of age at death. *American Journal of Physical Anthropology* 68:15–28.

Lovejoy, C. O., R. S. Meindl, T. R. Pryzbeck, T. S. Barton, K. G. Heiple, and D. Kotting
1977 The palaeodemography of the Libben site, Ottawa County, Ohio. *Science* 198:291–93.
1985 Multifactorial determination of skeletal age at death: A method and blind tests of its accuracy. *American Journal of Physical Anthropology* 68:1–14.

Lozada, M. C., D. Blom, and J. E. Buikstra
1996 Evaluating Verticality through Cranial Deformation Patterns in the South Andes. Paper presented at the 61st Annual Meeting of the Society for American Archaeology, New Orleans.

MacCurdy, G. G.
1923 Human skeletal remains from the highlands of Peru. *American Journal of Physical Anthropology* VI(3):217–329.

Macho, G. A., and J. Moggi-Cecchi
1992 Reduction of maxillary molars in Homo sapiens sapiens: A different perspective. *American Journal of Physical Anthropology* 87(2):151–60.

Masset, C.
1989 Age estimation on the basis of cranial sutures. In *Age Markers in the Human Skeleton*, edited by M. Y. Isçan, pp. 71–105. Charles C. Thomas, Springfield, IL.

Menezes, D. M., T. D. Foster, and C. L. B. Lavelle
1974  Genetic influences on dentition and dental arch dimensions: A study of monozygotic and dizygotic triplets. *American Journal of Physical Anthropology* 40(2):213–19.

Mensforth, R. P., and C. O. Lovejoy
1985  Anatomical, physiological, and epidemiological correlates of the aging process: A confirmation of multifactorial age determination in the Libben skeletal population. *American Journal of Physical Anthropology* 106:68–87.

Miles, A.
1962  Assessment of the ages of a population of Anglo-Saxons from their dentitions. *Proceedings of the Royal Society of Medicine* 55:881–86.
1963  The dentition in the assessment of individual age in skeletal material. In *Dental Anthropology*, vol. V, edited by D. R. Brothwell, pp. 191–209. MacMillan Company, New York.
1978  *Teeth as an Indicator of Age in Man. Development Function and Evolution of Teeth.* Academic Press, New York.

Milner, G. R.
1984  Dental caries in the permanent dentition of a Mississippian period population from the American Midwest. *Coll. Anthropology* 8:77–91.
1992  *Determination of Skeletal Age and Sex: A Manual Prepared for the Dickson Mounds Reburial Team.* Dickson Mounds Museum, IL.

Mincer, H. H., E. F. Harris, and H. E. Berryman
1993  The A.B.F.O. study of third molar development and its use as an estimator of chronological age. *Journal of Forensic Sciences* 37:1068–75.

Molnar, S., J. K. McKee, I. M. Molnar, and T. R. Pryzbeck
1983  Tooth wear rates among contemporary Australian aborigines. *Journal of Dental Research* 62:562–65.

Moorrees, C. F. A., E. A. Fanning, and E. E. Hunt
1963  Age formation by stages for ten permanent teeth. *Journal of Dental Research* 42:1490–1502.

Moss, M.
1958  The pathogenesis of artificial cranial deformation. *American Journal of Physical Anthropology* 16:269–86.

Ortner, D. J., and W. G. J. Putschar
1985  *Identification of Pathological Conditions in Human Skeletal Remains.* Smithsonian Institution Press, Washington, D.C.

Ossenberg, N.
1970  The influence of artificial cranial deformation on discontinuous morphological traits. *American Journal of Physical Anthropology* 33:357–72.

Patterson, D. K.
1984  *A Diachronic Study of Dental Paleopathology and Attritional Status of Prehistoric Ontario Pre-Iroquois and Iroquois Populations.* Archaeological Survey of Canada, Mercury Series, Paper 122. Ottawa.

Phenice, T.
1969  A newly developed visual method of sexing the os pubis. *American Journal of Physical Anthropology* 30:297–301.

Platt, T.
1986  Mirrors and maize: The concept of yanantin among the Macha of Bolivia. In *Anthropological History of Andean Polities*, edited by J. Murra, N. Wachtel, and J. Revel, pp. 228–59. Cambridge University Press, Cambridge.

Powell, M. L.
1985  The analysis of dental wear and caries for dietary reconstruction. In *The Analysis of Prehistoric Diet*, edited by R. I. Gilbert and J. H. Mielke, pp. 307–38. Academic Press, Orlando, Florida.

Proulx, D.
1989  Nasca trophy heads: Victims of warfare or ritual sacrifice? In *Cultures in Conflict: Current Archaeological Perspectives*, edited by D. C. Tkaczuk and B. C. Vivian, pp. 73–85. University of Calgary Archaeological Association, Calgary.

Pucciarelli, H. M.
1974  The influence of experimental deformation on neurocranial Wormian bones in rats. *American Journal of Physical Anthropology* 41:29–37.

Redfield, A.
1970  A new aid to aging immature skeletons: Development of the occipital bone. *American Journal of Physical Anthropology* 33:217–20.

Reichs, K. J.
1986  *Forensic Osteology: Advances in the Identification of Human Remains.* Charles C. Thomas, Springfield, IL.

Roth, E. A.
1992  Applications of demographic models of palaeodemography. In *Skeletal Biology of Past Peoples: Research Methods*, edited by S. R. Saunders and M. A. Katzenberg, pp. 175–88. Wiley-Liss, New York.

Ruff, C. B., and W. C. Hayes
1983a  Cross-sectional geometry of Pecos Pueblo femora and tibiae—a biomechanical investigation. *American Journal of Physical Anthropology* 60:359–81.
1983b  Cross-sectional geometry of Pecos Pueblo femora and tibiae—a biomechanical investigation: II. Sex, age and side differences. *American Journal of Physical Anthropology* 60:383–400.

Schutkowski, H.
1987  Sex determination of fetal and neonate skeletons by means of discriminant analysis. *International Journal of Anthropology* 2:347–52.
1993  Sex determination of infant and juvenile skeletons: 1. Morphognostic features. *American Journal of Physical Anthropology* 90(2):199–206.

Scott, E. C.
1979a  Dental wear scoring technique. *American Journal of Physical Anthropology* 51:213–18.

1979b Increase of tooth size in prehistoric coastal Peru, 10,000 BP–1,000 BP. *American Journal of Physical Anthropology* 50:251–58.

Scott, G. R.
1973 Dental Morphology: A Genetic Study of American White Families and Variations in the Living Southwest Indians. PhD dissertation, Arizona State University, Tempe.

Shapiro, H. L.
1928 A correction for artificial deformation of skulls. *Anthropological Papers* 30:3–38. American Museum of Natural History, New York.

Sheridan, S. G., D. M. Mittler, D. P. V. Gerven, and H. H. Covert
1991 Biomechanical association of dental temporo-mandibular pathology in a medieval Nubian population. *American Journal of Physical Anthropology* 85(2):201–7.

Sjøvold, T.
1984 A report on the heritability of some cranial measurements and non-metric traits. In *Multivariate Statistical Methods in Physical Anthropology*, edited by G. N. VanVark and W. W. Howells. D. Reidel Publishing Company, Dordrecht.

Smith, B. H.
1984 Patterns of molar wear in hunter-gatherers and agriculturalists. *American Journal of Physical Anthropology* 63:39–56.

Souri, S. J.
1959 A morphological study of the fetal pelvis. *Journal of the Anatomical Society of India* 8:45–55.

Stanish, C.
2003 *Ancient Titicaca. The Evolution of Complex Society in Southern Peru and Northern Bolivia*. University of California Press, Berkeley.

Stanish, C., and A. Levine
2011 War and early state formation in the northern Titicaca Basin, Peru. *Proceedings of the National Academy of Sciences* 108(34):13901–6.

Steele, D. G., and C. A. Bramblett
1988 *The Anatomy and Biology of the Human Skeleton*. Texas A&M University Press, College Station, Texas.

Stewart, T. D.
1931 Dental caries in Peruvian skulls. *American Journal of Physical Anthropology* 15:315–26.
1943 The circular type of cranial deformity in the United States. *American Journal of Physical Anthropology* 28:343–51.

Stewart, T. D., and M. T. Newman
1950 *Physical Anthropology: Skeletal Remains of South American Indians. Anthropometry of South American Indian Skeletal Remains*. Handbook of South American Indians 6. Smithsonian Institution Bureau of American Ethnology, Bulletin 143, Washington, D.C.

Stuart-Macadam, P. L.
1985 Porotic hyperostosis: Representative of a childhood condition. *American Journal of Physical Anthropology* 66:391–98.

Suchey, J. M., P. A. Owings, D. V. Wiseley, and T. T. Noguchi
1984 Skeletal aging of unidentified persons. In *Human Identification: Case Studies in Forensic Anthropology*, edited by T. A. Rathburn and J. E. Buikstra, pp. 278–97. Charles C. Thomas, Springfield, IL.

Sutter, R. C., and L. Mertz
2003 Nonmetric cranial trait variation and prehistoric biocultural change in the Azapa Valley, Chile. *American Journal of Physical Anthropology* 123(2):130–45.

Tello, J. C.
1918 *El uso de las cabezas humanas artificialmente momificados y su representación en el antiguo arte Peruana*. Ernesto R. Villerán, Lima, Peru.
1928 La medicina y la antropología en la educación médica. *Revista Universitaria* 1:121.

Todd, T.
1921a Age changes in the pubic bone. 1: The male white pubis. *American Journal of Physical Anthropology* 3:285–334.
1921b Age changes in the pubic bone. III: The pubis of the white female. *American Journal of Physical Anthropology* 4:26–39.

Trotter, M., and G. C. Gleser
1958 A re-evaluation of estimation of stature based on measurements of stature taken during life and of long bones after death. *American Journal of Physical Anthropology* 16:79–123.

Turner, C. G.
1979 Dental anthropological indications of agriculture among Jomon people of central Japan. *American Journal of Physical Anthropology* 51:619–36.

Turner, C. G., C. R. Nichol, and G. R. Scott
1991 Scoring procedures for key morphological traits of the permanent dentition: The Arizona State University dental anthropology system. In *Advances in Dental Anthropology*, edited by M. A. Kelley and C. S. Larsen. Wiley-Liss, New York.

Ubelaker, D. H.
1989a *Human Skeletal Remains: Excavation, Analysis, Interpretation*. Taraxacum, Washington, D.C.
1989b The estimation of age at death from immature human bone. In *Age Markers in the Human Skeleton*, edited by M. Y. Isçan, pp. 55–70. Charles C. Thomas, Springfield, IL.

Uhle, M.
1914 *The Nasca Pottery of Ancient Peru*. Davenport Academy of Sciences, Davenport, Iowa.

Verano, J. W.
1995 Where do they rest? The treatment of human offerings and trophies in ancient Peru. In *Tombs for the Living: Andean Mortuary Practices*, edited by T. D. Dillehay, pp. 189–227. Dumbarton Oaks Research Library and Collection, Washington, D.C.

Vlahos, O.
1979 *Body: The Ultimate Symbol*. J. B. Lippincott Co., New York.

Walker, P. L., F. Drayer, and S. K. Siefkin
1996 *Malibu Skeletal Remains: A Bioarchaeological Analysis*. Resource Management Division, Department of Parks and Recreation, California.

Walker, P. L., G. Dean, and P. Shapiro (editors)
1991 *Estimating Age from Tooth Wear in Archaeological Populations*. Wiley-Liss, New York.

Walker, P. L., J. Johnson, and P. Lambert
1988 Age and sex biases in the preservation of human skeletal remains. *American Journal of Physical Anthropology* 76:183–88.

Weaver, D. S.
1980 Sex differences in the ilia of a known sex and age sample of fetal and infant skeletons. *American Journal of Physical Anthropology* 52:191–95.

Webb, P. A., and J. M. Suchey
1985 Epiphyseal union of the anterior iliac crest and medial clavicle in a modern multiracial sample of American males and females. *American Journal of Physical Anthropology* 68:457–66.

Wells, C.
1964 *Artificial Interference in Bones, Bodies and Disease*. F. A. Praeger, Washington, D.C.

Williams, S. R., K. Forgery, and E. Klarich
2001 *An Osteological Study of Nasca Trophy Heads Collected by A.L. Kroeber during the Marshall Field Expeditions to Peru*. Fieldiana Anthropology. Field Museum of Natural History, Chicago, IL.

# Chapter 10

# Ritual Use of Isla Tikonata in Northern Lake Titicaca

*Cecilia Chávez Justo and Charles Stanish*

## Introduction

A group of eight post-Tiwanaku mummified bodies were found in a cave on the small island of Tikonata in the district of Ccotos in northern Lake Titicaca. These mummies are similar to other post-Tiwanaku burials in the region. In addition to these mummies, Tiwanaku ceremonial objects were discovered in another location a few hundred meters from the cave. Significantly, all of the Tiwanaku-style ceramics are locally produced. Isla Tikonata is one of several islands in the lake with Tiwanaku and Pucara materials. The nature of these materials and their context suggests a ritual use of the island, reinforced most likely by the island's capacity to grow maize in this highland region. In this chapter, we present the data from Tikonata and suggest that many maize-producing islands in the lake were used by Tiwanaku and later peoples as a pilgrimage and/or as a string of sacred places, creating a pan-regional system of ritual associated with the concept of "uma" or water.

## Isla Tikonata

Isla Tikonata is located approximately one-half kilometer from the tip of the Capachica Peninsula (Fig. 10.1). Around the year 2005, local residents of the island discovered and removed eight mummy bundles from a narrow cave on the island's southeast side. They also recovered a number of objects putatively associated with the mummies. After contacting the local archaeological authorities, who told them to stop any more unauthorized excavations, they carefully protected the mummies and objects in a storage building on the island. A little later, an NGO arrived and provided funds for a hostel and a small museum, and then contracted the first author to evaluate the materials and create an exhibit of these materials on the island.

The island is very small at approximately 315 ha in total area and measuring 700 m at its maximum extent (Fig. 10.2); it belongs to the community of Ccotos immediately adjacent to the Capachica Peninsula. There are no villages or permanent residents on the island. However, the land is parceled out to individual families who work the land and graze animals, and there are temporary houses used by people whose main residence is in Ccotos.

The island is notable in that it is extremely fertile on the east side where maize can be grown, along with dozens of other Andean plants and European imports (Fig. 10.3). Maize is a plant that normally does not grow well in the region. However, under certain climatic and geographical conditions, such as islands (which, being surrounded by water, have elevated ambient temperatures), maize can be grown. The significance of maize in Andean ritual life cannot be overstated. Tikonata is an agriculturally rich island ideally suited to grow this important crop in the high and cold Titicaca region.

*184    Advances in Titicaca Basin Archaeology–III*

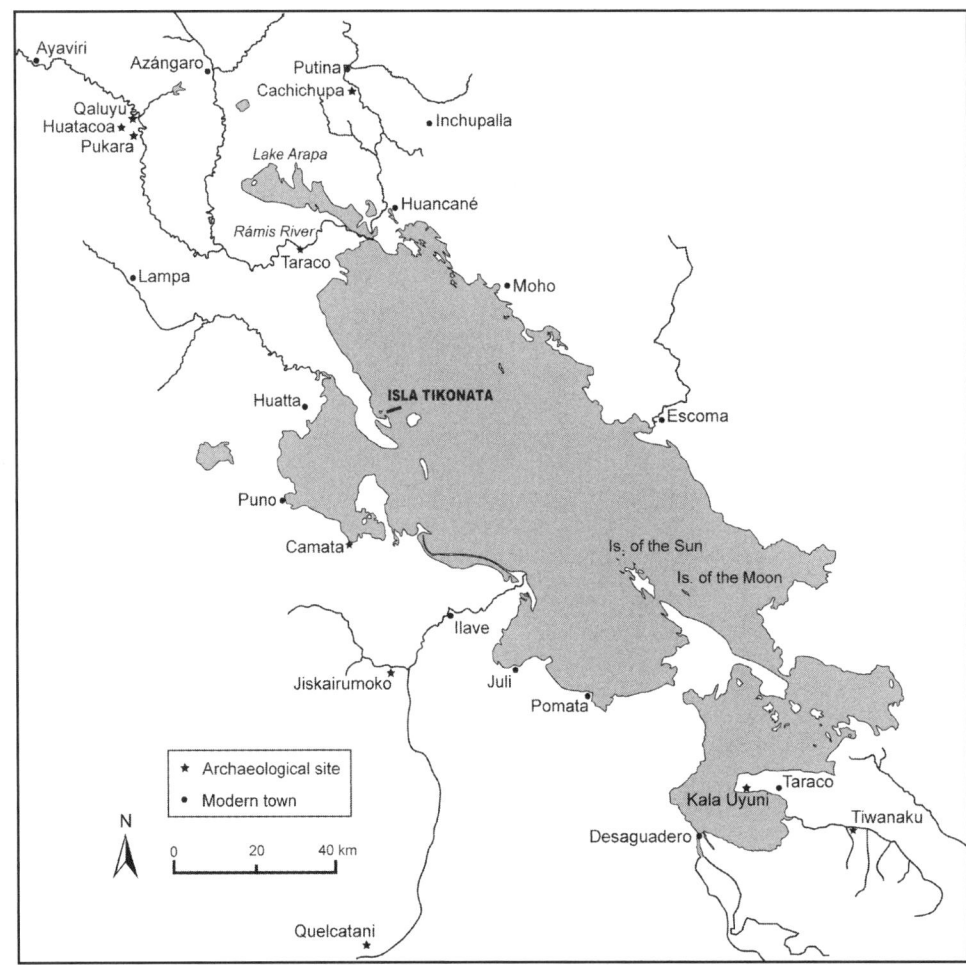

Figure 10.1. Map of Lake Titicaca showing location of Isla Tikonata.

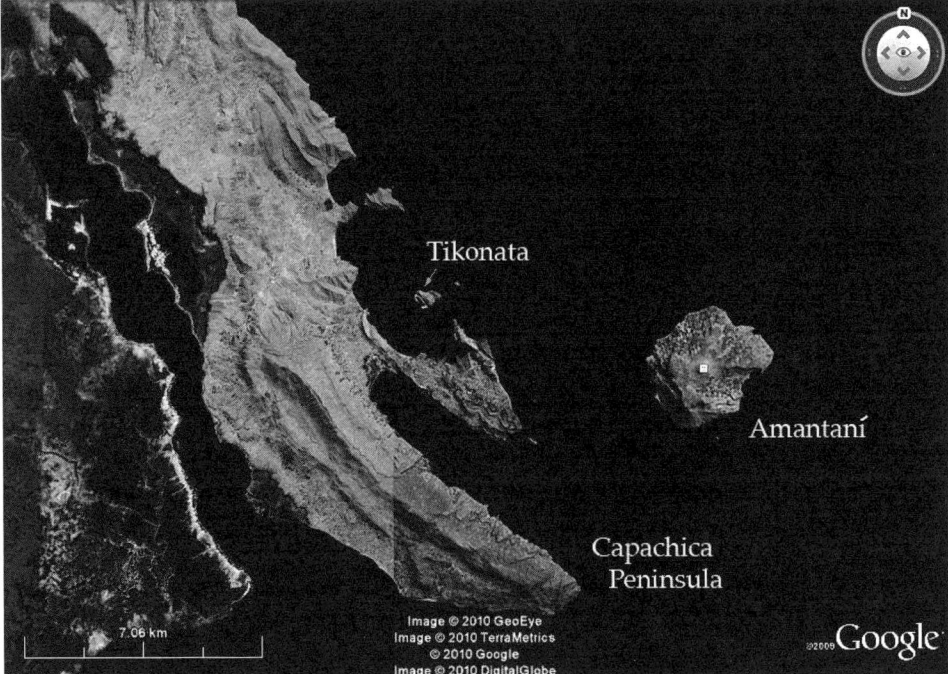

Figure 10.2. Google image of the Capachica Peninsula and precise location of Isla Tikonata.

Figure 10.3. Maize growing on the east side of the island during March. Photo courtesy of C. Stanish.[1]

Community members recovered eight mummy bundles in a typical altiplano style known as basket burials from a limestone cave on the southeast side of the island (Figs. 10.4, 10.5). They say there was a platform that they used for temporary activities, such as sleeping and eating, while working their fields. One day, some rocks moved and exposed a second platform where the mummies were located. The mummies were then removed and stored by the community. The information provided by the community members implies that the mummies were located in a lower level of the cave that over time had been covered by modern activities and natural sedimentation.

The dead were placed in a seated position in the cave. They were arranged in a half-moon shape as if they were seated around a traditional altiplano communal meal. According to one of the members who recovered the mummies, they were positioned to the southeast looking out of the cave entrance. There was no mention of artifacts found with the mummies by this informant. It is not possible to determine if certain remains were missed or thrown away since this was not a scientific excavation.

Apparently, the use of caves for burials extends back to the early Archaic periods and goes up to at least the Altiplano period in this region. These data suggest that in these early periods, prior to the development of above-ground chulpas (see Stanish, this volume), collective burials were associated with mobile agropastoral lifestyles (Frye and de la Vega 2005). The bodies were interred in vegetal fiber baskets (Fig. 10.6), in a flexed position, covered with textiles. Studies indicate that the majority of the bodies were infants—like those found on the coast—although adults of both sexes were also buried in this manner throughout the altiplano. Several of these eight individuals show signs of cranial deformation and are associated with a funerary context composed usually of Altiplano period pottery (Sillustani, Collao, Allita Amaya, etc.). It is significant that in some cases (Niño Korin, Molino Chilacachi) there are ritual ceramic vessels such as keros and hallucinogenic Tiwanaku artifacts (Wassén 1972; de la Vega et al. 2005). This suggests some kind of continuity with Tiwanaku traditions, or at the very least the use of curated heirlooms in the collective burials.

### Tiwanaku and Pucara Remains on the Island

Community members also discovered a number of artifacts as a result of agricultural land use and adobe manufacture. The pre-Tiwanaku evidence is light, with just a few puma faces that are almost certainly Pucara in date. On the other hand, there are some magnificent Tiwanaku ceremonial ceramic objects found by the community members (Figs. 10.7–10.10).[2] The Capachica area, where the island is located, has previously reported Tiwanaku sites (Erickson 1988). Therefore, we can conclude that Isla Tikonata was part of a larger Tiwanaku occupation of the region.

The Tiwanaku ceramic assemblage is composed of incensarios and keros manufactured locally. The incensarios have pedestaled bases, scallops on the rim and a lateral handle. In general terms, the incensarios use exterior painted motifs and molded figures.

Figure 10.4. The cave entrance where the mummies were found. Photo courtesy of C. Stanish

Figure 10.5. Two of the mummies found in the cave seen in Figure 10.4. Photo courtesy of E. de la Vega.

Figure 10.6. A typical, well-preserved basket (*serón*) burial found at the cave site of Molino-Chilacachi. Photo courtesy of C. Stanish.

Figure 10.7. A Tiwanaku incensario found on the eastern side of the island. Photo courtesy of C. Stanish.

The motifs use geometric designs (lines, steps, squares) in black, orange, white, and yellow over red. The molded appliqués represent feline heads. Vertical burnishing was used on the wet clay. On the other hand, the keros are not decorated but some are banded under the neck. They are orange slipped with vertical burnishing. In general terms, these vessels have a decoration that combined the exterior painting with plastic applications.

These two vessel types were used in ceremonial rituals and their presence on Tikonata indicates some kind of ritual use on the island. The materials associated with Tiwanaku were recovered on terraces as well as in a cave located on the northeast side of the island. In this latter cave, there is standing water and the local residents say that there are still more feline heads inside. This raises the possibility that this *pukio* or cave spring was used as a place for offerings to water and therefore linked to the lake.

## Altiplano (Late Intermediate) Period Remains on the Island

The eight basket mummies are typical of the region, and a number of similar finds have been documented in area limestone or volcanic rockshelters. Several reports document the presence of this kind of burial in the northern Titicaca Basin in the Omasuyu region (Nordenskiöld 1953; MacBain 1959; Rydén 1947), in the Callawaya area (Oblitas Poblete 1953 and see Wassén 1972), in the south in the Mallku territory (Berberián and Arellano López 1980; Arellano López and Berberián 1981; Arellano López and Kuljis 1986), in the Colla territory to the northwest at Sillustani (Ayca 1995), and in the western Lupaqa territory (de la Vega et al. 2005). As with the Tiwanaku period, there was a very substantial Altiplano period occupation in the region (Erickson 1988; de la Vega et al. 2005). The community

Figure 10.8. A Tiwanaku-style kero found on the eastern side of the island. Photo courtesy of E. de la Vega.

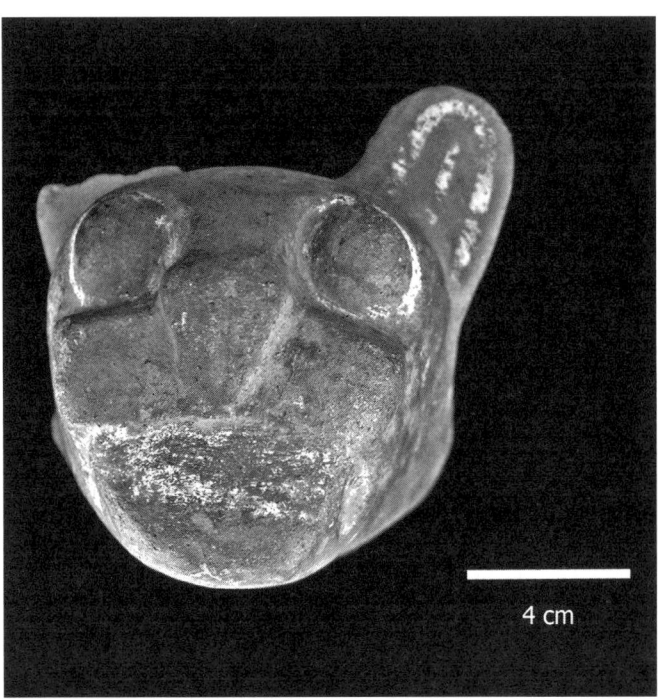

Figure 10.9. A possible Tiwanaku- or Pucara-style puma head from an incensario found on the eastern side of the island. Photo courtesy of E. de la Vega.

Figure 10.10. Detail of an incensario fragment found on the island. Photo courtesy of C. Stanish.

Figure 10.11. An Altiplano period-style kero found on the eastern side of the island. Photo courtesy of E. de la Vega.

Figure 10.12. An Altiplano period-style olla found on the eastern side of the island. Photo courtesy of E. de la Vega.

Figure 10.13. Altiplano period-style jars found on the eastern side of the island. Photo courtesy of E. de la Vega.

on the island found a number of Altiplano period ceramic objects, including jars, bowls, miniatures, and an Altiplano period kero (Figs. 10.11–10.13). Miniatures are usually associated with funerary or other ceremonial contexts.

Individual objects include medium and small jars, almost all plainwares, with only one example of a decorated one. This jar is a black-and-red on orange ware with geometric lines; it was slipped in orange and has an appended lizard facing upward. The miniatures include plainware jars and bottles plus an olla with exterior painted decoration in white over red, with geometric undulating lines under the rim. An interesting observation is that there were neither large vessels, nor any used for storage, preparation or consumption (pitchers, ollas, bowls or tazones). This suggests a largely ritual assemblage associated with the burials (particularly miniatures) and possibly lake offerings given that the local residents claimed that the objects were found in the same cave as the Tiwanaku objects described above.

The mummies, as mentioned, were Altiplano period in style. The adults have been provisionally sexed and all are female with ages between 12 and 35; the infant was 3 years old or less (Silvia Velásquez, pers. comm., 12 March 2010). One mummy was reportedly found with a vegetal fiber cap, as seen in Figure 10.14. Perhaps the most significant observation is that none of these individuals had typical cranial deformation seen in other mummies recovered from similar contexts. This raises the possibility that these females were not from the region. It could also be that these mummies are not even Altiplano period in date and are from a time when cranial deformation was not practiced. Obviously, more intensive study is needed to determine the reason for why these individuals did not have typical cranial deformation of the region.

### Inca Period Remains on the Island

There is a massive Inca presence in this region as there is throughout the Titicaca Basin, and community members found a few Inca ceramic objects. They also found a number of stone objects, including an Inca bowl, escudilla, stone mace heads, and some porras (Fig. 10.15). The ceramic sample is scarce and includes a medium-sized bowl with painted decoration on the interior in black over red with geometric motifs (lines and triangles) that cover the entire inside of the vessel. The vessel was burnished. There was also a bird head decorated with black lines on a red slip. This bird imagery is characteristic of Inca period bowl appendages.

These examples came from the same site as the Tiwanaku and Altiplano period objects. It is interesting to note that no closed vessels such as ollas, pitchers, jars or glasses in this period were found. Nevertheless, the bowls are open forms associated with food consumption. What is apparent is that this assemblage confirms a ritual use of Tikonata from at least Tiwanaku up to the Inca presence on the island.

Figure 10.14. Fiber cap reportedly found on this mummy. Photo courtesy of E. de la Vega.

Figure 10.15. An Inca-style mace head found on the island. Photo courtesy of C. Stanish.

## Interpretation

At present, we know of Tiwanaku remains on several islands in the lake. The largest and most famous is that of the Islands of the Sun and Moon complex (Bauer and Stanish 2001). A substantial Tiwanaku occupation characterized both islands. Numerous residential sites were located among ceremonial centers (Seddon 1998). The first pilgrimage center on the Islands of the Sun and Moon was established in Tiwanaku times. The ceramic assemblage included a number of incensarios and finely made keros.

Other islands in the lake have Tiwanaku remains including Pariti (Pärssinen 2005; Sagárnaga 2007), Amantaní (Niles 1987), Khoa (Ponce et al. 1992), Isla Esteves in the Puno Bay (Nuñez and Paredes 1978), Isla Paco or Suriqui (Estevez and Escalante 1994) and possibly Isla Soto (Myres and Paredes 2005). Altiplano and Inca period remains are found on all of these islands as well, plus a number of others such as Taquile, Amantaní, and some smaller islands near the Island of the Sun, such as Pallalla and Chuyu. Archaeologists to date have intensively investigated none of these other islands.

It is significant that Tikonata does not have any chulpas because chulpas are abundant throughout the region. A very quick walk around the island did not discover any chulpas or chulpa bases. This is not to say that these may not be found in future surveys, but unlike the other major islands with standing chulpas, Tikonata does not have any large and impressive ones like those found elsewhere. It is also significant that the island has been little disturbed by looting or other agricultural activities. Therefore, if the island had had the distinctive large chulpas, then they would have been obvious to the casual observer.

Also significant is the fact that the Tiwanaku pieces recovered are generally rare in the region. Recently completed work by the authors in the Taraco area indicates that incensarios make up a very small percentage of the total assemblage. Keros, on the other hand, are more common but also are essential components of ritual practices. Whether there is a major domestic component on the island remains to be discovered. However, we can say with some certainty, even with these limited data, that ritual was conducted on the island during the Tiwanaku period.

The Altiplano and Inca period occupations are likewise unknown without intensive survey. However, it is clear from the mummy bundles that stylistically date to this period that at least one cave held a very important burial of many individuals. The fact that all of the adults are female is extremely significant as well. The cave burials at Molino-Chilacachi had individuals of both sexes, and there was a second layer of mummies. It is possible that the cave on Tikonata has more than one level as well. Also, it is possible that there are burials in the other caves on the island.

In short, we find that Tikonata, like several other islands in the lake, has ceremonial objects associated with burials and other ritual practices. We argue that the Tiwanaku peoples created a series of ceremonial sites on islands as part of a pilgrimage focused on the lake. This would correspond to the well-known dual concept of "uma" and "urqu" (Bouysse-Cassagne 1986) that dominated the ideological views of the Titicaca peoples at the time of Spanish conquest. We suggest a bifurcated pilgrimage route, beginning in Ayaviri where the Inca royal road split between the Urqusuyu and Umasuyu segments (Cieza de León 1984). Parallel to this road system was a ritual pilgrimage that also bifurcated here. The probable route would have been through Asillo, Azángaro, Taraco, Huancané and to Carpa by land, and then a water route through the various islands of which Tikonata was one principal stop. Amantaní is one or two hours away by balsa raft in good weather, and it is likely that significant habitation sites are on that island. We also suggest that the Inca likewise had a bifurcated pilgrimage route indicating continuity of this ritual practice.

In this light, the capacity of this island to grow maize is extremely significant. Maize cultivation was possible at least on the Island of the Sun, Pariti, Amantaní, and Tikonata. Maize from special places like these was considered sacred in the Inca period, and we can project this to earlier periods. We suggest that this was a major factor in the use of Tikonata as a pilgrimage destination and/or ceremonial location. We also recognize the brilliant suggestion of Alexei Vranich (pers. comm., April 2010) that the lack of elite Tiwanaku burials across the region could be explained by their focus on islands. In this hypothesis, Tiwanaku elite chose to be buried on sacred islands, like Tikonata, Pariti, the Island of the Sun and so forth. This intriguing proposition deserves much more future research.

## Notes

1. The photographs in this chapter were taken on the island under suboptimal conditions.
2. The puma head in Figure 10.9 may be Pucara style. It is difficult to determine without more of the vessel.

## References Cited

Arellano López J., and E. E. Berberián
1981    Mallku, el señorío post-Tiwanaku del altiplano sur de Bolivia. *Bulletin de l'Institut Français d'Etudes Andines* 10(1/2):51–84.

Arellano López, J., and D. Kuljis
1986    Antecedentes preliminares de las investigaciones arqueológicas en la zona circumtiticaca de Bolivia sector (occidental sur). *Prehistóricas: Revista de la Carrera de Antropología y Arqueología de la Universidad Mayor de San Andrés* 1:9–28. La Paz.

Ayca Gallegos, O.
1995    *Sillustani*. Instituto de Arqueología de Sur, Tacna, Peru.

Bauer, B., and C. Stanish
2001    *Ritual and Pilgrimage in the Ancient Andes: The Islands of the Sun and Moon*. University of Texas Press, Austin.

Berberián, E., and J. Arellano López
1980    Desarrollo cultural prehispánico en el altiplano sur de Bolivia. *Revisto do Museu Paulista*, Nova Serie, vol. XXVII. São Paulo.

Bouysse-Cassagne, T.
1986    Urco and uma: Aymara concepts of space. In *Anthropological History of Andean Polities*, edited by John V. Murra, Nathan Wachtel, and Jacques Revel, pp. 201–27. Cambridge University Press, Cambridge.

Cieza de León, P. de
1984 [1553]   *La crónica del Perú*, facsimile ed. Historia 16. Madrid.

de la Vega, E., K. L. Frye, and T. Tung
2005    The cave burial from Molino-Chilacachi. In *Advances in Titicaca Basin Archaeology–1*, edited by Charles Stanish, Amanda B. Cohen, and Mark S. Aldenderfer, pp. 185–95. Cotsen Institute of Archaeology, University of California, Los Angeles.

Erickson, C. L.
1988    An Archaeological Investigation of Raised Field Agriculture in the Lake Titicaca Basin of Peru. PhD dissertation, Department of Anthropology, University of Illinois, Urbana-Champaign.

Estevez Castillo, J., and J. Escalante Moscoso
1994    *Investigaciones arqueológicas en la Isla Pako (a. Suriqui)*. Documentos Internos INAR. La Paz, Bolivia.

Frye, K. L., and E. de la Vega
2005    The Altiplano period in the Titicaca Basin. In *Advances in Titicaca Basin Archaeology–1*, edited by C. Stanish, A. B. Cohen, and M.S. Aldenderfer, pp. 173–84. Cotsen Institute of Archaeology, University of California, Los Angeles.

MacBain Chapin, E. H.
1961    *The Adolph Bandelier Archaeological Collection from Pelechuco and Charassani, Bolivia*. Universidad Nacional del Litoral, Facultad de Filosofía y Letras, Argentina.

Myres, J., and R. Paredes
2005    Pukara influence on Isla Soto, Lake Titicaca, Peru. In *Advances in Titicaca Basin Archaeology–1*, edited by Charles Stanish, Amanda B. Cohen, and Mark S. Aldenderfer, pp. 95–102. Cotsen Institute of Archaeology, University of California, Los Angeles.

Niles, S.
1987    The temples of Amantaní. *Archaeology* 40(6):30–37.

Nordenskiöld, E.
1953 *Investigaciones arqueológicas en la región fronteriza de Perú y Bolivia*. Biblioteca Paceña, La Paz, Bolivia.

Núñez Mendiguri, M., and R. Paredes
1978 Estévez: Un sitio de ocupación Tiwanaku. In *III congreso Peruano del hombre y la cultura Andina*, 2, edited by Ramiro Matos M., pp. 757–64. Lima, Peru.

Oblitas Poblete, E.
1953 Discurso de clausura de la exposición de motives Kallawayas. *Boletín Municipal de La Paz* 1040:5–6.

Pärssinen, M.
2005 Tiwanaku: Una cultura y un estado andinos. In *Pariti: Isla, misterio y poder*, edited by Antti Korpisaari and Martti Pärssinen, pp. 17–37. República de Bolivia and the government of Finland, La Paz, Bolivia.

Ponce S., C., J. Reinhard, M. Portugal, E. Pareja, and L. Ticlla
1992 *Exploraciones arqueológicas subacuáticas en el Lago Titicaca*. Editorial La Palabra, La Paz, Bolivia.

Rydén, S.
1947 *Archaeological Researches in the Highlands of Bolivia*. Elanders Boktryckeri Aktiebolag, Göteborg, Sweden.

Sagárnaga, J.
2007 Investigaciones arqueológicas en Pariti (Bolivia). *Anales del Museo de América* 15:67–88.

Seddon, M.
1998 Ritual, Power, and the Formation of a Complex Society: The Island of the Sun and the Tiwanaku State. PhD dissertation, Department of Anthropology, University of Chicago, IL.

Wassén, S. H.
1972 *A Medicine-Man's Implements and Plants in a Tiahuanacoid Tomb in Highland Bolivia*. Etnologiska Studier, vol. 32. Goteborgs Etnografiska Museum, Göteborg, Sweden.

Chapter 11

# Late Tiwanaku Mortuary Patterns in the Moquegua Drainage, Peru

Excavations at the Tumilaca la Chimba Cemetery

*Nicola Sharratt, Patrick Ryan Williams, María Cecilia Lozada, and Jennifer Starbird*

The collapse of the Tiwanaku state is a subject that has commanded significant interest in recent years (Bermann et al. 1989; Goldstein 2005; Kolata 1993; Owen 2005; Sims 2006; Williams 2002). Goldstein and Owen have both argued that Tiwanaku expansion represents a folk dispersion of altiplano peoples across the south-central Andes (Goldstein 2005; Owen 2005). Owen (2005) argues that the collapse of the highland state led to a second diaspora, composed of Tiwanaku refugees fleeing from the centers of state control. The Moquegua Valley, located in southern Peru 300 km from the site of Tiwanaku, was one of the most important centers of Tiwanaku culture (Fig. 11.1). In Moquegua, the late manifestation of Tiwanaku (post-AD 1000) has been termed Tumilaca, after the type site of Tumilaca la Chimba (Bawden 1989). Despite considerable research on settlement patterns, architecture and material culture from the Tumilaca phase (Bawden 1989; Goldstein 1989; Owen 1993, 1996; Sims 2006; Stanish 1985), questions remain about the cultural genesis of Tumilaca and the biological relatedness of Tumilaca populations to antecedent Tiwanaku populations. In this chapter, we suggest that mortuary data are central to ongoing understandings of who the inhabitants of Tumilaca sites were. Following a brief summary of current interpretations of the period, we present results from excavations undertaken in the cemetery sector of Tumilaca la Chimba in 2006.

**Tumilaca Phase in Moquegua**

The end of Tiwanaku influence across the south-central Andes was accompanied by the destruction of monumental architecture and the cessation of particular icons of the state, most notably the staff god image (Janusek 2004). Changes in material culture and shifts in settlement patterns in both the altiplano and more distant colonies followed (Bermann et al. 1989; Goldstein 2005; Janusek 2005). In Moquegua, Tumilaca ceramics show greater variation from altiplano types in both form and decoration than earlier Tiwanaku vessels. Iconography is more abstract than during the earlier phases, with greater use of geometric designs (Goldstein 1985, 1989, 2005). Recent analysis of surface material from Tumilaca sites links this material to Late Tiwanaku V material from the altiplano (Janusek 2003).

Settlements with Tumilaca-style ceramics are also more variable than their classic Tiwanaku counterparts and are found in more dispersed ecological zones than earlier Tiwanaku settlements. Goldstein (1985) ascertained Tumilaca presence in the area of previous Tiwanaku occupation of the middle valley (1000–1500 masl), specifically at the site Omo M11, but Owen (1993, 1996) also documents several late Tiwanaku settlements in the coastal Moquegua valleys as well as in the upper valley reaches (2000–2500 masl), and Stanish (1985) identified a pioneering Tumilaca settlement in the Otora Valley.

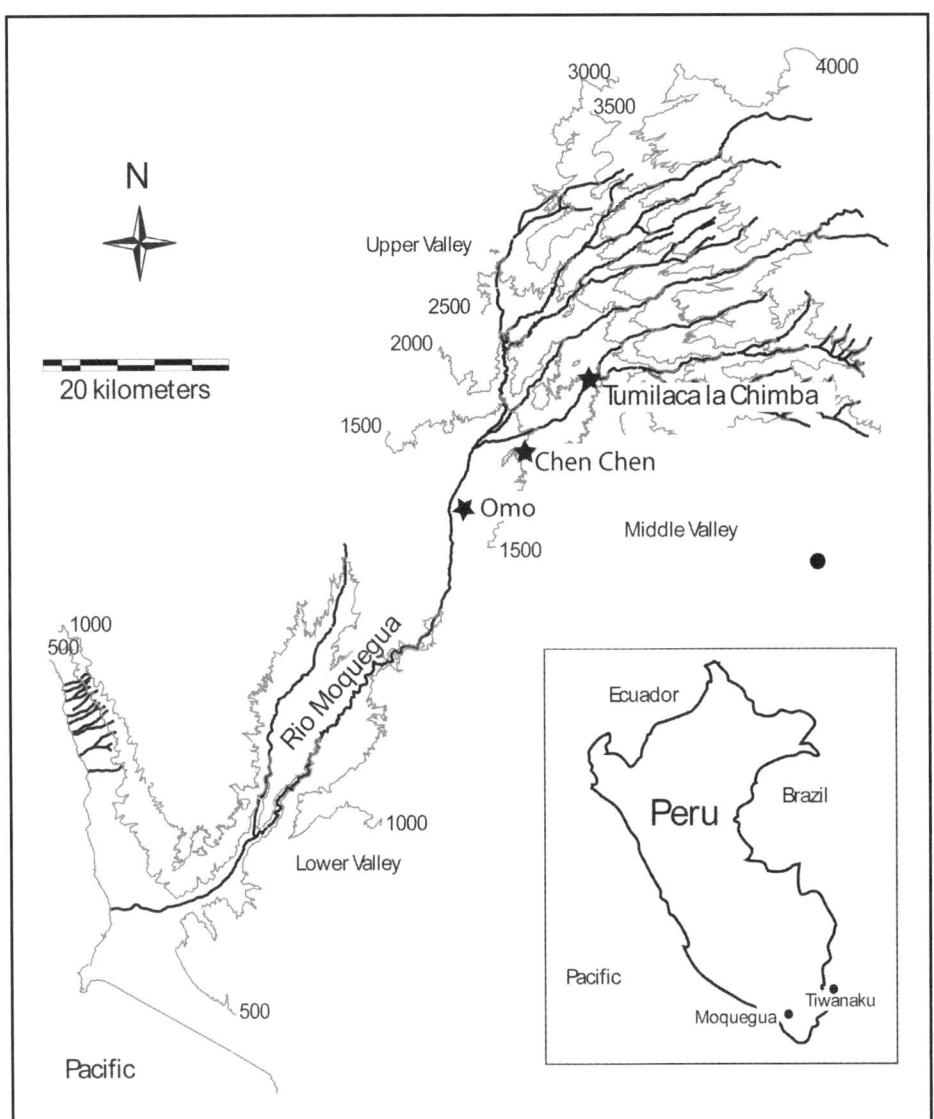

Figure 11.1. Map of the Moquegua Valley.

Settlements are typically located in less accessible locations than the classic period Tiwanaku sites. Architectural changes between the phases are apparent. Evidence from Tumilaca la Chimba indicates that inhabitants of Tumilaca phase sites maintained classic Tiwanaku residential practices, continuing to construct residential units with internal spatial differentiation and behavioral separation (Bawden 1989). However, while the classic period Omo complex is known for its temple (Goldstein 1989), Tumilaca sites are notable for their absence of nondomestic architecture (Bawden 1989).

## Mortuary Data for Tumilaca

Despite these advances in our understanding of Tumilaca settlements and material culture, there is a paucity of excavated mortuary data. To date, excavated burials for the phase include some 20 to 30 excavated by Owen (1993) in the coastal Osmore drainage, as well as 14 intact tombs excavated at Tumilaca la Chimba by Pari (1980). Skeletal remains from the latter excavations are unavailable for study. The relative absence of Tumilaca mortuary remains contrasts with the extensive mortuary collections recovered for the period of classic Tiwanaku in Moquegua, which count over 4000 tomb contexts and over 400 intact in-

Figure 11.2. Site of Tumilaca la Chimba.

terments (Owen 1997; Vargas 1988). The skeletal and cultural material excavated from Chen Chen provides evidence that populations at Chen Chen were immigrants from the altiplano, who were both biologically related to altiplano populations and who expressed cultural affiliation with the Tiwanaku capital (Blom 1999; Blom et al. 1998). Mortuary data for the Tumilaca phase will prove equally important in explaining who these later populations were. In particular, comparisons with the biological and cultural data from the Chen Chen cemeteries will illuminate whether these populations continued to identify themselves as Tiwanaku in the later years of Tiwanaku influence.

We propose several hypotheses regarding the origins of these late Tiwanaku peoples.

(1) Tumilaca peoples are actually the biological descendants of the pre-Tiwanaku inhabitants of the coastal valleys; these peoples adopted Tiwanaku pottery and some other material culture, but were rooted in the original Formative populations to occupy these valleys.

(2) Tumilaca populations are the direct descendants of altiplano peoples, as were their Chen Chen predecessors. A subsidiary hypothesis is that inhabitants of Tumilaca sites were actually descended from the populations interred at Chen Chen. This hypothesis corresponds most closely with Owen's suggestion of a second Tiwanaku diaspora.

(3) The Tumilaca are of mixed descent that may include Tiwanaku altiplano, local Wari groups, and coastal predecessors.

To evaluate these hypotheses, excavations are underway in the Tumilaca phase cemetery at the site of Tumilaca la Chimba.

## The Tumilaca la Chimba Site

The Tumilaca la Chimba site lies about 15 km up-valley from the modern city of Moquegua (Fig. 11.2). In the 1980s, Programa Contisuyo researchers defined a large cemetery associated with a defended town on a ridge above the Tumilaca River and identified late Tiwanaku-style material (Bawden 1989) (Fig. 11.3). Overlying part of the Tumilaca town are later Estuquiña (AD 1200–1500) constructions. The cemetery extends down both the east and west slopes of the ridge, covering an area of almost 3300 m². A conservative estimate, based on the excavated sample, suggests that there are as many as 300 burials in the western slope cemetery alone. Tombs are arranged on artificial terraces, likely a mechanism for coping with the extreme gradient of the slope. Mortuary contexts at the site have been badly disturbed by modern looting; the surface is littered with ceramic fragments and, to a lesser degree, human bone.

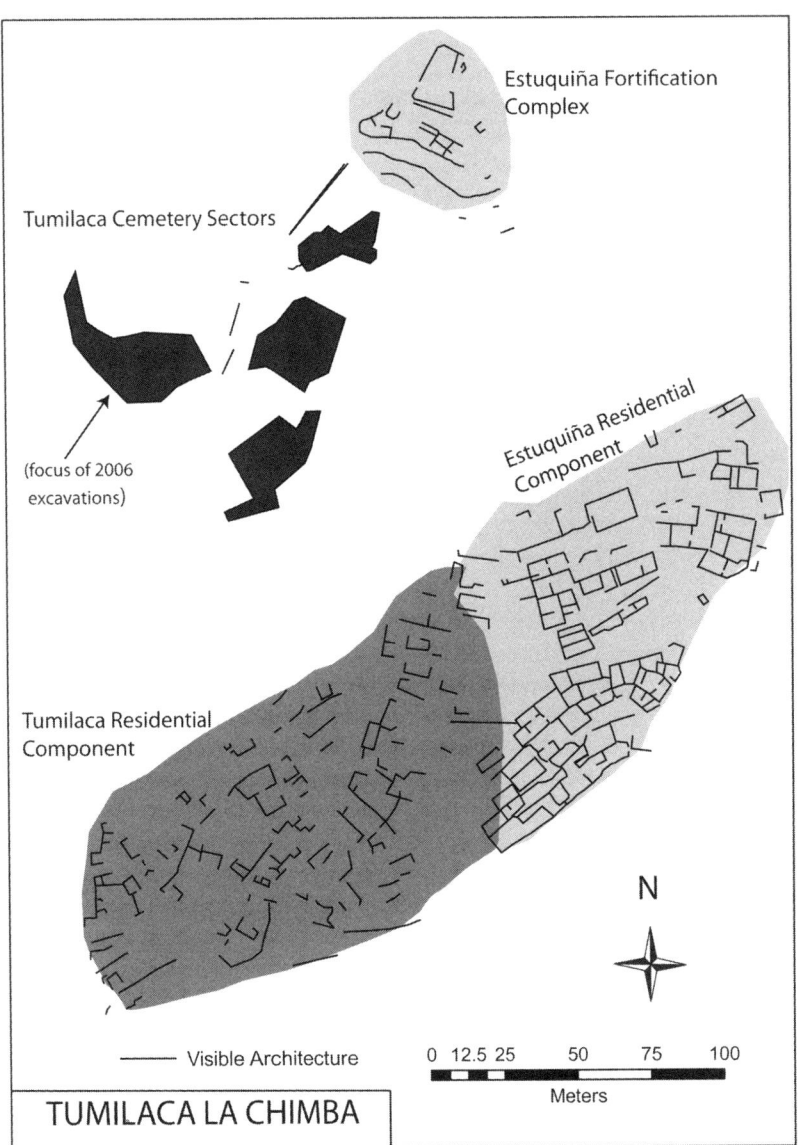

Figure 11.3. Map of Tumilaca la Chimba.

Based on visible tomb architecture, the cemetery has been separated into four sectors: three on the eastern slope of the ridge, and one on the western slope. The excavations discussed in this chapter were undertaken on the western slope, where the cemetery covers almost 1130 m². During the 2006 season, we excavated 120 m², essentially cutting a transect from the upper to lower areas of the ridge, and encountered approximately one tomb per 4 m². A total of 27 tombs were excavated, and despite the looting, the excavations furnished interesting data. Looting had largely been restricted to cultural materials. Six (22%) excavated tombs were determined to be intact, and even those that had been damaged revealed information on grave architecture and body position. Laboratory analysis of both cultural and biological materials is ongoing. However, observations in the field allow us to comment upon several aspects of mortuary behavior at Tumilaca la Chimba. In this chapter we deal specifically with grave architecture, interment treatment, and grave goods, and compare the evidence with that from earlier and later cemeteries in Moquegua.

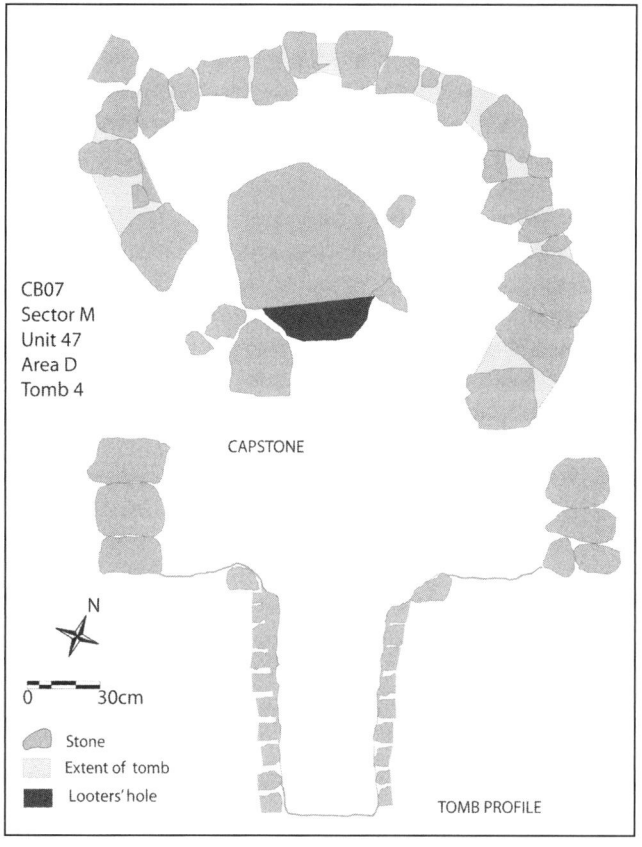

Figure 11.4. Stone-lined tomb, Tomb 4.

Figure 11.5. Stone-lined tomb, Tomb 15.

## Results

### Grave Architecture

Considerable variation in grave architecture is evident. All excavated tombs were roughly cylindrical in shape. All were subterranean, reaching an average depth of 1 m, although many had above-ground markers. Tombs were classified into three categories, based on wall construction: 11 were stone lined (*tumba*) (Figs. 11.4, 11.5); 10 were partially stone lined (*hoyo con alguna construcción de piedras*) (Figs. 11.6, 11.7); and 6 were unlined (*hoyo sin revestimiento*) (Figs. 11.8, 11.9). There appears to be no spatial variation in tomb types, as variation in wall construction was evident throughout the western slope, and tombs of differing wall construction are found in association with one another.

Fifteen tombs were further distinguished by an outer ring (Figs. 11.10, 11.11). These encircle the subterranean structure and reach a height of approximately 0.5 m. Outer rings are not exclusively associated with one type of wall construction, as examples of outer rings were found with all three tomb types. However, there does seem to be a spatial component to the distribution of outer rings, as outer rings were far more common in the middle or the bottom of the slope. The only example found in the upper slope was unusual in that it encircled two separate juvenile burials, whereas in all other cases the ring enclosed a single tomb.

The capstones of many tombs had been removed. Where present, they were often composed of several stones, rather than just one large slab. Floors were untreated in all but two cases. In these two cases, both infant burials, the individual had been placed in a seated position on a flat rock.

Variation in tomb structure not only crosscuts space, but also age at death. Adults, juveniles and infants were all found in the three different tomb categories, and outer rings were associated with both adults and children.

Grave architecture from Tumilaca la Chimba makes for an interesting comparison with that encountered at both the Chen Chen site and Late Intermediate sites in the Moquegua Valley. At Chen Chen, Owen (1997) reports cists (cylindrical tombs lined with stones, a few of which had a stone placed on the floor) and hoyos (also cylindrical tombs but with no stone lining). Both of these tomb types (in addition to partially lined tombs) were identified at Tumilaca la Chimba. Owen does not report outer rings. However, outer rings are mentioned by Williams et al. (1989)

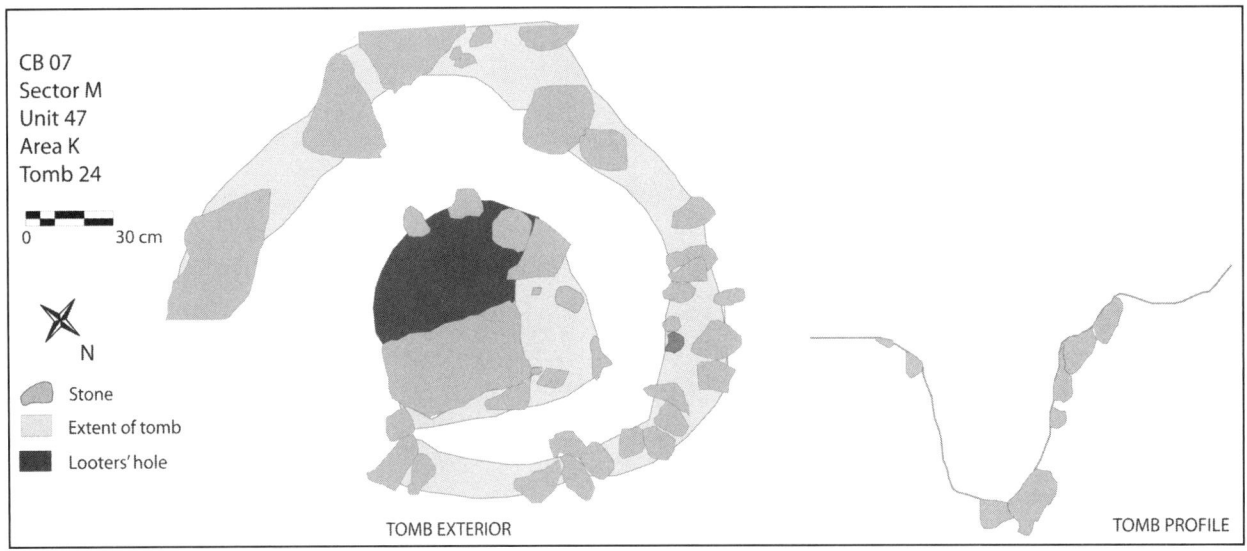

Figure 11.6. Partially stone-lined tomb, Tomb 24.

Figure 11.7. Partially stone-lined tomb, Tomb 16.

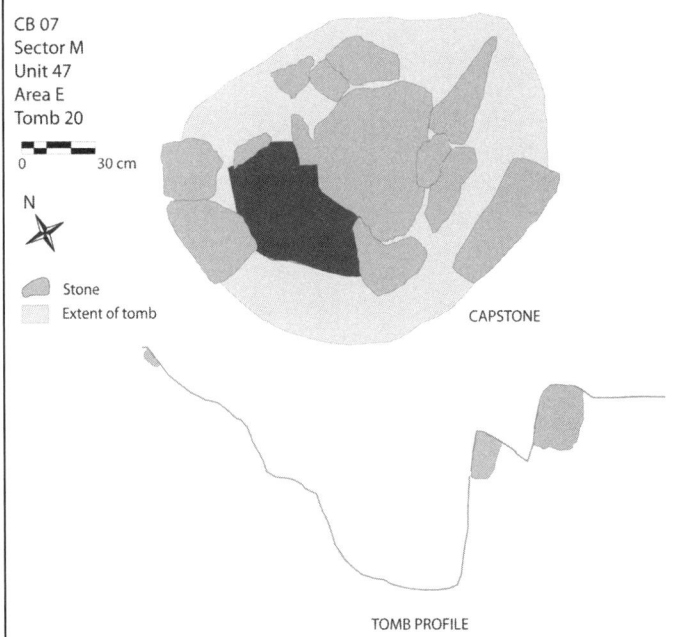

Figure 11.8. Tomb with no stone lining, Tomb 20.

Figure 11.9. Tomb with no stone lining, Tomb 20.

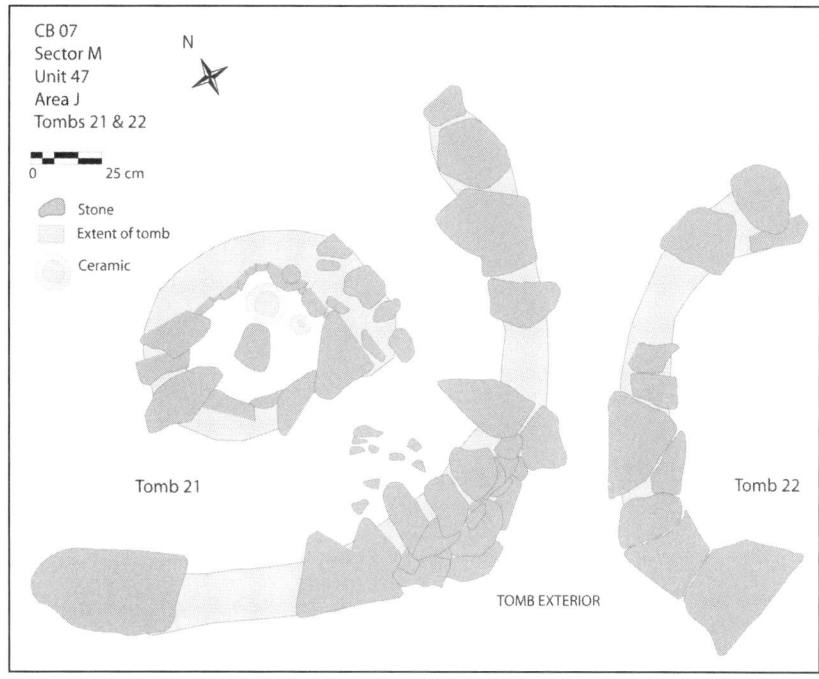

Figure 11.10. Outer rings surrounding Tombs 21 and 22.

Figure 11.11. Outer rings surrounding Tombs 21 and 22.

for the Late Intermediate period site of Estuquiña. Both those discussed by Williams et al. and those at Tumilaca la Chimba differ from the collared tombs reported by Stanish (1985).

Three types of tomb are evident at Tumilaca la Chimba, although all three forms have the same roughly cylindrical shape, and all are subterranean. There is no difference in the spatial distribution of tomb types, but there does appear to be a clear spatial distribution of outer rings. Examination of construction phases at Tumilaca la Chimba may elucidate whether the different tomb types represent a temporal shift, rather than act as indicators of individual status or identity. Elements of classic period Tiwanaku tomb construction clearly continued into the Tumilaca phase, but there is also evidence for the introduction of new forms, which arguably continued into the Late Intermediate period in Moquegua.

*Interment Treatment*

Human remains were identified in 25 of the excavated tombs. All remains were skeletal. Initial analysis demonstrates that a broad age range, as well as both biological sexes, is represented in the western cemetery. Infants, children, and juveniles accounted for 59% of individuals. There was also one fetal skeleton, three adolescents, four young adults and one older adult. Of the adults, there were two males, two females and a possible female. Pathologies included evidence for cribra orbitalia in nine individuals and possible tuberculosis in two. Degenerative joint disease affected one, while two demonstrated robust muscle attachments, likely a result of activity during life.

Interment treatment crosscut age and sex distinctions, as did grave architecture. Excellent preservation of original body position was encountered, even in most of the looted tombs. All burials were of single individuals. The 2006 excavations revealed no multiple burials. In all cases in which body position could be determined, individuals were in a flexed position. Nearly all individuals were seated, although two were lying on their right sides (CB06-47-0075 and CB06-47-0081). Given the shape of the tomb and evidence for decomposition, we are confident that at least one of these individuals was interred lying on their side. All individuals, without exception, were facing toward the east (Fig. 11.12), or, in two examples, southeast. This pattern of interment positioning illustrates strong continuities with the classic Tiwanaku cemeteries, where individuals are also interred in a flexed seated position facing east (Goldstein 2005).

Although conditions in the upper valley mean that preservation is not as good as at middle valley sites, such as Chen Chen, there is evidence that individuals were buried with woolen textiles and likely wrapped in fiber rope. Fragments of brown woven woolen cloth were found in 4 tombs. Braided fiber rope was in two contexts. In one of these (CB06-47-0081), the rope appeared to have been wrapped around the left arm; in the other (CB06-47-0078), the rope was by the top of the vertebral column, as well as by the arms and feet. Given that traces of rope have been found around the arms and shoulders of skeletons, we suggest that the body was held in a flexed position by the rope. This would mirror practices at Chen Chen where better preservation has revealed seated, flexed individuals wrapped in woven cloth and held in position by braided fiber rope (Owen 1997). Interment treatment practices are consistent across the western cemetery areas;

Figure 11.12. Individual facing east, Tomb 1.

again, investigation into the eastern areas will illuminate whether they were standard for the entire cemetery at Tumilaca la Chimba. Further, interment treatment practices appear to have been maintained from the classic Tiwanaku period into the Tumilaca phase.

*Grave Goods*

Looting at the Tumilaca la Chimba cemetery has affected cultural materials. Most ceramics retrieved during excavations were recovered through surface collection. Forms included *keros*, *tazones*, and jars. A fragment of an elaborately decorated painted zoomorphic *incensario* was found lying on the surface. Four complete vessels were recovered from intact contexts (two *keros*, a *tazon*, and a jar). Ceramics include both plain and decorated shards. Decorated ware was red-slipped with black, white and orange paints used in decoration (Fig. 11.13). Geometric designs predominated, but one *kero* (CB06-47-0026) interred in an intact infant burial was decorated with a stylized trophy head (Fig. 11.14). The material recovered here is comparable to that found by Pari (1980) in mortuary contexts on the eastern slope of the ridge. It is evident that the practice of including ceramic vessels in graves crosscut the cemetery, and ceramics were associated with adults and juveniles, as well as with all three types of tombs. Offerings were not ubiquitous, however. Four intact contexts included no ceramic offerings at all.

At Chen Chen, individuals were typically interred with one or two ceramic vessels, sometimes a wooden spoon, and occasionally other types of material (Owen 1997). At Tumilaca la Chimba, there was evidence for wooden fragments in 6 of the tombs excavated in 2006, and it is reasonable to suggest that these were also spoons. Preservation issues make it likely that they were included in other graves but did not survive, particularly given the disturbed nature of many contexts. As at Chen Chen, there is evidence that spoons were placed inside ceramic vessels.

Figure 11.13. *Kero* with black and orange geometric design, Tumilaca la Chimba.

Figure 11.14. *Kero* with depiction of stylized trophy head, Tumilaca la Chimba.

## Summary and Discussion

The large cemetery at Tumilaca la Chimba has great potential for informing investigations into late Tiwanaku populations in Moquegua. Although considerable evidence has been gathered on the settlement patterns and material culture of the Tumilaca phase, it is only recently that scholars have focused specifically on investigating who these people were biologically and to what extent they continued to express an affiliation with earlier Tiwanaku populations (Sharratt 2011; Sutter 2010). Mortuary data have proved instrumental to understanding classic period Tiwanaku in Moquegua (Blom et al. 1998). Biological and cultural data from Tumilaca la Chimba can similarly help answer questions about both the biological ancestry of late Tiwanaku populations and the social identity of those populations. Such investigations are central to understanding the implications of state collapse on regions that had been subsumed within the Tiwanaku polity.

We suggest that mortuary behavior at Tumilaca la Chimba was a combination of both tradition and innovation. Significant continuity from the classic period, as indicated by comparison with Chen Chen, is evident in interment treatment of individuals. As in the classic phase, individuals were buried in a seated, flexed position facing east, arguably wrapped in similar textiles and bound by braided fiber rope. Notions about appropriate grave goods were maintained—at least some individuals were accompanied by one or two ceramic vessels, and possibly wooden artifacts. However, mortuary behavior at Tumilaca la Chimba was not simply a seamless continuation of earlier practices. The ringed tombs suggest changes in, at very least, grave architecture. These are especially interesting, given their apparent similarity to those found at the Late Intermediate period cemetery at Estuquiña (Williams et al. 1989). Ongoing investigations into the relative chronology of different tomb forms, particularly the outer rings, will contribute to a clearer understanding of grave differentiation at the site.

As the largest Late Tiwanaku cemetery in the Moquegua Valley, Tumilaca la Chimba has the potential to answer questions about the biological heritage and cultural identity of Tumilaca populations, and by so doing to shed light on the effects of the end of Tiwanaku influence in the south-central Andes. The data discussed here will be supplemented by further investigations throughout the cemetery.

## Acknowledgments

Support for the excavations at Tumilaca la Chimba was provided by Dumbarton Oaks and the National Endowment for the Humanities grant to the Cerro Baúl Project, directed by Ryan Williams, Mike Moseley, and María Elena Rojas Chávez. We thank Donna Nash, Karl La Favre, Sabrina Scholtz, and Sofía Chacaltana for assistance in the field. Work was permitted by the Instituto Nacional de Cultura del Perú by RDN 1208/INC dated 26 July 2006. All errors or omissions are the responsibility of the authors.

## References Cited

Bawden, G.
1989 The Tumilaca site and post-Tihuanaco occupational stratigraphy. In *Ecology, Settlement and History in the Osmore Drainage, Peru*, edited by Don S. Rice, Charles Stanish, and Phillip R. Scarr, pp. 287–302. British Archaeological Reports, International Series, vol. 545(i), Oxford, U.K.

Bermann, M., P. Goldstein, C. Stanish, and L. Watanabe M.
1989 The collapse of the Tiwanaku state: A view from the Osmore drainage. In *Ecology, Settlement and History in the Osmore Drainage, Peru*, edited by Don S. Rice, Charles Stanish, and Phillip R. Scarr, pp. 269–86. British Archaeological Reports, International Series, vol. 545(i), Oxford, U.K.

Blom, D.
1999 Tiwanaku Regional Interaction and Social Identity. PhD dissertation, Department of Anthropology, University of Chicago, IL.

Blom, D., B. Hallgrímsson, L. Keng, M. C. Lozada, and J. E. Buiskra
1998 Tiwanaku 'colonization': Bioarchaeological implications for migration in the Moquegua Valley, Peru. *World Archaeology* 30(2):238–61.

Goldstein, P.
1985 Tiwanaku Ceramics of the Moquegua Valley, Peru. Master's thesis, Department of Anthropology, University of Chicago, IL.
1989 Omo: A Tiwanaku Provincial Center in Moquegua, Peru. PhD dissertation, Department of Anthropology, University of Chicago, IL.
2005 *Andean Diaspora: The Tiwanaku Colonies and the Origins of South American Empire*. University of Florida Press, Gainesville.

Janusek, J. W.
2003 Vessels, time and society: Toward a ceramic chronology in the Tiwanaku heartland. In *Tiwanaku and Its Hinterland: Archaeology and Paleoecology of an Andean Civilization*, edited by A. L. Kolata, pp. 30–91. Urban and Rural Archaeology, vol. 2. Smithsonian Institution Press, Washington, D.C.
2004 *Identity and Power in the Ancient Andes*. Routledge, London.
2005 Collapse as cultural revolution: Power and identity in the Tiwanaku to Pacajes transition. In *Foundations of Power in the Prehispanic Andes*, edited by K. J. Vaughn, D. Ogburn, and C. A. Conlee, pp. 175–210. American Anthropological Association, Arlington, Virginia.

Kolata, A.
1993 *Tiwanaku: Portrait of an Andean Civilization*. Blackwell, Cambridge.

Owen, B.
1993 A Model of Multiethnicity: State Collapse, Competition, and Social Complexity from Tiwanaku to Chiribaya in the Osmore Valley, Peru. PhD dissertation, University of California, Los Angeles.
1996 *Inventario Arqueológico del Drenaje Superior del Río Osmore: Informe del Campo y Informe Final*. Report submitted to the Instituto Nacional de Cultura del Perú.
2005 Distant colonies and explosive collapse: The two stages of the Tiwanaku diaspora in the Osmore drainage. *Latin American Antiquity* 16(1):45–80.

Pari Flores, R. E.
1980 Excavación Arqueológica en la Necropolis de Tumilaka–Moquegua. Bachelor's thesis, Universidad Católica Santa María, Arequipa, Peru.

Sharratt, N.
2011 Social Identities and State Collapse: A Diachronic Study of Tiwanaku Burials in the Moquegua Valley, Peru. PhD dissertation, Department of Anthropology, University of Illinois at Chicago, IL.

Sims, Kenny
2006 After state collapse: How Tumilaca communities developed in the Upper Moquegua Valley, Peru. In *After Collapse*, edited by Glenn M. Schwartz and John J. Nichols, pp. 114–36. University of Arizona Press, Tucson.

Stanish, Charles
1985 Post-Tiwanaku Regional Economics in the Otora Valley, Southern Peru. PhD dissertation, Department of Anthropology, University of Chicago, IL.

Sutter, R., and N. Sharratt
2010 Continuity and transformation during the Terminal Middle Horizon (A.D. 950–1150): A bioarchaeological assessment of Tumilaca origins within the Middle Moquegua Valley, Peru. *Latin American Antiquity* 21(1):67–86.

Vargas, V. B.
1988 *Rescate arqueológico del cementerio de Chen Chen*. Report submitted to the Instituto Nacional de Cultura del Perú.

Williams, P. R.
2002 Rethinking disaster-induced collapse in the demise of the Andean highland states: Wari and Tiwanaku. *World Archaeology* 33(3):361–74.

Williams, S. A., J. E. Buikstra, N. R. Clark, M. C. Lozada C., and E. Torres Pino
1989 Mortuary site excavations and skeletal biology in the Osmore project. In *Ecology, Settlement and History in the Osmore Drainage, Peru*, edited by D. Rice, C. Stanish, and P. Scarr, pp. 329–46. British Archaeological Reports, International Series, vol. 545(i), Oxford, U.K.

# Chapter 12

# Above-Ground Tombs in the Circum-Titicaca Basin

*Charles Stanish*

**Introduction**

For millennia throughout the south central Andes, people buried their dead exclusively in below-ground tombs. Around the twelfth century AD, a new practice spread throughout the region—people began to bury some of their dead in above-ground tombs. Not only were these visible markers on the landscape, but they also became places of repeated ritual use. Over time, above-ground tombs became more elaborate as true mausoleums of large groups of people, presumably kin groups. Simultaneously, the majority of people continued to bury their dead in below-ground cist tombs holding at most two people, and usually only one. This chapter explores this phenomenon. I describe the above-ground tomb types so far recorded in the south central Andes and seek to understand what kinds of changes in twelfth-century society led to this radical transformation in the treatment of the dead in the ancient south central Andes.

The most famous above-ground tombs in the region are called "chulpas" or "chullpas" (Hyslop 1977). The term "chulpa" is most likely of Aymara origin. It appears in Bertonio's Aymara-Spanish dictionary and is defined as a "grave or large basket where they placed their dead" (Bertonio [1612] 1956: 2nd vol.). Over the last generation, we have discovered quite a few mummies wrapped in baskets, usually found in caves.

According to Stig Rydén, the original meaning of the term "chulpa" signified a "basket and the corpse enclosed within it," most certainly reflecting these basket burials. "Chulpa" has since come to mean virtually any above-ground ancient grave or even cave site with burials (Rydén 1947:330–31).[1] Bertonio ([1612] 1956: bk 1, p. 218) lists another word that is most likely a more accurate term to describe the above-ground stone burial towers. The Aymara word "amaya uta" means "house of the soul" and refers to the above-ground tombs at least in the Titicaca Basin. This word is probably a more appropriate term than chulpa, but the latter is so deeply entrenched in the literature that it is best left unchanged.

Alongside chulpas are a variety of above-ground tomb types that are found throughout the south central Andes, most notably in the Titicaca Basin (Figs. 12.1, 12.2). In this chapter, I describe these various types and try to locate them in space and time, and I propose that the emergence of above-ground burials was linked to the collapse of the Tiwanaku state circa AD 900–1000. The key function of the more elaborate chulpas was the formation of elite alliances while other tomb types were used to house corporate groups, usually families in agro-pastoral societies. These more humble tomb types functioned to mark territory and to provide a locus for periodic pilgrimages by small family groups or ayllu to their ancestral lands.

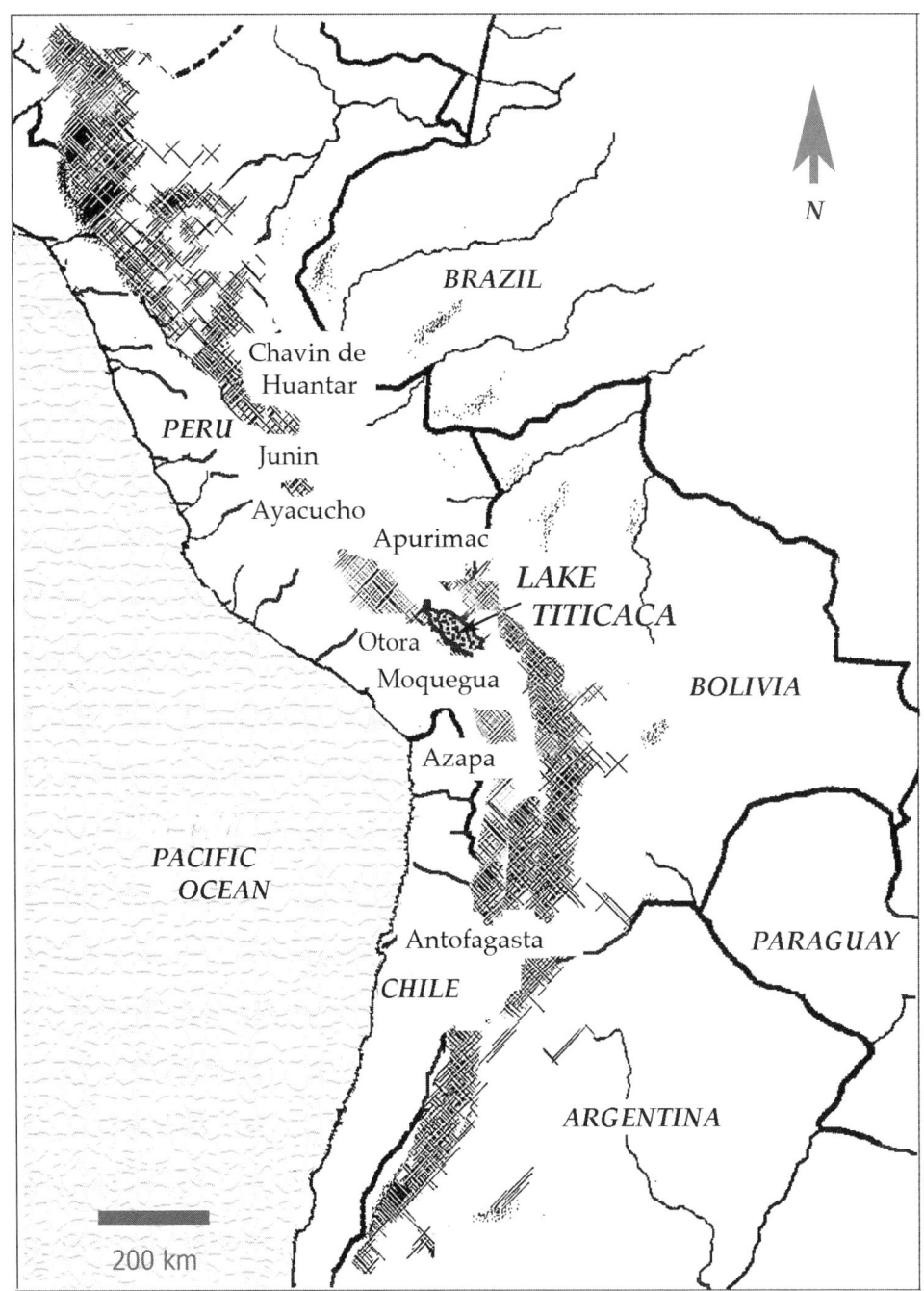

Figure 12.1. The south central Andes.

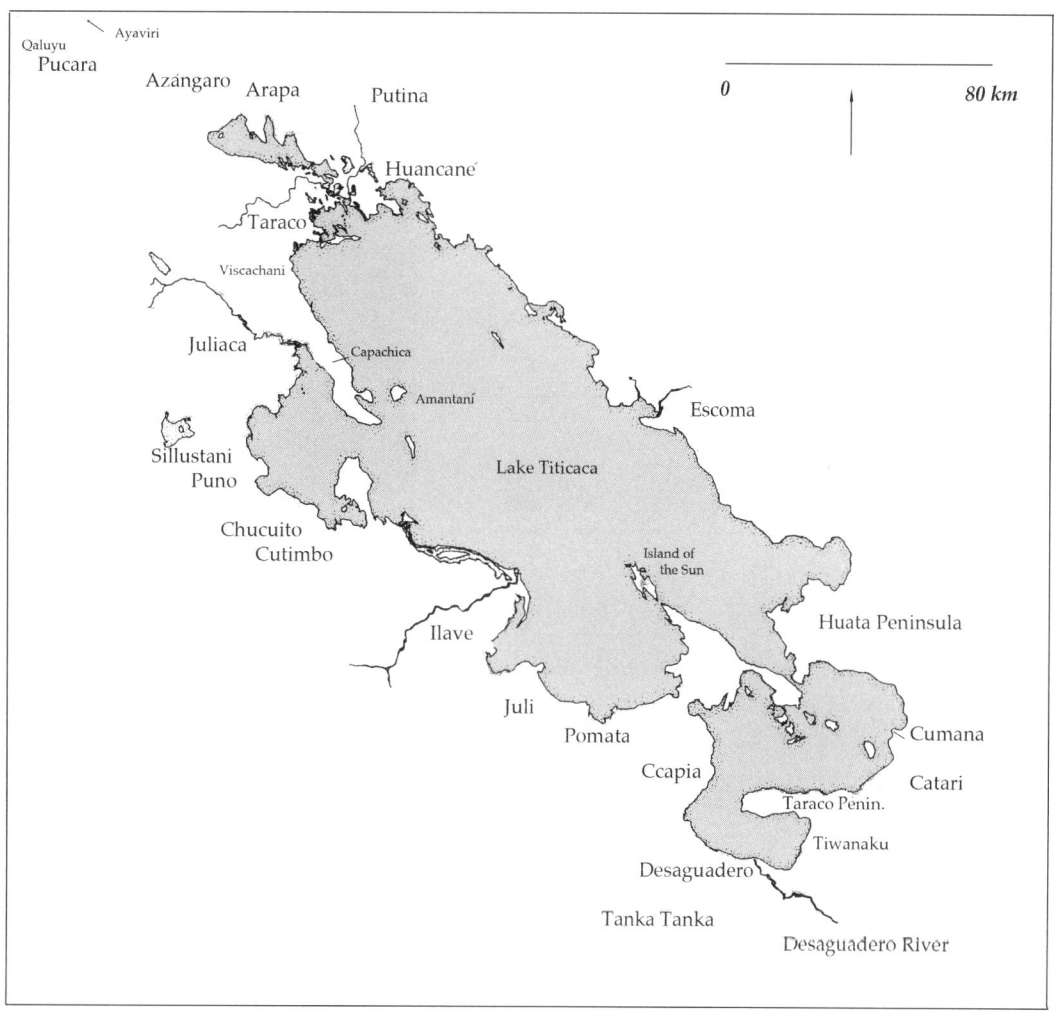

Figure 12.2. The Titicaca Basin.

## Above-Ground Tomb Types

The above-ground burial towers were some of the first monuments to attract the attention of the chroniclers who traveled through the south central Andes. Chulpas were noted by the early naturalists—such as Squier (1870, 1877), Nordenskiöld (1906a, 1906b), Conway (1899) and Bandelier (1905), to name a few—who explored the Andes.

Chulpa architecture varies throughout the central Andes. The most elaborate are the classic examples found at the site of Sillustani in the northwest side of the Titicaca Basin, or at the site of Cutimbo in the west (Figs. 12.3, 12.4). These towers are square or round and reach several meters in height. Some are built with finely carved Inca-style masonry, particularly those at Sillustani, a fact that suggests a Late Horizon construction date. Most other chulpas are more modest in construction and are built out of fieldstones or adobe (Bandelier 1905; Hyslop 1976, 1977; Vásquez 1937a). Variations include the smaller Type 3 chulpa of Tschopik (1946:16), Hyslop's "igloo shaped" chulpas, his "transitional" types (Hyslop 1977:154) (Figs. 12.5, 12.6), "roofed" chulpas (Fig. 12.7) and the ubiquitous small chulpas (Fig. 12.8). Larger chulpas are also constructed out of adobe (Figs. 12.9–12.12), well-fitted fieldstones, poorly fitted fieldstones (Fig. 12.13) and cut blocks. In the circum-Titicaca region, major chulpa sites include Viscachani (Tschopik 1946:6), Tanka Tanka (Hyslop 1976:334; Vásquez, Carpio, and Velazco 1935), the Cumana Peninsula, Cutimbo, a number of areas around Ayaviri, and the flanks of the Río Desaguadero.

Chulpas are found in abundance throughout the entire central Andes and have been reported as far north as Huancavelica (Matos 1960:316–17) and Chavín de Huantar (Burger 1982) and as far south as the Río Loa in Antofagasta (Aldunate and Castro 1981). Gisbert (1994) and Kesseli and Pärssinen (2005) illustrate some beautiful adobe chulpas in south central and southern Bolivia. Numerous chulpas are also found in the Cusco area (Kaufmann-Doig 1983:538), in Apurímac (Arrendo 1942),

(*above*) Figure 12.3. Chulpa at the site of Cutimbo, Puno. Photo: C. Stanish.

(*right*) Figure 12.4. Chulpa at the site of Cutimbo, Puno. Photo: C. Stanish.

(*below*) Figure 12.5. Fieldstone chulpa at the site of AR-1062, near Arapa, Peru. Photo: A. Umire.

(*top*) Figure 12.6. Large fieldstone chulpa at the site of Yacari-Tuntachawi, near Juli. Photo: C. Stanish.

(*middle*) Figure 12.7. Roofed chulpa from Carabaya, above Ollachea. Photo: C. Stanish.

(*bottom*) Figure 12.8. Small chulpa in the high puna, near Mazocruz. Photo: E. de la Vega.

Figure 12.9. Adobe chulpas from Sillustani. Photo: C. Stanish.

Figure 12.10. Adobe chulpa from the site of AR-1374, near Arapa, Peru. Photo: A. Umire.

Figure 12.11. Adobe chulpa from the site of AR-1172, near Arapa, Peru. Photo: A. Umire.

Figure 12.12. Adobe chulpa from the site of AR-1374, near Arapa, Peru. Photo: A. Umire.

Figure 12.13. Chulpa from the site of HU-532, near Huancané, Peru. Photo: C. Stanish.

in the Ayacucho Valley, and in other areas throughout the central Andes. We can presently identify more than a dozen chulpa types in the Titicaca Basin.

Apart from chulpas, there are several other above-ground and visible types including collar tombs (Stanish 1992:121–36) (Fig. 12.14), slab-cist tombs (Tschopik 1946:19), hillside tombs, stone fence graves (Rydén 1947:362), and tumuli (Focacci and Erices 1971; Goldstein 2000; Muñoz 1996). Collar tombs are described below but essentially consist of a below-ground cist tomb surrounded by a low circular wall. Slab-cist tombs are very common in the Titicaca region. They generally range in diameter from 2 to 5 m. Some can be quite large, as seen in Figure 12.15, while others are more modest (Figs. 12.16–12.18). The limited evidence indicates that they contained numerous individuals.

Squier illustrates one rather large slab-cist tomb with a corbelled roof (Squier 1870:3). He is not the most accurate of nineteenth-century naturalists and one has to take his drawings with some skepticism; it is likely that the human figure used as a scale was smaller than the "original." However, his drawing of a very large slab circle at Sillustani is generally accurate.

Hillside tombs are rarely reported in the area, most likely because they have been heavily looted. The ones seen in Figures 12.19 and 12.20 are associated with pottery styles from all time periods in the region and a definitive date cannot be determined for these at the present time. Tumuli, also discussed below, are found in at least Ilave in the Lake Titicaca drainage and in the western valleys of Moquegua and Azapa. Their former distribution was most likely much larger.

Figure 12.14. Collar tomb from the site of P-4, Otora, Peru. Excavations by R. Pari. Photo: D. Jessup.

Figure 12.15. Large slab-cist tomb near the town of Caya Caya, Peru. Photo: A. Umire.

(*top*) Figure 12.16. Several slab-cist tombs on the site of AR-1100, near Arapa, Peru. Photo: A. Umire.

(*middle*) Figure 12.17. A modest slab-cist tomb at the site of TA-706, near Taraco, Peru. Photo: A. Umire.

(*bottom*) Figure 12.18. Slab-cist tombs on a ridge at the site of AR-1104, near Arapa, Peru. The location of slab cists in clusters on ridges is a common find in the region. Photo: A. Umire.

Figure 12.19. Hillside graves in a rockshelter at the site of AR-1112, near Arapa, Peru. Photo: A. Umire.

Figure 12.20. Hillside graves in a rockshelter at the site of AR-1112, near Arapa, Peru. Photo: A. Umire.

## Chulpa Function

Throughout the nineteenth and early twentieth centuries, most scholars accepted the Spanish chroniclers' interpretation that the massive chulpas at sites such as Sillustani were indeed graves or mausoleums for the dead, particularly the dead elite (Hutchinson 1875; Rivero and Tschudi 1855:292; Squier 1877:388). Three of the major Spanish chroniclers—Bernabé Cobo (1956), Pedro Cieza de León (1967) and Felipe Guamán Poma de Ayala (1980:262–65, 268–72)—provided descriptions and/or drawings of chulpas as burial chambers. Cobo even noted that indigenous graves vary throughout the Andes and that the above-ground chulpas are most typical of the Colla in the Titicaca Basin (Rydén 1947:408–9). The early Spanish travelers and crown officials originally described the stone and adobe towers that they encountered as "mausoleums" for dead nobility. Cieza de León also commented that these towers were most remarkable in the Titicaca Basin and unequivocally described them as tombs: "the most notable thing to see in Collao, in my view, are the graves of the dead . . . made of small, four-cornered towers, some of stone and others of earth and stone, some wide and others narrow" (quoted from Rydén 1947:407). Bernabé Cobo also ascribed the chulpas to the Colla and describes them at great length as burial towers (Cobo 1956: vol. IV).

The available evidence suggests that all chulpas and most slab-cist tombs were burials for corporate groups and not individuals. The first controlled excavations of chulpas were conducted by Erland Nordenskiöld (1906b) in the early part of the twentieth century. This pioneering naturalist worked in the northeast side of Lake Titicaca in the high valleys of the altiplano (Aldunate and Castro 1981:86). One of the most striking results of Nordenskiöld's excavations was the discovery of collective burials in the chulpas, in some cases totaling as many as 200 individuals (Aldunate and Castro 1981:86). Later excavations by other scholars also supported the interpretation that chulpas functioned primarily as multiple burial chambers. Ryden's (1947:343–61) work in circum-Titicaca Basin "grave houses" produced numerous instances of multiple burials in stone and adobe chulpas. In spite of the fact that all the chulpas excavated by Ryden were looted, numerous human skeletal remains were still present. Similarly, Arrendo notes that in a site in the Department of Apurímac each tomb had "a great number of mummies" that presumably were destined for a family with "no individual tombs evident" (Arrendo 1942:58).

John Hyslop further argues that chulpas were elite constructions associated with an increasing importance of "ancestor-related religious or ceremonial rites" after the collapse of Tiwanaku hegemony (1977:169–70). He also references historical reports suggesting a field boundary function of chulpas—that is, the burial chambers may delineate agricultural fields or pasture lands. Hyslop then offers a hypothetical link between elite control of agricultural land and chulpa distribution, offering a model relating the collapse of Tiwanaku power, the development of independent polities, elite control of land and the emergence of chulpas (Hyslop 1977:160).

A notable exception to the interpretation of chulpas as burial chambers was offered by Adolph Bandelier (1905), who concluded that some of the large chulpas at Sillustani were Inca storehouses or colcas. George Serracino (1979) has also argued that some chulpas in the circum-Puno area were used for storage and not as tombs. Other interpretations of chulpas include their use as residential dwellings (Gutiérrez N. 1935, 1937; Vásquez, Carpio, and Velazco 1935:243). In a review of the existing literature, Ryden noted that Middendorf and Bennett used the term "chulpa" to refer to habitations in the Callejón de Huaylas and that Gutiérrez N. (1935) used the term for prehistoric round structures in Junín (Ryden 1947:449).

Carlos Aldunate and Victoria Castro excavated eleven smaller chulpas in the Río Loa drainage in northern Chile. Unlike previous investigators, they did not discover significant human remains in the excavated structures. In their principal publication on this work (1981) and in subsequent articles (Aldunate, Berenguer, and Castro 1982; Berenguer, Aldunate, and Castro 1984) they concluded that the chulpas were not used as tombs, but instead functioned as ceremonial loci for rituals similar to those practiced in the region today. While agreeing that the chulpas were primarily ceremonial in nature, they offer the first comprehensive archaeological evidence against interpretations of some chulpas as burials (see Castro and Aldunate 2003).

## Dates for Above-Ground Tombs in the Circum-Titicaca Basin

John Hyslop carried out the first systematic reconnaissance of a Titicaca Basin region just over one decade ago. His survey of the Lupaqa region dates all chulpa types firmly after the collapse of Tiwanaku power in the region coincident with major shifts and changes in settlement patterns and artifact styles. Intensive surveys in the Juli-Pomata area in the west and in the northern Titicaca Basin located the remains of numerous above-ground tombs (Stanish et al. 1997). Virtually all of these tombs were associated with habitation sites or had pottery nearby that dated to the Late Intermediate period, Late Horizon and/or Early Colonial period.

Virtually all objects recovered from above-ground tombs in the circum-Titicaca region are post-Tiwanaku in style. However, there are a few notable exceptions. Erland Nordenskiöld was one of the first to report several ceramic types from chulpa graves that Ryden characterized as "Decadent Tiahuanaco" (in Ryden 1947:444). Likewise, Paul Goldstein convincingly argues that the Putuni chamber tombs at Tiwanaku were "the first chulpas" (2005:258). He furthermore reports that a small but significant percentage of cist tombs in the Tiwanaku colony of Omo in Moquegua had collars or rings of stone to mark the surface (Goldstein 2005:247). Also significant is his observation that in some instances at least, Tiwanaku cist tombs were marked with wooden poles in places such as Azapa, San Pedro de Atacama and Omo itself (Goldstein 2005:246).

Goldstein furthermore reports that the Huaracane occupations in the Moquegua region had tumuli, similar to those found in the

Azapa. He dates these three-meter-high constructions to the last three centuries BCE (Goldstein 2000:349). Similar dates were obtained for the northern Chilean tumuli where they are Alto Ramirez in tradition (Muñoz 1996). Similar tumuli were found in the Titicaca Basin in the Ilave River by the author of this chapter in 1997. We therefore see that the above-ground burial tradition began in the Upper Formative, reaching a zenith in the Late Intermediate and Late Horizon periods.

### The Otora Valley: Settlement and Funerary Data

Otora is one of four major sierra tributaries (2500–3000 masl) of the Moquegua (Osmore) drainage (Fig. 12.21) located in the extremely arid Peruvian south (70° latitude × 17° longitude). Like so many of the valleys of the western slopes in the south central Andes, Otora has a number of above-ground tombs associated with prehispanic settlements. Survey indicated that many of these sites also have below-ground tombs in domestic areas and in nearby cemeteries. The Otora drainage is small and the total number of sites limited. There is a sequence of sites from the Tiwanaku period up to the Inca and Colonial periods. Each of these sites has burials. The data, therefore, allow us to reconstruct burial patterns through time, at least in this valley.

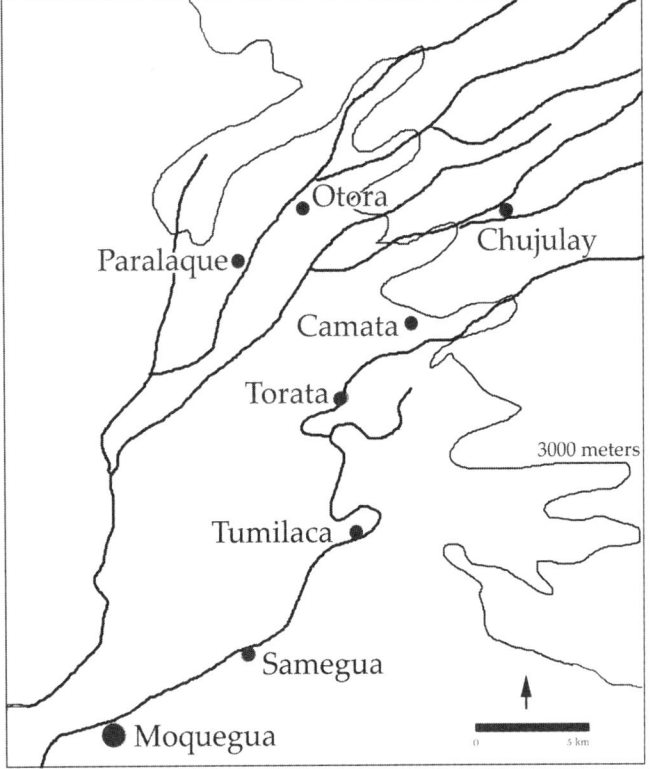

Figure 12.21. The location of the Otora Valley, Peru.

An intensive surface survey located thirteen sites in the immediate Otora Valley (Fig. 12.22). Five prehispanic periods were defined (Stanish 1985, 1992). The earliest settlement in Otora was represented by a single hamlet (P-5) dated to a post-Tiwanaku period known locally as Tumilaca (Bermann et al. 1989:273). This period is hypothesized to represent a local polity that controlled the entire Moquegua drainage immediately after the collapse of Tiwanaku control of the region. The Tumilaca period would immediately postdate the Tiwanaku 5 period in the region, known locally as the Chen Chen phase (Goldstein 1989:237). The evidence for this model of a localized polity includes ceramic and architectural data from P-5 as well as other sites in the drainage.

All tombs associated with late Tiwanaku and Tumilaca period sites in the Moquegua drainage are stone-lined cist types, ranging from 35 to 85 cm in mouth diameter and between 50 and 200 cm in depth. Most tombs contain one or two bodies that were buried in a flexed position, wrapped and mummified. The burials were usually accompanied with offerings such as ceramic vessels, gourds, foodstuffs, baskets, wooden spoons, rapé tablets and other utilitarian and/or ritual objects. Cist tombs are the exclusive burial mode in the Tiwanaku V and Tumilaca period in the Osmore drainage.

The following Otora period in the Otora Valley typifies the dramatic cultural change that occurred after the collapse of the local Tumilaca period settlement system in the drainage. Five sites (P-4, P-7, P-8, P-9 and P-12) have been dated to this period using several independent lines of evidence, including stylistic comparisons of ceramics to established sequences, architecture, and existing $^{14}$C dates from similar sites in the region (Stanish 1991, 1992). Two of these sites (P-4 and P-8) represent colonial extensions of coastal Chiribaya (P-4) and northern Titicaca Basin polities (P-8) respectively. A third (P-7) is best interpreted as an indigenous settlement developing out of the earlier Tumilaca period site of P-5. It is also possible that P-7 is a Tumilaca period site, but if this is the case, it would not alter the funerary pattern data. The remaining sites are small, specialized, and nonresidential. The Otora period in the Otora Valley, in fact, represents a classic case of multiethnic colonization and land use of an upper sierra valley as hypothesized by Murra for the Chillón Valley in the late sixteenth century (Stanish 1992:136).

Collar or ring tombs first appear in the valley during the Otora period at the sites of P-4 and P-8 (see Williams et al. 1989:333–37 and Sharratt et al., this volume); they combine elements of both below-ground cists and completely above-ground chulpas. Collared and ring tombs are essentially composed of a traditional cist tomb with a low stone wall, approximately 2.0 m in diameter, surrounding a prepared floor above the capstones (Williams et al. 1989:333). The wall height was not determined, but it was probably not more than 50–100 cm and there is no evidence for a roof. The mummified bodies of both males and females were placed in the cist while offerings of ceramic vessels, guinea pigs and possibly other objects were left inside the walled area on the surface. No grave goods were found inside the cist itself. While the actual body was apparently treated no differently from that

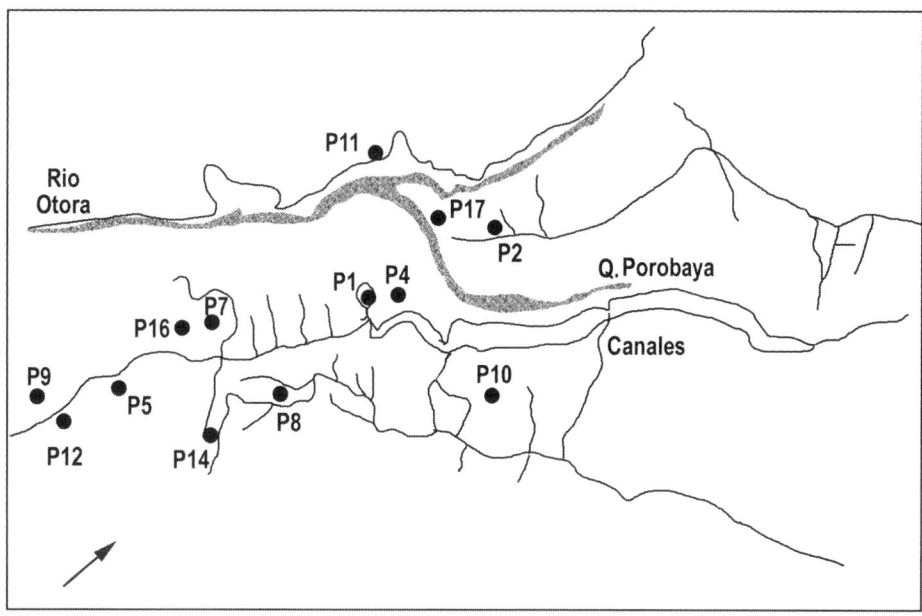

Figure 12.22. Sites located on survey in the Otora Valley, Peru.

in earlier cist tomb practices, the interment area was visible and constructed to allow permanent access. Visibility of funerary architecture and permanent access to the burial area are the essential features that distinguish completely above-ground chulpas from other types of below-ground burials.

Collared tombs are found on the sites of P-8 and P-4. All of these were looted. Most of the looting occurred prior to the eruption of the volcano Huaynaputina in February of 1600. The volcanic ash layer above the looted tombs determines this date. At P-4, these collar tombs coexisted with below-ground tombs and chulpas in a cemetery area adjacent to, but away from, the habitation. P-4 also had cist tombs under residential floors in the residential area. At P-8, three collared tombs were located in the site's residential area while at least three cist tombs were located in a cemetery area away from the site. Excavations of the collar tombs revealed the presence of human remains, llama phalanges, pottery, maize and cuy remains (Stanish 1985: appendix 7). At P-8, an AMS date for a domestic structure associated with the collar tombs was 945 +/- 20 BP. This calibrates to 2-sigma AD 1027–1155.

One possibly significant feature of P-8 is that the three collar tombs were associated with a single room block. As seen in Figure 12.23, there were four blocks of structures that most likely represented different social groups. One interpretation is that the collar tombs were adopted by the group represented by the nearby architectural block while the rest of the people in other room groups continued to bury their dead in the "traditional" below-ground manner.

The following Estuquiña and Estuquiña-Inca periods are characterized by the adoption of fortification walls (Moseley 1990:243), a shift to strategic hilltops, population increases, agricultural intensification, the rise of social hierarchies, and the appearance of completely above-ground chulpas. Several sites in the Otora Valley date to these two periods. Principal residential sites include Porobaya (P-1), Colana (P-2), Sajena (P-3) and Paralaque (P-6). These sites are dated by the presence of Sillustani-, Gentilar-, and Inca-style ceramics in various domestic and non-domestic contexts. Sillustani and Gentilar begin in the pre-Inca (ca. AD 1300–1400) periods in the region and continue into the Late Horizon (Lumbreras and Amat 1968; Lumbreras 1974). Both pre-Inca and Late Horizon variants are found in the Estuquiña and Estuquiña-Inca sites in Otora. One $^{14}$C date of 490 +/- 80 BP (2-sigma AD 1295–1631) from a house floor on P-1 is consistent with Estuquiña and Estuquiña-Inca periods.

Several independent lines of evidence strongly suggest that these Estuquiña settlements represent an indigenous sierra culture that developed out of the earlier multiethnic sites in the valley of the Otora period (Stanish 1992:170–74). These data strongly suggest that the Estuquiña sites were not altiplano colonies (specifically Lupaqa), as has been hypothesized previously for the region (e.g., Murra 1968; Mujica, Rivera, and Lynch 1983:94), but were politically autonomous settlements maintaining extensive exchange relationships with both the coast and the puna. There is, in fact, absolutely no evidence of significant external colonization of the Moquegua sierra during this period.

There were several hundred looted cist tombs on the Estuquiña sites. As with below-ground tombs in general throughout the Moquegua drainage, there are rarely more than two individuals interred in any single below-ground grave. Usually, cist tombs contain only one body. Discrete cemeteries are located on the site

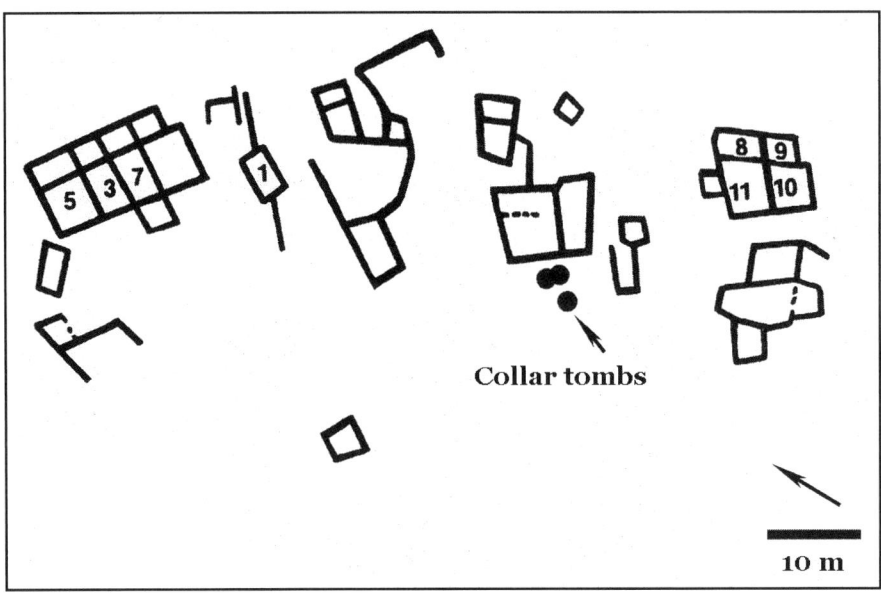

Figure 12.23. The site of P-8 with three collar tombs located next to a cluster of rooms.

peripheries, both inside and outside the major defensive walls. Individual cist tombs are also found under habitation floors.

At the largest site of Porobaya (P-1), a major cemetery is located on a hilltop approximately 75 m away from the site's main residential area. There are two groups of chulpas in this cemetery, containing five and four graves respectively. A series of cist tombs are located on a low terrace immediately below one of these groups. With one possible exception, there are no chulpas located on the residential area of the site.

The chulpas in this cemetery, as well as those in the other Estuquiña and Estuquiña-Inca period sites, are completely above ground. They would correspond to Hyslop's "early" or "transitional" types (Hyslop 1977:157) in the altiplano (ca. AD 1200). The Estuquiña period chulpas have a base diameter of 2.0–2.5 m, are constructed of fieldstone masonry, and have east-facing "doors" or open niches. All of the chulpas in Otora were looted, and many were destroyed prior to AD 1600.[2] At the single-component Estuquiña period site of P-2, there were several chulpas on, or near, the residential area. More chulpas were located at the "entrance" of the site in an open plaza area between two main defensive walls. One chulpa was built on a small promontory on the site's northern side while another group was built below the site's southern side, between two sets of agricultural terraces. All other major Estuquiña and Estuquiña-Inca period sites in the Moquegua drainage had chulpas similar to those investigated at Porobaya.

Excavations of the chulpas revealed a full suite of grave goods including wooden spoons, baskets, cuy remains, camelid phalanges, pottery, combs, and textiles. One chulpa that had been looted prior to AD 1600 had two floors. The upper floor had been completed removed. About 75% of the lower floor was intact. This slightly ovoid, fieldstone chulpa was approximately 2.3 × 2.0 m at the base with an interior chamber of between 70 and 100 cm. We estimate its height originally at around 2.0–2.5 m. It was in a group of eight other chulpas of similar construction.

The remains inside this chulpa (identified as "P1-ch2" in Stanish 1985: appendix 7) included at least five humans—three adults, one child and one infant.[3] Other grave goods included: 76 llama phalanges representing 27 articulated feet, cuy bones (MNI = 14), 12 maize cobs, gourd fragments, textile fragments, wood fragments, freshwater shrimp, a wooden spoon, marine shell (minimum 3), cactus spine needles (minimum 15), cuy feces, a cryptocrystalline quartz knife, and a ceramic jar. This of course represents just a part of one floor. It is likely that the chulpa contained several times more individuals and contents in antiquity. The importance of this excavation is that it was an intact context. Virtually all chulpas are looted and many were reused for rituals. The objects in this one were those placed there at the time of interment and use.

The Inca period occupation of the Otora Valley was characterized by the abandonment of the hilltop, fortified locations and a resettlement to lower, valley bottom hamlets dispersed along the modern canals. Most sites are small sherd scatters without surface architecture. They generally have evidence of extensive Spanish Colonial and Republican occupations. Being adjacent to the canals, they are also favored locations for modern farming settlements and have therefore been severely disturbed for centuries.

One Late Horizon site (P-13) remains relatively intact without any post-Hispanic occupations or major disturbances. This site is located high up in the Otora Valley near the Estuquiña-Inca period site of Sajena (P-3). It has approximately 12 rooms built in a local architectural style that incorporated Inca-style wall niches. This site most likely represents a local, Late Horizon population

Figure 12.24. Modern cemetery from the Mazocruz area. Photo: E. de la Vega.

and may be seen as an example of the other now-destroyed Inca period sites lower in the valley.

There are no above-ground tombs at P-13 and no evidence for below-ground cist tombs either in peripheral cemetery areas or under domestic residences. Cist tombs are associated with some local Late Horizon sites in the mid-Moquegua Valley, however, although no chulpas have been found near these sites. One exception is Camata, an Estuquiña, Estuquiña-Inca and Inca period site in the Chujulay drainage (Mathews 1989:429). At this site, chulpas very similar to those found at Porobaya (P-1) are associated with Late Intermediate period and Late Horizon settlements, including colcas. Unfortunately, it is difficult to determine if these chulpas were constructed in the Late Horizon or earlier Late Intermediate period. Round structures that are located at the large Inca administrative site of Torata Alta were originally interpreted as above-ground burial structures (Stanish and Pritzker 1990) although limited test excavations have since suggested a storage function. In general, it would appear that chulpa building ceases in the Moquegua drainage during the Late Horizon, while below-ground cist tombs continued as the predominant form of burial for the population.

## Conclusions

Above-ground burial styles started in the Upper Formative periods of the region, well before Tiwanaku expanded. During Tiwanaku, the use of above-ground tombs appears to be restricted, perhaps to some kind of sociopolitical or religious elite. The use of above-ground tombs rapidly increased in the aftermath of the collapse of Tiwanaku. The classic "chulpa" tradition began in earnest during the Late Intermediate period.

The data from the circum-Titicaca Basin indicate that slab cists, collar tombs and chulpas are predominantly burial structures, usually containing multiple interments, that first developed in the early Late Intermediate period in the circum-Titicaca region. They are best interpreted as the burial locus for corporate groups that developed in the aftermath of Tiwanaku control of the area, though data from Moquegua indicate that there may have been an elite above-ground burial tradition during the Tiwanaku occupation of that valley.

Chulpas varied considerably in architectural style, but the essential principle behind chulpa building remained constant: above-ground tombs became a locus of ritual surrounding corporate groups and their ancestors. The doors and wall niches in chulpas suggest that, unlike below-ground cist tombs, they were designed for continual ceremonial reuse and possibly numerous episodes of interment as individuals within the group died. Traditional below-ground cist tombs, on the other hand, were used for one event and were permanently covered, often under the floor of a domestic structure or in cemeteries. They reflect traditional ideologies associated with treatment of the dead.[4]

The development of above-ground tomb styles in the south central Andes can only be understood as part of the larger cultural processes operating in the region after the retraction of the Tiwanaku state. The more humble above-ground tombs marked areas on the landscape where corporate groups could periodically return and reaffirm social bonds and ties with ancestors. The modern tombs seen in Figure 12.24 are located in the Mazocruz area of the western Titicaca region in the high puna. They were built by agro-pastoral peoples and are revisited periodically. They are also the loci of ritual, as evidenced by the remains found at such tombs. The tombs also serve to mark territory that is used by these groups.

Some scholars have seen these phenomena as ayllu-based reactions to supra-community pressures, particularly the state (e.g., Isbell 1997; Gil 2001; Tantaleán 2000). I share Goldstein's view—that the chulpa phenomenon was a way in which newly-emergent societies of the post-Tiwanaku periods drew on an elite burial practice of Tiwanaku to establish links across political and cultural space. Goldstein (2005:247) aptly notes that "the spread of post-Tiwanaku collared tombs represents the appearance of new status markers of a locally constituted elite in the face of state collapse." These practices were clearly ancestor-worship centered, as the dead were constantly revisited and the tombs were the focus of ritual.

The post-Tiwanaku political landscape throughout the area may be viewed as one in which smaller political units sought to reestablish regional exchange systems after the collapse of a state system. From this perspective, chulpas represent a classic example of a status-validation marker for prominent lineage heads seeking to establish regional political alliance and economic exchange systems. They act "to discriminate the ruling elite and to mark them as a people apart" in a manner quite similar to what Earle has proposed for iconography and style in general for the origins and maintenance of political complexity in chiefly societies (Earle 1990:76). The mutual adoption of similar above-ground burial practices can be understood as one means of reinforcing new alliance systems between these emergent elite lineages, most likely by drawing on, and intensifying, ancient ancestor-worship traditions by certain prominent families.

## Acknowledgments

This article is dedicated to the memory of my fellow graduate student, colleague, and friend David Jessup. David spent a week with me in the field in 1984. He helped excavate some tombs and rooms and, most importantly, he was a gracious friend and inspiring colleague. He is missed.

The Otora research was supported by the Henry and Grace Doherty Foundation, the National Science Foundation, the University of Chicago, Robert and Irene Pritzker, the late Victor Barua R., Lucy Barua, the Instituto Nacional de Cultura, the Museo Peruano de Ciencias de la Salud, the Heinz Trust of Pittsburgh, and the Tinker Foundation. Our Titicaca Basin research has been extensively supported by the National Science Foundation, the Wenner-Gren Foundation for Anthropological Research, the Field Museum of Natural History, the College of Letters and Sciences at UCLA, the Cotsen Endowments, and Ms. Patricia Dodson. Their support is deeply appreciated.

My thanks to Don Rice, Michael Moseley, the Barua family, Joyce Marcus, Luis Lumbreras, Robert McC. Adams, Luis Watanabe, Robert Feldman, James Richardson, Manuel García, Adán Umire, James Mathews, Gloria Salinas, Pat Dodson, Edmundo de la Vega, Antonio Oquiche, Cecilia Chávez J., Alexei Vranich, Elizabeth Klarich, the faculty of the Universidad Católica "Santa María" and many other colleagues. Manuel García supervised the excavation of the chulpa on Porobaya. Marc Bermann conducted the osteological and faunal analyses of the chulpa contents. Errors are my own responsibility.

## Notes

1. The etymology of the word "chulpa" is treated at length in Aldunate and Castro (1981), Bandelier (1905), Hyslop (1977), Rydén (1947), and Tschopik (1946).

2. This is based upon the stratigraphic position of the AD 1600 volcanic ash fall from Huaynaputina, located near Omate in the Tambo drainage.

3. The human osteological and faunal analyses were kindly conducted in 1984 by Dr. Marc Bermann, currently at the University of Pittsburgh.

4. Goldstein interprets the cist tombs with capstones differently, arguing that they were "sealed chambers with visible capstones that permitted future access to the deceased" (Goldstein 2005:244).

## References Cited

Aldunate, C., and V. Castro
1981 *Las chullpas de Toconce y su relación con el poblamiento altiplánico en el Loa superior período tardío*. Ediciones Kultrun Ltda, Santiago.

Aldunate del S., C., J. Berenguer R., and V. Castro R.
1982 La función de las Chullpa en Likan. In *Actas del VIII Congreso de Arqueología Chilena*, pp. 129–80. Kultrun Ltda, Santiago.

Arrendo, Sofía
1942 Las ruinas de Marcansaya. *Revista del Instituto Arqueológico* 4(10/11):52–65. Cuzco.

Bandelier, A.
1905 The aboriginal ruins at Sillustani, Peru. *American Anthropologist* n.s. 7(1):49–69.

Berenguer, J., C. Aldunate del Solar, and V. Castro R.
1984 Orientación orográfica de las chulpas en Likan: La importancia de los Cerros en la fase Toconce. In *Simposio, culturas Atacameñas*. Universidad del Norte, Arica.

Bermann, M., P. S. Goldstein, C. Stanish, and L. Watanabe M.
1989 The collapse of the Tiwanaku state: A view from the Osmore drainage. In S*ettlement, History and Ecology in the Osmore Drainage*, edited by D. Rice, C. Stanish, and P. Scarr, pp.

269–85. British Archaeological Reports, International Series, Oxford, U.K.

Bertonio, L.
1956 [1612] *Vocabulario de la lengua Aymara*. CERES, La Paz.

Burger, R. L.
1982 Pójoc and Waman Wain: Two Early Horizon villages in the Chavín heartland. *Ñawpa Pacha* 20:3–40.

Castro, V., and C. Aldunate
2003 Sacred mountains in the highlands of the south-central Andes. *Mountain Research and Development* 23:73–79.

Cieza de León, P.
1967 [1533] *El señorío de los Incas: Segunda parte de la crónica del Perú*, edited by C. Aranibar. Instituto de Estudios Peruanos, Lima.

Cobo, B.
1956 *Historia de Nuevo Mundo* (1653), edited by F. Mateos. Biblioteca de Autores Españoles. Ediciones Atlas, Madrid.

Conway, M.
1899 Explorations in the Bolivian Andes. *The Geographical Journal* 14:14–31.

Earle, T.
1990 Style and iconography as legitimization in complex chiefdoms. In *The Uses of Style in Archaeology*, edited by Margaret Conkey and Christine Hastorf, pp. 73–81. Cambridge University Press, Cambridge.

Focacci, G., and S. Erices
1971 Excavaciones en tumulos de San Miguel de Azapa (Arica, Chile). In *Actas del VI Congreso Nacional de Arqueología Chilena*, pp. 47–62. Museo de la Serena, Chile.

Gil G., F. M.
2001 Ideología, poder, territorio. Por un análisis del fenómeno chullpario desde la arqueología de la percepción. *Revista Española de Antropología Americana* 31:59–96.

Gisbert, T.
1994 El señorío de los Carangas y los chullpares del Río Lauca. *Revista Andina* 2:427–85.

Goldstein, P.
1989 Omo, a Tiwanaku Provincial Center in Moquegua, Peru. PhD dissertation, Department of Anthropology, University of Chicago, IL.
2000 Exotic goods and everyday chiefs: Long-distance exchange and indigenous sociopolitical development in the south central Andes. *Latin American Antiquity* 11:335–61.
2005 *Andean Diaspora: The Tiwanaku Colonies and the Origins of South American Empire*. University Press of Florida, Gainesville.

Guamán Poma de Ayala, F.
1980 *El primer nueva corónica y buen gobierno*. Siglo Veintiuno, Mexico, D.F.

Gutiérrez Noriega, C.
1935 Jatun Malka. *Revista del Museo Nacional* 4(1):105–10. Lima.
1937 Ciudadelas chullparias de los Wankas. *Revista del Museo Nacional* 6(1):43–51. Lima.

Hutchinson, T. J.
1875 Explorations amongst ancient burial grounds, chiefly on the sea coast valleys of Peru. *The Journal of the Anthropological Institute of Great Britain and Ireland* 4:2–13.

Hyslop, J.
1976 An Archaeological Investigation of the Lupaca Kingdom and Its Origins. PhD dissertation, Department of Anthropology, Columbia University, New York.
1977 Chulpas of the Lupaca zone of the Peruvian high plateau. *Journal of Field Archaeology* 4:149–70.

Isbell, W.
1997 *Mummies and Mortuary Monuments*. University of Texas Press, Austin.

Kaufmann-Doig, F.
1983 *Manual de arqueología Peruana*. Kom Pak Tos, Lima.

Kesseli, R., and M. Pärssinen
2005 Identidad étnica y muerte: Torres funerarias (chulpas) como símbolos de poder étnico en el altiplano Boliviano de Pakasa (1250–1600 d.C). *Bulletin de l'Institut Français d'Études Andines* 34(3):379–410.

Kolata, A. (editor)
1989 *Arqueología de Lukurmata*, vol. 2. Editorial Sui Generis, La Paz.

Lumbreras, L. G.
1974 Los reinos post-Tiwanaku en el área altiplánica. *Revista del Museo Nacional* 40:55–85. Lima.

Lumbreras, L., and H. Amat
1968 Secuencia arqueológica del altiplano occidental del Titicaca. *37th International Congress of Americanists, Actas y Memorias* 2:75–106. Buenos Aires.

Mathews, James
1989 Dual systems of Inka agricultural production: Evidence from the Osmore drainage, southern Peru. In *Settlement, History and Ecology in the Osmore Drainage*, edited by D. Rice, C. Stanish, and P. Scarr, pp. 415–34. British Archaeological Reports, International Series, Oxford, U.K.

Matos M., Ramiro
1960 Informe sobre trabajos arqueológicos en Castrovirreyna, Huancavelica. In *Antiguo Peru: Espacio y tiempo*, edited by Ramiro Matos M., pp. 313–24. Editorial Juan Mejía Baca, Lima.

Moseley, M. E.
1990 Fortificaciones prehispánicas y la evolución de tácticas militares en el Valle de Moquegua. In *Trabajos arqueológicos en Moquegua, Peru*, vol. 1, edited by Luis Watanabe, Michael E. Moseley, and Fernando Cabieses, pp. 237–52. Programa Contisuyo del Museo Peruano de Ciencias de la Salud, Southern Peru Copper Corp., Lima.

Mujica, E., M. Rivera, and T. Lynch
1983 Proyecto de estudio sobre la complementaridad económica Tiwanaku en los valles occidentales del centro-sur andino. *Chungará* 11:85–109.

Muñoz, I.
1996 Poblamiento humano y relaciones interculturales en el valle de Azapa; Nuevos hallazgos en torno al período Formativo y Tiwanaku. In *Prehistoria del norte de Chile y del desierto de Atacama: Simposio homenaje a Percy Dauelsberg Hahmann*, pp. 241–78. *Diálogo Andino*, nos. 14–15. Universidad de Tarapacá, Arica.

Murra, J. V.
1968 An Aymara kingdom in 1567. *Ethnohistory* 15:115–51.

Murra, J. V., N. Wachtel, and J. Ravel (editors)
1986 *Anthropological History of Andean Polities*. Cambridge University Press, Cambridge.

Nordenskiöld, E. F.
1906a *Arkeologiska Undersökninear I Perus och Bolivias Gränstrakter*. Almquist and Wiksell, Uppsala.
1906b Travels on the boundaries of Bolivia and Peru. *The Geographical Journal* 28:105–27.

Rice, D. S., C. Stanish, and P. Scarr (editors)
1989 *Settlement, History and Ecology in the Osmore Drainage*. British Archaeological Reports, International Series, Oxford, U.K.

Rivero, M. E., and J. J. von Tschudi
1855 *Peruvian Antiquities*, translated by F. L. Hawks. Putnam and Co., New York.

Rydén, S.
1947 *Archaeological Researches in the Highlands of Bolivia*. Elanders Boktryckeri Aktiebolag, Göteborg, Sweden.

Serracino, G.
1979 Relaciones interregionales en los Andes meridionales 1000–1200 D.C. Paper presented at the XLIII International Congress of Americanists, University of British Columbia, Vancouver.

Sever, J.
1921 Chullpas des environs de Pucará (Bolivie). *Société des Américanistes* 13:55–58. Paris.

Shimada, I.
1982 Horizontal archipelago and coast-highland interaction in north Peru: Archaeological models. In *Senri Ethnological Studies 10*, edited by Luis Millones and Hiroyasu Tomoeda, pp. 137–210. University of Tokyo, Tokyo.

Squier, E.
1870 The primeval monuments of Peru compared with those in other parts of the world. *The American Naturalist* 4(1):1–7.
1877 *Peru: Incidents of Travel and Exploration in the Land of the Incas*. Harper and Brothers, New York.

Stanish, C.
1985 Post-Tiwanaku Regional Economies in the Otora Valley, Southern Peru. PhD dissertation, Department of Anthropology, University of Chicago.
1987 Agroengineering dynamics of post-Tiwanaku settlements in the Otora Valley, Peru. In *Pre-Hispanic Agricultural Fields in the Andean Region*, edited by William M. Denevan, Kent Mathewson, and Gregory Knapp, pp. 337–64. British Archaeological Reports, International Series, vol. 359(i), Oxford, U.K.
1989a An archaeological evaluation of an ethnohistorical model in Moquegua. In *Settlement, History and Ecology in the Osmore Drainage*, edited by D. Rice, C. Stanish, and P. Scarr, pp. 303–20. British Archaeological Reports, International Series, Oxford, U.K.
1989b Household archeology: Testing models of zonal complementarity in the south central Andes. *American Anthropologist* 91(1):7–24.
1991 *A Late Pre-Hispanic Ceramic Chronology for the Upper Moquegua Valley, Peru*. Fieldiana Anthropology, New Series 16. Field Museum of Natural History, Chicago.
1992 *Ancient Andean Political Economy*. University of Texas Press, Austin.

Stanish, C., E. de la Vega, L. H. Steadman, C. Chávez J., K. L. Frye, L. Onofre, M. Seddon, and P. Calisaya Chuquimia
1997 *Archaeological Survey in the Juli-Desaguadero Region of Lake Titicaca Basin, Southern Peru*. Fieldiana Anthropology, New Series 29. Field Museum of Natural History, Chicago.

Stanish, C., and I. Pritzker
1990 Reconocimiento arqueológico en el sur del Perú. In *Trabajos arqueológicos en Moquegua, Perú*, vol. 3, edited by L. Watanabe, M. Moseley, and F. Cabieses, pp. 167–76. Programa Contisuyu, Lima.

Tantaleán, H.
2006 Regresar para construir: Prácticas funerarias e ideología(s) durante la ocupación Inka en Cutimbo, Puno-Perú. *Chungará* 38:129–43.

Tantaleán, H., and C. Pérez Maestro
2000 Muerte en el altiplano Andino: Investigaciones en la necrópolis Inka de Cutimbo (Puno, Perú). *Revista de Arqueología* 228:26–37.

Tschopik, M.
1946 *Some Notes of the Archaeology of the Department of Puno, Peru*. Papers of the Peabody Museum of American Archaeology and Ethnology, Harvard University, vol. 27, no. 3. Cambridge, MA.

Vásquez, E.
1937a Sillustani: Una metrópoli pre-Incasica. *Revista del Museo Nacional* 6(2):278–90. Lima.
1937b Las ruinas de Kachakacha. *Revista del Museo Nacional* 6(1):52–57. Lima.

Vásquez, E., A. Carpio, and D. E. Velazco
1935 Informe sobre las ruinas de Tankatanka. *Revista del Museo Nacional* 4(2):240–44.

Williams, S., J. E. Buikstra, N. Clark, M. Lozada C., and E. Torres P.
1989 Mortuary site excavations and skeletal biology in the Osmore project. In *Ecology, Settlement and History in the Osmore Drainage*, edited by D. Rice, C. Stanish, and P. Scarr, pp. 347–70. British Archaeological Reports, International Series, Oxford, U.K.

Chapter 13

# The Ancient Raised Fields of the Taraco Region of the Northern Lake Titicaca Basin

*D. Michael Henderson*

The landscape around Lake Titicaca today displays evidence of a once intensive agricultural system known as raised field farming. Raised fields are basically large, elevated planting platforms surrounded by water-filled channels that moderate the moisture, temperature and soil conditions of the difficult altiplano environment. Since abandonment, the platforms have eroded somewhat and the channels have filled with sediment. Thus, the original channel depths of typically one meter have been reduced to as little as 10 centimeters in many cases. Yet the evidence in the form of residual or "relict" raised fields is surprisingly easy to identify, both on the ground and in aerial photos. Using aerial photos, Smith et al. (1968) were the first to report the broad extent of the raised fields around Lake Titicaca (82,000 ha). Today, over 120,000 hectares have been identified in five major zones: Juliaca and Pomata in Peru and Tiwanaku, Catari and Desaguadero in Bolivia (Díaz Zeballos and Velasquez 1992; Kolata and Ortloff 1996a; Bandy 2005). The massive Juliaca complex running from Juliaca to Paucarcolla is by far the largest with more than 50,000 hectares.

Two areas in particular have been the subject of a large number of detailed studies. These studies provide valuable insight into the nature, organization and operation of raised fields around Lake Titicaca. In the north, Erickson centered his efforts around Huatta on the Juliaca plain. His work focused on "the determination of original raised field morphology, origins and evolution of the system, carrying capacity and population dynamics, field functions, and crops cultivated" (Erickson 1994:111) (also see Erickson 1985, 1987, 1988, 1992, 1993, 1998, 1999, 2000; Erickson and Candler 1989). In the south around Tiwanaku and the nearby Catari Basin, the work of Kolata and colleagues had a broad scope as well—"the long-term human-environment interactions in the southern Lake Titicaca basin, with a focus on the technology and organization of agricultural production in the prehispanic Andean state of Tiwanaku" (Kolata 1996:2) (also see Kolata 1986, 1991, 1993; Kolata and Ortloff 1989, 1996a, 1996b; Kolata, Rivera, Ramírez and Gemio 1996; Janusek and Kolata 2004).

The focus of the present work is the Taraco alluvial plain located on the northwest shore of Lake Titicaca between Río Ramis and the lake (Fig. 13.1). Recent research suggests that Taraco was the major regional center during the late Qaluyu and early Pukara periods from about 500 BC to AC 100 (Plourde and Stanish 2006; Chávez and Plourde 2008; Levine 2008). The goal is to present an in-depth picture of the ancient raised field system and water resource management around Taraco that will contribute to understanding the evolution of the sociopolitical complexity that occurred in this region.

Relict raised fields were identified south of Taraco alongside the lake in the above-mentioned surveys but were listed under the "scattered" category in comparison to the major zones (also see Denevan 1970). Aside from this early survey work, however, this region has not been the subject of detailed studies as with Huatta

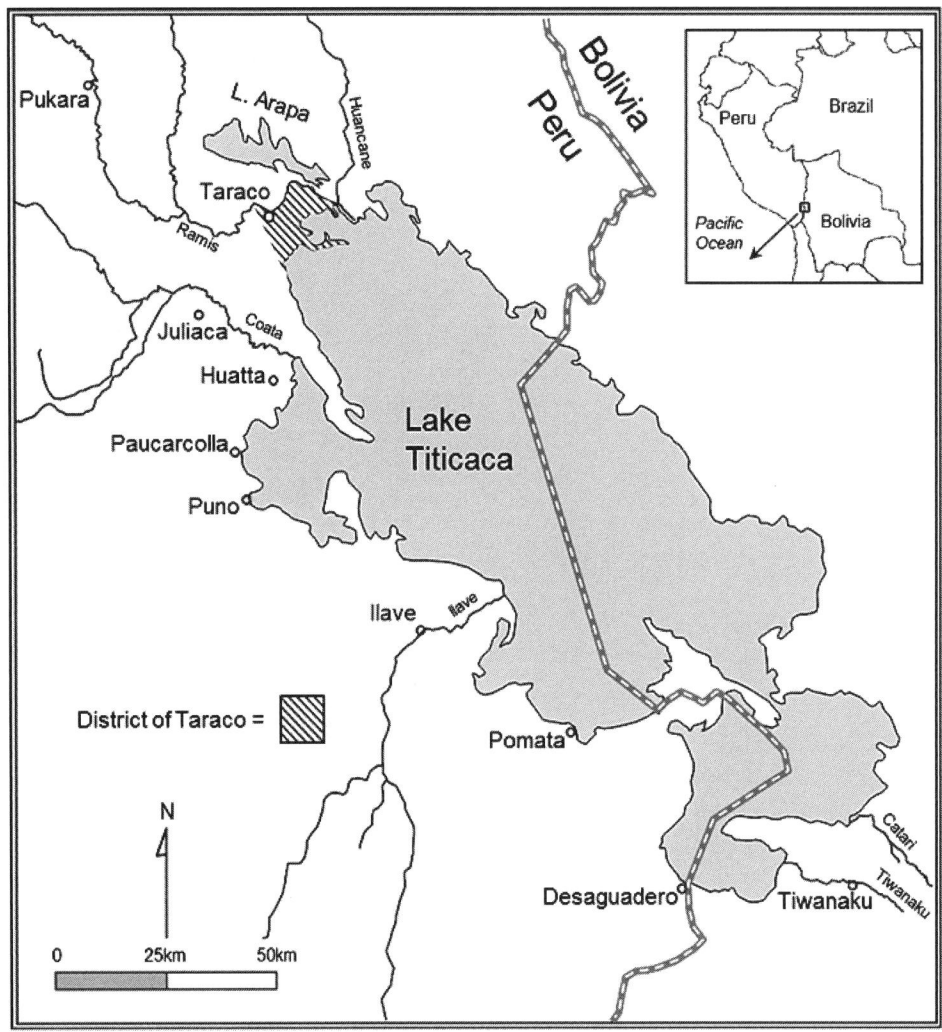

Figure 13.1. Lake Titicaca region showing the district and town of Taraco as well as locations and major rivers discussed in this chapter. All illustrations by author.

and Tiwanaku. The results of the current work carried out over four field seasons from 2004 to 2007 that included both ground and aerial photographic surveys are presented in this chapter. The photos used have higher resolution than those in the original work in 1968. In many areas, the fields have become highly degraded by contemporary farming. Yet, evidence of earlier raised field farming often appears on the higher resolution aerial photos in a fashion akin to a palimpsest in which earlier writing shows through later writing placed above it. These newly identified fields escaped attention in earlier studies. A detailed survey using 41 aerial photos has been carried out. The resulting assessment shows much broader ancient raised field coverage around Taraco than previously pictured. From 5500 ha to 7500 ha of raised fields existed around Taraco versus perhaps 1000 ha previously identified. With this new assessment, it is now recognized that the Taraco region was a major raised field complex comparable in size and complexity to those of Pomata, Tiwanaku, Catari and Desaguadero.

An important objective of this work is to gain an understanding of the water management practices used by the region's early farmers and hydraulic engineers. Today, in many areas of the alluvial plain, there is a complete absence of any modern infrastructure for water management. In these areas, the current inhabitants do not utilize modern equipment in the excavation of wells and *qochas*[1] or in the construction and maintenance of canals and levees. They rely solely on manual labor. They must also rely on gravity flow of water alone since electrical or mechanical pumps are absent. Thus, by studying these areas, it is hoped that insight into practices used by earlier farmers and hydraulic engineers will be gained. The timing is important as electrification of the countryside has been initiated in the last few years. The current practices will certainly change in the coming years.

To help in this understanding, modeling of water sources for farming in the region is carried out. There are two sources, the Río Ramis and rainfall runoff, both of which are seasonal. Lake water for both farming and domestic use is ruled out as a source due to its high salt content. As the typical depth of the water table at its highest—judged from observations of wells and qochas—is one to two meters, the direct filling of the channels with groundwater is ruled out in most cases. There are no artesian springs or other year-round sources around Taraco. The modeling is guided by archaeological evidence that is present on the landscape as well as by an understanding of the local terrain and topographic features. Hydraulic calculations link the sources with the fields. To this end, monthly precipitation and Río Ramis discharge records for Taraco over the last 40 years were obtained from the Servicio Nacional de Metrología e Hidrología, Lima (SENAMHI).[2] The runoff calculations also rely on evaporation and soil absorption data from the Oficina Nacional de Evaluación de Recursos Naturales, Puno (ONERN 1985). It is found that less than 15% of the raised fields could have been supported by rainfall runoff alone. These fields were principally located at the base of Cerro Imarocus, a chain of hills about 250 m high that run alongside the west side of the alluvial plain from Taraco to the lake.

The Río Ramis is the only source with sufficient water for supplying the large area of fields around Taraco. Aerial photos and ground surveys reveal numerous portions of abandoned watercourses on the alluvial plain—both natural (meander scars) and human-made (canals). It is believed they were once part of an ancient hydraulic system that supplied the raised fields, not unlike the evidence found around Tiwanaku of a once sophisticated hydraulic system there: river canalization, canals, aqueducts, dikes, and so on (Kolata and Ortloff 1996b).

Several authors have analyzed the flow in such canals based on so-called "open channel flow" analysis (Farrington and Park 1978; Farrington 1980, 1983; Ortloff et al. 1982, 1983; Ortloff 1996). To model this flow, a specific canal that runs from the Río Ramis to the lake was selected. This canal, called Canal Ramis, was chosen because we believe it once supplied ancient raised fields. From this calculation, it is found that the Río Ramis could easily have supplied the large area of fields found around Taraco. The basic operation, control and maintenance of the ancient canals supplying the raised fields are examined through comparison of the Canal Ramis with a similar canal near Tiwanaku discussed by Ortloff (1996).

A map of the hydraulic features on the alluvial plain (river courses, canals, meander scars and qochas) is presented, which displays their relationship to the raised fields. In addition, a mapping of ancient site locations across the region has recently become available (Chávez and Plourde 2008). Overlaying these ancient sites on the map of hydraulic features provides additional insight into the overall understanding of raised field farming around Taraco.

## The Taraco Region Today

The Taraco district is currently a community of about 16,500 Quechua inhabitants located on the broad alluvial plain adjacent to Lake Titicaca. Online census data list 91% of the population as rural. The heart of the region is the small town of the same name. The town's infrastructure includes running water, electricity and a sewage system. The countryside is organized into sectors and districts or *barrios*. Sectors have 300 to 400 people each, organized into four to six barrios per sector. Individual farmsteads are dispersed across the fields on the sparsely populated alluvial plain (Fig. 13.2). There are typically two to six structures for housing and storage on a given farmstead. The vast majority of farmsteads do not have electricity although a program to electrify the countryside is underway. None have running water or sewage systems.

The following water management practices on the plain are carried out today in the absence of modern infrastructure:

- Water for animals and domestic use is obtained solely from the aquifer using manually excavated wells and qochas.
- Rain-fed agriculture is the norm at this time.[3]
- Manually constructed levees along rivers and drainage canals for control of runoff are in evidence.

The region's canals and levees are constructed of sod blocks known locally by the Quechua word *champa*. They are readily obtained from simple quarries found throughout the region, as seen in Figure 13.3. The canal walls are constructed of sod blocks alone while the larger levees have sod block walls with fill in their interior. The buildings of the region are constructed of either adobe or sod blocks. There are two distinct types of domiciles. The first and most common type is a simple, rectangular structure of adobe walls on a stone foundation with a thatched roof constructed of totora reeds, cebada and grasses. Corrugated metal roofing is beginning to replace thatched roofs. The second, called a *putuco*, is a more primitive type found throughout the region. It is constructed solely of sod blocks arranged in a truncated pyramidal shape. This design avoids the need for the ridge beam of adobe structures as the putuco's steep roof is also made of sod blocks. Each succeeding layer slightly overhangs the previous layer similar to the construction of a "corbelled hall." Adobe lacks the strength for this type of construction. Today, putucos are most commonly used for cooking (a putuco can be seen in the foreground of Figure 13.3, with an adobe structure behind it).

Erickson (1988) has demonstrated the effective use of ancient Andean tools in cutting such sod blocks in the construction of raised fields. Thus, is it clear that the early inhabitants had available the tools and materials for water management seen on the alluvial plain today.

Figure 13.2. View looking south across the alluvial plain. See Figure 13.4 for location and orientation of photograph. All photographs by author.

Figure 13.3. Contemporary sod block (champa) structures found throughout the alluvial plain.

## Geography

Four main geographical features define the Taraco region (Fig. 13.4):

- An alluvial plain that constitutes the largest area of the region.
- A continuous range of hills (Cerro Imarocus) about 200 m to 250 m in elevation above the plain that starts south of the river near the town and runs in a southeasterly direction to the lake.
- Lake Titicaca, which is located about 12 km to the southeast.
- Río Ramis, which runs across the middle of the plain within 100 m of the town.

In the early quaternary period, the region was occupied by the lake, which was gradually filled in. The alluvial-lacustrine plain consists of deposits of fine sediment in the form of sand, mud, clay and gravel. To these are added coarser rocks from local, as well as distant, sources that have been torn away and transported to the plain by water (ONERN 1985). The topography is quite flat. In the middle of the plain, the overall slope of the terrain is < 1:1000 (that is, less than 1 m fall over 1 km distance). Even though the plain is quite flat, there is still micro-topography present with local variations of a meter or so. Typically, this type of terrain has been shaped by meandering rivers changing courses over time across a plain, often abandoning earlier features that become part of the micro-topography. Seasonal distributaries also shape the land.

The alluvial plain is of vital economic importance for the farming conducted there. Almost every available hectare is used for farming or herding. Cattle and sheep have replaced llamas and alpacas that are so prevalent in other regions of the altiplano. In fact, the region prides itself on being the "Dairy Basin of the Altiplano," reportedly producing 30,000 liters of milk a day. The main growing season is from October to April. The top five crops of the region are: potatoes, quinua, cebada, avena and habas. In addition, two crops grow during the drier periods. The first crop is alfalfa, which is planted around February and can withstand the water deficiency of the soil during the dry period from May to September. The second is again cebada, which is planted in August alongside the river and harvested in December before the river rises to a level to destroy the crops. No terrace farming was found today nor was there evidence of past terrace farming in this region.

The continuous range of hills have folded strata approaching vertical that give rise to the mountain-like topography seen in Figures 13.2 and 13.4. Erosion has created a gently sloping rise along their base that extends onto the alluvial plain. These hills are a local source of flooding because of annual runoff. An extensive drainage system has been constructed to deal with the runoff.

Also important to the region are wetlands at the edge of the lake and major qochas (Fig. 13.25) that provide an important en-

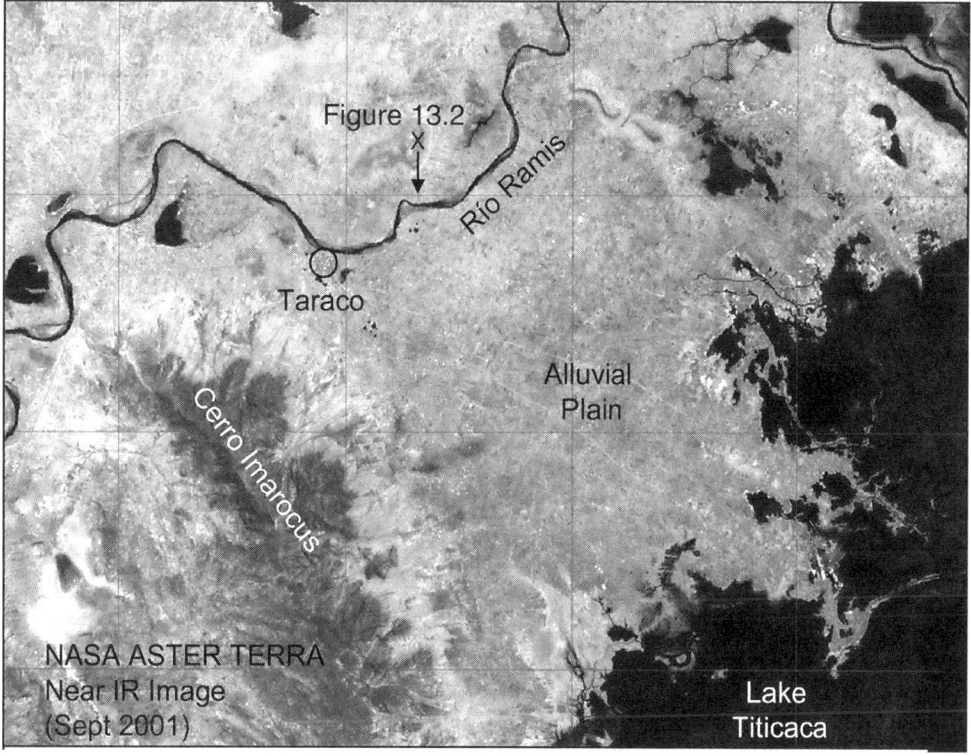

Figure 13.4. Satellite image[4] of the Taraco region showing major geographical features. The "x" and black arrow mark the location and orientation from which Figure 13.2 was taken.

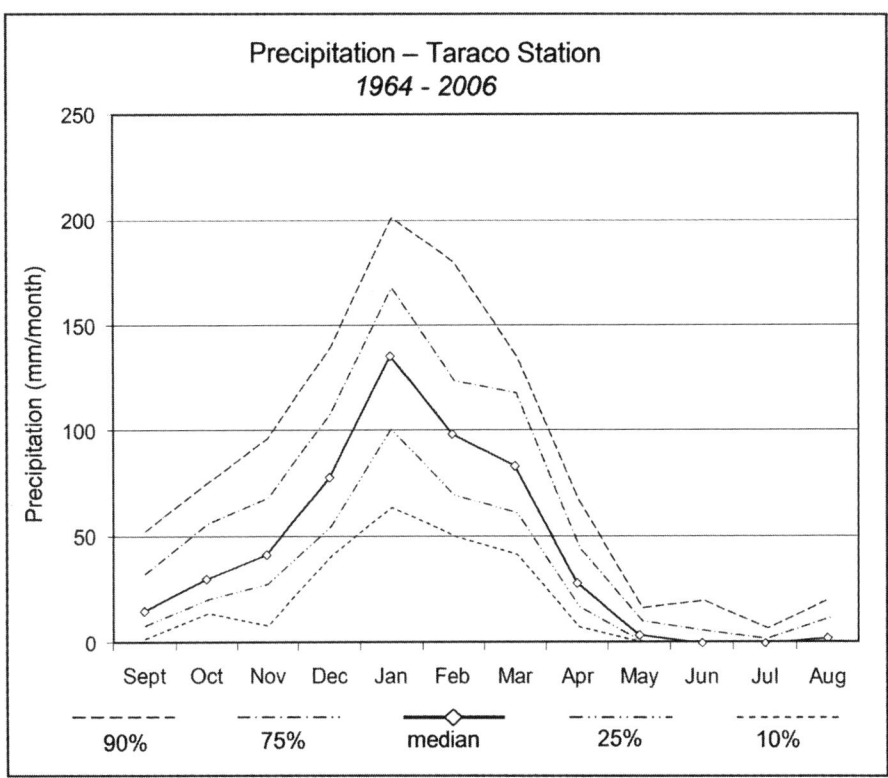

Figure 13.5. Annual rainfall statistics for the Tararco region for the period 1964–2006 (SENAMHI). The percentages represent the portion of the period in which the rainfall was less than the value shown. For example, for 25% of the period the rainfall in January was less than 100 mm/month. The value of 50% represents the median rainfall for the period.

vironment for fish and waterfowl as well as for the all-important totora reed used in roof, raft and mat construction. Totora also serves as fodder for cattle.

### Water Resources

All water resources in the Taraco region have their origin in highly seasonal rainfall over the Lake Titicaca Basin. Direct rainfall on the fields from September to April supports farming. The variation of annual rainfall is shown in Figure 13.5. The runoff from higher in the Andes feeds the rivers and streams that flow into Lake Titicaca. In addition, these rivers and streams charge an aquifer underlying the alluvial plain that is critical to the region. No artesian springs were identified in the area.

There is substantial variability in rainfall from year to year, which causes the lake level to rise and fall. Records of lake level over the last 100 years show a maximum drop in lake level of -3.72 m in December, 1943, and a maximum increase of +2.65 m in April, 1986. Severe flooding resulted from the 1986 lake level rise. The town of Taraco is about 12 km from the lake and about 5 m higher in elevation than the high water lake level in 1986. Accordingly, the town avoided flooding from the rising lake level.

The lake is not the only potential source of flooding in this area. The Río Ramis is the largest of all rivers terminating in Lake Titicaca and provides more than a quarter of the total runoff into the lake. Figure 13.6 shows the annual flow of the Ramis. The river flows year-round, albeit with more than a 95% reduction in the dry season compared to the peak flow. The cresting of the Río Ramis is a major problem near Taraco and it occurs at a very inopportune time. Unlike Egypt, where flooding of the Nile occurred after harvest in ancient times and was beneficial to reconstituting the soil, flooding at Lake Titicaca occurs at the peak of the growing season. Such flooding would ruin the crops. Today, a massive earthen levee exists alongside Río Ramis. The inner levee was manually constructed using sod block construction while the newer, outer levee was constructed with machine help in the 1990s. The levee contains the river at high stage; however, occasional breaching does occur (Fig. 13.7).

The predominantly clear aquifer flows from the mountains into the lake. Its contribution to the overall level of the lake is quite small (< 1% of water into the lake annually). Despite the small contribution to the lake, it is critical to the region's livelihood. Water for animals and domestic use comes from the aquifer for all except those few who live close to the river. The depth of the

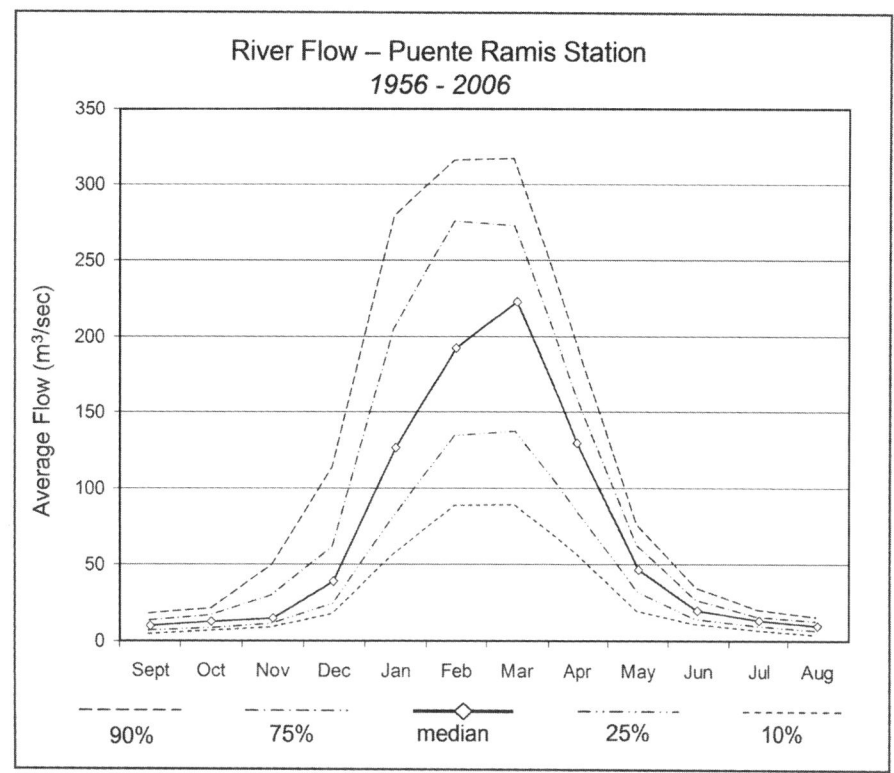

Figure 13.6. Annual flow for the Río Ramis near Tararco from 1956 to 2006 (SENAMHI). See Figure 13.5 for discussion of percentages shown.

Figure 13.7. Massive levee located alongside Río Ramis near the town of Taraco. It is composed of two parts: a lower, inner levee and a higher, outer levee.

water table typically varies from about 1 m to 2 m at its highest to more than 8 m below the plain. This depth, as well as the conductance of the wells and qochas, is more than sufficient in most areas to meet the minimal demands placed upon the aquifer by animal and domestic needs on this sparsely populated plain. However, during the 2005 field season, which was a particularly dry year, it was noted that shallower qochas in some areas were dry although they had provided water for animals only the year before. It became necessary for the affected farmers to use water from their deeper wells for their herds.

The straightforward construction of the wells and qochas also accounts for their widespread usage. A typical well is about 1 m × 1.5 m and 10 m deep. It can be excavated by two men in two days. In many barrios, the water is still extracted from wells manually with a simple bucket and rope. In other areas, mechanical displacement pumps are becoming the norm. A typical qocha of about 7 m to 8 m in diameter and up to 7 m deep can be excavated by four men in three days. These are large enough for livestock to enter to reach the water table.

## Raised Field Survey

### Background

Raised fields consist of a series of elevated planting platforms created by excavating ditches adjacent to the platforms that later become water-filled channels. They are found in areas of waterlogged soil or areas subject to seasonal flooding. The morphology of raised fields is well documented from earlier work (Kolata and Ortloff 1996a; Erickson 1994). The dimensions vary widely. Platform widths range in size from 2 m to 10 m. Channel depths vary from 0.5 m to 3 m with a typical depth of 1 m. From 30% to 60% of the field area is given over to platforms. The length of individual platforms varies dramatically as well, going from perhaps 10 m to more than several hundred meters. Three examples of raised fields found around Taraco are shown in Figure 13.8. The first is actually a contemporary raised field constructed during a period of rehabilitation in the 1980s and 1990s (Erickson 1998; Kolata et al. 1996). Only a few such fields were constructed around Taraco and all have been abandoned.[5] The latter two photos are of relict raised fields. The channel depths in many cases have been reduced to as little as 10 cm yet they can be identified easily by variations in vegetation and/or elevation. When dealing with relict raised fields, it is difficult to determine separately the widths of the original platforms and channels because of platform erosion and channel in-filling. It is easy, however, especially with aerial photos, to determine the wavelength (that is, the combined width of platform and adjacent channel) assuming nearby platforms eroded similarly. In general, the wavelengths range from 5 m to 12 m across the plain. Characteristic raised field patterns have been classified by geometric shapes and orientations of platforms (Smith et al. 1968; Denevan 1970, 2001). The most common type found around Taraco is the "open checkerboard." The term "open" indicates the platforms are not continuous so water can flow freely through the checkerboard arrangement of channels (Fig. 13.11a).

Extensive contemporary farming in the region has disturbed evidence of the earlier raised field farming. This makes it difficult, but not impossible, to identify relict raised fields in many areas of the alluvial plain. In the pioneering work of Smith et al., relict fields were indeed identified near Taraco but mainly alongside the lake where farming had not reached (in the vicinity of Fig. 13.11a) (also see Denevan 2001). The fields in this region also are atypically large, making them easier to see. Regarding the inland area, they stated (Smith et al. 1968:355–56):

> It seems anomalous that there should be few traces of ridge field patterns . . . in the pampas of Taraco . . . in contrast to their abundance in the [nearby] Juliaca plain.
>
> The pampas of Taraco . . . are occupied by indigenous Indian communities and carry some of the highest rural population densities in the Peruvian sierra.
>
> It seems likely that any traces of former field systems will have been destroyed.

With higher resolution aerial photos not available to these early investigators, it is possible to identify relict raised fields across almost all the alluvial plain in spite of disturbance by farming.

The proposed chronologies for raised field development differ between northern and southern Lake Titicaca.[6] In the north, Erickson's evidence from Huatta (Erickson 1987) based on thermoluminescence dating of seven ceramic samples along with comparative dating of ceramics suggests that raised fields were originally developed in the Formative period sometime before 1000 BC. The activity reached its peak around 600 to 800 BC and subsequently the fields were abandoned sometime after AD 300. A second phase involving reconstruction and reutilization occurred around AD 1000 and lasted until the Inca conquest.

The chronology for the south developed by Kolata and colleagues is based on extensive excavation in the Catari Basin (Janusek and Kolata 2004). Twenty-five mollusk shells and organic carbon samples were radiocarbon dated. They conclude that while raised field farming was likely to have been developed during the Late Formative period, no evidence was found earlier than AD 600. It flourished on a large scale only after AD 600 and declined after AD 1150. Excavations in the Taraco region could provide an additional view of the chronology.

### Survey Methodology

This survey comprises both ground and aerial photographic components. The ground portion, which was carried out over four field seasons from 2004 to 2007, had two objectives. The first was an understanding of water management on the plain today through numerous interviews with local farmers. The second was validation of water features identified in the aerial photos

Figure 13.8. Three views of raised fields around Taraco district: *a*, a contemporary (but abandoned) raised field; *b*, a relict raised field alongside the lake with salt deposits in the channels; *c*, a relict raised field inland from the lake.

(relict raised fields, canals and meander scars on the landscape). In fact, in many cases, the ground survey was instrumental in interpreting the aerial photos. It provided confidence that the raised field areas identified from the air in the 1970 flights are indeed relict raised fields. In every case, relict fields identified in the ground survey were apparent in the aerial photos. The converse was not true. Many times, the fields found in the aerial photos had been destroyed by deep plowing or construction of farmsteads. Thus, these 1970 aerial photos are important not only because they allow rapid surveying of large areas, but in this case because they display patterning that has subsequently been destroyed.

The parameters of three aerial surveys carried out around northern Lake Titicaca are given in Table 13.1. In the original survey of Smith et al. (1968), aerial photos were used to identify fields throughout the greater basin. The locations of the sites identified in the photos were then transferred to a base map of the region with scale 1:200,000. Lennon (1983) focused on a much smaller area. His interest was in studying raised field patterning around Huatta using the higher resolution photos available in 1983 than those used in the original work. He was able to make quantitative measurement of relict raised field dimensions by enlarging the photos and overlaying them with a mylar grid with 0.01" graduations. An impressive 1.5-m minimum sample size was achieved.

In this chapter, both a large area survey to identify relict raised fields and detailed quantitative measurements of small field dimensions are of interest. With the digital scanning tools available today, both large and small measurements can be carried out in a straightforward fashion. High-resolution aerial photos from Servicio Aerofotográfico Nacional (SAN) are used.[7] These photos are scanned to generate a grayscale bit map of the photo. The scan density is an important consideration in order to minimize scan artifacts, provide adequate resolution and still yield a reasonable file size. As a test of the scan density, an area of contemporary fields shown in Figure 13.9 was selected. Parallel contrasting terrain bands from plowing are seen in the photos; wavelengths (combined width of a dark and a light band) as small as 2.4 m are visible. A scan density of 600 lines/inch was selected for the survey because (1) it is large enough to avoid the scan artifacts seen at 300 lines/inch, (2) it provides adequate resolution for this study of raised fields with wavelengths ~ 4 m and larger, and (3) it yields a file size (~ 25 MB) four times smaller than a 1200 lines/inch file.

In general, relict raised fields lack the strong contrast seen in the newly plowed fields of Figure 13.9. A typical region on the Taraco plain is shown in Figure 13.10 from two different aerial photographic flights. In the higher resolution photos from the 1970 flight (scale 1:17,000), the relict fields are easily seen, while they are very difficult to identify in the lower resolution 1955 flight of the early studies (scale 1:65,000). Note, however, that relict raised fields can have high contrast when the channels either contain water or highly reflective salt deposits (Figs. 13.8$b$, 13.11$a$). In these cases, they are easy to identify both in aerial photos and on the ground.

The next step in processing the photos is to register them to UTM coordinates so that relict fields identified in the photos can be transferred to a base image of the region (near IR satellite image). This is accomplished with a software package called Global Mapper[8] using GPS reference points taken in the field. Stable

Table 13.1. Comparison of three aerial photographic surveys of northern Lake Titicaca.

|  | Author(s) | | |
|---|---|---|---|
|  | Smith et al. | Lennon | Present Study |
| year | 1968 | 1983 | 2010 |
| survey location | greater Lake Titicaca Basin | Huatta | Taraco district |
| survey area | basin wide | 400 ha | 35,000 ha |
| aerial photos: | | | |
|   year | 1955 | unstated | 1970 |
|   scale | 1:65,000 | 1:15,000 | 1:17,000 |
| methodology: | | | |
|   for locating fields | by transfer from aerial photos to topographic map | – | by transfer from aerial photos to satellite image |
|   for measurement | – | photo enlargement with mylar overlay | electronic scanning of photos (bit map) |
|   photo size |  | 18" × 18" | 9" × 9" |
|   graduations |  | 0.01" (mylar overlay) | 0.0016" (600 lines/inch) |
| smallest unit of measurement | – | ~ 1.4 m | ~ 0.72 m (pixel size) |

geographic landmarks such as road intersections and prominent buildings served as reference points in the field. By identifying three or more reference points in a given photo, a UTM coordinate grid is superimposed on the photo that has been appropriately scaled and oriented by the software. A total of 41 high-resolution photos from the 1970 flight series were processed, covering the area from Lago de Arapa south to Lake Titicaca and from Cerro Imarocus east to the lake.

The final, albeit lengthy, step is to search each of the 41 registered photos for evidence of relict raised fields. This is done by enlarging the registered photo so that a 0.5 km × 0.5 km region fills the computer screen (equivalent to a photographic enlargement of about seven times). The entire photo is searched with each identified relict raised field block highlighted (Fig. 13.12).[9]

As previously stated, relict fields are easy to identify when they have not been disturbed by farming (Fig. 13.11a, near the lake). Going inland, however, it is more difficult as there is clear evidence of disturbance (Fig. 13.11b–c). Thus, it becomes necessary to distinguish the relict fields from contemporary fields. To this end, four criteria are used; high confidence that a given area once contained relict raised fields is realized if there are parallel bands of contrasting terrain that have:

(1) the appropriate dimensions (wavelength, length),
(2) platform definition that is not "sharp,"
(3) some areas with "patchwork quilt" patterns, and
(4) some "palimpsest" evidence.

The first criterion simply requires that the dimensions of a candidate field be consistent with the range of values from the literature discussed above. The second criterion, while admittedly subjective, is important to rule out contemporary fields as seen

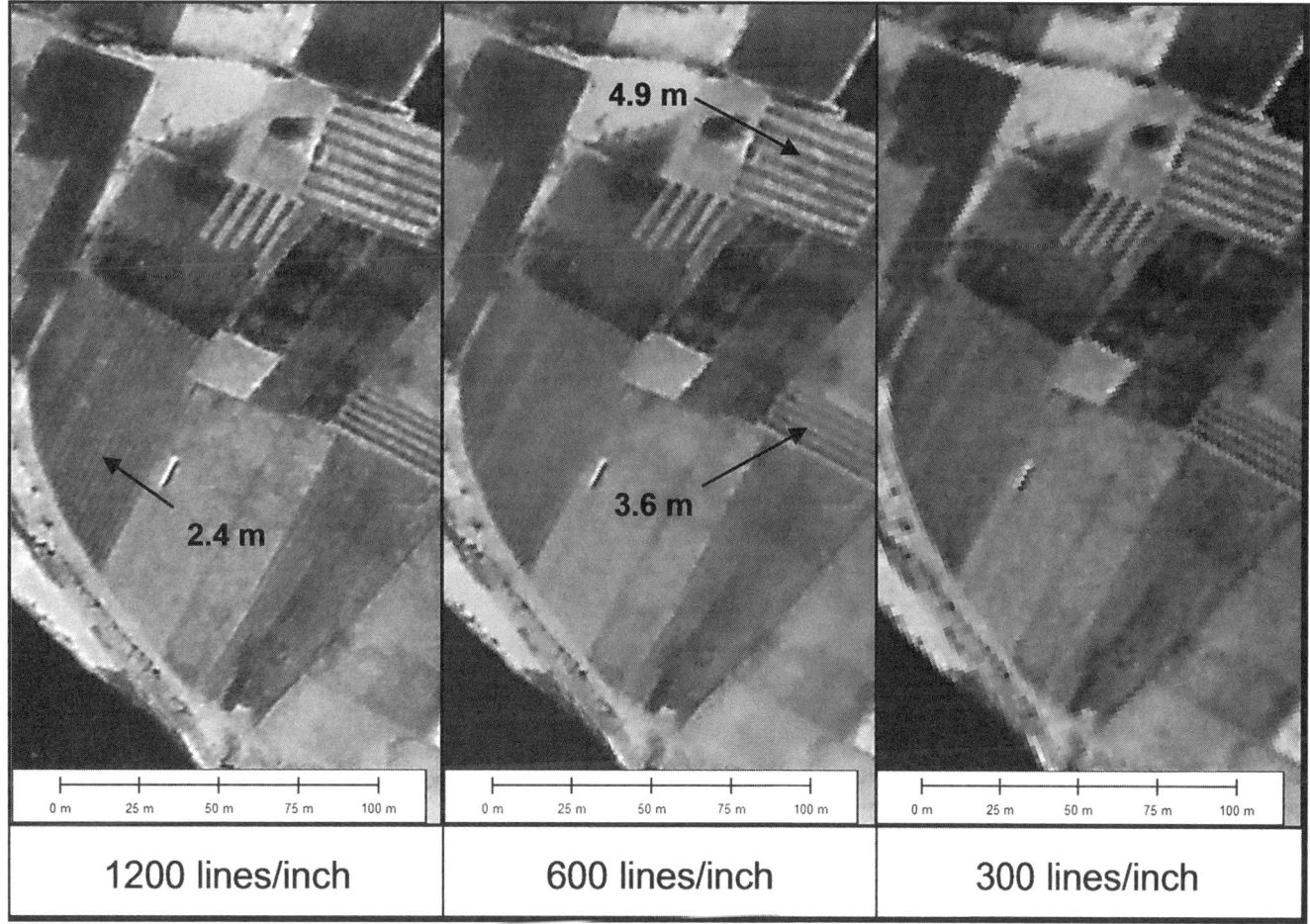

Figure 13.9. Enlargements of an aerial photo (SAN #411) showing contemporary fields scanned with three different scan densities. A density of 600 lines/inch was chosen for this survey.

Figure 13.10. Aerial photos of a typical region of relict raised fields taken from two different flights. The relict fields are easily seen in the 1970 flight but are very difficult to see in the 1955 flight.

in Figure 13.9, which have not been eroded over time. The one exception to this rule is when the channels contain water as they then have sharp channel definition. In the third criterion, the term "patchwork quilt" is used to include various raised field patterns (such as the "open checkerboard") that are distinguishable from contemporary farming. The final criterion relies on the fact that the relict raised fields were present before the contemporary fields were plowed. In these cases, the relict fields have the appearance of a palimpsest with the earlier features showing through the modern ones. A key indicator is the presence of raised field features that do not conform to contemporary ones like roads or field boundaries but cut across them, as clearly seen in Figure 13.11b–c. When all four criteria are met, the appropriate regions of the photo are highlighted for later incorporation on the regional satellite image (an example of such a highlighted photo is shown in Fig. 13.12).

There are two cases—both occurring in highly disturbed areas—in which identification becomes more difficult and could lead to false positive identifications. The first is when contemporary farming is so extensive that the only evidence that remains is in small isolated areas containing platforms of a single size and orientation. In this case, there is insufficient evidence to apply criteria (3) and (4). From the ground, it is still possible to ascertain their validity as relict fields because of their characteristic elevation variations. Such small, isolated relict fields were indeed identified in the ground survey. In the aerial photos, however, elevation information is lost so only the first two criteria can be evaluated. Thus, identification in this case lacks the degree of confidence found when all four criteria are used. In order to minimize false positives, it is required that for a region to be identified with high confidence as once containing raised fields, it must have at least a *core* that meets all four criteria listed above. Once a core is established, then isolated blocks in the vicinity (typically within 1 km) are considered part of that region. In the absence of a core, the isolated blocks are ignored. A region that has been highly disturbed could be overlooked in this approach

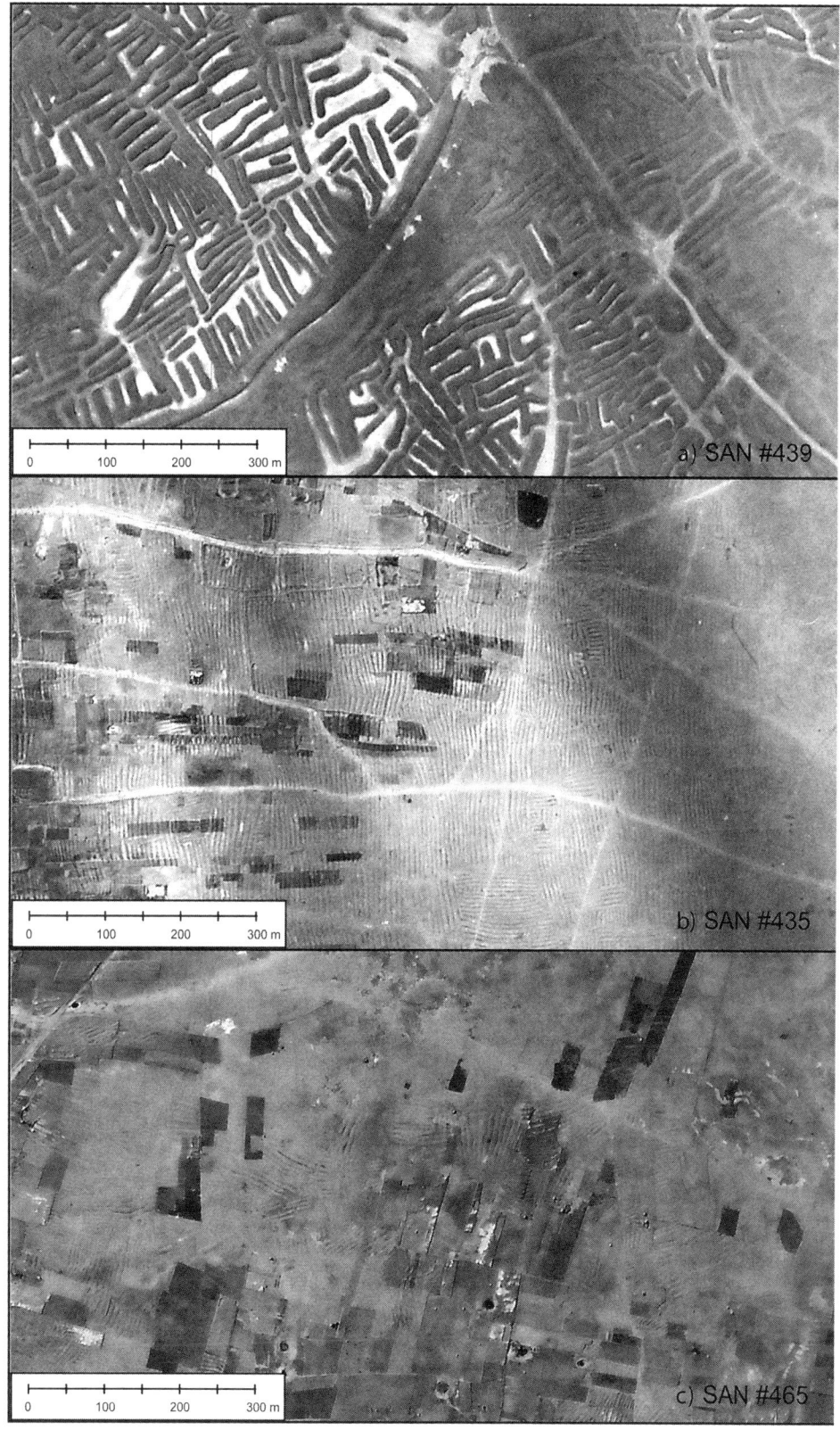

Figure 13.11. Examples of relict raised fields. The fields in (*a*) are alongside the lake and have not been disturbed by modern farming. The fields further inland seen in (*b*) and (*c*) have been disturbed. Nevertheless, the relict raised fields can still be identified.

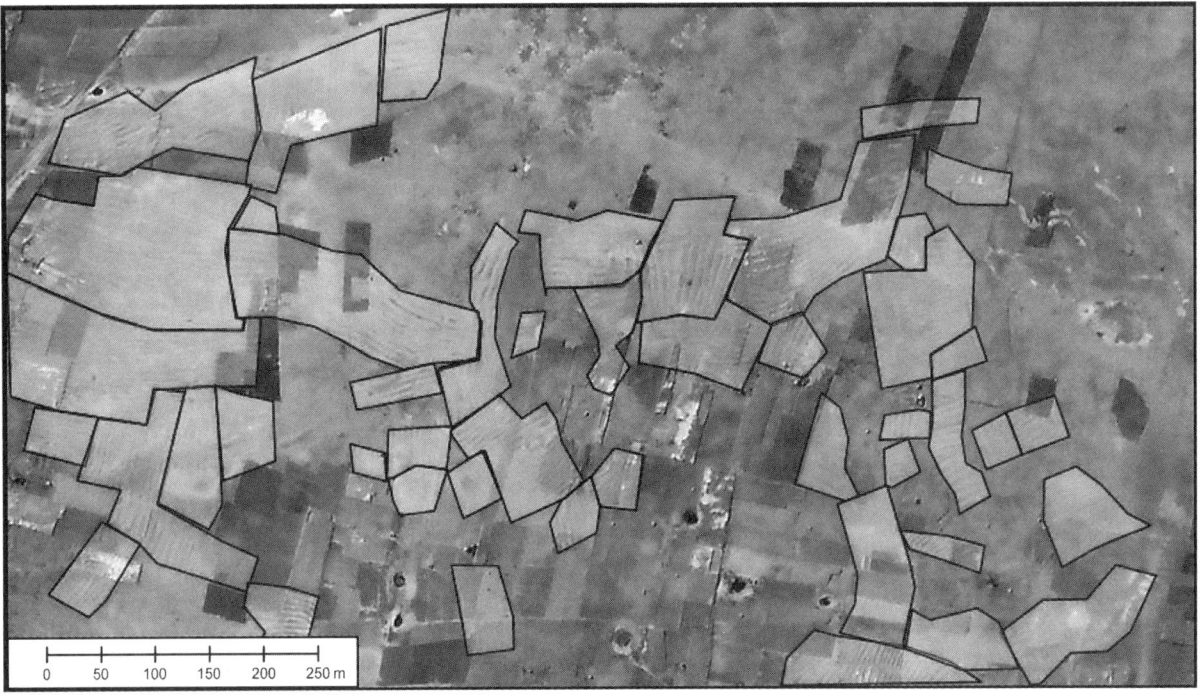

Figure 13.12. The terrain features in Figure 13.11c that meet the criteria for relict raised fields have been highlighted.

Figure 13.13. The identification of relict fields in highly disturbed areas is less certain.

if it contains only isolated fields. However, this choice is knowingly made in order to minimize false identifications. The other case also involves highly disturbed areas as shown in Figure 13.13. Here there are more than single, isolated blocks but with their present condition it is difficult to say with the same high confidence as Figure 13.11 that they represent relict raised field patterning. In these cases, the blocks are highlighted differently, indicating they are regions of possible relict raised fields.

*Survey Results*

*Fields North of Río Ramis*

The results of the aerial photographic survey for the region north of Río Ramis are presented first. This is because the analysis of the relict fields in this area is much simpler due to the fact that there are no canals from the Río Ramis, either natural or human-made. All water for the fields comes from rainfall. The identified fields are shown in Figure 13.14 in which all photos within the dashed perimeter have been scanned and searched. The identified relict raised fields have been circled in black.

The character of the fields in this area is best described by Smith et al. (1968:355) who stated "there are also many small and scattered pockets, none larger than 1000 hectares, and occurring mainly in marshy depressions or on valley floors, often set back from the river course itself, and adjacent to the sharp break of slope at the valley side to mountainous terrain." It was determined from the ground survey that the fields in locations N4 and N5 are located in marshy depressions near large qochas. Locations N2 and N3 are at the base of local hills and receive runoff from them. Perhaps the most interesting are in location N1, which is "pockmarked" with small qochas. An enlargement of the region (Fig. 13.15) clearly shows a typical "open checkerboard" pattern within small qochas. Such qochas were identified from the ground survey as well. While this is the only region near Taraco with such utilization of small qochas, they are in fact quite common northwest of Taraco and represent a different form of agriculture intensification once used in this difficult environment (Flores Ochoa 1987; Flores Blanco et al. 2008).

It is important to recognize that all the raised field regions north of the river represent the simplest of hydrological circumstances as infrastructure and labor were not required to bring the water to these fields because rainfall naturally settles in depressions due to runoff. The fields there are quite small as well when compared to those located south of the river. Thus, they would have been quite amenable to household or village level construction, operation and maintenance. From the chronology discussed above, it has been suggested that "raised field technology undoubtedly developed out of the knowledge and practices of local groups, perhaps during the Formative Period" (Janusek and Kolata 2004:425). The early raised fields could well have been developed in such areas as early farmers explored ways to deal with waterlogged soils. Their success led to large-scale intensification as seen on the alluvial plain south of the river.

Also, during periods of abandonment of large raised field complexes, these smaller, more easily managed fields could well have continued to operate.

*Fields South of Río Ramis*

The situation south of the river is dramatically different from the north, as seen in Figure 13.16. Both areas of high confidence patterning (solid black) and other areas of possible ancient raised field farming (white) are shown. Eight separate high confidence areas have been identified based on their geographical location and relationship to water sources. It is evident from the photo and ground survey that runoff from Cerro Imarocus fed fields in regions S1 and S2 although it will be shown that region S2 was also supplied from the Río Ramis. Region S6 is also indicative of runoff from hills similar to those to the north but was probably supplied from the river as well. Region S7 and possibly S8 would appear to be in depressions near large qochas, also similar to the north. This leaves the large regions S3, S4, S5, S9 and parts of S2 that most likely were supplied by the Río Ramis. The alluvial plain is crisscrossed with numerous canals that were instrumental in providing water to these fields. In the next section the physical landscape, both natural and human-made, that supports the delivery system is described.

There is an absence of high confidence identifications on the central plain S9. There are, however, a number of small areas indicated in white that meet the first two raised field criteria. All four criteria could not be evaluated because the fields in these areas are more highly disturbed than elsewhere. It is possible that ancient raised field farming took place on the central plain but the disturbance by contemporary farming is greater here than elsewhere. As will be seen in the next section describing the physical landscape, there are also numerous "relict canals" in this area. This evidence, in conjunction with the raised field evidence that does exist, increases the confidence that raised field farming occurred on the central plain as well.

Thus, this survey has revealed that extensive raised fields once existed on the alluvial plain of Taraco. Based on the data of Figure 13.16, it is concluded with high confidence that more than 5500 ha of fields occupied the plain in the past and that the extent was probably as large as 7500 ha. In either case, this places Taraco on par with the complexes of Pomata (4000 ha), Tiwanaku (6000 ha), Desaguadero (6000 ha) and Catari (7000 ha) although smaller than the huge, nearby Juliaca complex.

*Lakeshore Fields*

The physical characteristics of the relict raised fields in region S3 alongside the lake are markedly different from all other areas of the plain. As noted earlier, this was the region near Taraco identified by Smith et al. in their 1968 publication. The fields here are atypically large (Fig. 13.17). The difference in size can easily be seen in the aerial photos of Figure 13.11, which all have the same scale. Clearly, the sizes of the platforms and canals from S3 (shown in Fig. 13.11*a*) are much

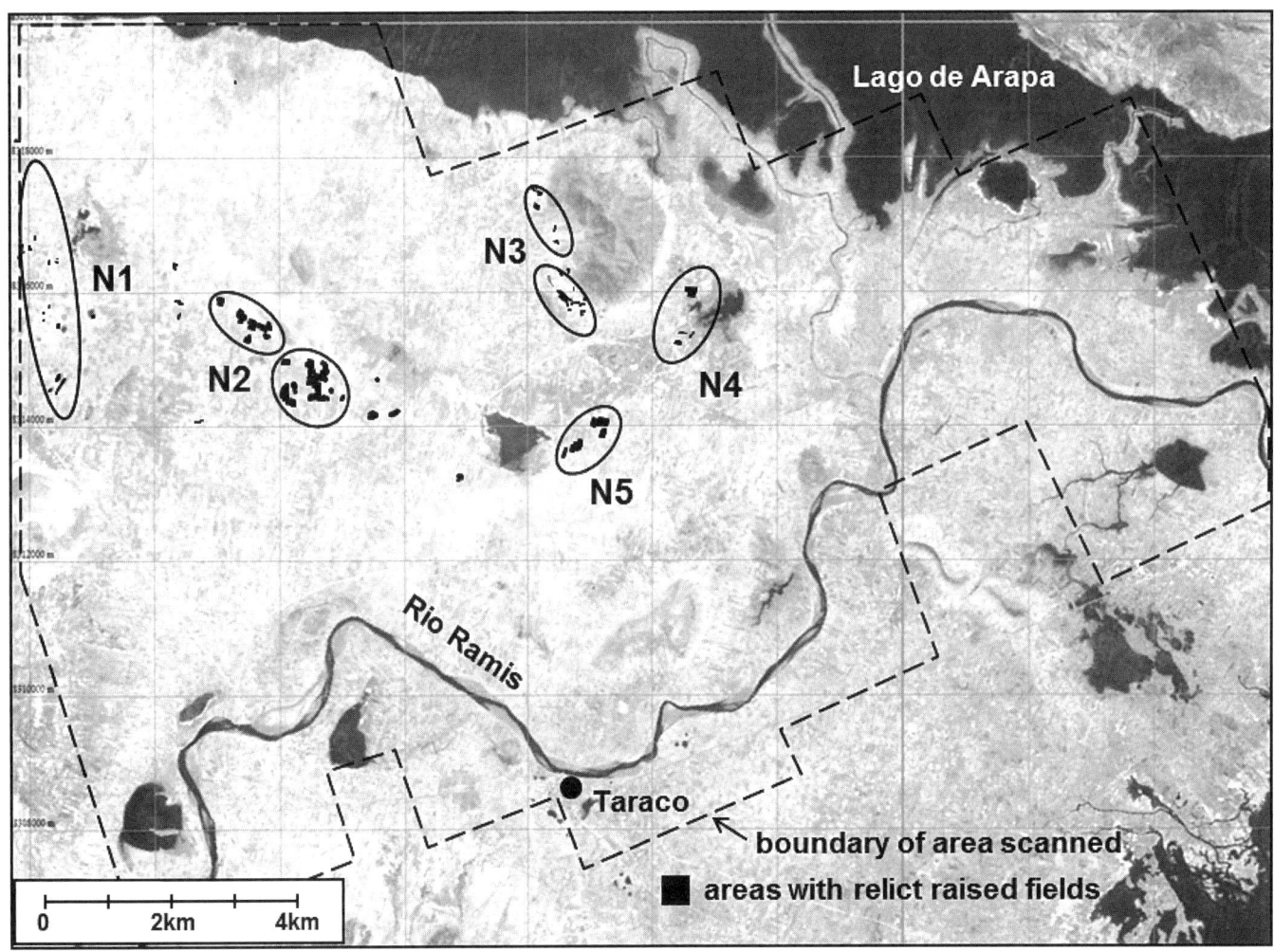

Figure 13.14. Relict raised fields north of Río Ramis identified with high confidence are shown overlaid on the ASTER satellite image. The geographic locations of these fields (N1 to N5) have been called out.

larger than those from inland fields (shown in Fig. 13.11b–c). These differences have been quantified in Figure 13.18, which shows the wavelength distributions from fields alongside the lakeshore (S3) as well as from four inland areas in regions S1, S2 and S5. These data were compiled by selecting a 1 km × 1 km reference square within each of five aerial photos from high confidence regions of relict raised fields. Within each reference square, individual fields that contain a unique period and orientation were identified as in Figure 13.12. The wavelength and area of each individual field were tabulated. From these data, the area-weighted frequency of occurrence of fields in a given region is plotted on the $y$ axis versus wavelength on the $x$ axis (Fig. 13.18).[10] The difference between the two spectra is strik-

ing. Less than 30% of the fields within the reference square in S3 alongside the lake fall within the nominal range of 5 m to 12 m for the inland fields. Conversely, no fields with wavelengths greater than 15 m were found anywhere on the entire plain except for region S3. It is seen in Figure 13.18b that there are both significant short wavelength and long wavelength contributions alongside the lake that are completely absent inland. The situation is even more intriguing when it is recognized that in many locations the small wavelength fields are located between large platforms (Fig. 13.19). Clearly, a different land use strategy was employed by the ancient farmers and hydraulic engineers for the fields located alongside the current lakeshore than for the fields inland.

Figure 13.15. Enlargement of region N1 showing raised field patterns within individual qochas.

A different strategy between inland and lakeshore has been noted by previous authors. Lennon (1983:195) studied the physical characteristics of raised fields for both river and lake regimes in his study in the Juliaca complex; he found in general that "the river area contains larger field patterns overall and the lake regime is consistently smaller in dimensions with the exception of the land to water proportion [field area given over to platforms]." The lake regime fields were about 25% smaller in his study. He attributes the result to differences in drainage of the soil in the two regions, with larger dimensions in areas with better drainage. He did note, however, that "within the high water availability lake edge area, there is an emphasis towards proportionally larger means to be grouped closer lakeside and the smaller means to be found further from the lake" (Lennon 1983:191). While the latter observation suggests larger fields lakeside, the wavelengths of the fields he reported (mean values from 5.7 m to 7.9 m) are well within the nominal range in Figure 13.18b. It is clear that the very long wavelength fields of region S3 around Taraco (some wavelengths > 30 m and some platform widths from 15 m to 20 m) are inherently different than the lake edge fields reported by Lennon.

Denevan (2001:262) has described very large platforms near Pomata (widths averaging from 15 m to 25 m, occasionally reaching 35 m) in what he called a "ladder pattern." He described these as platforms rather than the ridges of raised fields. They are arranged into "parallel groups of ladders separated by troughs and occasionally stone or adobe walls" (Denevan 2001:262). He suggested that they simply represent practices of land division. The large platforms alongside the lake near Taraco are clearly not of the ladder type. We are unaware of other regions around Lake Titicaca with such large platforms in the "open checkerboard" pattern, especially ones enclosing very small wavelength fields.

It is possible that these large fields were reconstructed from smaller fields. Erickson (1987) reported evidence from his excavations of raised fields modified after a period of abandonment. They were made larger by filling alternating canals to increase the field surface from 5 m wide to more than 10 m. Janusek and Kolata (2004:419) have reported modified fields with multiple periods (different times) of construction as well. In their excavation in the Catari Basin, only 7% of the fields demonstrated such modifications but significantly, "most multiple-period fields [different times] were located near the lake or in areas of high

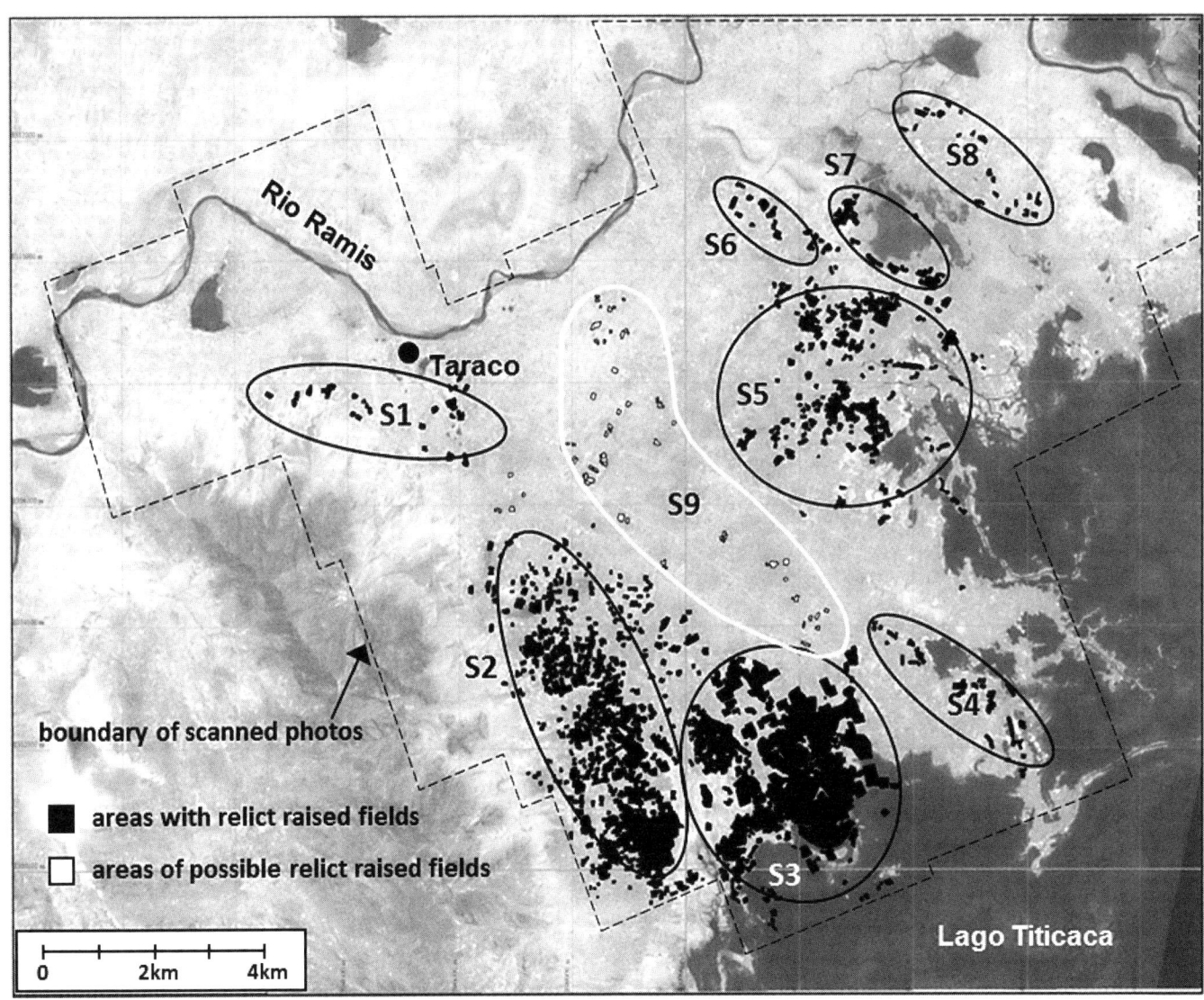

Figure 13.16. Relict raised fields south of Río Ramis are shown overlaid on the ASTER satellite image (Fig. 13.4). Areas of high confidence are indicated in solid black while areas of lower confidence are in white. The geographic locations of these fields (S1 to S9) have been called out. In area S9, only sparse, lower confidence identifications were found.

Figure 13.17.
Photograph of author among very large raised fields in area S3 alongside lake.

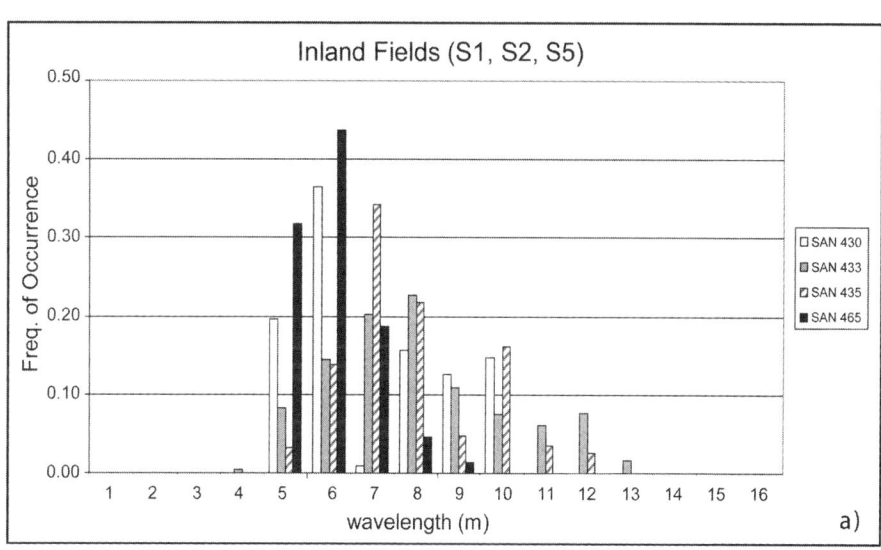

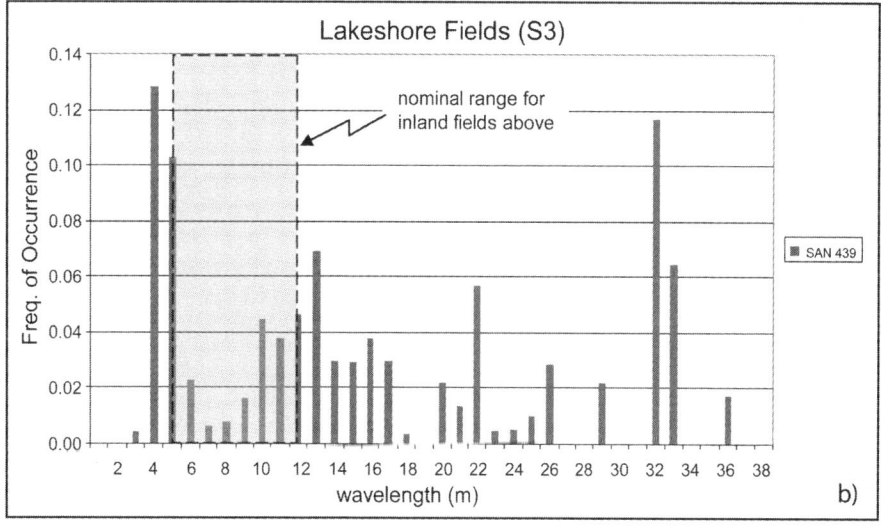

Figure 13.18.
Comparison between the wavelength characteristics of four inland fields shown in (a) and those of the lakeshore fields of region S3 shown in (b). The frequency of occurrence on the y axis is a measure of the contribution to the total from the wavelength range on the x axis. For example, 20% of the area of identified fields in the 1 km × 1 km reference from SAN 430 is composed of fields with wavelengths between 4.5 and 5.5 m.

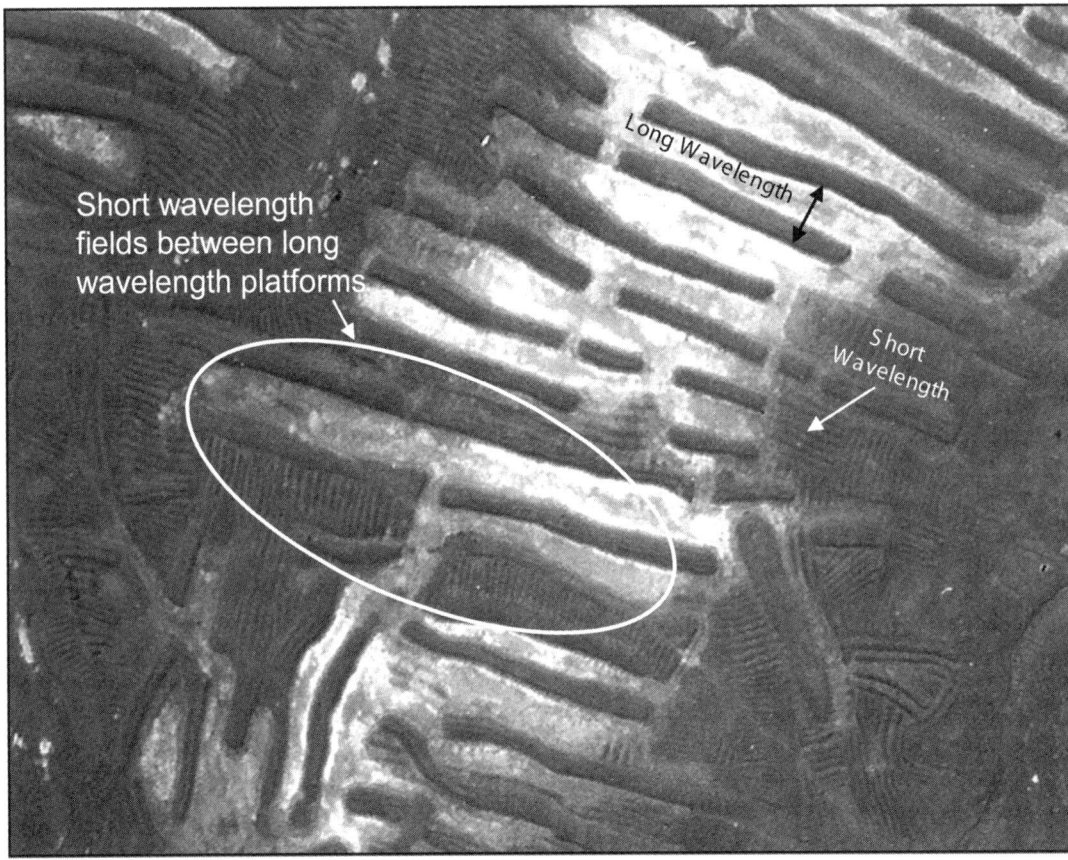

Figure 13.19. Enlargement of photo (SAN 439) of fields alongside the lakeshore in region S3 showing the close spatial relationship of the small wavelength and large wavelength components of Figure 13.18*b*.

groundwater" (Janusek and Kolata 2004:419). Of particular interest is their Figure 9*c*, which shows new, larger, elevated field beds (platforms) reconstructed on top of earlier, smaller beds.

Kolata and Ortloff (1989:249) have modeled raised fields taking into account "salinization of field growing zones by incursion of saline Lake Titicaca water [for cases for which the lake level (temporarily) exceeds the local (fresh) water table height or the water table recedes due to drought conditions leading to saline water intrusion]." They conclude that "to a certain degree, salinization (or incursion of lake-borne concentrates), heat storage, and distance from roots to water table surface can be regulated by artificial mounding and elevation of planting surfaces. This control can be exercised if fill is available for transport or can be obtained from further swale [channel] dredging" (Kolata and Ortloff 1989:250). Certainly fill was available from the large channels seen in Figure 13.19. This suggests a possible reason for field modification. The obvious next step in determining the nature of the large fields alongside the lake is trenching to reveal their morphology and, in particular, the presence or absence of modified fields.

## Raised Fields and the Physical Landscape

The distribution of raised fields depicted in Figure 13.16 can best be understood from their relationship to the physical landscape of the region. Two landscape features, Río Ramis and Cerro Imarocus with its attendant runoff, are central to this understanding as they were the main sources of water for the fields. The landscape today shows evidence of both natural and human-made canals and watercourses that once flowed across the alluvial plain linking the fields with these sources. Some of these canals are still in use for controlling the runoff from Cerro Imarocus. Other canals are idle and have been disturbed by contemporary farming, as have the raised fields themselves. In many cases, only partial canal sections remain and have become, in effect, "relict canals." However, there is ample evidence on the landscape to describe the hydrological system that supplied the ancient fields.

An overview of the main hydrological features around Taraco is shown in Figure 13.20. The topographic map of the Taraco region (1:25,000) served as the base map onto which features

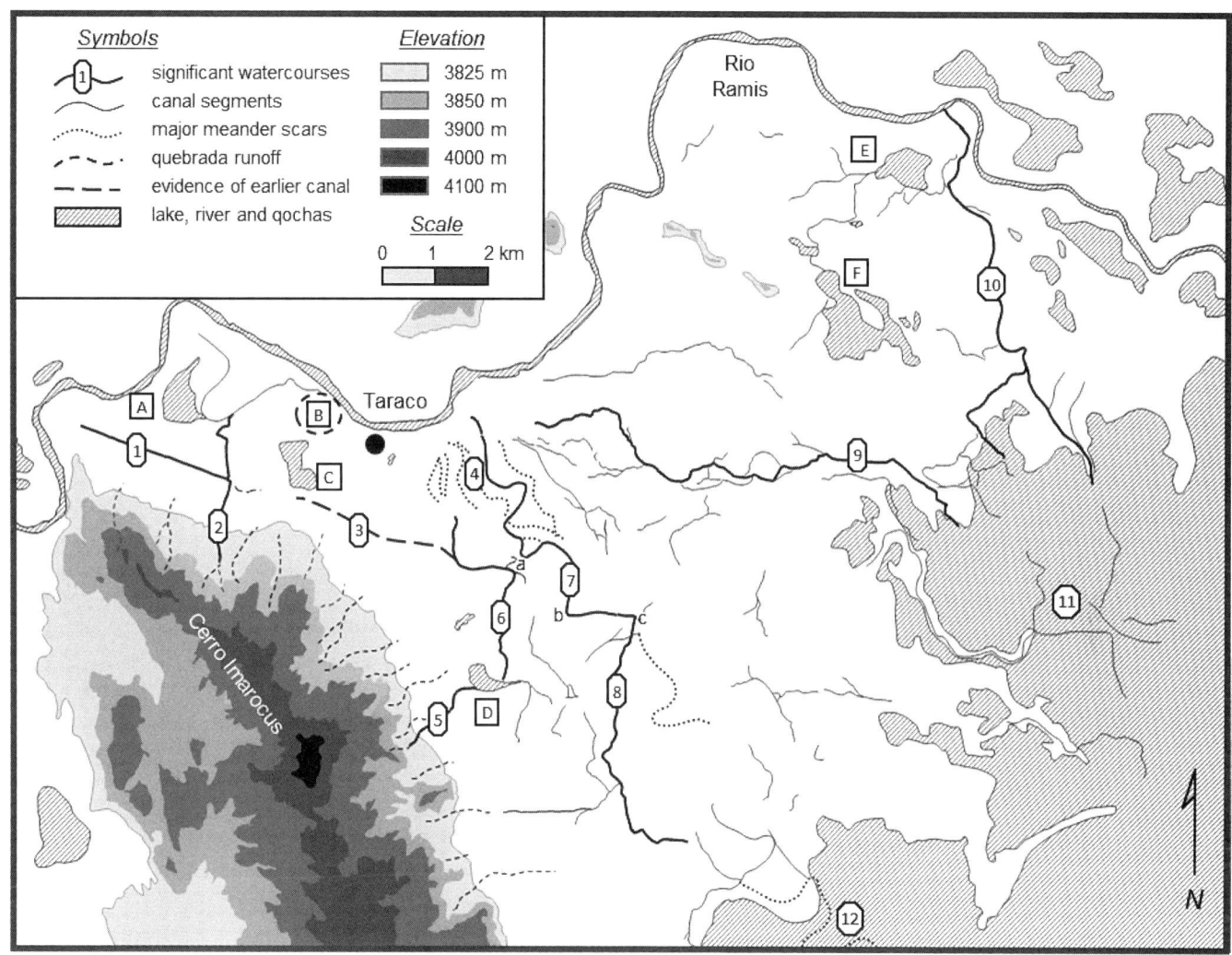

Figure 13.20. Composite map showing the location of major hydrological features on the alluvial plain. Note that offshore watercourses that are evident in aerial photos and satellite imagery have been included. Items discussed in text are:

| | | |
|---|---|---|
| 1: Canal Antiguo Taraco | 7: Upper Río Anta | A: Qocha Pucachoca |
| 2: Canal Huarisán | 8: Lower Río Anta | B: Pampa Huito |
| 3: Earlier canal extension | 9: Río Jarinmayo | C: Qocha Chuno Macha |
| 4: Meander scars | 10: Canal Ramis | D: Qocha Quechuata |
| 5: Canal Quechuata | 11: Offshore canals | E: Qocha Camilaca |
| 6: Río Binogache | 12: Offshore meander | F: Qocha Uyasi |

Points a, b and c along Río Anta are also discussed.

from aerial photos and satellite imagery[11] were transferred. The transfer was straightforward as the photos and imagery were previously registered to UTM coordinates using Global Mapper software. In this fashion, small canal sections not present on the topographic map but noted in the aerial photos were transferred to the base map. Canals visible offshore in aerial photos and satellite images were also included. In Figure 13.21 the locations of the raised field areas from Figure 13.16 have been overlaid onto the same base map. Areas S1 through S8 have been identified with high confidence as containing relict raised fields. Area S9 was identified as having possible relict fields in its northern and southern parts. Numerous canal segments are seen in this latter area. The presence in this area of both canals and relict raised fields together provides a stronger case for raised field farming in S9 even though these fields are more highly damaged than elsewhere. Area S10 offshore has been added as another

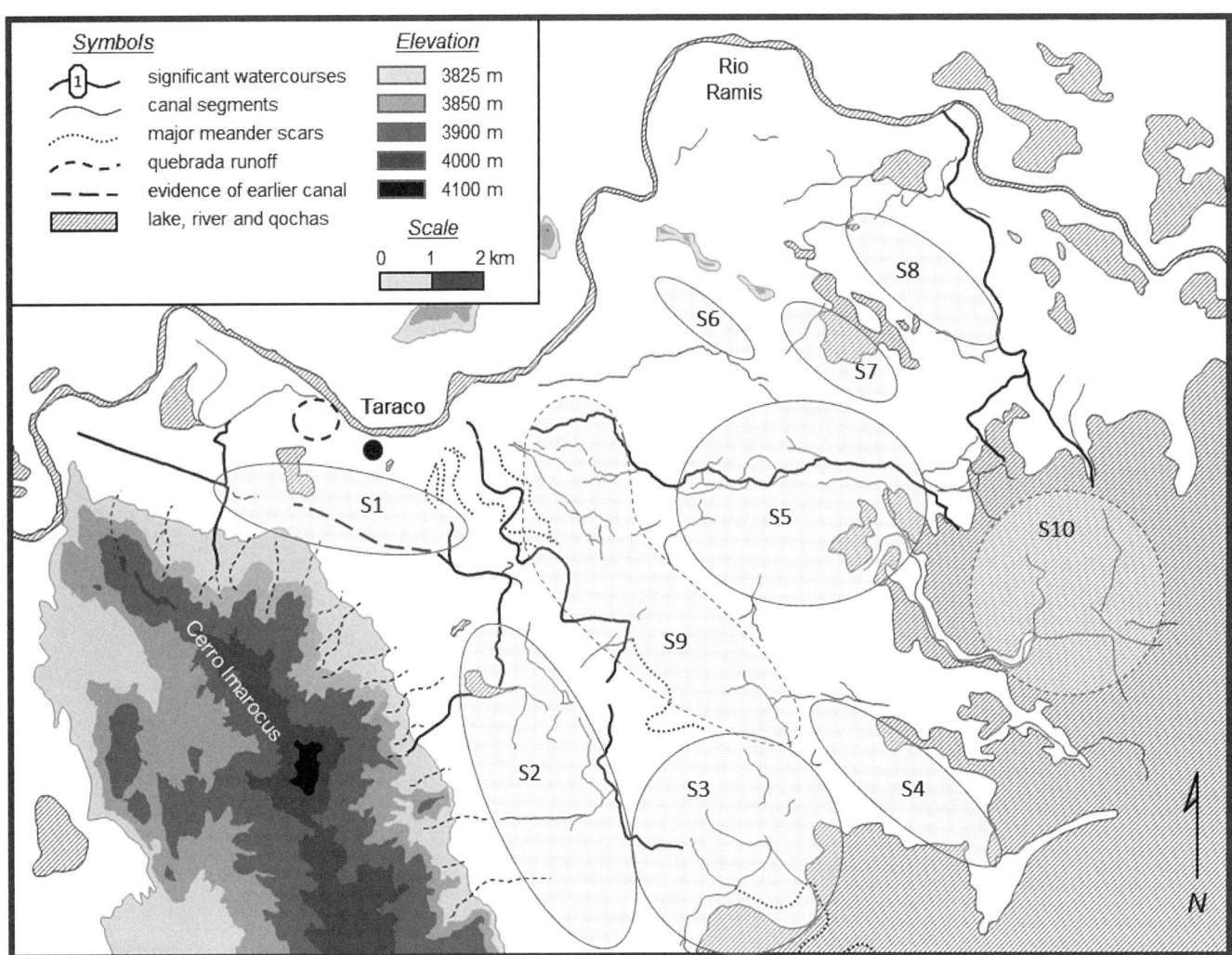

Figure 13.21. The identified relic raised field areas of Figure 13.16 labeled S1 thru S9 have been overlaid on the map of hydrological features shown in Figure 13.20. An additional area, S10, is suggested by the offshore canal segments.

possible area of raised field agriculture based on analysis of the canal geometry of Figure 13.20. The relationship of raised fields to the watercourses and canals is now discussed.

### Natural Watercourses

There are natural watercourses found on the plain that were instrumental in raised field water management. To identify natural courses, the principles used by Adams (1981:8) in his extensive work in analyzing the landscape of Mesopotamia have been invoked: (1) sinuosity and meander suggest a prevailing natural regime and (2) meander wavelength is closely proportional to stream discharge (but may vary somewhat in different settings). There are numerous meander scars indicative of natural courses on the pampa immediately to the east of Taraco near a sharp northward bend in the Río Ramis (Figs. 13.20 [item 4], 13.22a). It is significant that they appear on the inside (concave) bend in the river. These features display the classic morphology of meander scarring caused by bank overtopping during flooding. Russell (1967:71) has described the process of their origin as follows:

> Under natural conditions, flood-overtopping of natural levees occurs when bank-full stage is reached. Most crevasses occur across concave-bank levees, where they divert sediment in suspension, rather than bed load. The amount diverted is a relative small fraction of the total load. If bank-full stage lasts for a considerable time, crevasse channels may become fairly deep and divert a portion of each high-stage flow for several years or decades, in which case they become more or less permanent distributaries. Sooner or later, however, meandering [of the parent river] ordinarily causes course modifications . . . and the distributary is sealed off by natural levee deposition.

There is evidence on the landscape of a major distributary originating in this area that at one time flowed southeast to the lake. The upper portion, called Río Anta on topographic maps (Figs. 13.20 [item 7], 13.22*a*), is the most prominent and deepest of the meander courses in the upper half of the plain today. The most distant portion of the distributary is actually best seen by a meander course offshore (Figs. 13.20 [item 12], 13.22*b*) as it travels almost 5 km into Lake Titicaca. It can be detected by overexposing either the satellite or aerial photographic imagery to bring out the course in the totora reeds offshore (Fig. 13.22*b*). It is hypothesized that these were the two ends of a single distributary. Another smaller course travels eastward from the same general area to the lake (Figs. 13.20 [item 9], 13.22*c*). It is called Río Jarinmayo on topographic maps. Today no water from the Ramis flows in either of these courses due to the large levee system alongside the river (water seen in Fig. 13.22*c* is not from the river, but from the lake).

The role of these watercourses can best be seen in the overlay of raised field areas in Figure 13.21. The Río Jarinmayo was the likely source for the fields of area S5. A separate canal north of the Jarinmayo likely supplied area S6. Río Binogache supplied water to area S2 although this area also received runoff from Cerro Imarocus. The situation for the Río Anta is less straightforward. Evidence on the terrain suggests that the course of the Anta was modified by human agency. During the field survey, the entire course from Taraco to the lake was walked. There are distinctive differences between the upper and lower Anta (Fig. 13.20 [items 7, 8]). In the upper portion, the course is about 20 m wide with gently sloping sides and is about 0.5 m to 1 m deep. The broad meandering course is evident and easy to follow (Fig. 13.23). This radically changes beginning at the point marked "b" in Figure 13.20. At this point, the course takes a sharp turn and enters a lateral stretch in which the walls become steeper and the depth quickly lowers to almost 2 m. As it approaches point "c," it gradually rises to a depth of only a few tens of centimeters. The course then takes a sharp (> 90°) turn to avoid a roadbed. Beyond this point, its character changes dramatically. This new portion is described as the lower Río Anta. It is much shallower and no longer exhibits broad meanders. At places, it is difficult to follow, even being masked by plowed fields. The natural river course that created the upper Anta could not have created the circumstances surrounding the lower Anta. Only controlled flow that limited the volume would have allowed water to negotiate this modified course. It had to have been created by human agency.

A probable explanation for these circumstances is that the Anta, along with the other courses (Jarinmayo and Binogache), were adopted and modified by early farmers and hydraulic engineers as conduits to carry water from Río Ramis to the raised fields. Adams (1981) has described just such usage of natural watercourses by the early irrigationists of Mesopotamia. Another course, the Canal Ramis (discussed in the next section), also suggests there was controlled flow from the Ramis. Such a strategy would have likely required modification of the natural levees originally alongside the river to control the volume of flow in these watercourses as well as to stop overtopping at high stage in wet years. Such modification is clearly evident today with the large, manually constructed levees alongside the Ramis that effectively contain the river, even in the wettest years (Fig. 13.7).[12] Kolata (1991:116) has described similarly large levees (3 m high and 5 m wide) alongside ancient watercourses around Tiwanaku. Unfortunately, there is no direct material evidence around Taraco today that points to a period of time in antiquity when (or even if) such modifications took place. However, the circumstantial evidence of controlled flow in these canals is substantial and points to the early modifications of the natural levees.

The rationale for the specific modifications to the Anta can only be speculated. From Figure 13.20 it is seen that lateral extension ("b" to "c"), which was probably modified by human agency, would have allowed the lower Anta to supply fields further south in area S2 and the western portion of S3 alongside the lake. Also note that another possible modification by human agency near point "a" would have joined the upper Anta to the Binogache to provide water that flowed to Qocha Quechuata and then to the fields of S2.

Only partial evidence of a major meander course on the lower half of the alluvial plain that would have linked the upper Río Anta to the offshore meander course is present on the terrain. This seems consistent with the greater damage to surface evidence around area S9 than elsewhere. The central plain (eastern portion of S3, S4 and lower portion of S9) was likely fed by water from Río Anta based upon the geometry of the meander scars and the small canal segments in this region (Fig. 13.21).

*Canals*

There are canals in use today to control runoff from Cerro Imarocus. Numerous *quebrada* or ravines descend from the hills to the plain, thereby creating drainage paths for rain falling on the hills (the major quebrada are shown by dashed lines in Fig. 13.20). Extensive effort is spent today constructing and maintaining a number of canals below them to avoid flooding of fields. The flows from the largest quebrada are canalized using sod block construction. Two examples, Canal Huarisan and Canal Quechuata,[13] are highlighted in Figure 13.24*a–b*. These are very large canals about 4 m to 5 m in width and 0.5 m to 1 m in depth. This runoff is not used for irrigation. It is carried directly from the hills to terminal catchments to avoid flooding. Runoff on the north side terminates in low-lying catchments alongside or near the Río Ramis. For example, the runoff from Canal Huarisan terminates in Qocha Pucacoha and Pampa Huito. Runoff to the northeast finds its way to Río Binogache, which then carries it to Qocha Quechuata. This qocha is distinctly different from others in the area. It is very shallow (only 1 to 2 m deep) and consequently dries out each summer (when local inhabitants use it as a soccer field) (Fig. 13.25). During most rainy seasons, it overflows with the runoff then making its way to Lake Titicaca. Canal Quechuata flows directly to Qocha Quechuata while run-

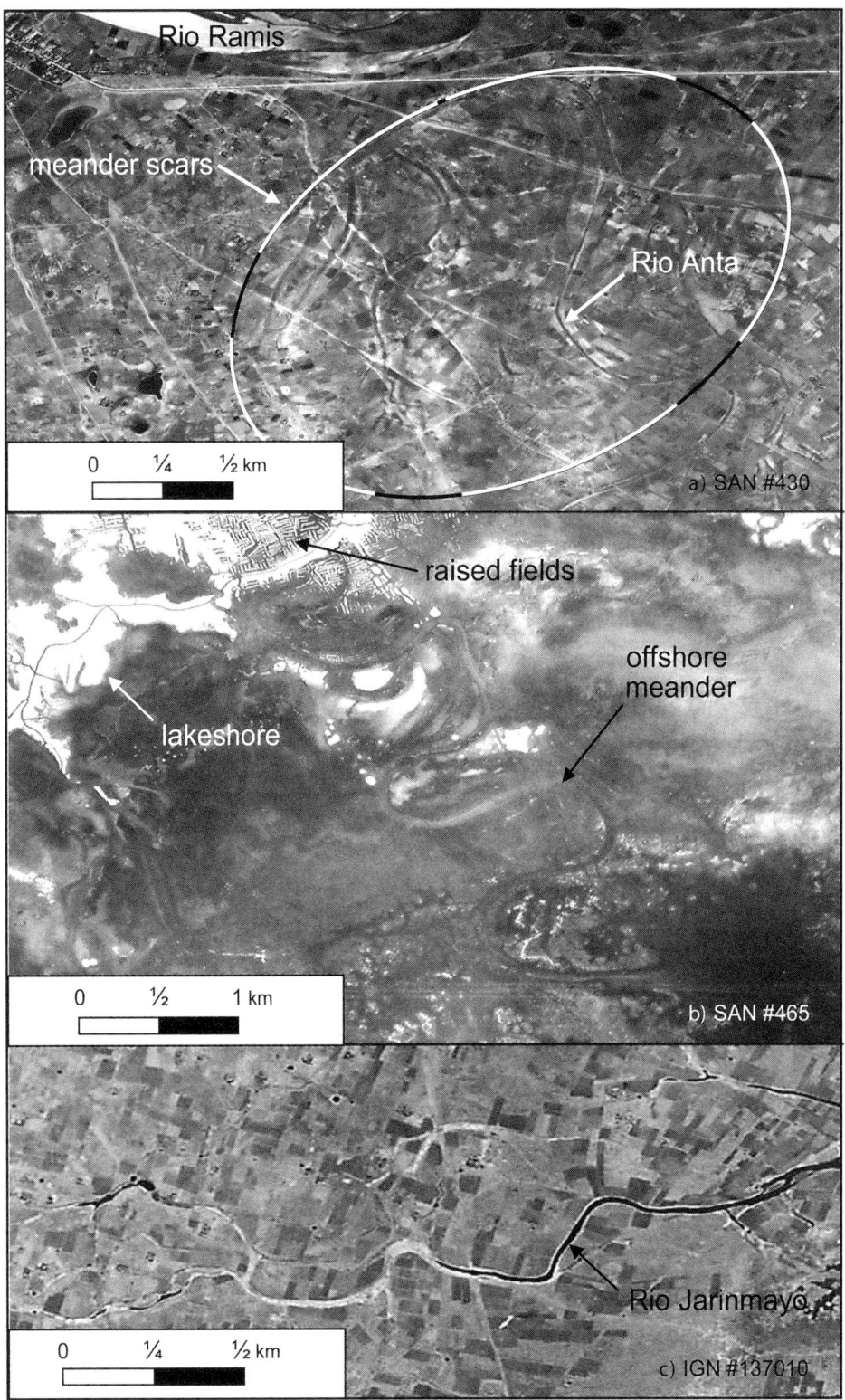

Figure 13.22. Evidence of meander scarring in three different areas around Taraco. See Figure 13.20 for exact locations. In (*b*) the meander actually is seen offshore in Lake Titicaca; in (*c*), lake water is present in the eastern portion of the river course.

Figure 13.23. Evidence of natural watercourses that once flowed across the alluvial plain. The direction of meander is shown by black arrows. The white path in (b) is marked by salt deposits that remain after water entering from the lake during the wet season has evaporated.

Figure 13.24. Canals in use today in controlling the runoff from Cerro Imarocus. Two views of Canal Antiguo Taraco are shown with (d) being further east and deeper than (c).

Figure 13.25. Comparison between deeper Qocha Camilaca and shallower Qocha Quechuata in the dry season (August 2006).

off from quebrada further south flows to the lake without any intermediate catchment.

Still other canals feed the canalized quebrada runoff. The most important one feeding Canal Huarisan is called Canal Antiguo Taraco in this report.[13] This name is selected to stress the fact that circumstantial evidence suggests that it is ancient in origin. The canal runs in an east-southeasterly direction below the hills in a straight path for more than 5 km with no sinuosity whatsoever (Fig. 13.20). It collects a large quantity of water, gaining size as it travels to the east (Fig. 13.24c–d).[14] This runoff then joins the runoff from Canal Huarisan and flows to its terminal catchment. Today, the canal flows no further east than Canal Huarisan. There are anecdotal reports from local inhabitants that the Canal Antiguo Taraco once flowed past this point all the way to Lake Titicaca via Qocha Quechuata. However, there is scant evidence on the ground today of it traveling further east than Canal Huarisan. This is because numerous farmsteads and plowed fields now occupying this area have made it difficult to detect evidence of a watercourse from the ground. Yet close inspection of both the satellite and aerial photographic imagery does reveal an indication of an earlier course. Figure 13.26 shows the aerial photograph of the region of interest from 1970. The course seen in the photo that could well have been an earlier extension of Canal Antiguo Taraco is highlighted. This course would have united the current Canal Antiguo Taraco with Río Binogache so flow indeed would have traveled to the lake via Qocha Quechuata. Such an extension would have been an integral part in the water management of the raised fields below Cerro Imarocus.

It is seen in Figure 13.21 that the extension canal would have run through the middle of area S1. The raised fields in this area could only have been supplied by runoff as they are at an elevation above any flow from Río Ramis. It is interesting to note that during the ground survey one farmer complained that in spite of all the canals today carrying away runoff, this area in particular is annually subject to flooding up to 1 m deep. As discussed above, areas subject to seasonal flooding are natural locations for raised fields and the extension canal would have been crucial to their operation. It would have been a water supply source as it collected runoff from a large area below the hills and, of equal importance, it would have drained excess water during especially wet years. Based on this photographic evidence of the extension and its location relative to the relict raised fields, it is concluded that most likely Canal Antiguo Taraco did extend to Río Binogache and was an integral part of water management in this region.

There is still another watercourse further east from Taraco, the Canal Ramis[13] that originated at the Ramis and flowed to the lake (Fig. 13.20). The canal was clearly manually constructed using sod block construction (Fig. 13.27). It is a very large canal measuring 10 m wide and 1 m deep with earthen levees of about 0.5 m in height. It was capable of carrying a huge volume of water. It is even bigger than the canals shown in Figure 13.24 that have to transport large quantities of runoff from torrential rains over Cerro Imarocus. Yet today there is no requirement for such a large canal in this flat region. It does have a small annual flow described by nearby residents as resulting from *filtración*, which refers to seepage from the high water table in the area. However, the canal's size is much larger than needed for this purpose, which suggests that the need for such a large canal was based on an earlier requirement. Ortloff (1996) has described the water management system for the raised fields around Tiwanaku. Central to the water management system was Canal Waña Jawira,

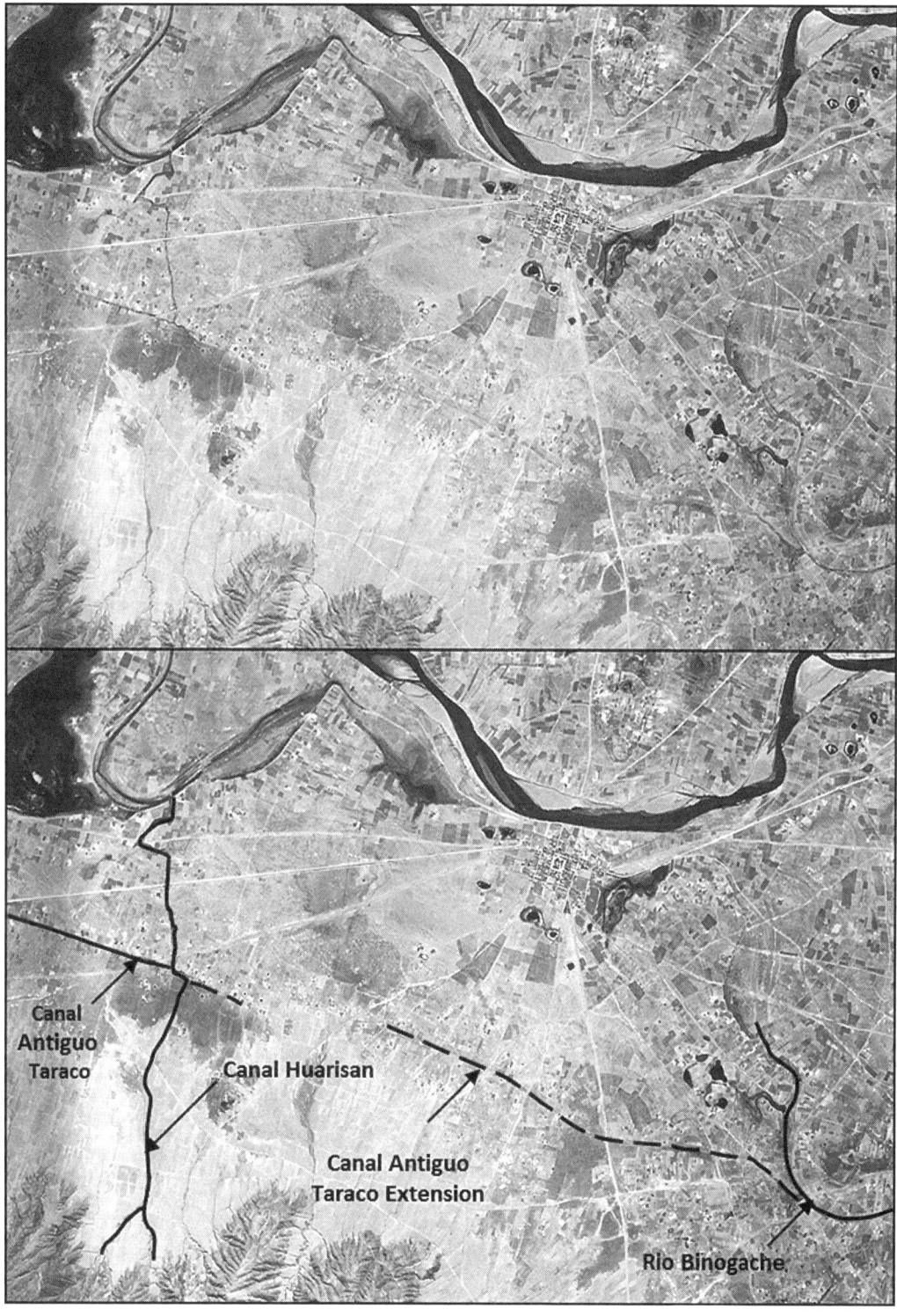

Figure 13.26. An aerial photograph (IGN 15222) of the area below Cerro Imarocus showing the major canals discussed in the text. The two photos are identical. In the lower photo, the canals have been highlighted for clarity.

Figure 13.27. Two views of Canal Ramis: *a*, looking northwest to the levee alongside Río Ramis; *b*, looking southeast to the lake. A rod one meter in length has been placed in the center of the canal with the darker end pointing north.

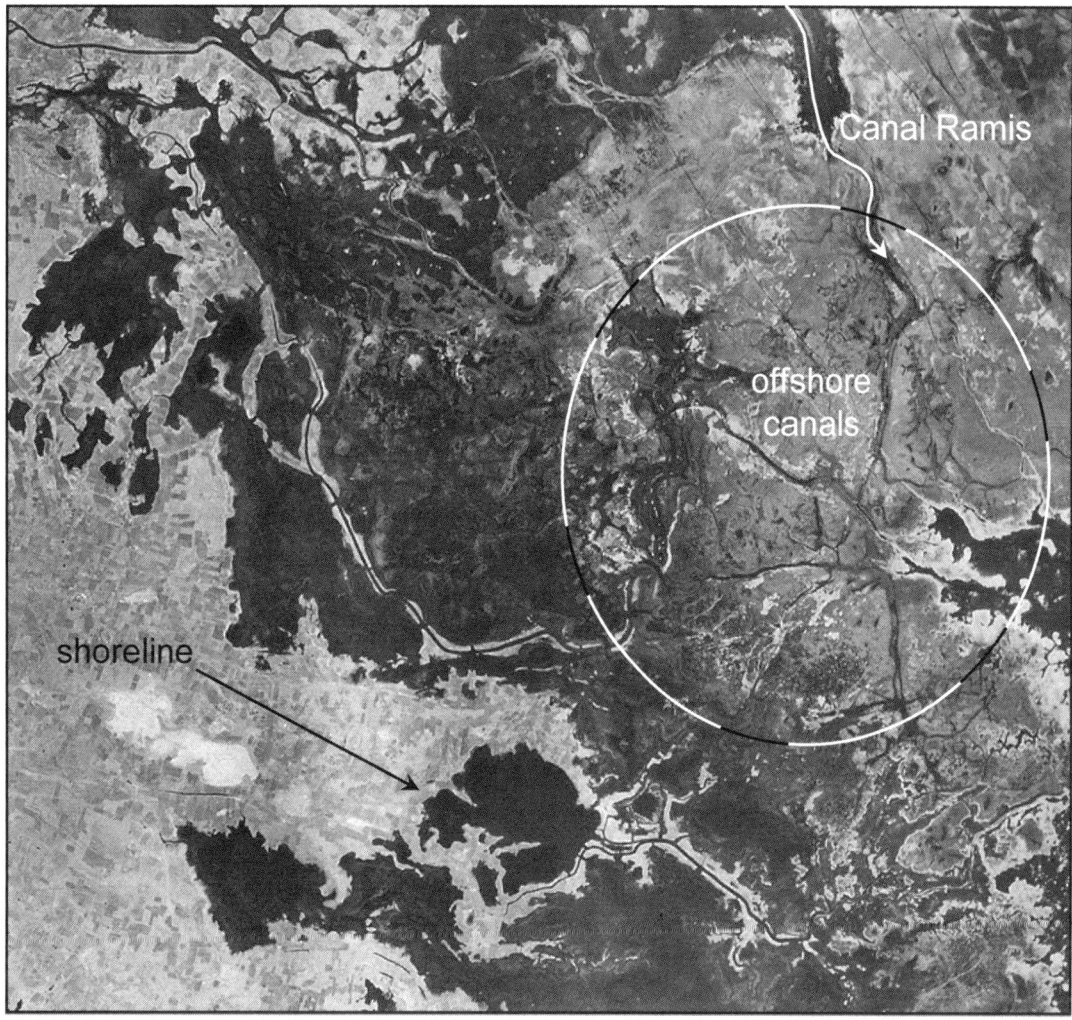

Figure 13.28. Offshore canals visible within dashed circle were supplied by Canal Ramis (IGN 15220). See area S10 in Figure 13.21 for location.

which took water from an intake on the Tiwanaku River to the raised fields to the west. It is of the same construction type and has comparable dimensions (as wide as 9.2 m) to Canal Ramis. The similar size suggests an earlier use of Canal Ramis for supplying raised fields. Note that its path can be traced offshore into the lake using aerial photos (Fig. 13.20 [item 10]). In Figure 13.28, it is seen that the canal is part of a network of other offshore canals. Based on these observations, it is concluded that this area was once indeed a site of raised field farming supplied by Canal Ramis at an earlier time when the lake level was lower.

In spite of relict raised field and canal deterioration and destruction in many areas due to farming, this survey of landscape features including human-made canals and human-modified natural watercourses has been most beneficial. It has shown that ancient farmers and hydraulic engineers utilized different sources of water (river water, runoff and groundwater from qochas) as the situation presented itself. The relationship between the raised field areas seen in Figures 13.16 and 13.21 and these sources is summarized in Table 13.2. This estimate of raised field coverage is a conservative one as some fields probably existed between the different areas and have not been included in the totals. In the case of area S9, which contains more highly disturbed relict fields than other areas, the presence of canals there further substantiated the existence of raised field agriculture in that area. The canal

Table 13.2. A detailed summary of relict raised field areas discussed in the text specifying the basic source of water and principal delivery means for each area. Areas S1–S8 and N1–N5 were identified with high confidence based on relict raised field patterning alone. Additional evidence provided by canal locations supports areas S9 and S10 as also once being sites of raised field farming.

| Area | Location | Size (ha) | Elevation (m) | Source | Delivered by |
|---|---|---|---|---|---|
| South | | | | | |
| S1 | Taraco (west) | 200 | 3818–3819 | runoff | Canal Antiguo Taraco |
| S1 | Taraco (south) | 200 | 3816.5–3817 | runoff | Canal Antiguo Taraco |
| S2 | around Qocha Quechuata | 300 | 3813–3813.5 | runoff + Río Ramis | Río Binogache + direct runoff |
| S2 | Qocha to lakeshore | 1200 | 3811–3813 | runoff + Río Ramis | Qocha overflow + direct runoff + Anta |
| S3 | lakeshore (large period) | 1200 | 3810–3811 | Río Ramis | probably canals from Anta |
| S4 | lakeshore (east) | 400 | 3809–3810 | Río Ramis | probably canals from Anta |
| S5 | Río Jarinmayo | 1200 | 3811–3812 | Río Ramis | Río Jarinmayo |
| S6 | Cerro Puquis | 200 | 3812–3813 | runoff + Río Ramis | direct runoff + delivery canal north of Jarinmayo |
| S7 | Qocha Uyasi | 200 | 3909–3010 | qocha + possibly Ramis | qocha + possible canals north of Jarinmayo |
| S8 | Qocha Camilaca | 400 | 3809–3810 | qocha + possibly Ramis | qocha + possible canals from Canal Ramis |
| sub-total | | 5500 | | | |
| S9 | central plain (N) | 500 | 3813–3814 | Río Ramis | canals from Río Ramis |
| S9 | central plain (S) | 500 | 3811–3812 | Río Ramis | probably canals from Anta and Jarinmayo |
| S10 | offshore | 1000 | below 3809 | Río Ramis | Jarinmayo and Canal Ramis |
| total south | | 7500 | | | |
| North | | | | | |
| N1 | Pampa Quejón Moco | small qocha | 3822–3824 | fields within small qocha | no delivery canal |
| N2 | Cerro Camijachi | 150 | 3818–3820 | runoff | no delivery canal |
| N3 | Cerro Chucaripo | 100 | 3811–3813 | runoff | no delivery canal |
| N4 | Pampa Anamoco | 100 | 3811–3812 | qocha + minor runoff | no delivery canal |
| N5 | Pampa Saitococha | 100 | 3812–3813 | qocha + minor runoff | no delivery canal |
| total north | | 450 | | | |

geometry also suggests that fields once existed offshore when the lake level was lower, such as area S10. Thus, the preponderance of evidence presented here points to an extensive system of water management across the entire alluvial plain covering as much as 7500 ha.

*Human Occupation and the Physical Landscape*

Physical landscape plays an important role in determining site location around Taraco. Thanks to recently available survey data reported by Chávez and Plourde (2008), it is possible to relate the location of ancient sites to contemporary ones. Marked differences between the two reflect different land use strategies at work. Today, habitation sites are found across the alluvial plain from corner to corner. While the population density there is low in comparison to the town (see Fig. 13.2), there is hardly any area above the lake level that is not occupied or farmed. The construction of the large levees along the Río Ramis has enabled this usage. Also of note is the absence of sites on the gently sloping ground below Cerro Imarocus because this area has been totally devoted to farming following the construction of the irrigation canal (out of operation since 2000) mentioned above.

The locations of ancient sites around Taraco are taken from the much larger surface survey of northwest Lake Titicaca Basin reported by Chávez and Plourde. Information such as site type, topography and area characteristics has been recorded. Surface artifacts have been identified by period—Formative, Tiwanaku, Altiplano and Inca as well as the local Huana style that overlaps the late Formative and Tiwanaku periods. In Figure 13.29, the sites covering all periods have been overlaid on Figure 13.21

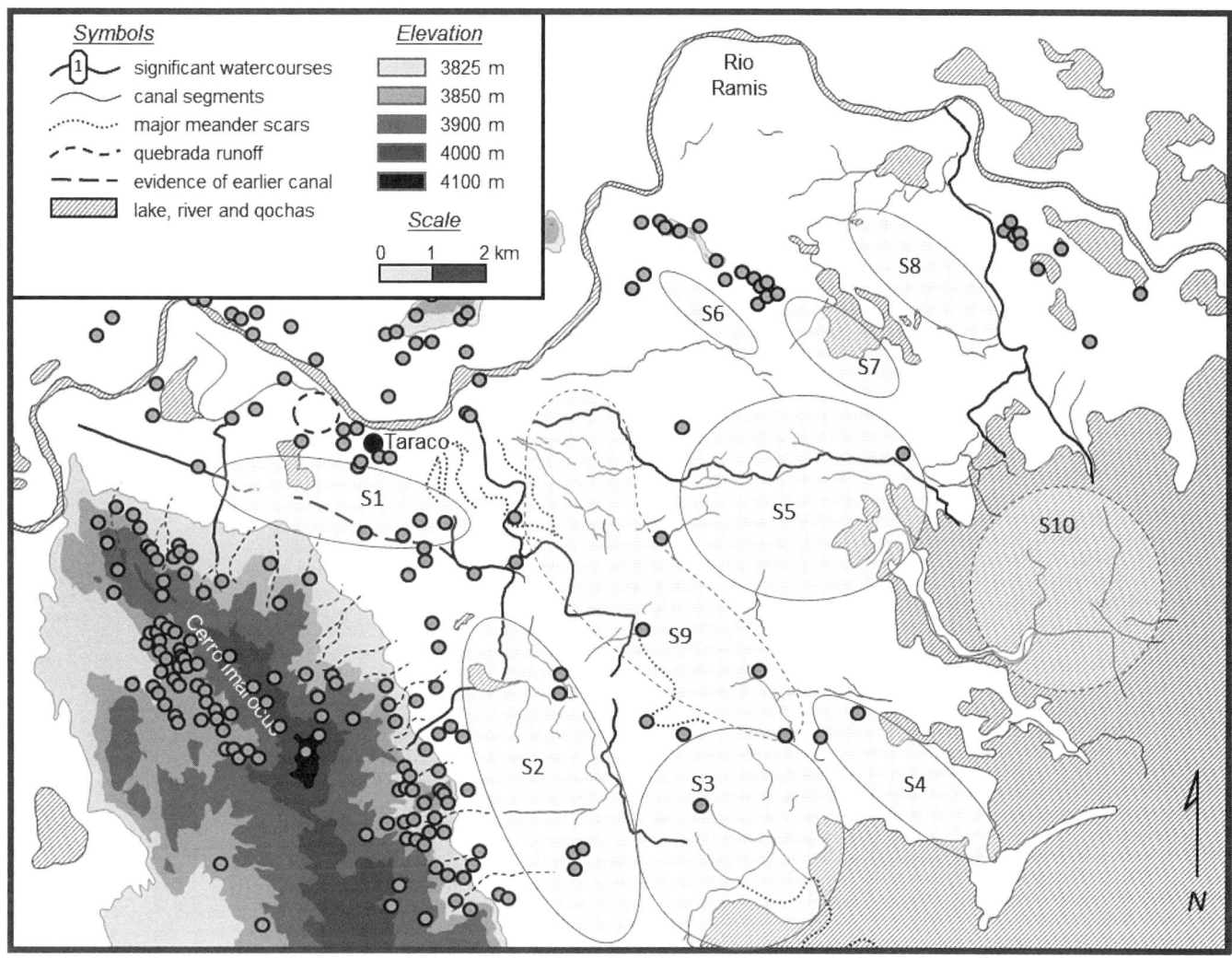

Figure 13.29. Occupation sites identified around Taraco by Chávez (Chávez and Plourde) indicated by the small circles have been overlaid on Figure 13.21 showing the major zones of raised field farming around Taraco.

showing the major raised field farming zones around Taraco (the sites are indicated by small circles). For the Taraco district east of the Cerro Imarocus ridge line, there are more than 150 sites. The majority (67%) are located above the alluvial plain either on the hills in the region or immediately below the hills at elevations above the plain. The preference for sites above the alluvial plain is clear—they are not subject to flooding due to their elevation. A number of other sites (23%) are located near the river and qochas of the region. There is a comparative dearth of identified sites on the alluvial plain itself (10%).

These data present a dramatically different picture of land utilization. Most notable is the absence of a large number of sites among the raised fields on the alluvial plain. In carrying out population estimates for the Juli-Pomata region with its large raised field complex, Stanish (1994) assumed sites within 1 or 2 km of the fields were associated with raised field land usage because they allowed a short walk to the fields. As shown in Figure 13.29, fields in zones S1, S2, S6, S7, and S8 are within 2 km of the numerous sites at the base of Cerro Imarocus. But there is an absence of a comparable density of ancient sites near the major raised field zones on the alluvial plain (S3, S4, S5 and S9). It is instructive to note that of the 16 sites identified on the alluvial plain, 13 sites are located on small mounds known as *monticulos*. They have an average site size of 4 ha. Furthermore, all 13 of these sites show evidence of continuous occupation from the Formative through Inca periods. Clearly, these sites were desirable in antiquity because of their elevation. Prior to the human augmentation of natural levees, this area was a flood plain with large areas of waterlogged soil not conducive to year-round occupation except for the mounds. Augmentation of the natural levees is suggested by the network of canals on the plain (discussed above). The area was then dedicated to extensive raised field farming, which again was not conducive to year-round occupation. The mounds were the only choice.

Kolata (1991:115) has reported a similar situation on the Pampa Koani, which was supplied by Río Catari. He states "small house mounds physically associated or structurally merged with the raised-field segments were the residences of rural families engaged in primary agricultural production. In demographic terms, there are simply insufficient numbers of human settlements of the Pampa Koani proper to account for the virtually continuous expanse of raised fields and associated hydraulic structures in the region" (Kolata 1991:115). He concludes that the labor must have come from a wider, non-local region. While labor may well have come from a wider region, it is not clear how many of the fields were in operation at any one time so it is not clear how much labor was needed at any given point.

Modern farming has also had a major impact on land use strategy. In most cases, the mounds have been abandoned and in some cases they are actually just another part of plowed terrain as they can be easily plowed by tractor. Also, as noted, farming has taken over the gently sloping hills below Cerro Imarocus, which earlier would have been a preferred area for habitation.

Finally, it is also important to recognize that the occupation sites on mounds do not necessarily imply that their sole purpose was for raised field farming. The surface survey showed that these sites were continually occupied, even during the period in which Erickson believes the fields were abandoned (from about AD 300 to AD 1000). The sites would have been desirable for rainfall farming or for smaller scale raised field farming (household level as seen north of the river) as well as for large-scale raised field farming. This situation points to the importance of trenching the raised fields, which is the only accurate way to establish periods of operation.

## Hydrology

In this section, the raised field water sources are examined in more detail, including the capacity and timing of both rainfall runoff from Cerro Imarocus and river water from the Ramis. The goal is to understand the capability and limitations of each source. It is shown that the limited rainfall in the region restricted the size of raised fields supplied by runoff alone to about 1000 ha of the 5500 to 7500 ha identified in the last section. On the other hand, modeling of the Canal Ramis shows that the Río Ramis could have easily supplied the fields on the alluvial plain under normal conditions. Canal Ramis is also compared to Canal Waña Jawira, which supplied the raised fields near Tiwanaku, to gain insight into the basic operation, control and maintenance issues of the canals supplying the fields.

A flow chart of the approach used in these calculations is shown in Figure 13.30; the calculations are based on hydrological data from ONERN (1985) and SENAMHI as well as on field measurements of the terrain parameters. Both calculations rely on the continuity equation for continuous steady flow that relates the flow rate $Q(m^3/sec)$ to the velocity $v(m/sec)$ and cross-sectional area of flow $A(m^2)$ by:

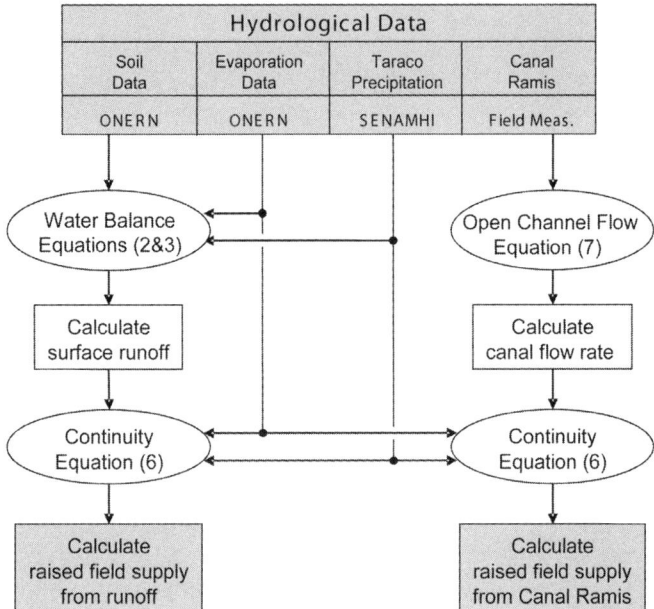

Figure 13.30. Flow chart of hydrological calculations used to calculate the filling of raised fields from the two sources discussed in the text.

$$Q = A \cdot v \qquad (1)$$

The objective here is to gain a qualitative understanding of these sources rather than quantitative detail. Accordingly, average values for related parameters are used. As discussed earlier, from 30% to 60% of the field is given over to cultivation. Denevan (2001:277) states that 50% represents a good compromise value. Consequently, the area occupied by channels is taken to be 50% of the total surface area ($A_t$). Similarly, a typical canal depth of 1 m is used. The channel is considered full when the water height in the channel ($h_{ch}$) reaches 80% of maximum. This allows margin against overtopping due to additional direct rainfall over the fields. Since the height of water and area of the channels are linearly related to the flow, the results can be easily scaled to other values if desired.

### Runoff from Cerro Imarocus

The first order of business is to determine just how much of the rain falling on the terrain actually ends up as runoff rather than going to soil saturation and evaporation. With this information, the area of raised fields supplied by this runoff can be determined. ONERN (1984) has calculated just such runoff for a region alongside the lake just south of Puno about 60 km south of Taraco. To carry out the calculation, the region's soil retention properties were measured. The approach uses the equilibrium or water balance condition in which input flow $<Q_{in}>$ is equated to the output $<Q_{out}>$ where:

$$<Q_{in}> = <Q_{rain}> \quad \text{and} \quad (2)$$

$$<Q_{out}> = <Q_{evaporation}> + <Q_{soil\ retention}> + <Q_{runoff}> \quad (3)$$

The brackets indicate that the values are monthly averages. Runoff occurs once the soil is saturated and rainfall exceeds evaporation. The ONERN calculation (1984:29) for station Ganja Salcedo, a small agricultural community 3 km south of Puno and about 1.5 km from the lake, has been reproduced. As Figure 13.31 indicates, runoff (mm/month) occurs from December through March when rainfall exceeds evaporation and the soil is saturated. Beginning in April, evaporation exceeds rainfall so moisture is released, thereby drying out the soil. Starting in September, rainfall exceeds evaporation and soil moisture is recovered to the point of saturation in late November when runoff is initiated once again. The calculation was then repeated using the median rainfall data for Taraco (Fig. 13.5). The runoff values, shown by the left-hand axis of Figure 13.32, indicate that runoff peaks at about 100 mm/month for the month of January. For future reference, it is noted that this value equates to a steady flow rate of ~ 0.04 m³/km²/sec for the month.

Of interest are the raised fields below Cerro Imarocus that were supplied by runoff. When filling a container of cross-sectional area A, the flow velocity can be treated as vertical so v = dh/ht where h is the height of water in the container. Therefore, equation (1) can be expressed as:

$$dh(t)/dt = (1/A) \cdot [Q_{in}(t) - Q_{out}(t)] \quad \text{or} \quad (4)$$

$$h(t) - h(0) = (1/A) \int_0^t [Q_{in}(t) - Q_{out}(t)]\, dt \quad (5)$$

where the net flow ($Q_{in} - Q_{out}$) has been used. In equations (4) and (5), only the vertical velocity of flow has been considered. Obviously, the filling of a container involves a three-dimensional flow. But since the flow in transverse directions is generally much faster than the vertical direction, the filling can be viewed as uniform across the container with equation (4) describing flow in the vertical direction. To estimate the filling of raised fields, a sequential filling of the fields is envisioned with blocks small enough that the uniform assumption holds in a given block. Therefore, the total area $A_t$ filled to a level $h_{ch}$ after a time T is:

$$A_t(T) = (1/h_{ch}) \int_0^T [Q_{in}(t) - Q_{out}(t)]\, dt \quad (6)$$

The input into the raised field channels is composed of two sources: runoff and direct rainfall over the channels. The area has been adjusted in the calculation to account for the fact that the channels comprise only 50% of the fields. The output loss is due to evaporation and soil seepage. Evaporation is dependent upon temperature, solar irradiation levels and hours of sunshine a day. These parameters have been collected by ONERN (1984: Annex 2, p. 16) for the Puno station. These data are taken as the best available estimates for evaporation around Taraco. Seepage beyond the soil saturation of the ONERN data is unknown. Any additional deep seepage has not been accounted for. However, since raised fields are in areas of highly saturated soils to begin with, it is believed that this is not a dominant loss mechanism. Another needed parameter in the calculation is the runoff catchment size. Using aerial photos, it is estimated that the total catchment area around Cerro Imarocus is about 6000 ha with one-third supplying raised field area S1 to the north and two-thirds supplying area S2 to the east. Rain falling over this area becomes concentrated in the quebrada and delivered to the fields by the series of canals previously discussed. The runoff naturally flows into the low-lying areas where the raised fields were located. Of course, not all runoff was captured in the raised fields. However, the water captured is believed to be a significant fraction of the total since water lost by evaporation and soil seepage has already been taken into account. Only water trapped in isolated depressions not used for raised fields is lost. A range of possible collection efficiencies of 12.5%, 25% and 50% have been used in the calculation of Figure 13.32 (the figure's right-hand axis shows the results). This efficiency represents the fraction of the runoff that actually fills the raised field channels. For 50% collection efficiency, by the end of January about 800 ha of raised fields were filled below Cerro Imarocus, and, by the end of February, about 1200 ha. The values drop accordingly with the smaller collection efficiencies.

It is interesting to note that the timing seen in Figure 13.32 is consistent with reports by a local farmer who managed one of the demonstration raised fields in the early 1990s. He reported during the ground survey that:

- He planted in October/November to allow the rain of September/October to percolate the soil.
- The raised field channels filled with runoff in January and February.
- The crops were harvested in March ahead of the frost.

The calculated areas are now compared to the earlier identified fields in Figure 13.33 and Table 13.2. The value of 1000 ha for 50% efficiency is used in the figure as the size of fields filled by mid-February (500 ha for 25% and 250 ha for 12.5%). Thus, additional water beyond mid-February values (the remainder

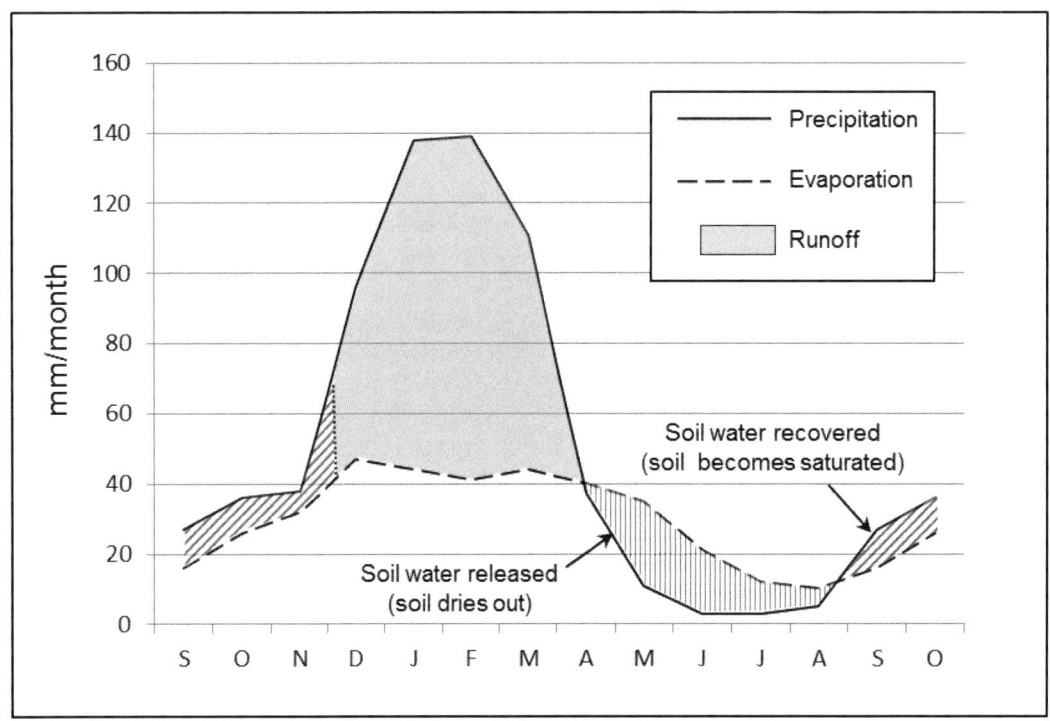

Figure 13.31. Calculation by ONERN (1984) of seasonal rainfall runoff in mm/month for the Granja Salcedo region alongside Lake Titicaca.

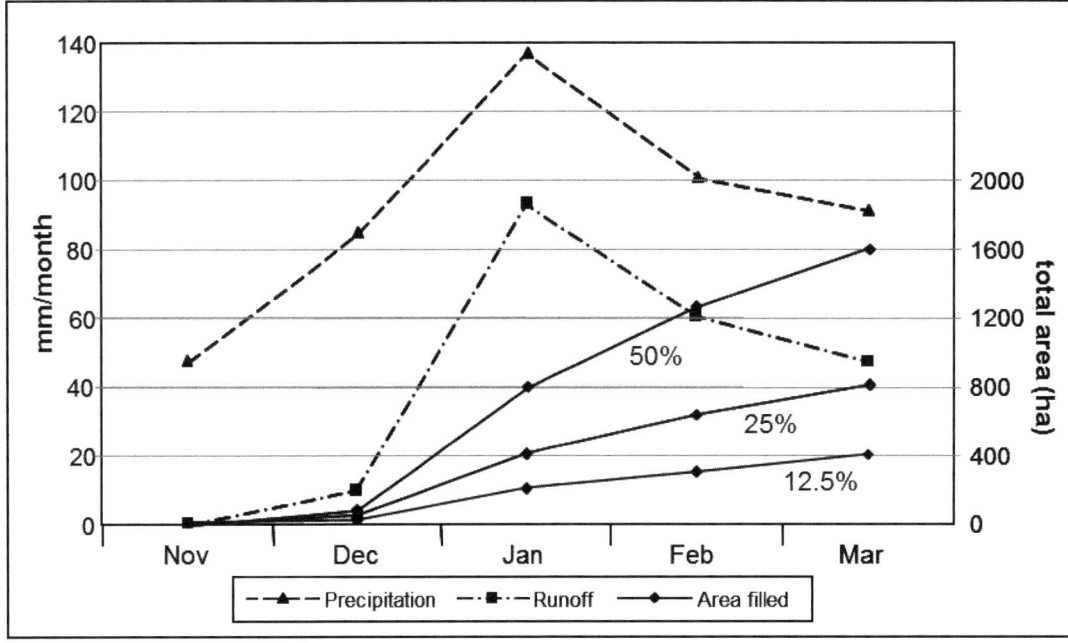

Figure 13.32. Precipitation and runoff in the Taraco region using the methodology of Figure 13.30 are given by the left-hand axis. The calculated area of raised fields filled by this runoff using equation (6) is given by the right-hand axis. The data points represent the total amount of rainfall, runoff and area for the given month. The parameters of the calculation are: catchment area = 6000 ha; collection efficiency = 12.5%, 25% and 50%; channel depth = 1.0 m; water height = 80% of depth; channel fraction = 50% of total field area. The median precipitation from Taraco region has been used while evaporation and soil data are from Granja Salcedo.

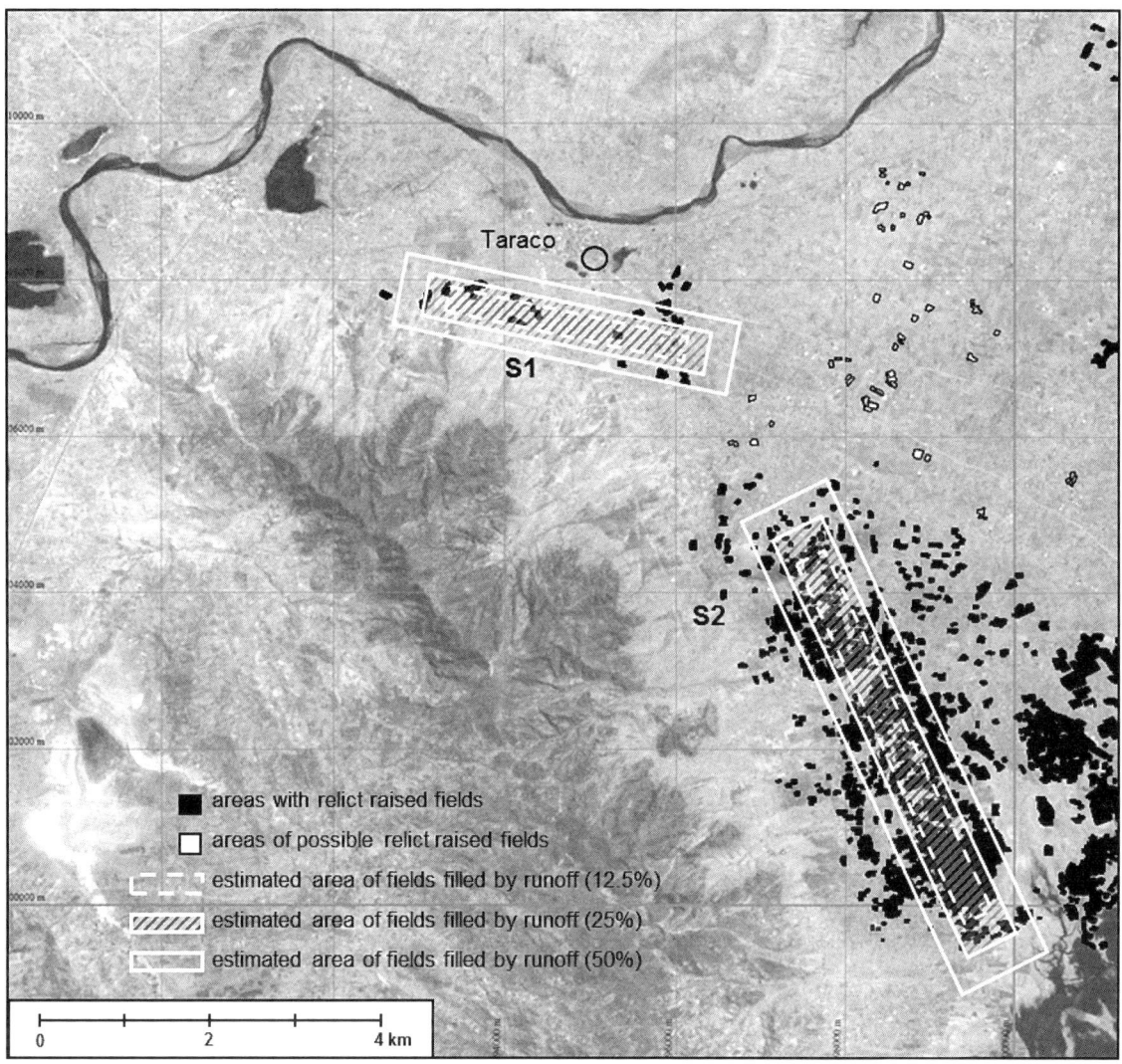

Figure 13.33. The estimated area of raised fields supplied by runoff from Cerro Imarocus is indicated by the rectangular boxes for runoff collection efficiencies of 12.5%, 25% and 50%. The total area enclosed is 333 ha, 500 ha and 1000 ha, respectively, with one-third being in the runoff catchment to the north supplying area S1 while two-thirds are to the south supplying S2.

of February and March) does not contribute to enlarging of the fields. The additional water can contribute to the transevaporation needs of crops planted on the platforms[15] and/or simply be allowed to flow past the fields into the lake. In Figure 13.33, rectangular boxes for the three efficiencies are shown with one-third of the area to the north and two-thirds to the south.

Area S1 is interesting because it could have been supplied only by runoff as it is at an elevation above the Río Ramis. The three rectangles (Fig. 13.33) contain 333 ha, 167 ha and 83 ha for the three efficiencies. These values compare to the earlier estimate of 400 ha from Table 13.2. Hence, the calculation shows that runoff was indeed the main source for these fields and suggests that high collection efficiency was achieved.

The situation is different with area S2. These fields appear to have also been supplied by canals from the river. This calculation shows, however, that a significant area of raised fields was supplied by runoff from Cerro Imarocus as well. The important conclusion is that there was insufficient rain to supply the large areas further inland on the alluvial plain, even with high collection efficiencies. The source for these fields was the Río Ramis.

## Fields Supplied by Río Ramis

Numerous canals from Río Ramis leading to the raised fields were identified earlier. Canal Ramis is particularly useful for modeling because it demonstrates gravity flow from the river to the lake as this canal can be traced all the way back to the river's edge. Today, the other courses fall short of the river, making it difficult to determine just how high the river must rise before water would have flowed in these canals.

The discharge in such a canal is described by open channel hydraulics. The analysis is simplified by assuming uniform flow in which the depth, water area, and velocity are constant with the canal being straight or having wide, gentle curves. Previous related works include Farrington's analysis (1980, 1983) of costal Peru's irrigation canals and Ortloff's analysis (1996) of the Waña Jawira canal supplying raised fields near Tiwanaku. In this approach, the flow rate is expressed in metric units by the continuity equation in the form (Chow 1959:98):

$$Q = A \cdot \{R^{2/3} \cdot S^{1/2} / n\} \qquad (7)$$

where the bracketed term is the well-known Manning formula for the flow velocity. The term R is the hydraulic radius (ratio of water area to wetted perimeter), S is the slope of the canal bed and n is a coefficient of roughness of the canal surfaces known as Manning's roughness factor. From equation (7), the canal discharge ($Q_{ca}$) can be found in terms of the flow height ($h_{ca}$) and canal width (w). As a qualitative understanding is the goal, Canal Ramis (Fig. 13.27) is modeled as a simple rectangular channel 1 m deep and 10 m wide. The hydraulic radius therefore becomes R = ($h_{ca}$w)/(w + 2 $h_{ca}$). The discharge has been calculated using a typical roughness factor value of n = 0.025. The bed slope value was equated to the slope of the alluvial plain (S = 0.0006) as determined from elevation data on the topographic map of the region. Equation (7) can be solved numerically. The resulting flow rates are shown in Table 13.3.

The table demonstrates the canal was capable of handling huge discharges. As an example, the flow rate is 1.27 m³/sec when the canal is 30% full. Relating this to the earlier reference flow rate of ~ 0.04 m³/km²/sec for January runoff from Cerro Imarcus shows the canal capacity at this level is equivalent to carrying all the runoff from the 60 km² catchment with the 50% collection efficiency used earlier (0.04 · 60 · 0.5 = 1.2). This means that for a fixed height of 0.3 m, the raised field channels would fill at the same rate as shown in Figure 13.32 in the month of January with 50% collection efficiency (i.e., fill about 800 ha during the month). But the height of water in the canal will increase with time under normal conditions. The flow rate is about three times larger when the canal is 60% full and almost six times larger when 90%. Thus, it is clear that the canal was capable of rapidly filling large raised field areas once water from the Río Ramis had risen to the level of the canal. Only a few canals would have been needed to supply the area of raised fields identified in Figure 13.16, although it is unlikely that all of these fields were in operation concurrently due to the need for fallowing. Saltation of the fields after prolonged use could also have led to abandonment of some fields.

Table 13.3. Hydraulic parameters for Canal Ramis for assumed flow heights. The parameters were calculated for w = 10 m, S = 0.0006 and n = 0.025. A Froude number < 1.0 indicates the flow is subcritical, resulting in a stable flow.

| Flow Height (m) | Discharge (m³/sec) | Velocity (m/sec) | Froude Number |
|---|---|---|---|
| 0.15 | 0.41 | 0.27 | 0.22 |
| 0.30 | 1.27 | 0.42 | 0.25 |
| 0.45 | 2.45 | 0.54 | 0.26 |
| 0.60 | 3.99 | 0.65 | 0.27 |
| 0.75 | 5.54 | 0.74 | 0.27 |
| 0.90 | 7.51 | 0.83 | 0.28 |

The next subject to address is the timing of the rising river. The elevation profile of Canal Ramis relative to the river is shown in Figure 13.34. The bed of the 1-m-deep canal is only 0.76 m above the dry season low in these measurements taken in August 2006. The Río Ramis hydrological data of Figure 13.6 are given in terms of discharge, not river height. The two parameters are related by the continuity equation. As shown above, it is possible to relate the two for uniform flow by equation (7). As the direction and cross section of the Río Ramis change near Canal Ramis, the exact application of equation (7) is ruled out because uniform flow requires more gradual changes. It is useful, however, to consider the relationship from a *theoretical* point of view for a hypothetical river course that does meet the normal flow conditions and has the temporal discharge properties of the Ramis. This will contribute to the *qualitative* understanding of the timing of the river rise. A closed-form solution to equation (7) can be obtained if it is assumed that the height of the water in the river above the low stage, $h_{ri}$, is much smaller than the river width W (that is, $h_{ri}/W \ll 1$). This approximation holds since the river width at Canal Ramis is ~ 110 m. This simplification leads to R ~ $h_{ri}$. Thus, the height is given in terms of the flow $Q_{ri}$ by:

$$h_{ri} = H \cdot [(Q_{ri}^{3/5} - Q_{low}^{3/5})/(Q_{high}^{3/5} - Q_{low}^{3/5})] \qquad (8)$$

where $Q_{high}$ refers to the discharge at high stage in March and $Q_{low}$ to the low stage in September. The total change in river height between stages is H. It is seen that the height varies as the 3/5 power of the discharge.

The values in this equation are instantaneous ones while those given in Figure 13.6 are monthly averages. Fortunately, recent data are available from SENAMHI for the instantaneous Ramis discharge under conditions described as "normal" (Fig. 13.35). By comparing monthly averages to the instantaneous flow, it is

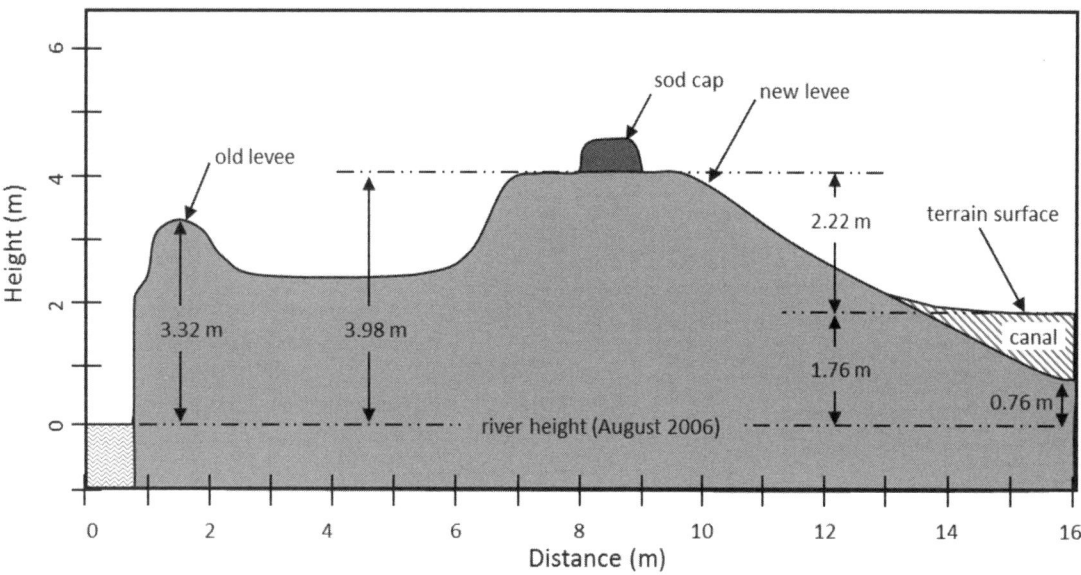

Figure 13.34. Elevation profile of levees alongside Río Ramis at the location of Canal Ramis. A sod block cap of ~ 0.5 m tops the new levee. Note canal bed was measured to be 0.76 m above the river during the dry season (August 2006).

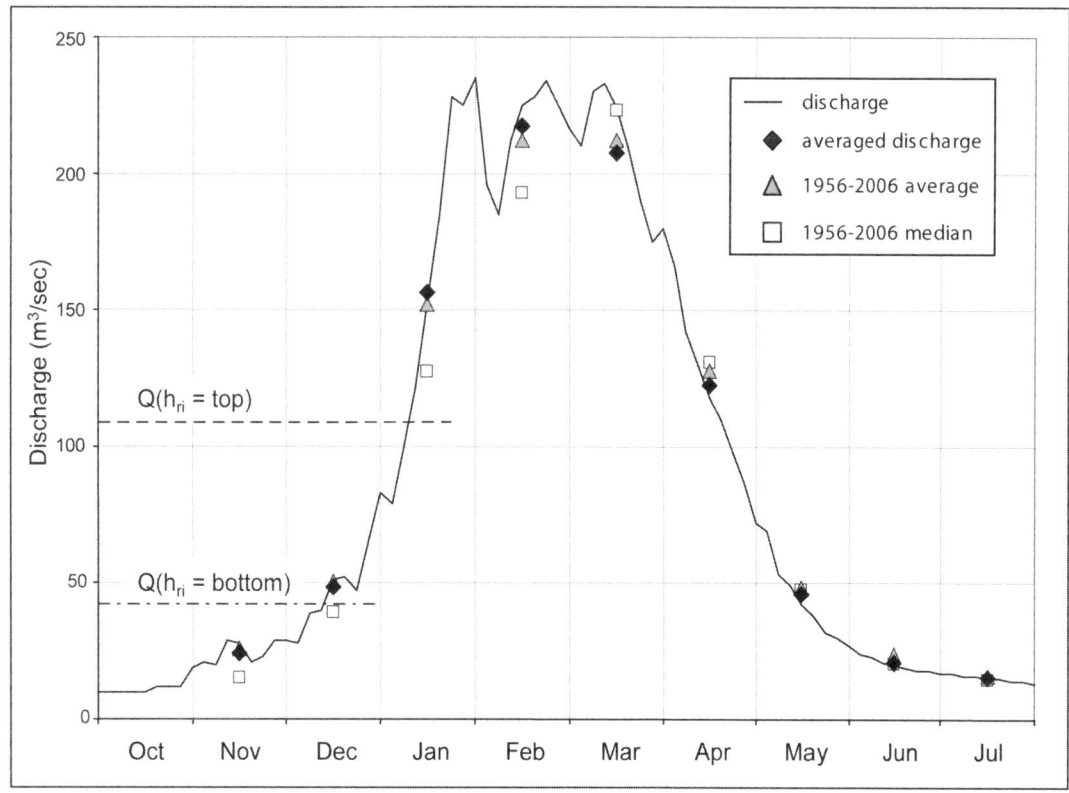

Figure 13.35. The normal discharge of Río Ramis at Puente Ramis as described by SENAMHI (2005). The long-term average and median discharges from 1956 to 2006 are shown for comparison. The discharge values, Q, from equation (8) corresponding to the river height at the bottom and top of Canal Ramis are also shown on the left.

seen that this recent instantaneous "normal" flow is closely related to the longer term (1956–2006) monthly averages of Figure 13.6 as shown by the individual data points. The values of Río Ramis discharge from equation (8) are shown in the figure when the river height rises to the bottom of the canal (canal bed) and the top. In this calculation, $Q_{high}$ = 225 m³/sec and $Q_{low}$ = 10 m³/sec from Figure 13.6 for a median year have been used. A value of H = 3 m is used, which is a conservative value in a normal year as it is reported that in a typical year the river height approaches the top of the old levee (~ 3.3 m). It is seen in the figure that the river approaches the canal bottom by mid-December and is well above the top (1-m-high canal) by mid-January for the hypothetical river course. Gravity flow in the canal could have started any time after mid-December depending upon the input control to the canal. Because of the rapid rise in river height seen in Figure 13.35, the canal will fill rapidly once the flow begins. This rapid rise along with the large capacity of the canal from Table 13.3 would have led in turn to rapid filling of the raised fields in January and February. This conclusion applies as well to the canals near Taraco leading to the raised fields on the alluvial plain. A more detailed modeling of the river is needed to determine the quantitative details, but the qualitative picture presented here of the filling of Canal Ramis from the rapid river rise during normal conditions will certainly dominate a more exact calculation as well.

More exact modeling will be especially important in understanding performance in drier years when the river rise is much less than the normal conditions. For example, the uniform flow assumption would suggest that even in the driest one-of-ten years (curve marked 10% in Fig. 13.6) gravity flow to the fields could still have occurred, although starting later in the year. This would have made water available to the crops during time of drought, possibly using the "splash irrigation" technique described by Erickson and Candler (1989:240). However, small differences between the approximate and exact calculations become much more significant in this case and such a general statement cannot be made at this time. For this reason, a refined understanding of performance during drier years is a subject of ongoing research.

*Comparison with Canal Waña Jawira*

Comparing the properties of Canal Ramis to those of Canal Waña Jawira that supplied raised fields in the Tiwanaku Valley (Ortloff 1996) can provide insight into the operation, control and maintenance issues associated with the canals supplying raised fields near Taraco. The two canals have several properties in common. First is their physical size. As noted earlier, Canal Ramis is about 10 m wide and 1 m deep while Canal Waña Jawira varies from 5 m to 9 m wide with a comparable depth. The terrain slope in both cases is shallow, although the slope around Taraco (S = 0.0006) is somewhat less than around the Tiwanaku Valley (S = 0.0014). As a consequence of this difference, the discharges of Canal Ramis in Table 13.3 are about 15% less than the values calculated for Canal Waña Jawira (see Ortloff 1996: Table 6.3). Another common property is a relatively low flow velocity as a consequence of the shallow bed slopes. In canal design, hydraulic engineers attempt to achieve a flow velocity fast enough to avoid silt deposition while at the same time slow enough to avoid bed and sidewall erosion. The maximum velocity is dependent upon the materials making up the canal bed and sidewalls but in alluvium the values ranges from about 1 to 1.5 m/sec (Farrington 1980:292). Farrington also describes a minimum desired velocity that ranges from about 0.5 to 0.9 m/sec. From Table 13.3, it is seen that the flow velocity is clearly slow enough that erosion is not a problem. However, because the minimum desired velocity is marginal, silting could have been a problem. In fact, Ortloff (1996:164) has reported finding evidence of "multiple cleaning episodes" of Canal Waña Jawira. During the ground surveys of the present work, discussions with local workers who manage the canals carrying runoff below Cerro Imarocus also revealed silting as a concern. They complained of the need to clean out the canals near the terminal catchment at Pampa Huito about every three years. They were unhappy with the situation but resigned to it as there is no alternative due to the shallow bed slopes in the region.

There are differences between the canals as well: (1) the distance today from the base of the canal inlet to the current dry season river, (2) the size of the river in relation to the canal size, and (3) the height of the levees alongside the canals. Ortloff (1996:162) states "the present canal inlet stands about 2.5 meters above the current dry-season river height, indicating that the Tiwanaku River has downcut substantially since the canal was abandoned during the Tiwanaku V period." The situation for Río Ramis is much different. As seen in Figure 13.34, the base of Canal Ramis is only 0.76 m above the dry season low. The Ramis has not downcut and, if anything, has aggraded. Aggraded channels provided the basis for early gravity-fed irrigation in Mesopotamia (Adams 1981). Aggradation, along with natural levees, resulted in stable courses with high stage water levels elevated above the surrounding land surfaces. Adams (1981:8) states that "fairly short, shallow cuts in its banks are sufficient, therefore, to bring water out onto the backslopes at or above the land's level, establishing 'command' of it for irrigation." We believe this was also the basis for gravity flow to the canals supplying the raised fields of Taraco.

The lack of downcutting around Taraco is not surprising due to the suspended sediment and bed load carried by the river. When a river terminates in a large body of water like Lake Titicaca, large quantities of material are brought to the shoreline that result in new land formation. The formation process is a complicated one but it can be seen at work in Figure 13.36, which shows the termination of Río Ramis into Lake Titicaca just below the point of confluence with Río Huancané. The presence of the sediment load is readily visible. The extension of land into the lake is not unlike delta formation when a river empties into coastal waters (Schumm 1977; Way 1977). Schumm (1977:297) states that "channel aggradation [is] due to progressive extension of a delta into the sea (the increased length of the stream requires aggradation to maintain the gradient upstream)." This follows since the

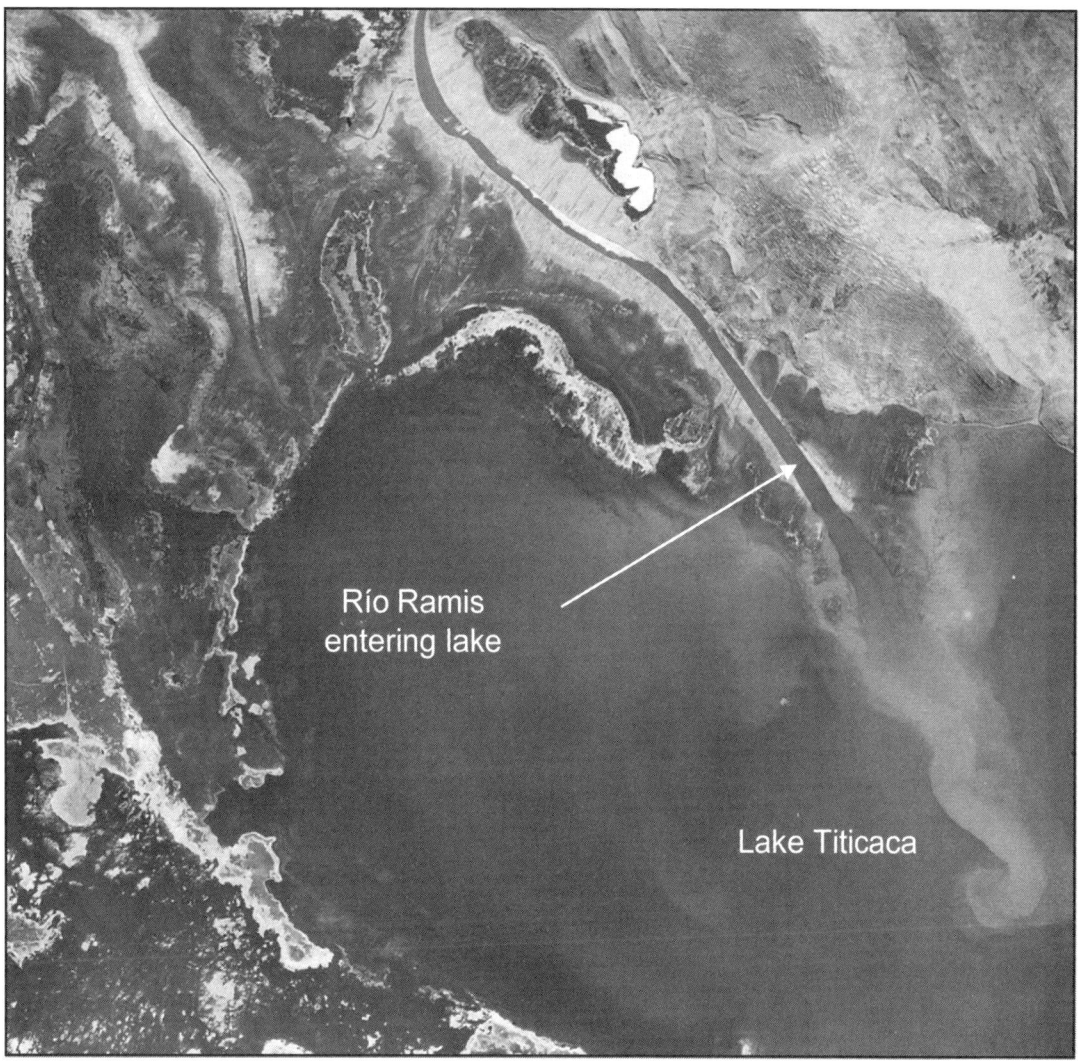

Figure 13.36. Aerial photo (IGN 15218) showing the entrance of Río Ramis into the lake near its confluence with Río Huancane. The sediment load carried by the rivers is clearly seen extending into the lake.

course needs to maintain the same gradient because it continues carrying the same sediment load despite the increased length.

It is possible that the Ramis could have aggraded over the period of usage possibly as long as 3000 years.[16] With an older, deeper riverbed, the river would have had to rise to a higher level before gravity flow commenced. This would have meant a delay in the initiation of flow from that of Figure 13.35. But since the Ramis rises rapidly, the delay would have been comparatively short. For example, a 0.5-m lowering of the riverbed would have delayed initiation of flow by about two weeks for the normal flow of Figure 13.35. In dry years, the consequences would have been much more significant. Interestingly, it also would have meant that the human-made levees that contain flooding would not have needed to be as tall as they are today.

The critical issue of control of the input to Canal Ramis also needs to be discussed. Adams described shallow extraction cuts in the natural levees of Mesopotamia. This approach would have been problematic for extraction from the Ramis. For a "shallow" cut of 1 m in the old levee, the flow for Canal Ramis would have commenced in mid-January. There was adequate time to fill the fields in normal years due to the high discharge capacity of the feeder canal (Table 13.3). But what about other years with the higher or lower flows as seen in Figure 13.6? In dry years, the river height could have fallen short of the bottom of the shallow cut so flow to the fields would not have commenced. Yet the river height could still have been above the bed of the feeder canals and have provided gravity flow to the raised fields if only the extraction cuts were made deeper. In very wet years, the natural levee would have been overtopped, flooding the fields. Both of these situations point to the need for control of the input by the ancient hydraulic engineers.

The input situation for the Canal Waña Jawira near Tiwanaku is considered next. This canal is quite interesting as it had the dual purposes of drainage and distribution "implementing either a water-distribution or a water-extraction strategy" (Kolata 1991:117). It carried water to the raised fields in the water-distribution mode and provided a shunt to Río Tiwanaku in the water-extraction mode similar to the dual purposes of Canal Antiguo Taraco (Fig. 13.26). Ortloff (1996:163) states that "the width of the canal intake is such that the *entire flow* of the Tiwanaku River could have been diverted to adjacent Tiwanaku raised fields systems." If the entire flow were to be contained, it would have required large levees alongside Canal Waña Jawira, possibly as high as those of the river itself. Again, these levees would have been especially important in wet years. Ortloff (1996:163) does describe "large earthen levees built over the existing ground surface [alongside Canal Waña Jawira] that served to contain the extracted flow."

The relative size of the extraction canal to the river itself is much different near Taraco. Rather than being the same size as the river with Canal Waña Jawira, Canal Ramis is less than one-tenth the width of Río Ramis. Thus, only a small portion of the river flow entered the canals near Taraco. Today there are massive levees alongside Río Ramis constructed to contain the river in wetter years (Figs. 13.7, 13.34). The inner levee is ~ 1.5 m above the terrain surface while the outer levee is more than 2.2 m above. If Río Ramis discharge were to have entered the Canal Ramis *unconstrained*, as suggested for Canal Waña Jawira, then similarly large levees would have been needed alongside Canal Ramis for containment in wetter years as it made its way across the alluvial plain to the raised fields. Yet the levees alongside are comparatively small (~ 0.5 m high). In fact, no large levees were noted on any of the ancient conduits from the Ramis (including Ríos Anta, Jarinmayo and Binogache).

There are several possible reasons for the absence of large levees across the plain. The first is that they once existed but have been destroyed. This possibility is ruled out because in this region with very slowly changing terrain features (aside from farming), at least some evidence surely would have survived somewhere on the alluvial plain. Yet there is none. This leads to the conclusion that they never existed. In the absence of large levees alongside the Ramis controlling the intake, water would have flowed in an unconstrained manner from the distributaries (Anta and Jarinmayo), creating a flood plain across large areas. Walker (2011) has described such raised field farming along the Iruyañes River in the Amazon. While the initial stages of raised field farming may well have started on the margins of such waterlogged areas, the extensive network of canals found across the entire plain, not just at the margins, suggests that the flow was constrained at the intake. With such constrained flow, large levees across the plain were simply not needed. Constraining the flow would have required large levees alongside the Ramis.

Unfortunately, the original canal intakes and control configurations of both Canal Waña Jawira and Canal Ramis have all been destroyed by erosion and/or new levee construction. Thus, any extraction and control methods used by the ancient hydraulic engineers are not known. A fixed, passive input to the canal could have been designed on the basis of a "worst case" river discharge to constrain the input so that the capacity of the primary canal was not exceeded, even during the wet years. This means, however, that the flow during normal years, and especially dry years, would be less than the values of Table 13.3. During dry years, it would have been very easy to make the extraction cut deeper to permit gravity flow when the cut of nominal depth was insufficient. The deeper opening would have had to been closed before the next rainy season. During the ground survey of the present work, such a closing of a large levee using traditional sod blocks to repair a breach was observed. It is clear that a more rapid, active response to deal with changes in the river level would have been the preferred method. Kolata (1991:117) has suggested that at least the *secondary* canals fed by Canal Waña Jawira may have been actively controlled. He stated that "during the rainy season, or an inundation event, the intakes of the secondary distribution canals could have been blocked with some form of formal or informal sluice gates" (Kolata 1991:117). The more difficult job of controlling the input to primary canals was not discussed. Therefore, there is a need to better understand these control mechanisms given their importance to a robust system of raised field agriculture that could have dealt with the hydrological variation in rainfall and river discharge that occurred around Lake Titicaca.

**Conclusion**

This work has focused on identifying and understanding ancient raised field farming around Taraco, and has presented the first extensive survey of relict raised fields in this area. The survey relies on aerial photos from 1970 and digital scanning techniques available today, neither of which were available to earlier researchers. With these tools, relict raised fields have been identified across a much greater area of the alluvial plain than previously thought. Prior to this survey, the Taraco area was considered only a minor location for raised field agriculture. It was listed in the "scattered" category in comparison to the major areas of Juliaca, Pomata, Tiwanaku, Catari and Desaguadero. It is now understood that Taraco was a major site in its own right—as large as or larger than all but the massive Juliaca complex.

An understanding of the size and complexity of the water management system around Taraco has been gained through examination of hydraulic features on the alluvial plain (river courses, canals, meander scars and qochas) using aerial photographs, satellite imagery and ground surveys. The ground survey of these surface features was instrumental in interpreting aerial and satellite imagery. Also, many interviews were conducted with local farmers who provided valuable information into water management practices around Taraco today. From this work, a picture has emerged of a network of canals and natural watercourses across the plain to support ancient raised field farming. The key hydrological features are captured in Figure 13.21. This network is not unlike that around Tiwanaku described by Kolata and colleagues. The comparison between Canal Ramis around Taraco and Canal Waña Jawira around Tiwanaku has been described in detail.

Issues of water management including the basis of operation, control and maintenance have been addressed through hydrological calculations and comparisons of the Taraco system to the similar system near Tiwanku. The goal of the calculations to this point has been to gain a qualitative understanding of these issues. It was clearly shown that rainfall runoff was sufficient to supply the fields below Cerro Imarocus but was in no way sufficient for the vast area of fields on the alluvial plain. Modeling of canals from the river showed that in median years, the river rapidly rises in December and January and could have easily supplied the canals leading to the fields on the plain. A more exact model of the river is needed to treat the drier years when the river rise is less. Because these would have been the most important years to the inhabitants of Taraco, additional modeling to better understand the river rise in dry years is continuing. This consideration is even more relevant if the river has aggraded and the river bottom was at a lower level in antiquity.

Different chronologies of ancient raised field farming have been proposed by Erickson for the north side of the lake and by Kolata for the south. They have also shown that trenching is the only way to get to needed archeological evidence for dating ancient raised fields as surface surveys alone do not provide a reliable picture. Time is of the essence for such work around Taraco. This survey has identified the locations of relict raised fields across almost the entire alluvial plain. The aerial photos from 1970 were crucial as many areas seen in the photos have been, and continue to be, destroyed by modern farming. This is especially true closer to the town of Taraco where only a handful of small, isolated fields remain. Such a project of trenching could provide an independent look at the chronology in the north. Additionally, it could help in understanding the dramatically different raised field construction employed along the lakeshore (the very large platforms) versus that used inland.

It is hoped that this new understanding of ancient raised field farming and water resource management in the region will contribute to ongoing research into the evolution of sociopolitical complexity around Lake Titicaca.

## Acknowledgments

The author gratefully acknowledges support from the Cotsen Endowments and Programa Collasuyu. Charles Stanish, Edmundo de la Vega and Cecilia Chávez require special mention for their continued support and encouragement throughout the project. Also, special thanks go to Edgar Ulises Choque Paricela, a Taraco resident and member of the project team, who enabled the interviews with the Quechua residents of the region.

## Notes

1. *Qocha* is a Quechua word meaning "container of water." It is a generic term that applies to water sources both large and small whether human-made or of natural origin (Flores Ochoa 1987). The deeper qochas of the region encounter the aquifer so they contain water throughout the year. The shallower qochas are seasonal as they are filled only by rain runoff, which evaporates during the dry season.

2. Servicio Nacional de Meterologia e Hidrologia del Perú (SENAMHI), Jr. Cahuide 785 Jesús María, Lima 11, Perú. Also, online data hydrological data are available at www.senamhi.gob.pe.

3. There is a 20-km-long irrigation canal constructed in 1966 that is capable of irrigating the portion of the plain along the base of Cerro Imarocus from Saman to Pusi. However, the pump that brought water up from the Río Ramis to the canal head malfunctioned in the year 2000. The system has been out of operation since as no funds have been identified to repair/replace the pump.

4. Satellite imagery was purchased from the U.S. Geological Survey EROS Data Center, Sioux City, South Dakota.

5. For discussions of the abandonment of the raised field rehabilitation projects, see Erickson 2001 and Bandy 2005.

6. The periods covered in this paper are: Middle Formative (1300–500 BC), Late Formative (500 BC–AD 400), Tiwanaku (AD 400–1100), Altiplano (AD 1100–1450) and Inka (AD 1450–1533).

7. Aerial photos were obtained from two sources: (1) Servicio Aerofotográfico Nacional (SAN) in Surquillo, Peru, and (2) Instituto Geográficio Nacional (IGN), Lima, Peru. The SAN series is from the May 1970 flight #176-70. Throughout this document, these photos are identified by the photo number from that flight (e.g., SAN 435). The IGN photos are from flights in 1955 and are identified similarly. Note that the SAN photos have four times the resolution of the older IGN series. A comparison of the two is shown in Figure 13.10. It is important to recognize the value of the photos from older flights because surface evidence on the terrain has suffered additional damage since the flights were made. Many times during the ground survey, areas were witnessed in which relict raised field features evident in the 1970 photos had been destroyed due to deep plowing or construction of new farmsteads.

8. Global Mapper is a software package for accessing, editing and displaying multiple types of imagery, topographic maps and gridded terrain data. It was selected for this project because of its ability to process the NASA TERRA ASTER imagery in the "hdf" format. It also proved valuable in rectifying the aerial photos. It is available from Global Mapper Software LLC, Olathe, KS.

9. In a recent investigation of raised fields in the southwestern Amazon, Walker (2011) used ArcGIS with digitized aerial photograph to display and categorize raised field platforms. The term "platform groups" defined by Walker is comparable to the blocks in Figure 13.12.

10. The bar chart in Figure 13.18*a* is based on 212 measurements from S1 (SAN 430), S2 (SAN 433 and 435) and S5 (SAN465); Figure 13.18*b* is based on 127 individual measurements from region S3 (SAN 439).

11. In addition to the ASTER satellite imagery from 2001, earlier declassified CORONA imagery from 1966 was used to identify meander courses. This imagery was helpful because it has higher resolution and better contrast than ASTER. Although it has somewhat worse resolution than the aerial photos, the CORONA imagery provided a valuable independent look at features of interest. Also, it was found that Google Earth imagery was not particularly useful in preparing Figure 13.20. This is because many features of interest have been destroyed by modern farming, and for those that have not, the contrast with surrounding terrain is weak.

12. Flooding does occur occasionally around Taraco but it is reported to be due to an uncontrolled breach in the levee, not overtopping.

13. The local Quechua names for three canals discussed in this report are not known to the author at this time. They have been given names that reflect neighboring communities and/or landmarks. They are: Canal Quechuata, Canal Ramis and Canal Antiguo Taraco (see Fig. 13.20 [items 1, 3, 5, 10]).

14. Water collected in the western portion of the canal flows to the west. It collects a far smaller amount of water than the eastern part discussed in the text. The western portion terminates in a modest-sized qocha located on the plain about 0.7 km from Río Ramis, and about 8 m above it.

15. There are two passive mechanisms by which water from the channels can provide sustenance to the crops on the platforms: capillary action and condensation (dew) during the cold altiplano nights. Also, Erickson and Candler (1989) have discussed actively transferring water from the channels to the crops in times of drought by "splash irrigation."

16. See Farabaugh and Rigsby (2005) for a detailed discussion of the fluvial history of the Río Ramis.

## References Cited

Adams, Robert McC.
1981 *Heartland of Cities: Surveys of Ancient Settlement and Land Use on the Central Floodplain of the Euphrates*. University of Chicago Press, Chicago.

Bandy, Matthew S.
2005 Energetic efficiency and political expediency in Titicaca Basin raised field agriculture. *Journal of Anthropological Archaeology* 24:271–96.

Binford, Michael W., Alan L. Kolata, Mark Brenner, John W. Janusek, Matthew T. Seddon, Mark Abbot, and Jason H. Curtis
1970 Climate variation and the rise and fall of an Andean civilization. *Quaternary Research* 47:235–48.

Chávez, Cecilia, and Aimée Plourde
2008 El desarrollo del complejo ceremonial Formativo en la Cuenca Norte: Evidencia nueva de los sitios Anta Moc'o y Huayra Mocco. Presented at the 72th Annual Meeting of the Society for American Archaeology, Vancouver.

Chow, V. T.
1959 *Open Channel Hydraulics*. McGraw-Hill, New York.

Díaz Zeballos, C., and E. Velasquez Coaquira
1992 Inventario de infraestructuras agrícolas Andinas in Puno, Peru. In *Avances de investigacion sobre la tecnologia de Waru Waru I: Infraestructura*, pp. 17–38. PELT/INADE–COTESU, Puno, Peru.

Denevan, William M.
1970 Aboriginal drained-field cultivation in the Andes. *Science* 169:647–54.
2001 *Cultivated Landscapes of Native Amazonia and the Andes*. Oxford University Press, Oxford.

Erickson, Clark L.
1985 Applications of prehistoric Andean technology: Experiments in raised field agriculture, Huatta, Lake Titicaca. In *Prehistoric Intensive Agriculture in the Tropics*, edited by I. S. Farrington, pp. 209–32. British Archaeological Reports, International Series, vol. 232, Oxford, U.K.
1987 The dating of raised field agriculture in the Lake Titicaca Basin, Peru. In *Pre-Hispanic Agricultural Fields in the Andean Region*, edited by W. M. Denevan, K. Mathewson, and G. Knapp, pp. 373–84. British Archaeological Reports, International Series, vol. 359, Oxford, U.K.
1988 Raised field agriculture in the Lake Titicaca Basin. *Expedition* 30(3):8–16.
1992 Prehistoric landscape management in the Andean highlands: Raised field agriculture and its environmental impact. *Population and Environment* 13(4):285–300.
1993 The social organization of prehispanic raised field agriculture in the Lake Titicaca Basin. In *Research in Economic Anthropology: Economic Aspects of Water Management in the Prehispanic New World*, edited by V. L. Scarborough and B. L. Isaac, pp. 369–426. JAI Press, Greenwich, CT.
1994 Methodological considerations in the study of ancient Andean field systems. In *The Archaeology of Garden and Field*, edited by Naomi F. Miller and Kathryn L. Gleason, pp. 111–52. University of Pennsylvania Press, Philadelphia.
1998 Applied archaeology and rural development: Archaeology's potential contribution to the future. In *Crossing Currents: Continuity and Change in Latin America*, edited by Michael W. Whiteford and Scott Whiteford, pp. 34–45. Prentice Hall, Upper Saddle River, NJ.
1999 Neo-environmental determinism and agrarian 'collapse' in Andean prehistory. *Antiquity* 73:634–41.
2000 The Lake Titicaca Basin: A precolumbian built landscape. In *Imperfect Balance: Landscape Transformations in the Precolumbian Americas*, edited by David L. Lentz, pp. 311–56. Columbia University Press, New York.
2001 Agricultural Landscapes as World Heritage: Raised Field Agriculture in Bolivia and Peru. Proceedings of the 4th Annual US/ICOMOS International Symposium, Philadelphia, 6–8 April.

Erickson, Clark L., and Kay L. Candler
1989 Raised field and sustainable agriculture in the Lake Titicaca Basin of Peru. In *Fragile Lands of Latin America: Strategies for Sustainable Development*, edited by J. Browder, pp. 230–48. Westview Press, Boulder, CO.

Farabaugh, Renee L., and Catherine A. Rigsby
2005 Climatic influence on sedimentology and geomorphology of the Río Ramis Valley, Peru. *Journal of Sedimentary Research* 5:255–68.

Farrington, I. S.
1980 The archaeology of irrigation canals, with special reference to Peru. *World Archaeology* II(3):287–305.
1983 The design and function of the intervalley canal: Comments on a paper by Ortloff, Moseley and Feldman. *American Antiquity* 48:360–75.

Farrington, I. S., and C. C. Park
1978 Hydraulic engineering and irrigation agriculture in the Moche Valley, Peru: c. 1250–1532. *Journal of Archaeological Science* 5:255–68.

Flores Blanco, Luis, Silvia Román, and Mark Aldenderfer
2008 El origen de qochas en la cuenca del Ramis y su repercusión en el surgimiento de la complejidad social. Presented at the 72th Annual Meeting of the Society for American Archaeology, Vancouver.

Flores Ochoa, Jorge A.
1987 Cultivation of the qocha of the south Andean puna. In *Arid Land Use Strategies and Risk Management in the Andes: A Regional Anthropological Perspective*, edited by David L. Browman, pp. 271–96. Westview Press, Boulder, CO.

Janusek, J. W., and Alan L. Kolata
2004 Top-down or bottom-up: Rural settlement and raised fields agriculture in the Lake Titicaca Basin, Bolivia. *Journal of Anthropological Archaeology* 23:404–30.

Kolata, Alan L.
1986 The agricultural foundations of the Tiwanaku state: A view from the heartland. *American Antiquity* 51(4):13–28.
1991 The technology and organization of agricultural production in the Tiwanaku state. *Latin American Antiquity* 2:99–125.
1993 *The Tiwanaku*. Blackwell, Cambridge.
1996 Proyecto Wila Jawira: An introduction to the history, problems and strategies of research. In *Tiwanaku and Its Hinterland: Archaeology and Paleoecology of the Andean Civilization*, edited by Alan L. Kolata, pp. 1–22. Smithsonian Institution Press, Washington, D.C.

Kolata, Alan L., Oswaldo Rivera, Juan Carlos Ramírez, and Evelyn Gemio
1996 Rehabilitating raised-field agriculture in the southern Lake Titicaca Basin of Bolivia: Theory, practice and results. In *Tiwanaku and Its Hinterland: Archaeology and Paleoecology of the Andean Civilization*, edited by Alan L. Kolata, pp. 203–30. Smithsonian Institution Press, Washington, D.C.

Kolata, Alan L., and Charles R. Ortloff
1989 Thermal analysis of Tiwanaku raised field systems in the Lake Titicaca Basin of Bolivia. *Journal of Archaeological Science* 16:233–63.
1996a Tiwanaku raised-field agriculture in the Lake Titicaca Basin of Bolivia. In *Tiwanaku and Its Hinterland: Archaeology and Paleoecology of the Andean Civilization*, edited by Alan L. Kolata, pp. 109–52. Smithsonian Institution Press, Washington, D.C.
1996b Agroecological perspectives on the decline of the Tiwanaku State. In *Tiwanaku and Its Hinterland: Archaeology and Paleoecology of the Andean Civilization*, edited by Alan L. Kolata, pp. 181–202. Smithsonian Institution Press, Washington, D.C.

Lennon, Thomas J.
1983 Pattern analysis of prehistoric raised fields of Lake Titicaca, Peru. In *Drained Fields of the Americas*, edited by J. P. Darch, pp. 183–300. British Archaeological Reports, International Series, vol. 189, Oxford, U.K.

Levine, Abigail
2008 Competition and Cooperation in the Formative Lake Titicaca Basin: New Insights from Taraco, Peru. Presented at the 72th Annual Meeting of the Society for American Archaeology, Vancouver.

Oficina Nacional de Evaluacíon de Recursos Naturales (ONERN)
1984 *Inventario y evaluación e integración de los recursos naturales de la micro-región Puno*. ONERN, Puno.
1985 *Inventario, evaluación semidetallada de los recursos naturales de suelo, uso actual de la tierra e hidrología de la micro-región Puno*. ONERN, Puno.

Ortloff, Charles R.
1996 Engineering aspects of Tiwanaku groundwater-controlled agriculture. In *Tiwanaku and Its Hinterland: Archaeology and Paleoecology of the Andean Civilization*, edited by Alan L. Kolata, pp. 153–80. Smithsonian Institution Press, Washington, D.C.

Ortloff, Charles R., and Alan L. Kolata
1993 Climate and collapse: Agro-ecological perspectives on the decline of the Tiwanaku state. *Journal of Archaeological Science* 20:195–221.

Ortloff, Charles R., Michael E. Moseley, and Robert A. Feldman
1982 Hydraulic engineering aspects of the Chimu Chicama-Moche intervalley canal. *American Antiquity* 47(3):572–95.
1983 The Chimu Chicama-Moche intervalley canal: Social explanations and physical paradigms. *American Antiquity* 48:375–89.

Plourde, Aimée M., and Charles Stanish
2006 The emergence of complex society in the Titicaca Basin: The view from the north. In *Andean Archaeology III: North and South*, edited by William Harris Isbell and Helaine Silverman, pp. 237–57. Springer, New York.

Russell, Richard J.
1967 *River Plains and Sea Coasts*. University of California Press, Berkeley.

Schumm, Stanley A.
1977 *The Fluvial System*. Wiley, New York.

Smith, C. T., W. M. Denevan, and P. Hamilton
1968 Ancient ridged fields in the region of Lake Titicaca. *Geographical Journal* 134:353–66.

Stanish, Charles
1994 The hydraulic hypothesis revisited: Lake Titicaca Basin raised fields in theoretical perspective. *Latin American Antiquity* 5(4):312–32.

Walker, John H.
2011 Social implications from agricultural taskscapes in the southern Amazon. *Latin American Antiquity* 22(3):275–95.

Way, Douglas S.
1977 *Terrain Analysis: A Guide to Site Selection Using Aerial Photographic Interpretation*. McGraw-Hill, New York.

# Chapter 14

## The Archaeology of Northern Puno

### Late Sites in Sandia and Carabaya, Peru

*Luis Flores Blanco, César Cornejo Maya, and Daniel Cáceda Guillén*

The provinces of Sandia and Carabaya represent the accessways to the forest zone for the altiplano of Puno. The importance of this area is even greater if one takes into account the political and economic strategy of the control of vertical ecological zones as understood by John Murra (1975).

Lawrence Coben and Charles Stanish (2005) suggested that the Carabaya region was an area where gold was extracted by both the Spaniards and the Inca Empire. We believe that the Sandia region could also have fulfilled this role, which implies that the eastern Puno region was a strategic geopolitical and economic area for the stability and growth of the Inca Empire. Likewise, it would have been an equally important area for the complex agro-pastoral societies of the Altiplano period as defined by Stanish (2003).

Yet, in spite of the importance of this area for Andean archaeology, the northern and eastern sides of Puno are, at present, a virtually unknown territory. In this chapter we emphasize the potential that this inhospitable region has for providing a perspective from the periphery on questions on the development of complex societies of the Late Intermediate and the imperial strategies of the Inca in Puno.

Ethnohistorical accounts, oral histories and local histories agree in affirming that the Carabaya and Sandia regions, along with Larecaja in northern Bolivia, were the territories of a nation called Callahuaya, whose people were known as pastoralists, travelers and, most notably, curanderos. Their lands were famous for gold deposits—so important that the Incas included these lands in the quarter of Antisuyu and the Spanish Crown, during the colonial period, explored and exploited these territories (Ávila 2005; Dueñas Tovar 1975).

As mentioned, in spite of its great importance, there have been virtually no investigations in this region, with the exception of Coben and Stanish (2005), who conducted some explorations in Carabaya. Before this recent work, there were visits by Antonio Raimondi, Sir Clements R. Markham, Erland Nordenskiöld (1953), Augusto Weberbauer, and J. C. Spahni (1971), among the most prominent. We also have the work of individuals and people—such as José Franco Inojosa (1936); Nicolás Luna Peralta (1999); Juan Palao Berastain (1991); Amador Quispe, Lorgio Quispe, and José Quispe (1995); Félix Tapia (1985); Benjamín Dueñas (1975); and Walter Ávila (2005)—who want to know the history of their region.

This chapter represents an attempt, using surface reconnaissance, to understand a bit more of the ancient history of Carabaya and Sandia. We do not claim that this survey is representative given the small number of sites visited, nor did we recover much material. This was merely a brief visit to some sites easy to access from the road to obtain insight into the scientific and tourist potential of the region as well as to gather data for a future research project. Therefore, the work consisted only of obtaining surface descriptions of the sites, locating them in space with a GPS, calculating the total site area, creating a sketch map and taking photographs (Flores and Cáceda 2004a; Cornejo and Flores 2004).

We were able to register ten sites, four of which were in the province of Sandia and the other six in Carabaya. While small, this sample gives us an idea of the existence of extensive sites and of a complex spatial organization (Fig. 14.1), the same that has been noted by the few investigators who have been interested in this region (Conlee, Dulanto, Mackey, and Stanish 2004; Coben and Stanish 2005:243).

The complex spatial organization that we see in these sites from the eastern Puno regions, we believe, reflects a complex social organization that was set up to exploit the region's resources. To understand the organization of the settlements that we studied, we created three levels of analysis. First, we studied each of the buildings or minimum architectural units (the domestic unit, public building, plaza, colcas, chulpas, and so on). Second, we analyzed the global organization of the settlement formed as an aggregation of the minimum architectural units. Finally, we looked at the location of the sites in their landscape. Note that we have divided the sites into their respective political divisions for strictly analytical purposes; this does not reflect the ancient sociocultural reality.

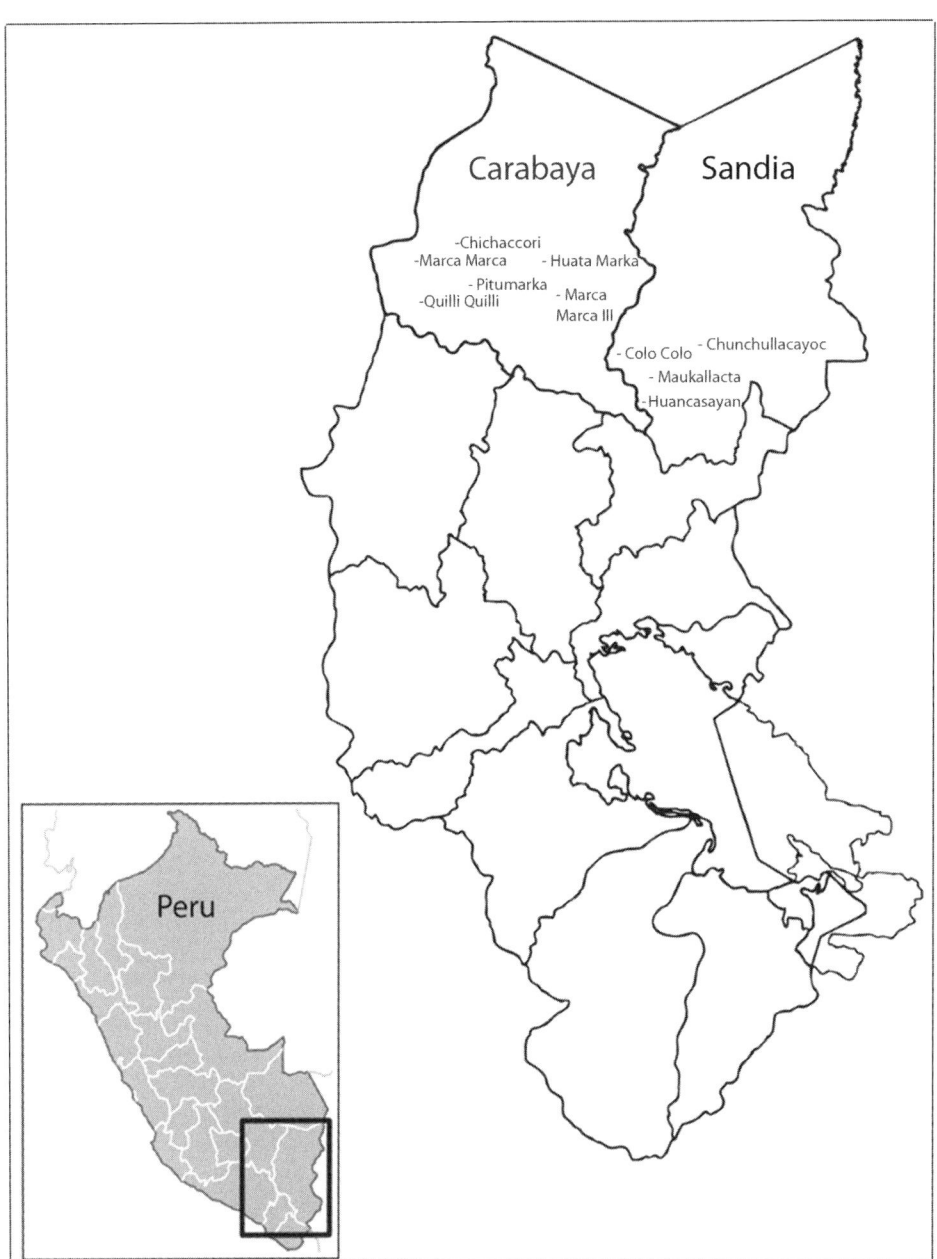

Figure 14.1. Location map of the sites registered in Carabaya and Sandia.

## Sandia and Carabaya: Geography

The Department of Puno is 72,382 km$^2$ of which 70% is in the altiplano of Collao, which has been the focus of archaeological research to date. The other 30% is composed of the cordillera and the forested zone with borders in Madre de Dios. The forest zone is separated from the altiplano by the cordillera of Carabaya that divides the drainage between the south toward Lake Titicaca and the Inambari drainage to the north that ultimately goes into the Amazonian drainage (PEISA 2004; Ávila 2005).

Our reconnaissance covered four tributaries of the Inambari drainage including the rivers Sandia, Usicayos, Coasa, Ayapata and San Gabán or Ollachea. We did not survey other tributaries such as the Upina and Blanco Rivers. We believe that in the future we should cover surveys in each of the tributaries of the Inambari, which, in our view, are the true political and economic corridors into the selva.

This vast region has many ecological floors. From the south to the north, it is divided into mountains with very sharp relief, such as Macusani, covered with extensive forests and zones characterized as subalpine pluvial plateaus. There is also a narrow band of quechua zone (agriculturally-rich valley areas), then the rainy yunga zones open up into the humid matorrales (dense shrubland) and forest of Sandia and Ollachea. After this, we immediately arrive at the rain forests of the montaña or rupa rupa, such as San Juan de Oro and Masiapo in Sandia, and into the low very humid subtropical forests such as Lanlacuni Bajo in Carabaya and Oroya and Candamo in Sandia, to name just a few examples (PEISA 2004; Ávila 2005).

## Archaeology of Sandia

We visited the Sandia area and registered four archaeological sites, all of distinct sizes of which only the largest in area (Maukallacta) demonstrated open spaces and areas for specialized public ceremonies and distinct domestic zones. The majority of the others are cemeteries or domestic settlements. It is interesting that all the sites are located on top of terraced hillsides or leveled peaks on hills, and all are within forty minutes to one hour of a stream or waterfall. We did not find a single diagnostic ceramic fragment, most likely due to the fact that the sites are near roads and villages.

### *Maukallacta*

This site sits on the hill of Cerro Chinchanaco, at 2850 masl, on the left margin of the Sandia River, south of the Chichanaco quebrada and 1.5 km to the southwest of the present town of Sandia. The site is also called Ch'iara-Pata (Nalvarte M. 1983:123).

The site of Maukallacta covers an area of approximately 469,691 m$^2$ (approximately 47 ha) and can be divided into four sectors (Fig. 14.2).

*Sector A* is formed from 6 funerary structures, commonly called "chulpas" in the Andes. Each is rectangular in shape with straight corners but with curved interior finishing. Each structure is approximately 9 m$^2$ in interior space with stone walls about 2 m high. The roof is made in a false dome technique with stones that overhang 80 cm past the walls. All the tombs have only one small access and in some cases there are platforms made with large slabs that rise 60 cm from the walls. In these structures one can see various disturbed human remains that indicate that multiple mummies were interred (Fig. 14.3).

*Sector B* corresponds to larger structures, among which is found a sunken plaza that is in the shape of an irregular oval. Also, there are a number of walls with one or two faces and quadrangular structures. In this sector, apart from the plaza, there is a small quadrangular enclosure that has a door, three windows and a niche, which is circumscribed in another structure (Fig. 14.4).

The presence of a sunken plaza and the quadrangular structure with niche probably indicates that public performances were conducted here (in the plaza) as well as private ones in the larger enclosure. Also, given the presence of some very well made quadrangular enclosures near the public areas, we suggest the possibility of associated elite residences.

*Sector C* is formed with more than 15 quadrangular structures and sub-quadrangular structures concentrated in a cluster. In general, these structures are slightly larger than those in Sector A. The function of this area is unknown but it is possible that these are domestic residences and storage units. Only detailed excavations of the floors will tell us more about this.

*Sector D* is found in the extreme northeast of the site and is composed of large retention walls, similar to the large walls that surround this part of the settlement. Likewise, one can identify some structures similar to those in Sector C. The spatial layout of Maukallacta demonstrates an architectural hierarchy among various sectors and a preoccupation to defend the site with large walls. Also, it was important for the people at the site to have a public space in which to gather, possibly for festivals linked to the mallquis, an interpretation that would explain the proximity of the chulpas to the plaza.

### *Chunchulacalloc*

This is a settlement found on the sides of the Cerro Queneque, at 1950 masl, located at the confluence of the Sandia River and the Cahuanchaca quebrada. The site is 56,630 m$^2$ (more than 5 ha) in size and is about 6.7 km northeast of the town of Sandia. It is also known as Q'awan-Chaka (Nalvarte M. 1983:122).

Because of architectural plan, the site has been divided into three sectors created principally by habitation units and possibly some administrative buildings (Fig. 14.5). We were not able to identify a cemetery area but it is possible, as mentioned by Sr. Luis Cabrera, vice mayor of the area, that it is found to the south of the site in the nearby hillsides.

*Sector A* is composed of approximately 17 quadrangular and sub-quadrangular structures 3 × 3 m on a side in average. The

268　　　　　　　　　　　　　　　　　　　*Advances in Titicaca Basin Archaeology–III*

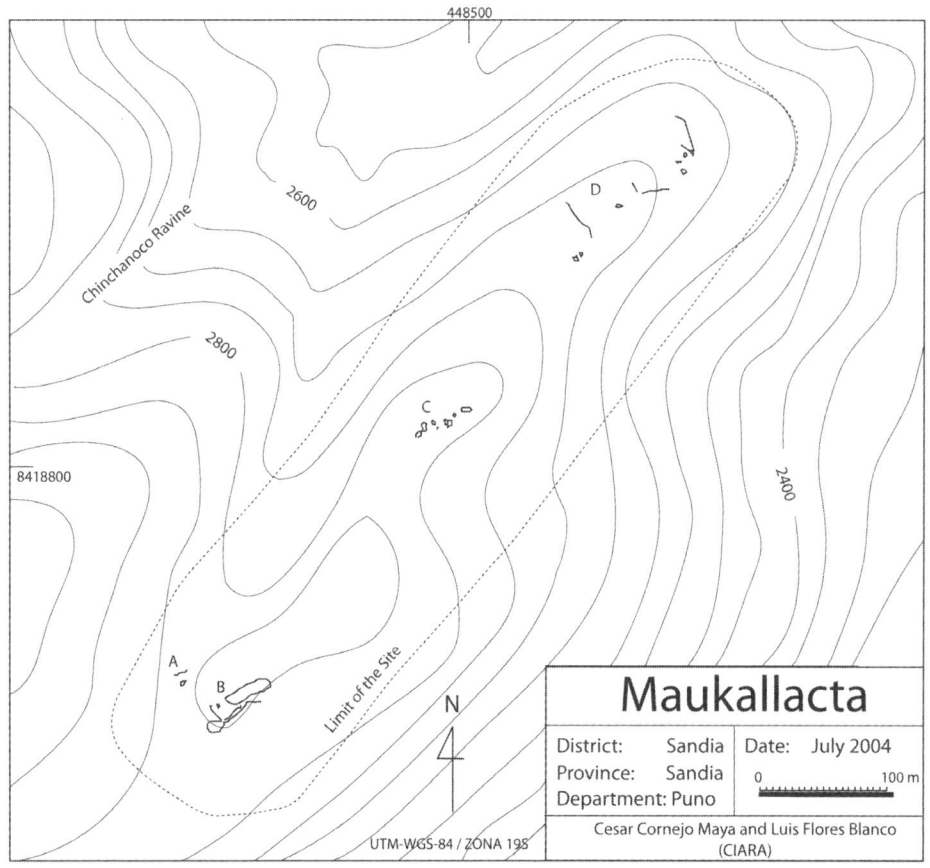

Figure 14.2. Plan of Maukallacta.

Figure 14.3. Circular structures (chulpas) in Maukallacta.

Figure 14.4. Quadrangular structures with niches in Maukallacta.

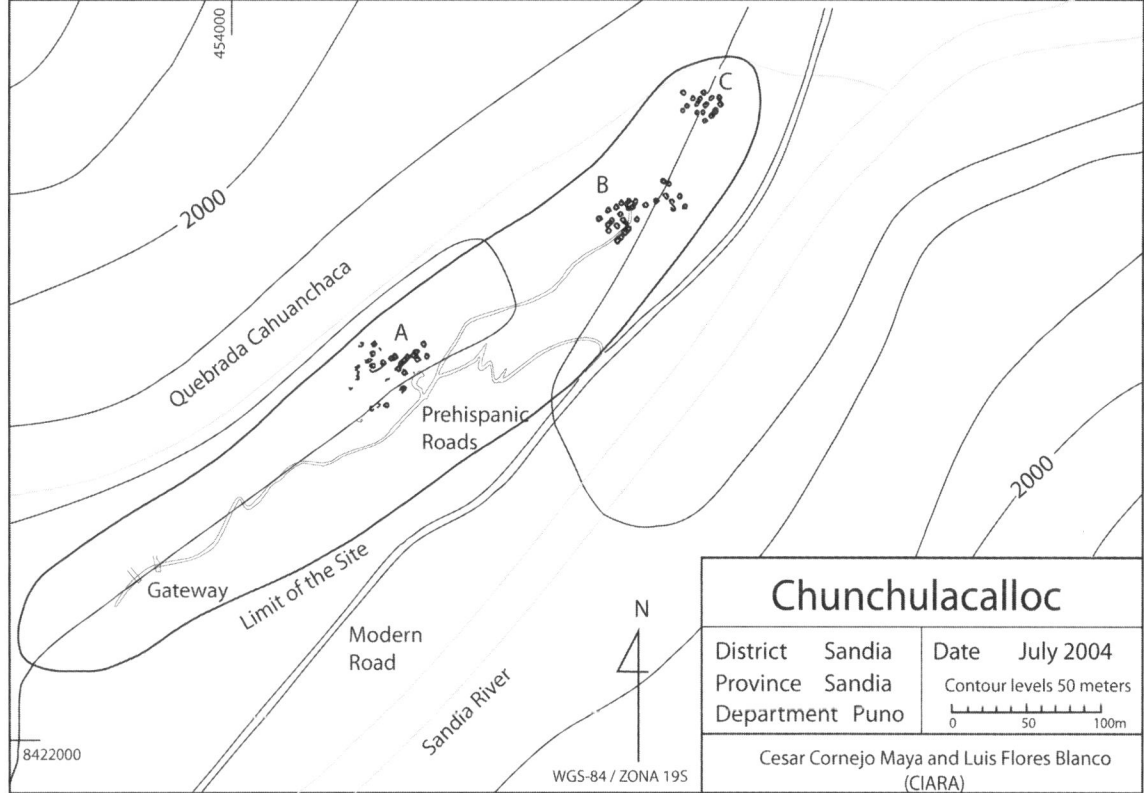

Figure 14.5. Plan of Chunchulacalloc.

Figure 14.6. Semi-subterranean structure in Chunchulacalloc.

structures are generally contiguous and placed on low terraces. The lowest terrace is notable in that it has a complex of 7 structures, all of them surrounding a plaza. The structures have cut stone pirca walls and are still preserved up to 1.67 m. Some of the walls have a niche and in one case there is a shared window between two contiguous rooms. Of these only one preserves its original roof, which is conical in shape and slightly elevated (Figs. 14.6, 14.7).

Another type of construction can be seen in the 5 structures that abut the hill, on the southeast side, and that are made with just one or two walls, similar to corrals. Also, there are 2 structures that do not conform to the observed patterns. They are similar to the Inca pattern and have a rectangular form while the other appears to be 2 contiguous structures that share a central accessway.

There is a paved stone road about 2 m wide that goes toward the entrance of the site in the southeast. The entrance has two large doors more than 2 m in height.

The B Sector is connected with the A Sector by this road. In Sector B, the road is 1.1 m wide on average. This is, in reality, a bifurcation of the road that goes from the site entrance to the southeast of Sector A while another one goes to the modern road. Sector B is comprised of 20 structures similar to those in Sector A. Although there is a high quantity of similar structures, these are more concentrated and some of them are located on the edge of an escarpment that faces the Sandia River.

We did not visit Sector C for lack of time, but from Sector B we were able to observe at least 7 structures similar to those found in Sectors A and B. These were located at a lower altitude on the promontory that is at the confluence with the Cahuanchaca quebrada and the Sandia River.

Chunculacayoc is the only site with a formal entrance, which indicates a concern with protection. Likewise, the existence of only one paved road in the entire site area indicates some kind of control of traffic. These features would usually indicate that there was a defensive wall associated with the settlement, particularly to the south and east, but we did not find evidence for these. It is possible that the construction of the Sandia-San Juan del Oro road destroyed this evidence. Certainly, the north and west sides of the site were naturally protected by the abrupt cliffs.

Sector A was the best documented area of the site where we were able to note three types of constructed spaces. One of these types deserves mention: it is an aggregation of enclosures, many of them contiguous, next to a common patio used by a domestic group. This pattern is similar to that recorded by Lavallée and Julien (1983:49); they called it "alveolar (socket) units" in the case of Asto in the central sierra. Apart from these small patios, we did not identify open spaces of significant size that could be considered an area of supra-domestic use.

Figure 14.7. Quadrangular structure in Chunchulacalloc.

### Huancasayan or Wanka-Sayani

This is a small site located next to the quebrada Soniapo, on the left side of the Río Nacroreque, near the village of Huancasayani. It is located approximately 17 km south of the town of Sandia, at an elevation of 3700 masl.

The site is relatively small, about 3836 m² (about half a hectare), and is composed of 10 individual rectangular structures that in average measure 2.5 to 4.5 m².

The structures are very well preserved and one can reconstruct the construction process at the site. They first constructed a solid platform filled with rocks and soil, raising it about 1 m above the ground. Then, they placed large slabs for a floor that hung over the platform. Finally, they raised the walls with medium-sized rocks using clay mortar mixed with some small, ground stones. They finished the construction with a conical roof and a slightly arched surface made with overlapping stones (Fig. 14.8).

The site was organized spatially with tomb structures next to an open area that functioned as a plaza. Huancasayan is linked with other settlements via a road that runs through its western side.

### Colocolo

The site of Colocolo is located on the sides of Cerro Pojoni, on the left margin of the Río Patambuco at 3300 masl.

The archaeological complex measures approximately 35,508 m² (3.5 ha) and is composed of approximately 80 structures built on terraces, supported by stone walls. Each terrace has open spaces, entrances and passages that permit access between the structures across the site. Some of the funerary structures were constructed on rocky promontories on the highest area of the site (Fig. 14.9).

The structures are semi-quadrangular and on average measure 3 m on a side with small open spaces (vanos) oriented largely toward the hills to the northeast with a few toward the valley and others facing each other. All the structures were plastered with red clay. The majority of the structures have preserved roofs, which are convex in form and reach up to 1 m high (Fig. 14.10).

There are similar structures on the hillsides, which are difficult to reach and, for lack of time, we did not record them.

Between the Río Patambuco and the modern road there is a recently abandoned village. There is evidence of buried structures that suggests that this was an ancient village, perhaps the one that Nalvarte M. (1983:125) called Mayo-Pampa.

It is generally thought that these structures were used exclusively as chulpas but it is worth investigating through excavations and precise surface analysis whether the site had other activities.

It is noteworthy that Colocolo did not have a plaza like Maukallacta and Huancasayan. This lack of public space is common and can be explained if the structures were used exclusively for

Figure 14.8. Complex of chulpas in Huancasayan.

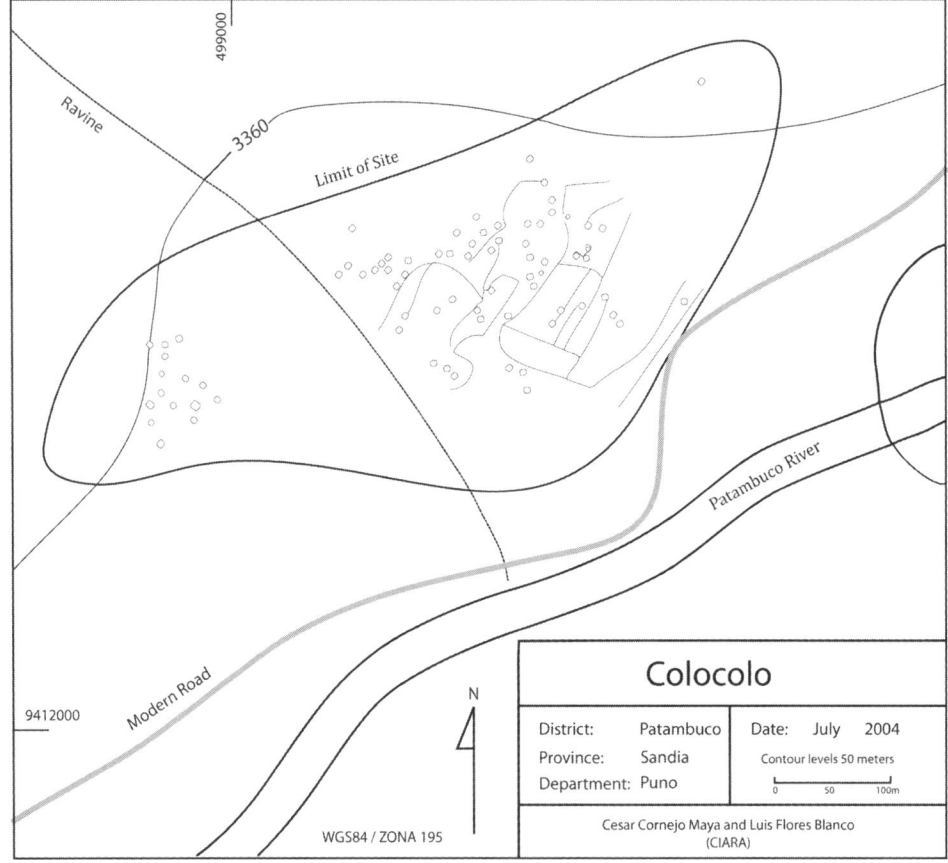

Figure 14.9. Plan of Colocolo.

Figure 14.10. View of a pair of structures in Colocolo.

funerary or domestic purposes, and there were no communal activities. It is also possible that the public activities were segmented. This would explain the existence of structure complexes (the domestic group) sharing limited open space on a terrace for domestic, ritual and/or funerary activities.

*Other Archaeological Sites in Sandia*

We are aware of many other sites in the region. For example, in the Sandia district, there is evidence of chulpas in Q'awan-Chaka, Pata-Laqueque, Qéusani and Ñacoreque-Chico; in Wayra-Ph'auchinta there are reports of rock art (Nalvarte M. 1983:122–23). In the Cuyo Cuyo district, we have reports of a pre-Inca settlement (ciudadela) called Ph'utuni-Pata (Nalvarte M. 1983:124). In the Patambuco district, we have various settlements reported with characteristics of "forts" such as Pukara-Pata and Chuncho-Pukara. There are also chulpas and large monoliths in the vegetation at the site of Tira-Waka. Finally, in the site of Harawaña, there are chulpas, andenes and monoliths. In the Phara district there are reports of small habitations, chulpas and corrals that look like fortification walls in Chamapola (Nalvarte M. 1983:127). In Limbani, in the site of Mauq'a-Limbani, we find pirca constructions, huts with gabled roofs and chulpas with slab roofs (Nalvarte M. 1983:127). In the Quiaca district we also have evidence of chulpas at the site of Pukara-Pata or Miraflores (Nalvarte M. 1983:128).

## Archaeology of Carabaya

Our reconnaissance of the province of Carabaya allowed us to visit six of the ten districts of Carabaya (Macusani, Corani, Ollachea, Ayapata, Coasa, Usicayos). The major concentration of the registered sites were in the Ollachea Valley or San Gabán, such as Marca Marca de Tantamaco, Quilli-Quilli and Chichac-cori. In the Ayapata Valley, we visited only the site of Pitumarca that, for its complexity, is similar to the sites of Larecaja in Bolivia. In Coasa we visited Chulpas de Esquena and the site of Huatamarca. Finally, in Usicayos we reconnoitered the site of Marca Marca III.

Like Sandia, in Carabaya all the sites that we explored are found on terraced hillsides or on flat hilltops near small rivers that flow below. Unlike Sandia, the sites in Carabaya had some diagnostic ceramic fragments on the surface and in the storerooms of the municipality of Usicayos (Fig. 14.11). The majority of the fragments were Altiplano period or Inka in date. One piece that was notable was a wooden spoon with a feline motif that had Tiwanaku characteristics.

We note, but do not discuss, the great quantity of rock art that has been reported for Carabaya (Hostnig 2003, 2004; Flores and Cáceda 2004b).

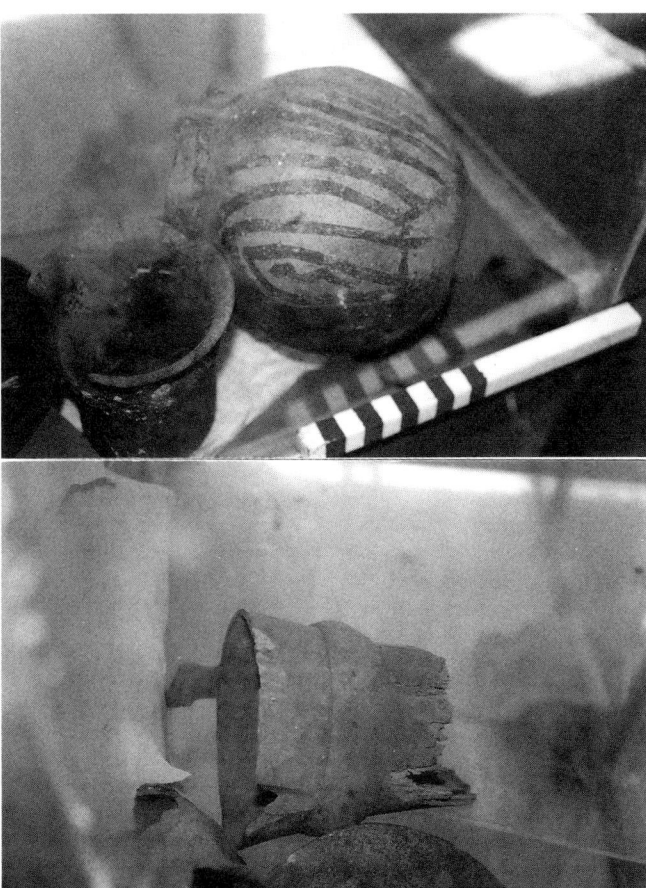

Figure 14.11. Photograph of some archaeological material in the museum cases in the Municipal Museum of Usicayos.

## Marca Marca de Tantamaco

This site is located to the north and above the village of Tantamaco at 4241 masl, and is located on a terraced area. The structures are constructed with cut stone with a clay mortar. The structures have circular, semicircular (appears to be local) and rectangular plans (Inka).

The archaeological reconnaissance was able to define four sectors:

*Sector A.* This is a large plaza with a rectangular structure with internal measurements of 13.80 × 5.50 m. Some of the internal niches are trapezoidal in form, measuring 0.38 × 0.55 m and 0.30 m in depth. Other rectangular structures are found associated with this plaza. The architectural elements indicate that this sector has Inka influence. This area functioned to host public and administrative activities.

*Sector B.* On the edges of the plaza of Sector A, on the north side, there are circular houses that in average reach 3.30 m in diameter. The distribution of the structures is both isolated and agglutinated. In this last case, we find small passages that allow access between these structures.

*Sector C.* This is composed of a large rock on the highest part of the site. The inhabitants of Tantamaco have placed a Christian cross here. This rock is 5 m long and 2.5 m wide on one side and 0.60 m on the other. It is 2.0 m at the highest point. There are the remains of small niches formed by medium-sized rocks located on one of the highest areas of the rock. Nearby the rock there are buildings, both open and closed, divided and defined by stone walls.

By this evidence, we believe that this sector was reserved for magico-religious ceremonial activities. The characteristics of these open spaces suggest the concentration of a considerable number of people in this area of the site.

*Sector D.* This sector is defined as an area of funerary chambers at the base of the rock outcrops. There is local Inca pottery on the surface, characterized by bowls with Cuzco type B designs.

Finally, there is a stratified midden deposit at the edge of the site. The strata are dark brown in color, typical of organic decomposition. The deposit is about 0.6 m in width and contains ceramic fragments, textiles, camelid bone and various botanical materials.

## Quilli-Quilli

Thirty minutes to the north of the community of Tantamaco is the archaeological site of Quilli-Quilli. It is located on some rocky promontories on the right side of the quebrada of the same name at the base of the Cerro Quilla Quillisenja.

The site is spread over the terraced hillside on a very abrupt side at 3942 masl. The majority of the buildings are rectangular and quadrangular in plan, with patios and plazas delimited by walls that reach up to 1.40 m in thickness (Fig. 14.12).

The survey was able to distinguish two large sectors or halves, divided by a street 1.5 × 2.0 m wide in a north-south direction. Three roads came together to form this road, one from the north (probably from the selva), another from the west from Corani, and the last from Tantamaco (Quispe et al. 1995:47).

*Sector A or the lower half.* This is composed of many wide plazas that are associated with rectangular or quadrangular structures that appear to be administrative or ceremonial.

*Sector B or the upper half.* In the area closest to the road, toward the highest part of the site, a series of structures are concentrated near the small, round plazas. Above this area we found a series of funerary chambers made by excavating holes at the base of the natural rock outcrops. Here, the mummies were placed in the holes as if they were caves associated with patios and small terraced plazas defined by double-faced walls. This use of space suggests that there were ceremonies associated with the dead, possibly at a regular period of time, with the goal of worshipping and asking for well-being, but mainly to bring the ancestors into the group's social life.

Coben and Stanish (2005:274) indicated that this spatial differentiation of the two halves, also noted by us, suggests an occupation and remodeling by the Inca at the site. Within this surface material we have identified ceramic fragments of a red-orange paste and one with only a brown paint. The red-orange is an Inca diagnostic, supporting the interpretation of an Inca reuse of the area.

Figure 14.12. Panoramic view of Quilli-Quilli covered with grass.

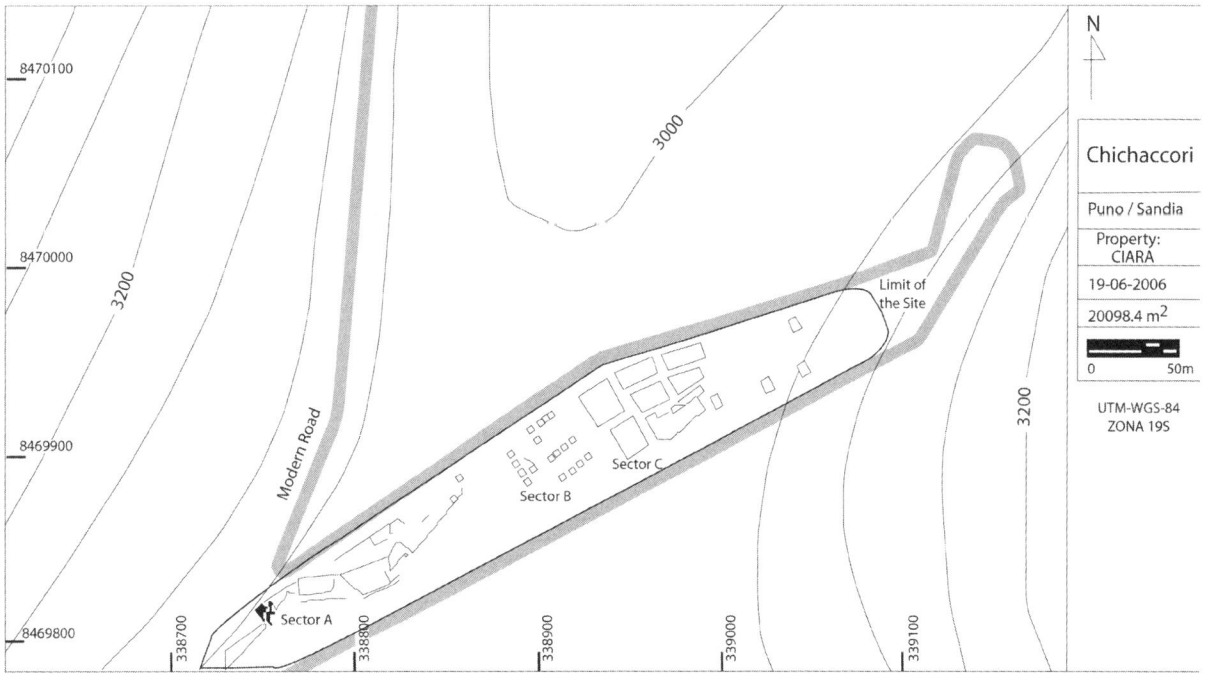

Figure 14.13. Plan of Chichaccori.

*Chillacori or Chichaccori*

The site is found at the side of the Macusani-Ollachea highway on the right side of the San Gabán River. The site is located at an altitude of 3082 masl.

The surface of the site was terraced in order to build structures. This is a common architectural technique to adapt the steep land for habitation, one that we have seen in other prehispanic sites in northeast Puno (Fig. 14.13).

The reconnaissance differentiated three sectors that cover about 20,098 m² (a little more than 2 ha).

*Sector A.* This is composed of large rectangular plazas built on a layered set of terraces that can reach up to 2 m high. These terraces are accessed by corridors, stairways and open

Figure 14.14. One of the chulpas at Chichaccori.

niches. Without doubt these were built to host large numbers of people.

There are two rocky promontories that overlap the plazas on which the people built chulpas. These funerary structures have only one walled access that measures 1.7 m wide. The walls are up to 1.6 m high, built with cut stones with a beige clay mortar mixed with straw and small stones. The roof is built in the false arch (false corbel) technique with large slabs in the interior. These slabs overlap the walls, like a cornice, for 0.70 m. The wall was decorated with a red mortar (Fig. 14.14).

The presence of chulpas in a Late Intermediate period style suggests to us a possible pre-Inka occupation, but one that was totally remodeled by the Inka.

*Sector B*. This is located in the center of the site. Here we find the remains of rectangular structures that have gabled roofs. The walls climb over 2.5 m high. Here, we registered smaller semi-rectangular structures, but all placed regularly along shared patios.

*Sector C*. This area is composed of a complex of large plazas, some of which have extensive platforms that create two interior levels. The plazas are interconnected by wide, open niches that can be up to 2.30 m thick and as high as 2.4 m.

Within these we identified 3 structures in an Inka style, with a rectangular plan and gabled roofs and a small window some centimeters below the angle of the gable. The accessways have a slight trapezoidal form. The largest and most central structure is built on a platform of rock. In the interior, there are benches and a small space that could be a storage unit. In the highest part of the corners there are four angular slabs that have some kind of architectural function (Fig. 14.15).

To the west of the above structure there is a smaller one, with the same style. The internal space of this structure is plain, without any additional architectural element.

On the opposing side, toward the east, the inhabitants had attached a new structure some time after the earlier buildings were in use. This structure has benches in the interior, and in the eastern half, a hollow platform that could have functioned as a storehouse. In the corners we once again see four angular slabs.

By the characteristics of the structures, the use of space, the existence of a prehispanic road that goes toward the west, and the existence of a nearby site (Illingaya) also linked to the Inca occupation (Coben and Stanish 2005:256–57), we suggest that we have an important Inca enclave, settling and remodeling an Intermediate period site, located strategically at the beginning of the selva with the intent to control the trade of goods such as gold and coca.

### Pitumarka

The site is found leaving the village of Ccochauma, in Ayapata, toward the Ccañocota Lake. It takes about one hour of travel, arriving at a flat area where a prominent rock outcrop is found and at the base of which is another lake called Allpicota. The site of Pitumarka is found on the mesa at an altitude of 4008 masl. The site is spread over an area of 36,752 $m^2$ or about 3.7 ha.

The entrance to the site is by an open niche about 1.70 m wide with jambs that reach 2 m in width.

The site has a regular architectural plan that centers on a street that leaves from Sector A and crosses the site from south

Figure 14.15. Quadrangular structure in Chichaccori.

to north toward Sectors C and D and from there goes in three branches toward the other sectors of the site. There are other smaller streets that come out of the main ones (Fig. 14.16). We have identified seven sectors:

*Sector A*. This is located in the far south of the site. The site is dominated by a rectangular structure approximately 333 m$^2$ in size. Some of the most notable elements are lateral platforms. Judging by the characteristics of the area, this architectural complex not only controlled the entrance of the site, but was the most important space in the community. Behind this building are a series of minor rooms with benches and low platforms. This sector had a public ceremonial function.

*Sector B*. This sector is located to the north side of Sector A, and is composed of large rectangular structures, about 11 m$^2$ in interior size and distributed regularly around the principal street that crosses the site. A prehispanic canal runs through this sector. Due to the regular plan of these structures and the fine architectural features of the buildings, we suggest that these areas were the residences of the elite.

*Sector C* is defined by the two highest points of the settlement, on which have been found adjacent rectangular structures.

*Sector D* is composed of rectangular structures that are located to the east side of the settlement, below Sector C. This sector does not show as much architectural order and is characterized by narrow, crowded streets. This appears to be an area of lower status residences than that of Sector B.

*Sector E* is composed of 6 rectangular structures, separately arranged in an irregular row. There is a seventh structure complex that is associated with a patio.

*Sector F* is located at the north end of the settlement, on a terrace 10 m below Sector E. Here you can see 3 or 4 rectangular structures that are poorly preserved. Sector F may be accessed from the bottom of the site though not from the top, where we have not been able to identify any form of access (Fig. 14.17).

*Sector G* is the set of compounds that are distributed throughout the lower and western side of the settlement, east of the small Lake Allpicota. Some of the structures are spatially restricted while others are corrals.

Also, we observed from a distance a number of chulpas in the hilltops located to the west of the site, and in the climb up to the hill there are a number of zoomorphic rock art panels painted in red (Flores and Cáceda 2004).

## Chulpas of Esquena

These structures are found about 100 m from the Esquena-Coasa highway at about 3694 masl. Some are located on small natural embankments while others are attached to the walls of a cliff. To access them you must descend from the road over rugged and steep terrain that increases toward the riverbed.

One of the identified chulpas has a rectangular shape, and a false dome vault. This was built with a series of flat slabs that overlap and are plastered with mud mortar to form a solid dome. This type of chulpa architecture has been recorded for other sites like Chichaccori and Marca Marca III.

The first chulpa that was sighted was painted red and measured 1.7 m on a side and was 1.6 m high.

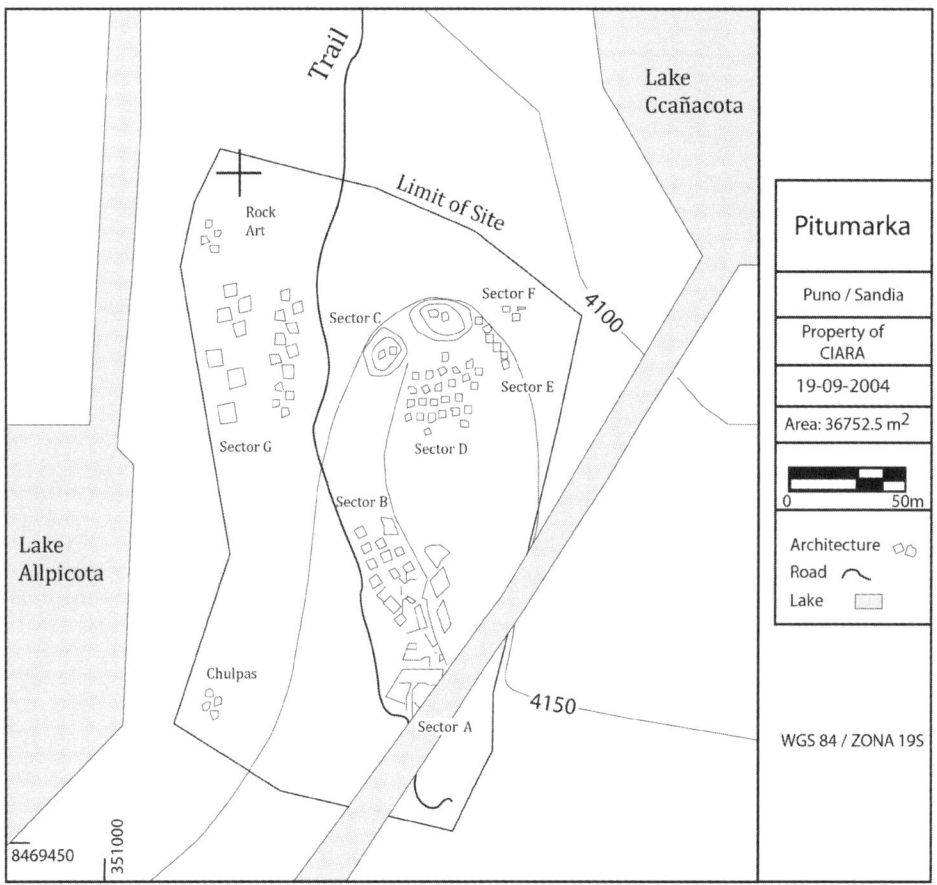

Figure 14.16. Plan of Pitumarka.

Figure 14.17. General view of the lower sector at Pitumarka.

Five meters down the steep cliff, one finds a multiple burial chamber largely destroyed by looting and seismic activities that have shattered much of the rock that supports it. Inside are four chambers in which funeral bundles were deposited; based upon the surface evidence, we could determine that there were individuals of both sexes, each with associated offerings such as ceramic vessels.

In front of these chulpas, on the other side of the ravine, is an archaeological site called Huatamarca that we could not visit. Local people describe it as a large and well-made site, two hours by road from the village of Esquena. Ávila (2005:108) tells us that there are double-story chulpas at this site.

## Marca Marca III

This site is located on the crest of a hill, at 3883 masl, on the left side of the river Pacchani, across from the village of Usicayos about one hour away.

The settlement is oriented from west to east and is dominated by a complex system of terraces that extend from the top of the hill to the bed of the quebradas. The site is crossed by an Inca road, which has some preserved sections of pavement. This road enters the site from the west on the terraces and continues up to a plaza, then continues its course to the northwest toward the modern district of Coasa. The total site area, including much of the andenes, is 259,413 m², or nearly 26 ha. The actual architectural core of the site is 69,316 m² (about 7 ha) (Fig. 14.18).

Formally, the rooms are rectangular and are arranged on terraces. The building material consists of elongated stones, heavily worn and placed over clay mortar. No differences were observed regarding the construction technique, or the shape of the buildings, except in the case of Sector A, which reminds us of Late Intermediate period sites. This architectural homogeneity reflects the fact that the site is fundamentally Inka in construction.

Seven sectors are identified on the site, which are linked by a series of streets and alleys, deriving from a main road that crosses the settlement from east to west.

*Sector A* consists of chulpas that are located on the lower north side of the settlement along the road leading to the modern district of Coasa. These chulpas are rectangular, 1.3 to 1.7 m on a side and 1.5 to 1.8 m high, plus 1 m of a high dome-shaped roof. Each chulpa was constructed with a base of elongated stones placed in clay with straw, and then painted first yellow and then red. Inside some of the chulpas, two slabs were placed in a transverse position, which possibly served as shelves on which to place offerings to the bodies that it housed.

*Sector B* is found on the highest part of the site, facing the west. This position visually dominates the entire settlement, the river and the agricultural terraces in the lower parts. Also, three small spaces have been identified that were used for observation or surveillance.

*Sector C* is located east of sector B and is composed of a complex of structures including terraces and small houses that are associated with Plaza 2.

*Sector D* is located northeast of Sector C and consists of large rectangular structures densely aggregated around patios. The structures have gables and in some cases have windows, entrances and trapezoidal niches and walls that exceed 3 m high (Fig. 14.19).

*Sector E* encompasses the entire northeastern flank of the site. There are smaller structures in greater quantities than those in Sector D, but they maintain the same ordered use and distribution of space. These are associated with the main street that cuts through the site from east to west.

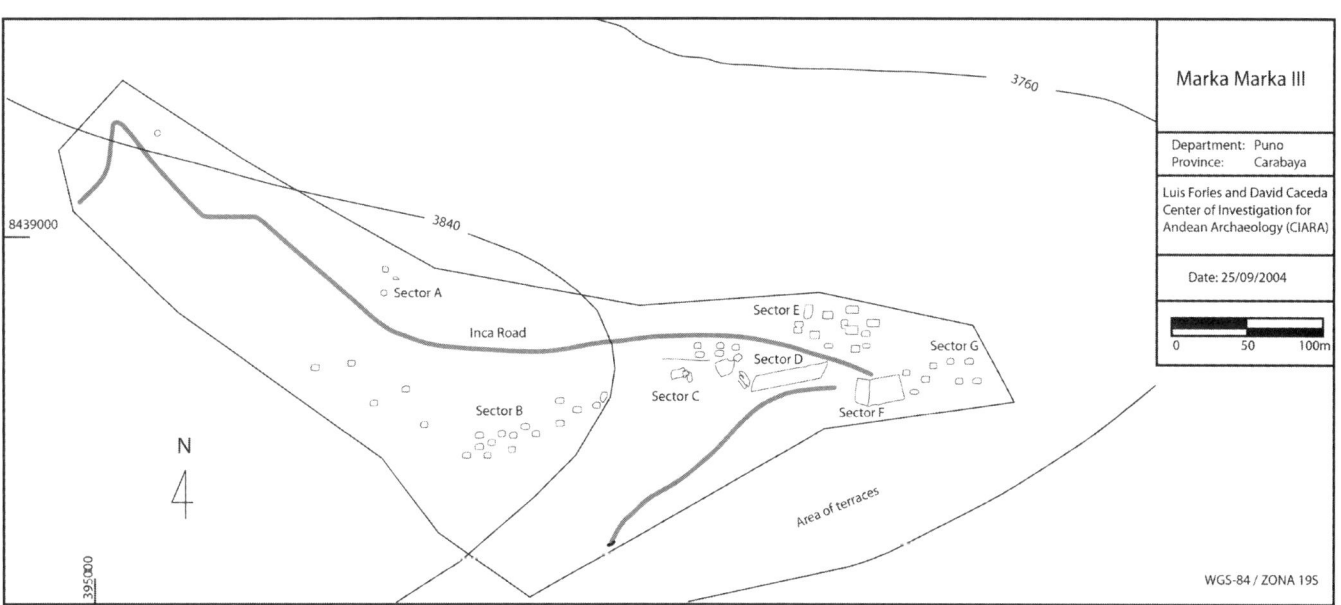

Figure 14.18. Plan of Marka Marka III.

Figure 14.19. View of the entrance at Marka Marka III.

*Sector F* is a plaza with two lateral structures, one on each side and facing each other. These structures have a rectangular plan and are gabled and there are trapezoidal niches in their interiors.

The Inca road that rises from the river Pacchani enters the south side of the square, so that everyone who walked this path must necessarily enter this settlement. This is where the people at the site possibly were able to exercise control of the movement toward that zone that today is modern Coasa.

*Sector G* is the set of terraces and structures that are substantially agglutinated, which are found on the eastern end of the settlement.

### Other Archaeological Sites in Carabaya

There are other sites that have been reported: Illingaya in Ollachea; Oja T'oqo in Ituata; Khurkutra, Qoa Qoa in Coaza; and Phushka, Oqosiri, Sucha Ccucho, and Phisca Phichu Puncu in Usicayos (Ávila 2005:108–9; Dueñas 1975:20).

### A Brief Characterization of the Archaeology of Northern Puno

The cultural affiliation of sites in Carabaya Sandia has been difficult to assess due to the kind of surface survey that we have done, the scarcity of ceramic materials on the surface, and the lack of archaeological information about these regions that would allow us to more fully understand our evidence.

However, from these few data and the similarities such as the presence of funerary constructions called chulpas (which in the typology of Marion Tschopik [1946:15–16] would be Type 3), we suggest that most of the sites described originally belonged to the Late Intermediate period and were united by a common cultural background. This begs the question: Who constructed the architecture described here? Was it a local population of the eastern part of Puno? Perhaps it was a group that came from the altiplano to exploit the different ecological floors in the region? Or, perhaps it was people from both groups? This proposal would not be so far from the truth if we consider that linguists include the northwest, north and northeast of the plateau as the speech range associated with the cultural group Pukina Colla (Torero 1987, 2005).

The Inka presence is more easily understood. We recorded Inka architectural features at three sites: Marca Marca de Tantamaco, Chichaccori in Ollachea and Marka Marca III in Usicayos. But there is also evidence of the imposition of Inca control, including both architectural and ceramic data, on Late Intermediate period sites such as Quilli-Quilli, Marca Marca de Tantamaco and possibly Maukallacta in Sandia.

All of these propositions regarding chronology are still very preliminary; only future systematic surveys and excavations will illuminate the archaeology of northern Puno. We have no doubt that the region was very important economically for the pre-Inca cultures, the Inca Empire and the Spaniards. The area was rich in resources such as precious metals (especially gold) and exotic species, which explains why the region has such an extensive network of roads linking mountains and forest.

[Translated by C. Stanish]

## Acknowledgments

This article is the result of a strong collaboration with the Centro de Investigación de Arqueología Andina (CIARA) with logistical and financial help from local authorities during the months of July and October 2004. For this we remain very grateful to the authorities of the Province of Sandia, especially Mayor Dr. Enrique Quilla Gómez and the Teniente-Alcalde Luis Abel Cabrera Cárdenas. For our work in Carabaya, we are eternally grateful to Sr. Alcalde Michel Portier Ballano, the Teniente-Alcalde Julio Juno Minaya, Sra. Nilo Maque Huayta and Prof. Nicolás Luna Peralta, who were always ready to help. Their love of their local history and their constant support made us feel as if we were at home and we always left with the wish to return.

## References Cited

Ávila Quispe, Walter M.
2005 *Carabaya. Historia general*, Tomo I. Arequipa, Peru.

Coben, Lawrence, and Charles Stanish
2005 Archaeological reconnaissance in the Carabaya region, Peru. In *Advances in the Archaeology of the Titicaca Basin-1*, edited by Charles Stanish, Amanda B. Cohen, and Mark S. Aldenderfer, pp. 243–66. Cotsen Institute of Archaeology, University of California, Los Angeles.

Conlee, C. J., J. Dulanto, C. Mackey, and C. Stanish
2004 Late prehispanic sociopolitical complexity. In *Andean Archaeology*, edited by H. Silverman, pp. 209–36. Blackwell Publishing Ltd., Malden, MA.

Cornejo, César, and Luis Flores
2004 Evaluación preliminar del potencial científico y turístico de los principales monumentos arqueológicos de La Provincia de Sandia. Informe Final presentado a la Municipalidad Provincial de Carabaya.

Dueñas Tovar, Benjamín
1975 *Ensayo monográfico de la provincia de Carabaya*. Editorial Los Andes, Puno, Perú.

Flores, Luis, and Daniel Cáceda
2004a Evaluación del potencial científico y turístico de los principales recursos culturales de la Provincia de Carabaya, Puno. Informe Final presentado a la Municipalidad Provincial de Carabaya.
2004b Arte rupestre en la Provincia de Carabaya, Puno: Estableciendo una secuencia temporal relativa. Presented in "I Simposio Nacional de Arte Rupestre," Cusco, November 2004.

Franco Inojosa, José María
1936 Exploraciones arqueológicas en el Perú: Departamento de Puno. *Revista del Museo Nacional* 5(2):157–83. Lima.

Hostnig, Rainer
2003 *Arte rupestre del Perú. Inventario nacional*. Consejo Nacional de Ciencia y Tecnología, Lima, Perú.
2004 Las maravillas de Macusani y Corani. *Rumbos* IX(40):1–6.

Lavallée, Danièle, and Michèle Julien
1983 Modelos de asentamiento y habitat. In *Asto: Curacazgo prehispánico de los Andes centrales*, by D. Lavallée and M. Julien, pp. 47–107. Arqueología, 7. Instituto de Estudios Peruanos, Lima, Peru.

Luna Peralta, Nicolás
1999 *Ensayo monográfico del Distrito de Corani—Carabaya*. Editorial Área del Desarrollo Educativo-Enlace, Macusani.

Murra, John V.
1975 *Formaciones económicas y políticas del mundo andino*. Instituto de Estudios Peruanos, Lima, Perú.

Nalvarte Maldonado, Nicolás
1983 Panorama turístico de la Provincia de Sandia. In *Álbum de Oro*, edited by Frisancho Pineda, tomo X, pp. 119–30. Puno.

Neira Avendaño, Máximo
1967 Informe preliminar de las investigaciones arqueológicas en el Departamento de Puno. *Anales del Instituto de Estudios Socio Económicos* 1(1):107–64. Universidad Técnica del Altiplano, Puno.

Nordenskiöld, Erland
1953 *Investigaciones arqueológicas en la región fronteriza de Perú y Bolivia*. Upsala/Estocolmo (1906); Biblioteca Paceña. Alcaldía Municipal, La Paz, Bolivia.

Palao Berastain, Juan B.
1991 *Arte rupestre pictórico de Tantamayo—Puno, Perú* (resumen).

PEISA ediciones
2004 *Tomo 7: Puno. Atlas regional del Perú. Imagen geográfica, estadística, histórica y cultural*. Lima, Perú.

Quispe Aragón, Amador, Lorgio V. Quispe Aragón, and José P. Quispe Aragón
1995 *Macusani. Capital de la Provincia de Carabaya*. Macusani, Puno.

Spahni, J. C.
1971 *Semblanza de los pueblos del Perú*. Peruano Suiza S.A., Lima.

Stanish, Charles
2003 *Ancient Titicaca. The Evolution of Complex Society in Southern Peru and Northern Bolivia*. University of California Press, Berkeley.

Tapia, Félix
1985 *Contribución a la investigación arqueológica en los valles de Sandia y Carabaya, en el departamento de Puno–Perú*. Grupo de Arte Utaraya, s/n, Puno.

Tschopik, Marion H.
1946 *Some Notes on the Archaeology of the Department of Puno, Peru*. Papers of the Peabody Museum of American Archaeology and Ethnology, Harvard University, vol. 27, no. 3. Cambridge, Massachusetts.

Torero, Alfredo
1987 Lenguas y pueblos altiplánicos en torno al siglo XVI. *Revista Andina* 5(2):329–68. Cusco.
2005 *Idiomas de los Andes. Lingüística e historia*. Instituto Francés de Estudios Andinos (IFEA) y editorial Horizonte, 2nd ed., Lima.

Chapter 15

# The Late Intermediate Period Occupation of Pukara, Peru

*Sarah J. Abraham*

Across much of the Andes, the Late Intermediate period (AD 1100–1450) was a time of factionalism as polities fought to fill the power vacuum created by the political collapse of Wari and Tiwanaku. In the Titicaca Basin of south central Peru, the Colla were one of the groups that rose to predominance during this time. Much of our understanding of the Colla comes from ethnohistory but a growing body of archaeological research is both expanding and refining our knowledge of this culture. This chapter presents the results of recent research on the Collao occupation at Pukara. Although this site is best known for its Late Formative (500 BC–AD 200) occupation, excavations have uncovered a Late Intermediate period non-fortified habitational area, a site type relatively unknown in the northern Titicaca Basin. Using ceramic and architectural data, this chapter examines the nature of the Collao[1] occupation of Pukara and its place in the regional chronology during a dynamic period in Andean prehistory.

### The Late Intermediate Period in the Titicaca Basin

Although it spanned hundreds of years, the Late Intermediate period is an understudied era in Titicaca Basin prehistory and our knowledge is based on limited archaeological research and historic documents. Shifting settlement patterns show that after the fall of Middle Horizon states, major population centers in the altiplano were abandoned as populations dispersed across the basin into agro-pastoral zones and shifted economic focus to animal husbandry (Frye and de la Vega 2005:177). People moved away from rich agricultural lands to settle in defensive sites high on hills and ridges, and in many places they built *pukaras*,[2] or hilltop forts and refuges, to provide protection in times of conflict. Although the impressive forts have been the focus of much of Collao archaeology, most Late Intermediate period sites were not fortified, as the majority of the Colla lived in small villages and hamlets at the base of or close to the *pukaras* (Stanish 2003:209). Unfortunately, there are few published data on these smaller sites in the Collao region.

The ethnohistoric record provides a wealth of information on how altiplano polities responded to Inca conquest, including detailed accounts of the Colla during this period. According to the chronicles, the Colla resisted Inca imperial expansion with both sides fighting with "equal courage" and with "much fury and persistence" (Cobo [1653] 1979:140). Sarmiento ([1572] 1999) reported as many as three Collao uprisings after Pachacuti's initial conquest. They were described as protracted conflicts in which each side incurred great losses. One battle waged for years as the imperial army chased the Colla from *pukara* to *pukara* until the Inca finally emerged triumphant. One of the last clashes took place at Pukara, where the Colla had fled for protection from the empire.

Data from the archaeological and ethnohistoric records also can help reconstruct the sociopolitical organization of the Colla

*283*

and other polities in the basin during the Late Intermediate period. The chronicles depict the Colla as a unified kingdom, with various authors referring to the Colla as a series of kingdoms, nations, and other terms that suggest a high political complexity. Cieza identifies them, along with the Lupaqa, as the dominant groups during this time and characterizes them as powerful, arrogant, and tyrannical ([1553] 1984:356). He mentions that both these two groups had their own leaders and tells of their exploits:

> Before the Inca reigned, according to many Indians from Collao, there were in their province two great lords, one named Zapana and the other Cari, and they conquered many pucaras that are their fortifications. [Cieza (1553) 1984:356]

Sarmiento de Gamboa ([1572] 1999:111) describes the Colla leader in particular as "increased in power and wealth among those nations of Collasuyu, [and] that he was respected by all the Collas, who called him Inca Ccapac." In sum, the ethnohistoric record depicts the Colla unified under a single leader, Zapana, and equally unified in its response to the Inca imperial expansion.

Conversely, the archaeological data suggest that the Late Intermediate period was not a time of political unification but of fragmentation. Frye and de la Vega (2005:173) argue that persistent warfare and factional competition over resources during this period would have prevented political unification in the basin. Although there is little doubt that altiplano polities allied with their neighbors from time to time, some do not believe that the Collao people were ever under the leadership of a single leader (Frye and de la Vega 2005:184). Moreover, Stanish (2003:14) argues that the Late Intermediate period settlement pattern does not demonstrate a high level of sociopolitical organization. Nor is there evidence of monumental architecture or other markers of social complexity in the basin at this time (see Frye 1997). Thus, many believe that the statelike characteristics attributed to these polities in the historical documents were the result of Inca reorganization and that the Late Intermediate period polities were probably simple chiefdoms (Stanish 2003:14; Graffam 1992:887). Recent work by Arkush (2008) confirms these observations.

Although seemingly contradictory, the archaeological and ethnohistoric lines of inquiry might actually be complementary. While it is likely that the Titicaca Basin was politically fragmented during most of the Late Intermediate period, the political landscape may have been changing just prior to Inca conquest. Some suggest that on the eve of the Late Horizon (AD 1450–1532), some *pukaras* became "centers of political and economic activity and most likely headed by an emerging elite group, which expanded its political and economic influence through feasting ceremonies and political alliances" (Frye and de la Vega 2005:184). Thus, the ethnohistoric record might be capturing this transitional period from small, rival polities in the Late Intermediate period to Inca imperialism.

## History of Colla Archaeology

Colla archaeology has a long and sporadic history. One of the first inquiries was Bandelier's 1905 article on Sillustani, a site occupied during the Late Intermediate period, with a large cemetery that is well known for its *chulpas*, or burial towers. This was followed in 1943 by Kidder's report presenting the results of his survey of the northern basin. He recorded many sites with Collao ceramics, expanding the previously defined boundaries of Collao territory. Shortly after, Tschopik's *Some Notes on the Archaeology of the Department of Puno* (1946) provided a detailed inventory of Collao sites and their associated artifacts. In her report, Tschopik presented stylistic typologies of ceramics, defining the Collao Plain and Collao Black on Red styles along with other Late Intermediate period ceramic types found in the basin. This seminal work continues to serve as the principal guide to ceramics in the northern basin.

These initial investigations were followed by Julien's research at the site of Hatuncolla and Carlevato's work at Pukara. Based on the ethnohistoric data, Hatuncolla has been described as the capital of the entire Collao polity and the site of a later Inca provincial center. While excavations at Hatuncolla uncovered a substantial Late Horizon site occupation, Julien found no evidence that the site was ever the Collao capital and in fact suggests it was founded after the Inca conquest (Julien 1983). Carlevato's investigations into the Late Intermediate period and Late Horizon occupation of Pukara provide the first in-depth analysis of Collao pottery (Carlevato 1988). Using collections from Kidder's 1939 excavations, Carlevato has been able to characterize ceramic pastes, identify clay minerals and inclusions, and reconstruct firing technology. She believes there was a strong continuity of Late Intermediate period ceramic technology into the Late Horizon, with local products coexisting with Inca craft production. According to Carlevato, the function of Pukara changed over time and it served as a Formative capital, a large local center during the Late Intermediate period, and a royal Inca *tambo*.

More recently, Stanish's survey in the northern and northeastern basin and Arkush's research in the northern basin have expanded our understanding of the Collao polity. In particular, the latter study has challenged traditional views of a monolithic Late Intermediate period in the northern basin. Using data collected from survey and test excavations, Arkush has established a chronology of *pukara* use in the northern basin during the Late Intermediate period. Results suggest that *pukaras* were built and inhabited mostly between AD 1275 and the late 1400s and not immediately after the fall of Tiwanaku (Arkush 2005:317). Thus, political collapse alone did not cause the major settlement shift to hilltop sites that characterized the Late Intermediate period. Instead, the Collao settlement pattern can be explained as the result of a combination of environmental, political, and economic factors. This new research also supports recent arguments that depictions of an integrated Colla polity fostered by the ethnohistoric record are incorrect and that survey data suggest the northern basin was home to many Collao polities with their own centers and even pottery styles (Arkush 2005:4).

## The Collao Occupation of Pukara

At 3871 meters above sea level, the site of Pukara is located in the northern Lake Titicaca Basin just south of the modern town of Pucará.[3] Pukara is best known for its monumental architecture, which includes the Kalasaya, a series of large terraces and multiple sunken courts. This architectural core was constructed by the Pukara culture and served as the center of the polity. Dense habitational areas have been found in the surrounding pampa along with a few adjacent artificial mounds that may hold additional sunken courts. However, the occupational history of Pukara postdates the Kalasaya by over a thousand years.

Around AD 100, the Kalasaya was "rapidly and peacefully" abandoned and was left uninhabited until the beginning of the Late Intermediate period (Wheeler and Mujica 1981). Collao sherds blanket much of the site's surface, suggesting that the whole area was occupied during the Late Intermediate period. Although focused on the Late Formative occupation of the site, research conducted by Kidder in 1939 and COPESCO in the 1970s found evidence of a Collao occupation on the Kalasaya, the slopes at the foot of the El Peñon outcrop behind the site, the nearby Calvario Hill, and the pampa in front of the Kalasaya (Wheeler and Mujica 1981; Carlevato 1988:40; Paredes 1985:38). Wheeler and Mujica (1981) report that the southwest corner of one of the Kalasaya platforms was used as a Collao cemetery. However, no associated Late Intermediate period architecture has been documented. The Collao occupation ended with Inca conquest, when the site became a royal *tambo*, or way station. The remains of that final pre-Columbian occupation are now underneath the modern town of Pucará. Like the Colla, the Inca also modified the Kalasaya, constructing buildings over the original Pukara architecture.

## Excavation Results

The data presented were recovered in 2001 by the Pukara Domestic Archaeology Project. While looking for Late Formative elite domestic contexts on the open pampa below the terraces, the project found substantial Late Intermediate period deposits. One of the excavation units, Block 1, had multiple strata and architecture and was selected as the focus of this study (Fig. 15.1). The topmost stratum was a Late Intermediate period fill that covered the entire unit (Fill Episode 1). However, once this layer was removed, the western and eastern halves of the unit had different stratigraphy. On the western half, the top fill was preceded by another fill (Fill Episode 2). Below these two fills, there were two occupation levels. The earliest Late Intermediate period deposit appears to be a fill that served to level the immediate area in order to build architectural features (Fill Episode 3). On the eastern half of the block, the Late Intermediate period presence begins initially with the leveling that created Fill Episode 3. On top of this deposit, the Collao built several architectural features that were assigned Occupation 1. These features in turn were covered in wall fall that is absent on the western half of Block 1 (Wall Fall 1).

While our knowledge of Colla settlements and architecture has been limited to hilltop sites, Block 1 is situated on the open pampa and represents one of a small handful of examples of non-hilltop Collao architecture. Excavations uncovered a large meter-wide wall (labeled as architectural subdivision 2, or ASD 2) running north/south across the block (Fig. 15.2). The wall was originally constructed during the Formative period and the Colla added large slabs and widened the wall (Fig. 15.3). As Klarich (2005) notes, both the Formative and Late Intermediate period wall represent a substantial investment in labor. On the eastern side of the wall, there were foundations of circular structures, roughly 2–3 m in diameter, which consisted of a single course of double-faced walls. The structures were built around the same time as ASD 2 and, based on their shape, are believed to be domestic in nature. At some point, the Collao wall was destroyed and most of the wall fell to its eastern side, covering the circular structures. Klarich (2005) interprets this wall fall pattern as evidence that the wall was intentionally destroyed. On the western side of the wall, there were smaller walls running parallel and perpendicular to ASD 2; they may have been part of a rectangular building.

In general, Late Intermediate period houses were round structures. Research in the Lupaqa region (Hyslop 1977) and the Colla region (Arkush 2005) has found that these circular dwellings were usually larger than 2 m in diameter and averaged about 3 to 4 m. This description is similar to those found in the ethnohistoric documents (see Cobo 1990:192–93). Structures smaller than 2 m in diameter are also found at Late Intermediate period sites and are interpreted as storage structures; recent excavations in the Lupaqa region validate this explanation (Stanish et al. 1993; Frye and de la Vega 2005). Finally, rectangular houses have been found at Late Intermediate period sites but their distribution appears to be restricted to the area around Vilquechico, Moho and Conima in the northeastern basin (Arkush 2005:169). Though relatively small, the circular structures found in Block 1 can be interpreted as habitational. However, determining the function of ASD 3 on the western side of the block is not as straightforward.

## Ceramic Analysis

Ceramic analysis was conducted to address the function of the Collao structures over space and time and to assist in developing a local chronology for post-Formative pottery. Questions included whether the circular and rectangular structures were functionally distinct, if there is a change in function over time in Block 1, and if there exist any changes in the ceramic assemblage over time. All diagnostic sherds (mainly rim sherds and decorated

Figure 15.1. Map showing location of Block 1 in relation to the Kalasaya and other sites mentioned in the text.

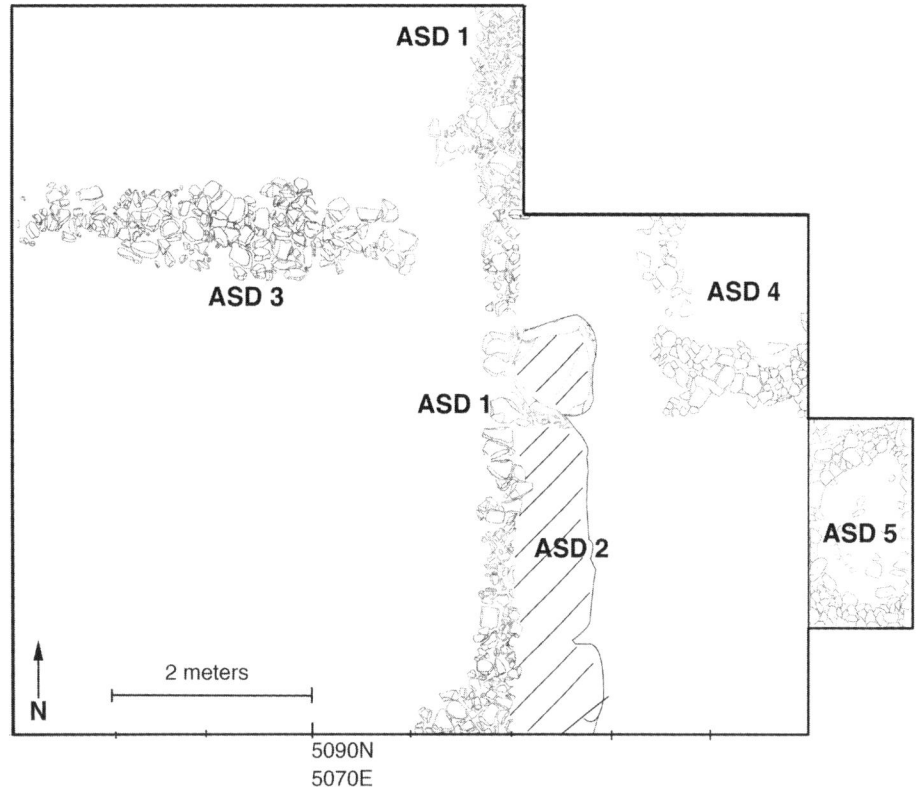

Figure 15.2. Block 1 showing architectural subdivisions (ASD) 1–5 (from Klarich 2005).

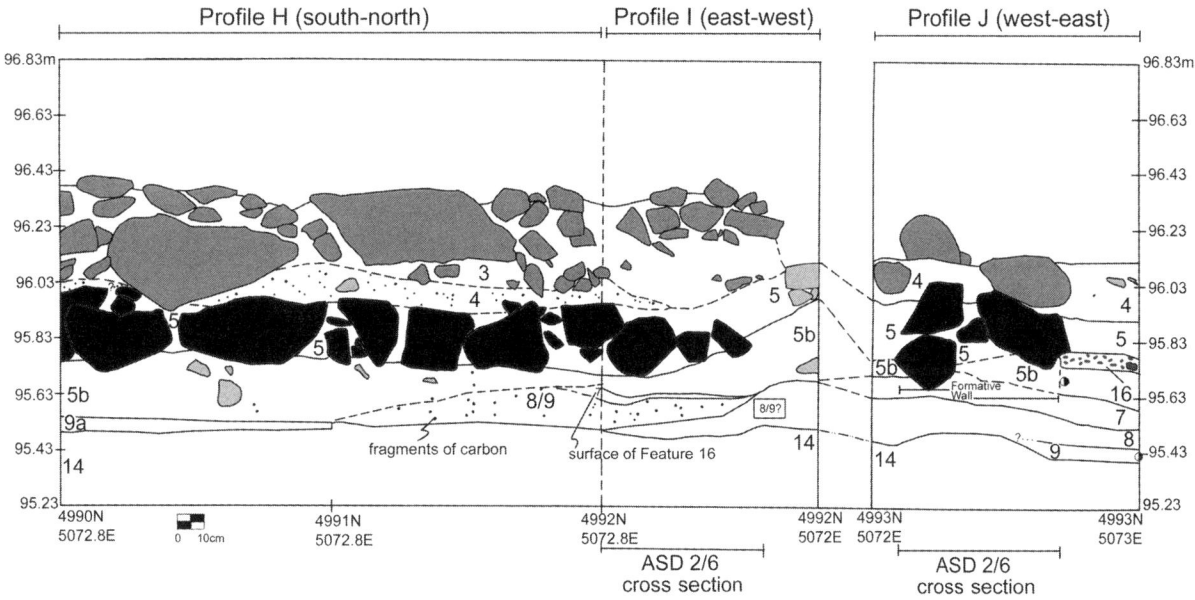

Figure 15.3. Profile of Collao wall in Block 1 (from Klarich 2005).

body sherds) were analyzed, and, due to time constraints, nondiagnostic sherds were counted and weighed. Attribute analysis was conducted using a 10× hand lens on a cleanly broken sherd profile and included the following:

*Vessel Form.* Sherds were sorted into basic restricted and unrestricted vessel categories. When possible, rim orientation, diameter, and rim percentages were recorded. Ceramic tools and other non-vessel artifacts (spindle whorls, scrapers, and so on) were also documented. Assigning vessel form was at times difficult because of the scarcity of complete or re-constructable vessels found during excavation. Only four complete Late Intermediate period vessels were recovered but they were associated with burials from Block 3.

*Paste Composition.* For each sherd, paste inclusions were recorded by size—small (<1 mm), medium (1–2 mm), and large (2–5 mm)—and by material. In addition, clay color was documented using a Munsell Soil Color book.

*Surface Treatment.* Surface treatments—including wiped/smoothed, burnished, polished, and eroded—were recorded for each surface (Table 15.1). Interior and exterior surface colors were determined using a Munsell Soil Color book. The colors of slips and paints were also noted, along with any other decorative techniques (punctate, appliqué, and so on). Sherds that were too eroded or had motifs that were too fragmentary to confidently identify were not included in this analysis.

*Collao, Late Horizon, and Transitional Types*

### Collao

The most predominant ceramic type found in Block 1 is classic Collao pottery, described by Tschopik (1946) and Carlevato (1988). Common vessel types are beakers/tumblers, one-handled jars, two-handled jars, and deep bowls. Miniature bowls and jars were also found. In addition, spindle whorls, scrapers, figurines, and all other non-vessel ceramic artifacts found in Block 1 had Collao paste and thus are dated to the Late Intermediate period. Collao paste is coarse with large inclusions including talc schist, phyllite, and magnetite/hematite (Carlevato 1988:43). These inclusions create a pitted and lumpy surface. Carlevato (1988:43) reports that Collao clay is usually highly oxidized and fired below 900–1000°C. Collao pottery ranges in color from brick red, to orange-red, to pale orange. Some are self-slipped (usually bowls) and the surface is usually smoothed or lightly burnished.

Traditionally, the Collao ceramic type has been broken down into two principal subtypes based on decoration. Collao Plain ceramics lack painted motifs (and sometimes slips as well) and Collao Black on Red ceramics have matte black decoration on a red slip (Figs. 15.4–15.7). Collao Black on Red sherds have linear and curvilinear designs around the necks and bodies of jars, cup exteriors, and bowl interiors. The designs are made of lines of uneven density and often have irregular margins and dripping lines (Tschopik 1946). The decoration is applied with a very thin and weak black paint that is easily removed with

Table 15.1. Surface treatment by ceramic type.*

|  | No Treatment | Wiped/ Smoothed | Burnished | Polished |
|---|---|---|---|---|
| Collao | 5 | 109 | 278 | 40 |
| Transitional | 0 | 12 | 45 | 23 |
| Late Horizon | 0 | 7 | 48 | 47 |

*Eroded/undetermined not included

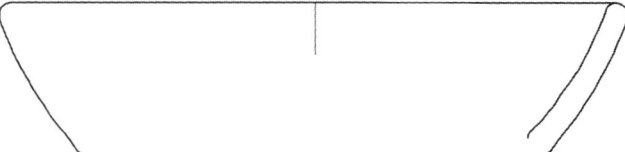

1804/8, d=15 cm, interior and exterior 5YR 6/4 (light orange)

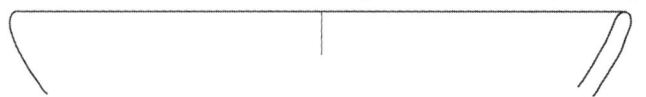

474/2, d=15 cm, interior 2.5YR 6/8 (dark orange), exterior 2.5YR 6/6 (dark orange)

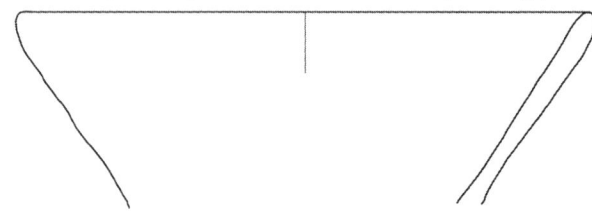

1509/1, d=14 cm, interior and exterior 2.5YR 6.6 (dark orange)

418/1, d=10 cm, interior 5YR 6/6 (light orange), exterior 5YR 6/4 (light orange)

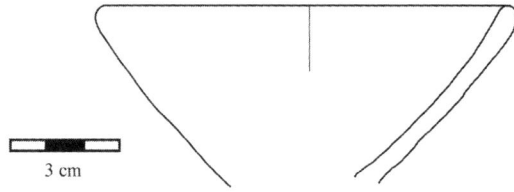

3 cm

Figure 15.4. Collao bowls.

water. Several motifs are found repeatedly on Collao wares. A single undulating line around the interior bowl rim is fairly common. Striped and crosshatched butterfly designs are very frequent around necks, exterior jar rims, and bodies of jars. A ladder motif is also regularly used to decorate the interior rims of bowls. Other decorations include fillets of clay with a row of punctate incisions around bases, appliqué animal figures

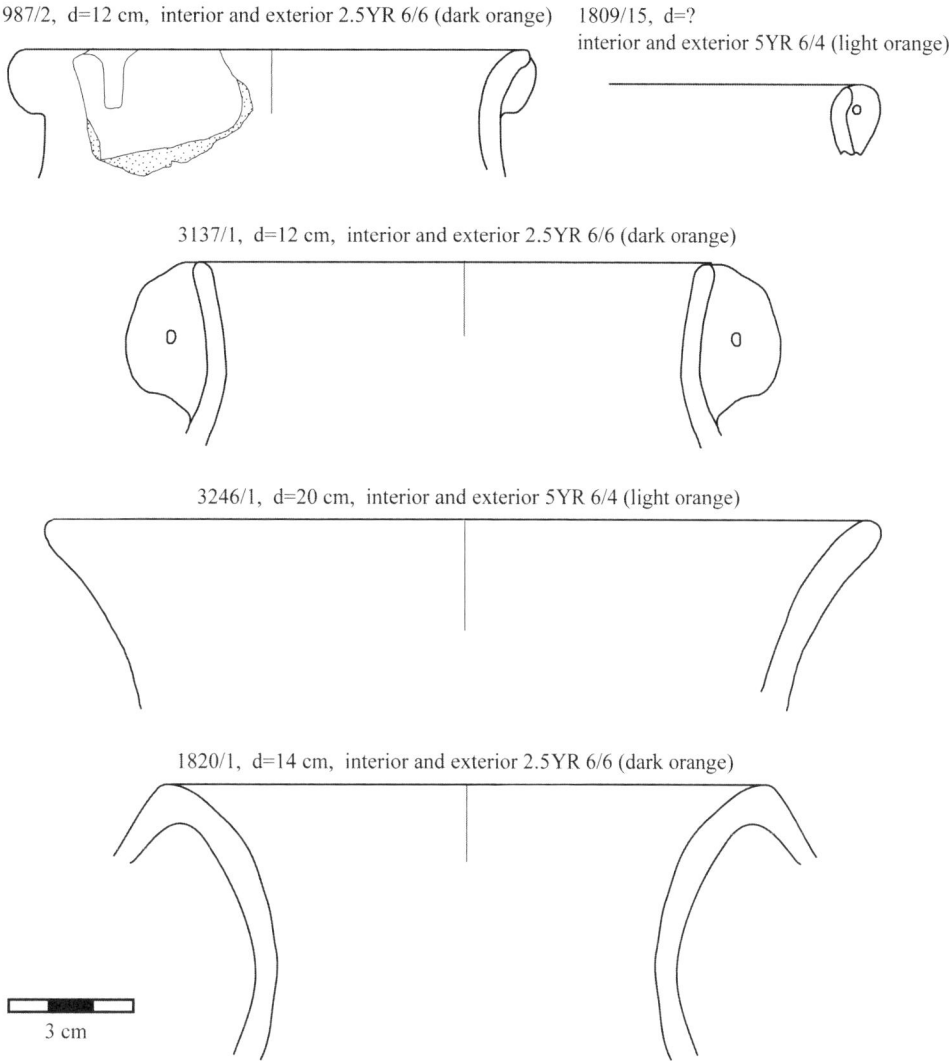

Figure 15.5. Collao jars.

attached to bowl rims and the necks of jars, and handles with incisions (Fig. 15.8).

Asillo ware, a newly defined Collao pottery subtype, was found in the Block 1 assemblage. This ware is most common in the area near Asillo and Azángaro, although the full extent of its distribution is not yet known. Asillo wares are tentatively restricted to jars. As described by Arkush (2005:660), this ware can be distinguished from Collao wares by two characteristics. First, Asillo jars commonly have a branching plant motif that travels down from the rim to the neck. This motif also occurs on handles (Fig. 15.9). Secondly, this motif is frequently accompanied by vertical and horizontal appliqué bands with angular punctate. Asillo wares from Block 1 are made of Collao paste and received little surface treatment.

*Late Horizon*

Late Horizon sherds were also present in the Block 1 assemblage. Vessel forms include shallow bowls, aryballos, and jars. The paste is finer with fewer, smaller inclusions and a small subset was made from fine kaolin paste. The surfaces are either burnished or polished. Late Horizon wares are characterized by well-executed motifs on the interior of bowls and the exterior of jars. Various slip colors are used and polychrome decoration is common. Most motifs fall into the Sillustani, Chucuito, and local

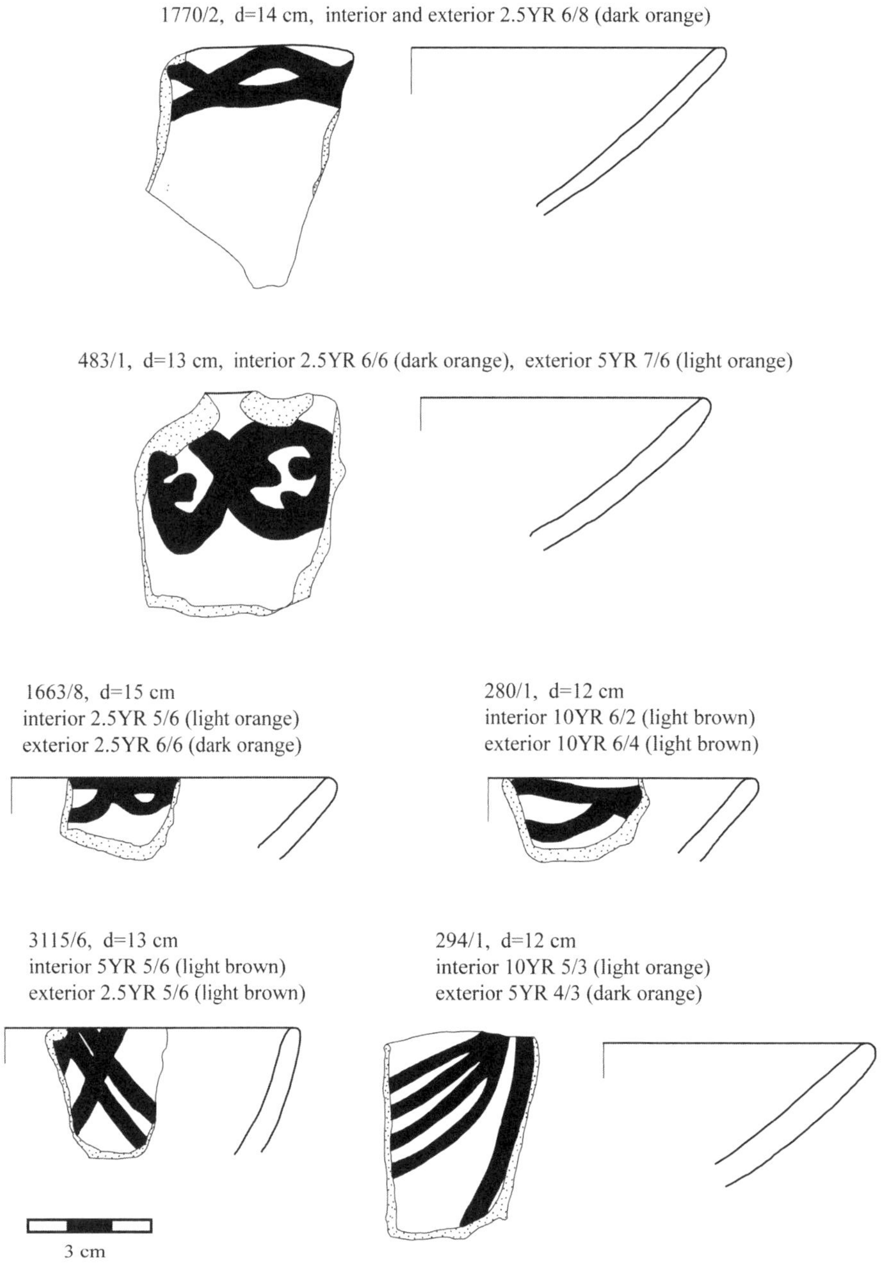

1770/2, d=14 cm, interior and exterior 2.5YR 6/8 (dark orange)

483/1, d=13 cm, interior 2.5YR 6/6 (dark orange), exterior 5YR 7/6 (light orange)

1663/8, d=15 cm
interior 2.5YR 5/6 (light orange)
exterior 2.5YR 6/6 (dark orange)

280/1, d=12 cm
interior 10YR 6/2 (light brown)
exterior 10YR 6/4 (light brown)

3115/6, d=13 cm
interior 5YR 5/6 (light brown)
exterior 2.5YR 5/6 (light brown)

294/1, d=12 cm
interior 10YR 5/3 (light orange)
exterior 5YR 4/3 (dark orange)

3 cm

Figure 15.6. Collao Black on Red bowls.

3039/2, d=13 cm, interor and exterior 10R 6/4 (red brown)

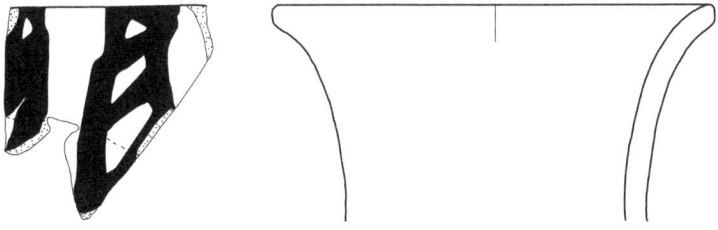

3741/9, interior 5YR 6/6 (light orange), exterior 2.5YR 5/8 (dark orange)

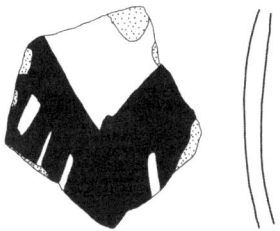

3025/6, interior 5YR 4/1 (dark brown), exterior 5YR 6/6 (light orange)

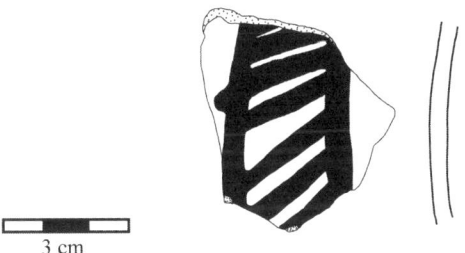

136/4, d=14 cm, interior and exterior 2.5YR 5/8 (dark orange)

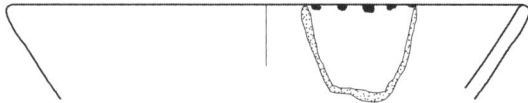

439/3, d=12 cm, interior and exterior 2.5YR 5/8 (dark orange)

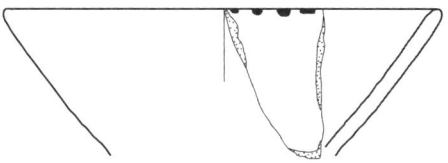

3021/4, interior 10R 6/4 (light brown), exterior 5YR 7/2 (light orange)

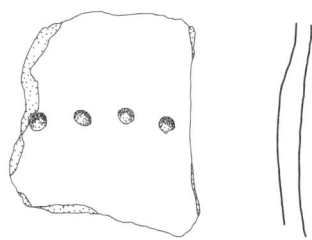

3065/5, interior and exterior 10R 6/4 (red brown)

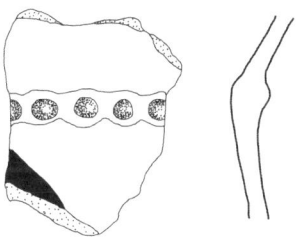

1775/19, interior 2.5YR 5/6 (light orange), exterior 2.5YR 6/6 (light orange)

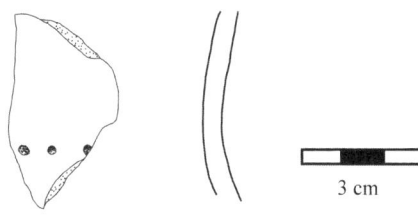

Figure 15.7. Collao Black on Red jars.

Figure 15.8. Collao pottery: rim tics and punctates.

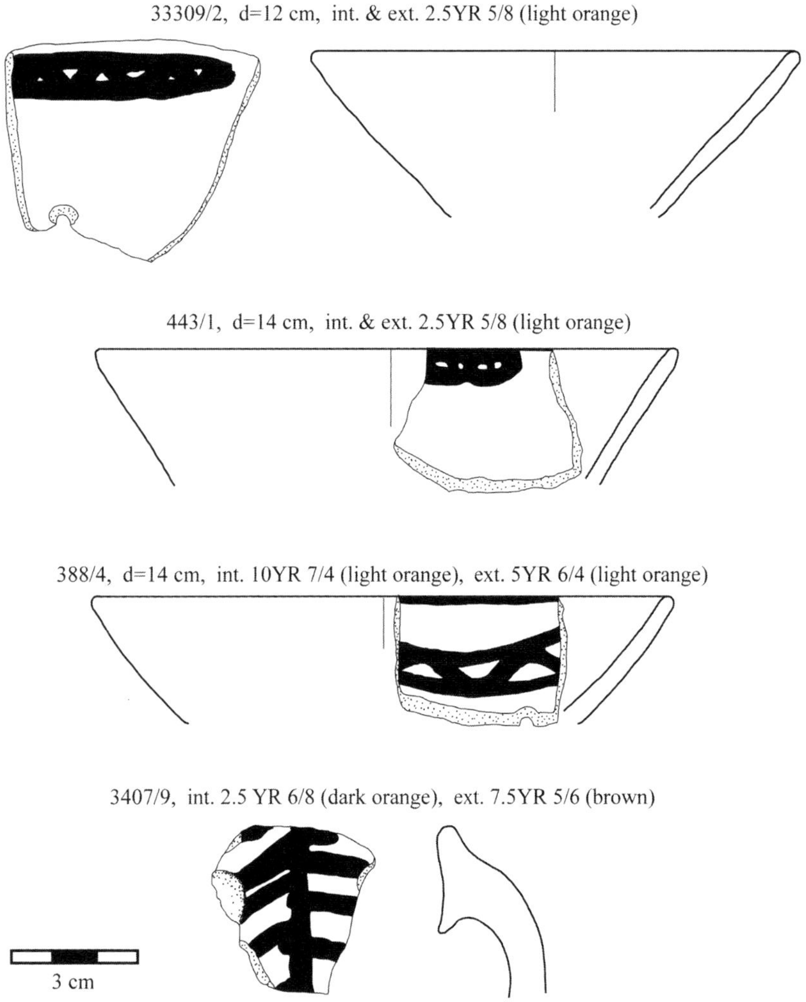

33309/2, d=12 cm, int. & ext. 2.5YR 5/8 (light orange)

443/1, d=14 cm, int. & ext. 2.5YR 5/8 (light orange)

388/4, d=14 cm, int. 10YR 7/4 (light orange), ext. 5YR 6/4 (light orange)

3407/9, int. 2.5 YR 6/8 (dark orange), ext. 7.5YR 5/6 (brown)

3 cm

Figure 15.9. Asillo pottery.

Inca substyles. Fillets, punctate, and incisions are not common and no examples were found in the Pukara collection. No Cusco Inca sherds were found and there were very few local Inca pieces. The Late Horizon assemblage clearly differs from Collao pottery in paste, finish, decoration, and overall execution.

*Transitional*

There is a third group of sherds that are not clearly Collao or Late Horizon. In fact, these sherds, provisionally labeled Transitional, seem to fall between these two well-documented wares in a few ways. While no complete vessels were found, deep bowl and jar fragments were uncovered (Figs. 15.10, 15.11). In general, the sherds are burnished and often polished while the paste is finer than Collao but not as fine as Late Horizon sherds. The decoration is better executed than the Collao wares and consists of linear and curvilinear motifs that more closely resemble Collao designs than Late Horizon ones.

*Summary of Attribute Analysis*

Based on the ceramic types and their associated attributes, some general trends can be discerned from the Block 1 ceramic assemblage. First, each ware had a relatively limited distribution of forms. Most bowls were medium in size and came in deep and shallow varieties. The range of bowl rim diameters remained fairly constant over time at 11–16 cm (Fig. 15.12). Block 1 also had a handful of jar varieties, including a few Inca aryballo jars.

Secondly, in terms of paste, the Collao, Transitional, and Late Horizon wares were fairly consistent, with only minor variations in inclusion size. The most marked change in paste over time was a decrease in inclusion size from the coarser Collao to the finer Inca. Some paste recipes excluded mica and black inclusions but there were no temporal, spatial, or functional patterns associated with their distribution. The only exception was the small handful of Late Horizon kaolin paste sherds.

Thirdly, there was a wide range of surface treatments represented in the Block 1 assemblage. The majority of the sherds were smoothed or burnished. Most Collao pottery was either smoothed or burnished while the majority of Transitional and Late Horizon wares were either burnished or polished. The number of smoothed and burnished sherds decreases over time as the quantity of polished sherds increases. Thus, pottery in Block 1 received more intensive surface treatment over time. Decoration became more refined over time as well. The majority of the decorated wares from Block 1 had motifs executed in a weak black paint. Over time, other colors were introduced and polychrome pottery became more abundant by the Late Horizon.

*Temporal and Spatial Distributions*

In Block 1, Collao pottery dominates the post-Formative assemblages in every event horizon (Table 15.2). However, the percentage of the Transitional wares increases over time, as does the percentage of Late Horizon sherds. This suggests that the Transitional wares could be placed temporally between the Collao and the Late Horizon and may represent a later Late Intermediate period ware. The small proportion of Late Horizon sherds was not entirely surprising considering most of the Inca occupation was located under the modern town of Pucará.

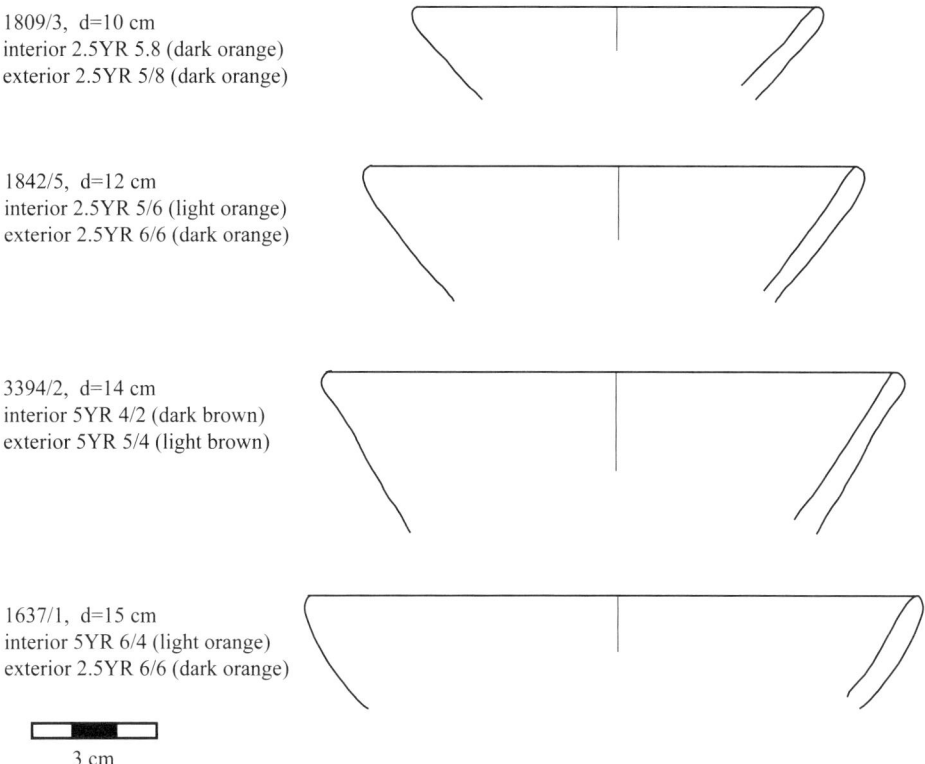

Figure 15.10. Transitional period bowls.

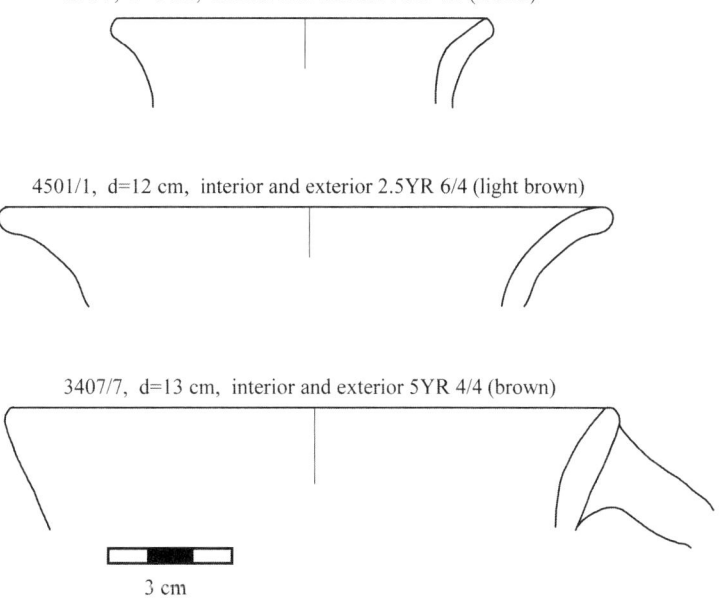

Figure 15.11. Transitional period jars.

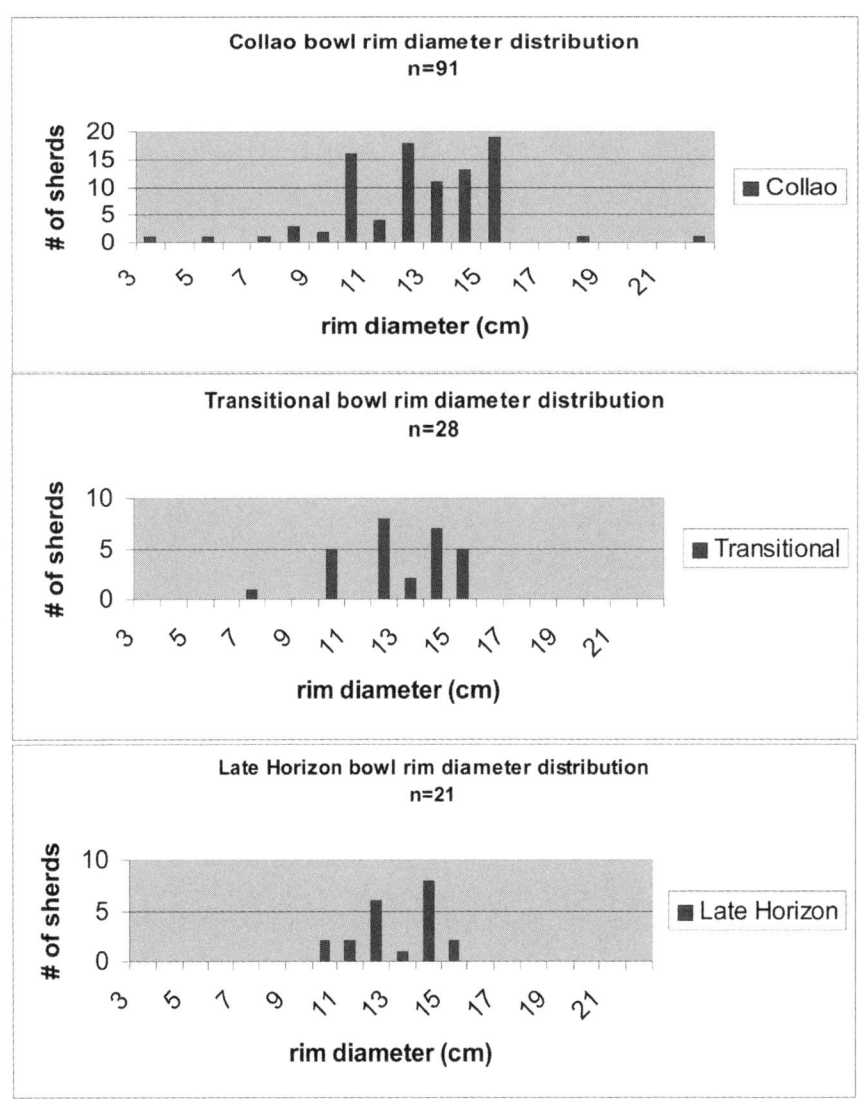

Figure 15.12. Bowl rim diameter distribution.

Although Transitional and Late Horizon wares were introduced over time, they never replaced Collao pottery. The high proportion of Collao ceramics throughout the post-Formative occupation of Block 1 supports Carlevato's argument that Collao ceramic technology (paste type and vessel form) remained fairly consistent over time and even after the Late Intermediate period (see Carlevato 1988).

The Transitional wares also fall between Collao and Late Horizon types in terms of form distribution (Table 15.3). The Collao sub-assemblage comprises around 62% bowls and 38% jars but during the Late Horizon, these percentages change to 90% and 10%, respectively. The Transitional wares fall between that range with 77% bowls and 23% jars. The different proportions of bowls to jars over time are statistically significant ($\chi^2 = 35.184$, $p < .001$). These differences in form distribution between wares suggest that the Collao and the Transitional wares were probably used in a different context than the Late Horizon wares. The Late Horizon form distribution suggests an emphasis on activities involving bowls, such as food service and feasting instead of food storage or preparation. The different distribution of vessel forms between the Collao and the Transitional may bolster Frye and de la Vega's proposal that an elite group had emerged late in the Late Intermediate period and gained influence through feasting ceremonies. In addition, there is evidence that the relative frequencies of different functional classes changed over time. Bowls make up the bulk of all event assemblages (60–80%). In

Table 15.2. Temporal distribution of the Pukara ceramic assemblage.

|  | Collao | Transitional | Late Horizon | Other | Total |
|---|---|---|---|---|---|
| Fill Episode 1 | 154 | 38 | 35 | 7 | 234 |
| Fill Episode 2 | 207 | 27 | 41 | 11 | 286 |
| Occupation 1W | 68 | 19 | 12 | 7 | 106 |
| Occupation 1E | 16 | 3 | 0 | 4 | 23 |
| Occupation 2 | 63 | 8 | 11 | 1 | 83 |
| Fill Episode 3 | 16 | 5 | 3 | 0 | 24 |

Table 15.3. Distribution of vessel forms by ceramic types.

|  | Bowls | Jars |
|---|---|---|
| Collao | 278 (62%) | 170 (38%) |
| Transitional | 72 (77%) | 21 (23%) |
| Late Horizon | 94 (90%) | 10 (10%) |

Table 15.4. Temporal distribution of vessel forms.

|  | Block 1 Western Side | Block 1 Eastern Side |
|---|---|---|
| bowls | 266 (68%) | 81 (56%) |
| jars | 110 (28%) | 59 (41%) |
| other | 13 (4%) | 5 (3%) |

fact, the percentage of bowls increases over time as jars drop out. This could indicate changes in activity patterns or function, change in the use of or need of one form over the other.

Combining the architectural and ceramic data from Block 1 generates a number of spatial and temporal patterns. Although the western and eastern sides of the wall have different architectural styles, the ceramic data suggest that both sides were occupied at the same time. This is based on the observation that they have almost identical distributions of Collao, Transitional, and Late Horizon wares. So, if the difference in architectural style is not temporal, a functional explanation can be suggested. Additional support for this interpretation comes from comparing the form distribution of these two areas. The western side has 68% bowls and 28% jars whereas the eastern side has 56% bowls and 41% jars (Table 15.4). This difference is statistically significant ($\chi^2 = 7.6635$, $.05 > p > .02$) and suggests that the eastern side had a greater focus on storage, cooking and the range of domestic tasks than did the western side. The western side's assemblage can be associated more with a serving function. However, these distinctions need further investigation.

Finally, Carlevato's work suggests an increase in textile production during the Late Intermediate period at Pukara. Carlevato (1988) reports an increase in the quantity of spindle whorls at Pukara during the Late Intermediate period and believes that this relates to an increase in textile production. She links this to an increased access to camelid fibers during this period of pastoralism. Although Collao spindle whorls were found in Block 1 ($n = 5$), there are not enough data to support or contradict that argument.

## Discussion

Artifact and architecture data from Block 1 offer a number of insights into the Colla, including the post-Formative occupation of Pukara as well as the sociopolitical development of the polity during the Late Intermediate period. With the reuse of a major Formative center and its impressive monumental architecture, the Late Intermediate period occupation of Pukara was unlike any other known Collao site. Ceramic data point to a change in activity over time in Block 1: an increased focus on food serving and possibly feasting within the Late Intermediate period. This finding supports the hypothesis that a Collao elite emerged late in the Late Intermediate period. However, further excavation and investigation are needed to clarify these questions of site use and corresponding issues of sociopolitical complexity.

Block 1 also provides data on Pukara's place in the northern Lake Titicaca Basin settlement pattern during the Late Intermediate period. While *pukaras*, small habitational clusters, and cemeteries are the most common Collao site types, Pukara cannot be easily classified as one of these. It may be a habitational cluster, but one much larger than those that have been recorded. It is possible that Pukara was a Collao center during the Late Intermediate period; the wide distribution of Late Intermediate period artifacts on the surface does imply a substantial Collao presence at Pukara although the full extent of that occupation is unclear. Unfortunately, a paucity of published reports makes comparisons with similar sites difficult. The question of when Collao occupied Pukara remains undecided but based on Arkush's and Frye and de la Vega's work, it might have emerged late in the Late Intermediate period along with other large sites in the region.

Lastly, the ceramic data from Block 1 contribute to our understanding of the post-Formative chronology of the northern basin and of Pukara in particular. Although Tiwanaku artifacts have been recorded in the region, there is no evidence of a Middle Horizon occupation at Pukara (see Stanish 2003:186–89). Nor were there any Huaña artifacts found, although this ceramic type and culture is provisional (see Stanish 2003:198). This supports the argument that after the fall of the Pukara culture, the site was abandoned for hundreds of years, until the Collao occupation. In addition, the Transitional wares may help further refine our understanding of the Late Intermediate period. Though once conceived as a long epoch of homeostasis, this period likely encompassed gradual shifts in sociopolitical complexity. The Transitional wares may correspond to that change but the nature of that change and how it corresponds to emerging elite class remains unclear.

## Conclusion

Excavations at Pukara have revealed a little-known Late Intermediate period site type as well as a new transitional ceramic style that falls between the classic Collao and the later Late Horizon traditions. Analysis of the ceramic assemblage indicates a shift in activity in Block 1 from one of food production and storage to one of serving and feasting. Along with recent investigations in the basin, this chapter suggests that toward the end of the Late Intermediate period in the northern Titicaca Basin, an elite class emerged through ceremonial feasting and the creation of political alliances. It is these more sociopolitically complex groups— that later fiercely fought against Inca attempts to conquer this region—that have been well documented in the ethnohistoric record. As part of a growing body of Late Intermediate period research, the study of the Collao occupation of Pukara contributes to the changing perceptions of this complex and volatile era in Andean prehistory.

## Notes

1. "Colla" refers to the ethnic and political group whereas the term "Collao" is used when referring to aspects of that culture.

2. Although they share the same name, fortified hilltop sites, or *pukaras*, are distinct from the Pukara culture and the archaeological site of Pukara.

3. The modern town is Pucará but the archaeological site and culture are called Pukara.

## References Cited

Arkush, Elizabeth
2005   Colla Fortified Sites: Warfare and Regional Power in the Late Prehispanic Titicaca Basin, Peru. PhD dissertation, Department of Anthropology, University of California, Los Angeles.
2008   War, chronology, and causality in the Titicaca Basin. *Latin American Antiquity* 19(4):339–73.

Bandelier, Adolph
1905   The aboriginal ruins at Sillustani, Peru. *American Anthropologist* 7(1):49–69.

Carlevato, Denise
1988   Late ceramics from Pucara, Peru. *Expedition* 30(3):39–45.

Cieza de León, Pedro
1984 [1553]   *La crónica del Perú. Crónicas de America 4*, edited by Manuel Ballesteros. Historia 16. Madrid.

Cobo, Bernabé
1979 [1653]   *History of the Inca Empire*, translated and edited by Roland Hamilton. University of Texas Press, Austin.
1990 [1653]   *Inca Religion and Customs*, translated and edited by Roland Hamilton. University of Texas Press, Austin.

Frye, Kirk Lawrence
1997   Political centralization in the Altiplano period in the southwestern Titicaca Basin. In *Archaeological Survey in the Juli-Desaguadero Region of Lake Titicaca Basin, Southern Peru*, edited by C. Stanish, E. de la Vega, L. Steadman, L. Onofre, C. Chávez Justo, P. Calisaya, K. Lawrence Frye, and M. Seddon, pp. 129–41. Fieldiana no. 29. Field Museum of Natural History, Chicago.

Frye, Kirk, and Edmundo de la Vega
2005   The Altiplano period in the Titicaca Basin. In *Advances in Titicaca Basin Archaeology–1*, edited by C. Stanish, A. Cohen, and M. Aldenderfer, pp. 173–84. Cotsen Institute of Archaeology, University of California, Los Angeles.

Graffam, Gray
1992   Beyond state collapse: Rural history, raised fields, and pastoralism in the South Andes. *American Anthropologist* 94(4):882–904.

Hyslop, John
1977   Hilltop cities in Peru. *Archaeology* 30(4):218–25. New York.

Julien, Catherine
1983   *Hatunqolla: A View of Inca Rule from the Lake Titicaca Region*. University of California Publications in Anthropology, vol. 15. University of California Press, Berkeley.

Kidder, Alfred II
1943 *Some Early Sites in the Northern Lake Titicaca Basin*. Papers of the Peabody Museum of American Archaeology and Ethnology, Harvard University, vol. 27, no. 1. Cambridge, MA.

Klarich, Elizabeth
2005 From the Monumental to the Mundane: Defining Early Leadership Strategies at Late Formative Pukara, Peru. PhD dissertation, Department of Anthropology, University of California, Santa Barbara.

Paredes, Rolando
1985 Excavaciones arqueológicas en Pukara, Puno. Thesis, Universidad Nacional, San Antonio Abad de Cusco.

Sarmiento de Gamboa, Pedro
1999 [1572] *History of the Incas*, translated and edited by Sir Clements Markham. Dover Publications, Mineola.

Stanish, Charles
2003 *Ancient Titicaca: The Evolution of Complex Society in Southern Peru and Northern Bolivia*. University of California Press, Berkeley.
2009 The Tiwanaku occupation of the northern Titicaca Basin. In *Andean Civilization: A Tribute to Michael E. Moseley*, edited by J. Marcus and P. R. Williams, pp. 145–64. Cotsen Institute of Archaeology Press, University of California, Los Angeles.

Stanish, Charles, Amanda Cohen, Edmundo de la Vega, Elizabeth Arkush, Cecilia Chávez, Aimée Plourde, and Carol Schultze
2005 Archaeological reconnaissance in the northern Titicaca Basin. In *Advances in Titicaca Basin Archaeology–1*, edited by C. Stanish, A. Cohen, and M. Aldenderfer, pp. 289–316. Cotsen Institute of Archaeology, University of California, Los Angeles.

Stanish, Charles, Edmundo de la Vega, and Kirk Lawrence Frye
1993 Domestic architecture on Lupaqa area sites in the Department of Puno. In *Domestic Architecture in South Central Andean Prehistory*, edited by M. Aldenderfer, pp. 83–93. University of Iowa Press, Iowa City.

Tschopik, Marion
1946 *Some Notes on the Archaeology of the Department of Puno, Peru*. Papers of the Peabody Museum of American Archaeology and Ethnology, Harvard University, vol. 27, no. 3. Cambridge, MA.

Wheeler, Jane, and Elías Mujica
1981 *Prehistoric Pastoralism in the Lake Titicaca Basin, Peru, 1979–1980 Field Season*. Report submitted to National Science Foundation, grant no. BNS 7015119.

# Chapter 16

# The Development of Society and Status in the Late Prehispanic Titicaca Basin (circa AD 1000–1535)

R. Alan Covey

## Introduction

As archaeologists develop more dynamic perspectives on archaic states, it is increasingly apparent that the tempo and scale of state growth, consolidation, and decline are influenced by negotiations of unity and diversity. At their capitals, states simultaneously promote a shared civic identity and a set of power relations of unprecedented unevenness. Beyond the core, the administrative relationships between local elites and state rulers often more closely resemble a crazy quilt of personality-driven policies—and ad hoc solutions to their unanticipated consequences—than a well-executed blueprint for regional political and economic efficiency. The dynamics of these interactions may confound the expectations of evolutionary typologies, but they are critical to understanding the long-term development of statecraft, as well as local constructions of society and status.

The Titicaca Basin represents a particularly well researched region where new archaeological data can be brought to such questions. From AD 1000 to 1535, the region experienced (1) the widespread local rejection of state institutions that had developed within the basin over centuries of local elaborations of complexity, (2) the reemergence of new political arrangements and individual status configurations, and (3) local accommodation and exploitation of foreign rule. This chapter first presents region-wide archaeological data at multiple scales of analysis for each period in question, and then concludes with a consideration of important developments.

## The Tiwanaku-Altiplano Transition (ca. AD 1000–1200)

During the Middle Horizon, the Tiwanaku state established relationships of varying intensity with local societies in the Titicaca Basin and nearby regions. These included direct administration, hegemony, and co-option or alliance-building using "soft power"—as seen in the acceptance or emulation of Tiwanaku material culture and religious practices (Goldstein 2005; Stanish 2003:165–203; for a discussion of soft power, see Nye 2004). While areas near the state capital underwent major economic and political reorganization at all levels of their regional settlement systems, other parts of the Titicaca Basin experienced Tiwanaku state influence through existing configurations of complexity.

The regional interconnectedness forged by Tiwanaku began to dissolve around AD 1000. All parts of the Titicaca Basin experienced profound changes at this time, brought on by the universal failure of state economic networks and political administration, as well as the perceived bankruptcy of state-influenced ideology, iconography, and religious values (Janusek 2004a:249–73, 2004b). At the same time, the nature, tempo, and intensity of local transitions away from the Tiwanaku world reflected the cultural and environmental diversity of the Titicaca Basin. While post-Tiwanaku conditions in many parts of the basin exhibit a radical shift away from well-established settlement and subsistence systems (Bandy 2001:235; cf. Stanish 1994:322), such changes should not be viewed as coping mechanisms by survivors of the state, but rather as innovative responses to unpredictably changing political and natural climates.

*Regional Perspectives*

Generally, Altiplano period (ca. AD 1100–1450) survey data indicate a shift from existing settlement hierarchies and established resource management regimes to a more dispersed and shifting use of a wide range of environmental zones (Fig. 16.1; Table 16.1). Major Tiwanaku sites experienced a significant reduction in population and cessation of centrally coordinated political and ritual activity (Bermann 1994; Janusek 2004c). The apparent growth in post-Tiwanaku settlement in the Tiwanaku Valley may be due to dispersal of population from the site of Tiwanaku to dispersed settlements that shifted over time during the Altiplano period. While the Tiwanaku Valley itself saw a marked *increase* in settled area in the Altiplano period (Albarracin-Jordan and Mathews 1990), nearby areas saw considerable declines (Bandy 2001; Bauer and Stanish 2001; Janusek and Kolata 2003; Stanish and Bauer 2004:38–39; cf. Lémuz 2006). Beyond the Tiwanaku heartland, an increase in settled area has been observed in the Altiplano period settlement patterns of the Juli-Pomata and Chucuito-Cutimbo study areas, while the Huancané-Putina region experienced a 760% increase in Altiplano period site counts.

In terms of site counts, settlement continuity is actually high in the Tiwanaku Valley (90.3%, or 306/339 Tiwanaku V sites) and the Katari Valley (77.1%, or 37/48 sites), while it is markedly lower in other areas with a demonstrated Tiwanaku influence, including the Taraco Peninsula (39.1%, or 27/69 sites) and the Island of the Sun (40%, or 10/25 sites). Farther away, the Juli-Pomata survey region saw just under half of Tiwanaku sites continuing to be occupied (48.8%, or 20/41), while preliminary results from the Puno Bay (Schultze and Sosa Alcón 2003) indicate a dispersal of settlement from large sites near the lakeshore or important trade routes. Such patterns contrast significantly with results from the Huancané-Putina survey region, where all Tiwanaku period habitation sites have an Altiplano period component (*n* = 57).

Stanish (2003:216) has noted the proliferation of hamlets and dispersed villages in the Altiplano period, concomitant with a marked reduction of mean site size and the flattening of regional settlement hierarchies throughout the basin (Albarracin-Jordan 1992:277; Albarracin-Jordan and Mathews 1990:191–92; Bandy 2001:235; Frye 1997; Frye and de la Vega 2005:176–80; Hyslop 1976:132; Mathews 1992; Stanish 1992:86–97, 1994, 2003:204–35; Stanish and Bauer 2004:37–39; Stanish et al. 1997:55–57). Regional projects have also identified new settlements in previously unoccupied environmental zones, especially higher elevation agricultural zones and pasturelands at a distance from the lakeshore. This is frequently considered to constitute an economic response to fluctuating (and generally drier) climatic conditions, with intensive production regimes and political hierarchies abandoned in favor of localized kin-based systems focused on local subsistence self-sufficiency through the management of herding and broad-spectrum horticulture. The decline of political economy in the Titicaca Basin did not mean the complete cessation of intensive production—raised field agriculture continued to be practiced in some parts of the basin during the Altiplano period, although it appears to have ceased by the time of the Inka occupation (Albarracin-Jordan 1992:282; Erickson 1999; Graffam 1994; Janusek 2004c:196; Stanish 2006).

The regional data signal the failure of the Tiwanaku state, the abandonment of its monumental constructions and state iconography, and the dissolution of interregional arrangements throughout the Titicaca Basin. Given the local variations in Tiwanaku power throughout the basin, it is significant that virtually all local societies broke with established hierarchies and economic practices rather than coalescing into secondary states to challenge Tiwanaku's regional preeminence. This does suggest that fluctuating precipitation, temperatures, and lake levels at this time were intense enough across the basin to promote new risk-management regimes based on kin affiliation rather than social or political inequality. While some areas (namely, the Taraco Peninsula and the Island of the Sun) appear to have experienced population declines, the population levels and settlement dispersal indicate that this transition reflects an embrace of heterarchy (and not anarchy), and was sufficient for maintaining significant population levels in the Titicaca Basin in the centuries that followed.

*Site Layout*

The shift to household- or kin-based subsistence management is seen not only in regional patterning, but also in how settlements were laid out and occupied. The dispersed villages and hamlets typical of the early Altiplano period lack evidence of central planning (for example, formal streets or accessways, public spaces) and internal specialization or hierarchy. Of course, it is difficult to do more than comment on the absence of such characteristics, as almost all sites are identified through surface ceramics rather than well-preserved architecture. During the Tiwanaku-Altiplano transition, the most significant distinction between settlements would be between (1) new hamlets and villages established for localized economic activities and (2) small populations continuing to occupy parts of local centers or administrative sites that no longer functioned as such. It is possible that hilltop refuges were established to provide defense in areas where social transformations were associated with violent conflict—these would have been modest precursors to the *pukara* (hill-fort) sites of the late Altiplano period.

*Domestic and Special-Purpose Construction*

More excavation work is needed to articulate the changes in household composition and domestic economy occurring in the Tiwanaku-Altiplano transition. Bermann's excavations at Lukurmata suggest a shift from extended family households under

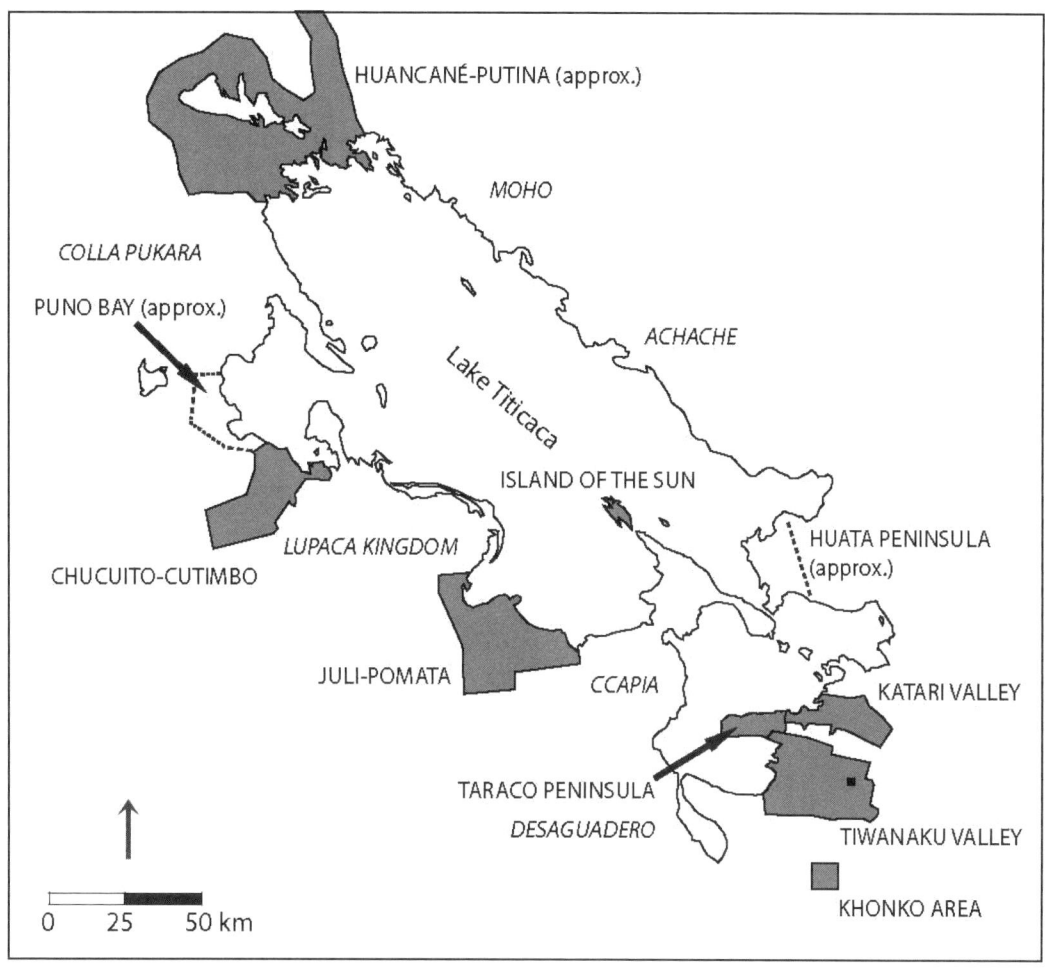

Figure 16.1. The Titicaca Basin, with systematic regional survey regions shaded. Approximate areas of regional reconnaissance projects are noted in italics.

Table 16.1. Major Titicaca Basin survey regions, with site counts for Tiwanaku, Altiplano, and Inka period occupations.

| Survey Region | Area (km²) | Tiwanaku | Altiplano | Inka | References |
| --- | --- | --- | --- | --- | --- |
| Tiwanaku Valley | 400 | 339 | 964 | 492 | Albarracin-Jordan and Mathews 1990 |
| Katari Valley | 102 | 48 | 145 | 79 | Janusek and Kolata 2003; Bandy and Janusek 2005 |
| Taraco Peninsula | 85 | 69 | 83 | 125 | Bandy 2001 |
| Island of the Sun | 21 | 25 | 22 | 78 | Stanish and Bauer 2004 |
| Juli-Pomata | 360 | 41 | 140 | 242 | Stanish et al. 1997 |
| Chucuito-Cutimbo | 200 | 22 | 52 | 110 | Frye 2005 |
| Huancané-Putina | ~1000 | 57 | 433 | 319 | Stanish and de la Vega 2004 |

Tiwanaku to single-family residences (1993:235). Evidence from the Tiwanaku Valley indicates that houses were often built of perishable materials, or with stone that was removed from Tiwanaku constructions (Albarracin-Jordan 1992:277–84). Low investments in house construction are consistent with excavation evidence for shorter duration of occupation (Janusek 2004c:199), indicating a much more shifting settlement pattern. There is considerably more evidence for discussing domestic architecture and special-purpose constructions toward the end of the Altiplano period (below).

*Burial Patterns*

Burial practices show significant changes following the decline of the Tiwanaku state. Elite shaft tombs and sacrificial burials described at the state capital (e.g., Couture 2004) are not reported for the succeeding Altiplano period, although low-status cist tombs with few or no grave offerings are common before and after the Tiwanaku-Altiplano transition. The proliferation of above-ground mortuary constructions (*chullpa* structures and slab-cist tombs) is a post-Tiwanaku innovation (e.g., Frye and de la Vega 2005:180–83; Stanish 2003:200) that is most easily addressed in the discussion of the later Altiplano period (below).

*Ceramic Production and Distribution*

As state institutions failed, Tiwanaku state styles were gradually replaced by a more localized pattern of ceramic production and distribution in the Titicaca Basin (Fig. 16.2). As Janusek (2004c:196) notes, state iconography and the assemblage used for public eating and drinking events disappeared, while the decorative focus shifted to personal bowls, small pitchers, and other modest-sized vessels that reflect local production and distribution. The diversification of black-on-red and tricolor styles during the Altiplano period is comparable to similar developments occurring throughout the Andean highlands after AD 1000 (see Covey 2008). Several local styles dating to the Altiplano period have been identified throughout the Titicaca Basin, including Kekerana, Asillo, Collao, Sillustani, Pucarani, Kelluyo, and Early Pacajes (Arkush 2005a:291–301; Albarracin-Jordan 1992:272–73; Bandy 2001:230–32; Bennett 1950; Frye and de la Vega 2005:176–77; Lumbreras and Amat 1966; Mathews 1992:186–87; Rivera 1991:34–38; Rydén 1947; Schiappacasse et al. 1989; Stanish et al. 1997; Tschopik 1946). The distribution of these styles is fairly localized, with overlapping distribution areas of perhaps 50 km or so (Arkush 2005a; Bermann 1993:132).

The emergence of multiple local styles reflects less specialized craft production (but see Albarracin-Jordan 1992:272–73), as well as regional economies characterized by limited long-distance exchange. Titicaca Basin pottery is found infrequently at sites on the Pacific and Amazonian slopes, and limited amounts of pottery from those regions are found in the altiplano.

Figure 16.2. Altiplano period ceramic styles. Distribution of these styles is generally restricted to 50 km or so of the location of production.

*Other Material Culture*

The Tiwanaku-Altiplano transition is noteworthy for the disappearance of other artisan products and long-distance exchange goods. Stone sculptures and monoliths cease to be produced, and goods such as hallucinogenic paraphernalia are not known following the Tiwanaku collapse.

**Late Altiplano Period Developments (ca. AD 1300–1450)**

According to Colonial documentary sources, Inka incursions into the northwestern Titicaca Basin began in the late fourteenth century or early fifteenth century, and several generations of conquest and repression of local insurrection were required for the consolidation of imperial administration over the basin by the late fifteenth century. Inka informants describe imperial expeditions against centralized Aymara states or regional confederations united under the rulers of groups such as the Colla, Lupaqa, and Pacaje, and archaeologists have generally accepted the basic outline of these narratives. Arkush's (2005) study of fortified sites (*pukaras*) in the Colla region has generated invaluable data challenging the Inka characteristic of their Titicaca Basin rivals, and her radiocarbon dates from several *pukaras* (2005:720–26) indicate a late intensification of regional conflict and fortification construction. On the basis of this and other studies, the classic manifestations of Altiplano period societies—defensive *pukara* settlement and widespread use of *chullpa* structures for mortuary remains—are treated here as characteristic of the latter part of the period (ca. AD 1300–1450) rather than the period as a whole.

## Regional Perspectives

The emergence of major *pukaras*—well-fortified sites on hilltops or ridges with permanent settlement—may represent the most significant transformation of the regional settlement systems established in the early Altiplano period (from AD 1000 to 1200) (Fig. 16.3). Radiocarbon dates now indicate that while refuge sites and small *pukaras* were present earlier on, it was only after around AD 1300 that major investments in fortification were made at sites reaching impressive sizes (Arkush 2005a:278; Frye and de la Vega 2005:178; Zovar 2007a). Increases in population size, intensification of conflict, and prioritized investment in defense are not limited to the Titicaca Basin, but are part of a pattern seen in many parts of the Andean highlands in the century or so leading up to the earliest Inka imperial campaigns (see Covey 2008). The residential areas of the largest *pukara* sites are large enough to signify the emergence of local centers dominating a number of modest local settlement hierarchies (Arkush 2005a; Frye 1997; Frye and de la Vega 2005; Hyslop 1976; Stanish 2003; Stanish et al. 1997). The distribution of large *pukaras* suggests that these sites provided defense—and probably managed local economies more centrally—for people living within a few hours' walk (perhaps about 10 km) of the fortified center. The distribution of major *pukara* sites reflects the divergence of local settlement trajectories in the Titicaca Basin throughout the Altiplano period. The major *pukaras*, which may number in the dozens (Stanish 2003:213), are more common in the Colla and Lupaqa territories than in the former Tiwanaku heartland (Albarracin-Jordan and Mathews 1990:279; Bandy 2001:233; Bauer and Stanish 2001:155; Janusek and Kolata 2003:155). Bennett (1933, 1950) has reported *pukara* sites with several hundred houses in the Achache area on the Omasuyu side of the lake.

## Site Layout

The construction of fortifications stands out as one of the few corporate investments of labor beyond the level of the family or king group during the Altiplano period. The most modest examples include refuges where natural defenses were augmented by limited wall construction, as well as minor *pukaras*—sites with more substantial defensive wall construction, but with limited evidence for sustained habitation (Albarracin-Jordan 1992:282; Arkush 2005a:249–70; Hyslop 1976; Stanish 2003:209–10, 214–16). Such sites may have been established to protect local populations from seasonal raiding throughout the Altiplano period (and earlier in some areas, as evidenced by Formative dates and ceramics). As population grew in parts of the Titicaca Basin in the second half of the Altiplano period, raiding gave way to more intensive and destructive warfare, and Arkush (2005a) argues that the monumentality and complexity

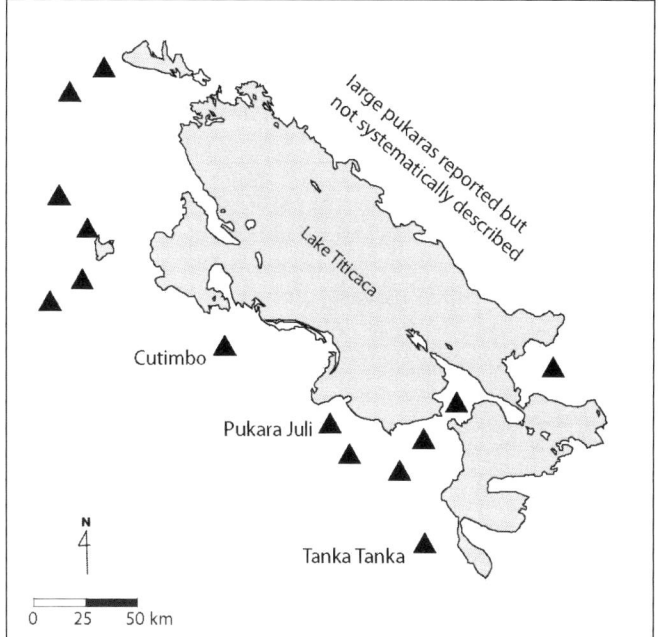

Figure 16.3. Major *pukara* locations, based on Arkush 2005a (Category 5 and 6), Hyslop 1976, and Stanish 2003. Map does not show all possible major *pukara* sites.

of major *pukara* defenses may be read as a measure of the threat posed by intergroup warfare.

Major *pukaras* include defenses (walls, gateways, parapets) that were built to enclose and protect more than just the resident population—at some sites, the walls enclose cemeteries, pasturelands, and agricultural terraces (e.g., Stanish 2003:209). Ringed defensive walls frequently employ a sophisticated combination of natural terrain and built features to protect against attacks, and non-domestic areas sometimes show sectoring that may have been intended to segregate camelid herds or distinguish between the planting areas of different kin groups. Inside the walls, however, the protected interior spaces typically exhibit the absence of a centrally-planned layout of domestic and mortuary areas (Arkush 2005a:221–45, 2006; Frye 1997; Hyslop 1976:341–47; Stanish 2003:211–14). The largest habitation areas are more than 20 ha and have upwards of 500 houses (Arkush 2005a:249–70; Frye 1997:133; Hyslop 1976), and some of these have streets or informal accessways that subdivide domestic areas. Even at sites that appear to have had populations numbering in the low thousands at times, there is evidence for only modest public spaces, while special buildings (palaces, temples) are virtually absent.

## Domestic and Special-Purpose Construction

The residential architecture at late Altiplano period sites in the Titicaca Basin is consistent with broader regional patterning in many neighboring parts of the south-central Andean highlands (Chacama 2005; Covey 2008; Dean 2005; Rivera 1991:34–38,

1993; Schiappacasse et al. 1989; Wernke 2003). Except for the north side of the lake (Bennett 1933, 1950; Tschopik 1946:6–7), houses are almost always single-room circular constructions grouped on terraces or around patio spaces to comprise households (Arkush 2005a:177–81; Beaule 2002; de la Vega 1990; Frye and de la Vega 2005:178; Hyslop 1976; Rydén 1947; Stanish et al. 1993; Bermann 1993:132–33). Houses are invariably of modest size—with diameters of 2 to 7 m—and descriptions of household clusters often have difficulty distinguishing between elite and commoner households (Arkush 2005a:231–38; Bennett 1933; Frye and de la Vega 2005:178; Hyslop 1976; Zovar 2007a). Such distinctions derive from building size and number of structures in a household cluster, as well as masonry techniques used in construction (fieldstones, or in very rare cases, cut stone) and the overall use of stone (that is, slab foundations, lower wall courses, or complete walls). While stone architecture is clearly linked to the *pukara* phenomenon seen in the northern and western part of the Titicaca Basin, surveyors in the former Tiwanaku heartland report very little architecture at their sites.

Non-domestic construction includes storage structures, defensive works, special-purpose buildings, and tombs. Small circular structures that may have been used for storage are present within household clusters at several *pukara* sites, indicating subsistence management at the level of the household rather than the polity (Arkush 2005a; Frye and de la Vega 2005:178–79; Hyslop 1976). While families managed the preservation and consumption of food surpluses at *pukara* sites, they joined other households and kin groups to construct massive defensive works (Arkush 2005a; Hyslop 1976; Stanish 2003:214–16). As noted above, defenses could be quite massive, and the necessary construction labor would have required repeated organization of a site's population (and in some cases, populations from nearby areas that presumably relied on the *pukara* as a refuge) (Arkush 2005a). While warfare united the various groups residing in large communities, there is little evidence of other civic institutions at the largest Altiplano period sites. Special buildings (larger than average, with unique plans) are present at some of the later *pukara* sites, and platforms have been identified both at *pukaras* and valley-bottom settlements (e.g., Albarracin-Jordan and Mathews 1990:142; Arkush 2005a:240–43). The variability in special architecture throughout the Titicaca Basin suggests localized religious or political practices and the absence of an integrated elite stratum at the regional level.

*Burial Patterns*

By the late Altiplano period, regional burial patterns were quite different from what is known for Tiwanaku times. While individual cist burials continued to be made, the mortuary emphasis shifted to group burials, including (1) burials in caves or rock outcrops; (2) slab-cist tombs, consisting of an underground crypt marked on the surface by a circle of upright slabs; and (3) above-ground mortuary structures of a number of different construction types (typically lumped together under the term *chullpa*) (Albarracin-Jordan 1992:310; Arkush 2005a:181–84, 238–40; de la Vega et al. 2005; Frye and de la Vega 2005:180–83; Hyslop 1976, 1977; Stanish 2003:229–35; Tschopik 1946). The shift to above-ground facilities and group burials shows a continuing concern on the part of kin groups for asserting their place on a landscape where populations were growing and economic production required adequate resources for grazing camelids and cultivating small plots of land. Such practices are part of larger regional shifts in burial practice and group identity in the south-central Andean highlands and beyond (Covey 2008; Isbell 1997).

Although the *chullpa* is often treated as a hallmark of Altiplano period groups in the Titicaca Basin, there is evidence that mortuary patterns varied over time and space. *Chullpas* are not common in the former Tiwanaku heartland (Albarracin-Jordan 1992:309), and Arkush notes that slab-cist tombs may be a more common burial type in the Colla region (2005a:238–40). As discussed below, *chullpa* use continued in Inka and early Colonial times, while mortuary patterns that may be strictly pre-Inka were abandoned (see Frye and de la Vega 2005:180–83; Stanish 2003). The broad distribution of mortuary structures includes most of the Titicaca Basin and nearby highland regions, but there are regional variations in construction that may signify temporal developments and local variations in group identity (Stanish 2003:230–35; see also Hyslop 1976:119–21, 1977; Isbell 1997; Kesseli and Pärssinen 2005; McAndrews et al. 1997:158, 168; Neira 1967; Rivera 1991:34–38; Rossi et al. 2002; Schiappacasse et al. 1989; Stanish 1985; Stanish 2003:230–34; Tschopik 1946; Wernke 2003). Mortuary structures are built of mud brick, fieldstones, and cut stone, and are of varying scale, with heights ranging from 1 to 5 m. Plans are both round and circular, with crypts that may be underground or contained within the above-ground architecture (Stanish 2003:230–35; for other typologies, see Hyslop 1976, 1977; Tschopik 1946). As discussed below, the most elaborate of these structures appear to date to the Inka occupation of the Titicaca Basin, when local elites introduced Inka architectural elements (cut stone, rectangular plan) to monuments at existing cemeteries.

*Ceramic Production and Distribution*

As discussed above, the decline of the Tiwanaku state coincided with more local patterns of ceramic production and distribution. Because the Altiplano period is not clearly subdivided in local sequences, it is difficult to assess changes occurring throughout the period, although it is worth noting that the pottery found in association with occupations of the fourteenth or fifteenth century is similar to what is seen in the same area at sites where habitation continued from Tiwanaku times. It is also significant to note that decorated pottery is found at large numbers of small hamlets, suggesting that household access to craft goods was fairly even during this period (a broader distribution of archaeological diagnostics could also explain some of the increases in site count in the Altiplano period).

## Inka Imperial Transformations (ca. AD 1450–1535)

At the time of the European invasion, the Titicaca Basin was one of the wealthiest Inka provinces, and its imperial administrators and local elites were responsible for managing the lands, camelid herds, and labor tribute for the basin and neighboring regions. These three resource bases were considerable, but each presented a challenge for the rapidly expanding Inka state: fluctuating temperatures and precipitation contributed to regular crop failure, llama and alpaca herds grew slowly and could easily be hidden from state officials, and local resistance to (and exploitation of) imperial settlement and labor policies imposed high direct administration costs. The availability of a wide range of documentary sources has led to careful documentary studies aimed at reconstructing provincial order in the region (e.g., Julien 1983; Spurling 1992; see Stanish 2003 for an excellent synthesis of the ethnohistory and archaeology). Space constraints preclude a comprehensive treatment of documentary content and historiographic issues; in the interests of continuity, the present discussion considers the archaeological features of the Inka provincial apparatus and the development of local societies and identities under Inka rule.

### Regional Perspectives

The Inka incorporation of the Titicaca Basin brought significant changes as imperial administrative strategies were introduced and modified. One of these is a population growth of a scale consistent with the influx of new settlers (Stanish et al. 1997:58–59). Settled area under Inka rule was 200–300% of the levels seen for the Altiplano period in most survey regions, with the notable exceptions of the Tiwanaku Valley, where it declined to 53% of previous levels (excluding the occupation of Tiwanaku), and the Huancané-Putina area, where only about three-quarters of Altiplano period sites remained occupied and few site locations were established in the Inka period. The Inka occupation of the Huancané-Putina region involved strong continuity of existing settlements (99% of Inka sites have an Altiplano period component), which is also seen in the Tiwanaku Valley, where 90% of Inka sites represent continuing occupation. Such patterns contrast dramatically with other survey regions, where most Inka settlements were established as new occupations—this is true for the Island of the Sun (14% of Inka sites have an Altiplano component), the Taraco Peninsula (24%), and the Juli-Pomata region (29%).

Along the southern side of Lake Titicaca, settlement discontinuities are consistent with a shift to larger sites located in close proximity to the lake and to new Inka highways traversing the area. This has been reported for the Puno Bay (Schultze and Sosa Alcón 2003), while published data indicate a significant increase in mean site size in the Chucuito-Cutimbo area (47% increase), the Juli-Pomata area (39% increase), and the Taraco Peninsula (55% increase). Stanish et al. (1997:119) note that 50% of the sites in the Juli-Pomata area lie within 500 m of the Inka road. These parts of the basin transitioned into more hierarchical settlement systems located near imperial infrastructure (cf. Lémuz 2006). The regional data show an increased Inka economic coordination of these areas, targeting local resources for intensification or central management. Regional settlement patterns display an ecological variability suggesting that some areas saw Inka population increases in herding areas, while others saw an influx of settlement in lakeside terrace areas.

In contrast, areas where the Inka elite established patronage over religious sites and pilgrimage routes do not see the same growth in average site size. For example, on the Island of the Sun, Inka mean site size decreases to 56% of the Altiplano period average. The Tiwanaku Valley provides an interesting illustration of these forces at work—average site size in the lower valley (closer to the lake) grew by 22% in the Inka period, while it remained virtually unchanged in the middle valley (as the site of Tiwanaku was resettled under Inka patronage and reached a size of 50 ha or more).

### Site Layout

Inka site planning has been well documented for the largest administrative centers in the Titicaca Basin, which are clustered in the Colla and Lupaqa territories, surrounding the Bay of Puno (e.g., Hyslop 1990:195–97; Julien 1983; Stanish 2003:238–51), and contrasts qualitatively with *pukara* occupations known for the last decades of the Altiplano period (Fig. 16.4). At 50–80 ha, the largest Inka sites (Hatunqolla and Chucuito) are substantially larger than major *pukara* sites, and they exhibit the kind of central planning that is absent at such sites (Hyslop 1990:195–97; Julien 1983:89–93). While little architecture remains at the largest sites, researchers have noted the presence of formally laid out plaza spaces and principal roadways, establishing a new urban grid plan. Inka-style masonry is found distributed through the modern communities that overlie the Inka settlements, with remains of finely worked cut stone masonry reflecting different statuses or functions for some parts of these sites. Storage structures, which are common at Inka administrative centers, are not well documented for Inka sites in the Titicaca Basin, although storehouses have been identified on the hillside above Hatunqolla (Hyslop 1990:196). It is possible that storage architecture has been mistaken for *chullpas* in some parts of the Titicaca Basin, but also that storage facilities were built within sites rather than as disembedded complexes at the margins of way stations and administrative centers.

A grid plan was established at Hatunqolla and Chucuito, as well as at some other important administrative sites (e.g., Carpa, Paucarcolla), but does not represent typical settlements throughout the basin (see Stanish et al. 2005:298, 305). It is clear that in areas most heavily affected by imperial occupation, new settlements were established on or near the imperial highway, with central plaza spaces laid out at the site center. Most small villages and hamlets lacked any formal site planning.

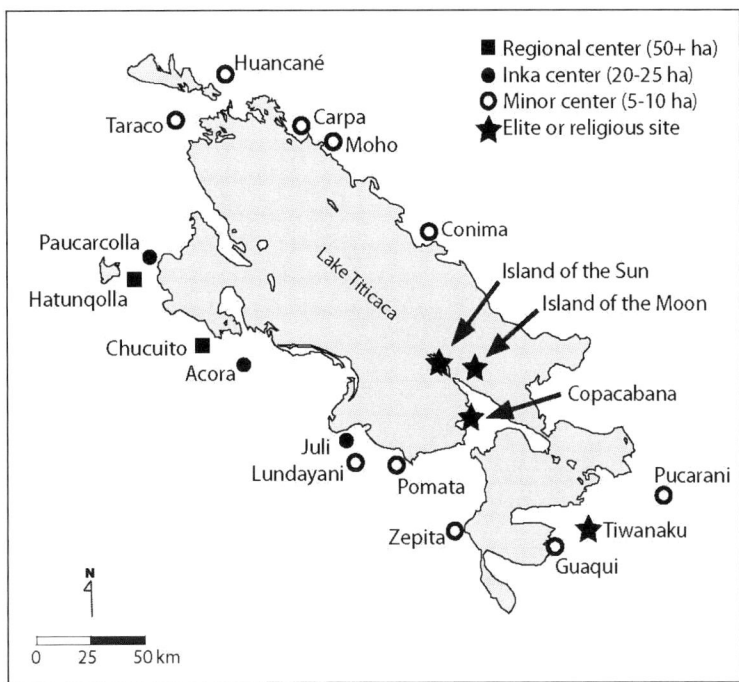

Figure 16.4. Important Inka sites, following Stanish (2003).

## Domestic and Special-Purpose Construction

During the Inka occupation, circular house forms continued to be common, but rectangular houses are also noted (e.g., Hyslop 1976:152–53; Rydén 1947; Zovar 2007b). The rectangular form is also used for special religious and administrative architecture (e.g., Bauer and Stanish 2001; Bauer et al. 2004; Yaeger and López Bejarano 2004). The production of cut stone masonry, which virtually ceased during the Altiplano period, was reestablished during the Inka occupation, for use in special-purpose buildings and in elite tombs. Masonry blocks are noted at Inka administrative centers, as well as at lower order sites (e.g., Albarracin-Jordan and Mathews 1990:162–64). Similar techniques were employed in carved rock outcrops and minor shrine sites distributed throughout the basin (Arkush 2005b).

## Burial Patterns

From what is known of Inka period mortuary contexts, local groups continued to practice their existing burial patterns, with slight modifications. Under Inka rule, Colla elites constructed larger mortuary towers at the site of Sillustani (e.g., Ayca Gallegos 1995; Bandelier 1905), incorporating Inka masonry techniques in the monumental constructions. Lupaqa elites presumably residing at Chucuito continued to bury their dead in impressive mortuary towers at the abandoned *pukara* site of Cutimbo during the Inka occupation (Frye 2005:203; Hyslop 1976:158–64, 1977). Studies of *chullpa* architecture (e.g., Arkush 2005a; Frye 2005:202; Hyslop 1976:118, 120, 1977) have observed instances of Inka pottery and masonry in the mortuary sectors of several fortified hilltop sites, indicating continued use of burial facilities under imperial rule. Inka period *chullpa* sites have also been identified near Acora and Pomata (Stanish 2003:271).

Given the conclusion that the Inka occupation involved substantial state-directed immigration, it is important to consider the breadth of known mortuary contexts in the Titicaca Basin at that time. Hyslop (1976:153–55) notes a paucity of mortuary remains in Inka villages in the Lupaqa area, suggesting that local people continued to bury their dead at or around their now-abandoned *pukara* sites, while labor colonists brought to the region by the state were either not present long enough or were not commonly buried away from their homelands.

## Ceramic Production and Distribution

One of the most significant changes in local material culture throughout the Titicaca Basin under Inka rule is the widespread distribution of Inka polychromes, which are found at all levels of local settlement hierarchies (Albarracin-Jordan and Mathews 1990; Bandy 2001; Hyslop 1976; Stanish et al. 1997). Documentary sources indicate the placement of specialized communities of potters in certain locations in the basin (see Julien 1993; Spurling 1992). The ubiquity of Cusco-style polychromes stands in marked contrast with what has been described for many Inka regions, where imperial ceramics are found at administrative centers and in tombs, but rarely in local domestic contexts.

The proliferation of Inka design motifs and vessel forms did not wholly replace local ceramic traditions (Fig. 16.5). There are fewer local ceramic styles in the basin than in the Altiplano period, but these styles show a much wider distribution reflecting more lively exchange networks, as well as the increased influence of certain local elites (Stanish et al. 1997:47–49; Mathews 1992:192). In some cases, this pottery is thought to represent Inka resettlement of Titicaca Basin populations (e.g., Cohen 2005:322; Covey 2000). The Sillustani, Chucuito, and Pacajes Inka styles show a continuity from earlier ceramic traditions (e.g., Albarracin-Jordan 1992:313–15, 319; Mathews 1992:191–92), and in the case of the former two are distributed around the administrative sites where the Colla and Lupaca resided (especially Hatunqolla and Chucuito). By contrast, Taraco and Urcosuyu pottery shows much stronger Inka influence and may have been produced by potters placed in local communities by the Inka state (Julien 1993; Spurling 1992).

## Other Material Culture

Evidence for metalworking has been tentatively identified at Paucarcolla (Stanish 2003:242), as well as

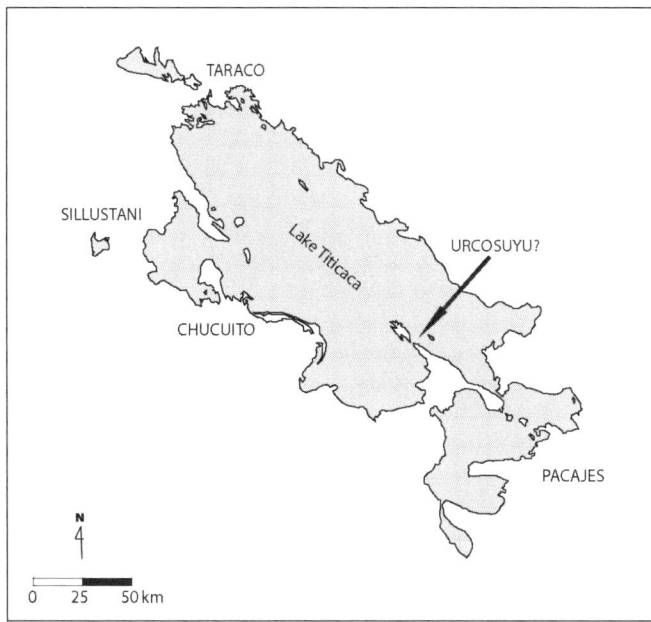

Figure 16.5. Inka period local ceramic styles.

at the site of Pilag Patag (Hyslop 1976:178–79). Documentary sources describe the Inka use of Titicaca Basin populations for mining gold on the Amazonian slope, and the immersion of the Titicaca Basin into the imperial economy appears to have increased local access to common and precious metal objects, which are found in burials and offerings (e.g., Bandelier 1910; Bauer et al. 2004; Reinhard 1992).

## Discussion

The long-term consideration of society and status in the late prehispanic Titicaca Basin offers valuable perspectives on the development of society and status outside of state heartlands. The decline of the Tiwanaku state affected the region in different ways—based on local ecology and social organization—but the shift from polity to kin group appears to have been widespread, if not universal. Secondary state formation did not occur, and local groups turned outward from Lake Titicaca to disperse into the horticultural and grazing resources that lay in unsettled areas. Although ephemeral settlement patterns may distort population levels in the early Altiplano period, it is clear that the rejection of Tiwanaku state institutions was not devastating for the new social groups that emerged at that time. Instead, the focus on population dispersal, broad-spectrum horticulture, and small-scale herding permitted substantial populations to thrive throughout the basin.

New regional data and radiocarbon dates from major *pukaras* dramatically alter the interpretation of the Altiplano period in the Titicaca Basin. It is now possible to assess the differing degrees of social disruption as the Tiwanaku state order fragmented, and to understand radical reconfigurations of economic and social arrangements in a broader context. The rejection of state mechanisms for risk management was a drastic social measure that over the long term proved to be a successful one. Areas close to the Tiwanaku capital may have experienced emigration and the dysfunctions attendant to political fragmentation, but at the time of the Inka conquest this region sustained a sizeable population that was capable of cooperating at least in mutual interests of defense. In other parts of the Titicaca Basin, population increased throughout the Altiplano period, to the point where demographic and ecological pressures led to the elaboration of new patterns of group integration shaped around resource management and defense (e.g., Arkush 2005a:322ff). The reemergence of hierarchy in the late Altiplano period represents an avenue toward complexity that is clearly distinct from Tiwanaku institutions, which focused on intensive agriculture, interregional exchange, and the spread of religious values and worldview. The major *pukara* pattern represents a conservative response to resource management—one where social networks and agropastoral diversity are key tools for managing production fluctuations, and where civic coordination emphasized safeguarding subsistence and human resources rather than increasing them.

The archaeological evidence of the Inka occupation of the Titicaca Basin complements the rich documentary record for the region. Imperial occupation wrought profound changes to settlement systems, local hierarchies, and the expression of social and ethnic identities. Under imperial rule, the Inka state promoted centralized herding and integrated Titicaca Basin populations into a broader imperial political economy (Stanish 1997b). These developments permitted some local elites to become more wealthy and powerful, adopting Inka construction techniques and material culture styles to assert their status, and using imperial administrative policies to extend their kin and ethnic networks to the Pacific and Amazonian slopes (e.g., Covey 2000; Stanish 1985). The source of local elite power shifted from resource management and defense leadership to canny exploitation of imperial hegemony. The uneven provincial landscape in the Titicaca Basin and the increased means for expressing status and identity appear to have accentuated ethnic identities and shaped local narratives of interactions with the empire. The most powerful Aymara elites in the Titicaca Basin were not those living in the former Tiwanaku heartland (which came to be dominated by Inka elites and facilities aimed at promoting imperial creation mythology), but rather those in highly populated *pukara* zones.

Recent research has encouraged some important revisions in documentary interpretations of late prehispanic social organization and individual status in the Titicaca Basin. Longitudinal archaeological perspectives demonstrate the capacity of local leadership to adapt to (and at times, exploit) strong state policies, and to formulate new arrangements as alternatives to unsustainable state practices. Both possibilities involved radical shifts toward new configurations of power, accommodating substantial changes in wealth availability, local supernatural concerns, and the frequency and intensity of violent conflict. Where conditions favored a more conservative and managerial elite, kin groups assumed greater importance than civic identity, and political divisions and social statuses were more muted in material culture. Conversely, conditions promoting intensification, surplus production, and regional trade sustained clearer social divisions and broader ranges of social status.

## References Cited

Albarracin-Jordan, J.
1992 Prehispanic and Early Colonial Settlement Patterns in the Lower Tiwanaku Valley, Bolivia. PhD dissertation, Department of Anthropology, Southern Methodist University, TX.

Albarracin-Jordan, J., and J. E. Mathews
1990 *Asentamientos prehispánicos del valle de Tiwanaku, Vol. I*. La Paz, Bolivia.

Arkush, E. N.
2005a Colla Fortified Sites: Warfare and Regional Power in the Late Prehispanic Titicaca Basin, Peru. PhD dissertation, Department of Anthropology, University of California, Los Angeles.
2005b Inca ceremonial sites in the southwest Titicaca Basin. In *Advances in Titicaca Basin Archaeology–1*, edited by C. Stanish, A. B. Cohen, and M. S. Aldenderfer, pp. 209–42. Cotsen Institute of Archaeology, University of California, Los Angeles.
2006 Collapse, conflict, conquest: The transformation of warfare in the late prehispanic Andean highlands. In *The Archaeology of Warfare: Prehistories of Raiding and Conquest*, edited by E. N. Arkush and M. W. Allen, pp. 286–335. University Press of Florida, Gainesville.

Ayca Gallegos, O.
1995 *Sillustani*. Instituto de Arqueología del Sur, Tacna, Peru.

Bandelier, A. F. A.
1905 The aboriginal ruins at Sillustani, Peru. *American Anthropologist* 7(1):49–69.
1910 *The Islands of Titicaca and Koati*. Hispanic Society of America, New York.

Bandy, M. S.
2001 Population and History in the Ancient Titicaca Basin. PhD dissertation, Department of Anthropology, University of California, Berkeley.

Bandy, M. S., and J. W. Janusek
2005 Settlement patterns, administrative boundaries, and internal migration in the early Colonial period. In *Advances in Titicaca Basin Archaeology–1*, edited by C. Stanish, A. B. Cohen, and M. S. Aldenderfer, pp. 267–88. Cotsen Institute of Archaeology, University of California, Los Angeles.

Bauer, B. S., R. A. Covey, and J. Terry
2004 Excavations at the site of Iñak Uyu, Island of the Moon. In *Archaeological Research on the Islands of the Sun and Moon, Lake Titicaca, Bolivia: Final Results from the Proyecto Tiksi Kjarka*, edited by C. Stanish and B. S. Bauer, pp. 139–73. Cotsen Institute of Archaeology Press, Los Angeles.

Bauer, B. S., M. Futrell, L. Cipolla, R. A. Covey, and J. Terry
2004 Excavations at Inca sites on the Island of the Sun. In *Archaeological Research on the Islands of the Sun and Moon, Lake Titicaca, Bolivia: Final Results from the Proyecto Tiksi Kjarka*, edited by C. Stanish and B. S. Bauer, pp. 43–82. Cotsen Institute of Archaeology Press, Los Angeles.

Bauer, B. S., and C. Stanish
2001 *Ritual and Pilgrimage in the Ancient Andes: The Islands of the Sun and Moon*. University of Texas Press, Austin.

Beaule, C. D.
2002 Late Intermediate Period Political Economy and Household Organization at Jachakala, Bolivia. PhD dissertation, Department of Anthropology, University of Pittsburgh, PA.

Bennett, W. C.
1933 Archaeological hikes in the Andes. *Natural History* 33(2):163–74.
1950 Cultural unity and disunity in the Titicaca Basin. *American Antiquity* 16(2):89–98.

Bermann, M.
1993 Continuity and change in household life at Lukurmata. In *Domestic Architecture, Ethnicity, and Complementarity in the South-Central Andes*, edited by M.S. Aldenderfer, pp. 114–35. University of Iowa Press, Iowa City.
1994 *Lukurmata. Household Archaeology in Prehispanic Bolivia*. Princeton University Press, Princeton, NJ.

Chacama, J.
2005 Patrón de asentamiento y uso del espacio. Precordillera de Arica, extreme norte de Chile, siglos X–XV. *Bulletin de l'Institut Français d'Études Andines* 34(3):357–78.

Cohen, A. B.
2005 Future directions in Titicaca Basin research. In *Advances in Titicaca Basin Archaeology–1*, edited by C. Stanish, A. B. Cohen, and M. S. Aldenderfer, pp. 317–23. Cotsen Institute of Archaeology, University of California, Los Angeles.

Couture, N.
2004 Monumental space, courtly style, and elite life at Tiwanaku. In *Tiwanaku: Ancestors of the Inca*, edited by M. Young-Sánchez, pp. 126–49. Denver Art Museum, Denver, and University of Nebraska Press, Lincoln.

Covey, R. A.
2000 Inka administration of the far south coast of Peru. *Latin American Antiquity* 11(2):119–38.
2008 Multi-regional perspectives on the archaeology of the Andes during the Late Intermediate period (c. AD 1000–1400). *Journal of Archaeological Research* 16:287–338.

Dean, E. M.
2005 Ancestors, Mountains Shrines, and Settlements: Late Intermediate Period Landscapes of the Southern Vilcanota River Valley, Peru. PhD dissertation, Department of Anthropology, University of California, Berkeley.

de la Vega, E.
1990 Estudio arqueológico de pucaras o poblados amurallados de cumber en territorio Lupaqa: El caso de Pucara-Juli. Tesis bachiller, Universidad Católica Santa María, Peru.

de la Vega, E., K. L. Frye, and T. Tung
2005 The cave burial from Molino-Chilacachi. In *Advances in Titicaca Basin Archaeology–1*, edited by C. Stanish, A. B. Cohen, and M. S. Aldenderfer, pp. 185–95. Cotsen Institute of Archaeology, University of California, Los Angeles.

Erickson, C. L.
1999 Neo-environmental determinism and agrarian 'collapse' in Andean prehistory. *Antiquity* 73(281):634–42.

Frye, K. L.
1997 Political centralization in the Altiplano period in the southwestern Titicaca Basin. In *Archaeological Survey in the Juli-Desaguadero Region of Lake Titicaca Basin, Southern Peru*, edited by C. Stanish et al., pp. 129–41. Field Museum of Natural History, Chicago, IL.
2005 The Inca occupation of the Lake Titicaca region. In *Advances in Titicaca Basin Archaeology–1*, edited by C. Stanish, A. B. Cohen, and M. S. Aldenderfer, pp. 197–208. Cotsen Institute of Archaeology, University of California, Los Angeles.

Frye, K. L., and E. de la Vega
2005 The Altiplano period in the Titicaca Basin. In *Advances in Titicaca Basin Archaeology–1*, edited by C. Stanish, A. B. Cohen, and M. S. Aldenderfer, pp. 173–84. Cotsen Institute of Archaeology, University of California, Los Angeles.

Goldstein, P. S.
2005 *Andean Diaspora: The Tiwanaku Colonies and the Origins of South American Empire*. University Press of Florida, Gainesville.

Graffam, G.
1994 Beyond state collapse: Rural history, raised fields, and pastoralism in the south Andes. *American Anthropologist* 4:882–904.

Hyslop, J.
1976 An Archaeological Investigation of the Lupaca Kingdom and Its Origins. PhD dissertation, Department of Anthropology, Columbia University, New York.
1977 Chulpas of the Lupaca zone of the Peruvian high plateau. *Journal of Field Archaeology* 4:149–70.
1990 *Inka Settlement Planning*. University of Texas Press, Austin.

Isbell, W. H.
1997 *Mummies and Mortuary Monuments: A Postprocessual Prehistory of Central Andean Social Organization*. University of Texas Press, Austin.

Janusek, J. W.
2004a *Identity and Power in the Ancient Andes: Tiwanaku Cities through Time*. Routledge, New York.
2004b Tiwanaku and its precursors: Recent research and emerging perspectives. *Journal of Archaeological Research* 12(2):121–83.
2004c Collapse as cultural revolution: Power and identity in the Tiwanaku to Pacajes transition. In *The Foundations of Power in the Prehispanic Andes*, edited by K. J. Vaughn, D. E. Ogburn, and C. A. Conlee, pp. 175–209. Archaeological Papers of the American Anthropological Association 14. American Anthropological Association, Washington, D.C.

Janusek, J. W., and A. L. Kolata
2003 Prehispanic rural history in the Río Katari Valley. In *Tiwanaku and Its Hinterland: Archaeological and Paleoecological Investigations of an Andean Civilization*, vol. 2, edited by A. L. Kolata, pp. 129–71. Smithsonian Institution Press, Washington, D.C.

Julien, C. J.
1983 *Hatunqolla: A View of Inca Rule from the Lake Titicaca Region*. University of California Publications in Anthropology, vol. 15. University of California Press, Berkeley.
1993 Finding a fit: Archaeology and ethnohistory of the Incas. In *Provincial Inca: Archaeological and Ethnohistorical Assessment of the Impact of the Inca State*, edited by M. A. Malpass, pp. 177–233. University of Iowa Press, Iowa City.

Kesseli, R., and M. Pärssinen
2005 Identidad étnica y muerte: Torres funerarias (chullpas) como símbolos de poder étnico en el altiplano boliviano de Pakasa (1250–1600 d.C.). *Bulletin de l'Institut Français d'Études Andines* 34(3):379–410.

Lémuz A., C.
2001 Patrones de asentamiento arqueológico en la Península de Santiago de Huatta, Bolivia. Licenciatura thesis in archaeology, Universidad Mayor de San Andrés, La Paz.
2006 Patrones de asentamiento arqueológico en el área de influencia del Sitio de Khonkho Wankane. In *Khonkho Wankane: Segundo informe preliminar del proyecto arqueológico Jach'a Machaca*, edited by J. W. Janusek and V. Plaza Martínez, pp. 5–44. Report submitted to the Bolivian Vice-Ministry of Culture, National Archaeology Unit of Bolivia.

Lumbreras, L. G., and H. Amat O.
1966 Secuencia cronológica del altiplano occidental del Titicaca. In *Actas y memorias del XXXVII Congreso Internacional de Americanistas* 2:75–106. Buenos Aires.

Mathews, J.
1992 Prehispanic Settlement and Agriculture in the Middle Tiwanaku Valley, Bolivia. PhD dissertation, Department of Anthropology, University of Chicago, IL.
2003 Prehistoric settlement patterns in the middle Tiwanaku Valley. In *Tiwanaku and Its Hinterland: Archaeology and Paleoecology of an Andean Civilization. 2: Urban and Rural Archaeology*, edited by A. Kolata, pp. 112–28. Smithsonian Institution Press, Washington, D.C.

McAndrews, T. L., J. Albarracin-Jordan, and M. Bermann
1997 Regional settlement patterns in the Tiwanaku Valley of Bolivia. *Journal of Field Anthropology* 24(1):67–83.

Neira A., M.
1967 Informe preliminar de las investigaciones arqueológicas en el Departamento de Puno. *Anales del Instituto de Estudios Socio-Económicos* 1(1):107–63. Puno.

Nye, Jr., J. S.
2004 *Soft Power: The Means to Success in World Politics*. Public Affairs, New York.

Reinhard, J.
1992 Underwater archaeological research in Lake Titicaca. In *Ancient America: Contributions to New World Archaeology*, edited by N. J. Saunders, pp. 117–43. Oxbow Monograph 24. Oxbow Books, Oxford.

Rivera, M.
1991 The prehistory of northern Chile: A synthesis. *Journal of World Prehistory* 5:1–47.
1993 South-central Andean domestic architecture: A view from the south. In *Domestic Architecture, Ethnicity, and Complementarity in the South-Central Andes*, edited by M. S. Aldenderfer, pp. 147–52. University of Iowa Press, Iowa City.

Rossi, M. J., R. Kesseli, P. Liuha, J. Meneses, and J. Bustamente
2002 Preliminary archaeological and environmental study of pre-Columbian burial towers at Huachacalla, Bolivian altiplano. *Geoarchaeology* 17(7):633–48.

Rydén, S.
1947 *Archaeological Researches in the Highlands of Bolivia*. Elanders Boktryckeri Aktiebolag, Göteborg, Sweden.

Schiappacasse, V., V. Castro, and H. Niemeyer
1989 Los desarrollos regionales en el norte grande (1000–1400 d.C.). In *Culturas de Chile. Prehistoria desde sus orígenes hasta los albores de la conquista*, edited by J. Hidalgo, V. Schiappacasse, H. Niemeyer, C. Aldunate, and I. Solimano, pp. 181–220. Editorial Andrés Bello, Santiago.

Schultze, C. A., and F. J. Sosa Alcón
2003 *Proyecto Wayruro: Reconocimiento [arqueológico] sistemático e intensivo [de la] Bahia de Puno, Lago Titicaca, Perú*. Field report presented to the National Institute of Culture.

Spurling, G. E.
1992 The Organization of Craft Production in the Inka State: The Potters and Weavers of Milliraya. PhD dissertation, Department of Anthropology, Cornell University, Ithaca, New York.

Stanish, C. S.
1985 Post-Tiwanaku Regional Economies in the Otora Valley, Southern Peru. PhD dissertation, Department of Anthropology, University of Chicago.
1989 Household archeology: Testing models of zonal complementarity in the south central Andes. *American Anthropologist* 91(1):7–24.
1991 *A Late Pre-Hispanic Ceramic Chronology for the Upper Moquegua Valley, Peru*. Fieldiana Anthropology, New Series 16. Field Museum of Natural History, Chicago.
1992 *Ancient Andean Political Economy*. University of Texas Press, Austin.
1994 The hydraulic hypothesis revisited: Lake Titicaca Basin raised fields in theoretical perspective. *Latin American Antiquity* 5(4):312–32.
1997a The settlement history of the southwestern Titicaca Basin. In *Archaeological Survey in the Juli-Desaguadero Region of Lake Titicaca Basin, Southern Peru*, edited by C. Stanish et al., pp. 113–19. Fieldiana Anthropology, New Series 29. Field Museum of Natural History, Chicago.
1997b Nonmarket imperialism in the prehispanic Americas: The Inka occupation of the Titicaca Basin. *Latin American Antiquity* 8(3):195–216.
2003 *Ancient Titicaca: The Evolution of Complex Society in Southern Peru and Northern Bolivia*. University of California Press, Berkeley.
2006 Prehispanic agricultural strategies of intensification in the Titicaca Basin of Peru and Bolivia. In *Agricultural Strategies*, edited by J. Marcus and C. Stanish, pp. 364–97. Cotsen Institute of Archaeology Press, Los Angeles.

Stanish, C., and B. S. Bauer
2004 The settlement history of the Island of the Sun. *Archaeological Research on the Islands of the Sun and Moon, Lake Titicaca, Bolivia: Final Results from the Proyecto Tiksi Kjarka*, edited by C. Stanish and B. Bauer, pp. 23–42. Monograph 52. Cotsen Institute of Archaeology, University of California, Los Angeles.

Stanish, C., A. B. Cohen, E. de la Vega, E. Arkush, C. Chávez, A. Plourde, and C. Schultze
2005 Archaeological reconnaissance in the northern Titicaca Basin. In *Advances in Titicaca Basin Archaeology–1*, edited by C. Stanish, A. Cohen, and M. Aldenderfer, pp. 289–316. Cotsen Institute of Archaeology, University of California, Los Angeles.

Stanish, C., and E. de la Vega
2004 *Informe Final: Prospección arqueológica del sector bajo de la Cuenca del Ramis (Ríos Azángaro y Ramis), Puno*. Report submitted to the National Technical Commission of Archaeology, National Institute of Culture, Peru.

Stanish, C., E. de la Vega, and K. L. Frye
1993 Domestic architecture on Lupaqa area sites in the Department of Puno. In *Domestic Architecture in South Central Andean Prehistory*, edited by M. Aldenderfer, pp. 83–93. University of Iowa Press, Iowa City.

Stanish, C., E. de la Vega M., L. Steadman, C. Chávez Justo, K. L. Frye, L. Onofre Mamani, M. T. Seddon, and P. Calisaya Chuquimia
1997 *Archaeological Survey in the Juli-Desaguadero Region of Lake Titicaca Basin, Southern Peru*. Fieldiana Anthropology, New Series 29. Field Museum of Natural History, Chicago.

Tschopik, M. H.
1946 *Some Notes on the Archaeology of the Department of Puno*. Papers of the Peabody Museum of American Archaeology and Ethnology, Harvard University, vol. 27, no. 3. Cambridge, MA.

Wernke, S. A.
2003 An Archaeo-History of Andean Community and Landscape: The Late Pre-Hispanic and Early Colonial Colca Valley, Peru. PhD dissertation, Department of Anthropology, University of Wisconsin-Madison.

Yaeger, J., and J. M. López Bejarano
2004 Reconfiguración de un espacio sagrado: Los inkas y la pirámide pumapunku en Tiwanaku, Bolivia. *Chungará* 36(2):337–50.

Zovar, J. M.
2007a Excavaciones arqueológicas en la Pukara de Khonko. In *Khonkho e Iruhito: Tercer Informe Preliminar del Proyecto Jach'a Machaca (Investigaciones en 2006)*, edited by J. W. Janusek and V. Plaza Martínez, pp. 203–11. Field report posted online at http://khonkhowankane.org/sitebuildercontent/sitebuilderfiles/janusek_plaza_martinez_2007.pdf.
2007b Investigaciones arqueológicas en Ch'auch'a de K'ula Marka. *Khonkho e Iruhito: Tercer Informe Preliminar del Proyecto Jach'a Machaca (Investigaciones en 2006)*, edited by J. W. Janusek and V. Plaza Martínez, pp. 212–15. Field report posted online at http://khonkhowankane.org/sitebuildercontent/sitebuilderfiles/janusek_plaza_martinez_2007.pdf.

# Index

*Page numbers in italics refer to illustrations. Page numbers followed by* t *or* tt *refer to tables; those followed by* n *refer to notes.*

above-ground tombs. *See* tombs, above-ground
Abraham, Sarah, 7. *See also* Pukara's Late Intermediate occupation
Achachiwa (near Cabanaconde), 152
Adams, Robert McC., 242–43, 258–59
Aguirre stelae, 130, *134*
Aldenderfer, Mark, 1, 91, 145, 147–48, *147*
Aldunate, Carlos, 213
altiplano burials. *See* Tikonata
Altiplano kingdoms, 73, 77–78, 168–69, 170*t*, 174, 195, 284. *See also* Late Intermediate period
Amantaní Island, 5, 7, 190–91
Amat, Hernán, 44
amaya uta (house of the soul), 203. *See also* chullpas
Andean archaeology, twenty-first century: chronology of Titicaca Basin, 4–9 (*see also* ceramic sequence); future of, 9; map of Lake Titicaca, *2*; northern Titicaca Basin, 3–4; years of exploration, 1
Arapa (lake), 231
Arapa (town), 3, 4, 124–25, *206, 208–9, 211–12*

Arapa stela, 121, 124
Arizaca, Eduardo, 49, *73*, 73–74
Arkush, Elizabeth, 1, 284, 289, 295–96, 302–4, *303*
Arrendo, Sofía, 213
Asana site (Moquegua), 91, 148–49
Asaro, Frank, 158n1
Asillo pottery, 289, *292*
ASTER satellite imagery, 262n11
Ávila, Walter, 265, 279
Ayacwira pottery, *60–61*, 72, *72*
Ayaviri zone, 72, 191, 205. *See also* Balsaspata

Balsaspata (Ayaviri), 3, 49–74; Ayacwira pottery at, *60–61*, 72, *72*; Collao pottery at, *53, 68*, 69; Cusipata pottery at, *73*; Inca pottery at, *73*; location/geography of, 4, 50, *50–51*; map of, 50, *51*; methodology used at, 50, 52; occupations of, 4, 49, 71–74; overview of, 4, 49; Pukara pottery at, *56, 61*, 69–70, *71*, 72–74; Pukara-style stela at, 4; Qaluyu pottery at, *53, 57–62, 64–65, 67–68*, 72, 72–73; raised fields near, 4, 71–72; stone buildings at, 4; stone walls at, 72, *72*; tombs at, 74; Unit 01 description, 52, *52–64*, 54; Unit 02 description, 64, *64–66*; Unit 03 description, 66; Unit 04 description, 66, *67–68*; Unit 05 description, 68, *68–69*; Unit 06 description, 69; Unit 07 description, 69–70, *70–72*; Unit 08 description, 70

*311*

Bandelier, Adolph, 1, 205, 213, 284
Bandy, Mathew S., 124
barter exchange, 150–51
Beck, Robin A., 92–94, 102
Bennett, Wendell C., 213, 303
Bermann, Marc, 218n3, 300, 302
Bertonio, Ludovico, 203
bows and arrows, 151
Brooks, Sarah O., 152, 158n1
Buikstra, Jane E., 165, 197, 199
Burger, Richard L., 72, 74n3, *142–43*, 149–50, 158n1
burials: in baskets, 185, 187, *187* (*see also* chullpas); in caves, 185, *186*; development of patterns of, 302, 304, 306; of mummies, 187 (*see also* Tikonata); ritual/sacrificial, 166; by Tiwanaku, 191. *See also* human remains; tombs, aboveground; tombs, below-ground; Tumilaca la Chimba cemetery

Cabrera, Luis, 267
Cáceda Guillén, Daniel, 7. *See also* Puno
Cachichupa (Putina Valley), corporate architecture at, 4, 91–102; appearance/development of, 91–94, 102; for ceremonies, 91, 100, 102; for defense, 102; discovery of Cachichupa, 94; Formative period pottery at Cachichupa, 94, 96; function of, 102; location of Cachichupa, 94, *96*, 102; monumental terracing, 91, 94, 96, *97–99*, 99*t*, 100, 102; occupations of Cachichupa, 94; overview of, 4–5, 91; pit feature, 100; Qaluyu pottery at Cachichupa, 100; ritual structures, 94; similarity to Pucara, 102; site map of Cachichupa, *97*; terrace function at, 100, 102
Calero Flores, Jorge, 49, *60, 72*
Calisaya Chuquimia, Percy, 305
Callahuaya (Kallawaya), 265
camelid bone, in excavations, 52, 54, 64, 66, 68, 70–71, 216, 274
camelid herds, 3, 7, 77, 81, 157–58, 303–5
Canal Antiguo Taraco, *245*, 246, 262n14
canal flow velocity, 258. *See also* raised fields
Canal Huarisan, 243, *245*, 246
Canal Quechuata, 243, *245*
Canal Ramis, 223, *241*, 243, 246, *248–49*, 249, 252, 256–60, 256*t*, *257*
Canal Waña Jawira, 246, 249, 252, 258–60
Cancha Cancha Asiruni, 3; statues at, 124–25
Candler, Kay L., 258, 262n15
Carabaya (Puno); archaeology overview for, 273, *273–74*; Chichaccori, 275–76, *275–77*, 280; chulpas in, *207*, 277, 279; importance of, 265–67; location of, *266*; Marca Marca de Tantamaco, 273–74, 280; Marka Marka III, 274, 279–80, *279–80*; Pitumarka, 273, 276–77, *278*; Quilli-Quilli, 274, *275*, 280; Usicayos, 273, *274*, 280
caravan transport, 94, 141, 143, 150–51, 157–58
Cari, 77–78, 284
Carlevato, Denise, 284, 288, 294–95
carved stones, 121–39; Aguirre stelae, 130, *134*; Arapa stela, 121, 124; associated with political centers, 138; carved architectural slabs, 130, *133–34*, 135, *136*, *139*; carved portable stones, 135, 138, *138–39*; carved statues (stelae), 121–25, *124*, *126–27*, *134–35*, *137–39*; classification of, 121; Cornejo stela, 125, *126*; figurines, 124; of Huancané/Juliaca, 5; lintels/building stones, 135, *137*; materials used in, 124; miscellaneous, 138, *139*; overview of, 5, 121; sites where found, 124–25; standing, in situ, 124–25, *128*; Tacca stela, 130, 135, *135*; Thunderbolt stela, 121; of Tiwanaku/Huatta, 5; uncarved architectural slabs, 135, *136*; uncarved statues, 123, 125, *128–32*, 130; Yaya-Mama stela, 135, *137*
Castro, Victoria, 213
Catari (Bolivia), 221, 237, 240
ceramic sequence (Pukara site), 13–47; appliquéd vessels, *41–43*, 45; appliquéd vessels (exterior), 32–33, *43*; bowls, 23, *24–26*, 28–29; chronology of Titicaca Basin, *14*; closed vessels, 23, *27–28*; correlation of formal categories to decoration, 33, 44; Cusipata style, *34–35*, 44; decorative categories for, overview of, 29; distribution of wares by strata, 46*t*; earliest, 45, 46*tt*; formal variations in, 28–29; Huaña I style, 45, 47; incised vessels, *41–43*, 45; incised vessels (exterior), 32–33, *36–40*; incised vessels (interior), 30, *31–33*, 33, *43*; jars, 23, *27*, 29, *29*; lattice motifs, *34*, 44; location/description of site, 13–15, *15*; ollas, 23, *27–28*, 28–29; open vessels, 23, *24–26*; original contexts of, 17–22, *18–22*; overview of, 13, 47; painted vessels, *41*, *43*; painted vessels (exterior), 30, *30*, 32–33, *34*, *39–40*, *42–43*; painted vessels (interior), 30, *30–33*, 33, *42–43*; paste analysis of, 45; plant motifs, 32, *38*; plates, 23, *24–25*; Pucara Pampa style, *31–33*, *39*, *43*, 44; Qaluyu style, *34*, *36–37*, 44, 47; Ramis style, *33*, *37–38*, 44–45; rhomboid motifs, 32, *34–35*; small X motifs, 32, *41*; spiral motifs, 32, *36–37*; square motifs, 32–33, *41*, *43*; step motifs, 30, *30–33*, 32, *39*, *43*; strata descriptions for, 21–22
Cerro Cupe, 82
Cerro Imarocus runoff, 223, 235, 240, *245*, 252–53, *255*, 255–58
Cerro Sechín (Peru), 4
champas (sod blocks), 223, *224*
Charasuta (near Lari), 152
Chávez, Karen Mohr, 1, 44, 72, 74n3, *108*, 121, *138*
Chávez, Sergio, 1, 72, 74n3, 121, 125
Chávez Ballón, Manuel, 114, 125
Chávez Justo, Cecilia, 4, 5, 7, 47n3, *95*, *170–172*, 250, 305. *See also* Tikonata
Chen Chen (Moquegua), 195, 197, 200, 214
Chichaccori (Carabaya), 275–76, *275–77*, 280
Chinchorro burials (Chile), 151
Chiripa public architecture, 92–94
Chivay obsidian, 4, 5, 72, 141–58; by blocks of the study region, 143–44, *145*, *148*, 152; ceramic period distributions from survey, 151–52; ceramic period evidence from the Colca, 152; chemical variability in, 153; clarity of, 153; consumption site altitudes for, *143*; Early and Middle Archaic use of, 142, 148–49, *149*; by ecological zone, 143; evidence from procurement of, 148–49, *149*; flake size, 153, *155–56*, 157; inclusions in artifacts, 153; Late and Terminal Archaic evidence from source area, 142, 150–51; Late and Terminal

Archaic use of, 142, 147, 150–51; local consumption vs. workshop production of, 153, *154*, 154*t*; location of source, 141; low-quality, 141–42, 158n2; map of sites with, *142*; in the Maymeja quarry area, 143–44, *144*, *146*, 149, 152–53, 157; overview of, 141–45, *142–43*, 158n1; procurement of, 141, 157; for projectile points (*see* projectile points); regional demand guiding workshop production of, 155, *156*, 157; and regional interaction/exchange relationships, 157–58; road from the quarry pit, 144–45; summary of survey evidence, 152–53; temporal distributions around, 145, *147–49*, 147–53; transportation's impact on availability of, 157; variability at source of, 157–58

Choquehuanca structure (Chiripa), 92

Chucuito, 8, 289, 292, 305–6

chullpas (chulpas), *8*, 85, 185, *206–9*, 284, 302–6; architecture of, 205, *206–13*; as ceremonial, 5, 213; at Chichaccori, *276*, *276*; definition of, 203; development of, 304; elites' use of, 6; of Esquena, 277, 279; Estuquiña period, 216; excavations of, 213; function of, 203, 213, 217–18; grave goods from, 216; in Huancasayan, 271, *272*; Inka pottery/masonry in, 8; locations of, 205, 210; looting/destruction of, 216, 218n2; at Marka Marka III, 279; in Maukallacta, 266–67, *268*; multiple burials in, 5, 213, 217; origin of term, 203; at Porobaya, 216; in Sandia, *272*, 273; Tikonata's lack of, *7*, 190. *See also* tombs, above-ground

Chunchulcalloc (Sandia), 267, *269–71*, 270

Cieza de León, Pedro, 213, 284

cist tombs, 5, 197, 203, 210, 213–17, 218n4

Clark, Niki R., 197, 199

Coben, Lawrence, 265, 274

Cobo, Bernabé, 213

Cohen, Amanda, 4, 72, 124, 135

Colana, 215

Colla, 2; elite of, 295; at Hatuncolla, 85; vs. Inca, 283; vs. Lupaca, 77, 284; mortuary towers constructed by, 8; sociopolitical organization of, 283–84. *See also* Pukara's Late Intermediate occupation

Collao paste, 288, 292

Collao pottery: at Balsaspata, *53*, *68*, 69; at Paucarcolla-Santa Barbara, 81; at Pukara, 115, 288–89, *288–91*, 288*t*, 292, 294, *294*, 295*tt*

collar tombs, 5–6, 210, 214–18, *216*

Collasuyu, 2, *6*, 7, 77

Colocolo (Sandia), 271, *272–73*, 273

Copesco Project, 15, *16*, 93, 105, 115, *116*

cordillera zone, 4, 82, 85, 92, 94, 102, 267

Cornejo Maya, César, 7

Cornejo stela (Arapa area), 125, *126*

CORONA satellite imagery, 262n11

corporate architecture. *See* Cachichupa's corporate architecture

Covey, R. Alan, 7. *See also* society/status, development of

cranial deformation, 164–65, *166*, 167, 171, *172*, 174, 189. *See also* cranial deformation, intentional

cribra orbitalia, 166, 173

Cusipata pottery, *34–35*, 44, 73

Cutimbo, 8, 205, *206*, 306

Cuyo Cuyo (Sandia), 273

Dean, Emily, 92

Decapitator (Ñakaj) style, 73, 74n2. *See also* Pukara pottery

degenerative joint disease, 173

de la Vega, Edmundo, 284, 294–96, 305

Denevan, William M., 221, 228, 235, 237

dental development and health, 170*t*, *171*, 174

Desaguadero (Bolivia), 221

Drayer-Verhagen, Francine, 5. *See also* human remains

Dueñas, Benjamín, 265

Earle, Timothy, 218

Early Formative period, 54, 71, 78, 91, *93*, *107*, 123, 141, 151, 153

Early Huaña culture, 74

Erickson, Clark: on raised fields, 4, 71, 221, 228, 237, 252, 261; on splash irrigation, 258, 262n15; on tools for cutting sod blocks, 223

Escalera, 145

Estuquiña, 197, 199, 215, 217

Farrington, Ian S., 258

fiber-tempering, 124

Flores, Luis, 119n9

Flores Blanco, Luis, 7. *See also* Puno

forest zone, 267

forts. *See* pukaras

Franco Inojosa, José, 265

Franquemont, Edward, 73

frog motif, 125, *126*

Frye, Kirk, 284, 294–96, 305

gato de agua motif, 125

Gemio, Evelyn, 221, 228, 230

Gentilar, 215

Giesso, Martín, 158n1

Gisbert, Teresa, 205

Glascock, Michael D., 149, 158n1

Global Mapper, 230–31, 261n8

Goldstein, Paul, 5, 193, 213–14, 218n4

Google Earth imagery, 262n11

GPS data, 107, 112, *112–13*

Guamán Poma de Ayala, Felipe, *6*, 7, *8*, 213

Gutiérrez Noriega, Carlos, 213

Hastorf, Christine A., 92, 102, 124

Hatuncolla, 1, 8, 77, 85, 121, 124–25, 284

Henderson, Michael, 7. *See also* raised fields

house construction, development of, 300, 302–4, 306

Huaña culture, 74, 250

Huaña I pottery, 45, 47, 130

Huancané-Putina River valley: corporate architecture in, 102 (*see also* Cachichupa's corporate architecture); location/geography of, *92*, 94; Middle Formative sites in, 94, *95–96*; pre-Columbian trade in, 94; settlement pattern in, 102, 300, *301*, 305

Huancanewichinka (near Huancané), 3, 125, *128*

Huancasayan (Sandia), 271, *272*

Huatacoa (Ayaviri area), *2*, 4, 72

Huatta area, 81–82, 221, 228, 230

human remains (Taraco), 163–75; age determination for, 163–64, 166–69; Burial 1, 163, *164*, 165–67, 174–75; Burial 2, 163, *164*, 167, 173–75; Burial 2a, 163, 167, 175; Burial 3, 163, *164*, 167–75, *168*, *170–72*; cranial deformation in, intentional, 165, *166*, 167, 171, *172*, 174; cranial traits in, discrete, 174; cranial traits in, nonmetric, 165; dental attrition/wear, ascertaining, 165, 169, 170*tt*, *171*, 174; dental development and health, 170*t*, *171*, 174; dental health and disease, ascertaining, 165; descriptions of, 165–69, *166*, *168*, 169–70*tt*, *170–72*, 171; facial/cranial indices of time periods, 169, 169*t*; general health of the occupants, 173–74; health and disease, ascertaining, 165; methods for analyzing, 163–65; odontometric methods used, 165; odontometrics of, 173; osteometric methods used, 165; osteometrics and activity patterns of, 169*t*, 171, 173; overview of, 5, 163, *164*; sex determination for, 164–65, 167–68, 171; trophy heads, 174–75

human remains (Tumilaca). *See* Tumilaca la Chimba cemetery

Humboldt, Alexander von, 1

hypoplasias, 173–74

Hyslop, John, 213, 306

Illingaya (Carabaya), 276, 280

Inca-Cuzco tombs, 74

Inca Empire: administration by, 85; burial customs in quarters of, 7 (*see also* tombs, above-ground); vs. Colla, 283; and the Colla vs. the Lupaca, 77–78; imperialism of, 284–85; population growth in, 305. *See also* Carabaya; Sandia; Tikonata

Inca pottery, *73*, 81, *90*

incensarios, 80–82, 185, 187, *187–88*, 190, 200

Inojosa, Franco, 13

Instituto Geográfico Nacional (IGN), *232*, 261n7

Instituto Nacional de Cultura del Perú (INC), 49

irrigation, splash, 258, 262n15

Isla Estévez, 7, 82, 85, 190

Islands of the Sun and Moon, 1, 6–7, 190

Isla Tikonata. *See* Tikonata

Janusek, John W., 221, 237, 240, 302

Johnson, Ilana, 4. *See also* Paucarcolla-Santa Barbara

Juliaca (Peru), 221, 251

Julien, Catherine, 1, 270, 284

Julien, Michèle, 270

Kalasasaya Complex (Pucara), 80–82, *84*, 285

Kala Uyuni, *2*, 124

keros (drinking beakers): appearance/use of, 80; on the Islands of the Sun and Moon, 6–7; on Tikonata, 185, 187, *188*, 189–90; at Paucarcolla, 82; at Tumilaca, 200, *201*

Khurkutra (Coaza), 280

Kidder II, Alfred, 1, 14, *16*, 105–6, *108*, *110–11*, 114–15, *116*, 121, 125, 284–85

Klarich, Elizabeth, 5, 13, 44–45, 115, 218, 285

Klink, Cindy, 145, 147, *147*

Kolata, Alan L., 1, 221, 228, 230, 237, 240, 243, 252, 260–61

Lagunita Mound (Pukara), 13, 15, *114*, 114–15, 119n7

Lake Titicaca, map of, *122*

Lake Titicaca Basin. *See* Titicaca Basin

Larecaja (Bolivia), 265, 273

Late (Upper) Formative period, 3; arthritis in women of, 169, 173; cranial indices of, 169, 169*t*; cultures of, *93*; dates of, 123; dental health in, 174; dental wear in, 169, 170*tt*; elites of, 4; health in, 173–74; otitis media in, 174; tooth size in, 173; tympanic dehiscences in, 174. *See also* human remains; Pukara; Pukara's Late Intermediate occupation

Late Horizon pottery, 288*t*, 289, 292, 294, *294*, 295*tt*

Late Intermediate (Altiplano) period, 77; above-ground slab-cist tombs of, 85, *87–88*, 304; agro-pastoralism in, 169; cranial indices of, 169, 169*t*; dental health in, 174; dental wear in, 169, 170*tt*; factionalism of, 283–84; health in, 173–74; otitis media in, 174; society/status, development of, 302–4; Tiwanaku-Altiplano transition, 299–302, *302*; tooth size in, 173; tympanic dehiscences in, 174. *See also* Pukara's Late Intermediate occupation; Tikonata

lattice ceramic motifs, *34*, 44

Lavallée, Danièle, 270

Lennon, Thomas J., 230, 237

Levine, Abigail, 4

long-distance exchange, 150–51

Lozada, María Cecilia, 5, 197, 199. *See also* Tumilaca la Chimba cemetery

Lukurmata, 1, 302

Lumbreras, Luis, 44, 50, 218

Luna Peralta, Nicolás, 265

Lupaqa (Lupaca), 8, 77, 187, 189, 213, 284–85, 303, 305–6

Lynch, Thomas, 93

Machacamarca (Hu-316): as a Formative and Huaña I period center, 125, 130; statues at, 125, *129–30*, 130; sunken court at, *129*

Mackay, Alex, 5. *See also* Chivay obsidian

Macusani (Puno), 267

maize, *6*, 7, 183, *185*, 191

Maravillas, 74

Marca Marca de Tantamaco (Carabaya), 273–74, 280

Marcavalle pottery, 4, 44, 72

Marka Marka III (Carabaya), 274, 279–80, *279–80*

masonry blocks, 8, *8*

Maukallacta (Sandia), 267, *268–69*, 280

Mauq'a-Limbani (Sandia), 273
Maymeja quarry area (Chivay), 143–44, *144*, *146*, 149, 152–53, 157
Mayo-Pampa, 271
metalworking, 306–7
Middle Formative period, 3; cultures of, *93*; dates of, 13, *14*, 123; vs. Early Formative period, 91, *93*; elites of, 47; Huancané-Putina River valley sites from, *95*. *See also* Cachichupa's corporate architecture; Pukara
monoliths. *See* carved stones
Monte Albán (Mexico), 3–4
monuments, 5, 8, *8*. *See also* carved stones
mortuary patterns/structures, 304, 306. *See also* chullpas; tombs, above-ground; tombs, below-ground; Tumilaca la Chimba cemetery
mountain worship, 92
Mujica, Elías, 13, 15, 17, 44, 119n2, 285. *See also* Copesco Project
mummies. *See* Tikonata
Murra, John, 214, 265
mutualism, 148, 150–51

Ñacoreque-Chico (Sandia), 273
Ñakaj (Decapitator) style, 73, 74n2. *See also* Pukara pottery
Nakandakari, 15, 17
Nalvarte Maldonado, Nicolás, 271
Nordenskiöld, Erland F., 205, 213, 265
Northern Mound at Pukara, 13, 15, *114*, 115

Oaxaca Valley (Mexico), 3–5
Oberti, Italo, 49
obsidian. *See* Chivay obsidian
odontometrics/odontometric methods, 165, 173
Oja T'oqo (Ituata), 280
Omo complex, 194
ONERN, 252–53, *254*
Onofre Mamani, Luperio, 305
open channel flow analysis, 223
Oqosiri (Usicayos), 280
Ortloff, Charles R., 221, 240, 246, 258, 260
Oshige Adams, David, 4. *See also* ceramic sequence
osteoarthritis, 173
osteometrics/osteometric methods, 165, 169t, 171, 173
otitis media, 174
Otora Valley settlement/funerary data, *214–15*, 214–17
Owen, Bruce, 193–95, 197

Pachacuti Inca, 78, 283
Palao, Juan, 265
Pampa Koani, 252
Paralaque (upper Moquegua drainage), 215
Paredes, Rolando, 49, 149, 285
Pari Flores, Romulo E., 194, 200
Pärssinen, Marti, 205

pastoralism, 150–51, 158, 295
Pata-Laqueque (Sandia), 273
Paucarcolla-Santa Barbara, 77–90; above-ground slab-cist tombs at, 85, *87–88*; carved stone stelae at, 79; ceramic distribution at, 81, *82*; Colla pottery at, 81; data analysis and chronology of, 78–81; data recovery at, 78; elites at, 4, 78–79, 81–82, 85, 90; in the Inca period, 81; in the Late Intermediate period, 81, 85, *87*; location of, 78, *80*, 82, 85; in the Middle Formative period, 79, 81, 85; in the Middle Horizon, 80, 82; occupation of, 78, 81–82, 85; overview of, 4, 77–78; polychrome elite wares of, 79; as a provincial center, 85; Pucara pottery at, 81, *83*; as a Qaluyu center, 81–82; Qaluyu pottery at, 79, 81, *83*; religion/ritual at, 82, 85, 90; sunken court complexes at, 79, 82, *84*; Tiwanaku ceramics/artifacts at, 80, 82, 85, *86–87*; in the Upper Formative period, 79–82, 85; zone-incised pottery at, 79–81
Pérez Maestro, Carmen, 4, 49
periostitis, 169, 173
*Peru: Incidents of Travel and Exploration* (Ephraim Squier), 1
Phisca Phichu Puncu (Usicayos), 280
Phushka (Usicayos), 280
Ph'utuni-Pata (Sandia), 273
pilgrimages, 6–7, 183, 190–91
Pitumarka (Carabaya), 273, 276–77, *278*
Pizarro, Francisco, 1
Plourde, Aimée, 4, 250. *See also* Cachichupa's corporate architecture
Pomata (Peru), *2*, 7, 222, 235, 237, 251, 260
Porobaya (upper Moquegua drainage), 215–16
porotic hyperostosis, 166, 173
projectile points: chronology of, 145, 147, *147–48*; from small obsidian nodules, 157; types/distribution of, *149*, 150–51
Pucaorqo (Pukara), 115, *116–17*
Pucara Pampa pottery, *31–33*, *39*, *43*, 44
Pukara (Pucara), 105–19, 119n3, 119n9; aerial photos of, 112–15, *113*, *116*; carved slab at, 130, *133*; chronology of, *107*; Collao sherds at, 115; corporate constructions at, 93; elites at, 82; fall of, 73–74, 82; in the Formative period, 113–15, 117; function of, 118; future research on, 117–18; growth of, 81, 105; influence of, 105; lagoon at, 114–15; location of, *108*, 285; middens of, 13; mounds at, 115, *116*; occupations of, 93, 105, 113–15; overview of, 5, 105–6; project methods at, 106–7, *110–13*, 112–13; project results for, *113*, 113–15, 119n6; Pucaorqo at, 115, *116–17*; Pukara Archaeological Project mapping/excavation of, 119n8; pyramids of, 13–15, *16–18*, 28; Qalasaya structure at, 115; size/boundaries of, 5, 105–6, *109*, 113, 115, 117, *118*; statues at, *124*, 124–25; sunken courts at, 130, *133*, 135 (*see also* White and Red Temple); vs. Taraco, 3; uncarved slabs at, *133*, 135; zone-incised pottery of, 80. *See also* ceramic sequence; Lagunita Mound; Northern Mound; Pukara's Late Intermediate occupation
Pukara Domestic Archaeology Project, 285
Pukara-Pata/Miraflores (Quiaca), 273
Pukara period, divisions of, 119n2

Pukara pottery: at Balsaspata, *56*, *61*, 69–70, *71*, 72–74; characteristics of, 105; at Paucarcolla-Santa Barbara, 81, *83*
pukaras (hilltop fortifications), 77, 283–84, 295, 300, 302–4, *303*
Pukara's Late Intermediate occupation, 283–96; Asillo pottery of, 289, *292*; attribute analysis of pottery, 292; ceramic analysis for, 285, 288–89, 288*t*, *290–93*, 292, 294–95, 295*t*; by Colla, 283, 285; Collao pottery of, 288–89, *288–91*, 288*t*, 292, 294, *294*, 295*tt*; excavation results for, 285, *286–87*, 296; history of Colla archaeology, 284–85; houses/structures of, 285; Late Horizon pottery of, 288*t*, 289, 292, 294, *294*, 295*tt*; overview of, 7, 283–84; temporal/spatial distribution of ceramics of, 292–95, *294*, 295*tt*; Transitional pottery of, 288*t*, 292, *293–94*, 294, 295*tt*
Pukara statues, 122–24
Puno, 265–80; characterization of archaeology of, 280; gold deposits in, 265, 280; location/geography of, *266*, 267; overview of, 7, 265–67. *See also* Carabaya; Sandia
Putina statues, 125, *128–29*
putucos (adobe structure), 223, *224*

Qalasasaya complex, 105
Qalasasaya pyramid, 13–15, *16–18*
Qaluyu, 3; location of, 93; Stanish's inspection of, 93; sunken courts at, 93–94; terracing at, 93–94
Qaluyu period, 71–72
Qaluyu pottery: at Balsaspata, *53*, *57–62*, *64–65*, *67–68*, *72*, 72–73; at Cachichupa, 100; at Paucarcolla-Santa Barbara, 79, 81, *83*; at Pukara, *34*, *36–37*, 44, 47
Qaluyu statues, 122–24, *129*
Qaqachupa, 4, 71
Q'awan-Chaka (Sandia), 273
Qéusani (Sandia), 273
Qillqatani, 148–49
Qoa Qoa (Coaza), 280
Qocha Quechuata, 243, 246, *246*
qochas (cocha), 222, 228, 235, *237*, 261n1
Quebrada Jaguay, 149
quechua zone, 267
Quelcatani cranial deformation, 174. *See also* cranial deformation, intentional
Quilli-Quilli (Carabaya), 274, *275*, 280
Quispe, Amador, 265
Quispe, José, 265
Quispe, Lorgio, 265

Raimondi, Antonio, 265
raised fields (Taraco), 221–62; aerial photos of, 221–23, 228, 230, *230–32*, 246, *247*, 260–61, 261n7; Canal Antiguo Taraco, *245*, 246, 262n14; Canal Huarisan, 243, *245*, 246; Canal Quechuata, 243, *245*; Canal Ramis, 223, *241*, 243, 246, *248–49*, 249, 252, 256–60, 256*t*, *257*; canals for runoff control, 223, 240–41, *241*, 243, *245*, 246, *247–49*, 249–50; Canal Waña Jawira, 246, 249, 252, 258–60; of Catari, 221, 237, 240; Cerro Imarocus runoff, 223, 235, 240, *245*, 252–53, *255*, 255–58; chronologies for, 228, 261, 261n6; of Desaguadero, 221; farming in the region, 225, 228, 235, 250–52, *251*, 261; flooding/lake level in the region, 226, 262n12; geography of the region, *224–25*, 225–26; human occupation and the physical landscape, 250–52, *251*; hydrological features, generally, 223, 240, *241*, 252, *252*, 261; of Juliaca, 221, 251; lakeshore vs. inland, *233*, 235–37, *239–40*, 261n10; and land formation, 258, *259*; modern, 228, *229*, *231*, 231–32; north of Río Ramis, 235, *236–37*; overview of, 7, 221–23, *222*; and the physical landscape, overview of, *238*, 240–42, *241*; of Pomata, 221, 237, 251; and Qocha Quechuata, 243, 246, *246*; rainfall in the region, 226, *226*, 252–53, *254*; Río Ramis's flow/levees, 226, *227*, *243*, 250, 256, *257*, 258–60, 262n12; Río Ramis-supplied, 223, 235, 255–56, 256*t*, *257*, 258; satellite imagery of, 240–41, 260–61, 262n11; south of Río Ramis, 235, *238*; survey background, 228, *229*, *233*; survey methodology, 228, 230–32, 230*t*, *231–34*, 235, 260–61, 261n9; Taraco region today, 223, *224*, 261n3; of Tiwanaku, 221; watercourses (meanders) of the region, 223, *241–42*, 242–43, *244–45*; water management for, generally, 7, 222, 224, 246, 249–50, 261, 261n3, 262n15; water resources of the region, 223, 225–26, *226–27*, 228, 249, 250*t*, 261n1
Ramírez, Juan Carlos, 221, 228, 230
Ramis canal (Taraco), 7
Ramis pottery, *33*, *37–38*, 44–45
rhomboid ceramic motifs, 32, *34–35*
ritual use of Isla Tikonata. *See* Tikonata
Rivera, Oswaldo, 221, 228, 230
Roddick, Andrew, 124, 135
Román Bustinza, Nancy, 5
Rowe, John, 115
Rydén, Stig, 203, 213

Sajena (Upper Moquegua), 215–16
Salas, Guido, 158n1
San Bartolomé-Wiskachani, 91–92
Sandia (Puno): archaeology overview for, 267, 273; Chunchulacalloc, 267, *269–71*, 270; Colocolo, 271, *272–73*, 273; geopolitical importance of, 265; Huancasayan (Wanka-Sayani), 271, *272*; location of, *266*; Maukallacta, 267, *268–69*, 280
Sandweiss, Daniel H., 149
Sandweiss, M. del Carmen, 149
San José Mogote (Mexico), 3
San Martín Tilcajete (Mexico), 3
Santiago area (at Chiripa), 92
Schumm, Stanley A., 258
Seddon, Matthew T., 305
SENAMHI, 252, 256, *257*, 258
Serracino, George, 213
Servicio Aerofotográfico Nacional (SAN), 230, *232*, 261n7
Sharratt, Nicola, 5. *See also* Tumilaca la Chimba cemetery
Sillustani: as burial center for elites, 85, 213; dates for, 215; mortuary towers at, 8, *8*, 284 (*see also* chullpas)
Sillustani-Inca pottery, 81, 85, *90*

skeletal remains. *See* human remains; Tumilaca la Chimba cemetery
slab-cist tombs, 85, *87–88*, 210, *210–11*, 217, 302, 304
slabs, architectural. *See* carved stones
Smith, C. T., 221, 228, 235
society/status, development of, 299–308; burial patterns, 302, 304, 306 (*see also* tombs, above-ground); ceramic production/distribution, 302, *302*, 304, 306, *307*; domestic/special-purpose construction, 300, 302–4, 306; Inka imperial transformations, 305–7, *306*; Late Altiplano period developments, 302–4; overview of, 7–9, 299, *301*, 301*t*; regional perspectives, 300, 303, 305; site layout, 300, 303, 305, *306*; Tiwanaku-Altiplano transition, 299–302, *302*
Spielmann, Katherine A., 148
spindle whorls, 71, 295
spiral ceramic motifs, 32, *36–37*
splash irrigation, 258, 262n15
square ceramic motifs, 32–33, *41*, *43*
Squier, Ephraim George, 124–25, 205, 210; *Peru: Incidents of Travel and Exploration*, 1
Stanish, Charles: on Altiplano hamlets/dispersed villages, 300; on Carabaya, 265, 274; on collared tombs, 199; on cooperation, 4; on elites' burial customs, 7; on Juli-Pomata sites, 305; on the Late Intermediate period settlement pattern, 284; northern and northeastern basin surveyed by, 284; on Pukara occupations, 117; on Pukara's size, 105–6; Qaluyu inspected by, 93; on raised fields, 4, 71, 251; on sunken court architecture, 91–92; on Tumilaca settlement in Otora Valley, 193. *See also* carved stones; Tikonata; tombs, above-ground
Starbird, Jennifer, 5. *See also* Tumilaca la Chimba cemetery
statues. *See* carved stones
status via ceremonial/religious rites, 4. *See also* society/status, development of
Steadman, Lee H., 44–45, 305
stelae. *See* carved stones
step ceramic motifs, 30, *30–33*, 32, *39*, *43*
stone raw materials. *See* Chivay obsidian
stones, carved. *See* carved stones
Stross, Fred, 158n1
Sucha Ccucho (Usicayos), 280
sunken courts, 3; earliest, 92; at Machacamarca, *129*; at Maukallacta, 267; at Qaluyu, 93–94

Tacca stela, 130, 135, *135*
Tantaleán, Henry, 4. *See also* Balsaspata
Tapia, Félix, 265
Taraco: vs. Pukara, 3; as a regional center, 221, 260; statues at, 124–25, *126*, *128*, *130*; stone "altar" at, 138, *139*; uncarved slabs at, *136*. *See also* human remains; raised fields
*Tasa de Toledo* (1572), 7
temporomandibular joint disease, 173–74
Terminal Archaic period, *93*
terracing: at Cachichupa, 91, 94, 96, *97–99*, 99*t*, 100, 102; for the dead, 93; earliest, 102; at Qaluyu, 93–94

TerraSync, 107, 112, *112*
textiles, 71
Thunderbolt stela (Tiwanaku), 121
Tikonata, 183–91; Altiplano period remains on, 187, *188–89*, 189; ceremonial incensarios and keros on, 185, 187, *187–88*, 190; chulpas lacking on, 190; Inca period remains on, 189, *190*; interpreting, 190–91; location/geography of, 183, *184*; maize on, 183, *185*, 191; mummies on, 183, 185, *186*, 187, 189–90, *190*; overview of, 5, 183–85; as a pilgrimage site, 183, 190–91; Tiwanaku and Pucara remains on, 183, 185, *187–88*, 190–91
Tira-Waka (Sandia), 273
Titicaca Basin: administrative centers in, 7–8; chronology of, 4–9, *14*, *93*, *107* (*see also* ceramic sequence); European invasion of, 7; Inka occupation of, 7–9; maps of, *15*, *79*, *92*, *106*, *122–23*, *205*; northern, archaeology of, 3–4; occupation of, 3; size of, 3; society/status development in (*see* society/status, development of); wealth of, 7
Titicaca Basin Type obsidian. *See* Chivay obsidian
Tiwanaku: burials by, 191; collapse of, 85, 193, 217–18, 300, 307; elite wares from, 80; expansion of, 74, 82, 193, 195; interment treatment at, 200; in Moquegua, 193 (*see also* Tumilaca la Chimba cemetery); obsidian used in, 152; raised fields of, 221; remains, locations of, 6–7, 190 (*see also* Tikonata); resource areas controlled by, 151–52; Tiwanaku-Altiplano transition, 299–302, *302*
Tiwanaku/Huatta carved stones, 5
tombs, above-ground, 203–18; ancestor worship at, 5–6; ceremonial use of, 5, 217; collar, 5–6, 210, 214–18, *216*; for corporate groups, 213, 217–18; cultural/political processes involving, 5–6; dates for, 213–14, 217; hillside, 210, *212*; locations of, 6–7; mausoleums, 203, 213; modern, *217*, 218; multiple interments in, 5, 217; Otora Valley settlement/funerary data, *214–15*, 214–17 (*see also* Tumilaca la Chimba cemetery); overview of, 5–6, *6*, 203; at Paucarcolla-Santa Barbara, 85, *87–88*; slab-cist, 85, *87–88*, 210, *210–11*, 217, 304; tumuli, 210, 213–14; types of, 203, 205, *206–12*, 210 (*see also* chullpas)
tombs, below-ground: vs. above-ground, 5, 217; cists, 5, 197, 203, 210, 213–17, 218n4; collared, 199; with outer rings, 197, 199, *199*, 201; stone-lined, 197, *197–98*
Torata Alta (Moquegua), 217
Torres Pino, Elva, 197, 199
trade, cooperation due to, 4
Transitional period pottery, 288*t*, 292, *293–94*, 294, 295*tt*
Tripcevich, Nicholas, 5. *See also* Chivay obsidian
trophy heads, 174–75
trophy heads/skulls, 3
Tschopik, Marion, 205, 280, 288; *Some Notes on the Archaeology of the Department of Puno*, 284
Ttacca, Honorato, 115
Tumilaca la Chimba cemetery (Moquegua Valley, Peru), 193–201; excavations at, 196; grave architecture at, 197, *197–99*, 199, 201; grave goods at, 200, *201*; interment treatment at,

*200*, 200–201; location/geography of, 195, *195–96*; looting at, 200; map of Moquegua Valley, *194*; mortuary data from, 193–94, 201; number of burials at, 195; overview of, 5, 193; Tumilaca phase in Moquegua, 193–94

uma and urco (urqu), 7, 183, 191
Umire, Adán, 130, 135, *135*
Upper Formative period. *See* Late Formative period
urbanism, 4. *See also* Cachichupa's corporate architecture; Pukara
Usicayos (Carabaya), 273, *274*, 280

Valcárcel, Luis E., 121, 125
Viracocha Inca, 77–78
Vranich, Alexei, 191

Walker, John H., 260, 261n9
Waña Jawira canal (Tiwanaku), 7, 246, 252, 256–61

war, cooperation due to, 4
Wari, 151–52
weaving, 71
Weberbauer, Augusto, 265
wells, 222, 228
Wernke, Steven, 152
Wheeler, Jane, 44, 285
White and Red Temple (Pukara), 14–15, *16*
Williams, Patrick Ryan, 5. *See also* Tumilaca la Chimba cemetery
Williams, Sloan A., 197, 199

Yaya-Mama stela (original), 135, *137*
Yaya-Mama style, 100, 124
yunga zones, 267

Zapana, 77, 284
Zapotec, 5, 7
zone-incised pottery, 79–81